The United Nations and Mozambique, 1992-1995

The United Nations
Blue Books Series, Volume V

The United Nations and
Mozambique
1992-1995

**With an introduction by
Boutros Boutros-Ghali,
Secretary-General of the United Nations**

Department of Public Information
United Nations, New York

Published by the United Nations
Department of Public Information
New York, NY 10017

Editor's note:

Each of the United Nations documents and other materials reproduced in this book ("Texts of documents", pages 93-310) has been assigned a number (e.g. Document 1, Document 2, etc.). This number is used throughout the Introduction and other parts of this book to guide readers to the document texts. For other documents mentioned in the book but not reproduced, the United Nations document symbol (e.g., A/479/69-S/24065) is provided. With this symbol, such documents can be consulted at the Dag Hammarskjöld Library at United Nations Headquarters in New York, at other libraries in the United Nations system or at libraries around the world which have been designated as depository libraries for United Nations documents. The information contained in this volume is correct as at 1 May 1995.

The United Nations and Mozambique, 1992-1995
The United Nations Blue Books Series
Volume V
ISBN 92-1-100559-0
United Nations Publication
Sales No. E. 95.I.20

Printed by the United Nations Reproduction Section
New York, NY

Contents

Section One:
Introduction by Boutros Boutros-Ghali, Secretary-General of the United Nations

Section Two:
Chronology and Documents

Section One
Introduction

I   Overview

1   Over a three-day period from 27 to 29 October 1994, Mozambique conducted the first free and fair multi-party elections in the country's history. The elections brought together in an open democratic contest the ruling Frente da Libertação de Moçambique (FRELIMO) and the Resistência Nacional Moçambicana (RENAMO), the country's two major political parties and former foes, after a long-running conflict that had claimed the lives of hundreds of thousands of people, driven millions from their homes and destroyed much of Mozambique's economic and social infrastructure. Against this tragic background, the elections symbolized a new spirit of reconciliation among the people of Mozambique. The elections were also the culmination of a major success story in United Nations peacemaking, peace-keeping, and humanitarian and electoral assistance. Through a complex, multifaceted and highly innovative strategy which broke new ground in how the United Nations dealt with parties in a conflict situation, a formerly socialist Government, committed to a one-party State, negotiated with an armed, rebellious group to create peace for their country.

2   The inauguration of the victor of the presidential election, Mr. Joaquim Alberto Chissano, on 9 December 1994 formally ended the two-year mandate of the United Nations Operation in Mozambique (ONUMOZ). When the last ONUMOZ contingents departed Mozambique in January 1995, they had overseen a remarkable transformation, from the ravages of civil war to the implementation of democratic government and the creation of a peaceful environment in which economic activity could once again flourish. The strong commitment of the major participants to peace, along with firm support from the international community, was the central prerequisite that enabled the United Nations to help bring about this dramatic transition. Neighbouring States also played a vital role, first in bringing the major participants to the negotiating table and then in helping to sustain the peace process under ONUMOZ. Their endeavours have helped to bring peace to the entire southern African region, which in early 1995 faced a brighter future after more than 30 years of bitter conflict.

3   ONUMOZ was a complex operation involving peace-keeping, the demobilization of armed forces, the provision of humanitarian relief, electoral support and the return of millions of refugees. One of its most important aspects was the emphasis placed on peace-building—in helping to ensure that the laying down of guns would create a durable peace. The Organization's unprecedented endeavours were concentrated not only in its oversight of the electoral process but also in channelling efforts by the international community to strengthen the organizational capability of parties contesting the election.

4   In a significant development for peace-keeping operations, in May 1993, the United Nations established a trust fund to help RENAMO transform itself from a military movement into a political party. The transformation of a guerrilla force, experienced only in war, into a political entity with a stake in the democratic process, is one of the most significant legacies of the United Nations operation. Another such fund was established to provide training, logistical support and other forms of assistance to other opposition parties. These efforts were crucial to the effective participation of all parties in the October 1994 election and hence to the establishment of sustained peace in Mozambique.

5   The mandate of ONUMOZ was to verify and monitor the implementation of the General Peace Agreement for Mozambique, signed by the Government of Mozambique and RENAMO in Rome on 4 October 1992.[1] The peace accords required the United Nations to supervise the cease-fire between the two parties, provide security for key transport corridors, monitor a comprehensive disarmament and demobilization programme, coordinate and monitor humanitarian assistance operations throughout the country and provide assistance and verification for national elections. ONUMOZ subsequently undertook a number of additional tasks at the request of the parties. In 1993, the United Nations assumed the chairmanship of the commission responsible for the formation of the new Mozambican Defence Force (FADM).[2] In 1994, the mission's scope was expanded further with the addition of a large civilian police (CIVPOL) component, which monitored the neutrality of the Mozambican police and helped protect the rights and liberties of Mozambican citizens, especially during the election period.[3]

6   The General Peace Agreement provided a clear and precise, if nevertheless complex, set of tasks for the United Nations. The Rome accords envisaged a one-year timetable for the accomplishment of the peace process. From the outset, however, this was recognized as unrealistic and all parties involved showed pragmatism in agreeing to an evolving implementation schedule. This adherence to an established and agreed plan—despite some differences in interpretation—was a vital factor in the success of ONUMOZ, even though the mission required two years instead of one to complete its mandate.

7   The United Nations chairmanship of the commissions established to supervise the implementation of the General Peace Agreement allowed ONUMOZ to maintain the momentum of the peace process, especially whenever either party showed reluctance to move to the next stage. Patient but active diplomacy, with the constant involvement of the

1/Document 12
See page 105

2/Document 38
See page 189

3/Document 57
See page 228

international community, helped to overcome the deep distrust that initially divided the two main parties and to defuse a number of potential crises. Most importantly for the achievement of an atmosphere of genuine peace in Mozambique, the two parties respected the cease-fire without serious breaches.

8   The principal problems confronting ONUMOZ concerned the long delay in the initial deployment of the peace-keeping contingents; the question of territorial and administrative control over certain areas of the country which had been contested during the war; the additional demands made by the different parties, especially RENAMO, which led to serious delays in the demobilization of the armed forces; and the many logistical constraints which made more difficult the task of closely coordinating the various aspects of the operation and which were compounded by delays in the start of the vitally important programme of mine clearance. By October 1993, disagreements on a number of aspects of the electoral process and on other issues had created a deadlock that threatened the entire peace process, and I was compelled to visit Maputo, the capital of Mozambique, where I was able to persuade all parties to work on negotiating a solution to outstanding issues.

9   One of the keys to the success of the ONUMOZ operation was the United Nations humanitarian assistance programme, which helped to build a climate of trust and cooperation between the contending parties. In October 1992, immediately upon the signing of the peace accords, the Office of the United Nations High Commissioner for Refugees (UNHCR) began delivery of food relief to Tete Province, establishing a pattern of increasing relief activity in areas that had been under RENAMO control. In 1993, humanitarian efforts centred on the return of refugees; indeed, the Mozambican repatriation was one of the largest such operations ever undertaken by UNHCR in Africa. By the time the ONUMOZ mandate ended in December 1994, the country's humanitarian crisis was considerably eased. Some 4 million refugees and displaced persons had gained sufficient confidence to travel to their home areas and resume farming and other economic activities.

10   Although both the General Peace Agreement and the ONUMOZ mandate were successfully implemented, a number of concerns remained at the time of the mission's conclusion. These included, on the security front, the continuing need to train and equip the new integrated armed forces and to collect and dispose of all outstanding caches of weapons. There was also a need to strengthen Mozambique's democratic institutions and to promote economic and social reconstruction so that peace, democracy and development could be sustained.

11   This Introduction traces the origins of the war, the peace negotiations and the period of the ONUMOZ mandate. Part II of the Introduction reviews the background to the Mozambican conflict and

the involvement of the United Nations during the 1980s in helping to relieve the mounting humanitarian crisis. Part III describes the process of negotiations to end the war and outlines the key elements of the General Peace Agreement. Part IV covers the first year of ONUMOZ, concluding with the agreement of the parties to follow a revised timetable for the remainder of the peace process during 1994. Part V recounts the process of demobilization, and Part VI surveys the improvements in the humanitarian situation. Part VII provides an account of the election process and its aftermath, including the termination of the mandate of ONUMOZ. Part VIII sums up the contribution of the United Nations to the implementation of the General Peace Agreement and to efforts to consolidate the peace as the Mozambican people embark on a new and more hopeful future.

12 The collection of documents in Section Two represents a comprehensive record of the involvement of the United Nations in Mozambique. Included are the complete text of the General Peace Agreement, resolutions of the General Assembly and the Security Council, reports to the Security Council on ONUMOZ, correspondence between myself and some of the parties involved, and other United Nations materials relevant to the resolution of the conflict.

II   The war and its humanitarian consequences

13   From the time of its independence from Portugal in 1975, Mozambique enjoyed few periods of peace. Committed as it was to the end of the minority regimes in neighbouring Southern Rhodesia and South Africa, the new Government immediately faced bitter enemies on its borders. The conflict quickly spread to Mozambican territory when, with external support, the Resistência Nacional Moçambicana (RENAMO) was established. During the course of the 16-year civil war RENAMO gradually gained de facto control of wide parts of the country. The conflict significantly destabilized the Government and drained its resources. Neither side, however, was able to achieve a military victory. Amid a deepening humanitarian crisis—the result of the protracted civil war exacerbated by periodic droughts—the Government and then RENAMO began efforts to resolve the stalemate through negotiation.

A long history of conflict

14   Mozambique's colonial experience had been marred by massive human rights abuses, racial conflict and instability. As the anti-colonial tide swept across the African continent in the 1960s, Portugal denied the legitimacy of Mozambican demands for independence and continued to encourage increased settlement by Europeans.

15   In defiance of Portuguese policy, various independence movements were established. In June 1962, three of these groups merged to form the Frente da Libertação de Moçambique (FRELIMO), under the leadership of Dr. Eduardo Mondlane. From bases in the United Republic of Tanzania, FRELIMO launched an armed struggle for Mozambique's independence in September 1964 and quickly succeeded in loosening Portugal's hold on much of the north of the country. However, the movement suffered set-backs, including the assassination of Dr. Mondlane in February 1969.

16   In April 1974, a group of military officers took power in Lisbon. Under an agreement signed on 7 September 1974, the new Government of Portugal handed the administration of Mozambique to a FRELIMO-dominated transitional Government, with Mr. Joaquim Chissano as Prime Minister. This move prompted a mass exodus of

Mozambique

Mozambique's geographical position has made it of vital concern to neighbouring countries, who depend on it for access to the sea. Bringing peace to Mozambique therefore was important for the entire southern Africa region.

Portuguese settlers. When FRELIMO, under the leadership of President Samora Machel, assumed the mantle of government at independence on 25 June 1975, the country was sorely depleted of the managerial and professional skills needed for its economic development.

The rise of RENAMO

17   The new Mozambique Government's strong opposition to minority rule in both Southern Rhodesia and South Africa attracted the fierce hostility of these two regimes, and the former began providing armaments and training to anti-FRELIMO forces inside Mozambique. In 1976, in active support of the Zimbabwean National Liberation struggle, Mozambique closed its transport routes to land-locked Southern Rhodesia. When in 1977 FRELIMO declared itself to be a Marxist-Leninist party and the Government signed aid agreements with the Union of Soviet Socialist Republics (USSR) and Cuba, covert assistance from the minority regime in Southern Rhodesia was stepped up and directly channelled to a group that began to operate openly under the name Mozambican National Resistance (initially referred to as MNR, but subsequently as RENAMO, after its Portuguese name—Resistência Nacional Moçambicana).

18   Mr. André Matsangaissa was RENAMO's first leader, having escaped to Southern Rhodesia from a FRELIMO re-education camp in Sacuze following accusations that he had engaged in theft while in the army. After receiving training from Southern Rhodesian forces at Odzi, near Mutare, the group prepared to undertake armed actions inside Mozambique. When Mr. Matsangaissa was killed in action in Mozambique in October 1979, his associate, Mr. Afonso Macacho Marceta Dhlakama, became president of RENAMO.

19   RENAMO adopted tactics designed to inflict damage on the economic and social infrastructure of Mozambique and to disrupt production. Road, rail and power links were frequently damaged, and towns and villages were attacked.

20   After 1980, following the independence of Zimbabwe, the support previously given to RENAMO by Southern Rhodesia ceased while that from South Africa and some groups in Western countries increased substantially. RENAMO grew rapidly in size and in military effectiveness, which enabled it to destroy the social and economic infrastructure through wide areas of the country. Between 1980 and 1982, RENAMO's strength increased from less than 1,000 to an estimated 8,000 fighters, and its operations spread from the central provinces of Manica and Sofala into the southern provinces of Gaza and Inhambane. But South Africa's aggression against Mozambique was not limited to

arming and training RENAMO: the apartheid regime in South Africa also undertook its own direct commando and air force raids on Mozambique between 1981 and 1983.

21   RENAMO's disruption and destruction of Mozambique's transport and supply facilities, and in particular the Beira and Limpopo corridors, aroused the concern of Zimbabwe and Malawi, which depended on these routes for much of their foreign trade. In November 1982, with the consent of the Mozambique Government, Zimbabwe sent more than 10,000 troops to protect the Beira transport corridor. A smaller contingent of troops from the United Republic of Tanzania was sent to patrol the Nacala transport route in the north. These three neighbours of Mozambique also began to host increasing numbers of refugees who had fled their homes in the wake of RENAMO attacks.

22   Large areas of the countryside soon became dangerous for the movement of both military and civilians. The spread of violent conflict disrupted agricultural production and drove many rural dwellers into the principal cities of Beira and Maputo. The onset of drought between 1982 and 1984 accelerated a mounting shortage of food. In the 1983/84 growing season, a famine in Gaza and Inhambane provinces killed tens of thousands of people. Across the country, agricultural and industrial production slumped and the economy went into rapid decline.

First negotiations fail

23   On 16 March 1984, the Mozambique Government made an unsuccessful bid for peace. At the border town of Nkomati, President Machel signed an "Agreement on Non-Aggression and Good-neighbourliness" with the South African Prime Minister, P. W. Botha, whereby South Africa undertook to halt its support for RENAMO and Mozambique agreed to close down the military operations of the African National Congress (ANC). South Africa then proceeded to mediate the first attempt at negotiations between FRELIMO and RENAMO in Pretoria in October 1984 but these talks soon collapsed. While Mozambique largely stood by the commitment it had made at Nkomati, documents captured from RENAMO bases showed that the South African military was continuing to provide support for the movement by direct airlifts and the occasional use of supply lines through Malawi.

24   Moreover, instead of reducing its armed actions after the Nkomati Agreement, RENAMO intensified its campaign, provisioning itself from the local population and replenishing its arms with weaponry captured from the Mozambique Armed Forces (FAM). In 1985 and 1986, RENAMO opened new fronts in Tete and Zambézia provinces.

When RENAMO began to threaten Zambézia's capital, Quelimane, the war reached a new pitch.

25   Mozambique's hard-pressed armed forces had to rely on the support of Tanzanian and Zimbabwean troops in its defensive campaigns in Zambézia, Manica and Sofala provinces. Zimbabwe's armed forces, originally deployed to protect the Beira corridor, were now drawn directly into the escalating civil conflict within Mozambique. In August 1985, a joint FAM-Zimbabwean force conducted a major operation to capture RENAMO's headquarters in Gorongosa district in Sofala Province; the base changed hands several times in the months that followed, although RENAMO eventually re-established its hold. On 19 October 1986, the Government of Mozambique suffered a major blow when President Machel died after his aircraft crashed on its return to Maputo following a regional summit meeting in Zambia. Mr. Joaquim Chissano, then the Minister for Foreign Affairs, was appointed President in November.

26   The conflict in Mozambique reached its widest extent in 1987, when RENAMO made gains in Tete, Nampula and Niassa provinces and undertook actions in the south of the country. An attack on the town of Homoine, Inhambane Province, on 18 July 1987 killed some 400 people. Later in the same year, there were massacres at Manjacaze, Gaza Province, and on Route Number 1, the national highway about 80 kilometres north of Maputo. There were widespread atrocities during the conflict, most of which were attributed to RENAMO, although there were also alleged abuses by Government troops acting outside the orders of their commanders.

27   By this time, the war had devastated the Mozambican economy, and the country had become increasingly dependent on foreign assistance. At this juncture the Government decided to undertake far-reaching economic reforms, abandoning its former Marxist philosophy in favour of political liberalization and a more market-oriented approach. By 1990, the principles of a multi-party system and other reforms had been enshrined in a new constitution. The Government's moves in this direction helped to win further financial and political support from Western Governments and kept RENAMO politically isolated. Still, the Government, its resources dissipated by years of war and the destabilization efforts of South Africa, was incapable of imposing a military solution to the conflict.

28   RENAMO, too, it was clear, did not have the sustained military capability to achieve its goal of bringing down the Government, even though, by 1988, it controlled wide areas of the countryside and one large town, Inhaminga in Sofala Province. With this military impasse, the possibility of a political solution gradually gained strength.

The deepening humanitarian tragedy

29   The war in Mozambique, which was already one of the world's poorest nations, had tragic consequences for its civilian population. RENAMO attacks on villages and towns often resulted in large numbers of civilian deaths, while others were forcibly evicted from their homes. RENAMO's policy of destroying the economic and social infrastructure—including roads, factories, schools, hospitals and clinics—and disrupting agricultural production resulted in widespread malnutrition, famine and death.

30   Hundreds of thousands of Mozambicans died as a result of the war, whether from direct or indirect causes. In addition, by late 1986, at least 3.2 million Mozambican rural dwellers had been displaced or otherwise affected, the number rising to 4.6 million by 1989 as many families from rural areas of Zambézia, Tete, Sofala and Manica provinces found relative safety in district towns and the Beira corridor. By this time, more than 1 million Mozambicans had fled to Malawi, the United Republic of Tanzania, Zambia and Zimbabwe to escape the fighting. International agencies estimated that about 250,000 children had been either orphaned or separated from their parents. School enrolment was reduced by an estimated 500,000 and medical facilities serving approximately 5 million people were destroyed, according to a study published by the United Nations Economic Commission for Africa.

31   In many parts of the country where RENAMO raids were most frequent, or where land-mines had made road travel dangerous, air transport remained the only viable means of providing the local population with its basic needs. RENAMO attacks in Maputo and Gaza provinces in 1989 and 1990 frequently targeted food relief convoys.

32   The United Nations mobilized and coordinated emergency assistance to alleviate the human suffering. A major international appeal for emergency assistance to Mozambique, launched in Geneva in February 1987, yielded over $330 million, including the monetary equivalent of 755,100 tons of food aid. The appeal coincided with the Government's inauguration of an ambitious structural adjustment and rehabilitation programme that focused on macroeconomic policy reforms. A United Nations Special Coordinator for Emergency Relief Operations was appointed for Mozambique in 1987 to integrate the objectives of the emergency programme with those for economic rehabilitation and development.[4]

4/Document 18
See page 131

33   At a meeting held in November 1989, the World Bank's Consultative Group for Mozambique agreed to expand the scope of the economic rehabilitation programme in order to alleviate poverty and war-related suffering. By 1990, virtually all the major United Nations agencies were active in Mozambique, in addition to other multilateral agencies, bilateral donors and official agencies from 35 countries and numerous external non-governmental organizations (NGOs) from 23 countries. An inter-agency mission to assess the situation in February 1990 noted that, among other things, RENAMO's targeting of the economic and social infrastructure had paralysed the country's productive capacity, leaving Mozambique dependent on external aid for 90 per cent of its cereal needs.

34   By 1990, Mozambique's annual per capita income was estimated at $150, very nearly the lowest in the world, and infant mortality was the world's second highest, with one out of every three children dying before reaching the age of five. The impressive social gains made by the FRELIMO Government in the first years of independence had been wiped out and, in fact, reversed.

35   As drought took hold in large areas of Mozambique over the next two years, the number of internally displaced persons needing emergency assistance continued to grow. The threat of famine and mass starvation was particularly severe for the rapidly growing numbers of displaced persons who sought refuge either along the protected Beira and Limpopo corridors or in neighbouring countries—which were themselves feeling the effects of a drought that was afflicting the entire subregion. The cost of Mozambique's 1992/93 emergency assistance programme, now targeted to 3.1 million people, amounted to more than $400 million.

36   Security considerations severely constrained the delivery and distribution of relief supplies. When the Tete corridor came under attack by RENAMO in early 1991, traffic between Zimbabwe and Malawi had to be re-routed through Zambia, causing delays in delivery and huge increases in costs. By late 1992, supply convoys to 74 of Mozambique's 128 districts needed armed escorts to ensure delivery. Numerous trucks were destroyed and many drivers were killed. Such conditions hindered any increase in relief operations, although a wide variety of donors remained strongly committed to assistance to alleviate Mozambique's human tragedy.[5]

5/Document 18
See page 131

III   Negotiations and agreement

37   For the FRELIMO Government, negotiation with a group it considered an externally inspired "bandit" force bent on seizing power through terror and destruction was generally considered an unacceptable course of action. But the devastation of the civil war—made more tragic by drought—coupled with the military impasse compelled a re-evaluation of this view. The Government's economic and political reforms also enhanced the prospects of accommodation. For its part, RENAMO, at a similar military stalemate, as well as organizationally weak and with the degree of its external material support uncertain, was also being pushed towards negotiations.

38   Tentative negotiations through Catholic Church intermediaries began in 1988 and rapidly involved African Governments—initially Kenya and Zimbabwe, and subsequently Botswana, Malawi and other members of the Front-line States, as well as South Africa. After indirect contact was made between the Government and RENAMO in late 1989, the process gained momentum gradually and came to be supported by the efforts of Italy, Portugal, the United Kingdom of Great Britain and Northern Ireland and the United States of America, as well as the United Nations.

39   The United Nations lent its advice and expertise, especially in the final stages of the negotiations in Rome beginning in June 1992. By this point it had become clear that the United Nations, being the only mutually acceptable—as well as the most appropriate—body to ensure implementation of the emerging General Peace Agreement for Mozambique, was the key to the successful culmination of the negotiations. The Organization was eventually asked to monitor and guarantee implementation of the Agreement in all its important aspects.

The start of negotiations

40   Establishing a basis for negotiations between the Mozambique Government and RENAMO was one of the most difficult peacemaking challenges of the late 1980s. The rebels, while politically isolated at the international level, were still receiving clandestine help from elements of the South African military. They were increasingly self-sufficient and continued to inflict heavy damage on the Mozambican economy.

41   Having been tied almost exclusively to South Africa in the past, RENAMO's leaders were reluctant to travel abroad or to establish contact with other Governments that might be willing to offer their good offices to end the conflict. Eventually, meaningful contact with RENAMO was established by the Community of Sant'Egidio, a Roman Catholic lay organization dedicated to social concerns. The community was familiar with the Mozambican crisis through its long association with Don Jaime Gonçalves, a Mozambican priest who had become Archbishop of Beira in 1977. Members of Sant'Egidio had helped to negotiate the release of priests and nuns held by RENAMO in 1982 and had played a facilitating role between the Vatican and the FRELIMO Government in 1985.

42   In May 1988, Archbishop Gonçalves travelled to rebel head-quarters in Gorongosa to explore with the RENAMO leader, Mr. Afonso Dhlakama, the possibility of developing negotiations between RENAMO and the Government. Despite obstacles, the Archbishop persisted in his efforts, helping to arrange meetings between Mozambican church leaders and RENAMO in Nairobi in February and August 1989. At the second of these meetings, the church leaders presented the Mozambique Government's proposals for peace to Mr. Dhlakama, who reciprocated with his own proposals, which the church leaders conveyed back to President Chissano.

43   The search for common ground between the two parties showed that, while both had a strong interest in peace, each remained highly distrustful of the other and could not accept the other's claim to legitimacy. In particular, RENAMO's demand to be considered as having a status equal with that of the Government in any direct negotiations was unacceptable to the authorities in Maputo.

44   For negotiations to begin, it was also essential to identify mutually acceptable mediators. RENAMO was willing to consider mediation by Kenya, or alternatively Portugal, the former colonial Power. The Government favoured joint mediation by Zimbabwe and Kenya. A number of other Governments cautiously expressed interest in facilitating talks but, when an opening round of direct talks hosted by Malawi failed to start in June 1990, the Community of Sant'Egidio offered Rome as an alternative, with the approval of the Government of Italy. The offer was promptly accepted by both sides.[6]

6/Document 44
See page 200

Agreement on basic principles

45   The first direct meeting between delegations of the Mozambique Government and RENAMO took place from 8 to 10 July 1990 at the Convent of Sant'Egidio in Rome. The talks resulted in the adoption of a joint communiqué on 10 July, with both sides agreeing to set aside what divided them and to focus on what united them in their common

7/Document 12
See page 105

search for an end to the war.[7] Although this was little more than a statement of intent to start negotiations, it was an achievement that was immediately welcomed by the European Community, the United States and many other Governments. By November 1990 the two sides had agreed on four individual mediators, representing the Italian Government (Mr. Mario Raffaelli), the Sant'Egidio Community (Professor Andrea Riccardi and Don Matteo Zuppi) and Mozambique's Episcopal Conference (Archbishop Jaime Gonçalves). The Governments of Botswana and Zimbabwe, among those represented at the Rome talks, played significant roles in the negotiations at this stage.

8/Document 1
See page 93

46   Soon after the opening of formal talks, a partial cease-fire was agreed to on 1 December 1990.[8] Under its terms, RENAMO would cease its attacks on the Beira and Limpopo transport corridors in return for an agreement by the Zimbabwean troops in Mozambique to confine their operations to those routes. While this partial cease-fire agreement did not address the conflict that still raged in wide areas of the country, it sought to protect the highly vulnerable corridors. The guarantee of access to the corridors was to become of major importance for the movement of food relief during the drought that affected southern Africa in 1991 and 1992. The agreement also established the precedent of a joint commission to monitor the cease-fire. Members of the Joint Verification Commission were the Congo, France, Kenya, Portugal, the USSR, the United Kingdom, the United States and Zambia. RENAMO was permitted to send a representative to Maputo for commission meetings.

47   The partial cease-fire was not a success, as RENAMO, claiming that Zimbabwean troops were operating elsewhere in Mozambique, continued to attack the transport corridors. During 1991, progress towards a more substantial peace agreement was also slowed by RENAMO's refusal to recognize the legitimacy either of the Government or of its moves—first made in 1990—to institute multi-party democracy.

48   An agenda for full peace negotiations was eventually agreed upon on 28 May 1991, specifying six areas requiring agreement: the law on political parties, the electoral system, military issues, guarantees, a cease-fire and a donors conference. However, the issue of legitimacy continued to prevent any progress on these items until agreement was reached at the eighth round of talks, in Rome on 18 October, on Protocol I, what would become the "Basic principles" of the General

9/Document 12
See page 105

Peace Agreement.[9]

49   The first protocol settled two important issues that were to guide the negotiations over the next 12 months. The first of these was the question of the Mozambican Government's legitimacy. RENAMO agreed to respect the authority and institutions of the Government, to renounce the use of force and "to conduct its political struggle in

conformity with the laws in force" after the enactment of a cease-fire (Protocol I, point 2). In return, the Government promised to delay legislation on any issue under discussion until after democratic multi-party elections.

50   The other important issue to be settled was the principle of establishing a commission to supervise and monitor the peace process. Already at this stage, the negotiators felt that the United Nations would play a critical role, although its precise nature had yet to be fully clarified. The Protocol simply declared: "The commission shall be composed of representatives of the Government, RENAMO, the United Nations and other organizations or Governments to be agreed upon between the parties" (Protocol I, point 5).

51   Building on these "Basic principles", the mediators pursued the formulation of a full peace agreement over the next 12 months, with the increasingly active participation of the international community and with direct assistance from the Governments of Italy and the United States. Protocol II, on the "Criteria and arrangements for the formation and recognition of political parties", was signed in November 1991, and Protocol III, on "Principles of the Electoral Act", covering such issues as freedom of the press, freedom of association and expression and freedom of movement, as well as the principles of the country's electoral system, was signed in March 1992. Chapter VI of the Protocol called for international assistance in the electoral process, specifically from the United Nations and the Organization of African Unity.[10]

52   The parties then attended to the most difficult issues, including the formation of a new Mozambican army and other military matters, and guarantees covering the peace process and a cease-fire. The final four protocols (Nos. IV, V, VI and VII) were concluded only during the final rounds of negotiation in the second half of 1992 and were signed together on 4 October 1992.[11]

10/Document 12
See page 105

11/Document 12
See page 105

Involving the United Nations

53   In the course of the negotiations, the need to secure the services of the United Nations as an impartial guarantor of the peace process emerged only gradually. Initially, RENAMO was more in favour of the presence of the United Nations than was the Government, which viewed the war as having had an international dimension but also had deeply felt concerns about the implications that a United Nations presence would have in several areas relating to national sovereignty. The Government was also concerned by the possibility that RENAMO could improve its political status as a result of such United Nations involvement. However, consensus developed on the need for impartial manage-

ment of the peace process, and the United Nations was clearly the institution that could best provide this.

12/Document 2
See page 94

13/Document 3
See page 95

14/Document 4
See page 96;
Document 5
See page 96

54   On 28 May, I wrote to President Chissano offering the services of the United Nations in promoting an agreement between the Government and RENAMO.[12] On 1 June, President Chissano responded by outlining, in a letter to me, the elements of the agreements signed thus far which envisaged a role for the Organization. Specifically, the two parties intended, once a peace agreement was concluded, to formally invite the Organization to participate in a commission that would supervise and monitor compliance with the accord, and to provide assistance for the electoral process.[13] The latter invitation was received by the United Nations in July, following the Government's announcement of a plan to hold multi-party elections one year after the signature of the cease-fire agreement.[14]

55   In June 1992, United Nations military observers joined the Rome negotiations in an expert capacity, providing technical advice on cease-fire monitoring. By August, a United Nations Senior Political Affairs Officer was also present. For the United Nations itself, consideration of a peace-keeping operation in Mozambique required close study and consultation. A strong link was needed between the peace process and the delivery of humanitarian aid; roads required urgent repair and mine clearance; and the number of military observers would be influenced by the quantity and location of sites at which the troops of the two sides would assemble, an issue that had not yet been determined in Rome.

56   In July, a number of United Nations and international agencies, including the Office of the United Nations High Commissioner for Refugees (UNHCR), the World Food Programme (WFP) and the International Committee of the Red Cross (ICRC), assisted in the preparation of a Declaration on the Guiding Principles for Humanitarian Assistance, which was agreed to by the Government of Mozambique and RENAMO

15/Document 12
See page 105

and issued on 16 July.[15] The declaration established two important principles: that there should be no discrimination in delivering humanitarian assistance to affected Mozambicans, and that there would be freedom of movement throughout the country for humanitarian personnel or goods travelling under United Nations or ICRC flags. Both the Government and RENAMO also undertook not to derive military advantage from humanitarian assistance operations.

57   To follow up on the Declaration, a Committee for Humanitarian Assistance was established in Maputo, chaired by the United Nations Special Coordinator for Emergency Relief Operations and including representatives of United Nations agencies, the ICRC, neighbouring countries and major donor Governments. The committee negotiated with RENAMO on delivery of relief to areas under its control.

58   In a 4 July meeting with Zimbabwe's President Robert Mugabe and Botswana's President Sir Ketumile Masire in Gaborone, Botswana, Mr. Dhlakama declared his readiness to sign a cease-fire under the condition of guaranteed security for himself and RENAMO supporters and freedom for RENAMO to operate as a political party. After further meetings with President Mugabe, as well as with South Africa's President F. W. de Klerk, President Chissano agreed to meet with Mr. Dhlakama.

59   President Chissano and Mr. Dhlakama finally met face to face in Rome on 7 August 1992. There they signed a joint political declaration guaranteeing agreement on outstanding issues by 1 October 1992.[16] The Joint Declaration also committed the parties to "accepting the role of the international community, and especially that of the United Nations, in monitoring and guaranteeing the implementation of the General Peace Agreement, in particular the cease-fire and the electoral process".

16/Document 12
See page 105

60   On 19 August, I wrote to President Chissano detailing the arrangements for a United Nations operation to implement the General Peace Agreement, which included the appointment of a Special Representative and the creation of mechanisms to verify both military and civilian aspects of the peace process.[17] President Chissano requested that United Nations technical teams—one to evaluate the cease-fire arrangements, the other to assess the organization of the electoral process— arrive in Mozambique by 26 August. The Government wanted the cease-fire to commence no later than seven days after the signing of an agreement.[18]

17/Document 6
See page 97

18/Document 7
See page 100

61   By early September 1992, agreement between the two parties was close, but certain issues were holding up the conclusion of the remaining protocols. These included the precise details of the cease-fire, the role of the Government's security services and the control and administration of the territory claimed by RENAMO. President Chissano and Mr. Dhlakama met again on 18 September, this time in Gaborone. They reached agreement on most of these outstanding issues and announced that they would sign the final documents in Rome by 1 October. Despite this breakthrough, the drafting of texts posed a final challenge for the mediators, especially as RENAMO was reluctant to accept the legitimacy of the Government's territorial administration during the peace process.

62   In early September, I sent the two technical teams, on cease-fire arrangements and electoral organization, to Mozambique. On 10 September, I briefed the Security Council, noting that the Mozambican parties had been informed that the dispatch of the two teams did not imply United Nations agreement to assume the role desired of it. However, it was clear that if, as I hoped, the talks between the parties continued to progress, I would soon be recommending to the Council the establishment of a substantial new peace-keeping operation in Mozambique. On 22 September, President Chissano wrote to me requesting United Nations financial support in the areas of national reconstruction, reintegration of refugees and demobilized soldiers, formation of the new national army and organization of democratic elections.[19]

19/Document 8
See page 101

63   On 29 September, I sent a letter to the President of the Security Council in which I emphasized the importance of entrusting the chairmanship of the supervisory commissions to an impartial third party. I pointed out that "past experience has shown that such joint machinery functions best when the chairmanship is entrusted to an impartial third party, rather than alternating between the two protagonists".[20] Ultimately, the parties agreed to entrust the United Nations with chairmanship of the Supervisory and Monitoring Commission, which would monitor implementation of the entire Agreement, as well as of two subsidiary commissions, which would oversee implementation of the cease-fire. I also stressed the need for precision in determining the number and location of assembly points for the forces of the two sides, so that plans for the United Nations monitoring operation could be prepared. This last point remained under discussion even as the respective delegations arrived in Rome for the signing ceremony, and, in fact, no final decision was made on the number or location of the assembly points until after the General Peace Agreement was signed.

20/Document 10
See page 102

64   Mr. Dhlakama did not arrive in Rome until the evening of 1 October. It was apparent that before the General Peace Agreement could be finalized and signed, further negotiations were necessary on the issues of the security services, the police, the civilian administration and the assembly areas. In these last-minute talks, agreements were reached on the security services and police matters (Protocol IV, sections IV and V) and, finally, on a national commission on administrative matters to be formed by the two parties (Protocol V, section III, point 9). Much of these discussions concentrated on the role of the United Nations. The timing of the Organization's arrival on the ground was critical, with both parties expressing a desire to have a United Nations presence in Mozambique by 15 October, the date the cease-fire was to go into effect. My representative at the talks met both President Chissano and Mr. Dhlakama to address these concerns.

65   Once these outstanding issues—with the exception of the location of assembly areas—were resolved, the General Peace Agreement was signed on 4 October by both President Chissano and Mr. Dhlakama in the presence of the Presidents of Botswana and Zimbabwe, senior ministers from Kenya, Malawi and South Africa and representatives of the observers. At the Rome signing ceremony, President Chissano handed my representative a copy of the Agreement with a

letter formally requesting prompt and speedy United Nations implementation of the peace accords.[21]

21/Document 12
See page 105

An extensive United Nations role

66   The General Peace Agreement required the United Nations to perform a comprehensive range of tasks. The first and most urgent priority was that the Organization undertake verification of the cease-fire from the first day the Peace Agreement was to come into force (Protocol VI, section I, points 5 and 6, and Protocol VI, section II). In this connection, and also as a matter of priority, the United Nations was required to supervise the withdrawal of foreign troops from Mozambican territory, a measure that was intended to be achieved within one month of the start of the cease-fire (Protocol VI, section I, point 10 (*c*)).

67   Of equal importance was the invitation to the United Nations to undertake the overall supervision of the peace process. This was made specific in the declared commitment of the Government of Mozambique to "submit a formal request to the United Nations for its participation in monitoring and guaranteeing the implementation of the General Peace Agreement" (Protocol V, section III, point 1). United Nations supervision was clarified by the explicit commitment that the chairman of the Supervisory and Monitoring Commission (CSC), the body charged with overall responsibility for monitoring and supervising implementation of the Agreement, should be appointed by the Secretary-General of the United Nations (Protocol V, section II, points 1 and 2). This superseded the preliminary agreement, reached in 1991, that the United Nations should be merely a member of the CSC (Protocol I, point 5).

68   The General Peace Agreement also allocated to the United Nations the chairmanships of the Cease-fire Commission (CCF) and the Reintegration Commission (CORE), and further asked it to assist in the implementation, verification and monitoring of the entire demobilization process (Protocol IV, section VI (i), points 2 and 3). These points were again amplified in Protocol VI, which provided details of the cease-fire and its timetable (Protocol VI, section I, points 1, 2, 5, 6, 7 and 8, and section II). At the time the General Peace Agreement was signed, the annexes on assembly areas had not yet been provided; the locations of the assembly areas were only specified some weeks later.

69   In addition to the supervisory and military responsibilities, the General Peace Agreement assigned a number of other tasks to the United Nations. The parties agreed to seek the involvement of the competent United Nations agencies in drawing up and implementing the plan to return Mozambican refugees and displaced persons (Protocol III, section IV (*b*). They agreed to invite the United Nations to observe the electoral

process and to provide technical and material assistance for the holding of elections (Protocol III, section VI). They also empowered the Supervisory and Monitoring Commission to settle any disputes relating to the registration of political parties (Protocol II, point 5 (*d*)).

70   Although not all aspects of the General Peace Agreement specifically required United Nations monitoring, the supervisory role allocated to the Organization carried the implication of responsibility for the entire peace process in Mozambique. The implementation of each part of the process was likely to come under the purview of the Supervisory and Monitoring Commission and therefore of the United Nations.

71   The points contained in Protocol IV, which dealt with a range of military questions, were of special significance to the overall process. Among the protocol's requirements was the formation of three additional commissions: a Joint Commission for the Formation of the Mozambican Defence Force (CCFADM—Protocol IV, section I (iii)); a National Information Commission (COMINFO—Protocol IV, section IV, point 7), which was to monitor and investigate the functioning of the security police; and a National Police Affairs Commission (COMPOL—Protocol IV, section V, point 7).

72   Other commissions to be established under the terms of the General Peace Agreement included a National Elections Commission (CNE—Protocol III, section V, point 3) and one that was proposed for the facilitation of "collaboration and good understanding" between the Government and the administration in areas of Mozambique that were controlled by RENAMO (Protocol V, section III, point 9 (*d*)). The name of the latter commission was eventually established as the National Commission on Administration (CNA).

73   Immediately upon the signing of the peace accords on 4 October 1992, the United Nations moved to implement one of the most extensive peace-keeping operations in its history. The Organization was encouraged by the positive indications that Mozambicans were ready for peace after a decade and a half of war. Despite the problems being encountered at this time in the Angolan peace-keeping operation—important lessons from which were incorporated into ONUMOZ—hopes for a peaceful settlement were also strongly buoyed by political reforms taking place across the southern African subregion, particularly developments occurring inside South Africa.

IV Establishing ONUMOZ

74   The signing of the General Peace Agreement in Rome had triggered an immediate invitation from the Government of Mozambique to the United Nations to undertake a comprehensive peace-keeping operation that would guide the country from armed conflict to democratic and peaceful elections.[22]

22/Document 12
See page 105

75   As proposed in my 3 December report to the Security Council, which the Council approved on 16 December, ONUMOZ's mandate included four distinct, but interlocking, sets of objectives—political, military, electoral and humanitarian.[23] The overall success of the mission would be dependent on parallel progress in each of these sectors. As I stated in my report, the task facing the United Nations was large and difficult. In October 1992, neither the Government nor RENAMO nor the United Nations was in a position to begin fully implementing the provisions of the General Peace Agreement, and it became increasingly clear that the one-year timetable specified in the Rome accords was unrealistic. Nevertheless, from the outset of ONUMOZ many donor countries indicated their willingness to provide additional assistance, while the greatest assurance came from ordinary Mozambicans, who welcomed the arrival of peace in their country. For the United Nations, the most immediate objective was to build upon the achievements of the Rome Agreement. The Organization needed to instill confidence in both parties, and in the Mozambican population as a whole, the idea that the peace process could succeed.

23/Document 26
See page 149;
Document 27
See page 158

Sustaining the peace

76   In my first report to the Security Council on a possible United Nations operation in Mozambique, on 9 October 1992, I pointed out that only a token presence could be established in the country by 15 October, the date on which the cease-fire was due to become effective.[24] The viability of the cease-fire would therefore depend almost entirely on the political will of the two parties and their strict compliance with the terms of the Agreement.

24/Document 13
See page 126

77   The United Nations was quick to lend whatever support it could to keep the peace process on track. On 13 October, the Security Council approved my appointment of an interim Special Representative and the dispatch of a team of up to 25 military observers.[25] I appointed Mr. Aldo Ajello (Italy), a senior staff member of the United Nations

25/Document 16
See page 130

Development Programme (UNDP), as my Special Representative (initially on an interim basis) and asked him to proceed to Maputo to help the parties carry out the actions required of them at the beginning of the peace process.

78   The Special Representative and a team of 21 military observers arrived in Mozambique on 15 October as the General Peace Agreement came into force. On 20 October, two teams of military observers were deployed to Nampula and Beira. As I reported to the Security Council on 23 October, my Special Representative quickly set a precedent of regular meetings by visiting President Chissano (in Maputo) and Mr. Dhlakama (in Maringue, Sofala Province), and by establishing contact with their high-ranking representatives and those of the Organization of African Unity (OAU) and the diplomatic community in Maputo.[26] Key among the latter were the ambassadors of those States which had played a leading role in mediating or observing the peace negotiations.

26/Document 19
See page 141

79   The first major difficulty was encountered with RENAMO's wish to maintain its headquarters in Gorongosa, instead of relocating to Maputo, until the Government provided adequate logistic support, i.e. appropriate housing, transport and communications facilities as foreseen in the Agreement. RENAMO also lacked sufficient personnel able to deal with the complex machinery of the commissions, and thus had to train its people as well as identify new recruits. The Government, for its part, did not have the resources for the enormous task of setting up RENAMO in Maputo and the nation's provincial capitals. It took many months to resolve this problem satisfactorily. RENAMO's absence from the capital impeded the establishment of the monitoring and verification machinery that was specified by the General Peace Agreement. Thus, major violations reported in the days following the cease-fire could not be effectively investigated.[27] These violations prompted a statement of concern by the Security Council and, in order to overcome this immediate potential crisis, my Special Representative convened an informal meeting of the two parties, who responded by sending high-level delegations to Maputo on 29 October.[28] The meeting greatly helped to defuse the atmosphere of political and military tension, and no further major cease-fire violations occurred.

27/Document 19
See page 141;
Document 21
See page 144

28/Document 20
See page 143

80   Once the precedent of such meetings had been set, serious discussions between the parties' senior delegations could begin and the first cautious moves towards implementing the General Peace Agreement became possible. Although Mr. Dhlakama remained in Maringue, some of his senior colleagues took up residence in the capital. On 4 November, one month after the signing of the Agreement, the Supervisory and Monitoring Commission (CSC) was appointed and held its first meeting, at which the composition of the three main subsidiary commissions was

also agreed: the Cease-fire Commission (CCF), the Commission for Reintegration (CORE) and the Joint Commission for the Formation of the Mozambican Defence Force (CCFADM). The United Nations assumed chairmanship of the CSC, the CCF and the CORE but, in accordance with the terms of the Peace Agreement, was not at this stage requested to participate in the CCFADM.

81   In addition to the Government of Mozambique and RENAMO, the commissions chaired by the United Nations had the following members: CSC—France, Italy, Portugal, the United Kingdom, the United States and the OAU (with Germany invited to join later); CCF—Botswana, Egypt, France, Italy, Nigeria, Portugal, the United Kingdom and the United States (with Kenya and Zimbabwe invited to join later); CORE—Denmark, France, Germany, Italy, the Netherlands, Norway, Portugal, South Africa, Spain, Sweden, Switzerland, the United Kingdom, the United States and the European Community.[29]

29/Document 26
See page 149

Assessing the size of ONUMOZ

82   It was clear from the outset of the operation that a substantial United Nations presence was needed to ensure the success of the peace process. As the international community weighed the human and material resources that a United Nations operation in Mozambique would require, three parallel considerations had to be taken into account: the need for impartiality and support for the peace process; the responsibility of the international community in helping to rebuild a country devastated by war; and the insecurity still prevailing over wide areas of the country and, in particular, along the major transport corridors, which were of critical importance to humanitarian operations in southern Africa as a whole as well as to the economies of neighbouring countries. It was anticipated that large quantities of food and emergency assistance would need to be transported to countries throughout the subregion, which was threatened by its most severe drought in living memory.

83   The need to secure the corridors emerged as the principal determinant of the size of the military component of the operation. In order to protect the routes after the departure of the Zimbabwean and Malawian forces, at least five logistically self-sufficient infantry battalions were needed, assisted by the necessary support units, including engineering battalions, military logistic companies, military communications units, an aviation unit and a medical unit (see map, page 30). In recommending this requirement to the Security Council in the operational plan I presented on 3 December, I noted that it was critically important to deploy troops quickly in the Beira and Nacala corridors.[30] The 15 October deadline for the withdrawal of the troops from Malawi

30/Document 26
See page 149

and Zimbabwe had passed, and, in a 17 November letter to Prime Minister Giuliano Amato of Italy, I had appealed for an advance contingent.[31]

84   In my operational plan, I also noted the desirability of deploying a police monitoring unit to monitor human rights and liberties and to provide technical advice to the National Police Affairs Commission. The need for such monitors was rejected by the Government at the time, but was to be accepted eventually.[32] Another important role for the United Nations was the coordination of humanitarian activities in Mozambique with the priorities of the peace process. Assistance was required in resettling Mozambicans displaced by the war within and outside the country while maintaining ongoing drought and famine relief operations being undertaken throughout the southern African region.

85   It was apparent to all concerned that Mozambique's planned elections should not take place until the military aspects of the Agreement had been implemented. This conclusion was reinforced by the events following Angola's elections in the preceding weeks; there, the failure to complete demobilization had enabled the loser of the election to launch an all-out war. In Mozambique, demobilization of the two sides' forces would have to be vigorously pursued, and arrangements would have to be made for the control and disposal of weapons and ammunition. United Nations verification would be carried out by teams of military observers.

86   The electoral process itself, to be credible, required the establishment of an electoral division and extensive technical and logistic support as well as the services of a large number of international observers during the polling process. The broad range of needs included assistance in the drawing up of an electoral law and training for national election monitors.

87   In recommending these and other elements of the operation to the Security Council, I said: "In the light of recent experiences elsewhere, the recommendations in the present report may be thought to invite the international community to take a risk. I believe that the risk is worth taking; but I cannot disguise that it exists".[33]

88   On 16 December 1992, the Security Council approved the establishment of the United Nations Operation in Mozambique (ONUMOZ) and agreed to its mandate for the political, military, electoral and humanitarian objectives outlined in my report by a unanimous vote on resolution 797 (1992).[34]

89   The Security Council encouraged Member States to respond positively to requests for contributions of personnel and equipment. A donors conference on Mozambique was held on 15 and 16 December in Rome, at which the participants pledged nearly $400 million for an emergency reintegration programme.[35] The programme targeted

31/Document 24
See page 147;
Document 25
See page 148

32/Document 26
See page 149

33/Document 26
See page 149

34/Document 27
See page 158

35/Document 23
See page 146

26   THE UNITED NATIONS AND MOZAMBIQUE, *1992-1995*

displaced persons, returning refugees and demobilized soldiers and also provided for technical assistance for the electoral process.[36]

36/Document 28
See page 159

90   Despite the strong international support for ONUMOZ expressed by resolution 797 (1992), and despite the desire of both President Chissano and Mr. Dhlakama to get the peace-keeping operation under way, a significant delay occurred in securing definite commitments from Member States to contribute troops to the operation. Many national armed forces with peace-keeping experience were already heavily committed to other United Nations operations. Fortunately, Italy, following up its role as host and one of the initial mediators of the Rome accords, gave early indication of its support, confirming on 12 December its readiness to provide one self-sufficient infantry battalion. The unit itself would be able to control the Beira corridor, and its deployment would permit the withdrawal of the Zimbabwean forces. The first offers of other national contingents came during January 1993.

A slow beginning

91   Logistical and procedural problems were inevitable in establishing a military and administrative presence as complex as that to be undertaken by ONUMOZ. The Government also needed time to address concerns in the National Assembly about the implications for national sovereignty of such a large and comprehensive international operation. A further delay in the deployment of ONUMOZ forces was caused by the slow pace of negotiations to conclude a status-of-forces agreement between the United Nations and the Government, which would permit the movement of United Nations military personnel without prior approval of the authorities. This agreement was not signed until 14 May 1993.[37]

37/Document 33
See page 173

92   The delay in the deployment of peace-keeping troops made it necessary to retain the presence of Zimbabwean and Malawian forces along the vital transport corridors, despite the commitment in the peace accords to their early withdrawal. A precipitous withdrawal would have created a dangerous vacuum, leading to a deterioration in the security situation and thereby jeopardizing the entire peace process. At first, Mr. Dhlakama did not accept the need to keep the Zimbabwean and Malawian military in place until the arrival of the United Nations battalions. He finally agreed following a meeting with President Mugabe of Zimbabwe in Harare on 11 December, but also began to insist that he could not consent to the assembly and demobilization of RENAMO troops until 65 per cent of the planned ONUMOZ force had been deployed, particularly in RENAMO areas.[38] The Government, for its part, asked for wider deployment of ONUMOZ forces so that the

38/Document 29
See page 170;
Document 30
See page 171

movements of RENAMO and Government forces could be monitored equally.

93   Groups of military cease-fire observers, drawn from several different countries, began to arrive in February 1993. On 13 February, I appointed Major-General Lélio Gonçalves Rodrigues da Silva (Brazil) as Force Commander of ONUMOZ. By mid-March, 154 military observers drawn from 12 countries had been deployed, primarily in Maputo, Beira, Matola and Nampula. While the cease-fire held, demobilization of the two sides' armed forces remained stalled because of their continuing failure to supply complete lists of their troop strength, arms and ammunition, as they had originally pledged to do by 15 October 1992. The Joint Commission for the Formation of the Mozambican Defence Force (CCFADM) could not begin sitting, as the two parties had not named their respective delegations.[39]

39/Document 33
See page 173

94   A further hindrance to the start of demobilization was the unsuitability of the designated assembly points for the cantonment of troops. During November 1992, the Government had identified 29 assembly points and RENAMO had identified 20, but for many of them access, either for purposes of verification or for prolonged habitation, was difficult. They had been designated more for their strategic importance in controlling certain areas than for their suitability for cantonment. Some could be reached only by roads or tracks that were known to be mined; some had no access to water and therefore could not sustain temporary settlement. After investigating the sites with a view to preparing for the supply and well-being of troops once the assembly process began, the United Nations asked for several to be relocated.[40]

40/Document 33
See page 173

95   During the first three months of 1993, both the Supervisory and Monitoring Commission (CSC) and the Cease-fire Commission (CCF) held a number of meetings to establish procedural guidelines. The CCF was the most active commission, reviewing alleged violations of the cease-fire, including troop movements by both sides. It developed a national policy for clearing land-mines and established a plan for immediate mine-clearing activities on a number of roads that were essential for the provision of humanitarian assistance. The Reintegration Commission (CORE) held one session.[41]

41/Document 33
See page 173

96   The work of both the CSC and the CCF became stalled, however, after the departure from Maputo on 9 March of the head of the RENAMO negotiating team and its representative to the CSC, Mr. Raúl Domingos. RENAMO representatives to the other commissions—CCF and CORE—also returned to their headquarters in Maringue, paralysing the work of the commissions for more than three months, although RENAMO officials remained in communication with ONUMOZ. RENAMO's absence from the capital also meant that the subsidiary commissions covering the formation of the armed forces,

police affairs, territorial administration and the electoral process could not be established. The absence of the electoral commission, and a continuing failure to agree on an electoral law, had particularly serious implications for the one-year timetable for the peace process.

97   The official reason given by RENAMO for its absence from Maputo was a lack of logistical support from the Government. It maintained that international funding to help it become a political party had not materialized and cited a key clause of the General Peace Agreement in support of its claim (Protocol III, section V, point 7 (*b*) and (*c*)).[42] Some of these logistical problems would be addressed by a Trust Fund, established by the United Nations in May, which enabled RENAMO to settle in Maputo and other provincial capitals and to recruit new people and train them for assignment on the commissions.[43]

42/Document 12
See page 105

43/Document 37
See page 184

98   By the time I reported to the Security Council on 2 April 1993, it was evident that elections could not be held by October 1993.[44] Most authoritative estimates suggested a postponement of one year, in part because an election process could not be organized during the season of intense rainfall between November and March, but also because the demobilization of forces remained stalled. On 14 April, in its resolution 818 (1993), the Security Council expressed its concern at the delays in the implementation of major aspects of the Peace Agreement and urged the Government and RENAMO to take urgent and determined steps to comply with their commitments under the Agreement.[45]

44/Document 33
See page 173

99   The administration of ONUMOZ was meanwhile severely hampered by financial constraints which affected its recruitment and deployment of key personnel as well as its arrangements for accommodation and other essential services. After a start-up allocation of $9.5 million, the operation did not receive approval of its first interim budget, amounting to $140 million, from the General Assembly until 16 March 1993.[46]

45/Document 34
See page 180;
Document 35
See page 181

100   It was only between March and May 1993, as the five infantry battalions began to arrive, that ONUMOZ became a significant military presence in Mozambique. Each battalion was allocated a different transport corridor: Bangladesh along the Nacala-Malawi railway line; Botswana along the Tete road corridor between Malawi and Zimbabwe; Italy along the road, rail and pipeline corridor between Beira and Zimbabwe; Uruguay along the south-north Route Number 1, the national highway between Maputo and Beira; and Zambia along the Limpopo valley railway line connecting Maputo and Zimbabwe (see map, page 30). Italy's battalion, the first to be deployed, provided important logistical equipment, a medical element and an air wing. India provided logistics and engineering companies, Portugal provided a small signals battalion and Argentina sent a medical unit.

46/Document 33
See page 173

101   The stationing of Italy's ONUMOZ troops along the Beira corridor allowed for the withdrawal of Zimbabwean forces by 15 April, in

Initial ONUMOZ military deployment along transport corridors, May 1993

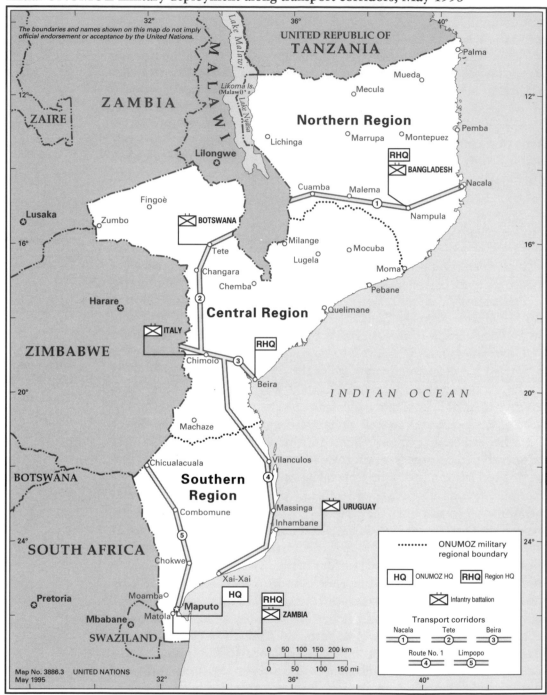

Providing security to Mozambique's vital transport corridors was a major factor in determining the initial deployment of ONUMOZ's military component. Deployment commenced in April 1993 and was largely completed within two months.

fulfilment of a key item in the General Peace Agreement.[47] Zimbabwe's withdrawal was followed in early June by the departure of the last Malawian troops from the Nacala corridor, where the Bangladesh troops were now stationed. Both withdrawals were verified by United Nations military observers. The other ONUMOZ battalions took up their positions along the designated corridors by early May. Deployment was completed over the following two months, and by the end of August 1993 the total number of troops was just over 6,000. ONUMOZ military strength remained at around this level until the middle of 1994, when a reduction of the military component commenced in anticipation of the winding down of the operation. The largest providers of military personnel at the end of August 1993 were Bangladesh (1,363), Italy (1,010), India (899), Zambia (831), Uruguay (816), Botswana (721) and Portugal (280).[48]

47/Document 37
See page 184

102 By August, the number of military observers numbered 303, provided by Bangladesh, Brazil, the Czech Republic, Egypt, Guinea-Bissau, Hungary, India, Malaysia, the Russian Federation, Spain, Sweden and Uruguay. The observers surveyed the assembly areas for demobilization and established a presence in those that were suitable; they also investigated reports of cease-fire violations. In the meantime, the United Nations contingents were able to provide logistic support both for the observers and for a range of humanitarian operations, including escorting food convoys and repairing and surveying roads.

48/Document 40
See page 190

Progress resumes

103 By mid-1993, peace was still being maintained in Mozambique, regardless of the slippage in the demanding timetable set by the General Peace Agreement. The spontaneous return of refugees from neighbouring countries, particularly from Malawi, continued as it had since the signing of the Agreement even though they faced the risk of land-mines and the absence of basic services in many areas of return. International agencies and donors had to move quickly to prepare large-scale programmes to improve the supply of food and services for returnees.

104 At the Donors Conference for Mozambique held in Rome in December 1992, participating countries had committed themselves to providing additional funds to support the democratic process in Mozambique.[49] On 10 May 1993, the United Nations established a Trust Fund for the Implementation of the Peace Agreement, with an initial contribution of almost $6 million from Italy.[50] Protocol III of the General Peace Agreement had enunciated the need to ensure that RENAMO had the facilities to carry out its political activities in all areas of the country and

49/Document 28
See page 159

50/Document 31
See page 172;
Document 32
See page 172

envisioned that the Government would seek support from the international community, particularly Italy, for this purpose. The Trust Fund was the response to this requirement and proved critical to the peace process, as it helped to finance the transformation of RENAMO from a rebel force into a political party that would be able to campaign effectively in the electoral process.[51]

51/Document 12
See page 105;
Document 37
See page 184

105   At the end of May, RENAMO met informally with my Special Representative and the Government to prepare to resume the work of the commissions. The first full meetings of the Supervisory and Monitoring Commission (CSC) and the Cease-fire Commission (CCF) to be held since early March were convened on 3 June 1993. Preparations were also made for the functioning of the other commissions, with the exception of the Electoral and State Administration commissions, which covered areas on which the Government and RENAMO continued to be divided.

106   The draft electoral law prepared by the Government was presented to Mozambique's other political parties on 26 March 1993. However, a multi-party meeting called by the Government on 27 April to discuss the draft failed to produce a consensus. RENAMO refused to attend and 12 other parties—which constituted the so-called "unarmed opposition"—walked out after presenting a number of demands, including one for financial support from the Government.[52] At the end of June,

52/Document 37
See page 184

at the Cairo Summit of the Organization of African Unity, I had the opportunity to discuss with President Chissano the issue of creating additional ad hoc funds, similar in purpose to the Trust Fund already established for RENAMO, to strengthen the campaigning capabilities of the other parties. In time, the Government announced that it was setting aside funding and housing for other opposition parties and in early April 1994, a special trust fund was established for other registered political parties.[53]

53/Document 63
See page 232

107   Establishment of an electoral law and training of the armed forces were two other issues which had to be resolved before the electoral process could move forward. By the end of June, it was broadly accepted that elections could not be held in Mozambique until September or October 1994 at the earliest. The Security Council, in resolution 850 (1993) of 9 July, also underlined the importance of holding the elections no later than October 1994.[54]

54/Document 38
See page 189

108   Under the terms of the General Peace Agreement, the formation of the new Mozambican army was to begin immediately after the cease-fire was established and was to be conducted simultaneously with the concentration, disarmament and integration into civilian life of the demobilized personnel. Each side was to contribute an equal number of troops. Following delays in this regard, the two parties—having earlier agreed that United Nations chairmanship would be most appropriate in

the event that either demobilization or the formation of the new army failed to get under way—decided to request my Special Representative to assume chairmanship of the Joint Commission for the Formation of the Mozambican Defence Force (CCFADM). In my 30 June report to the Security Council, I expressed readiness to accede to the request on the strict understanding that this would not entail any United Nations obligation to train or establish the armed forces.[55] In its resolution of 9 July, the Security Council approved my recommendation.[56]

55/Document 37
See page 184

56/Document 38
See page 189

109 The first meeting of the CCFADM, chaired by the United Nations, was held on 22 July, with its membership consisting of representatives of the two parties and the Governments that had agreed by that time to contribute to the formation of the new army (France, Portugal and the United Kingdom). The Joint Commission immediately decided to initiate training of instructors for the new Mozambican Defence Force (FADM) by sending 50 officers from the Government and 50 from RENAMO to attend the course run by the United Kingdom at the training facility at Nyanga, Zimbabwe. Additional officers would follow in due course. Other agreements covered the timetable for the formation of the FADM and the structure of its high command.[57]

57/Document 40
See page 190

Risks of confrontation

110 The cease-fire continued to be respected in most of Mozambique, but two potentially serious violations that came before the CCF during June and July 1993 were transferred to the CSC for consideration. Both incidents raised the issue of territorial and administrative control, which had been a sticking point in the negotiations over the General Peace Agreement and remained essentially unresolved. In the first incident, RENAMO detained 27 people in Maputo Province, claiming that they had been hunting in the area of RENAMO-controlled Salamanga without permission. Negotiations with RENAMO conducted by my Special Representative in conjunction with the head of the RENAMO delegation to the CSC, Mr. Raúl Domingos, succeeded in obtaining the prisoners' return to Maputo. In the second incident, the Government attempted to forcibly dislodge RENAMO from three villages in Tete Province and one in Gaza Province on the grounds that RENAMO had moved into these areas after the signing of the General Peace Agreement. The Government's action implied that it had the right to use force to reclaim territory that it considered to be under its control.[58]

58/Document 40
See page 190

111 My Special Representative, supported by other CSC members, declared that disputes of any kind could be resolved only within the mechanisms established under the General Peace Agreement. Hoping to defuse what was a potentially explosive issue, he formulated a set of rules to guide the CCF in dealing with troop movements. The rules separated the military and logistic aspects of troop movements from those relating to the administration of territory. They also defined as cease-fire violations all military movements conducted for the purpose of gaining new positions and required all troops moved for such purposes to be withdrawn. While RENAMO at first requested more time to approve the guidelines, it indicated a readiness to accept the principle of a single administration throughout the country.[59]

59/Document 40
See page 190

112   Appreciably greater progress was possible once Mr. Dhlakama took up residence in Maputo during August 1993, although he still did not move there permanently. For the first time since signing the General Peace Agreement, President Chissano and Mr. Dhlakama met on 23 August and were able to resolve some of the outstanding issues. Members were appointed to the National Commission on Administration (CNA), the National Information Commission (COMINFO) and the National Police Affairs Commission (COMPOL). The critical question of territorial administration was addressed and the parties agreed to integrate into the state administration all areas which had been under RENAMO control; the agreement provided for the appointment of RENAMO advisers to each provincial administration.[60]

60/Document 39
See page 190;
Document 40
See page 190;
Document 41
See page 196

113   On 10 September, Mozambique's Minister for Foreign Affairs, Mr. Pascoal Manuel Mocumbi, notified me that all the commissions under United Nations chairmanship were functioning, that refugees and displaced persons had begun to return to their home areas and that the training programme for the new armed forces was now under way in Zimbabwe. However, he added, demobilization had not yet started and little progress had been made in drafting an electoral law.[61] The Foreign Minister also requested that a United Nations police contingent be dispatched in order to address emerging problems in this area.

61/Document 42
See page 198

114   For some time, RENAMO had been voicing its concern over the role of the police, arguing that the Government was incorporating demobilized soldiers into their ranks. RENAMO called for United Nations monitoring of the police, warning that such a mechanism had to be in place before demobilization could begin. The Government and RENAMO agreed to ask the United Nations to monitor all police activities in the country, verifying that they were consistent with the General Peace Agreement, and to provide technical support to COMPOL.[62] In accordance with the Security Council's adoption of resolution 863 (1993) on 13 September, which requested my examination of United Nations monitoring of police activities in Mozambique, I sent a small survey team to Mozambique to assist me in making recommendations for the proposed ONUMOZ police contingent. Security Council resolution 882

62/Document 40
See page 190;
Document 41
See page 196;
Document 42
See page 198

(1993) of 5 November authorized the immediate deployment of 128 police observers.[63]

115   Despite progress in some areas, electoral issues remained deadlocked. Another multi-party conference was convened by the Government on 2 August but failed to resolve disagreement over the composition of the proposed National Elections Commission. The dispute revolved around the Government's insistence on retaining a majority in the 21-member body. Although, in its 13 September resolution, the Security Council urged all parties to reach agreement quickly on the electoral process, four days later the Government dissolved the multi-party conference and declared its intention to finalize the law through bilateral consultation with all interested parties.[64]

116   The main weakness in implementing the peace process continued to be the failure to start demobilization of the two sides' armed forces. Teams of ONUMOZ military observers had for some time been awaiting the beginning of the cantonment of troops, although only 34 of the 49 assembly areas had been approved as of September 1993.

117   On 24 September, the Government publicly declared its readiness to send its troops to the assembly areas as soon as RENAMO was prepared to do the same, and expressed frustration at what it perceived to be stalling tactics by RENAMO.[65] Although a return to war was not contemplated, the RENAMO leadership was reluctant to give up its military option, while still seeking to gain what it perceived as important political concessions. In a declaration adopted on 25 September, RENAMO reconfirmed its commitment to elections in October 1994 but suggested that they be held without completing the demobilization process. With the situation in Angola offering clear evidence of the dangers of this approach, my Special Representative reasserted ONUMOZ's determination to hold elections only after full demobilization had taken place. He publicly warned RENAMO that it could no longer try to preserve both a political and a military option.

A new timetable

118   The peace process was now badly stalled. In light of the gravity of the situation, I decided to visit Maputo in order to impress on President Chissano and Mr. Dhlakama the very real possibility of an ONUMOZ withdrawal and to urge both sides to find solutions to outstanding problems. Italy had already indicated its wish, for budgetary reasons, to reduce its troop contribution after its tour of duty expired on 31 October. Without a tangible commitment to maintaining the peace process, there was a danger that other troop-contributing countries would pull out or reduce their contingents.

63/Document 43
See page 199;
Document 49
See page 212

64/Document 43
See page 199

65/Document 45
See page 201

119 I visited Maputo from 17 to 20 October 1993. In an address carried on national television, I warned of a growing reluctance on the part of the international community to sustain the recent peace-keeping and peace-enforcement commitments: "Time is short. Solutions must now be found. While the international community continues to show a willingness to assist in the process of building peace, peace cannot be imposed from outside, nor can it be built where there is not sufficient political will to make peace."

120 Among the items which needed to be addressed during my visit were the failure of the parties to demobilize, questions of cease-fire guidelines and territorial control, approval of a draft electoral law, the appointment of the National Elections Commission and the ongoing dispute over chairmanships of the national commissions on police, information and administration. I met with both sides together on 20 October in order to break the impasse on these and other problems. In an impressive show of political will by both parties, compromise was reached on all the outstanding issues. The parties agreed that troops would start to move to assembly areas in November 1993. Demobilization of all troops, including paramilitary forces, militia and irregular troops, would begin in January 1994 and would be completed no later than May 1994.

121 The composition of the National Elections Commission (CNE) was also decided upon. It would include 10 members from the Government, 7 from RENAMO and 3 from other political parties, and an independent chairman selected by the members. President Chissano and Mr. Dhlakama also agreed that the draft electoral law would be examined at technical meetings between the parties with a view to submitting it to the National Assembly of the Republic by the end of November 1993. As for the remaining commissions, the National Commission for Administration would have two rotating chairmen—one appointed by the Government and one appointed by RENAMO. President Chissano would select the chairman of the National Police Affairs Commission, and Mr. Dhlakama would select the chairman of the Commission for Information. Lastly, both parties accepted new guidelines for the work of the Cease-fire Commission.[66]

66/Document 48
See page 205

122 As a follow-up to these decisions, on 22 October 1993 the Supervisory and Monitoring Commission approved and signed a revised timetable for the remainder of the peace process. The concentration of troops was to commence in November 1993, followed by the start of demobilization in January 1994. Demobilization was due to end in May 1994, by which time the demobilized soldiers would be returned to their home areas. The new Mozambican Defence Force was to be fully operational by September 1994. Voter registration was to be conducted between April and June 1994. The electoral campaign was to take place in

September and October in time for elections to be held by the end of October 1994.[67]

123   I was encouraged by the new timetable and stated at the time: "This new momentum will help me convince the Security Council to continue to give me a mandate to maintain the United Nations presence in Mozambique. This will help me obtain from the different financial institutions all over the world and from the donor countries, from the European Community, more assistance for Mozambique, because Mozambique has reached an agreement and Mozambique is activating the peace process".[68] On 29 October 1993, the Security Council extended ONUMOZ's mandate for an interim period until 5 November pending examination of my upcoming report.[69] On 5 November, the Council commended the latest agreements reached in Maputo and urged the parties to adhere to their new timetable, especially in the area of demobilization. It also renewed the mandate of ONUMOZ for a period of six months.[70] I notified President Chissano and Mr. Dhlakama of the ONUMOZ extension as well as of the Council's proviso that it would review the status of the mandate within 90 days, based on a report from me, and that henceforth I was to report every three months on whether the parties had made sufficient and tangible progress towards implementing the General Peace Agreement and meeting the new timetable.[71]

67/Document 48
See page 205

68/Document 46
See page 203

69/Document 47
See page 204

70/Document 49
See page 212

71/Document 50
See page 213;
Document 51
See page 214

V   Achieving demobilization

124   The new timetable agreed to during my visit to Maputo in October 1993 put the peace process back on track. Although a year had passed since the signing of the General Peace Agreement, demobilization was finally under way and the electoral process could begin.

125   In rapidly changing circumstances, the United Nations and the international community acted firmly, by means of the Supervisory and Monitoring Commission and the other commissions, to keep to the new timetable. By the time a Security Council mission visited Mozambique in August 1994, sufficient progress had been achieved to enable it to declare its cautious optimism about the prospects for a successful conclusion to the operation.[72]

72/Document 70
See page 258

Opening the assembly areas

126   After the failure of both sides to start demobilizing in 1993, the timetable agreed upon in October of that year demonstrated a new willingness on the part of both RENAMO and the Government to move forward.[73]

73/Document 48
See page 205

127   Demobilization was the most difficult and dangerous phase of the ONUMOZ mandate. There was considerable uncertainty about the numbers of troops to be demobilized, and both sides were reluctant to give up their best fighting units or to assemble their senior officers until the very end of the assembly and demobilization process. The agreed procedures laid down by the General Peace Agreement could not be followed; reinterpretation and occasional substantive changes were required.

128   To prepare for demobilization, the role of the Cease-fire Commission (CCF) was of critical importance. In addition to verifying the cease-fire and arranging for the clearance of land-mines, the CCF had the central responsibility for establishing procedures for the cantonment, assembly and demobilization of Government and RENAMO soldiers. The CCF also set itineraries for the movement of forces and approved rules of conduct for the assembly areas.

129   Preparations were made to supply the assembly areas with food, cooking equipment, tarpaulins, blankets, health care, water and civilian clothing. According to the plan, after a maximum of two months in the assembly areas, the soldiers being demobilized would receive severance payments, subsidies and assistance with transportation to their homes. Numerous donors and agencies made generous contributions to this programme.

130   Critical to the success of the assembly and demobilization of troops was the Technical Unit, a civilian team supporting the military observers. The unit, collaborating with the United Nations Office for Humanitarian Assistance Coordination (UNOHAC), was responsible for the distribution of food, medicines and other basic services to the assembly areas; the organization of a database and issuance of personal documents to demobilized soldiers; the supply of civilian clothing and the organization of transport of ex-combatants to their homes; and the establishment of a solid link with provincial and district authorities in the demobilization process.[74]

74/Document 26
See page 149

131   The principal outstanding difficulty was in reaching agreement on a final list of assembly areas. By November 1993, only 35 of the 49 areas (26 out of the 29 designated by the Government and 9 out of the 20 designated by RENAMO) had been approved. ONUMOZ military observers found several to be unacceptable because of inaccessibility, lack of basic security (especially because of the existence of land-mines) or the absence of basic infrastructure, especially water.

132   In addition, RENAMO still proved slow to cooperate in reconnaissance of the assembly areas and reluctant to request the Government to provide alternative sites to those rejected as unsuitable by ONUMOZ observers. For its part, the Government refused to grant ONUMOZ a presence at more than 14 of its sites until a greater number of RENAMO sites had also been allocated an ONUMOZ presence.[75]

75/Document 48
See page 205

133   ONUMOZ could still only estimate the total numbers of soldiers that it would have to register. Following the earlier registration of 13,717 Government soldiers who were demobilized before the signing of the General Peace Agreement, ONUMOZ broadly expected to register about 80,000 Government soldiers and about 21,000 from RENAMO.

134   The first 20 assembly areas were formally opened on 30 November 1993, followed by 15 more on 20 December 1993. Continuing disagreements between the two parties, however, delayed the opening of the remaining 14 sites. By 24 January 1994, 9,895 Government soldiers and 6,714 RENAMO troops had been assembled. The arrival of RENAMO troops in greater numbers than expected led to overcrowding and shortages of essential provisions in a few RENAMO assembly areas. Meanwhile, in some Government areas there were incidents of rioting by soldiers demanding back pay.[76]

76/Document 55
See page 216

135   After negotiations between my Special Representative and the two sides, the remaining 14 assembly areas were opened and became operational on 21 February 1994. The process then moved ahead, albeit at a slow pace. By mid-April 1994, more than 49,000 soldiers had

77/Document 63
See page 232

reported to assembly areas for cantonment, of which some 34,000 were from the Government and more than 14,000 were from RENAMO.[77]

Demobilization begins

136 Demobilization commenced formally on 10 March. Over the first three weeks, 12,195 Government and 561 RENAMO troops were given clothing, money and assistance with transport to their districts of choice. Arrangements were put in place for the full reintegration of demobilized soldiers in their home areas, under the supervision of the Reintegration Commission (CORE).[78] On 1 March 1994, I informed the Security Council of my decision to appoint Major-General Mohammad Abdus Salam (Bangladesh) as the new Force Commander of ONUMOZ.

78/Document 63
See page 232

137 Most of the assembled soldiers had to remain in the assembly areas much longer than they had expected. Serious tensions arose, resulting in about 20 violent incidents between January and March 1994. Initially, Government troops protested principally about arrears in their pay, while RENAMO troops refused to be demobilized until they received substantially greater benefits than were scheduled, following unrealistic promises made to them by their commanders. As the assembly period became more extended, troops from both sides began to demand immediate demobilization, including their severance pay. ONUMOZ had to work diligently to find solutions and defuse tensions.

138 On 8 April 1994, President Chissano and Mr. Dhlakama agreed on the need to speed up the assembly of Government forces and the demobilization of RENAMO troops. The two sides also agreed that some military personnel would not be moved to assembly areas but would be demobilized at their current locations, such as military hospitals, air bases or military headquarters.[79]

79/Document 63
See page 232

139 On 21 April, the Government delegation to the CCF presented a new figure for the total size of its forces, which at 64,110 was substantially lower than the 76,405 first declared in 1992. RENAMO refused to accept the new CCF figure, meaning that the matter had to be referred to the Supervisory and Monitoring Commission for a decision. Eventually, the Government revised its figure slightly upward to 64,466, which RENAMO agreed upon as a working estimate subject to CCF verification. The Government's explanation for the discrepancy was that its earlier figure had mistakenly included soldiers demobilized prior to the signing of the General Peace Agreement who were awaiting transportation home when the assessment was made in November 1992.[80]

80/Document 65
See page 242

140 On 5 May 1994, the Security Council adopted a resolution in which it urged the two parties to meet the target dates of 1 June for completion of the assembly of forces and 15 July for the end of demobilization.[81] The Government responded that it could not achieve these dates but said it would conclude assembly by 1 July and demobilization by 15 August. However, by 1 July, about 4,500 Government troops and 900 RENAMO troops had still not been assembled. The Government issued a statement protesting what it considered to be partiality by ONUMOZ, a long-held concern, claiming that while ONUMOZ had exerted considerable pressure on the Government for the cantonment of its troops, it had not done so with regard to RENAMO. My Special Representative had been urging the Government to demobilize some 23,000 remaining troops by its self-imposed deadline of 15 August in order to avoid another delay in the holding of elections. The Government's statement also cited RENAMO violations of the cease-fire.[82] Subsequently, it was agreed to increase the numbers of soldiers on both sides that were to be demobilized on site, without going to the assembly points.

141   On 19 July, the Security Council issued a statement again urging both sides to meet the 15 August deadline and stressing that elections should take place on 27 and 28 October.[83] On 4 August, the Council announced that it would send a mission to discuss with the parties how to ensure full and timely implementation of the General Peace Agreement.[84]

142   Continuing frustration among soldiers at their prolonged cantonment provoked further demonstrations and rioting, occasional attacks on United Nations personnel and looting of food and other supplies. As a precaution, on several occasions ONUMOZ troops were deployed around assembly areas.[85] Soldiers in a number of unassembled areas also protested, sometimes taking their commanding officers hostage to press their demands for rapid demobilization or more pay.

143   During July and August 1994 there was a series of protests by RENAMO troops demanding demobilization and/or financial compensation. These included a group of disabled fighters who blocked roads near Beira, a group of demobilized soldiers in Nampula Province and about 250 soldiers from one of the movement's unassembled points at Chinjale, Tete Province. In late August, demobilized RENAMO soldiers in Sofala Province took hostage the Minister of Construction and Water, Mr. João Salamão, and detained about 200 people at a roadblock, demanding transport to their home areas.

144   On 15 August, all assembly areas were officially closed to new entrants, and the 3,723 troops remaining at the assembly points on that day were quickly demobilized or recruited into the reconstituted Mozambican Defence Force. By late November 1994, demobilization accounted for a total of 57,540 Government and 20,538 RENAMO soldiers, a total of 78,078. These had been drawn from a total of 91,691 registered

81/Document 64
See page 241

82/Document 66
See page 248

83/Document 67
See page 250

84/Document 68
See page 251

85/Document 65
See page 242

troops (both assembled and unassembled, of which 67,042 were from the Government army and 24,649 from RENAMO), or 4,588 more than the figure of 87,103 that had been declared by both sides.[86] It was difficult for the CCF and ONUMOZ to keep an exact record of the numbers—the figures given by both the Government and RENAMO contained discrepancies—or to prevent abuses of the system by groups that reapplied for demobilization in the hope of getting a second package of benefits.

86/Document 90
See page 294

145   In mid-1994, CORE approved the creation of a provincial fund to provide small and medium-size grants to employ ex-soldiers and facilitate their participation in community-based economic activities. Other components of reintegration were: a support scheme providing each soldier with an 18-month subsidy in addition to his 6-month demobilization pay, career counselling and problem-solving services and an occupational-skills development programme.

Formation of the FADM

146   The Joint Commission for the Formation of the Mozambican Defence Force (CCFADM) faced the problem of identifying sufficient numbers of troops to form a new Mozambican army of the size that had been contemplated. Whereas the General Peace Agreement stipulated that the new armed forces required a troop strength of 30,000, comprising equal numbers from the Government and from RENAMO, only one third of this number volunteered for service.

147   By early July 1994, only 3,000 soldiers had completed training under the various programmes offered by France, Portugal and the United Kingdom. Another 1,000 were undergoing training. By late August, the new unified Mozambican Defence Force (FADM) totalled 7,806 soldiers, of which 4,263 were former Government troops and 3,543 former RENAMO fighters. By the end of the ONUMOZ mandate on 9 December 1994, a total of 11,579 soldiers had enlisted in the FADM.[87]

87/Document 90
See page 294

148   Owing to delays by both parties, the United Kingdom provided training for six FADM infantry battalions instead of the 15 originally planned. Portugal trained high-ranking officers, special forces and marines, and France trained teams in mine-clearance. Additional training support was provided by Zimbabwe, and Italy contributed financially to the rehabilitation of the training centres.[88]

88/Document 90
See page 294

149   Command of the FADM was shared jointly by officers from the Mozambique Armed Forces (FAM) and RENAMO—Lieutenant-General Lagos Lidimo and Lieutenant-General Mateus Ngonhamo, respectively—whose appointments were marked by a ceremony presided over by my Special Representative on 6 April 1994. With the establishment of the FADM, the military structures of the Government and

RENAMO were formally disbanded. The most senior officers on both sides were demobilized in August.

Post-demobilization verification

150 Teams comprising representatives of the Government, RENAMO and ONUMOZ began post-demobilization verification on 30 August 1994. A total of 722 former military positions or depots were declared to the CCF by the Government (435) and by RENAMO (287). In accordance with procedures approved by the CCF, the teams verified any information relating to the presence of unregistered troops and undeclared arms depots or weapons caches. The teams also examined 146 locations that had not been declared by either party.

151 Verification led to the discovery of substantial numbers of weapons, including tanks, anti-aircraft guns, mines, armoured personnel carriers and mortar bombs abandoned or stored throughout the country. A small number of previously unregistered military personnel were also identified at some Government and RENAMO bases.

152 The delays in demobilization and the parties' initial reluctance to participate fully in the verification meant that the process lagged behind schedule. It was not possible, therefore, to finish the checking of weapons before the expiry of the ONUMOZ mandate on 9 December 1994. At that point, United Nations teams had examined a total of 754 locations and had found 22,069 weapons, as well as large amounts of ammunition.[89]

See page 294

ONUMOZ *military and police components*

153 ONUMOZ military observers were closely involved in verifying the demobilization process, investigating complaints relating to the cease-fire and overseeing the collection of weapons before the electoral process entered its final phase.[90] After demobilization was nearly complete in September 1994, the number of military observers was reduced from 354 to 240.

See page 281

154 ONUMOZ military contingents continued to monitor security along the transport corridors, the airports, the depots of weapons collected from both parties and all United Nations properties and locations. The principal contingents serving with ONUMOZ in the first four months of 1994 were those of Bangladesh (1,371), Italy (953), India (894), Zambia (843), Uruguay (813), Botswana (736) and Portugal (274). During April, the Italian contingent was reduced by some 800 troops, leaving only a field hospital and a logistics element. In the

ONUMOZ military deployment at time of elections, October 1994

Starting in June 1994, ONUMOZ's military component was redeployed to provide wider coverage in anticipation of the October elections.

following month, the contingents from India, Bangladesh and Portugal were also substantially reduced, and nearly all of the Indian contingent was withdrawn by August 1994.[91]

155 To compensate for the departure of the Italian contingent, a self-contained Brazilian infantry company of 170 troops was deployed in Zambézia Province. There had previously been no ONUMOZ military presence in this densely populated but heavily war-damaged part of the country. Two Botswana companies and one Bangladeshi company were redeployed from their previous positions to replace the Italian contingent along the Beira corridor (see map, page 44).[92]

156 Because the phase of partial ONUMOZ troop reduction coincided with unrest among demobilizing soldiers and increasing banditry on Mozambique's roads, it was important to establish greater flexibility and wider coverage of various parts of the country.[93] With the Security Council's approval on 7 September of my recommendations in this regard, all ONUMOZ operations aimed at maintaining security, especially in the crucial period before, during and immediately after the elections, were stepped up.[94] The final withdrawal of the military component began on 15 November 1994, after the results of the elections were announced.

157 The deployment of international civilian police (CIVPOL) observers further compensated for the troop reduction which took place in May-June 1994.[95] The first 125 CIVPOL observers were deployed in Maputo and provincial capitals in November 1993. In addition to overseeing the neutrality of the Mozambican police, the mandate provided for the monitoring of respect for the rights and liberties of citizens, including during the election campaign. I proposed on 28 January 1994 that the total strength of the contingent should be established at 1,144, to be deployed no later than one month before the beginning of the electoral campaign in September 1994.[96] The Security Council authorized the establishment of a United Nations police component of ONUMOZ at the proposed level in resolution 898 (1994).[97]

158 With assistance from the Centre for Human Rights, CIVPOL monitors underwent an extensive human rights training programme, the first of its kind provided to a United Nations police force. By mid-May, the CIVPOL observers numbered 440, reaching a total of 1,095 in September 1994. Drawn from 29 Member States, they were widely deployed around the country at a total of 83 locations, of which 15 were in formerly RENAMO-controlled areas. CIVPOL personnel verified complaints of violations of political or human rights, including those made against the Mozambique police force and other security arms of the State such as the Rapid Intervention Force. The CIVPOL presence helped to check politically motivated breaches of these rights. By December 1994, CIVPOL had investigated 511 complaints, of which 61 related

91/Document 63
See page 232

92/Document 63
See page 232

93/Document 69
See page 251

94/Document 71
See page 267

95/Document 69
See page 251

96/Document 55
See page 216

97/Document 57
See page 228

98/Document 90
See page 294

to violations of human rights. Documentation on these complaints was forwarded to the National Police Affairs Commission (COMPOL), although the latter had taken no disciplinary or preventive action on them by the end of the ONUMOZ mandate.[98]

Territorial administration

159   The wide deployment of CIVPOL observers provided further evidence to the population of the role of ONUMOZ in the peace process as it moved towards elections, and also opened lines of communication in RENAMO areas where the Mozambique Government had yet to establish its own police or administrative presence.

160   Despite the beneficial effect of CIVPOL, the achievement of a unified territorial administration in Mozambique—a difficult issue throughout the peace process—remained to be resolved. It had been agreed by President Chissano and Mr. Dhlakama in September 1993 that all former RENAMO-controlled areas would be integrated into the State administration and that each provincial administration would have RENAMO advisers. But this agreement did not lead to a resolution of problems at the district level, where RENAMO was often reluctant to cede control.

161   The National Commission on Administration (CNA) made little progress at its meetings, and its work stalled when RENAMO boycotted the meetings after July 1994. The CNA was to determine which localities were under RENAMO control and to approve RENAMO-nominated administrators for them. Before the RENAMO boycott, the CNA had agreed on RENAMO control of five districts and 42 administrative posts, and administrators had been appointed for all of them. The status of numerous other districts and administrative posts remained undetermined.

VI The improving humanitarian situation

162   The years of war, compounded by a series of severe droughts—including the one in 1992, which was the worst to afflict the southern African region in a century—caused severe human suffering in Mozambique. Amid fears of mass starvation, humanitarian agencies faced the difficulties of providing relief in a war-torn country and ensuring that supplies quickly reached neighbouring countries through Mozambique's transport corridors. The decision to establish a humanitarian assistance component to ONUMOZ was supported by the Mozambican parties and was approved by the international community. In July 1992, the joint request of the Government and RENAMO that the United Nations coordinate the provision of humanitarian assistance became an integral part of the final peace accord.[99] On 12 October, after the signing of the General Peace Agreement, I appealed to President Chissano and Mr. Dhlakama to assure, on an urgent basis, access for relief aid to the millions of Mozambicans living under desperate and worsening humanitarian conditions.[100] Subsequently, the Security Council, in its resolution 797 (1992), endorsed the inclusion of the coordination of humanitarian assistance operations within the overall mandate of ONUMOZ, as delineated in my report of 3 December 1992.[101] International support for the humanitarian emergency was mobilized by the United Nations Department of Humanitarian Affairs.

99/Document 12
See page 105

100/Document 14
See page 129;
Document 15
See page 129

101/Document 26
See page 149;
Document 27
See page 158

163   Fortunately, shortly after Mozambicans began to return to their homes in late 1992, plentiful rain resulted in the best agricultural season in years. Production of food crops in 1993 reached 533,000 tons, compared with 133,000 tons the previous year. Even with the influx of returnees, the number of people requiring food aid fell from 3.1 million in late 1992 to a monthly average of 1.8 million in the 1993/94 period. This figure dropped to little more than 1 million in 1994/95, but even that figure meant that significant food imports needed to be continued.[102]

102/Document 73
See page 268

Gradual return to normality

164   The signing of the General Peace Agreement in October 1992 and the opening up of districts that RENAMO had controlled or held under siege prompted the spontaneous return of large numbers of displaced persons and refugees.

165   The Office of the United Nations High Commissioner for Refugees (UNHCR), in close cooperation with the Government's relief department and a non-governmental organization, delivered food to spontaneous returnees on a limited scale in RENAMO areas in Tete Province—the first direct delivery of United Nations assistance to a RENAMO area. The humanitarian effort thus contributed significantly to the wider peace process, building lines of communication and helping to foster trust. Operating as the humanitarian component of ONUMOZ, the United Nations Office for Humanitarian Assistance Coordination (UNOHAC) followed the twin principles of neutrality and freedom of movement. In all its operations, UNOHAC sought complete freedom of movement to deliver humanitarian assistance wherever it was required.

166   Under the terms of the General Peace Agreement, a Donors Conference for Mozambique was held in Rome on 15 and 16 December 1992 to address the country's humanitarian requirements and the needs of refugees and the displaced, those in severe distress and demobilized soldiers. Pledges in the amount of $450 million were made during and after the Conference.[103] On 19 May 1993, Italy deposited $10 million into a United Nations Trust Fund for Humanitarian Affairs, which in September 1994 had commitments of $50 million.[104] A humanitarian assistance programme for 1993/94, representing a shift in emphasis from emergency relief to reintegration and rehabilitation, was submitted at a follow-up Donors Meeting in Maputo on 8 and 9 June 1993 under the joint chairmanship of the United Nations and the Government of Italy. Additional pledges in the amount of $70 million were made. In June 1993, as political tensions mounted and access to RENAMO-controlled areas became increasingly difficult, my Special Representative and representatives of the International Committee of the Red Cross (ICRC) reached an agreement with RENAMO that humanitarian organizations be allowed unimpeded access to Mozambicans in need of assistance.[105]

167   The large-scale resettlement of refugees was another major achievement and provided a massive vote of confidence for the peace process. Between October 1992 and December 1994, approximately 4.3 million Mozambicans resettled voluntarily in different parts of the country, the great majority of them in their original home areas. Of the total number, 1.6 million were refugees who returned from camps or exile in neighbouring countries. About 200,000 were demobilized soldiers and their dependants, who were transported to their places of choice as part of the peace process.[106] The repatriation of Mozambican refugees was one of UNHCR's largest African operations and the successful accommodation of the returnees into their home areas one of the most significant achievements during ONUMOZ.[107]

103/Document 28
See page 159

104/Document 73
See page 268

105/Document 37
See page 184

106/Document 90
See page 294

107/Document 59
See page 230

168 Although most Mozambicans, apart from the demobilized soldiers, returned to their homes by their own means, some 300,000 refugees were transported by UNHCR's implementing partners. Of these, more than 200,000 were moved between July and December 1994 alone. In all, more than 700,000 Mozambican refugees returned from Malawi to their nearby homes in Tete, Zambézia and other northern and central provinces. Others travelled from South Africa, Zimbabwe, Zambia, Swaziland and the United Republic of Tanzania. An agreement, concluded in November 1993 between UNHCR and the Governments of Mozambique and South Africa, provided access to the refugees and formed the basis for a repatriation programme from South Africa. UNHCR focused its efforts on facilitating the repatriation by improving access to returnee areas, providing transport to those unable to organize their own movement and, most importantly, initiating programmes to strengthen the absorptive capacity of major returnee areas and facilitate reintegration. A Plan for Operations and subsequent appeal for a total of $200 million was presented in early 1993. The ongoing UNHCR reintegration programme in Mozambique focused on some 30 priority districts in Tete, Zambézia, Niassa, Cabo Delgado, Manica, Sofala, Gaza and Maputo provinces and aimed at improving roads, health facilities, schools, food production (through the distribution of seeds and tools) and access to safe water. In 1994, some 486 quick-impact projects were implemented through NGOs and the Government. More than 30 NGOs launched area-based programmes to reintegrate internally displaced people and demobilized soldiers. United Nations agencies, bilateral donors and NGOs supported many initiatives to rehabilitate social infrastructures as the first phase of longer-term reconstruction.

The humanitarian aspects of peace

169 The enormous movements of people throughout the period of the ONUMOZ mandate required UNOHAC to monitor closely their needs for food and essential services. UNOHAC had to establish and cultivate channels of communication between the Government and RENAMO, especially at local and provincial levels. Under UNOHAC chairmanship, provincial humanitarian assistance committees, with the participation of both the Government and RENAMO, were set up to plan the delivery of food and other relief and to promote the reconstruction and rehabilitation of basic services. UNOHAC also initiated tripartite discussions on social services, with a view to integrating RENAMO health personnel into the Government's health system and to expanding the provision of education in RENAMO areas. Donors channelled relief food aid through the World Food Programme (WFP) and NGOs.

170   There was considerable progress in providing assistance in RENAMO areas during the first year of the ONUMOZ mandate. As roads were opened and mines were cleared, deliveries to RENAMO areas increased steadily, particularly in Sofala Province. UNOHAC recorded 74,000 tons of food as having been distributed to RENAMO areas between October 1992 and May 1994. Across Mozambique, average standards of nutrition quickly recovered from the low levels brought about by prolonged war and drought. UNOHAC sent teams into RENAMO-controlled territory around Maringue, Sofala Province, to plan improvements in health, water supply and sanitation. Technical agencies from the Mozambican Government were frequently welcomed in districts that had been dominated by RENAMO. In some RENAMO areas, however, the need for mine, road or bridge clearance slowed delivery of humanitarian assistance. Occasionally, local RENAMO authorities were reluctant to permit the free movement of Government personnel who could contribute to the restoration of services.

171   Difficult security problems were experienced in Zambézia Province and other areas away from the transport corridors patrolled by ONUMOZ military contingents. The fact that the National Commission on Administration (CNA) did not begin to integrate RENAMO areas into the State administration until the second half of 1994 also delayed the reintegration of social services. In particular, United Nations agencies, such as UNHCR, with an extensive field presence in remote areas, experienced problems as a result of demobilized soldiers demanding assistance. On some occasions, staff were held or threatened, causing some assistance to be released on an ad hoc basis to defuse the situations.

172   UNOHAC coordinated more than 20 different agencies involved in the distribution of articles such as blankets, clothing, soap and kitchen utensils to 37 different districts previously under RENAMO control. Another project, in both Government and RENAMO areas, distributed items such as roofing sheets, kitchen sets and tents, as well as small generators and water tanks. The United Nations Children's Fund (UNICEF) was the leading international agency involved in providing water to combat the effects of drought and in assisting resettlement.

173   In addition to opening access to RENAMO areas, UNOHAC's special tasks included developing and coordinating the mine-clearance projects. Given the autonomous operation of many humanitarian agencies long established in Mozambique, the coordination of humanitarian assistance was an important challenge for UNOHAC. But UNOHAC eventually played a key role in more than 25 individual projects, while the actual implementation was handled by agencies such as the United Nations Development Programme (UNDP) and UNICEF.[108]

108/Document 73
See page 268

Reintegration of demobilized soldiers

174   A major UNOHAC function, reinforced by its chairmanship of the Commission for Reintegration (CORE), was planning, organizing and monitoring the economic and social reintegration of demobilized soldiers. Although many projects for demobilized soldiers were formalized under bilateral programmes and were outside CORE's control, CORE ensured that both the Government and RENAMO were fully consulted about reintegration issues. By the time demobilization began in 1994, all essential start-up projects were in place.

175   In addition to the six months' severance pay they received from the Government, the demobilized soldiers were provided with reintegration subsidy payments representing a further 18 months' pay. They were also entitled to use a country-wide information and referral service, an occupational skills development programme and a fund to promote their involvement in activities in their communities.[109] The programme was extended in June 1994 to include approximately 14,000 Government soldiers who had been demobilized before the General Peace Agreement was signed.

109/Document 63
See page 232

176   The Reintegration Support Scheme for demobilized soldiers was implemented by UNDP. Its budget eventually amounted to $31.9 million as a result of the demobilization of 20,000 more soldiers than the originally envisaged total of 57,103. By the end of the ONUMOZ mandate, however, only $8.9 million of the required amount had been received from donors, although a total of $27.6 million had been pledged.[110]

110/Document 90
See page 294

177   A number of international agencies became involved in the resettlement and counselling of Mozambique's child soldiers. A United Kingdom–based NGO, "Save the Children Fund", located the families of 8,000 children who had fought mostly for RENAMO, and in October 1994 it was still trying to trace the surviving families of another 4,000 such children. After the demobilization process, the ICRC also succeeded in reuniting 850 former RENAMO child soldiers with their families. The children were transported out of military zones and given psychological and social guidance under UNICEF supervision. Another 2,000 children separated from their families during the conflict were reunited with relatives by the ICRC.

Health and education

178   During the war, nearly half of Mozambique's rural health facilities were looted, destroyed or forced to close. After the signing of the peace accord, an immediate priority was to reactivate essential health services in those rural areas to which the population was beginning to return. By July 1994, at least 37 different agencies and NGOs were operating in the health sector in former RENAMO areas across 51 districts. Health posts in border areas were also rehabilitated to accommodate the reintegration of returnees. UNICEF actively supported the Government's 1994 health budget, which covered an expansion of the health network to include former RENAMO areas. Funds were allocated to help integrate the available health services in RENAMO areas into the national health system.

179   With less than half of Mozambique's children of primary-school age receiving any education by the time of the ONUMOZ mission, the reopening of schools became a major component of national reconstruction. About 1.2 million pupils and 20,000 teachers had been forced out of the schools between 1983 and 1991. In Tete, which had suffered the most in this regard, 98 per cent of primary schools had been closed or destroyed. After the peace accord was signed, hundreds of thousands of children returned to their home districts, increasing demands on the available infrastructure. In the six provinces for which UNOHAC had reliable data, more than 40 organizations were renovating or reconstructing a total of 790 classrooms by February 1995.[111]

111/Document 73
See page 268

Mine clearance

180   As the peace process took hold, it was known that thousands of kilometres of roads and tracks had been laid with land-mines. Although the actual number of mines was unknown, potentially hundreds of thousands of them presented a grave danger to the transport of passengers and goods, to farmers and rural dwellers and to the large numbers of refugees returning from neighbouring countries. The greatest concentrations of mines were in the central provinces, particularly Tete and Zambézia.

181   Bilateral agencies and donors participated in the de-mining of some 2,000 kilometres of road, particularly in the central and northern provinces. Norway, the United Kingdom and the United States operated independent programmes, while Italy, the Netherlands and Sweden financed mine clearance through a United Nations fund.

182   The first United Nations mine-clearance activities were initiated in late 1992 and early 1993 by the ICRC and WFP, with UNOHAC providing management and coordination. Programme management was the responsibility of UNDP. After long delays in getting a programme under way—partially the result of slow approval of the national mine-clearance plan by the Cease-fire Commission, as well as difficulties in identifying suitable contractors—an accelerated plan was put into place

in May 1994, and UNOHAC assumed responsibility for its coordination. A national land-mine survey by a United Kingdom NGO, the Halo Trust, was completed for UNDP in July 1994.[112]

183   A UNDP project for clearing 2,000 kilometres of priority roads—in addition to those de-mined by bilateral programmes—commenced in July 1994. UNOHAC established a national mine-clearance centre at Tete, and, by December 1994, the programme had trained some 450 Mozambicans to form de-mining teams, including supervisors, surveyors and instructors.[113]

184   Relying on funds from the ONUMOZ budget and on personnel provided by the Governments of Australia, Bangladesh, Germany, the Netherlands and New Zealand, the accelerated mine-clearance programme was expected to continue until November 1995. In my final report on ONUMOZ, I expressed the hope that agreement could be reached on the future of the programme before that time.[114] A comprehensive mine-clearance programme for Mozambique is expected to take between seven and 10 years to complete. All parties concerned shared the view that there was a need for the establishment of an entity at the national level to provide policy orientation, operational standards and coherence. At a meeting in Copenhagen during the March 1995 World Summit for Social Development, I assured President Chissano that the United Nations remained strongly committed to providing assistance to Mozambique for its reconstruction and for its mine-clearance efforts in particular.

Cyclone Nadia

185   In March 1994, cyclone Nadia caused heavy damage in Nampula and other northern provinces. The recorded death toll was 52, with 312 people injured. More than 900,000 people lost their crops or housing; many of those affected had been recently resettled. There was severe damage to schools, health posts and roads, and urban and nearby areas suffered cuts in power and water supplies. UNOHAC responded by organizing flights bringing in emergency relief supplies, including food, medicines, survival items, roofing sheets, tubes and generators, and United Nations troops assisted in the relief effort. The cyclone also destroyed large numbers of cashew trees, an important source of income in the northern provinces. Donor Governments and United Nations agencies pooled their efforts in mounting projects to limit the wider economic damage of the cyclone.[115]

112/Document 63
See page 232;
Document 65
See page 242;
Document 69
See page 251;
Document 73
See page 268

113/Document 90
See page 294

114/Document 90
See page 294

115/Document 63
See page 232;
Document 73
See page 268

Continuing commitments

186 The international community directly contributed more than 78 per cent of the approximately $650 million required to meet Mozambique's needs for humanitarian assistance during the period of the ONUMOZ mandate. United Nations organizations and agencies and international and Mozambican NGOs played an essential role in the design and implementation of individual and overall humanitarian programmes.

187 At the end of the ONUMOZ mandate, UNOHAC transferred its coordination responsibilities to the United Nations Resident Coordinator in Maputo. The ongoing mine-clearance programme became a joint responsibility of UNDP and the United Nations Department of Humanitarian Affairs.

188 The success of the humanitarian operation was critical to the peace process. Most significantly, it helped to maintain support in the country for the United Nations presence and demonstrated the potential advantages of sustained peace. Politically, the humanitarian effort enabled the Government and RENAMO to begin the necessary process of learning how to cooperate with each other. A crucial further step was to ensure that the significant inroads made in the context of the humanitarian assistance programme in Mozambique, particularly the initial rehabilitation operations, were sustained through longer-term development programmes.

VII   The holding of elections

189   The final and most crucial test of Mozambique's negotiated peace was the electoral process. Although the General Peace Agreement had envisaged elections within one year, a longer preparation period turned out to be necessary. The extension of the ONUMOZ mandate to two years allowed time for the peace process to mature, for the armed forces of both sides to demobilize and for political leaders to prepare for multi-party elections.

Establishing electoral machinery

190   Elections were held over the three days of 27 to 29 October 1994. The challenges leading up to that point included the need to establish a credible and independent electoral commission with an efficient secretariat, to train large numbers of election staff as well as monitors drawn from the political parties and to register the entire Mozambican electorate, many of whom had only recently returned from refugee camps in neighbouring countries. A major logistic challenge was also posed by the plan to deploy more than 2,300 international observers.

191   Implementing the electoral elements of the General Peace Agreement was a test of the authority of ONUMOZ and the Supervisory and Monitoring Commission. Following the issuance of a draft electoral law in March 1993, discussions repeatedly reached an impasse over the composition of the National Elections Commission (CNE). The Government tried throughout the year to convene meetings to discuss the draft. Finally, after my visit in October 1993, an agreement was reached; it was also decided that interested political parties would continue examining the remaining articles on technical matters.[116]

116/Document 48
See page 205

192   The differences between the Government and RENAMO focused on four points in the electoral law: voting rights for expatriate Mozambicans; the composition of provincial and district election commissions; the composition of the Technical Secretariat for the Organization of the Elections (STAE); and the establishment and composition of an electoral tribunal. Following a series of direct meetings between President Chissano and Mr. Dhlakama, which were held in close consultation with my Special Representative, these issues were resolved on 26 November 1993.

193   The Electoral Law was eventually approved by the National Assembly on 9 December 1993 and entered into force on 12 January

1994. The Law prescribed that the President should be elected by an absolute majority; if this was not obtained in the first round, a run-off would be held between the two candidates receiving the largest numbers of votes. The term of office for the President and the 250 members of the National Assembly would be five years. The number of deputies to the Assembly from each of the 11 electoral constituencies would be in proportion to the number of voters registered in that constituency. A system of proportional representation would be used to allocate the seats among the parties that received a minimum of 5 per cent of the vote nationally.[117]

117/Document 55
See page 216

194   The CNE was established on 21 January 1994 with 10 members nominated by the Government, 7 by RENAMO and 3 by the other political parties. The commission members selected as chairman Mr. Brazão Mazula, a respected Mozambican without affiliation to any political party. Starting its work on 15 February, the CNE quickly established a timetable for the entire electoral process, the main elements of which were: a period for voter registration between 1 June and 15 August; the electoral campaign, set for 10 September to 24 October; and the holding of presidential and assembly elections together on 27 and 28 October 1994.[118] The provincial and district election commissions were established in subsequent months. Although there was low representation initially from RENAMO and other parties, this increased in later months.

118/Document 63
See page 232

195   The CNE and its executive secretariat were responsible for the conduct, preparation and organization of the elections. The United Nations Development Programme (UNDP) coordinated international financial and material support and provided technical assistance throughout the entire electoral process in the areas of organization, training, civic education, jurisprudence, social communication and financial management.

196   This assistance entailed management, coordination and monitoring of a $64.5 million budget made up of contributions from 17 countries and international institutions. UNDP coordinated bilateral meetings with donors and periodic meetings with the Aid for Democracy Group (Maputo-based representatives of donors who were assisting the electoral process) to negotiate financial and material support, avoid gaps and duplication of effort and report to the donors on the progress of the elections. These frequent consultations with the donors ensured complete transparency of the management of funds and encouraged continued support of the electoral process even as it required additional expenditures, as became the case when the registration period was extended from 15 August to 20 August and then again from 24 August to 2 September.

197   The UNDP Chief Technical Advisor approved all expenditures and the micro-management of the budget, and careful account-

ability to donors ensured that resources were used effectively. The technical assistance included the training of 2,600 electoral officials at the national, provincial and district levels, 8,000 census agents, 1,600 civic education agents and 52,000 polling officers. In addition to a 12-person UNDP advisory team to the CNE, three to five United Nations Volunteers (UNVs) were assigned to each of the 11 electoral constituencies and worked closely with the provincial and district electoral authorities.

198   Under the supervision of the central technical team, these UNVs coordinated logistics and provided the technical and district electoral authorities with backup support and technical advice ensuring that the electoral process reached those remote and difficult-of-access areas that lacked such basic infrastructure as roads and bridges or that were surrounded by land-mines. The teams working on voter registration required shelter, water and basic foodstuffs, as well as registration materials. Extraordinary measures were taken by the advisory teams to make sure that these requirements reached the registration teams and that bottlenecks in the delivery of these items did not stall the electoral process.

199   The ONUMOZ electoral division established its own network of monitoring activities, with 148 officers stationed throughout the provinces to cover voter registration, civic education, political campaigns and political party access to, as well as impartiality of, the media, polling, vote counting and vote tabulation at the provincial counting centres. Complaints of alleged irregularities in the electoral process were to be transmitted to the CNE, while ONUMOZ was mandated to carry out separate investigations.

200   Agreement had been reached at the November 1993 meeting between President Chissano and Mr. Dhlakama on the establishment of a five-member Electoral Tribunal composed of two Mozambican judges and three international judges proposed by the United Nations. The Tribunal was to function as a court of appeal against decisions of the CNE.[119] After due consideration of candidates for the international members of the Tribunal, I appointed Michel Coat (France), Mariano Fiallos Oyanguren (Nicaragua) and João Moreira Camilo (Portugal), with Walter Ramos da Costa Porto (Brazil) and Juan Ignacio Garcia Rodriguez (Chile) as alternate members.[120] The members of the Electoral Tribunal were sworn in on 8 June 1994.

Voter registration

201   Registration of Mozambican voters began on schedule on 1 June 1994 with the deployment of 8,000 registrars and 1,600 civic education agents throughout the country. Good progress was made despite logistical bottlenecks and initial technical errors, such as the

119/Document 55
See page 216;
Document 65
See page 242

120/Document 61
See page 231;
Document 62
See page 232

improper filling in of forms, registration books and voter cards. Some registration teams encountered difficulties in gaining access to RENAMO-controlled districts—in some cases for political reasons, at other times for logistical reasons. The National Assembly twice decided to extend the registration process in order to guarantee that no groups of people were excluded from the electoral process, specifically populations in remote areas and returning refugees and demobilized soldiers. On 15 August, at the end of the initial registration period, 5,636,000 voters had been registered. On 20 August, at the end of the first extension, voter registration had risen to 6,034,066, and at the conclusion of the process on 2 September, 6,363,311 voters had been registered—81 per cent of the 7,894,850 estimated eligible voting population.

202   Registration totals by province demonstrated the electoral importance of Nampula, Zambézia, Cabo Delgado and Sofala. These four provinces had the highest numbers of registered voters and were allocated, between them, 146 of the 250 seats in the National Assembly.

Political parties

203   Although a number of political parties emerged, the electoral contest was dominated by FRELIMO and RENAMO. However, RENAMO continued to threaten delay. In part, this represented an attempt to extract new concessions from the Government on the electoral system under discussion, but it also reflected RENAMO's concern that without adequate resources it would not be able to mount an effective challenge to FRELIMO in the forthcoming elections. In December 1993, at a meeting of the Supervisory and Monitoring Commission, Mr. Dhlakama had made an urgent appeal for financial resources. Without them, he warned, RENAMO would be forced to abstain from the elections.

204   According to the Peace Agreement, RENAMO, as a partner in the peace process, was entitled to financial assistance for the process of

121/Document 12
See page 105

transforming itself from a military organization into a political party.[121] (Assistance to other political parties to meet the costs of the electoral campaign was dealt with in another section of the Agreement and ensured through an ad hoc trust fund; see paragraph 206.) The Peace Agreement stipulated that the Mozambique Government would provide the financing and, if lacking the necessary means, could appeal to the international community, in particular to Italy. The United Nations Trust Fund for the Implementation of the Peace Agreement in Mozambique, established in May 1993, was the main instrument for this critical task. Its creation was one of the most innovative features of the Mozambique operation and was a pivotal factor in maintaining the momentum of the peace process at this stage.

205   The Trust Fund, with an initial contribution from Italy of $5.7 million, amounted to $7.5 million at the end of 1993. Unfortunately, this amount was not sufficient. Given the primary role bestowed on Italy by the Peace Agreement, I wrote to the President of Italy's Council of Ministers, Mr. Carlo Azeglio Ciampi, stressing the urgency of ensuring that RENAMO had the necessary funds to fulfil its political role in the electoral process. Without such funding, I warned, the entire peace process could be destabilized. My letter focused on two issues. The first was quantitative: a total of at least $15 million was required. The second was qualitative: the rules governing United Nations administration of trust funds were too rigid to enable us to meet pressing needs. In this latter regard, I referred to the need to channel some $300,000 a month to RENAMO until the elections took place in October. In addition, a more flexible financial instrument would enable other nations to contribute to the fund. I therefore appealed to Italy to contribute $500,000 to meet immediate requirements; on 4 March, the Italian Government notified me of its positive response.[122] However, as I reported to the Security Council on 26 August, while $14.6 million had been pledged to the fund, contributions of only $13.6 million had been received, and I appealed to donors, through the Council, to fulfil their pledges.[123]

206   As important as the Trust Fund to assist RENAMO was a separate United Nations Trust Fund for Assistance to Registered Political Parties in Mozambique, launched following the establishment of the CNE, which had been given an important role in the distribution of its funds. This fund, designed to assist all political parties not signatories to the Peace Agreement in their preparations for the forthcoming elections, had pledges of $3.54 million, but had received only $1.88 million as of 26 August. I appealed to the donor community to honour these pledges. An initial sum of $50,000 had been given to each of the 16 parties on 19 August 1994; later, an additional $50,000 was given to those parties that could provide clear evidence that their spending of the first disbursal had only been for election-related requirements.[124] These trust funds were a vital element in the United Nations efforts to ensure a viable multi-party contest in which all the parties felt they had an adequate opportunity to present their views to the electorate.

Enhanced observation

207   Prior to the elections, a major effort was made to include the Mozambican parties themselves in observation of the elections. The

122/Document 54
See page 215;
Document 56
See page 227;
Document 58
See page 230

123/Document 69
See page 251;
Document 72
See page 268

124/Document 69
See page 251

United States Government funded a programme designed by ONUMOZ to provide training and monetary benefits for up to 35,000 monitors from different parties. The programme was implemented by the International Republican Institute, the International Organization for Migration and the Cooperative for American Relief Everywhere (CARE).

208   A parallel programme funded by the United Nations Trust Fund for Assistance to Registered Political Parties provided computer training to 78 representatives from all the political parties to enable them to verify the processing of election results at both provincial and national levels.

209   The involvement of Mozambican political party representatives was to complement the efforts of the international observers, whose presence was intended to be both substantial and visible. There were approximately 2,300 United Nations observers—570 from Member States, 279 from various United Nations offices, 934 directly from the ranks of ONUMOZ, 200 from the European Union and 278 from the diplomatic community in Maputo and non-governmental organizations (NGOs) working in Mozambique. The Organization of African Unity (OAU) and the Association of European Parliamentarians for Southern Africa also sent observers.[125]

125/Document 74
See page 281

The electoral campaign

210   In the weeks before the election campaign opened, some members of the international community began to recommend that President Chissano and FRELIMO reach an agreement with Mr. Dhlakama and RENAMO on some form of political accommodation before the elections, while others called for a political understanding that democratic rules would be observed after the elections.[126] The two men met twice during the week before the electoral campaign opened on 22 September, but failed to reach agreement on a post-election arrangement.

126/Document 70
See page 258

211   In view of the extension of time allotted for voter registration, it became necessary to shorten the campaign period from 45 to 35 days. As a result, the election campaign opened on 22 September 1994, little more than a month before the elections were to take place. Parties and presidential candidates were entitled to 5 minutes of radio broadcasting time each day on Radio Mozambique and 10 minutes per week on television. Few of the parties took advantage of the media access.

212   In August 1994, four opposition parties announced a formal coalition, called the União Democrática (UD). They were: Partido Liberal e Democrático de Moçambique (PALMO), Partido Nacional Democrático (PANADE), Partido Renovador Democrático (PRD) and Partido Nacional de Moçambique/Centro de Reflexão Democrática

(PANAMO/CRD), although PRD later dropped out. Other parties discussed joining this coalition or forming another, but did not do so. By the time of the elections, only two coalitions—the three-party UD and the two-party Patriotic Alliance (AP) of Movimento Nacionalista Moçambicano/Partido Moçambicano da Social Democracia (MONAMO/PMSD) and Frente de Ação Patriótica (FAP)—were operating.

213   Both principal presidential candidates, President Chissano and Mr. Dhlakama, undertook extensive tours of the country, focusing on the populous northern provinces. The campaign was largely conducted in an atmosphere of calm, albeit with considerable anxiety about the possibility of renewed conflict provoked by inflammatory rhetoric, occasional disturbances and even some physical attacks.[127]

127/Document 74
See page 281

214   Despite a number of such incidents and reports, I declared on 21 October that ONUMOZ did not believe that they posed a serious threat to the democratic electoral process.[128] On the same day, the Security Council appealed to the Mozambican parties to ensure that there would be no violence or threat of violence during the election days and their aftermath.[129] The Council's appeal underlined its determination to hold the parties to their obligation under the General Peace Agreement to abide fully by the results, should the United Nations declare the elections free and fair.

128/Document 74
See page 281

129/Document 75
See page 283

215   On 26 October, the day before the start of the elections, the leaders of the Front-line States—Angola, Botswana, Mozambique, the United Republic of Tanzania, Zambia and Zimbabwe—met in Harare, Zimbabwe, for discussions covering Mozambique, Angola and Lesotho. In their final statement they called for full respect for the 1992 peace accord.[130] They said that conditions existed for free elections and that the Front-line leaders would accept the result, but warned that they would take "appropriate and timely action" if it became necessary to keep the peace after the elections.

130/Document 76
See page 284

216   On the eve of the elections, there were 14 parties contesting the legislative election and 12 candidates seeking the presidency. Polling was to be conducted at 7,244 individual stations around the country. Approximately 52,000 polling officers and 35,000 party monitors had been given training in the agreed procedures. More than 2,300 international observers had reached the district capitals and were given the necessary transport to visit every polling-station in their jurisdiction at least once during the elections. In many places, the devastated urban and transport infrastructure had still not been repaired, and the risk of land-mines remained. Where land-mines threatened the safety of international observers, arrangements were made to transport them to remote polling-stations by helicopter.

RENAMO's boycott threat

217   Unexpectedly, late in the evening of 26 October, the day before the elections, Mr. Dhlakama announced in Beira that RENAMO would not participate in the polling, alleging that the Government was preparing to engage in massive fraud during the elections. The following morning, the RENAMO headquarters office in Maputo listed a number of demands. It wanted copies of the electoral registers—even though they had already been publicly displayed and the Electoral Law did not require them to be given to each party. It complained that transport to polling-stations had not been guaranteed for party agents and further demanded to know the exact location of the surplus ballot papers. RENAMO's complaints were formalized in a letter to the CNE that was also signed by three minor parties standing in the elections—the União Democrática (UD) coalition, the União Nacional Moçambicana (UNAMO) and the Partido de Convenção Nacional (PCN).

218   The CNE refuted each complaint and said that none of the questions raised by RENAMO contained anything that could call into question the holding of the elections or their results. The Commission pointed out that, under the Electoral Law, a presidential candidate who wished to withdraw from the polling was required to do so 15 days prior to the election; a party that wanted to pull out had to do so 72 hours beforehand. The CNE therefore concluded that both RENAMO and Mr. Dhlakama were still standing in the elections.

131/Document 77
See page 285

219   I myself had been immediately informed of the difficulties by my Special Representative, and I issued a statement emphasizing that the elections had to go ahead as planned.[131] The Security Council appealed directly to Mr. Dhlakama to reconsider RENAMO's decision to withdraw.[132]

132/Document 78
See page 285

220   On 27 October, the first day of elections, it was clear that the electorate was, in fact, proceeding to vote. The parties' election monitors, including those representing RENAMO, remained on duty at nearly all polling-stations throughout the country. In some districts, voters and election officials did not hear of RENAMO's announcement until the end of the day. Reports from ONUMOZ coordinators and observers indicated no major irregularities.

221   My Special Representative spoke on the telephone with Mr. Dhlakama in Beira on the morning of 27 October and urged him to return to Maputo. Mr. Dhlakama arrived in Maputo the same afternoon and negotiations went on until 2 a.m., when RENAMO agreed to resume its participation in the electoral process under certain conditions, which were immediately negotiated and agreed upon. A statement was drafted pledging that the members of the Supervisory and Monitoring Commission (CSC) would ensure that all potential irregularities were investigated

before the elections were declared free and fair. The Presidents of South Africa and Zimbabwe, as well as Don Matteo Zuppi of the Sant'Egidio Community, also lent their support to a resolution of the crisis which would allow the elections to go forward as planned.

222   On the morning of 28 October, Mr. Dhlakama announced the end of his party's boycott. In a statement issued simultaneously, the international CSC members and ONUMOZ reminded all parties that any evidence of significant electoral fraud would prevent them from declaring the elections free and fair.[133] They also welcomed Mr. Dhlakama's decision to participate fully in the elections and recommended that the CNE adopt a flexible approach to ensure that there was sufficient time to secure a high voter turnout.

133/Document 79
See page 286

223   The Electoral Law provided for a third day of polling if it proved necessary, and the CNE ordered an extension to 29 October. While most votes were cast during the first two days, the extension satisfied the parties that all those who wanted to vote had done so.

224   At every polling-station, the ballot boxes were sealed at the end of each day's voting. The final count at each site was signed by the polling-station staff and by all political party monitors present, whereupon the count was posted on a wall for the benefit of the public. Copies of each station's count were sent—escorted by Mozambique police and United Nations CIVPOL observers—to the relevant provincial commission, and thereafter to the CNE's head office in Maputo.

225   The overwhelming evidence provided by the international observers showed an election that was conducted peacefully, in which electoral officials followed procedures impartially and efficiently and in which the electorate participated patiently, seriously and with great dignity. By 31 October, ONUMOZ was able to declare the polling successful. It noted that some 90 per cent of the registered voters had cast their ballots.[134]

134/Document 80
See page 287

226   On 2 November, my Special Representative issued a preliminary statement asserting that Mozambique's first multi-party elections had been conducted peacefully, in a well-organized manner and without any major irregularities or incidents. He added that United Nations observation did not support any claim of fraud or intimidation, or any pattern of incidents that could affect the credibility of the elections. He promised to make an official pronouncement regarding the freedom and fairness of the entire electoral process following the completion of the count.[135]

135/Document 80
See page 287

227   The first indication of the final results, based on less than one third of the votes, was given by the CNE on 7 November. It indicated a lead for FRELIMO, with 52.17 per cent of the legislative votes, against RENAMO's 30.27 per cent. In the presidential election, Mr. Chissano had a lead of 62.61 per cent, against Mr. Dhlakama's 26.52 per cent.

Distribution of seats in the new National Assembly

Province	Total seats	FRELIMO	RENAMO	UD
Maputo City	18	17	1	0
Maputo Province	13	12	1	0
Gaza	16	15	0	1
Inhambane	18	13	3	2
Sofala	21	3	18	0
Manica	13	4	9	0
Tete	15	5	9	1
Zambézia	49	18	29	2
Nampula	54	20	32	2
Niassa	11	7	4	0
Cabo Delgado	22	15	6	1
Total	250	129	112	9

Source: National Elections Commission

One week later, it was apparent that RENAMO had received a larger share of the vote than these early indications had suggested. Final computing of the count took longer than anticipated, mainly out of concern for absolute accuracy and transparency and partly because of computer software problems. As a result, the announcement of the complete results was postponed until 19 November. In the meantime, on 14 November, Mr. Dhlakama telephoned me to tell me that, although he thought there had been irregularities, he was accepting the results.

228   Declaring the election results on 19 November, CNE Chairman Brazão Mazula said that Joaquim Chissano had received 53.30 per cent of the votes in the presidential election, while Afonso Dhlakama had received 33.73 per cent. A total of 5,402,940 people, representing 87.9 per cent of the electorate, had participated in the elections. In the legislative election, FRELIMO won 44.33 per cent of the votes, giving it 129 seats, while RENAMO received 37.78 per cent, giving it 112 seats. The three-party coalition, UD, received 5.15 per cent of the votes, entitling it to nine seats in the Assembly.[136]

136/Document 90
See page 294

137/Document 82
See page 289

229   On 19 November, in Maputo, my Special Representative welcomed the results with a formal declaration that the elections had been free and fair.[137] He said that although problems had occurred, no

event or series of events could affect the overall credibility of the elections. Both the OAU and the European Union also declared the elections to be free and fair. The observation mission of the European Union, which, with its Member States, defrayed about 80 per cent of the costs of the elections, expressed satisfaction that the results announced were correct and reflected the true outcome of the ballot.

230   Speaking as President-elect, Joaquim Chissano gave his assurance that the candidate who had come in second place should be given special status "as a necessary innovation to be introduced into the political customs and practices of the country". He also announced plans for democratic elections at the level of the local authorities. Mr. Dhlakama later declared that while he accepted the results, he continued to believe that the elections had not been fair.

231   Following the proclamation of the results, I made a statement congratulating the people and the leaders of Mozambique on the successful outcome of the elections. I called upon all Mozambicans to ensure that peace and stability prevailed in their country and region.[138] On 21 November, the Security Council endorsed the results and called on all parties to stand by their obligation to accept and fully abide by them.[139] On the same day, the President of the General Assembly stated that the elections had "enabled Mozambique to move irreversibly along the road to democracy", and that the Mozambican people would now be able to win the battle for the reconstruction and economic and social development of their nation.[140] On 14 December, the Security Council welcomed the inauguration of the new President and Assembly and expressed the hope that with United Nations assistance a national mine-clearance programme would be put in place prior to ONUMOZ's withdrawal.[141]

138/Document 83
See page 290

139/Document 84
See page 290

140/Document 85
See page 291

141/Document 88
See page 292

Winding up ONUMOZ

232   On 15 November 1994 the Security Council agreed to my recommendation that the mandate of ONUMOZ be extended for technical reasons until a new Government was installed in Mozambique, but not later than 15 December 1994.[142] The overall framework for the drawing down of ONUMOZ was not affected, although there were appropriate adjustments for the withdrawal schedule of military and police personnel.

233   The last meeting of the Supervisory and Monitoring Commission was held on 6 December 1994. At the meeting, the chairmen of the subsidiary commissions—Cease-fire Commission, Joint Commission for the Formation of the Mozambican Defence Force, Reintegration Commission, National Police Affairs Commission and National Informa-

142/Document 80
See page 287;
Document 81
See page 289

tion Commission—submitted their final reports. In a ceremony held on 7 December, my Special Representative handed those reports to Mr. Joaquim Chissano as President-elect, thus formally concluding the work of the commissions. The new Assembly of the Republic was installed on 8 December 1994.

234   The inauguration of the newly elected President of Mozambique on 9 December 1994 marked the expiry of the mandate of ONUMOZ, and my Special Representative left Mozambique on 13 December 1994.[143]

143/Document 90
See page 294

235   Reduction of the ONUMOZ military component began on 15 November, as scheduled in my report of 26 August 1994.[144] The residual operations and the liquidation phase of the mission were assisted by a limited force of four infantry companies, two from Bangladesh and two from Zambia, the Argentine field hospital, a skeleton headquarters staff, mine-clearance personnel and a small number of military observers. By 18 December 1994, 1,184 personnel from the military contingents and ONUMOZ headquarters and 157 military observers remained. The infantry units provided security for United Nations personnel and property until the withdrawal was completed at the end of January 1995. Thereafter, a small number of United Nations civilian logisticians remained in Mozambique for some weeks to deal with the disposal of ONUMOZ property and equipment and other residual duties.

144/Document 69
See page 251

236   On 27 January 1995, at the last meeting of the Security Council on the situation in Mozambique, Mozambique's Minister for Foreign Affairs and Cooperation, Mr. Leonardo Santos Simão, noted that considerable challenges of economic and social development awaited Mozambique, and he stressed the importance of strengthening democratic institutions and the need for the international community to continue to assist in the consolidation of peace and stability. A new era had begun in his nation, said the Foreign Minister, in which "violence and the use or threat of the use of force will be replaced by political dialogue and tolerance; an era in which the right to agree or disagree with one another must be respected by each and every person".[145]

145/Document 92
See page 300

VIII Conclusion

237 The United Nations operation in Mozambique stands as testimony to the ability of the international community to help build the foundation for sustained peace even in situations of seemingly intractable conflict. During its two-year mandate, the United Nations helped to achieve a remarkable transformation in Mozambique through one of the most complex operations the Organization has ever undertaken. The mission ensured the maintenance of a cease-fire, with few serious violations; undertook the disarming and demobilization of some 80,000 combatants and facilitated their return to civilian life; coordinated an enormous humanitarian relief effort, during which some 4 million refugees and displaced persons returned to their homes; and monitored an electoral process at the culmination of which 90 per cent of the electorate freely and democratically exercised their right to determine their future government.

238 Fundamental to this success was the deep desire of the Mozambican people—and of the principal parties involved in the process—for peace. The General Peace Agreement, signed in Rome in October 1992 after prolonged and difficult negotiations, provided the United Nations with a clear and precise plan which, though modified, was a prerequisite for ONUMOZ success. Once implementation began, the signatories to the accords remained committed to them; indeed, no effort at peace-building can succeed without such a commitment.

239 Inevitably in such a highly complex operation, logistical, political and other problems arose which required extended negotiation and modification of the plan. However, all parties displayed a welcome pragmatism concerning these changes, ensuring that the peace process remained on track. As provided for in the General Peace Agreement, the Supervisory and Monitoring Commission (CSC) became the key mechanism for sustaining both momentum and the involvement of the international community. The United Nations chairmanship of the CSC and the other commissions charged with implementing the accords greatly facilitated rapid, objective problem-solving. Whenever difficulties were encountered, the CSC was able to convene negotiations that succeeded in persuading the parties to adhere to their commitments. This form of collective oversight, involving the two parties, the United Nations, the Organization of African Unity and ambassadors of Mozambique's donor countries, allowed for flexible management and for adjustments to the timetable when such recourse became unavoidable.

240   In Mozambique, the United Nations role went beyond peace-keeping to the broader concern of assisting in the political evolution of a society previously riven by conflict. However deep the desire for peace, practical commitment to it depends on the belief that political goals can be realized through peaceful means. Reducing the level of distrust between former foes was therefore one vital function for ONUMOZ. Helping to establish the institutional framework for the democratic process was another—not only in terms of the Electoral Law but also, for example, in achieving an understanding on the role of the opposition in what had previously been a one-party system. The mobilization of resources that enabled RENAMO and new political groupings to organize themselves as parties and contest the elections in an effective manner was as crucial a factor as any in maintaining the peace process. Such peace-building was also essential to the successful implementation of the demobilization process.

241   The regional dimension was another crucial factor in the Mozambique peace process. The improved political environment in southern Africa from the end of the 1980s, which coincided with the end of the cold war, made possible the successful search for peace in Mozambique. A key element in this success was the active participation of Governments in the region in bringing peace negotiations to a fruitful conclusion in Rome. Their involvement, along with that of other members of the international community, throughout the implementation of the General Peace Agreement was equally vital to the success of ONUMOZ. The parallel efforts by the international community to bring peace to Angola had also provided many lessons for the operation in Mozambique, not least the necessity of complete demobilization before holding elections. In turn, the establishment of peace in Mozambique, along with the establishment of democratic rule in South Africa, has transformed the southern African region and, it is hoped, will enable the fledgling peace in Angola to become firmly established.

242   One of the most remarkable achievements during the two years of the ONUMOZ mandate was the voluntary resettlement of more than 4 million persons, some 1 million of whom had been refugees in neighbouring countries. The restoration of peace also facilitated Mozambique's rapid economic and social recovery from the effects of drought during 1991 and 1992. For its part, ONUMOZ coordinated and monitored humanitarian assistance operations, enabling them to reach RENAMO-controlled areas for the first time and providing the basis for the reconstruction of Mozambique's shattered hospitals, schools and other social facilities. Other vital humanitarian aspects of the peace process were also initiated, including the reintegration programme for demobilized soldiers and the training of Mozambicans to undertake long-term programmes to remove land-mines.

243   ONUMOZ succeeded admirably in all its objectives. It provided the vehicle with which Mozambicans could sustain their peace efforts, created an environment of security which allowed the cease-fire to hold, accomplished the demobilization of former combatants and, finally, provided the basis for democratic practices, rather than military confrontation, in the conduct of Mozambique's national affairs. But as the ONUMOZ mandate came to an end, it was evident that Mozambicans would need more time, with support from the international community, to entrench the democratic system they had adopted. The same was also true of other important aspects of nation-building in Mozambique, including the promotion of economic and social reconstruction, the continued integration of areas formerly under RENAMO control into the State administration, the training and provision of equipment for the newly unified armed forces and the national police, the safe-keeping of weapons collected by ONUMOZ and the systematic removal of land-mines and arms caches remaining from the war.[146]

146/Document 90
See page 294

244   ONUMOZ was one of the most effective peace-keeping operations in the history of the United Nations. It brought peace to Mozambique and, equally important, it contributed directly to the profound political transformation that has enabled Mozambique to set a firm course towards greater peace, democracy and development. As the last United Nations peace-keeping forces departed in January 1995, their colleagues from the development arms of the United Nations system remained in Mozambique, providing a strong international presence and bolstering the country's ongoing efforts to address the legacy of 16 years of civil war. As I indicated to President Chissano during my meeting with him at the March 1995 World Summit for Social Development in Copenhagen, the United Nations stands ready to provide its maximum support in these endeavours so that the Mozambican people can continue to build on the foundations of peace that have been laid over the past two years.

BOUTROS BOUTROS-GHALI

Section Two
Chronology and Documents

I Chronology of events

25 June 1962
The Frente da Libertação de Moçambique (FRELIMO) is founded with Dr. Eduardo Mondlane as its first president.

25 September 1964
FRELIMO launches an armed struggle to achieve independence from Portugal.

7 February 1969
FRELIMO president Eduardo Mondlane is assassinated by a parcel bomb delivered to him in Dar es Salaam.

21 December 1972
From bases in FRELIMO-controlled areas of Mozambique, the Zimbabwe African National Union (ZANU), led by Robert Mugabe, begins military operations against the minority Government of Southern Rhodesia.

April 1974
Southern Rhodesia's intelligence service establishes an armed group inside Mozambique to combat both FRELIMO and ZANU.

25 April 1974
A *coup d'état* in Portugal brings to power young officers who favour granting independence to the country's colonies in Africa.

7 September 1974
Portugal establishes a transitional Government in Mozambique; Joaquim Chissano serves as Prime Minister.

25 June 1975
On Mozambique's declaration of independence, Samora Machel, President of FRELIMO, is sworn in as the country's first President; Joaquim Chissano becomes Minister for Foreign Affairs.

March 1976
Mozambique closes its borders with Southern Rhodesia in support of the Zimbabwean nationalist struggle.

1977
The Southern Rhodesian Government is instrumental in the establishment of the Resistência Nacional Moçambicana (known initially as MNR but later as RENAMO) inside Mozambique to harass and destabilize the Government. FRELIMO declares itself to be a Marxist-Leninist party and signs aid agreements with the Union of Soviet Socialist Republics and Cuba.

October 1979
RENAMO's first leader, André Matsangaissa, is killed while leading a raid in the Gorongosa game park; he is succeeded by Afonso Macacho Marceta Dhlakama.

March 1980
Southern Rhodesia transfers control of RENAMO to the South African military.

April 1980
Zimbabwe achieves independence.

1981
South Africa undertakes military raids inside Mozambique. The Malawi-based Africa Livre movement, formerly known as UNAR, is absorbed into RENAMO.

1982
War intensifies in Mozambique; Zimbabwe sends troops to protect the Beira transport corridor. Severe drought and famine occur in the central provinces.

16 March 1984
President Machel signs a peace accord with South Africa's Prime Minister, P. W. Botha, at Nkomati, on the two countries' common border. South Africa agrees not to allow its territory to be used as a base for attacks against Mozambique and, for its part, Mozambique declares that it will not permit the African National Congress (ANC) to use its territory as a base for attacks against South Africa. RENAMO establishes new bases inside Mozambique.

August 1984
Mozambique joins the World Bank and the International Monetary Fund.

3 October 1984
Tentative peace talks between FRELIMO and RENAMO are held in Pretoria but are broken off by RENAMO.

April 1985
Attacks by RENAMO on convoys travelling between Maputo and Gaza Province kill more than 200 civilians.

June 1985
President Machel meets with Zimbabwe's Prime Minister Robert Mugabe and President Julius Nyerere of the United Republic of Tanzania in Harare, Zimbabwe; it is agreed that the two countries will support Mozambique and, in particular, that Zimbabwe will increase its military presence there.

August 1985
Joint military action is undertaken by Mozambican and Zimbabwean forces to capture RENAMO's headquarters in Gorongosa, Sofala Province; it is taken and retaken several times over the following months.

1986
Widespread RENAMO attacks in the northern provinces force tens of thousands of Mozambicans to flee to Malawi.

September 1986
President Machel meets President Hastings Banda of Malawi; after Malawi expels 12,000 RENAMO fighters, the movement launches a major offensive in the northern half of Mozambique.

19 October 1986
President Machel dies in a plane crash on his way back from consultations with other African heads of State in Lusaka.

3 November 1986
Joaquim Chissano is sworn in as President of Mozambique.

1987
Government forces, with the help of Zimbabwean troops, launch a counter-offensive against RENAMO between the coast and the Malawi border; the fighting forces additional hundreds of thousands of Mozambicans to flee to Malawi.

April 1988
The State Department of the United States of America issues a report attributing many of the worst atrocities to RENAMO and terming the war in Mozambique one of the most brutal holocausts since the Second World War.

May 1988
Archbishop Jaime Gonçalves of Beira meets RENAMO leader Afonso Dhlakama at his base in Gorongosa district to explore the possibility of negotiations.

September 1988
Pope John Paul II visits Mozambique. RENAMO leader Afonso Dhlakama visits the Federal Republic of Germany, where he meets senior Kenyan officials.

December 1988
Kenya's President Daniel arap Moi sends an envoy to meet Mr. Dhlakama in Gorongosa. The United Nations High Commissioner for Refugees (UNHCR), Mozambique and Malawi sign an agreement to promote the voluntary repatriation of Mozambican refugees in Malawi.

February 1989
Mozambican church leaders meet RENAMO leaders in Nairobi.

July 1989
The Mozambique Government issues a document outlining principles for dialogue with RENAMO. FRELIMO drops its designation as a Marxist-Leninist party. The Government undertakes a programme of political and economic liberalization.

August 1989
Mr. Dhlakama leads a RENAMO delegation to Nairobi for further meetings with Mozambican church leaders.

22 August 1989
Mr. Dhlakama announces the suspension of RENAMO attacks on the Nacala rail link to Malawi.

December 1989
Representatives of the Mozambique Government and RENAMO hold separate talks in Nairobi with the Kenyan Government.

January 1990
The draft of a new constitution is circulated for public review.

March 1990
Mr. Dhlakama visits Rome for talks with members of the Community of Sant'Egidio, a lay Roman Catholic organization, and with officials of the Italian Foreign Ministry.

12 March 1990
President Chissano meets President George Bush of the United States in Washington and affirms his Government's readiness to talk directly with RENAMO.

8-10 July 1990
The first direct meeting between delegations of the Mozambique Government and RENAMO takes place in Rome at the headquarters of the Community of Sant'Egidio. The two sides adopt a joint communiqué agreeing on their common interest in ending the war. *See Document 12, page 105*

31 July 1990
President Chissano announces the support of FRELIMO's political bureau for a multi-party political system.

11-14 August 1990
A second round of talks between the Government and RENAMO is held near Rome.

2 November 1990
The Mozambique Assembly approves the new Constitution, which introduces a multi-party system, universal suffrage, an independent judiciary, freedom of the press, the right to strike and a market economy; in a communiqué issued in Lisbon, RENAMO rejects the Constitution.

14 November 1990
As a third round of talks between Government and RENAMO delegations gets under way, Mr. Dhlakama meets the United States Assistant Secretary of State for Africa, Herman Cohen, in Rome.

1 December 1990
An agreement between the Government and RENAMO on a partial cease-fire, covering the key transport routes across Mozambique, is signed in Rome; an international Joint Verification Commission (JVC) is set up to monitor the agreement.
See Document 1, page 93

19 December 1990
With the inauguration of the JVC in Rome, it is agreed that future meetings will be held in Maputo, with support from a military verification committee.

22 December 1990
A law governing political parties is passed by the National Assembly in Maputo. Three new parties are formed.

6 May 1991
A new round of negotiations between the Government and RENAMO opens in Rome.

28 May 1991
An agenda for full peace negotiations is agreed upon at the Rome talks.

18 October 1991
In Rome, the Government and RENAMO sign the first protocol of their General Peace Agreement, covering the basic principles, asserting the legitimacy of the Mozambican Government and agreeing on the establishment of a commission — made up of representatives of the Government, RENAMO, the United Nations and other organizations or Governments — to supervise and monitor compliance with the General Peace Agreement.
See Document 12, page 105

13 November 1991
The second protocol of the General Peace Agreement, covering arrangements for the formation of political parties, including RENAMO, is signed in Rome.
See Document 12, page 105

10-15 December 1991
RENAMO holds a party congress in Gorongosa district; Mr. Dhlakama's position as president of the movement is confirmed.

12 March 1992
The third protocol of the General Peace Agreement, covering electoral matters, is signed in Rome.
See Document 12, page 105

28 May 1992
In a letter to President Chissano, Secretary-General Boutros Boutros-Ghali offers the services of the United Nations in promoting an agreement between the Government and RENAMO.
See Document 2, page 94

1 June 1992
In a letter to the Secretary-General, President Chissano outlines those elements of the Agreement which anticipate United Nations involvement, specifically participation in a supervisory and monitoring commission and observation of the elections.
See Document 3, page 95

10 June 1992
At a new round of negotiations in Rome, the parties approve the mediators' invitation to the United Nations, France, Portugal, the United Kingdom of Great Britain and Northern Ireland and the United States to act as observers.

28 June 1992
The Secretary-General sends military observers to participate in the talks.

4 July 1992
RENAMO president Afonso Dhlakama meets with President Robert Mugabe of Zimbabwe and President Sir Ketumile Masire of Botswana in Gaborone and declares his readiness to sign a cease-fire agreement in exchange for guaranteed security for himself and freedom for RENAMO to operate as a political party.

9 July 1992
The Government of Mozambique requests United Nations assistance for the electoral process.
See Document 4, page 96

16 July 1992
Government and RENAMO delegations in Rome sign the Declaration on the Guiding Principles for Humanitarian Assistance.
See Document 12, page 105

7 August 1992
Meeting in Rome, President Chissano and Mr. Dhlakama sign a Joint Declaration guaranteeing political freedoms and accepting the role of the United Nations in monitoring the General Peace Agreement.
See Document 12, page 105

19 August 1992
In a letter to President Chissano, the Secretary-General details modalities for a United Nations operation to implement the General Peace Agreement.
See Document 6, page 97

22 August 1992
President Chissano informs the Secretary-General that a cease-fire will commence seven days following the signing of a peace agreement and requests that United Nations technical teams on cease-fire arrangements and the electoral process arrive in Mozambique by 26 August.
See Document 7, page 100

10 September 1992
The Secretary-General briefs the Security Council on the dispatch of technical teams (which had been sent on 7 September) and the possibility that he will recommend a substantial peace-keeping operation in Mozambique.

18 September 1992
After a further meeting in Gaborone, President Chissano and Mr. Dhlakama announce their intention to sign the General Peace Agreement on 1 October.
See Document 9, page 101

22 September 1992
President Chissano requests United Nations financial support for the reintegration of refugees and demobilized soldiers, formation of the new army and the electoral process.
See Document 8, page 101

29 September 1992
The Secretary-General briefs the Security Council on the importance of the United Nations chairmanship of the supervisory commissions called for in the General Peace Agreement, on the need for precision in the number and location of assembly points for both sides' forces and on the humanitarian crisis, particularly in RENAMO-controlled areas.
See Document 10, page 102

4 October 1992
After a final round of negotiations, the remaining protocols of the General Peace Agreement are signed at a ceremony in Rome; the United Nations is formally invited to participate in monitoring and ensuring the Agreement's implementation.
See Document 11, page 104; and Document 12, page 105

9 October 1992
The Secretary-General reports to the Security Council on the signing of the General Peace Agreement for Mozambique and the request of the parties for a United Nations peace-keeping and electoral assistance operation.
See Document 13, page 126

12 October 1992
The Secretary-General requests President Chissano and Mr. Dhlakama to cooperate with the United Nations in bringing humanitarian relief to millions of Mozambicans facing the threat of famine.
See Document 14, page 129; and Document 15, page 129

13 October 1992
The Security Council adopts a resolution welcoming the signature of the General Peace Agreement for Mozambique.
See Document 16, page 130

15 October 1992
The Mozambique Government's publication of the General Peace Agreement, after approval by the National Assembly, marks the formal start of the cease-fire. The Special Representative of the Secretary-General, Mr. Aldo Ajello (Italy), appointed on **13 October,** arrives in Mozambique with a preliminary group of military observers drawn from other United Nations peace-keeping operations.

17-19 October 1992
Violations of the cease-fire are reported.

20 October 1992
Two teams of military observers are deployed to Nampula and Beira.

The Council of Ministers of Mozambique issues a communiqué reporting on the absence of RENAMO representatives in Maputo and on alleged cease-fire violations by RENAMO.
See Document 21, page 144

23 October 1992
The Secretary-General reports to the Security Council on the activities of his Special Representative for Mozambique and on reports of cease-fire violations and the urgent need to get a United Nations operation under way.
See Document 19, page 141

27 October 1992
The Security Council expresses concern at the continuing reports of major violations of the cease-fire in several regions of Mozambique.
See Document 20, page 143

4 November 1992
The Supervisory and Monitoring Commission, charged with overall responsibility for overseeing implementation of the Agreement, is established in Maputo; it holds its first meeting and appoints its subsidiary commissions.

17 November 1992
The Secretary-General appeals to Italy for advance deployment of troops to help protect Mozambique's vital transport corridors pending withdrawal of Zimbabwean and Malawian forces.
See Document 24, page 147

1 December 1992
The Secretary-General informs President Chissano about the status of preparations for a United Nations operation in Mozambique and expresses concern over reported cease-fire violations by Government troops.
See Document 25, page 148

3 December 1992
The Secretary-General outlines for the Security Council a mandate for a comprehensive United Nations operation in Mozambique.
See Document 26, page 149

10 December 1992
Mr. Dhlakama meets with President Mugabe of Zimbabwe in Harare and agrees to accept the continued presence of Zimbabwean troops along the Beira corridor until the arrival of United Nations forces.

15-16 December 1992
A special donors' conference in Rome agrees on a plan for humanitarian assistance to support the Mozambique peace process; pledges totalling nearly $400 million are made.
See Document 23, page 146; and Document 28, page 159

16 December 1992
The Security Council formally establishes the United Nations Operation in Mozambique (ONUMOZ) until 31 October 1993 with a mandate that includes monitoring the elections, tentatively scheduled for October 1993.
See Document 27, page 158

7 January 1993
Mr. Dhlakama informs the Secretary-General that cantonment and demobilization of RENAMO troops cannot begin until 65 per cent of United Nations troops have been deployed.
See Document 29, page 170

22 January 1993
The Secretary-General informs Mr. Dhlakama that 100 United Nations military observers will arrive in Mozambique within the week to verify the first phase of the assembly of Government and RENAMO troops and that the first ONUMOZ battalion will be installed by mid-February.
See Document 30, page 171

30 January 1993
The Italian Government requests the United Nations to establish a trust fund for the transformation of RENAMO into a political party called for by the General Peace Agreement.
See Document 31, page 172; and Document 32, page 172

9 February 1993
The first United Nations troops, from Italy, start to arrive in Mozambique.

14 February 1993
The ONUMOZ Force Commander, Major-General Lelio Gonçalves Rodrigues da Silva (Brazil), assumes his duties in Mozambique.

9 March 1993
RENAMO's chief negotiator in Maputo, Raúl Domingos, and other representatives depart for Maringue district, bringing the work of the joint commissions to a halt for many weeks to follow.

26 March 1993
The Government distributes a draft electoral law to RENAMO and other political parties.

1 April 1993
Italy's ONUMOZ battalion becomes fully operational in the Beira corridor.

2 April 1993
The Secretary-General reports to the Security Council that by mid-March some 154 military observers from 12 countries are engaged in verification of cease-fire violations and limited monitoring of assembly areas, but that there have been logistical delays in deployment of ONUMOZ military units.
See Document 33, page 173

11-15 April 1993
Zimbabwean troops are withdrawn from the Beira corridor.

14 April 1993
The Security Council urges the parties to take steps to comply with the commitments they have undertaken for the implementation of the Peace Agreement; and appeals to RENAMO to ensure effective functioning of the joint commissions and stresses to the Government the importance of the early signature of a status-of-forces agreement with the United Nations.
See Document 34, page 180

17 April 1993
ONUMOZ starts registering Government soldiers that were demobilized before the signing of the General Peace Agreement.

May 1993
All the main ONUMOZ infantry battalions — from Bangladesh, Botswana, Italy, Uruguay and Zambia — and support units from Argentina, Bangladesh, India, Italy, Japan and Portugal are deployed.

10 May 1993
A special United Nations trust fund is set up to help RENAMO establish itself as a political party.

14 May 1993
In New York, the United Nations and the Government of Mozambique sign a status-of-forces agreement covering the deployment of ONUMOZ troops.

3 June 1993
After a three-month absence from Maputo, RENAMO delegations resume attendance at meetings of the Supervisory and Monitoring Commission and the Cease-fire Commission.

8-9 June 1993
A follow-up donors' conference is held in Maputo under the joint chairmanship of the United Nations and the Government of Italy, increasing the pledges of humanitarian assistance made in Rome in December 1992 and after to a total of $520 million for the 12-month period from May 1993 to April 1994.

9 June 1993
Malawian troops are withdrawn from the Nacala corridor.

30 June 1993
The Secretary-General reports to the Security Council that while ONUMOZ's military component has been deployed and no major cease-fire violations have been reported, demobilization of troops is seriously delayed.
See Document 37, page 184

9 July 1993
The Security Council approves the Secretary-General's recommendation that the Joint Commission for the Formation of the Mozambican Defence Force be placed under United Nations chairmanship.
See Document 38, page 189

3 August 1993
A training programme under ONUMOZ for the new Mozambican Defence Force (FADM) begins in Nyanga, Zimbabwe.

23 August 1993
In Maputo, President Chissano and Mr. Dhlakama meet for the first time since the signing of the General Peace Agreement in Rome almost one year earlier. Mr. Dhlakama subsequently takes occupancy of a residence in Maputo (although he continues to spend long periods at his headquarters in Maringue district).
See Document 39, page 190

30 August 1993
The Secretary-General reports to the Security Council on the progress of talks between President Chissano and Mr. Dhlakama and in the establishment of assembly areas for the cantonment of Government and RENAMO troops.
See Document 40, page 190

2-3 September 1993
President Chissano and Mr. Dhlakama agree to integrate former RENAMO-controlled areas into the State administration; they also request the United Nations to monitor all police activities in Mozambique.
See Document 41, page 196

10 September 1993
The Government of Mozambique requests deployment of a contingent of United Nations civilian police.
See Document 42, page 198

13 September 1993
The Security Council, in its resolution 863 (1993), expresses concern over the continuing delays in the implementation of the General Peace Agreement and draws the parties' attention to the importance of demobilizing their troops and holding elections not later than October 1994.
See Document 43, page 199

24 September 1993
In response to Security Council resolution 863 (1993), the Government of Mozambique issues a statement addressing delays in demobilization, formation of the new army and drafting of an electoral law.
See Document 45, page 201

17-20 October 1993
The Secretary-General visits Maputo and meets with both President Chissano and Mr. Dhlakama. The Secretary-General attains the parties' agreement to begin demobilization of their forces in January 1994; the parties also reach agreement on police affairs and on the composition of the National Elections Commission (CNE).
See Document 46, page 203

22 October 1993
At a meeting of the Supervisory and Monitoring Commission in Maputo, the Government and RENAMO agree to a revised timetable for the implementation of the General Peace Agreement.

29 October 1993
The Security Council extends the mandate of ONUMOZ for an interim period until 5 November 1993.
See Document 47, page 204

1 November 1993
The Secretary-General reports to the Security Council on the new momentum in the implementation of the peace process in Mozambique.
See Document 48, page 205

5 November 1993
The Security Council authorizes the deployment of United Nations civilian police observers and extends the mandate of ONUMOZ until 30 April 1994, subject to the proviso that the Secretary-General would report every three months on whether the parties have made sufficient progress towards implementation of the Peace Agreement.
See Document 49, page 212

30 November 1993
As the first step in the revised demobilization programme, 20 assembly points are formally opened.

9 December 1993
The new Electoral Law is approved by the National Assembly in Maputo.

31 December 1993
The Mozambique Government reports to the Secretary-General that a large, heavily armed group has crossed the border from Malawi to Mozambique, posing a threat to the peace process.
See Document 52, page 214; and Document 53, page 215

12 January 1994
Preliminary demobilization begins, but is limited to paramilitary forces, militia and irregular troops.

14 January 1994
The Secretary-General appeals to Italy for additional resources for the trust fund established by the United Nations to finance the transformation of RENAMO into a political party.
See Document 54, page 215

21 January 1994
The National Elections Commission (CNE) is appointed. This permits the establishment of a United Nations Trust Fund for Assistance to Registered Political Parties in Mozambique, administered by the CNE.

28 January 1994
The Secretary-General reports to the Security Council that progress has been made in the assembly and demobilization of troops and in the electoral process and that resources are still needed for financial assistance to RENAMO.
See Document 55, page 216

15 February 1994
The CNE officially starts its work.

21 February 1994
The remaining assembly areas are opened, bringing the total to 49.

23 February 1994
The Security Council authorizes the establishment of a civilian police component of up to 1,144 personnel as an integral part of ONUMOZ.
See Document 57, page 228

1 March 1994
The Secretary-General appoints Major-General Mohammad Abdus Salam (Bangladesh) as new ONUMOZ Force Commander.

4 March 1994
Italy agrees to the Secretary-General's request for a further contribution to meet the needs of RENAMO in the electoral process and agrees that greater flexibility is needed in the administration of the Trust Fund.
See Document 56, page 227; and Document 58, page 230

10 March 1994
Full demobilization of forces begins.

6 April 1994
The joint High Commanders of the new FADM, General Lagos Lidimo for the Government and General Mateus Ngonhamo for RENAMO, are sworn in.

11 April 1994
President Chissano announces that general elections will take place on 27 and 28 October 1994.
See Document 60, page 231

27 April 1994
The Secretary-General appoints the international members of the Mozambique Electoral Tribunal.
See Document 61, page 231; and Document 62, page 232

28 April 1994
The Secretary-General reports to the Security Council that as of 18 April more than 49,000 soldiers from Government forces and RENAMO had reported to assembly areas and nearly 13,000 had been demobilized.
See Document 63, page 232

5 May 1994
The Security Council urges the parties to complete demobilization by 15 July and to support the electoral process. The mandate of ONUMOZ is extended until 15 November 1994.
See Document 64, page 241

June 1994
Mr. Dhlakama visits the United States and United Nations Headquarters.

1 June 1994
The registration of voters begins.

18 June 1994
The closure of the assembly areas begins.

24 June 1994
The registration of Government troops still stationed outside the assembly areas begins.

7 July 1994
The Secretary-General reports to the Security Council that while preparations for elections are proceeding in accordance with the established timetable, delays in the completion of the assembly and demobilization of troops, as well as in the formation of the new Mozambican Defence Force, are cause for serious concern. In a statement to the Cease-fire Commission, the Government of Mozambique protests what it claims is partiality by ONUMOZ towards RENAMO and cites RENAMO cease-fire violations.
See Document 65, page 242; and Document 66, page 248

19 July 1994
The Security Council urges both sides to meet the 15 August deadline for demobilization and stresses that elections should take place on 27 and 28 October.
See Document 67, page 250

7-12 August 1994
A Security Council mission visits Mozambique to discuss with the parties full implementation of the Peace Agreement.
See Document 68, page 251

16 August 1994
The Armed Forces of Mozambique (FAM) high command are demobilized; the authority, equipment and infrastructure of the FAM are transferred to the newly constituted FADM.

19 August 1994
The RENAMO military leaders are demobilized.

26 August 1994
The Secretary-General reports to the Security Council that the peace process is in its final phase and that preparations for the conduct of the elections are under way.
See Document 69, page 251

29 August 1994
The Security Council mission's report expresses cautious optimism about the pace of the peace process,

satisfaction with the progress of demobilization, and disappointment with the progress of mine clearance. It recommends that every effort be made to ensure that voter registration reaches all Mozambicans and that the Security Council encourage the international community to assist with reintegration programmes for demobilized soldiers and with the provision of additional trainers for the FADM.
See Document 70, page 258

30 August 1994
The demobilization process ends; follow-up verification begins.

2 September 1994
The registration of voters is concluded, with almost 6.4 million voters registered — 81 per cent of those eligible.

7 September 1994
The Security Council expresses satisfaction with the progress of the peace process in Mozambique.
See Document 71, page 267

22 September 1994
The electoral campaign begins; 12 presidential candidates and 14 political parties participate.

21 October 1994
The Secretary-General reports to the Security Council that the essential conditions now exist for holding free and fair elections in Mozambique. The Security Council calls for calm and responsible voting. United Nations electoral observers are deployed in Mozambique.
See Document 74, page 281; and Document 75, page 283

24 October 1994
The electoral campaign ends.

26 October 1994
On the eve of the elections, Mr. Dhlakama says RENAMO will not participate in the elections.

The Front-line States — six nations in the southern African region — meet in Harare, Zimbabwe, and call for full respect by foreign Powers of the General Peace Agreement.
See Document 76, page 284

27 October 1994
The Secretary-General says that the elections must proceed as planned, and the Security Council urges RENAMO to reconsider its decision to withdraw from the elections. Voting commences at most of the 7,244 polling-stations around the country.
See Document 77, page 285; and Document 78, page 285

28 October 1994
After meetings with the Secretary-General's Special Representative, the international members of the Supervisory and Monitoring Commission and senior officials of neighbouring Governments, Mr. Dhlakama announces that he will participate in the elections; the period of voting is extended one more day.
See Document 79, page 286

29 October 1994
Voting is completed.

9 November 1994
The Secretary-General recommends a technical extension of the mandate of ONUMOZ to continue its verification and monitoring activities until the new Government is installed.
See Document 80, page 287

15 November 1994
The Security Council extends the mandate of ONUMOZ until such time as a new Government is installed in Mozambique, but not later than 15 December 1994.
See Document 81, page 289

19 November 1994
The election results are declared by the CNE Chairman: Joaquim Chissano wins the presidential election and FRELIMO takes 129 seats in the new National Assembly, while RENAMO takes 112 seats and a coalition of three small parties 9 seats. Following a declaration by his Special Representative that the elections were free and fair, the Secretary-General congratulates the people of Mozambique.
See Document 82, page 289; and Document 83, page 290

21 November 1994
The Security Council calls on the Mozambican parties to stand by their obligation to accept the results of the elections. The President of the General Assembly expresses satisfaction with the conduct of the elections.
See Document 84, page 290; and Document 85, page 291

6 December 1994
The Supervisory and Monitoring Commission holds its final meeting.

8 December 1994
The new National Assembly is installed.

9 December 1994
The newly elected President of Mozambique, Joaquim Chissano, is inaugurated; the mandate of ONUMOZ expires.

14 December 1994
The Security Council welcomes the installation of the new President of Mozambique and the inauguration of the new Assembly.
See Document 88, page 292

23 December 1994
The Secretary-General reports to the Security Council that the withdrawal of ONUMOZ personnel has begun and will be completed by 31 January 1995.
See Document 90, page 294

January 1995
The withdrawal of ONUMOZ is completed. A small group of United Nations logisticians remains to deal with the disposal of property and equipment.

27 January 1995
The Security Council, in its final meeting on the situation in Mozambique, stresses the continued need for international assistance for Mozambique's reconstruction and development.
See Document 92, page 300

10 March 1995
The Secretary-General meets with President Chissano at the World Summit for Social Development in Copenhagen and reiterates the commitment of the United Nations to assist Mozambique in its recovery and long-term needs.

II List of reproduced documents

The documents reproduced on pages 93-310 include resolutions of the General Assembly and the Security Council, statements by the President of the Security Council, the General Peace Agreement for Mozambique, statements and other communications from Member States, reports and letters of the Secretary-General to the General Assembly and the Security Council, correspondence of the Secretary-General, and other communications.

1990

Document 1
Agreement on a partial cease-fire in Mozambique, signed by the Government of Mozambique and the Resistência Nacional Moçambicana (RENAMO) in Rome on 1 December 1990.
Not issued as a United Nations document.
See page 93

1992

Document 2
Letter dated 28 May 1992 from the Secretary-General to President Joaquim Alberto Chissano of Mozambique on United Nations participation in the peace talks.
Not issued as a United Nations document.
See page 94

Document 3
Letter dated 1 June 1992 from President Chissano to the Secretary-General on the progress of the peace talks between his Government and RENAMO.
Not issued as a United Nations document.
See page 95

Document 4
Letter dated 9 July 1992 from Mr. Pascoal Manuel Mocumbi, Minister for Foreign Affairs of Mozambique, requesting United Nations assistance for the electoral process.
Not issued as a United Nations document.
See page 96

Document 5
Letter dated 23 July 1992 from the Secretary-General to Mozambique's Minister for Foreign Affairs on the United Nations electoral assistance field mission.
Not issued as a United Nations document.
See page 96

Document 6
Letter dated 19 August 1992 from the Secretary-General to President Chissano on the role of the United Nations in the Rome peace talks; includes a "non-paper" on the modalities of United Nations verification of aspects of a peace agreement in Mozambique.
Not issued as a United Nations document.
See page 97

Document 7
Letter dated 22 August 1992 from President Chissano to the Secretary-General in response to the "non-paper" on United Nations verification of the General Peace Agreement.
Not issued as a United Nations document.
See page 100

Document 8
Letter dated 22 September 1992 from President Chissano to the Secretary-General on the United Nations electoral assistance technical mission in Mozambique.
Not issued as a United Nations document.
See page 101

Document 9
Letter dated 28 September 1992 from President Chissano requesting the Secretary-General's attendance at the signing of the General Peace Agreement.
Not issued as a United Nations document.
See page 101

Document 10
Letter dated 29 September 1992 from the Secretary-General to the President of the Security Council on United Nations involvement in implementation of the General Peace Agreement.
Not issued as a United Nations document.
See page 102

Document 11
Statement by the Secretary-General welcoming the signing of the General Peace Agreement in Rome on 4 October 1992.
UN Press Release SG/SM/4829, 5 October 1992
See page 104

Document 57
Security Council resolution authorizing the creation of a police component for ONUMOZ.
S/RES/898 (1994), 23 February 1994
See page 228

Document 58
Letter dated 4 March 1994 from the President of the Council of Ministers of Italy to the Secretary-General on Italy's further contribution to the United Nations Trust Fund.
Not issued as a United Nations document.
See page 230

Document 59
Letter dated 11 March 1994 from the United Nations High Commissioner for Refugees, Sadako Ogata, to the Secretary-General on repatriation of refugees to Mozambique.
Not issued as a United Nations document.
See page 230

Document 60
Letter dated 12 April 1994 from Mozambique concerning the holding of elections.
S/1994/419, 12 April 1994
See page 231

Document 61
Letter dated 21 April 1994 from the President of the Security Council to the Secretary-General regarding the appointment of international members of the Mozambique Electoral Tribunal.
S/1994/485, 21 April 1994
See page 231

Document 62
Letter dated 27 April 1994 from the Secretary-General to the President of the Security Council on the appointment of international members of the Mozambique Electoral Tribunal.
S/1994/514, 28 April 1994
See page 232

Document 63
Report of the Secretary-General on ONUMOZ.
S/1994/511, 28 April 1994
See page 232

Document 64
Security Council resolution renewing the mandate of ONUMOZ until 15 November 1994 and urging the Mozambican parties to allow ONUMOZ unimpeded access to the areas under their control.
S/RES/916 (1994), 5 May 1994
See page 241

Document 65
Report of the Secretary-General on ONUMOZ.
S/1994/803, 7 July 1994
See page 242

Document 66
Letter dated 7 July 1994 from Mozambique transmitting a statement of the position of the Government of Mozambique regarding the cantonment of troops.
S/1994/806, 9 July 1994
See page 248

Document 67
Statement by the President of the Security Council expressing concern at continuing delays in the implementation of the General Peace Agreement for Mozambique.
S/PRST/1994/35, 19 July 1994
See page 250

Document 68
Note by the President of the Security Council on the sending of a mission to Mozambique to convey the Security Council's concern at delays in the implementation of the General Peace Agreement.
S/1994/931, 4 August 1994
See page 251

Document 69
Further report of the Secretary-General on ONUMOZ.
S/1994/1002, 26 August 1994
See page 251

Document 70
Report of the Security Council Mission to Mozambique of 7 to 12 August 1994.
S/1994/1009, 29 August 1994
See page 258

Document 71
Statement by the President of the Security Council expressing cautious optimism that Mozambicans will fulfil the goals of the peace process.
S/PRST/1994/51, 7 September 1994
See page 267

Document 72
Letter dated 9 September 1994 from the Secretary-General to Italian Prime Minister Silvio Berlusconi on Italy's contribution to operations in Mozambique and to the Trust Fund for the Implementation of the Peace Agreement.
Not issued as a United Nations document.
See page 268

Document 89
General Assembly resolution concerning assistance to Mozambique.
A/RES/49/21 D, 20 December 1994
See page 293

Document 90
Final report of the Secretary-General on ONUMOZ.
S/1994/1449, 23 December 1994
See page 294

Document 91
Letter dated 26 January 1995 from President Chissano to the Secretary-General on the successful conclusion of ONUMOZ's mandate.
Not issued as a United Nations document.
See page 299

Document 92
Statements made by the Minister for Foreign Affairs and Cooperation of Mozambique and the representatives of Botswana, Germany, the Russian Federation, Italy, the United Kingdom, China, the United States, France, Brazil and Portugal at the final Security Council meeting on Mozambique (extract).
S/PV.3494, 27 January 1995
See page 300

The following is a breakdown, by category, of the documents reproduced in this book.

Resolution of the General Assembly
Document 89

Resolutions of the Security Council
Documents 16, 27, 34, 38, 43, 47, 49, 57, 64, 81, 84

Statement by the President of the General Assembly
Document 85

Statements by the President of the Security Council on behalf of the Council
Documents 20, 67, 71, 75, 78, 88

Peace agreements
Documents 1, 12

Statements and other communications from Member States
Documents 17, 21, 22, 23, 28, 41, 45, 60, 66

Reports and letters of the Secretary-General to the General Assembly and the Security Council
Documents 10, 13, 18, 19, 26, 33, 37, 40, 48, 55, 62, 63, 65, 69, 73, 74, 80, 90

Statements by the Secretary-General
Documents 11, 39, 44, 46, 77, 83

Statement by the Special Representative of the Secretary-General
Document 82

Correspondence of the Secretary-General
Documents 2, 3, 4, 5, 6, 7, 8, 9, 14, 15, 24, 25, 29, 30, 31, 32, 36, 42, 50, 51, 52, 53, 54, 56, 58, 59, 72, 86, 87, 91

Report of the Security Council Mission
Document 70

Provisional verbatim records of meetings of the Security Council
Documents 35, 92

Other
Documents 61, 68, 69, 76, 79

III Other documents of interest

Readers seeking additional information about the United Nations Operation in Mozambique (ONUMOZ) and the situation in Mozambique might wish to consult the following documents, which are available in the Dag Hammarskjöld Library at the United Nations Headquarters in New York City, at other libraries in the United Nations system or at libraries around the world which have been designated as depository libraries for United Nations documents. Other documents relevant to the United Nations Operation in Mozambique can also be obtained from the agencies and programmes of the United Nations system, in particular, the United Nations Development Programme, the United Nations Children's Fund (UNICEF), the Office of the High Commissioner for Refugees and the World Food Programme.

Financing ONUMOZ

Reports of the Secretary-General, of the Advisory Committee on Administrative and Budgetary Questions (ACABQ) and of the Fifth Committee (C.5) of the General Assembly
A/47/881/Add.1, 8 February 1993
A/47/896, 24 February 1993 (ACABQ)
A/47/906 (Part I), 11 March 1993 (C.5)
A/47/969, 28 June 1993
A/47/985, 27 July 1993 (ACABQ)
A/47/906/Add.1 (Part II), 10 September 1993 (C.5)
A/C.5/48/40, p.27, 9 December 1993
A/48/779, 17 December 1993 (ACABQ)
A/48/821, 23 December 1993 (C.5)
A/48/849, 17 January 1994
A/48/889, 2 March 1994 (ACABQ)
A/48/821/Add.1 (Part II), 4 March 1994 (C.5)
A/48/821/Add.2 (Part III), 21 March 1994 (C.5)
A/48/849/Add.1, 23 May 1994
A/48/956, 24 June 1994 (ACABQ)
A/48/821/Add.3 (Part IV), 20 July 1994 (C.5)
A/49/649, 8 November 1994
A/49/649/Add.1, 23 November 1994
A/49/817 (Part I), 22 December 1994 (C.5)
A/49/649/Add.2, 31 January 1995
A/49/849, 15 February 1995 (ACABQ)
A/49/817/Add.1 (Part II), 3 March 1995 (C.5)

Assessments of Member States' Contributions
ST/ADM/SER.B/406, 15 July 1994 (covering the period from 15 October 1992 to 30 June 1994)
ST/ADM/SER.B/448, 26 October 1994 (covering the period from 1 May 1994 to 15 November 1994).

Resolutions of the General Assembly
A/RES/47/224 A, 16 March 1993
A/RES/47/224 C, 14 September 1993
A/RES/48/240 A, 24 March 1994
A/RES/48/240 B, 29 July 1994
A/RES/49/235, 10 March 1995

Letter from Member State
A/C.5/48/70, 29 March 1994 (United States)

Special economic and disaster relief assistance

Reports of the Secretary-General
A/45/479, 9 October 1990
A/45/562, 10 October 1990

Reports of the Second Committee
A/45/856, 14 December 1990
A/47/727, 8 December 1992

Resolutions of the General Assembly
A/RES/45/227, 11 February 1991
A/RES/47/42, 9 December 1992
A/RES/48/249, 18 April 1994

Letter from Member State
A/48/249, 4 April 1994 (Mozambique)

Communications related to an alleged use of chemical weapons in Mozambique
A/47/78 - S/23490, 29 January 1992; Letter dated 27 January 1992 from Mozambique to the Secretary-General

S/24065, 12 June 1992; Report of the mission dispatched by the Secretary-General to investigate an alleged use of chemical weapons in Mozambique

Other resolution of the General Assembly
A/RES/44/221, 22 December 1989; Concerns cooperation between the United Nations and the Southern African Development Coordination Conference (SADCC)

Other communications from Member States
A/47/639, 6 November 1992; Letter dated 20 October 1992
from Mauritania, transmitting the communiqué adopted
at the ninth session of the OAU Ad Hoc Committee of
Heads of State and Government, held in Gaborone on
15 October 1992

A/49/87 - S/1994/263, 7 March 1994; Letter dated
2 March 1994 from Angola, Brazil, Cape Verde, Guinea-
Bissau, Mozambique, Portugal and Sao Tome and Prin-
cipe, transmitting the communiqué of the first meeting of
Ministers for Foreign Affairs of the Portuguese-speaking
countries, held in Brasilia on 10 February 1994

United Nations Development Programme (UNDP)
Report to the Governing Council of UNDP
DP/CP/MOZ/4, 31 March 1993; Fourth country pro-
gramme for Mozambique

Security Council: Provisional verbatim records
S/PV.3123, 13 October 1992 (Meeting at which the
    Council adopted resolution 782 (1992))
S/PV.3149, 16 December 1992 (resolution 797 (1992))
S/PV.3198, 14 April 1993 (resolution 818 (1993);
    extracts reproduced in this book as Document 35)
S/PV.3253, 9 July 1993 (resolution 850 (1993))
S/PV.3274, 13 September 1993 (resolution 863 (1993))
S/PV.3305, 5 November 1993 (resolution 882 (1993))
S/PV.3338, 23 February 1994 (resolution 898 (1994))
S/PV.3375, 5 May 1994 (resolution 916 (1994))
S/PV.3494, 27 January 1995 (extracts reproduced in this
    book as Document 92)

IV   Texts of documents

The texts of the 92 documents listed on the preceding pages are reproduced below. The appearance of ellipses (. . .) in the text indicates that portions of the document have been omitted. A subject index to the documents begins on page 311.

Document 1

Agreement on a partial cease-fire in Mozambique, signed by the Government of Mozambique and the Resistência Nacional Moçambicana (RENAMO) in Rome on 1 December 1990

Not issued as a United Nations document

Delegations of the Government of the Republic of Mozambique and RENAMO, led respectively by Armando Emilio Guebuza, Minister of Transport and Communications, and Raul Manuel Domingos, Head of the Department of External Relations, met in Rome at the Santo Egidio Community headquarters in the presence of the mediators, Mario Raffaelli, representative of the Government of the Italian Republic, Jaime Gonçalves, Archbishop of Beira, and Andrea Riccardi and Matteo Zuppi of the Community of Santo Egidio. Inspired by reciprocal commitment to and desire for the rapid attainment of a peaceful situation in Mozambique, they agreed on the need for immediate implementation of the understandings and conclusions reached in the discussion of point 1 of the agenda approved on 9 November 1990, "The presence and role of Zimbabwean Military Forces in the period preceding the Cease-fire Proclamation", in the following terms:

1. The Government of the Republic of Mozambique will agree with the Government of the Republic of Zimbabwe modalities for concentrating the Zimbabwean troops along the areas known as "The Beira Corridor" and "The Limpopo Corridor", to a minimum distance of 3 km outside the furthest edges of each corridor. This limit may be altered by a proposal from the Joint Verification Commission referred to in point 3, in conformity with criteria which will guarantee greater security and efficiency in verification. The concentration of the Zimbabwean troops in the above-mentioned corridors will begin at the latest 15 days after the signature of this Agreement and will be concluded by a deadline of 20 days after the time limit for beginning the concentration.

1.1. The Government of the Republic of Mozambique will inform the negotiating table of the maximum number of Zimbabwean troops to remain in the corridors.

1.2. The Zimbabwean troops may not be involved in military operations of an offensive nature while the concentration is under way.

2. To facilitate the peace process in Mozambique, RENAMO will end all offensive military operations and attacks on the Beira and Limpopo corridors, along the areas agreed in terms of point 1.

3. A Joint Verification Commission is created with the aim of invigilating the strict implementation of this Agreement. It comprises civilian and military representatives designated by the Government of the Republic of Mozambique and by RENAMO, three for each party, whose names will be given to the mediators within seven days of the signature of this Agreement. The Government of the Republic of Zimbabwe may also join the Joint Verification Commission and have three representatives.

3.1. The mediators or their representatives will also be members of the Joint Verification Commission and will chair it. Eight countries agreed between the parties will also be members.

3.2. The Joint Verification Commission will have its headquarters in Maputo. It will present reports to the negotiating table at regular intervals or whenever one of the parties so requests.

3.3. The Joint Verification Commission may create sub-commissions with the same composition, qualified to verify the implementation of this Agreement "in loco".

3.4. The members of the Joint Verification Commission will have diplomatic immunity. The Government of the Republic of Mozambique and RENAMO will guarantee the safety and free movement of the members of the Commission and its sub-commissions, as well as those of its emissaries, in any area subject to the application of this Agreement.

3.5. The Joint Verification Commission will agree the security measures necessary for its members at the due moment. The Government of the Republic of Mozambique will provide installations for the headquarters of the Joint Verification Commission as well as all the necessary logistic support for its operations.

3.6. The Joint Verification Commission will be sworn in up to 15 days after the signing of this Agreement, and will begin its work immediately. It will control the implementation of this Agreement for a period of six months, renewable by common agreement between the parties when necessary.

3.7. The Joint Verification Commission will submit the fundamental criteria that are to govern its activities to the negotiating table for approval as soon as it has been sworn in.

3.8. The delegations of the Republic of Mozambique and RENAMO request the Italian Government and other governments of the member countries of the Joint Verification Commission to make efforts at both bilateral and multilateral levels to guarantee the necessary financing and technical support for the efficient operation of the Joint Verification Commission created by this Agreement.

4. The parties undertake to avoid any activities that could directly or indirectly violate the spirit or letter of this Agreement. In the case of noting any unusual event of a military nature that could compromise the implementation of this Agreement, at the request of one of the parties the mediators may take practical initiatives to identify and overcome the problem.

4.1. The Government of the Republic of Mozambique and RENAMO, convinced that the signing and implementation of this Agreement will make a significant contribution to strengthening the climate of confidence necessary for dialogue, renew their commitment to continuing their analysis of the remaining points of the agenda aimed at establishing peace in Mozambique.

5. This Agreement comes into force on the date that it is signed.

For the delegation of the GRM:
Armando Emílio GUEBUZA

For the delegation of RENAMO:
Raul Manuel DOMINGOS

The mediators: Mario Raffaelli, D. Jaime Gonçalves, Andrea Riccardi, D. Matteo Zuppi

Done at Santo Egidio, Rome, on 1 December 1990

Document 2

Letter dated 28 May 1992 from the Secretary-General to President Joaquim Alberto Chissano of Mozambique on United Nations participation in the peace talks

Not issued as a United Nations document

The United Nations has been approached by the Santo Egidio Community on two separate occasions, in January of this year and today, regarding the peace talks being held in Rome between your Government and RENAMO. The Santo Egidio Community has provided me with a thorough briefing on the current status of the negotiations.

A particular concern of the Santo Egidio Community is the involvement of the United Nations, preferably as an observer, in the Rome talks, with a view to activating a United Nations role in the verification of the elections envisaged as part of the overall agreement between your Government and RENAMO.

In this connection the Community wished to be informed about United Nations participation in the next round of talks scheduled to commence in early June of this year. It has been brought to our attention that the third Protocol signed by the two parties on 12 March 1992 in Rome made provision for involvement by the United Nations.

I have been informed by Under-Secretary-General James O. C. Jonah, who discussed this matter with you on 14 October of last year in Maputo, that your Government is favourably disposed to United Nations involvement. However, to date no specific invitation or request has been received by the United Nations.

As you are aware I would like to be of assistance in promoting an agreement between your Government and RENAMO in the context of the talks being organized by the Santo Egidio Community. However, before indicating to the Community my reaction to their two demarches, I would be grateful if you could let me know whether your Government has the intention of issuing a formal written invitation for the involvement of the United Nations in the peace talks in Rome.

It is my fervent hope that peace and stability will soon return to your country. The United Nations stands ready at any time to assist in this process so that the work of reconstruction and rehabilitation can commence.

Please accept, Mr. President, the assurances of my highest consideration.

(*Signed*) Boutros BOUTROS-GHALI

Document 3

Letter dated 1 June 1992 from President Chissano to the Secretary-General on the progress of the peace talks between his Government and RENAMO

Not issued as a United Nations document; original in Portuguese

I have the honour to acknowledge receipt of Your Excellency's letter dated 28 May 1992. Allow me to welcome the readiness of and the interest of the United Nations to actively participate in the search for the so desired and urgent peace in my country. From the outset, the Government of the Republic of Mozambique welcomes and takes note of this expression, bearing in mind the evolution of the negotiation process and its next stages.

The very useful information Your Excellency so kindly conveyed to me in your letter brings up the need for some clarifications regarding the ongoing negotiation process, of which I have the honour to elaborate:

1. The negotiation process begun in July 8, 1990, at the Headquarters of the Santo Egidio Community, under the mediation of Mario Rafael, representative of the Italian government and coordinator of the mediators, D. Jaime Gonçalves, Archbishop of Beira, Mozambique, and Prof. Andrea Liccardi and Matteo Zuppi, of the Santo Egidio Community.

2. From July 8, 1990, to present date, a number of documents were signed. For the purposes of the present information, I wish to underline the 28 May 1991 Protocol, which contains the Agreed Agenda, and Protocol I on "The Fundamental Principles", both of which are annexed herewith.

As you may realize, the 28 May 1991 Protocol, envisages in its paragraph 5.b on "Guarantees", the establishment of a Political and Military Commission for the supervision of the cease-fire and monitoring of the compliance and implementation of future agreements.

On the other side, paragraph 4 of Protocol I lays down the principle that all subsequent Protocols to be agreed during the negotiations will form an integral part of the General Peace Agreement and, with the exception therein, that all Protocols will enter into force only on the date of the signing of the General Peace Agreement. Accordingly, this principle also applies to paragraph 5 of the same Protocol, which envisages the establishment of a Commission with the United Nations participation, for the supervision and control of compliance of the General Peace Agreement. Similarly, in the specific case of the electoral process, Protocol III of 12 March 1992, in its chapter VI, reaffirms the principle that there shall be an invitation to the United Nations as an observer, and a request for technical and material assistance. Finally, for the above mentioned purposes, the Protocol indicates in the same chapter that the Government shall submit a formal request to the United Nations. Like the preceding Protocols, this one shall be subject to the same principle as in paragraph 4 of Protocol I, on the "The Fundamental Principles", according to which it will only enter into force with the signing of the General Peace Agreement. Under these conditions, the best the Government could do was to inform the United Nations of the intentions and the agreements concluded between the parties, and of the permanent interest of the Government on the United Nations involvement. The Government has proceeded along these line.

3. I wish to reaffirm my Government's interest to benefit as soon as possible from the United Nations involvement in the Peace Process in Mozambique. I had the opportunity to express such an interest to Under-Secretary-General James Jonah during his last visit to Maputo. My Minister of Transport and Communications Armando Emilio Guebuza, head of the governmental delegation to the Peace Talks in Rome, had requested an appointment with you during his stay in New York last April. However, in view of impossibility of such an appointment with Your Excellency, he met with your deputy, Mr. James Jonah, followed by other meetings with Mr. Alvaro de Soto, Assistant Secretary-General in charge of El Salvador and Marrack Irvine Goulding, Under-Secretary-General in charge of peace-keeping operations.

In all those meetings Minister Guebuza had the opportunity to outline our interest in the United Nations involvement well before the signing of the General Peace Agreement, particularly as of the next round of talks which will be devoted to the discussion of military issues.

During those occasions we indicated that the United Nations involvement would only be possible after the conclusion of the discussion on the issue of observers to be involved in the current phase. This discussion will take place at the resumption of the talks in Rome, which will take place probably during the current month. Under these circumstances, without previous agreement between the parties, it is not possible to extend a formal invitation, either to the United Nations, or to any other country which we would like to see involved in the process. For this reason, we have not yet addressed any formal or written invitation to neither of the countries to whom we have already indicated our intention to invite them to participate as observers.

In conclusion, I wish to inform Your Excellency that the formal invitation for the United Nations involvement as an observer in the negotiations in Rome as of the current phase, will be extended to Your Excellency by the Government of the Republic of Mozambique, as soon as the necessary agreement is reached between the two delegations, which we hope, will happen at the beginning of the next round in Rome, when in principle, the question of observers is to be raised.

(*Signed*) Joaquim Alberto CHISSANO

Document 4

Letter dated 9 July 1992 from Mr. Pascoal Manuel Mocumbi, Minister for Foreign Affairs of Mozambique, requesting United Nations assistance for the electoral process

Not issued as a United Nations document

The government of the Republic of Mozambique is planning to hold multi-party elections, one year after the signature of the cease-fire Agreement between the government and RENAMO.

Aiming at organising and fair elections, taking into account the high costs involved and bearing in mind the experience as well as the possibilities and capacity of the United Nations, on behalf of the government of the Republic of Mozambique, I would like to request United Nations assistance for the electoral process.

Please accept, Your Excellency, the assurances of my highest consideration.

(*Signed*) Pascoal Manuel MOCUMBI

Document 5

Letter dated 23 July 1992 from the Secretary-General to Mozambique's Minister for Foreign Affairs on the United Nations electoral assistance field mission

Not issued as a United Nations document

I should like to thank you for your letter of 9 July 1992 in which you informed me of your Government's intention to hold multi-party elections one year after the signature of the cease-fire agreement between the Government of Mozambique and RENAMO. As you are aware, I designated an observer to attend the peace negotiations in Rome and I welcome the Joint Declaration which was recently signed there.

With reference to your request for United Nations assistance in the electoral process, I wish to inform you that I am asking UNDP and the Electoral Assistance Unit in the Department of Political Affairs to undertake a field mission to Mozambique in order to assess the nature of the assistance which the United Nations system could provide and its financial implications.

Accept, Excellency, the assurances of my highest consideration.

(*Signed*) Boutros BOUTROS-GHALI

Document 6

Letter dated 19 August 1992 from the Secretary-General to President Chissano on the role of the United Nations in the Rome peace talks; includes a "non-paper" on the modalities of United Nations verification of aspects of a peace agreement in Mozambique

Not issued as a United Nations document

I am writing regarding the talks in Rome and the role of the United Nations in the peace process in Mozambique.

I had a useful exchange of views on these subjects with Ambassador Afonso on the eve of his departure for Maputo. I was pleased to hear from him that you were satisfied with the contribution of the United Nations to the peace effort. As you may be aware, we have sent to Rome a Senior Political Affairs Officer to be available during the talks. It is my intention to send to Rome another official when the discussions move to military matters. The United Nations observers would continue to be available to provide technical advice and information to the parties regarding the modalities of United Nations involvement in the peace process but would not participate in any substantive discussions.

I understood from Ambassador Afonso that you would like to know my views regarding United Nations involvement in the verification and monitoring of the agreement both in terms of the cease-fire and the electoral process. With regard to the latter, I have already written to Foreign Minister Mocumbi about my intention to send a technical team to Mozambique to assess the nature of the United Nations assistance needed and its financial implications. I have the honour to enclose herewith a non-paper with its attachments which draws on our experience in other missions and explains in greater detail how the United Nations could be helpful to both parties in the implementation of agreements reached by them. I believe that this will represent a practical contribution to the peace process in Mozambique.

Accept, Mr. President, the assurances of my highest consideration.

(Signed) Boutros BOUTROS-GHALI

Non-Paper
Modalities of United Nations Verification of Aspects of a General Peace Agreement in Mozambique

In the joint declaration adopted in Rome on 7 August 1992 the Government of Mozambique and RENAMO bound themselves, *inter alia*, to "accepting the role of the international community, and especially that of the United Nations, in monitoring and guaranteeing the implementation of the General Peace Agreement, in particular the cease-fire and the electoral process". This non-paper gives a general description of the way in which the United Nations would carry out such a role.

As soon as further negotiations between the two sides have reached an outline agreement on those aspects of the General Peace Agreement (GPA), especially the cease-fire, which are to be verified by the United Nations, it would be desirable for a United Nations technical team to visit Mozambique in order to prepare recommendations on how the United Nations' role should be implemented ("the concept of operations"), to assess the resources required to implement that concept and to establish how many of the necessary goods and services could be obtained in Mozambique or neighbouring countries.

As soon as agreement is reached on all points in the GPA (but possibly before the GPA is actually signed), the Government of Mozambique would address to the Secretary-General of the United Nations a request that he obtain the Security Council's authority to make the arrangements necessary for the United Nations to carry out the role envisaged for it in the GPA. The Secretary-General would then submit to the Security Council a report describing his concept of operations and the resources required to implement it. The Security Council would be asked to approve the Secretary-General's recommendations and to authorise the establishment of the necessary United Nations operation in Mozambique.

As soon as the Security Council's approval had been given, a budget for the operation would be prepared by the United Nations Secretariat and submitted to the General Assembly for approval. As soon as the budget was approved, each Member State would be asked to pay its assessed share of the costs of the operation. The Member States would, however, expect the Government of Mozambique to do its utmost to make available goods and services (e.g. premises, local supplies) free of cost to the United Nations.

At the same time the Government of Mozambique would be asked to conclude with the Secretary-General an agreement defining the status, immunities and privileges of the United Nations operation.

Assuming that the United Nations would be asked

to verify both military and civilian aspects of the GPA, the Secretary-General would be likely to entrust the operation to a Special Representative who, acting under the authority and instructions of the Secretary-General, would direct the activities of all United Nations personnel involved in helping the Mozambican parties to implement the GPA. Under the Special Representative, who would reside in Maputo, there would be a Military Division and an Electoral Division, as well as political, legal, information and administrative staff. If, as has occurred in a number of other such operations in recent years, the United Nations was asked to monitor the local police forces during the implementation of the GPA, the United Nations operation could also include a Police Division. The Special Representative would also be responsible for coordinating any activities of the United Nations development and humanitarian agencies which were connected with implementation of the GPA.

The personnel of the Military Division would be provided by Member States at the request of the Secretary-General, after consultation with the parties, and with the approval of the Security Council. Any police personnel would also be provided by Member States. The civilian personnel would consist mainly of staff members of the United Nations Secretariat, though the Electoral Division would be reinforced by additional personnel made available by Member States at periods of peak activity.

It would be for the parties to the GPA to decide what joint bodies they might establish to assist implementation of the Agreement. Past experience in similar cases has shown that it is important that the Head of the United Nations operation should be a member of such bodies and that the best results are achieved if the chairmanship is entrusted to the United Nations rather than alternating between the two parties. Other Member States who have contributed to the peace process can also be members or observers in such bodies if the parties so desire.

As regards the cease-fire, a concept that has proved workable in other cases was communicated to the two sides in Rome in a document dated 13 August 1992, of which a copy is attached. For such an arrangement to work, it would be essential that both sides cooperate fully with the United Nations, respecting its international status and impartiality, allowing it full freedom of movement and providing it with the necessary information on the due dates. It would also be important for adequate arrangements to be made for the logistic support of the two sides' forces during the period in which they were concentrated prior to demobilisation.

As regards the elections, the United Nations' verification role would be in addition to any programme for the provision of technical assistance to the Mozambican electoral authorities by the United Nations. The United Nations' verification would cover the whole electoral process, including the establishment of the electoral authority, electoral legislation, registration of voters, registration of parties, the electoral campaign, the election itself, the counting of ballots and the announcement of the results.

The Secretary-General would report at regular intervals to the Security Council on the implementation of all aspects of the mandate entrusted to him by the Council at the request of the Government of Mozambique.

New York
18 August 1992

(*Original in Portuguese*)

Cease-fire

I. *Cessation of the armed conflict*

1. The cessation of the armed conflict (CAC) is a brief, dynamic and irreversible process of predetermined duration which must be implemented throughout the national territory of Mozambique.

The implementation of the process shall be the responsibility of the Government of the Republic of Mozambique and of RENAMO, acting within the framework of the Cease-fire Commission. The Cease-fire Commission is answerable to the Commission referred to in Protocol I of 10 October 1991, as the organ responsible for the overall political supervision of the cease-fire.

The Cease-fire Commission shall be composed of representatives of the Parties and of the United Nations whose representative shall preside.

The United Nations shall verify and monitor the implementation of the process.

2. The CAC shall begin on E-Day and end on E-Day + 180.

3. The CAC consists of 4 (four) phases:
    (a) cease-fire;
    (b) separation of forces;
    (c) concentration of forces;
    (d) demobilization.

4. *Cease-fire*

The Parties agree that:

(a) The cease-fire shall enter into force on E-Day (30 days after the signing of the General Peace Agreement);

(b) As of E-Day, neither of the Parties shall carry out any hostile act or operation by means of forces or individuals under its control. Accordingly, they may not:
 – carry out any kind of attack by land, sea or air;
 – organize patrols or offensive manoeuvres;
 – occupy new positions;
 – lay mines and prevent mine-clearing operations;

– interfere with military communications;

– carry out any kind of reconnaissance operations;

– carry out acts of sabotage and terrorism;

– acquire or receive lethal equipment;

– carry out acts of violence against the civilian population;

– restrict or prevent without justification the free movement of persons and property;

– carry out any other military activity which, in the opinion of the Cease-fire Commission and the United Nations, might jeopardize the cease-fire.

(c) On E-Day, the United Nations shall begin official verification of compliance with the undertaking described in paragraph (b), investigating any alleged violation of the cease-fire. Any duly substantiated violation shall be reported by the United Nations at the appropriate level;

(d) During the period between the signing of the General Peace Agreement and E-Day, the two Parties shall observe a cessation of hostilities and of the activities described in paragraph (b), in order to allow the United Nations to deploy its personnel in the territory to verify all aspects of the CAC as of E-Day. In performing its functions, the United Nations shall enjoy complete freedom of movement throughout the territory of Mozambique.

5. *Separation of forces*

The Parties agree that:

(a) The purpose of the separation of forces is to reduce the risk of incidents, to build trust and to allow the United Nations effectively to verify the commitments assumed by the Parties;

(b) The separation of forces shall last 6 (six) days, from E-Day to E-Day + 5;

(c) During this period, the FAM shall proceed to the barracks, bases, existing semi-permanent facilities and other locations listed in annex A;

(d) During the same period, the RENAMO forces shall proceed to the locations listed in annex B;

(e) The quantities indicated and the locations listed in the above-mentioned annexes are those agreed between the Parties and the United Nations;

(f) Accordingly, by 2400 hours on E-Day + 5, the FAM and the RENAMO forces must be in the locations listed in annexes A and B respectively;

(g) All movements shall take place under the supervision and coordination of the United Nations. Neither Party may do anything to prevent or jeopardize the movements of the other Party's forces. The United Nations shall supervise all the locations listed in annexes A and B and shall, in principle, be present 24 hours a day in each of those locations as of E-Day;

(h) During this period of 6 (six) days, no force or individual shall be able to leave the locations indicated, except to seek medical care or for other humanitarian reasons, and then only with the authorization and under the supervision of the United Nations. In each location, the commander of the troops shall be responsible for maintaining order and discipline and for ensuring that the troops conduct themselves in accordance with the principles and the spirit of this Protocol.

6. *Concentration of forces*

The Parties agree that:

(a) The concentration of forces shall begin on E-Day + 6 and end on E-Day + 30;

(b) During this period, the FAM shall concentrate in the normal peacetime barracks and military bases listed in annex C;

(c) During the same period, the RENAMO forces shall go to the assembly and billeting points listed in annex D;

(d) All movements shall take place under the supervision and coordination of the United Nations and shall be subject to the same conditions as those established for the separation of forces;

(e) Arrangements for the security of each area shall be agreed between the corresponding commander and the United Nations. The military unit stationed in each location shall provide its own security. Only the individual weapons and ammunition necessary for that local security service shall be distributed to personnel;

(f) The quantities indicated and the location listed in the above-mentioned annexes are those agreed between the Parties and the United Nations.

7. *Demobilization*

Shall take place as stipulated in item 3 (f) of the agreed agenda.

8. *Formation of the Mozambican Defence Force*

Shall take place as stipulated in item 3 (a) of the agreed agenda.

9. *Miscellaneous provisions*

(a) The Parties agree to the following:

1. To supply the United Nations with complete inventories of their troop strength, arms, ammunition, mines and other explosives on E-Day – 6, E-Day, E-Day + 6, E-Day + 30 and, thereafter, every 15 days;

2. To allow the United Nations to verify the aspects and data referred to in the preceding paragraph;

3. As of E-Day + 31, all collective and individual weapons, including weapons on board aircraft and ships, shall be stored in warehouses under United Nations control;

4. As of E-Day + 6, troops shall be able to leave their respective assembly and billeting points only with the authorization and under the supervision of the United Nations;

(b) As of E-Day, the naval and air force components of the FAM shall refrain from carrying out any offensive action. They may carry out only such non-hostile missions as are necessary for the discharge of their duties unrelated to the armed conflict. All air force flight plans must be communicated in advance to the United Nations. Aircraft may not, in any case, be armed and may not overfly assembly and billeting points;

(c) The foreign forces currently present in the territory of Mozambique must also respect the agreed cease-fire as if E-Day. In accordance with item 3 (b) of the agreed agenda, on E-Day the Government of the Republic of Mozambique shall communicate to the United Nations and the Commission referred to in Protocol I of 18 October 1991 the plans for the withdrawal of foreign troops from Mozambique. These plans shall include the numbers and equipment of such troops. Withdrawal shall begin on E-Day + 6 and end on E-Day + 30. All movements must be coordinated and verified by the United Nations;

(d) The Parties agree that, as of E-Day, they shall end all hostile propaganda, both internal and external;

(e) Border control as of E-Day shall be provided by the immigration services and the police.

II. *Operational timetable for the cease-fire*

E-Day – 30: Signing of the General Peace Agreement

E-Day: Entry into force of the cease-fire

Beginning of the cessation of the armed conflict (CAC)

Beginning of the separation of forces phase

E-Day + 5: End of the separation of forces phase

E-Day + 6: Beginning of the concentration of forces phase

E-Day + 30: End of the concentration of forces phase

E-Day + 31: Beginning of the demobilization phase

E-Day + 180: End of the demobilization phase and of the CAC.

III. *Release of prisoners, except for those being held for ordinary crimes*

1. On E-Day, all prisoners except for those being held for ordinary crimes shall be released by the Parties.

2. The International Committee of the Red Cross, together with the Parties, shall agree on the arrangements for and the verification of the process for the release of the prisoners referred to in paragraph 1.

Document 7

Letter dated 22 August 1992 from President Chissano to the Secretary-General in response to the "non-paper" on United Nations verification of the General Peace Agreement

Not issued as a United Nations document

It was with deep satisfaction, that I received your letter dated on the 19th August 1992, which I read with great interest, since it corresponds to the efforts being undertaken by my Government, in order to reestablish peace in Mozambique as soon as possible.

The Joint Political Declaration of Rome, signed on the 7th August 1992, opens great perspective for the end of the fight of the people and for the normalization of the living conditions of all the Mozambicans, based on a true National Reconciliation.

In this regard, it is with pleasure that I express the deep recognition and appreciation of my Government to the role and personal engagement of your Excellency and that of the organization under your guidance in the peace negotiations taking place in Rome.

The United Nations Organization's Commitment is witnessed by the prompt reaction of your Excellency to the preoccupations of my Government with the view to guarantee the fulfillment of the Rome Joint Declaration and the monitoring of the cease-fire.

In this view I have the honour to inform your Excellency that the United Nations Organization's Technical team, [to] which your Excellency has referred, is most welcomed in my country.

I propose that the teams, the one on elections and the other on the cease-fire, come by the 26 of August. It is important for the UN to have the first picture of the real situation from now so that the time frame for the procedures proposed in your letter and contained in the non-paper be shortened.

In due course we should agree, through the appropriate diplomatic channels, on the practical aspects of the mission.

The issues there mentioned are being already a subject of study and ponderation by the Government of the Republic of Mozambique. We are eager to discuss them with your mission since we think that the cease-fire should commence as soon as the legal procedures will be terminated by the National Assembly as foreseen in the Rome declaration of the 7th August.

We are working towards terminating the proceedings not longer than 7 days after the signing of the cease-fire agreement.

Please accept, Mr. Secretary General, the assurance of my Highest Consideration.

(Signed) Joaquim Alberto CHISSANO

Document 8

Letter dated 22 September 1992 from President Chissano to the Secretary-General on the United Nations electoral assistance technical mission in Mozambique

Not issued as a United Nations document; original in Portuguese

Following my letter of 22 August 1992, in response to your letter of 19 August, I have the honour to inform you that since 6 September a technical mission of the United Nations headed by Mr. Horacio Boneo has been in Maputo.

On 11 September, I received Mr. Horacio Boneo who stated that his mission had as its main objective to obtain information in order to envisage a "concept of operations" relating to electoral questions. He had working meetings with the Ministers of Finance, Information, Foreign Affairs and with the Technical Secretariat of the Ministerial Commission for the Elections.

In the aftermath of the information provided to me by Mr. Boneo, I reiterated the interest of my Government to see the United Nations involved in Mozambique as envisaged by the General Peace Agreement to be signed by 1 October, according to the provisions signed in Rome on 7 August by me and the RENAMO leader.

The main areas that need financial backing, and in which we would like to receive support from the United Nations, include:

- National reconstruction and the return to normality; this comprises the return of the refugees to the country and the reintegration of the displaced people and the military demobilized by the Government and by the forces of RENAMO;

- Formation of the new national army;

- The electoral process.

I am grateful for the personal interest you have been providing in order that peace in Mozambique will soon become a reality and I hope that the United Nations will help us find suitable solutions to overcome our material and financial problems with regard to the correct implementation of the National Peace Agreement.

(Signed) Joaquim Alberto CHISSANO

Document 9

Letter dated 28 September 1992 from President Chissano requesting the Secretary-General's attendance at the signing of the General Peace Agreement

Not issued as a United Nations document

To mark the end of hostilities between the parties in conflict in the Republic of Mozambique, the signing ceremony of the Cease-fire Agreement and the General Peace Accords will take place on the first October in Rome, the Capital of the Republic of Italy. This event marks the end of a long and hard process of negotiations, in which your personal support and that of the United Nations Organization that you represent was crucial and invaluable.

This Accord brings the hope of a new era of peace not only to Mozambique but also to the whole of Southern African countries whose peoples share with the Mozambican people the hardships caused by the war which thus comes to an end after seventeen years. It is a contribution for world peace and international cooperation.

It is my pleasure to request the honour of Your Excellency to attend to the Ceremony and share with the People of Mozambique this glorious and important moment of reconciliation and restoration of Peace.

Looking forward to see you soon, I avail myself of this opportunity to reiterate my highest esteem.

(*Signed*) Joaquim Alberto CHISSANO

Document 10

Letter dated 29 September 1992 from the Secretary-General to the President of the Security Council on United Nations involvement in implementation of the General Peace Agreement

Not issued as a United Nations document

It is my intention to keep you, and through you members of the Security Council, informed of current developments with regard to the situation in Mozambique, in view of the possible involvement of the United Nations in the implementation of the General Peace Agreement in that country.

When I last briefed the members of the Council on this matter, in informal consultations, on 10 September, I had just returned from Jakarta where I had engaged in discussions on the situation in Mozambique with President Mugabe of Zimbabwe and with Foreign Minister Pascoal Mocumbi of Mozambique. One of the immediate results of our discussions was the despatch, to which RENAMO concurred, of two technical teams, one to look into the question of electoral verification and assistance, the other to prepare an outline of an operational plan for a United Nations Verification Mission in Mozambique.

It was clearly indicated to the Mozambican parties that the despatch of the teams did not imply that the United Nations had agreed to assume the role desired of it, a decision which could only be taken by the Security Council.

You are no doubt aware that, notwithstanding the uneven pace in the talks between the two Mozambican parties, progress has been considerable. On 7 August 1992, in Rome, the parties signed the Joint Political Declaration by which they committed themselves to obtain agreement on all outstanding issues by 1 October 1992, so that the General Peace Agreement could be signed on that date. Both leaders agreed to accept "the role of the international community and especially that of the United Nations, in monitoring and guaranteeing the implementation of the General Peace Agreement, in particular the cease-fire and the electoral process".

According to our reports from Rome, a number of issues remained on which, up to mid-September, the divergence of views gave rise to concern that the 1 October target date might not be met. However, as a result of the summit meeting in Gaborone between the President of Mozambique, H.E. Mr. Joaquim Alberto Chissano, and RENAMO leader Dhlakama on 18-19 September, agreement was reached on a number of those issues and the two leaders committed themselves to conclude by 1 October the protocols concerning the "guarantees", the "cease-fire" and the "Donors Conference". It now appears likely that the peace agreement will be signed on 1 October or shortly thereafter.

I therefore feel it incumbent on me to give you an idea of where matters stand now, so that the Council might be able to take an early decision on a United Nations operation in Mozambique which is likely to be considerably larger than our involvement in Angola. My aim in this respect is to avoid any undue delay between the signing of the General Peace Agreement on 1 October and the commencement of United Nations operations in Mozambique.

The documents under discussion between the parties in Rome provide for the establishment of a number of joint bodies whose members would be the two parties and in some cases representatives of the United Nations and various of the Member States associated with the peace process. At the head of this structure there would be a "Commission to Supervise the Cease-fire and Monitor Respect for and Implementation of the Agreements between the Parties (CSC)". There would also be joint commissions for the formation of new armed forces, for the cease-fire, for demobilization, for the reintegration of ex-combatants and for various other aspects of the General Peace Agreement. Past experience has shown that such joint machinery functions best when the chairmanship is entrusted to an impartial third party, rather than alternating between the two protagonists. The Government and RENAMO have therefore been asked to consider entrusting to the United Nations chairmanship of the CSC and its subsidiary bodies responsible for activities which the United Nations would be directly monitoring. So far, it has been agreed that the United Nations should chair the cease-fire commission but not the other bodies.

The United Nations military observer who was present at the Rome talks from 28 June to 16 August has provided the parties, the mediators and the observers with advice on the technical aspects of establishing and monitoring cease-fires. Large parts of the cease-fire arrangements have already been agreed between the parties. Issues that remain to be settled include the number and location of the areas at which the forces of the two sides will be concentrated. Early precision is needed on this point so that plans for the United Nations monitoring operation can be prepared and estimates made of the human and material resources that will be needed.

The parties appear agreed on the need for the early withdrawal of the foreign forces currently deployed in Mozambique to protect the three corridors (Nacala, Beira and Limpopo) which are of crucial importance to the economies of the neighbouring countries. There is concern that, following the coming into effect of the cease-fire, these corridors should not become exposed to attacks by bandits or others. The latest drafts under consideration in the negotiations propose that the withdrawal of foreign forces commence after the entry into force of the cease-fire agreement and foresee that the CSC would assume responsibility for verification and security in assuming this role of protecting the corridors has been mentioned. This would greatly add to the size, complexity and cost of the proposed United Nations operation in Mozambique and would take several months to arrange. It is important that this question should be resolved before the General Peace Agreement is signed.

The timetable at present under discussion between the parties provides for the cease-fire to come formally into effect, under United Nations monitoring, 30 days after the General Peace Agreement is signed. During those 30 days it is expected that an informal cease-fire will be observed. The feasibility of such a timetable will be assessed as soon as the report of the Technical Team is available. But it is necessary to observe, at this stage, that if, as is hoped, the General Peace Agreement is signed on 1 October 1992, it would not be possible for the United Nations to establish more than a token presence in Mozambique within 30 days from that date. In this regard, it is to be noted that the situation in Mozambique is very different from that in Angola. At a similar stage of the peace process in Angola, detailed information was already available about the numbers and locations of the assembly areas agreed by the two sides and a United Nations peace-keeping operation (UNAVEM I) was deployed in that country and, being on the point of completing its mandate, was able to devote considerable resources to preparing, on the ground, the new tasks which it would assume under the Peace Agreements of Angola. These conditions do not, unfortunately, exist in the case of Mozambique where the details of the cease-fire agreement are not yet known and the United Nations operation would have to be established from scratch.

As I reported earlier, the technical team on electoral assistance visited Mozambique from 7 to 17 September, with the purpose of obtaining pertinent information on activities related to the organization of the electoral process by the Mozambican authorities and data required for drafting the terms of reference, the concept of operations and the staffing requirements of the electoral component of the verification mission. The mission also discussed the possibility of supporting the electoral organization in technical areas, ranging from comments on the draft electoral law, to suggestions on the budget or provision of specialized expertise in the evaluation of communication or computational requirements of the electoral operation. A statement of these requirements will be ready early in October.

As in other areas of conflict, Mozambique is suffering widespread food shortages exacerbated by the drought affecting the Southern African region. There has also been massive displacement of people within the country and an increasing flow of refugees to neighbouring countries. Over 35,000 persons crossed into Malawi and Zimbabwe in July and August alone exacerbating an already difficult situation in the host countries. It is widely considered that unless immediate action is taken to speed the delivery of relief food to the affected communities, a large-scale humanitarian disaster will result.

One of the major obstacles to expanding relief operations has been the inaccessibility of RENAMO-held territory to the United Nations due to the civil war. On 16 July, the Government and RENAMO issued a Declaration on the Principles Governing Humanitarian Assistance in which they agreed, in principle, to open all areas to relief operations. To follow up on the Declaration, a Committee for Humanitarian Assistance was established in Maputo. It is chaired by the United Nations Special Coordinator for Emergency Relief Operations and includes representatives of United Nations agencies, ICRC, neighbouring countries and major donor Governments.

On 11 September, the Humanitarian Committee presented a unified plan of action to the two sides. It proposes the delivery of humanitarian relief, to populations in need in specific destinations, by airlift and, more importantly, by truck convoys using overland routes.

While the Government accepted the package by the deadline of 14 September, RENAMO has still not consented to key components of the plan. Their latest official response to the Committee does not appear to give hope for a rapid resolution of this problem. RENAMO has been reluctant to open land routes in the areas under its control for fear that the Government would exploit the corridors for military advantage, as has in fact occurred in the past. In the meantime, the severity of conditions in the affected areas increases daily.

Two measures are now envisaged to remove the obstacles standing in the way of a more effective relief effort in Mozambique. Firstly, I am writing to RENAMO leader Dhlakama to appeal for immediate agreement on the unified plan of action. Simultaneously, a letter will be addressed to the President of Mozambique seeking strengthened cooperation between his Government and the United Nations on logistical arrangements for deliveries to Government-held areas.

Secondly, the Deputy to the Under-Secretary-General for Humanitarian Affairs will visit Mozambique next week to devise a more effective United Nations response to the emergency situation and to expedite the opening of the land corridors. He will be instructed to impress very forcefully upon all parties the urgent need to permit relief organizations direct and immediate access to the most vulnerable communities.

I shall keep you apprised of developments in this

regard. In the event neither of the above measures yields positive results, I may be required to seek the authorization of the Security Council for specific measures to ensure access to the populations in need. I feel strongly that the international community must act quickly and decisively to avert another large-scale humanitarian disaster in Africa.

As soon as the necessary detailed information is available about the tasks which the parties wish the United Nations to undertake in connection with the implementation of the General Peace Agreement, I shall present a report to the Security Council containing my recommendations on how the Council might respond to the parties' request. I envisage that, as in other such cases, I would appoint a Special Representative for Mozambique who would be in overall charge of the United Nations' activities in support of the General Peace Agreement and would also coordinate the humanitarian efforts of the United Nations system in Mozambique during the implementation of that Agreement.

Accept, Mr. President, the assurance of my highest consideration.

(*Signed*) Boutros BOUTROS-GHALI

Document 11

Statement by the Secretary-General welcoming the signing of the General Peace Agreement in Rome on 4 October 1992

UN Press Release SG/SM/4829, 5 October 1992

On behalf of the United Nations, I welcome the General Peace Agreement signed yesterday in Rome between President Chissano of Mozambique and RENAMO leader Dhlakama. The willingness of the two parties to put aside the animosities of the past and work for peace in their war-ravaged country is a most encouraging development. I commend the Italian Government and the other mediators for their persistence and commitment to bringing about this Agreement by helping the parties to reach this successful conclusion.

The General Peace Agreement envisages a central and large role for the United Nations in its implementation. The United Nations is again faced with an enormous challenge. The United Nations role will require greater effort and more resources than was the case in Angola.

But the international community, I believe, recognizes that these are sound investments. Peace is ultimately a far less expensive proposition than war.

At this critical moment, I call upon the parties to exercise maximum restraint in the period before the General Peace Agreement comes into force. I would hope that no actions would be taken which would call into question the seriousness and commitment of either party to the peace process.

This matter will be brought before the Security Council at the earliest possible moment so that the United Nations will be in position to carry out the extremely important responsibilities assigned to it by this Agreement.

Document 12

General Peace Agreement for Mozambique. Letter dated 6 October 1992 from Mozambique to the Secretary-General, transmitting a letter from President Joaquim Chissano of Mozambique requesting the participation of the United Nations in monitoring the General Peace Agreement; also contains the text of the General Peace Agreement, the joint communiqué of 10 July 1990, the Declaration on the Guiding Principles for Humanitarian Assistance of 16 July 1992 and the Joint Declaration signed in Rome on 7 August 1992

S/24635, 8 October 1992

Upon instructions from my Government, I have the honour to request Your Excellency that the letter dated 4 October 1992 and its annex, addressed to Your Excellency by H.E. Mr. Joaquim Alberto Chissano, President of the Republic of Mozambique, handed over to Mr. James O. C. Jonah, Under-Secretary-General for Political Affairs and special representative of the Secretary-General at the signing ceremony of the General Peace Agreement for Mozambique, in Rome last 4 October 1992, be circulated as an official document of the Security Council.

(Signed) Pedro Comissário AFONSO
Ambassador Extraordinary and Plenipotentiary
Permanent Representative to the United Nations

Enclosure

Letter dated 4 October 1992 from the President of the Republic of Mozambique addressed to the Secretary-General

I have the honour to convey to Your Excellency that the Government of the Republic of Mozambique and the Resistência Nacional Moçambicana (RENAMO) signed on 4 October 1992 a General Peace Agreement establishing the principles and modalities for the achievement of peace in Mozambique.

Accordingly, I would like to request Your Excellency to take appropriate action in order to ensure the participation of the United Nations in monitoring and ensuring the implementation of the General Peace Agreement and in assisting the Government by providing technical assistance for the General Elections and in monitoring these elections.

In this regard, I would also like to request the United Nations to chair the following Commissions:

(a) The Supervision and Control Commission of the implementation of the General Peace Agreement, as provided for in Protocol I;

(b) The Cease-fire Commission provided for in Protocol VI, and;

(c) The Reintegration Commission, provided for in Protocol IV.

I would equally like to request Your Excellency to inform the Security Council on the need to send a United Nations team to Mozambique to monitor the above-mentioned Agreement, until the holding of the General Elections, which, in principle, will take place one year after the signing of the General Peace Agreement.

The Agreement shall enter into force on the day of the publication of the legal instruments to be adopted by the Assembly of the Republic as envisaged in the Joint Declaration of August 1992. The publication of such legal instruments shall take place no later than 15 October 1992.

According to Protocol IV, the United Nations is expected to start its functions of verifying and monitoring the cease-fire on the day of entry into force of the General Peace Agreement.

Although the Agreement will come into force as indicated above, it would be our wish to see this monitoring mechanism established in the field as soon as possible, but not later than the date of the entry into force of this General Peace Agreement.

Attached please find the signed text of the General Peace Agreement.

(Signed) Joaquim Alberto CHISSANO
President of the Republic of Mozambique

Annex

General Peace Agreement for Mozambique

Rome, 4 October 1992

Joaquim Alberto Chissano, President of the Republic of Mozambique, and Afonso Macacho Marceta Dhlakama, President of RENAMO, meeting at Rome, under the chairmanship of the Italian Government, in the presence of the Minister for Foreign Affairs of the Italian Republic, Emilio Colombo, and in the presence of:

H.E. Robert Gabriel Mugabe, President of the Republic of Zimbabwe;

H.E. Ketumile Masire, President of the Republic of Botswana;

H.E. George Saitoti, Vice-President of the Republic of Kenya;

H.E. Roelof F. Botha, Minister for Foreign Affairs of the Republic of South Africa;

The Hon. John Tembo, Minister in the Office of the President of the Republic of Malawi;

Ambassador Ahmed Haggag, Assistant Secretary-General of OAU;

and of the mediators: Mario Raffaelli, representative of the Italian Government and coordinator of the mediators, Jaime Gonçalves, Archbishop of Beira, Andrea Riccardi and Matteo Zuppi of the Community of San Egidio;

and representatives of the observers: Dr. James O. C. Jonah, Under-Secretary-General for Political Affairs of the United Nations; H.E. Ambassador Herman J. Cohen, Assistant Secretary of State, for the Government of the United States of America; H.E. Ambassador Philippe Cuvillier for the Government of France; H.E. Dr. José Manuel Durao Barroso, Secretary of State for Foreign Affairs, for the Government of Portugal; and H.E. Sir Patrick Fairweather for the Government of the United Kingdom;

at the conclusion of the negotiating process in Rome for the establishment of a lasting peace and effective democracy in Mozambique, accept as binding the following documents which constitute the General Peace Agreement:

1. Protocol I (Basic principles);
2. Protocol II (Criteria and arrangements for the formation and recognition of political parties);
3. Protocol III (Principles of the Electoral Act);
4. Protocol IV (Military questions);
5. Protocol V (Guarantees);
6. Protocol VI (Cease-fire);
7. Protocol VII (donors conference).

They also accept as integral parts of the General Peace Agreement for Mozambique the following documents:

(a) The Joint Communiqué of 10 July 1990;

(b) The Agreement of 1 December 1990 [see Document 1];

(c) The Declaration of the Government of the Republic of Mozambique and RENAMO on guiding principles for humanitarian assistance, signed in Rome on 16 July 1992;

(d) The Joint Declaration signed in Rome on 7 August 1992.

The President of the Republic of Mozambique and the President of RENAMO undertake to do everything within their power for the achievement of genuine national reconciliation.

The above-mentioned Protocols have been duly initialled and signed by the respective heads of delegation and by the mediators. The present General Peace Agreement shall enter into force immediately upon its signature.

(*Signed*) Joaquim Alberto CHISSANO
President of the Republic of Mozambique

(*Signed*) Afonso Macacho Marceta DHLAKAMA
President of RENAMO

The mediators:

(*Signed*) Mario RAFFAELLI

(*Signed*) Jaime GONÇALVES

(*Signed*) Andrea RICCARDI

(*Signed*) Matteo ZUPPI

Signed at Rome on 4 October 1992

Protocol I

Basic principles

On 18 October 1991, the delegation of the Government of the Republic of Mozambique, headed by Armando Emílio Guebuza, Minister of Transport and Communications, and composed of Aguiar Mazula, Minister of State Administration, Teodato Hunguana, Minister of Labour, and Francisco Madeira, Diplomatic Adviser to the President of the Republic, and the delegation of RENAMO, headed by Raul Manuel Domingos, Chief of the External Relations Department, and composed of Vicente Zacarias Ululu, Chief of the Information Department, Agostinho Semende Murrial, Deputy Chief of the Political Affairs Department, and Joao Francisco Almirante, member of the President's cabinet, meeting at Rome in the context of the peace talks, in the presence of the mediators, Mario Raffaelli, representative of the Government of the Italian Republic and coordinator of the mediators, Jaime Gonçalves, Archbishop of Beira, Andrea Riccardi and Matteo Zuppi of the Community of San Egidio;

Determined to secure the higher interests of the Mozambican people, reaffirm that dialogue and collaboration are the indispensable means of achieving a lasting peace in the country.

Accordingly:

1. The Government undertakes to refrain from taking any action that is contrary to the provisions of the Protocols to be concluded and from adopting laws or measures or applying existing laws which may be inconsistent with those Protocols.

2. RENAMO, for its part, undertakes, beginning on the date of entry into force of the cease-fire, to refrain from armed combat and instead to conduct its political struggle in conformity with the laws in force, within the framework of the existing State institutions and in accordance with the conditions and guarantees established in the General Peace Agreement.

3. The two parties commit themselves to concluding as soon as possible a General Peace Agreement, containing Protocols on each of the items of the agenda adopted on 28 May 1991 and to take the necessary steps to that end. In that connection, the Government shall endeavour not to hamper international travel by representatives of RENAMO and external contacts of RENAMO in connection with the peace negotiations. Contacts within the country between RENAMO and the mediators or the members of the Joint Verification Commission shall likewise be permitted for the same purpose. Specific arrangements for such contacts shall be made on a case-by-case basis in response to requests by the mediators to the Government.

4. The Protocols to be concluded in the course of these negotiations shall form an integral part of the General Peace Agreement and shall enter into force on the date of signature of the Agreement, with the exception of paragraph 3 of this Protocol, which shall enter into force immediately.

5. The parties agree on the principle of establishing a commission to supervise and monitor compliance with the General Peace Agreement. The commission shall be composed of representatives of the Government, RENAMO, the United Nations and other organizations or Governments to be agreed upon between the parties.

For the delegation of the Government of the Republic of Mozambique:

For the delegation of RENAMO:

(*Signed*) Armando Emílio GUEBUZA

(*Signed*) Raul Manuel DOMINGOS

The mediators:

(*Signed*) Mario RAFFAELLI

(*Signed*) Jaime GONÇALVES

(*Signed*) Andrea RICCARDI

(*Signed*) Matteo ZUPPI

Done at San Egidio, Rome, on 18 October 1991

Protocol II

Criteria and arrangements for the formation and recognition of political parties

On 13 November 1991, the delegation of the Government of the Republic of Mozambique, headed by Armando Emílio Guebuza, Minister of Transport and Communications, and composed of Aguiar Mazula, Minister of State Administration, Teodato Hunguana, Minister of Labour, and Francisco Madeira, Diplomatic Adviser to the President of the Republic, and the delegation of RENAMO, headed by Raul Manuel Domingos, Chief of the External Relations Department, and composed of Vicente Zacarias Ululu, Chief of the Information Department, Agostinho Semende Murrial, Deputy Chief of the Political Affairs Department, and Joao Francisco Almirante, member of the President's cabinet, meeting in Rome in the context of the peace talks, in the presence of the mediators, Mario Raffaelli, representative of the Government of the Italian Republic and coordinator of the mediators, Jaime Gonçalves, Archbishop of Beira, Andrea Riccardi and Matteo Zuppi of the Community of San Egidio, took up item 1 of the Agreed Agenda of 28 May 1991, concerning "Criteria and arrangements for the formation and recognition of political parties".

At the conclusion of their talks, the parties agreed on the necessity of guaranteeing the workings of a multiparty democracy in which the parties would freely cooperate in shaping and expressing the will of the people and in promoting democratic participation by the citizens in the Government of the country.

In this connection, and bearing in mind the provisions of Protocol I on "Basic principles", the parties have agreed on the following principles:

1. *The nature of political parties*

(a) Political parties shall be independent, voluntary and free associations of citizens, national in scope, whose primary purpose shall be to give democratic expression to the will of the people and to provide for democratic participation in the exercise of political power in accordance with the fundamental rights and freedoms of citizens and on the basis of electoral processes at all levels of State organization.

(b) Associations whose primary purpose is to promote local or sectoral interests or the exclusive interests of a given social group or class of citizens shall be different from political parties and may not enjoy the status provided for by law for such parties.

(c) The Political Parties Act shall determine the conditions for the acquisition of the status of juridical person by political parties.

(d) Political parties shall be granted specific privileges, which shall be guaranteed by law.

(e) For the operation and full development of a multi-party democracy based on respect for and guarantees of basic rights and freedoms and based on pluralism of democratic political expression and organization under which political power belongs exclusively to the people and is exercised in accordance with principles of representative and pluralistic democracy, the parties must have fundamentally democratic principles by which they must abide in practice and in their political activities.

2. *General principles*

In their formation, structure and operations, political parties shall observe and apply the following general principles with the aim of controlling their actions:

(a) They must pursue democratic purposes;

(b) They must pursue national and patriotic interests;

(c) The political objectives pursued must be non-regional, non-tribal, non-separatist, non-racial, non-ethnic and non-religious;

(d) The members of political parties must be citizens of Mozambique;

(e) The parties must have a democratic structure and their internal bodies must be transparent;

(f) The parties must accept democratic methods for the pursuit of their aims;

(g) Joining a political party must be a voluntary act reflecting the freedom of citizens to associate with others who share the same political outlook.

3. *The rights of parties*

The purpose of the Political Parties Act shall be to protect the freedom of action and operation of political parties, with the exception of those which espouse antidemocratic, totalitarian or violent aims, or which conduct their activities in a manner contrary to law.

Parties shall enjoy the following rights:

(a) Equal rights and duties before the law;

(b) Every Party shall have the right freely and publicly to propound its policies;

(c) Specific guarantees shall be provided with respect to access to the mass media, sources of public funding and public facilities, in accordance with the principle of non-discrimination and on the basis of criteria of representativeness to be specified in the Electoral Act;

(d) Exemption from taxes and fees as provided for by law;

(e) No citizen shall be persecuted or discriminated against because of membership in a political party or political opinion;

(f) Other aspects specific to individual political parties shall be determined in their respective statutes or regulations, which must conform with the law. Public notice shall be given of such statutes or regulations.

4. *Duties of parties*

Political parties shall fulfil the following requirements:

(a) They shall be identified by name, acronym and symbol. The use of names, acronyms or symbols which may be considered offensive by the inhabitants or which incite to violence and may have divisive connotations based on race, region, tribe, gender or religion shall be prohibited;

(b) They shall not call into question the country's territorial integrity and national unity;

(c) They must establish their organs and organize their internal structure on the basis of the principle of democratic election and responsibility of all individuals holding party office;

(d) They must ensure that their statutes and programmes are approved by a majority of their members or by assemblies representing those members;

(e) As regards their internal organization, Parties must fully respect the principle of free adherence of their members, who may not be compelled to join or remain in a party against their will;

(f) They must be registered and disclose annually their accounts and sources of funding.

5. *Registration*

(a) The purpose of registration is to certify that the founding and existence of parties is in accordance with the applicable legal principles and, consequently, to confer on parties the status of juridical person;

(b) For the purposes of registration, each Party must have collected at least 2,000 signatures;

(c) Responsibility for registering parties shall rest with the Government;

(d) The Commission provided for in paragraph 5 of Protocol I on basic principles shall consider and settle any disputes which may arise in connection with the registration of parties. For that purpose the Government shall make available to the Commission the documents required by law.

6. *Implementation*

(a) The Parties agree that, immediately following the signature of the General Peace Agreement, RENAMO shall commence its activities as a political party, with the privileges provided for by law; it shall, however, be required to submit at a later date the documents required by law for registration;

(b) Pursuing the method of dialogue, collaboration and regular consultation, the parties agree to establish, in connection with the discussion of item 5 of the Agreed Agenda, the timetable of activities necessary for the proper implementation of this Protocol.

In witness whereof, the Parties have decided to sign this Protocol.

For the delegation of the Government of the Republic of Mozambique:

(*Signed*) Armando Emílio GUEBUZA

For the delegation of RENAMO:

(*Signed*) Raul Manuel DOMINGOS

The mediators:

(*Signed*) Mario RAFFAELLI

(*Signed*) Jaime GONÇALVES

(*Signed*) Andrea RICCARDI

(*Signed*) Matteo ZUPPI

Done at San Egidio, Rome, on 13 November 1991

Protocol III

On 12 March 1992, the delegation of the Government of the Republic of Mozambique, headed by Armando Emílio Guebuza, Minister of Transport and Communications, and composed of Aguiar Mazula, Minister of State Administration, Teodato Hunguana, Minister of Labour, and Francisco Madeira, Diplomatic Adviser to the President of the Republic, and the delegation of RENAMO, headed by Raul Manuel Domingos, Chief of the Organization Department, and composed of Vicente Zacarias Ululu, Chief of the Information Department, Agostinho Semende Murrial, Deputy Chief of the Organization Department, and Virgílio Namalue, Director of the Information Department, meeting in Rome in the context of the peace talks, in the presence of the mediators, Mario Raffaelli, representative of the Government of the Italian Republic and coordinator of the mediators, Jaime Gonçalves, Archbishop of Beira, Andrea Riccardi and Matteo Zuppi of the Community of San Egidio, took up the item of the agenda signed on 28 May 1991 concerning the Electoral Law and agreed as follows:

This Protocol sets forth the general principles which should guide the drafting of the Electoral Act and any possible amendments to the laws in connection with the conduct of the electoral process.

The Electoral Act shall be drafted by the Government, in consultation with RENAMO and all other political parties.

I. *Freedom of the press and access to the media*

(a) All citizens shall enjoy the right of freedom of the press and freedom of information. These freedoms shall encompass, specifically, the right to establish and operate newspapers and other publications, radio and television broadcasting stations and other forms of written or sound communication, such as posters, leaflets and other media.

These rights shall not be abridged by censorship.

(b) Administrative and tax regulations shall in no case be used to hamper or prevent the exercise of this right on political grounds.

(c) Freedom of the press shall also include freedom of expression and creation for journalists and the protection of their independence and professional secrecy.

(d) The Government-controlled mass media shall enjoy editorial independence and shall guarantee, in accordance with the specific regulations envisaged in section V.3.(b).1 of this Protocol, the right of all parties to access without political discrimination. Provision should be made in such regulations for access by all parties free of charge.

Advertisements which conform to the prevailing commercial practice may not be refused on political grounds.

(e) The mass media may not discriminate against or refuse on political grounds any party or its candidates the exercise of the right of reply or the publication of corrections or retractions. Access to the courts shall be guaranteed in cases of defamation, slander, libel and other press offences.

II. *Freedom of association, expression and political activity*

(a) All citizens shall have the right to freedom of expression, association, assembly, demonstration and political activity. Administrative and tax regulations shall in no case be used to prevent or hamper the exercise of these rights for political reasons. These rights shall not extend to the activities of unlawful private paramilitary groups or groups which promote violence in any form or terrorism, racism or separatism.

(b) Freedom of association, expression and political activity shall encompass access, without discrimination, to the use of public places and facilities. Such use shall be conditional on submission of an application to the competent administrative authorities, who must give a decision within 48 hours after the submission of the application. Applications may be rejected only for reasons of public order or for organizational considerations.

III. *Liberty of movement and freedom of residence*

All citizens shall have the right to move about throughout the country without having to obtain administrative authorization.

All citizens have the right to choose to reside anywhere in the national territory and to leave or return to the country.

IV. *Return of Mozambican refugees and displaced persons and their social reintegration*

(a) The parties undertake to cooperate in the repatriation and reintegration of Mozambican refugees and displaced persons in the national territory and the social integration of war-disabled.

(b) Without prejudice to the liberty of movement of citizens, the Government shall draw up a draft agreement with RENAMO to organize the necessary assistance to refugees and displaced persons, preferably in their original places of residence. The parties agree to seek the involvement of the competent United Nations agencies in the drawing up and implementation of this plan. The International Red Cross and other organizations to be agreed upon shall be invited to participate in the implementation of the plan.

(c) Mozambican refugees and displaced persons shall not forfeit any of the rights and freedoms of citizens for having left their original places of residence.

(d) Mozambican refugees and displaced persons shall be registered and included in the electoral rolls together with other citizens in their places of residence.

(e) Mozambican refugees and displaced persons shall be guaranteed restitution of property owned by them which is still in existence and the right to take legal action to secure the return of such property from individuals in possession of it.

V. *Electoral procedures: system of democratic, impartial and pluralistic voting*

1. *General principles*

(a) The Electoral Act shall establish an electoral system which is consonant with the principles of the direct, equal, secret and personal ballot.

(b) Elections to the Assembly of the Republic and for President of the Republic shall be held simultaneously.

(c) The elections shall take place within one year after the date of the signing of the General Peace Agreement. This period may be extended if it is determined that circumstances exist which preclude its observance.

2. *The right to vote*

(a) Mozambican citizens 18 years of age and over shall have the right to vote, with the exception of individuals suffering from certified mental incapacity or insanity.

(b) As envisaged by item 4 (a) of the Agreed Agenda, Mozambican citizens who are detained or have been sentenced to a prison term for a criminal offence under ordinary law shall not have the right to vote until they complete their sentence. In any event, this restriction shall not apply to individuals belonging to the Parties in respect of acts committed in the course of military operations.

(c) Exercise of the right to vote shall be conditional on registration in the electoral rolls.

(d) With the aim of promoting the broadest possible participation in the elections, the parties agree to encourage all Mozambican citizens 18 years of age and over to register and to exercise their right to vote.

3. *National Elections Commission*

(a) For the purpose of organizing and conducting the electoral process, the Government shall set up a National Elections Commission, composed of individuals whose professional and personal qualities afford guarantees of balance, objectivity and independence *vis-à-vis* all political parties. One third of the members to be appointed to the Commission shall be nominated by RENAMO.

(b) The Commission shall have the following functions:

1. To draw up, in consultation with the political parties, regulations governing election campaigning, regulations on the distribution of broadcast air time and regulations on the utilization of public and private places and facilities during the election campaign;

2. To oversee the compilation of electoral rolls, the legal filing of candidacies, the public announcement of candidacies and checking and recording the election results;

3. To monitor the electoral process and ensure compliance with the laws;

4. To ensure equality of treatment for citizens in all acts relating to the elections;

5. To receive, consider and settle complaints with respect to the validity of the elections;

6. To ensure equal opportunity and treatment for the different candidates;

7. To review the election accounts;

8. To draw up and have published in the national gazette (*Boletim da República*) the lists of the results of the final vote tally.

4. *Voting Assemblies*

(a) At each polling place there shall be a Voting Assembly composed of:
 – All citizens who are to exercise their right to vote at the given polling place;
 – representatives of the various candidates and parties.

(b) Each Voting Assembly shall be presided over by a Ballot Board composed of a Chairman, a vice-chairman-cum-secretary and tellers which shall oversee the electoral operations.

(c) The members of the Ballot Board shall be appointed from among the voters belonging to the Voting Assembly in question, with the agreement of the representatives of the various candidates.

(d) The Ballot Boards shall be responsible for monitoring all electoral operations and transmitting the results to the National Elections Commission.

(e) Delegates of the candidates or parties in the Voting Assembly shall have the right:

1. To monitor all electoral operations;

2. To examine the rolls compiled or utilized by the Board;

3. To be heard and to receive clarifications with respect to all matters relating to the conduct of the Assembly;

4. To submit complaints;

5. To occupy the places closest to the Assembly Board;

6. To initial and sign the official records of the Assembly and to monitor all acts related to the electoral operations.

(f) Any complaints shall be included in the official records and transmitted to the National Elections Commission.

5. Election to the Assembly of the Republic

(a) The country's provinces shall constitute electoral districts. The National Elections Commission shall decide on the apportionment of seats to each electoral district on the basis of population.

(b) The Electoral Act shall provide for an electoral system based on the principle of proportional representation for election to the Assembly.

(c) Parties which intend to stand jointly for elections to the Assembly must submit lists under a single emblem.

(d) Once the election campaign has begun, the combining of electoral lists for the purpose of pooling votes shall not be permitted.

(e) Citizens 18 years of age and over shall be eligible to stand for election to the Assembly of the Republic. The parties agree, however, on the desirability of raising the minimum age to 25 for the forthcoming elections as a transitional measure.

(f) A minimum percentage of votes cast nationwide shall be established, below which competing political parties may not have a seat in the Assembly. This percentage shall be agreed in consultation with all political parties in the country and shall not be less than 5 per cent or more than 20 per cent.

(g) Representatives of the parties in each electoral district shall be elected in the order in which they appear on the lists.

6. Election of the President of the Republic

(a) The President of the Republic shall be elected by an absolute majority of ballots cast. If no candidate obtains an absolute majority, a second ballot shall be held restricted to the two candidates who have received the highest number of votes.

(b) The second ballot shall take place within one to three weeks after the announcement of the results of the first ballot. Having regard to organizational considerations, the date of the ballot shall be indicated before the commencement of the election campaign.

(c) Individuals 35 years of age and over who are citizens and registered voters shall be eligible to stand for election to the office of President of the Republic.

(d) Candidacies for President of the Republic must have the support of at least 10,000 signatures of Mozambican citizens 18 years of age and over who are currently registered voters.

7. Financing and facilities

(a) The National Elections Commission shall guarantee the distribution to all parties competing in the elections, without discrimination, of subsidies and logistic support for the election campaign apportioned on the basis of the number of each party's candidates and under the supervision of all parties competing in the elections.

(b) The Government undertakes to assist in obtaining facilities and means so that RENAMO may secure the accommodation and transport and communications facilities it needs to carry out its political activities in all the provincial capitals, and in other locations to the extent that the available resources so permit.

(c) For these purposes the Government shall seek support from the international community and, in particular, from Italy.

VI. Guarantees for the electoral process and role of international observers

(a) Supervision and monitoring of the implementation of this Protocol shall be guaranteed by the Commission envisaged in Protocol I on "Basic principles".

(b) With a view to ensuring the highest degree of impartiality in the electoral process, the parties agree to invite as observers the United Nations, OAU and other organizations, as well as appropriate private individuals from abroad as may be agreed between the Government and RENAMO.

The observers shall perform their function from the commencement of the electoral campaign to the time when the Government takes office.

(c) With the aim of expediting the peace process, the parties also agree on the necessity of seeking technical and material assistance from the United Nations and OAU following the signature of the General Peace Agreement.

(d) The Government shall address formal requests to the United Nations and OAU in pursuance of the provisions of this section.

In witness whereof, the parties have decided to sign this Protocol.

For the delegation of the
Republic of Mozambique:
(*Signed*) Armando Emílio
GUEBUZA

For the delegation of
RENAMO:
(*Signed*) Raul Manuel
DOMINGOS

The mediators:

(*Signed*) Mario RAFFAELLI

(*Signed*) Jaime GONÇALVES

(*Signed*) Andrea RICCARDI

(*Signed*) Matteo ZUPPI

Done at Rome, on 12 March 1992

Protocol IV

On 4 October 1992, the delegation of the Government of the Republic of Mozambique, headed by Armando Emílio Guebuza, Minister of Transport and Communications, and composed of Mariano de Araújo Matsinha, Minister without Portfolio, Aguiar Mazula, Minister of State Administration, Teodato Hunguana, Minister of Labour, Lieutenant-General Tobias Dai, Francisco Madeira, Diplomatic Adviser to the President of the Republic, Brigadier Aleixo Malunga, Colonel Fideles De Sousa, Major Justino Nrepo, Major Eduardo Lauchande, and the delegation of RENAMO, headed by Raul Manuel Domingos, Chief of the Organization Department, and composed of José De Castro, Chief of the External Relations Department, Agostinho Semende Murrial, Chief of the Information Department, José Augusto Xavier, Director-General of the Internal Administration Department, Major-General Hermínio Morais, Colonel Fernando Canivete, Lieutenant-Colonel Arone Julai, Lieutenant Antonio Domingos, meeting at Rome in the presence of the mediators, Mario Raffaelli, representative of the Italian Government and coordinator of the mediators, Jaime Gonçalves, Archbishop of Beira, Andrea Riccardi and Matteo Zuppi of the Community of San Egidio, and the observers of the United Nations and the Governments of the United States of America, France, the United Kingdom and Portugal, took up item 3 of the Agreed Agenda of 28 May 1991, entitled "Military questions", and agreed as follows:

I. *Formation of the Mozambican Defence Force*

(i) *General principles*

1. The Mozambican Defence Force (FADM) shall be formed for service throughout the national territory.
2. The FADM:

(a) Has as its general purpose the defence and safeguarding of the country's sovereignty, independence and territory. During the period between the cease-fire and the time when the new Government takes office, the FADM may, under the FADM High Command, act in cooperation with the Police Command to protect civilian inhabitants against crime and violence of all kinds. Additional functions of the FADM shall be to provide assistance in crisis or emergency situations arising in the country as a result of natural disasters and to provide support for reconstruction and development efforts.

(b) Shall be non-partisan, career, professionally trained, and competent; it shall be made up exclusively of Mozambican citizens who are volunteers and are drawn from the forces of both Parties. It shall serve the country with professionalism and respect the democratic order and the rule of law. The composition of the FADM should preclude all forms of racial or ethnic discrimination or discrimination based on language or religious affiliation.

3. The process of forming the FADM shall begin after the entry into force of the cease-fire immediately following the inauguration of the Commission provided for in Protocol I of 18 October 1991, to be called the Supervisory and Monitoring Commission (CSC). This process shall be completed prior to the commencement of the election campaign.

4. The process of forming the FADM shall be conducted simultaneously with the concentration, disarmament and integration into civilian life of the personnel demobilized in stages as a result of the cease-fire. The Government and RENAMO shall be responsible for contributing units drawn from the existing forces of each side; this process shall proceed until the new units of the FADM have been formed, with all existing units being demobilized when the FADM has reached full strength.

5. The neutrality of the FADM during the period between the cease-fire and the time when the new Government takes office shall be guaranteed by the Parties through the Commission referred to in section I.iii.1.a of this Protocol.

6. By the time of the elections, only the FADM shall exist and shall have the structure agreed upon between the Parties; no other forces may remain in existence. All elements of the existing armed forces of the two Parties which are not incorporated into the FADM shall be demobilized during the period envisaged in section VI.(i).3 of this Protocol.

(ii) *Personnel*

1. The Parties agree that the troop strength of the FADM up until the time when the new Government takes office shall be as follows:

(a) Army: 24,000
(b) Air Force: 4,000

(c) Navy: 2,000

2. The personnel of the FADM in each of the service branches shall be provided by the FAM and the forces of RENAMO, each side contributing 50 per cent.

(iii) *FADM command structures* 1/

1. The parties agree to establish a Joint Commission for the Formation of the Mozambican Defence Force (CCFADM) on the following basis:

(a) CCFADM shall have specific responsibility for overseeing the process of forming the FADM and shall operate under the authority of CSC;

(b) CCFADM is the body responsible for the formation of the FADM until the time when the new Government takes office. FADM shall be headed by a High Command (CS), which shall be subordinate to CCFADM. After the new Government takes office, the FADM shall be placed under the authority of the new Ministry of Defence or any other body which the new Government may establish;

(c) CCFADM shall be composed of representatives of the FAM and the RENAMO forces as members, who shall be assisted by representatives of the countries selected by the Parties to advise in the process of forming the FADM. CCFADM shall be inaugurated on the date of the entry into force of the cease-fire (E-Day);

(d) CCFADM shall draw up directives on the phasing of the establishment of the FADM structures and shall propose to CSC:

– The rules governing the FADM;

– The budget to be provided for the FADM until the new Government takes office;

– The criteria for selection and the selection of FAM personnel and RENAMO forces for the formation of the FADM;

– The names of the commanding officers of the main commands.

2. FADM High Command

(a) The general mission of CS shall be to act on the directives issued by CCFADM, taking into account the establishment of the FADM structures and support for the FADM;

(b) Until the new Government takes office, the command of FADM shall be exercised by two general officers of equal rank, appointed by each of the Parties. Decisions of the command shall be valid only when signed by these two general officers;

(c) The FADM command structure shall be strictly non-political and shall receive directives and orders only through the appropriate chain of command;

(d) The FADM shall have a single logistics service for all three branches. To that end, a Logistics and Infrastructure Command shall be established, under the authority of the FADM High Command;

(e) Appointments to the FADM High Command and the commands of the three branches of the FADM and the Logistics Command shall be proposed by CCFADM and approved by CSC;

(f) Until the new Government takes office, the FADM High Command shall be assisted by the General Staff, with departments headed by general officers or senior officers proposed by CCFADM and approved by CSC.

3. Command of the Army, Air Force and Navy and the Logistics Command:

The FADM High Command shall have authority over the Commands of the three service branches (Army, Air Force and Navy) and the Logistics Command, which shall be organized as follows:

(a) Army Command

1. The structure of the Army Command shall encompass the military regions under the direct authority of the Army Commander, whose functions are to be determined but which may include the organization and preparation of forces, training, justice, discipline and logistic support to assigned forces.

2. Each military region shall have a commanding officer holding the rank of general, who shall be assisted by a deputy commander.

3. The headquarters of the military regions shall be proposed by the Commander of the Army and approved by CS.

(b) Air Force Command

The Air Force shall be formed having regard to the training and skills of the personnel of the existing Air Force and the existing RENAMO forces, in accordance with the provisions of the directives issued by CCFADM.

(c) Navy Command

The Navy shall be formed having regard to the training and skills of the personnel of the existing Navy and the RENAMO forces, in accordance with the provisions of the directives issued by CCFADM.

(d) Logistics and Infrastructure Command

1. A Logistics and Infrastructure Command shall be set up under the direct authority of the FADM High Command.

2. The Logistics and Infrastructure Command shall have the overall mission of planning and providing administrative and logistic support for the FADM (Army, Air Force and Navy) and ensuring delivery of such support through the FADM General Services. It shall, in particular, be responsible for production and procurement logistics.

3. The Logistics and Infrastructure Command shall be headed by a general, assisted by a deputy commander

1/ Annex No. 1.

and a general staff which shall, initially, include the following sections:

- Infrastructure;
- General services;
- Equipment;
- Finance.

4. The Logistics and Infrastructure Command shall have authority over such support units as may be assigned to it.

(iv) *Timetable for the process*

(a) The formation of the FADM shall commence with the appointment of the following:

- CCFADM, prior to the entry into force of the cease-fire (E-Day);
- The FADM High Command on E-Day + 1;
- The commanders of the three service branches and the logistics command;
- The commanders of the military regions;
- The unit commanders.

(b) General staffs shall be organized immediately following the appointment of each command.

(c) The system of administrative and logistics support shall be organized taking into account the new size of the FADM, in accordance with the principle of utilizing or transforming existing structures on the basis of the plans of the FADM High Command, as approved by CCFADM.

(v) *Technical assistance of foreign countries*

The parties shall inform the mediators within 7 (seven) days after the signing of the cease-fire protocol the countries which are to be invited to provide assistance in the process of forming the FADM.

II. *Withdrawal of foreign troops from Mozambican territory*

1. The withdrawal of foreign troops from Mozambican territory shall be initiated following the entry into force of the cease-fire (E-Day).

The Government of the Republic of Mozambique undertakes to negotiate the complete withdrawal of foreign forces and contingents from Mozambican territory with the Governments of the countries concerned.

The modalities and time-frame for the withdrawal shall not contravene any provision of the Cease-fire Agreement or the General Peace Agreement.

2. The Government of the Republic of Mozambique shall submit to CSC the deadlines and plans for implementation of the withdrawal, specifying the exact numbers of troops present in Mozambican territory and their location.

3. The complete withdrawal of foreign forces and contingents from Mozambican territory shall be moni-

tored and verified by the Cease-fire Commission (CCF) referred to in paragraph VI.(i).2 of this Protocol. CCF shall inform CSC of the conclusion of the complete withdrawal of foreign forces from the national territory.

4. In accordance with its mandate CSC, through CCF, will, following the withdrawal of the foreign troops, assume immediate responsibility for verifying and ensuring security of strategic and trading routes, adopting the measures it deems necessary for the purpose.

III. *Activities of private and irregular armed groups*

1. Except as provided in paragraph 3 below, para-military, private and irregular armed groups active on the day of entry into force of the cease-fire shall be disbanded and prohibited from forming new groups of the same kind.

2. CCF shall monitor and verify the disbanding of the private and irregular armed groups and shall collect their weapons and ammunition. CSC shall decide the final disposition of the weapons and ammunition collected.

3. CSC may as a temporary measure organize the continued existence of security organizations for the purpose of ensuring the security of specified public or private infrastructures during the period between the cease-fire and the time when the new Government takes office.

4. These security organizations may be authorized to use weapons in the discharge of their duties. The activities of these organizations shall be monitored by CCF.

IV. *Functioning of the National Service for People's Security*

1. The parties agree that it is essential that the State information service should continue to function during the period between the entry into force of the cease-fire and the time when the new Government takes office, in order to ensure that the strategic information required by the State is made available and for the purpose of protecting the sovereignty and independence of the Republic of Mozambique.

2. For the purposes indicated above, the Parties agree that the State Information and Security Service (SISE) established by Act No. 20/91 of 23 August 1991 shall continue to perform its functions under the direct authority of the President of the Republic of Mozambique and subject to the following principles:

3. SISE shall:

(a) perform its duties and functions strictly in accordance with the spirit and the letter of internationally recognized democratic principles;

(b) respect the civil and political rights of citizens, as well as the internationally recognized human rights and fundamental freedoms;

(c) be guided in the performance of its functions by the interests of the State and the common welfare, in a manner free from any partisan or ideological considerations or regard for social standing and from any other form of discrimination;

(d) act at all times and in all respects in conformity with the terms and spirit of the General Peace Agreement.

4. SISE shall be composed, at all levels of the service, of citizens selected on the basis of criteria that are in conformity with the principles specified above.

5. (a) The measures taken by SISE, as well as all actions of its agents, shall at all times be governed by the law in force in the Republic of Mozambique and by the principles agreed upon in the General Peace Agreement;

(b) The activities and prerogatives of SISE shall be confined to the production of information required by the President of the Republic, within the limits authorized by the juridical order and in strict respect for the principles of the State ruled by law and for human rights and fundamental freedoms. The information thus obtained may in no case be used to limit the exercise of the democratic rights of citizens or to favour any political party;

(c) In no case may police functions be assigned to SISE.

6. The Director-General and Deputy Director-General of SISE shall be appointed by the President of the Republic of Mozambique.

7. (a) For purposes of verifying that the actions of SISE do not violate the legal order or result in violation of the political rights of citizens, a National Information Commission (COMINFO) shall be established;

(b) COMINFO shall be composed of 21 members whose professional and personal qualities and past record afford guarantees of balance, effectiveness and independence *vis-à-vis* all political parties;

(c) COMINFO shall be established by the President of the Republic of Mozambique within 15 days following the entry into force of the General Peace Agreement and shall be composed of six citizens nominated by RENAMO, six nominated by the Government, and nine selected as a result of consultations to be held by the President of the Republic with the political forces in the country from among citizens meeting the requirements specified in subparagraph (b);

(d) COMINFO shall have full powers to investigate any matter relating to the activity of SISE that is held to be contrary to the legal order and to the principles specified in paragraphs 1, 2, 3 and 5. A request for investigation may be rejected only by a two-thirds majority of its membership;

(e) COMINFO shall provide CSC with the reports and clarifications called for by the latter Commission;

(f) COMINFO shall inform the competent State authorities of any irregularities detected, in order that they may take the appropriate police or disciplinary measures.

V. *Depoliticization and restructuring of the police forces*

1. During the period between the entry into force of the cease-fire and the assumption of power by the new Government, the Police of the Republic of Mozambique (PRM) shall continue to perform its functions under the responsibility of the Government.

2. The Police of the Republic of Mozambique shall:

(a) perform its duties and functions strictly in accordance with the spirit and the letter of internationally recognized democratic principles;

(b) respect the civil and political rights of citizens, as well as the internationally recognized human rights and fundamental freedoms;

(c) be guided in the performance of its functions by the interests of the State and common welfare, in a manner free from any partisan or ideological considerations or regard for social standing and from any other form of discrimination;

(d) act at all times in conformity with the terms and spirit of the General Peace Agreement;

(e) act at all times with impartiality and independence *vis-à-vis* all political parties.

3. The PRM shall be composed of citizens selected on the basis of criteria that are in conformity with the principles specified above.

4. The basic tasks of the PRM shall be:

(a) to ensure respect for and defence of the law;

(b) to maintain public order and tranquillity and to prevent and suppress crime;

(c) to guarantee the existence of a climate of social stability and harmony.

5. (a) The measures taken by the PRM, as well as all actions of its agents, shall at all times be governed by the law and the legislative provisions in force in the Republic of Mozambique and by the principles agreed upon in the General Peace Agreement;

(b) The activities and prerogatives of the PRM shall be exercised within the limits authorized by the juridical order, but with strict respect for the principles of the State ruled by law and for human rights and fundamental freedoms. These activities may not be directed towards limiting the exercise of the democratic rights of citizens or favouring any political party.

6. The Commander and Deputy Commander of the PRM shall be appointed by the President of the Republic of Mozambique.

7. (a) For purposes of verifying that the actions of

the PRM do not violate the legal order or result in violation of the political rights of citizens, a National Police Affairs Commission (COMPOL) shall be established;

(b) COMPOL shall be composed of 21 members whose professional and personal qualities and past record afford guarantees of balance, effectiveness and independence *vis-à-vis* all political parties;

(c) COMPOL shall be established by the President of the Republic of Mozambique within 15 days following the entry into force of the General Peace Agreement and shall be composed of six citizens nominated by RENAMO, six nominated by the Government, and nine selected as a result of consultations to be held by the President of the Republic with the political forces in the country from among citizens meeting the requirements specified in subparagraph (b);

(d) COMPOL shall have full powers to investigate any matter relating to the activity of PRM that is held to be contrary to the legal order and to the principles specified in paragraphs 1, 2, 4 and 5. On being apprised of a matter, the Commission shall conduct a preliminary internal analysis in order to determine whether it falls within the sphere of police activities. The Commission shall decide to proceed with the investigations if more than half of its members so agree;

(e) COMPOL shall submit systematic reports on its activities to CSC;

(f) COMPOL shall inform the competent State authorities of any irregularities detected, in order that they may take the appropriate judicial or disciplinary measures.

VI. *Economic and social reintegration of demobilized soldiers*

(i) *Demobilization*

1. Demobilization of the FAM and the forces of RENAMO means the process whereby, at the decision of the respective Parties, soldiers who on E-Day were members of those forces revert for all purposes to the status of civilians.

2. Cease-fire Commission

(a) On E-Day, the Cease-fire Commission (CCF) shall be established and begin its functions under the direct supervision of CSC.

(b) CCF shall be composed of representatives of the Government, RENAMO, the invited countries and the United Nations. CCF shall be presided over by the United Nations.

(c) CCF shall be based in Maputo and shall be structured as follows:
– Regional offices (North, Centre and South);
– Offices at the assembly and billeting locations of the two Parties.

(d) CCF shall have, *inter alia*, the function of implementing the demobilization process, with the following tasks:
– Planning and organization;
– Regulation of procedures;
– Direction and supervision;
– Registration of troops to be demobilized and issue of the respective identity cards;
– Collection, registration and custody of weapons, ammunition, explosives, equipment, uniforms and documentation; destroying or deciding on the other disposition of weapons, ammunition, explosives, equipment, uniforms and documentation as agreed by the Parties;
– Medical examinations;
– Issue of demobilization certificates.

(e) The United Nations shall assist in the implementation, verification and monitoring of the entire demobilization process.

3. Timetable

E-Day: Installation of CCF and commencement of its functions

E-Day + 30: Definition by both Parties of the troops to be demobilized; activation of demobilization structures and initiation of the process

E-Day + 60: Demobilization of at least 20 per cent of the total troops to be demobilized

E-Day + 90: Demobilization of at least a further 20 per cent of the total troops to be demobilized

E-Day + 120: Demobilization of at least a further 20 per cent of the total troops to be demobilized

E-Day + 150: Demobilization of at least a further 20 per cent of the total troops to be demobilized

E-Day + 180: End of demobilization of the troops to be demobilized.

(ii) *Reintegration*

1. The term "demobilized soldier" means an individual who:
– up until E-Day was a member of the FAM or the RENAMO forces;
– subsequent to E-Day was demobilized at the decision of the relevant command, and handed over the weapons, ammunition, equipment, uniform and documentation in his possession;
– has been registered and has received the relevant identity card;
– has received the demobilization certificate.

For all purposes, demobilized soldiers of both Parties shall become civilians and shall be accorded equal treatment by the State.

2. Reintegration Commission

(a) A Reintegration Commission (CORE) shall be established.

CORE shall operate under the direct authority of CSC and shall initiate its functions on E-Day.

(b) CORE shall be composed of representatives of the Government and RENAMO, representatives of the invited countries, a representative of the United Nations, who shall preside, and representatives of other international organizations.

(c) CORE shall be based at Maputo and shall be structured as follows:

– Regional offices (North, Centre and South);
– Provincial offices in each provincial capital.

(d) The assignment of CORE shall be to effect the economic and social reintegration of demobilized soldiers, and it shall for this purpose conduct the following tasks:

– Planning and organization;
– Regulation of procedures;
– Direction and supervision;
– Monitoring.

3. Resources

The economic and social reintegration of demobilized soldiers (demobilization allowances, technical and/or vocational training, transport, etc.) will depend on the resources made available within the framework of the Donors Conference as referred to in item 6 of the Agreed Agenda of 28 May 1991.

In witness whereof, the Parties have decided to sign the present Protocol.

*For the delegation of the
Government of the
Republic of Mozambique:*
(*Signed*) Armando Emílio
GUEBUZA

*For the delegation of
RENAMO:*
(*Signed*) Raul Manuel
DOMINGOS

The mediators:

(*Signed*) Mario RAFFAELLI

(*Signed*) Jaime GONÇALVES

(*Signed*) Andrea RICCARDI

(*Signed*) Matteo ZUPPI

San Egidio, Rome, 4 October 1992

Annex 1
Mozambican Defence Force

COMMAND STRUCTURE

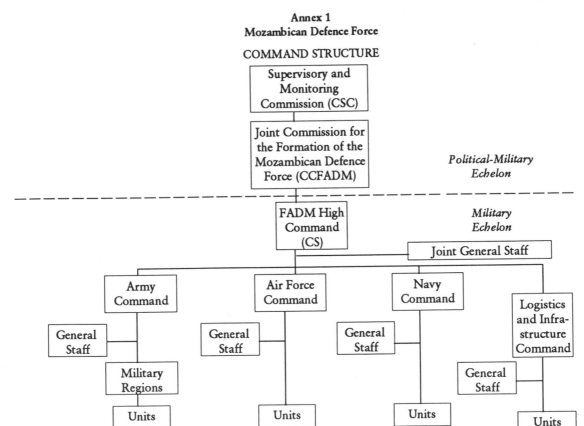

Protocol V

On 4 October 1992, the delegation of the Government of the Republic of Mozambique, headed by Armando Emílio Guebuza, Minister of Transport and Communications, and composed of Mariano de Araújo Matsinha, Minister without Portfolio, Aguiar Mazula, Minister of State Administration, Teodato Hunguana, Minister of Labour, Lieutenant-General Tobias Dai, Francisco Madeira, Diplomatic Adviser to the President of the Republic, Brigadier Aleixo Malunga, Colonel Fideles De Sousa, Major Justino Nrepo and Major Eduardo Lauchande, and the delegation of RENAMO, headed by Raul Manuel Domingos, Chief of the Organization Department, and composed of José De Castro, Chief of the External Relations Department, Agostinho Semende Murrial, Chief of the Information Department, José Augusto Xavier, Director-General of the Internal Administration Department, Major-General Hermínio Morais, Colonel Fernando Canivete, Lieutenant-Colonel Arone Julai and Lieutenant António Domingos, meeting at Rome in the presence of the mediators, Mario Raffaelli, representative of the Italian Government and coordinator of the mediators, Jaime Gonçalves, Archbishop of Beira, Andrea Riccardi and Matteo Zuppi, of the Community of San Egidio, and observers from the United Nations and the Governments of the United States of America, France, the United Kingdom and Portugal, took up item 5 of the Agreed Agenda of 28 May 1991, entitled "Guarantees", and agreed as follows:

I. *Timetable for the conduct of the electoral process*

1. The elections to the Assembly of the Republic and the post of President of the Republic shall be held simultaneously and shall take place one year after the date of signature of the General Peace Agreement, as provided for in Protocol III.

2. Further to the provisions set forth in Protocol III, the Parties also agree as follows:

(a) By E-Day + 60, the Government shall establish the National Elections Commission provided for in Protocol III;

(b) Immediately following the signature of the General Peace Agreement, the Government, for purposes of the provisions of Protocol III, shall request technical and material support from the United Nations and OAU;

(c) The Government shall draft the Electoral Act in consultation with RENAMO and the other parties within at most two months from the adoption by the Assembly of the Republic of the legal instruments incorporating the Protocols and guarantees, as well as the General Peace Agreement, into Mozambican law. The approval and publication of the Electoral Act shall take place within at most one month following the completion of its drafting;

(d) Within 60 days following the signature of the General Peace Agreement, the Government and RENAMO shall agree on the observers to be invited for the electoral process. The Government shall draw up the corresponding invitations;

(e) The election campaign shall begin 45 days before the date of the elections;

(f) By the date of commencement of the election campaign, all parties taking part must have been registered and have submitted their lists of candidates as well as their respective symbols;

(g) By the date of commencement of the election campaign, the candidates for the Presidency of the Republic must have submitted their candidacies in conformity with the legally prescribed requirements;

(h) The election campaign shall conclude 48 hours before the start of voting;

(i) The elected Assembly of the Republic shall take office 15 days after the publication of the lists giving the results of the election. The lists giving the results of the election shall be published not more than eight days after the closure of voting;

(j) The investiture of the elected President of the Republic shall take place one week after the elected Assembly of the Republic has taken office.

II. *Commission to supervise the cease-fire and monitor respect for and implementation of the agreements between the Parties within the framework of these negotiations: its composition and powers*

1. Pursuant to Protocol I, the Supervisory and Monitoring Commission (CSC) is established, which shall begin operating upon appointment of its Chairman by the Secretary-General of the United Nations.

2. This Commission shall be composed of representatives of the Government, RENAMO, the United Nations, OAU and the countries to be agreed upon by the Parties. The Commission shall be chaired by the United Nations and shall be based at Maputo.

3. The decisions of CSC shall be taken by consensus between the two Parties.

4. CSC shall draw up its own Rules of Procedure and may whenever it sees fit establish subcommissions additional to those provided for in paragraph II.7 of the present Protocol.

5. CSC shall in particular:

(a) Guarantee the implementation of the provisions contained in the General Peace Agreement;

(b) Guarantee respect for the timetable specified for the cease-fire and the holding of the elections;

(c) Assume responsibility for the authentic interpretation of the agreements;

(d) Settle any disputes that may arise between the Parties;

(e) Guide and coordinate the activities of the subsidiary commissions referred to in paragraph II.7 of this Protocol.

6. CSC shall cease to function when the new Government takes office.

7. CSC shall have under it the following Commissions:

(a) The Joint Commission for the Formation of the Mozambican Defence Force (CCFADM)

Its powers shall be those specified in Protocol IV, paragraph I (iii), on the formation of the Mozambican Defence Force. CCFADM shall be composed of representatives of the Parties and of the Governments selected by the Parties before the signing of the General Peace Agreement to provide assistance in the process of formation of the FADM in conformity with the provisions of Protocol IV, section I.

(b) The Cease-fire Commission (CCF)

Its composition and powers shall be those indicated in Protocol IV, section VI and Protocol VI, section I.

(c) Reintegration Commission (CORE)

Its composition and powers shall be those specified in Protocol IV, section VI.

III. *Specific guarantees for the period from the cease-fire to the holding of the elections*

1. The Government of the Republic of Mozambique shall submit a formal request to the United Nations for its participation in monitoring and guaranteeing the implementation of the General Peace Agreement, in particular the cease-fire and the electoral process, with immediate priority to coordinating and making available food, medical attention and all other forms of support necessary at the assembly and billeting locations for the forces as provided in Protocol VI.

2. With the means available to it and with the assistance of the international community, the Government of the Republic of Mozambique shall make available to CSC and its subsidiary commissions the logistical support required for their functioning.

3. The Government of the Republic of Mozambique shall send formal requests to the Governments and organizations selected by the two Parties to participate in the commissions agreed upon above.

4. The resources and facilities specified in Protocol III, paragraph 7 (b) shall be made available by the Government of Mozambique as from the date of incorporation of the General Peace Agreement into Mozambican law by the Assembly of the Republic. The major part of this process shall have been concluded by E-day.

5. The committee provided for in the Joint Declaration of 16 July 1992 shall exercise its functions before CSC takes office. CSC may if necessary decide to extend the activities of that committee, and establish guidelines for its operations to that end.

6. The Government of the Republic of Mozambique shall draw up in agreement with RENAMO and the relevant United Nations agencies, in accordance with Protocol III, the plan for assistance to refugees and displaced persons, which shall be submitted to the Donors Conference the holding of which is agreed upon in Protocol VII.

7. Between the entry into force of the cease-fire and the time when the new Government takes office, the entry of foreign troops or contingents into Mozambican territory shall not be permitted except in the cases agreed to by CSC.

8. RENAMO shall be responsible for the immediate personal security of its top leaders. The Government of the Republic of Mozambique shall grant police status to the members of RENAMO assigned to guarantee that security.

9. Guarantee of legality, stability and tranquillity throughout the territory of the Republic of Mozambique.

(a) The Parties recognize that the public administration in the Republic of Mozambique during the period between the entry into force of the cease-fire and the time when the new Government takes office will continue to obey the law in force and to be conducted through the institutions provided for by law.

(b) The public administration shall guarantee public tranquillity and stability, and seek to ensure the maintenance of peace and the creation of the climate required for the holding of fair and free general and presidential elections in accordance with the provisions of the General Peace Agreement and the Electoral Act.

(c) The two Parties undertake to guarantee that the laws and legislative provisions of the Republic of Mozambique, as well as the civil and political rights of citizens and human rights and fundamental freedoms, shall be respected and guaranteed in all parts of the national territory in conformity with Protocol I of 18 October 1991.

(d) In order to ensure greater tranquillity and stability in the period between the entry into force of the cease-fire and the time when the new Government takes office, the Parties agree that the institutions provided for by law for the conduct of the public administration in the areas controlled by RENAMO shall employ only citizens resident in those areas, who may be members of RENAMO. The State shall accord such citizens and the institutions staffed by them the respect, treatment and support required for the discharge of their duties, on the basis of strict equality and without any discrimination in relation to others performing similar functions and institutions at the same level in other areas of the country.

The relationship between the Ministry of State Administration and the administration in the areas controlled by RENAMO shall be conducted through a National Commission constituted by the Parties for the purpose of facilitating collaboration and good understanding. This Commission shall be composed of four representatives of each of the Parties and shall begin operating 15 days after the signature of the General Peace Agreement.

(e) The Government undertakes to respect and not antagonize the traditional structures and authorities where they are currently de facto exercising such authority, and to allow them to be replaced only in those cases where that is called for by the procedures of local tradition themselves.

(f) The Government undertakes not to hold local, district or provincial elections or elections to administrative posts in advance of the forthcoming general elections.

(g) The Parties undertake to guarantee throughout the national territory the exercise of democratic rights and freedoms by all citizens, as well as the performance of party work by all political parties.

(h) The Parties guarantee access by the Commissions provided for in the General Peace Agreement, the representatives and officials of the State institutions provided for by law and their officials to any part of the national territory to which they may need to proceed on official business, as well as the right to freedom of movement in all locations not restricted by any legislative measure, instrument or rule.

IV. *Constitutional issues*

The Joint Declaration of 7 August 1992 signed by Joaquim Alberto Chissano, President of the Republic of Mozambique, and Afonso Mecacho Marceta Dhlakama, President of RENAMO, constitutes an integral part of the General Peace Agreement. Accordingly, the principles embodied in Protocol I shall also apply with respect to the problem of constitutional guarantees raised by RENAMO and illustrated in the document submitted to the President of the Republic of Zimbabwe, Robert Gabriel Mugabe, at Gaborone, Botswana, on 4 July 1992. To this end, the Government of the Republic of Mozambique shall submit to the Assembly of the Republic for adoption legal instruments incorporating the Protocols, the guarantees and the General Peace Agreement into Mozambican law.

In witness whereof, the Parties have decided to sign the present Protocol.

For the delegation of the
Government of the
Republic of Mozambique:
(*Signed*) Armando Emílio
  GUEBUZA

For the delegation of
RENAMO:
(*Signed*) Raul Manuel
  DOMINGOS

The mediators:

(*Signed*) Mario RAFFAELLI

(*Signed*) Jaime GONÇALVES

(*Signed*) Andrea RICCARDI

(*Signed*) Matteo ZUPPI

San Egidio, Rome, 4 October 1992

Protocol VI

On 4 October 1992, the delegation of the Government of the Republic of Mozambique, headed by Armando Emílio Guebuza, Minister of Transport and Communications, and composed of Mariano de Araújo Matsinha, Minister without Portfolio, Aguiar Mazula, Minister of State Administration, Teodata Hunguana, Minister of Labour, Lieutenant-General Tobias Dai, Francisco Madeira, Diplomatic Adviser to the President of the Republic, Brigadier Aleixo Malunga, Colonel Fideles De Sousa, Major Justino Nrepo and Major Eduardo Lauchande, and the delegation of RENAMO, headed by Raul Manuel Domingos, Chief of the Organization Department, and composed of José De Castro, Chief of the External Relations Department, Agostinho Semende Murrial, Chief of the Information Department, José Augusto Xavier, Director-General of the Internal Administration Department, Major General Hermínio Morais, Colonel Fernando Canivete, Lieutenant Colonel Arone Julai and Lieutenant António Domingos, meeting at Rome in the presence of the mediators, Mario Raffaelli, representative of the Italian Government and coordinator of the mediators, Jaime Gonçalves, Archbishop of Beira, Andrea Riccardi and Matteo Zuppi, of the Community of San Egidio, and observers from the United Nations and the Governments of the United States of America, France, the United Kingdom and Portugal, took up item 4 of the Agreed Agenda of 28 May 1991, entitled "Cease-fire", and agreed as follows:

I. *Cessation of the armed conflict*

1. The cessation of the armed conflict (CAC) is a brief, dynamic and irreversible process of predetermined duration which must be implemented throughout the national territory of Mozambique.

The implementation of the process shall be the responsibility of the Government of the Republic of Mozambique and of RENAMO, acting within the framework of the Cease-fire Commission (CCF). The CCF is answerable to the CSC, the organ responsible for the overall political supervision of the cease-fire.

The CCF shall be composed of representatives of the Government, and countries accepted by them and a representative of the United Nations, who shall preside.

2. The CCF, which shall be structured as stipulated in Protocol IV, paragraph VI (i) (2), shall have the following functions:

– To plan, verify and guarantee the implementation of the cease-fire rules;
– To set itineraries for the movement of forces, in order to reduce the risk of incidents;
– To organize and implement mine-clearing operations;
– To analyse and verify the accuracy of the statistics provided by the Parties on troop strength, arms and military equipment;
– To receive, analyse and rule on complaints of possible cease-fire violations;
– To ensure the necessary coordination with organs of the United Nations verification system;
– The functions provided for in sections II, III and VI of Protocol IV.

3. The CAC shall begin on E-Day and end on E-Day + 180.

4. The CAC consists of 4 (four) phases:
– Cease-fire;
– Separation of forces;
– Concentration of forces;
– Demobilization.

5. The cease-fire

The Parties agree that:

(a) The cease-fire shall enter into force on E-Day.

E-Day is the day on which the General Peace Agreement is adopted by the Assembly of the Republic and incorporated into Mozambican law. The deployment of United Nations personnel in Mozambican territory to verify the cease-fire shall begin the same day.

(b) As of E-Day, neither of the Parties shall carry out any hostile act or operation by means of forces or individuals under its control. Accordingly, they may not:
– carry out any kind of attack by land, sea or air;
– organize patrols or offensive manoeuvres;
– occupy new positions;
– lay mines and prevent mine-clearing operations;
– interfere with military communications;
– carry out any kind of reconnaissance operations;
– carry out acts of sabotage and terrorism;
– acquire or receive lethal equipment;
– carry out acts of violence against the civilian population;
– restrict or prevent without justification the free movement of persons and property;
– carry out any other military activity which, in the opinion of the CCF and the United Nations, might jeopardize the cease-fire.

In performing their functions, the CCF and the United Nations shall enjoy complete freedom of movement throughout the territory of Mozambique.

(c) On E-Day, the United Nations shall begin official verification of compliance with the undertaking described in paragraph (b), investigating any alleged violation of the cease-fire. Any duly substantiated violation shall be reported by the United Nations at the appropriate level;

(d) During the period between the signing of the General Peace Agreement and E-Day, the two Parties agree to observe a complete cessation of hostilities and of the activities described in paragraph (b), in order to allow the United Nations to deploy its personnel in the territory to verify all aspects of the CAC as of E-Day.

6. Separation of forces

The Parties agree that:

(a) The purpose of the separation of forces is to reduce the risk of incidents, to build trust and to allow the United Nations effectively to verify the commitments assumed by the Parties;

(b) The separation of forces shall last 6 (six) days, from E-Day to E-Day + 5;

(c) During this period, the FAM shall proceed to the barracks, bases, existing semi-permanent facilities and other locations listed in annex A;

(d) During the same period, the RENAMO forces shall proceed to the locations listed in annex B;

(e) The locations listed in the above-mentioned annexes shall be those agreed to between the Parties and the United Nations no later than 7 (seven) days after the signing of the General Peace Agreement. The lists shall specify the name and site of the 29 assembly and billeting points for the FAM and the 20 such points for the RENAMO forces;

(f) Accordingly, by 2400 hours on E-Day + 5, the FAM and the RENAMO forces must be in the locations listed in annexes A and B respectively;

(g) All movements shall take place under the supervision and coordination of the United Nations. Neither Party may prevent or jeopardize the movements of the other Party's forces. The United Nations shall supervise all the locations listed in annexes A and B and shall in principle be present 24 hours a day in each of those locations as of E-Day;

(h) During this period of 6 (six) days, no force or individual shall be able to leave assembly and billeting points except to seek medical care or for other humanitarian reasons, and then only with the authorization and under the supervision of the United Nations. In each location, the commander of the troops shall be responsible for maintaining order and discipline and for ensuring that the troops conduct themselves in accordance with the principles and the spirit of this Protocol.

7. Concentration of forces

The Parties agree that:

(a) The concentration of forces shall begin on E-Day + 6 and end on E-Day + 30;

(b) During this period, the FAM shall concentrate in the normal peacetime barracks and military bases listed in annex C;

(c) During the same period, the RENAMO forces shall go to the assembly and billeting points listed in annex D;

(d) All movements shall take place under the supervision and coordination of the United Nations and shall be subject to the same conditions as those established for the separation of forces;

(e) All the main military facilities of the two Parties which cannot be moved to assembly and billeting points, such as military hospitals, logistical units and training facilities, shall be subject to verification *in situ*. These locations must also be specified no later than 7 (seven) days after the signing of the General Peace Agreement;

(f) Each assembly and billeting point shall be run by a military commander appointed by the corresponding Party. The military commander is responsible for maintaining the order and discipline of troops, distributing food and ensuring liaison with the organs for the verification and supervision of the cease-fire.

In the event of an incident or a cease-fire violation, the military commander must take immediate steps to avoid an escalation and put a stop to the incident or violation. Any incident or violation shall be reported to the senior level of the command structure and to the cease-fire verification and supervision organs;

(g) Arrangements for the security of each assembly and billeting point shall be agreed between the corresponding commander and the CCF, with the knowledge of the United Nations. The military unit stationed in each location shall provide its own security. Each assembly and billeting point shall cover an area with a maximum radius of five kilometres. Individual weapons and the necessary ammunition shall be distributed only to the security staff of assembly and billeting points;

(h) Each location must have the capacity to accommodate at least 1,000 soldiers.

8. Demobilization

Shall take place as stipulated in section VI of Protocol IV.

9. Formation of the FADM

Shall take place as stipulated in section I of Protocol IV.

10. Miscellaneous provisions

(a) The Parties agree to the following:

1. To supply the United Nations with complete inventories of their troop strength, arms, ammunition, mines and other explosives on E-Day – 6, E-Day, E-Day + 6, E-Day + 30 and, thereafter, every 15 days;

2. To allow the United Nations to verify the aspects and data referred to in the preceding paragraph;

3. As of E-Day + 31, all collective and individual weapons, including weapons on board aircraft and ships, shall be stored in warehouses under United Nations control;

4. As of E-Day + 6, troops shall be able to leave their respective assembly and billeting points only with the authorization and under the supervision of the United Nations;

(b) As of E-Day, the naval and air force components of the FAM shall refrain from carrying out any offensive operation. They may carry out only such non-hostile missions as are necessary for the discharge of their duties unrelated to the armed conflict. All air force flight plans must be communicated in advance to the United Nations. Aircraft may not, in any case, be armed and may not overfly assembly and billeting points;

(c) The foreign forces currently present in the territory of Mozambique must also respect the agreed cease-fire as of E-Day. In accordance with section II of Protocol IV, on E-Day the Government of the Republic of Mozambique shall communicate to the United Nations and the CSC the plans for the withdrawal of foreign troops from Mozambican territory. These plans shall include the numbers and equipment of such troops. Withdrawal shall begin on E-Day + 6 and end on E-Day + 30. All movements must be coordinated and verified by the CCF;

(d) The Parties agree that, as of E-Day, they shall end all hostile propaganda, both internal and external;

(e) Border control as of E-Day shall be provided by the immigration services and the police.

II. *Operational timetable for the cease-fire*

E-Day: Entry into force of the cease-fire and beginning of United Nations verification

Beginning of the cessation of the armed conflict (CAC)

Beginning of the separation of forces phase

E-Day + 5: End of the separation of forces phase

E-Day + 6: Beginning of the concentration of forces phase

Beginning of the withdrawal of foreign forces and contingents from the country

E-Day + 30: End of the concentration of forces phase

End of the withdrawal of foreign forces and contingents from the country

E-Day + 31: Beginning of the demobilization phase

E-Day + 180: End of the demobilization phase and of the CAC.

III. *Release of prisoners, except for those being held for ordinary crimes*

1. All prisoners who are being held on E-Day, except for those held for ordinary crimes, shall be released by the Parties.

2. The International Committee of the Red Cross, together with the Parties, shall agree on the arrangements for and the verification of the prisoner release process referred to in paragraph 1 above.

In witness whereof, the Parties have decided to sign this Protocol.

For the delegation of the Republic of Mozambique:
(*Signed*) Armando Emílio GUEBUZA

For the delegation of RENAMO:
(*Signed*) Raul Manuel DOMINGOS

The mediators:

(*Signed*) Mario RAFFAELLI

(*Signed*) Jaime GONÇALVES

(*Signed*) Andrea RICCARDI

(*Signed*) Matteo ZUPPI

San Egidio, Rome, 4 October 1992

Protocol VII

On 4 October 1992, the delegation of the Government of the Republic of Mozambique, headed by Armando Emílio Guebuza, Minister of Transport and Communications, and composed of Mariano de Araújo Matsinha, Minister without Portfolio, Aguiar Mazula, Minister of State Administration, Teodata Hunguana, Minister of Labour, Lieutenant-General Tobias Dai, Francisco Madeira, Diplomatic Adviser to the President of the Republic, Brigadier Aleixo Malunga, Colonel Fideles De Sousa, Major Justino Nrepo and Major Eduardo Lauchande, and the delegation of RENAMO, headed by Raul Manuel Domingos, Chief of the Organization Department, and composed of José De Castro, Chief of the External Relations Department, Agostinho Semende Murrial, Chief of the Information Department, José Augusto Xavier, Director-General of the Internal Administration Department, Major General Hermínio Morais, Colonel Fernando Canivete, Lieutenant Colonel Arone Julai and Lieutenant António Domingos, meeting at Rome in the presence of the mediators, Mario Raffaelli, representative of the Italian Government and coordinator of the mediators, Jaime Gonçalves, Archbishop of Beira, Andrea Riccardi and Matteo Zuppi, of the Community of San Egidio, and observers from the United Nations and the Governments of the United States of America, France, the United Kingdom and Portugal, took up item 6 of the Agreed Agenda of 28 May 1991, entitled "Donors Conference", and agreed as follows:

1. The Parties decide to request the Italian Government to convene a conference of donor countries and organizations to finance the electoral process, emergency programmes and programmes for the reintegration of displaced persons, refugees and demobilized soldiers.

2. The Parties agree to request that, of the funds provided by donor countries, an appropriate share should be placed at the disposal of political parties to finance their activities.

3. The Parties appeal for the donors conference to be convened no later than 30 days after E-Day. In addition to donor countries and organizations, the Government and RENAMO shall also be invited to send representatives.

In witness whereof, the Parties have decided to sign this Protocol.

For the delegation of the Republic of Mozambique:
(*Signed*) Armando Emílio GUEBUZA

For the delegation of RENAMO:
(*Signed*) Raul Manuel DOMINGOS

The mediators:

(*Signed*) Mario RAFFAELLI

(*Signed*) Jaime GONÇALVES

(*Signed*) Andrea RICCARDI

(*Signed*) Matteo ZUPPI

San Egidio, Rome, 4 October 1992

Joint communiqué

From 8 to 10 July 1990, at the headquarters of the Community of San Egidio, Rome, a direct meeting took place between a delegation of the Government of the People's Republic of Mozambique, headed by Armando Emílio Guebuza, Minister of Transport and Communications, and a delegation of RENAMO, headed by Raul Manuel Domingos, Chief of the External Relations Department.

Mario Raffaelli, representative of the Government of the Italian Republic, Andrea Riccardi and Matteo Zuppi, both of the Community of San Egidio, and Jaime Gonçalves, Archbishop of Beira, attended the meeting as observers.

The two delegations, acknowledging themselves to be compatriots and members of the great Mozambican family, expressed satisfaction and pleasure at this direct, open and frank meeting, the first to take place between the two parties.

The two delegations expressed interest and willingness to do everything possible to conduct a constructive search for a lasting peace for their country and their people.

Taking into account the higher interests of the Mozambican nation, the two parties agreed that they must set aside what divides them and focus, as a matter of priority, on what unites them, in order to establish a common working basis so that, in a spirit of mutual understanding, they can engage in a dialogue in which they discuss their different points of view.

The two delegations affirmed their readiness to dedicate themselves fully, in a spirit of mutual respect and understanding, to the search for a working basis from which to end the war and create the necessary political, economic and social conditions for building a lasting peace and normalizing the life of all Mozambican citizens.

At the close of the meeting, the two delegations decided to meet again in due course at Rome, in the presence of the same observers. They expressed satisfaction and gratitude for the spirit of friendship and the hospitality and support shown them by the Italian Government and by all those who helped make this meeting possible.

Done at San Egidio, Rome, on 10 July 1990.

For the delegation of the
Government of the People's   For the delegation of
Republic of Mozambique: RENAMO:

(Signed) Armando Emílio   (Signed) Raul Manuel
   GUEBUZA   DOMINGOS

Observers:
(Signed)

San Egidio, Rome, 10 July 1990

Declaration by the Government of the Republic of Mozambique and RENAMO on the guiding principles for humanitarian assistance

On 16 July 1992, the delegation of the Government of the Republic of Mozambique, headed by Armando Emílio Guebuza, Minister of Transport and Communications, and the delegation of RENAMO, headed by Raul Manuel Domingos, Chief of the Organization Department, in the presence of the mediators, of observers and of representatives of international organizations, agreed to adopt the following Declaration:

Considering that, for the population, the consequences of the armed conflict have been seriously aggravated by the worst drought in 50 years in the country and the region,

Determined to mobilize every resource to alleviate starvation and prevent deaths in Mozambique,

While pursuing efforts to reach a total peace agreement in Mozambique as soon as possible,

Reaffirming the principles for humanitarian assistance contained in resolution 46/182 of the United Nations General Assembly,

Reaffirming the understanding reached in December 1990 between the Government, RENAMO and the International Committee of the Red Cross on the principles of free movement of populations and assistance for all Mozambicans wherever they might be,

I. The Government and RENAMO solemnly agree and undertake to observe the following guiding principles for humanitarian assistance:

(a) Assistance shall go to all affected Mozambicans, freely and without discrimination;

(b) Freedom of movement and respect shall be guaranteed for persons and means which, under the flag of the United Nations or of ICRC, are engaged in humanitarian actions and are not accompanied by military escorts;

(c) The freedom and neutrality of humanitarian assistance shall be recognized and respected;

(d) Access shall be permitted to the entire affected population, using all means of transport;

(e) The use of all means for the rapid, expeditious distribution of humanitarian assistance shall be permitted and facilitated;

(f) Freedom of movement shall be guaranteed for all personnel who, under United Nations/ICRC auspices, are responsible for identifying populations in need, priority areas, means of transport and access routes and for supervising the distribution of assistance;

(g) Persons shall be allowed freedom of movement to enable them to have full access to humanitarian assistance.

II. In order to provide relief in situations of extreme urgency, which already exist in the country, the parties agree to:

(a) Immediately permit and facilitate air traffic to all points in the country, for transporting humanitarian assistance and whatever personnel is considered necessary and viable;

(b) To the same end, to permit and facilitate the immediate use and rehabilitation, where necessary, of other access routes to affected populations, including routes coming from neighbouring countries, as agreed to by the parties and communicated by the committee referred to in paragraph V of this Declaration.

III. In addition, the Government and RENAMO will continue their negotiations with a view to reaching, as soon as possible, an agreement on the opening of roads and the removal of all obstacles which might prevent the distribution of humanitarian assistance.

IV. The Government and RENAMO undertake not to derive military advantages from humanitarian assistance operations carried out under this Declaration.

V. Both parties agree that the coordination and

supervision of all humanitarian assistance operations carried out under this Declaration shall be the responsibility of a committee presided over by the United Nations. This committee shall be made up of the mediators, the observers to the Rome negotiations and ICRC. The mediators will also have the task of verifying respect for this Declaration and for bringing any complaints or protests to the negotiating table.

The committee will report to the parties, in due course, on the operational details.

VI. Both parties agree to participate and cooperate with the international community in Mozambique in formulating action plans, with a view to implementing such plans in accordance with this Declaration. The committee will coordinate such activities. To that end, RENAMO will appoint its representative in the framework of and in accordance with the procedures of the COMIVE, who shall have the status provided for therein.

VII. Both parties undertake to comply strictly with the terms of this Declaration and agree that any violation substantiated by the committee may be communicated to the international community.

VIII. This Declaration shall be disseminated as widely as possible in Mozambique.

For the delegation of the Government of the Republic of Mozambique:

(*Signed*) Armando Emílio GUEBUZA

For the delegation of RENAMO:

(*Signed*) Raul Manuel DOMINGOS

The mediators:

(*Signed*) Mario RAFFAELLI

(*Signed*) Jaime GONÇALVES

(*Signed*) Andrea RICCARDI

(*Signed*) Matteo ZUPPI

Done at San Egidio, Rome, on 16 July 1992

Joint declaration

We, Joaquim Alberto Chissano, President of the Republic of Mozambique, and Afonso Macacho Marceta Dhlakama, President of RENAMO,

Meeting at Rome in the presence of His Excellency Mr. Robert Gabriel Mugabe, President of the Republic of Zimbabwe; His Excellency Mr. Emilio Colombo, Minister for Foreign Affairs of the Republic of Italy; the representative of His Excellency the President of the Republic of Botswana, Ms. Gaositwe Keagakwa Tibe Chiepe, Minister for Foreign Affairs; the mediators of the peace process, Mario Raffaelli, representative of the Ital-ian Government and coordinator of the mediators, Jaime Gonçalves, Archbishop of Beira, Andrea Riccardi and Matteo Zuppi, of the Community of San Egidio,

Recognizing that

The achievement of peace, democracy and national unity based on national reconciliation is the greatest aspiration and desire of the entire Mozambican people,

In pursuit of this goal, the peace process was launched at Rome between the Government of the Republic of Mozambique and RENAMO, assisted by mediators from the Italian Government, the Community of San Egidio and the Catholic Church of Mozambique,

Important results have been achieved thus far, as exemplified and demonstrated by the signing of the partial cease-fire agreement of 1 December 1990 and the adoption of the following protocols and agreements:

(i) Agreed Agenda of 28 May 1991, and the amendments made thereto by the Act of 19 June 1992;

(ii) Protocol I "Basic principles", signed on 18 October 1991;

(iii) Protocol II "Criteria and arrangements for the formation and recognition of political parties", signed on 13 November 1991;

(iv) Protocol III "Principles of the Electoral Act", signed on 12 March 1992;

(v) Act of 2 July 1992 on improving the functioning of the COMIVE;

(vi) Declaration on guiding principles for humanitarian assistance, signed on 16 July 1992,

Supplementing these efforts in the search for peace, democracy and national unity based on reconciliation in Mozambique, a meeting was held at Gaborone, Botswana, on 4 July 1992 between His Excellency Mr. Robert Gabriel Mugabe, President of the Republic of Zimbabwe, and His Excellency Sir Ketumile Masire, President of the Republic of Botswana, on the one hand, and Mr. Afonso Macacho Marceta Dhlakama, President of RENAMO, on the other,

Following which the President of the Republic of Mozambique, Mr. Joaquim Alberto Chissano, was briefed in detail by the President of Zimbabwe on 19 July 1992,

Whereas Mr. Afonso Macacho Marceta Dhlakama declared his readiness to sign an immediate cease-fire if certain guarantees were provided and arrangements were made for the security of both himself and members of RENAMO, and if his party was given freedom to organize and campaign without interference or hindrance,

Considering his request for guarantees to enable RENAMO to operate freely as a political party after the signing of the General Peace Agreement,

Convinced that the suffering of the Mozambican people as a result of the war, exacerbated by the consequences of the worst drought in living memory, demands that rapid steps be taken to end the war,

Recognizing the need for the immediate restoration of peace in Mozambique,

Reaffirming the commitment of the Government of the Republic of Mozambique and of RENAMO to end the hostilities in Mozambique,

Determined to do everything possible to end the disaster brought about by the combined consequences of war and drought in our country,

Appreciating the progress made in the Rome peace negotiations between our respective delegations,

Considering the spirit of the Gaborone meeting of 4 July 1992,

Accordingly, commit ourselves to the following:

(i) To guarantee conditions permitting complete political freedom, in accordance with the internationally recognized principles of democracy;

(ii) To guarantee the personal safety of all Mozambican citizens and all members of political parties;

(iii) To accept the role of the international community, particularly the United Nations, in monitoring and guaranteeing the implementation of the General Peace Agreement, particularly the cease-fire and the electoral process;

(iv) Fully to respect the principles set forth in Protocol I, under which "the Government undertakes to refrain from taking any action that is contrary to the provisions of the Protocols to be concluded and from adopting laws or measures or applying existing laws which may be inconsistent with those Protocols" and "RENAMO undertakes to refrain from armed combat and instead to conduct its political struggle in conformity with the laws in force, within the framework of existing State institutions and in accordance with the conditions and guarantees established in the General Peace Agreement";

(v) To safeguard political rights, emphasizing that the principles set forth in Protocol I are valid and also relate to the problem of constitutional guarantees raised by RENAMO and dealt with in the document submitted to President Mugabe. To this end, the Government of the Republic of Mozambique shall submit to the Assembly of the Republic for adoption legal instruments incorporating the Protocols and guarantees, as well as the General Peace Agreement, in Mozambican law;

(vi) On the basis of the above principles and of our commitment made in this solemn Declaration, we, Joaquim Alberto Chissano, President of the Republic of Mozambique, and Afonso Macacho Marceta Dhlakama, President of RENAMO, hereby authorize and instruct our respective delegations participating in the Rome peace process to conclude, by 1 October 1992 at the latest, the remaining Protocols provided for in the Agreed Agenda, thereby permitting the signing of the General Peace Agreement by that date.

The signing of the General Peace Agreement and its adoption by the Assembly of the Republic as provided for in paragraph (v) [on this page] of this Declaration shall result in the immediate entry into force of the cease-fire agreed to under the General Peace Agreement.

(*Signed*) Joaquim Alberto   (*Signed*) Afonso Macacho
   CHISSANO   Marceta DHLAKAMA
President of the Republic   President of RENAMO
of Mozambique

(*Signed*) Robert Gabriel MUGABE
President of the Republic of Zimbabwe

Witnessed by:
(*Signed*) Gaositwe Keagakwa Tibe CHIEPE
Minister for Foreign Affairs of Botswana

and by the mediators:

(*Signed*) Mario RAFFAELLI

(*Signed*) Jaime GONÇALVES

(*Signed*) Andrea RICCARDI

(*Signed*) Matteo ZUPPI

Rome, 7 August 1992

Document 13

Report of the Secretary-General on the United Nations Operation in Mozambique (ONUMOZ)

S/24642, 9 October 1992

Introduction

1. On 4 October 1992 in Rome, Mr. Joaquim Alberto Chissano, President of the Republic of Mozambique, and Mr. Afonso Macacho Marceta Dhlakama, President of the Resistência Nacional Moçambicana (RENAMO), signed a General Peace Agreement (hereinafter referred to as "the Agreement") establishing the

principles and modalities for the achievement of peace in Mozambique. On the same day, President Chissano formally communicated the text of the Agreement to me under cover of a letter in which he requested me to take appropriate action to ensure the participation of the United Nations in monitoring implementation of the Agreement, in providing technical assistance for the general elections and in monitoring these elections. In the same letter President Chissano also asked me to inform the Security Council of his request that a United Nations team be sent to Mozambique to carry out the above functions until the holding of general elections which would take place one year after the signing of the Agreement. President Chissano's letter and its enclosures have been circulated to the Security Council as document S/24635.

I.   Principal features of the agreement

2. The General Peace Agreement consists of the Agreement itself and seven Protocols as follows:

(a)   Protocol I: basic principles;

(b)   Protocol II: criteria and arrangements for the formation and recognition of political parties;

(c)   Protocol III: principles of the Electoral Act;

(d)   Protocol IV: military questions;

(e)   Protocol V: guarantees;

(f)   Protocol VI: the cease-fire;

(g)   Protocol VII: donors conference.

The Agreement further specifies that four other documents form integral parts of it, as follows:

(a)   A Joint Communiqué of 10 July 1990;

(b)   An Agreement of 1 December 1990;

(c)   A Declaration by the Government of Mozambique and RENAMO on guiding principles for humanitarian assistance, signed in Rome on 16 July 1992;

(d)   A Joint Declaration, signed in Rome on 7 August 1992.

3. Implementation of the Agreement will begin with the cease-fire which is to come into effect on E-Day, the day on which the Agreement itself will enter into force following publication in the Official Gazette of the legal instruments adopted by the Assembly of the Republic. This is expected to take place not later than 15 October 1992. The cease-fire will be rapidly followed by the separation of the two sides' forces and their concentration in certain designated assembly areas. Immediately thereafter demobilization of these troops who are not to serve in the new Mozambican Defence Force (FADM) will begin and will be completed within six months of E-Day.

4. In parallel with these military arrangements, new political parties will be formed and preparations will be made for the election of a President and a legislative assembly which will take place simultaneously, one year after E-Day.

5. As mentioned in paragraph 2 above, the Declaration by the Government of Mozambique and RENAMO on guiding principles for humanitarian assistance, signed in Rome on 16 July 1992, as well as the Joint Declaration, signed in Rome on 7 August 1992, form an integral part of the Agreement. These commitments will need to be translated into concrete agreements for access to the affected areas and populations. This will need to be done with great urgency and in a manner which will ensure that all the activities of the United Nations in the political, security and humanitarian fields reinforce each other.

6. The implementation of the Agreement will be supervised by a Supervisory and Monitoring Commission (CSC), whose establishment and functions are provided for in part II of Protocol V. Its chairperson will be appointed by the Secretary-General of the United Nations and it will consist of representatives of the Government, RENAMO, the United Nations, the Organization of African Unity (OAU) and certain countries to be agreed between the parties. CSC's role will be:

(a)   To guarantee implementation of the provisions of the Agreement;

(b)   To guarantee respect for the timetable specified for the cease-fire and the elections;

(c)   To provide the authentic interpretation of the Agreement;

(d)   To rule on differences which may arise between the parties;

(e)   To guide and coordinate the activities of certain subsidiary commissions.

7. The subsidiary commissions of CSC will number three, as follows:

(a)   A Joint Commission for the Formation of the Mozambican Defence Force (CCFADM);

(b)   A Cease-fire Commission (CCF);

(c)   A Commission for the Reintegration of Demobilized Military Personnel (CORE).

II.   Role proposed for the United Nations

8. As indicated in President Chissano's letter of 4 October 1992, and as foreseen in the Joint Declaration of 7 August 1992 (S/24406), the United Nations is requested to undertake a major role in monitoring the Agreement. President Chissano has also conveyed to me his wish that United Nations monitoring mechanisms be established across the country as soon as possible.

9. In essence, the United Nations is asked to undertake certain specific functions in relation to the cease-fire, the elections and humanitarian assistance.

10. As regards the elections, the Organization is

requested both to monitor the whole electoral process and to provide technical assistance. This role is referred to in part VI of Protocol III.

11. As regards the cease-fire, the United Nations is asked to provide chairpersons for the two Commissions which will be charged with responsibility for the cease-fire itself (CCF) and for the reintegration of demobilized personnel (CORE). The functions of these two bodies are described in part VI of Protocol IV. CCF's role is similar to that entrusted to the United Nations in other recent cases where the Organization has monitored the implementation of a cease-fire, the separation and concentration of forces, their demobilization, and the collection and storage of weapons. CCF will also verify the existence of other armed groups, including irregulars, and will authorize security arrangements for vital public and private infrastructures. CORE will be responsible for planning, organizing and monitoring the economic and social reintegration of military personnel. All these and various other activities related to the peace process will depend on the resources made available by the international community on a voluntary basis. It is also to be noted that the viability of the agreed arrangements for the concentration of forces in assembly areas will depend critically on the readiness of the international community to provide the parties, from the very beginning, with the necessary provisions, medical care and other logistic support for their troops in the areas of concentration.

12. As regards humanitarian assistance, the Declaration of 16 July 1992 assigns to the United Nations responsibility for chairing a Humanitarian Assistance Committee for the coordination and monitoring of all humanitarian assistance operations.

III. Plan of action

13. The Agreement provides for the cease-fire to come into effect on E-Day which, as noted in paragraph 3 above, is expected to be not later than 15 October 1992. President Chissano's letter of 4 October 1992 states that the United Nations is expected to start its function of verifying and monitoring the cease-fire on that day.

14. As will be clear from my letter of 29 September 1992 to the President of the Security Council (at which time I was acting on the assumption that the Agreement would provide for the cease-fire to come formally into effect 30 days after signature), it will not be possible for the United Nations to establish more than a token presence in Mozambique by 15 October 1992. The viability of the cease-fire will therefore, in its early stages, depend critically on the political will and strict compliance of the two parties with the agreed modalities. It is to be noted that the parties have not yet reached agreement on loca-

tions for the assembly areas for the separation and concentration of forces which are to be specified in four annexes to Protocol VI, nor the access routes to them. It will also be necessary, as noted above, to ensure that adequate arrangements have been made for the logistic support of the troops in these areas. Adequate resources to ensure the rapid resettlement, reintegration and rehabilitation of the war-affected populations will also be critical to the successful implementation of the Peace Agreement.

15. Subject to the approval of the Security Council, it is my intention to appoint immediately an interim Special Representative who will be in overall charge of the United Nations activities in support of the Agreement, including the general function of monitoring its implementation and the specific tasks related to the military arrangements and the elections, and will also coordinate the humanitarian and other related efforts of the United Nations system in Mozambique during the implementation of the Agreement. As soon as appointed, my Special Representative will proceed to Maputo to assist the parties in setting up the joint machinery which is to be chaired by the United Nations, in finalizing the modalities and conditions for the military arrangements and in carrying out the various other actions which are required of them at the very beginning of the process. The Special Representative will also, as a matter of priority, take all necessary steps to ensure access for relief workers to all people in need of humanitarian assistance throughout the country.

16. The Special Representative will be supported in these initial tasks by a team of up to 25 military observers and necessary administrative support staff, whom I intend to send to Mozambique in the coming days. This team, whose military personnel will be drawn from existing peace-keeping missions, will establish their presence in Maputo, Beira and Nampula in order to carry out limited verification of the cease-fire arrangements; establish liaison with both parties in these regions and provide them with technical advice on the modalities for implementation of the Agreement; facilitate the build-up of the mission; and carry out reconnaissance and other required activities.

17. My Special Representative will be asked to send the earliest possible report on which I shall base recommendations to the Security Council for the deployment of a United Nations Operation in Mozambique (UNOMO) which, if approved by the Security Council, will, under the overall direction of my Special Representative, carry out the functions envisaged for the United Nations in monitoring and assisting the implementation of the General Peace Agreement.

Document 14

Letter dated 12 October 1992 from the Secretary-General to President Chissano expressing concern over the worsening humanitarian situation in Mozambique

Not issued as a United Nations document

The signing of the General Peace Agreement for Mozambique on 3 October was a truly historic event, and I commend your statesmanship which was so vital to the success of the negotiations. I have already brought this matter to the attention of the Security Council so that the United Nations will be in a position to carry out the extremely important responsibilities assigned to it in the Agreement.

I note that the Declaration of the Government of the Republic of Mozambique and RENAMO on guiding principles for humanitarian assistance, signed in Rome on 16 July 1992, is accepted as an integral part of the General Peace Agreement. It is in this context that I am writing to share with you my grave concern about the worsening humanitarian situation in Mozambique and to seek your continued cooperation in devising more effective means of bringing relief to the affected population.

As you are aware, millions of Mozambicans are facing a desperate situation and, unless humanitarian relief can be provided immediately, many will die. The United Nations and other relief organizations are committed to assisting your Government in responding to this challenge. As far as relief food is concerned, it appears that significant quantities have reached the country but distribution has been impeded by various logistical and organizational bottlenecks. These include administrative measures initiated by the Government which, while well intentioned, would increase the cost of importing and slow down the distribution of relief goods in Mozambique.

The Deputy to the Under-Secretary-General for Humanitarian Affairs has informed me and UN Headquarters about his recent mission to Mozambique and his productive meeting with you and other Government officials. I count on your continued active cooperation in these humanitarian efforts.

The full implementation of the General Peace Agreement will undoubtedly alleviate some of the hardships suffered by the people of Mozambique, but this will take time. Immediate action is required if a disaster is to be averted. I look forward to working closely with the Government to this end.

Accept, Mr. President, the assurances of my highest consideration and my warmest personal regards.

(*Signed*) Boutros BOUTROS-GHALI

Document 15

Letter dated 12 October 1992 from the Secretary-General to Mr. Afonso Dhlakama, the President of RENAMO, expressing concern over the worsening humanitarian situation in Mozambique

Not issued as a United Nations document

The signing of the General Peace Agreement for Mozambique on 3 October was a truly historic event, and I commend your statesmanship which was so vital to the success of the negotiations.

I note that the Declaration of the Government of the Republic of Mozambique and RENAMO on guiding principles for humanitarian assistance, signed in Rome on 16 July 1992, is accepted as an integral part of the General Peace Agreement. The Declaration represented a significant breakthrough in the efforts to expand emergency relief in Mozambique. However, it is only a first step towards the ultimate goal of bringing humanitarian assistance to all Mozambicans in need. It is now imperative that the remaining steps be completed without delay.

Large numbers of people, including those in various communities in RENAMO-held areas, are at risk of starvation. As you are aware, there has already been a significant movement of people from Manica and Sofala provinces to the Beira corridor. The United Nations and other relief organizations are prepared to expedite relief supplies to the vulnerable populations on a priority basis, which would have to include both air and land delivery. To delay these shipments would be a tragic disservice to the people of Mozambique.

I am writing to express my grave concern about the current situation in Mozambique and to seek your cooperation in assuring access to all affected communities.

The Humanitarian Committee established pursuant to the Declaration has presented a unified plan which, I believe, is a reasonable proposal which can be implemented without delay. If the land corridors proposed are not opened, the lives of thousands of Mozambicans will be in jeopardy and the confidence of donors in the future of Mozambique will be undermined.

The full implementation of the General Peace Agreement will undoubtedly alleviate some of the logistical difficulties in the distribution of humanitarian assistance. However, this will take time. Immediate action is required if a disaster is to be averted. I urge you to accept the plan presented by the Humanitarian Committee without delay.

(*Signed*) Boutros BOUTROS-GHALI

Document 16

Security Council resolution welcoming the signature of the General Peace Agreement for Mozambique

S/RES/782 (1992), 13 October 1992

The Security Council,

Welcoming the signature at Rome , on 4 October 1992, of a General Peace Agreement for Mozambique between the Government of Mozambique and the Resistência Nacional Moçambicana 1/,

Considering that the signature of the Agreement constitutes an important contribution to the restoration of peace and security in the region,

Taking note of the Joint Declaration signed at Rome on 7 August 1992 2/ by the President of the Republic of Mozambique and the President of the Resistência Nacional Moçambicana, in which the parties accept the role of the United Nations in monitoring and guaranteeing the implementation of the Agreement,

Also taking note of the report of the Secretary-General of 9 October 1992 on the United Nations Operation in Mozambique 3/ and of the request of the President of Mozambique 4/,

1. *Approves* the appointment by the Secretary-General of an interim Special Representative for Mozambique, and the dispatch to Mozambique of a team of up to twenty-five military observers as recommended in paragraph 16 of the report of the Secretary-General of 9 October 1992 on the United Nations Operation in Mozambique; 3/

2. *Looks forward* to the report of the Secretary-General on the establishment of a United Nations Operation in Mozambique, including in particular a detailed estimate of the cost of this operation;

3. *Decides* to remain actively seized of the matter.

1/ *Official Records of the Security Council, Forty-seventh Year, Supplement for October, November and December 1992*, document S/24635 and Corr.1, annex.

2/ Ibid., *Supplement for July, August and September 1992*, document S/24406, annex.

3/ Ibid., *Supplement for October, November and December 1992*, document S/24642.

4/ Ibid., document S/24635 and Corr.1, enclosure.

Document 17

Statement by Sir Ketumile Masire, the President of Botswana, at the signing of the General Peace Agreement for Mozambique

S/24687, 20 October 1992

The Permanent Mission of Botswana to the United Nations presents its compliments to the Secretary-General of the United Nations and has the honour to transmit for circulation the text of the statement by His Excellency Sir Ketumile Masire, President of the Republic of Botswana,

at the signing of the Mozambique Peace Accord on 4 October 1992 in Rome.

The Permanent Representative of Botswana would be grateful if the statement could be circulated as a document of the Security Council.

Statement by His Excellency Sir Ketumile Masire, President of the Republic of Botswana, at the signing of the Mozambique Peace Accord, Rome, 4 October 1992

The signing of this Peace Accord marks an important milestone not only for the people of Mozambique, but also for the people of southern Africa. It brings with it an opportunity for the people of Mozambique to taste the fruits of their independence and to direct their energies to national reconstruction and economic development. We feel honoured and privileged to bear witness to this historic occasion.

As we leave Rome to our respective destinations, we are fully conscious that the appendage of a signature alone does not and cannot bring about peace. Peace can only come about if there is mutual goodwill to sustain it. I would like to take this opportunity, therefore, to underscore the gravity of this undertaking which we have witnessed today. It is a commitment to peace, a responsibility to save lives in our region and a promise to work together as brothers and sisters in Mozambique. Let no man or woman look back to the past, let us look forward to work for national reconciliation and reconstruction in Mozambique. If there is any reason to look back, let it be for the sake of drawing lessons, to learn from past experience never to commit the same mistakes again. I urge the people of Mozambique to forge ahead with that which is good for their country and its people.

As the people of Mozambique turn a new leaf in their history, it is the responsibility of the international community to come to their help. The primary responsibility of the international community is the promotion of peace and security. We all have a community of interest to ensure that peace and development are achieved in Mozambique. All should make a contribution in this effort.

In conclusion, I would like to commend all those who have made it possible for peace in Mozambique to come about. I wish to congratulate the people of Mozambique on the successful conclusion of their two years of peace negotiations. The political will on both sides to negotiate has been the key in the whole process. I also wish to commend the Government and the people of Italy who have offered their country and its facilities for the negotiation process. I thank the mediators for the role they played in facilitating the countless meetings between the chief negotiators in the peace process. There are also countless heroes and heroines who will forever remain nameless and faceless who have contributed in their different ways in the whole process. I thank them just as well. Above all, I wish to assure the people of Mozambique that we are all with them; we shall do everything possible to help them in their effort to promote peace and development in their country.

Document 18

Report of the Secretary-General on special programmes of economic assistance to Mozambique

A/47/539, 22 October 1992

I. Introduction

1. By its resolution 45/227 of 21 December 1990 on assistance to Mozambique, the General Assembly, *inter alia*:

(a) Appealed to the international community to continue to provide relief aid, in particular urgent food aid and logistics support, so as to improve distribution capacity and prevent further widespread starvation;

(b) Drew the attention of the international community to the non-food sectors, the funding of which continued to lag, particularly in the areas of relief items, agriculture, health, assistance to returnees and institutional support;

(c) Called upon Member States, regional and interregional organizations and other intergovernmental and non-governmental organizations to provide and expand technical, financial and other material assistance to Mozambique wherever possible, and urged them to give priority to the inclusion of Mozambique in their development assistance programmes;

(d) Invited all appropriate organizations and programmes of the United Nations system to maintain and increase their current and future programmes of assistance to Mozambique;

(e) Requested the Secretary-General to continue his efforts to mobilize the financial, technical and material assistance required by Mozambique; to continue to coordinate the work of the United Nations system, in close cooperation with the Government of Mozambique, in the implementation of the country's emergency and rehabilitation programmes; and to prepare, on the basis of consultations with the Government of Mozambique, a report on the implementation of the emergency and rehabilitation programmes for that country and to submit the report to the General Assembly at its forty-seventh session.

2. The present report has been prepared in compliance with the latter request, and includes information communicated to the Secretary-General by entities of the United Nations system, Member States and other donors concerning assistance rendered by them under the terms of the resolution.

II. Role of the United Nations in support of Mozambique emergency programmes

3. The United Nations has played a lead role in the mobilization of international support for Mozambique for over a decade. The Office for Emergencies in Africa assisted in drawing international attention to the needs which arose as a result of the drought that affected Mozambique in 1983/84. By late 1986 the combined impact of natural disasters and civil strife had resulted in a situation where 3.2 million Mozambican peasants had been displaced or affected within the country. The provision of food and other basic commodities was necessary to avert widespread starvation. The Secretary-General, in response to the urgent request from the President of Mozambique early in 1987, launched an international appeal to support Mozambique. He also appointed the resident coordinator of the United Nations system's operational activities for development in Mozambique as the United Nations Special Coordinator for Emergency Relief Operations.

4. The Office of the Special Coordinator works closely with the Government and, in particular, with the National Executive Commission for the Emergency, which has established an Emergency Operating Committee chaired by the Commission Coordinator, the Vice Minister for Cooperation. The Office has aimed at integrating the objectives of the emergency programme with those for economic rehabilitation and development. While ensuring a certain degree of coordination within the donor community, it has continued its efforts to maintain a permanent dialogue among the Government, donors and the United Nations.

5. Supported by the United Nations Development Programme (UNDP) and the Department of Humanitarian Affairs of the United Nations Secretariat, the Office of the Special Coordinator, in partnership with the Government and United Nations agencies, carries out inter-agency assessments which form the basis for joint appeals that define the requirements of the emergency programme. To date, four such emergency appeals have been issued.

6. As part of an effort to promote the gradual integration of the emergency programme within the overall economic and social rehabilitation process, a programme of emergency requirements was prepared by the Government, in consultation with the United Nations, for presentation at the World Bank Consultative Group meeting on Mozambique, in December 1990. United Nations inter-agency missions also assisted in the preparation of the emergency programme document for the Consultative Group meeting in December 1991.

7. Immediately after the signing at Rome, on 4 October 1992, of the General Peace Agreement for Mozambique, a mission from the Department of Humanitarian Affairs was dispatched to Mozambique to establish a comprehensive mechanism that would ensure a more effective response to the emergency situation, especially in the light of new realities. The Peace Agreement promises not only an effective and expeditious expansion of the emergency programme but also its gradual merger into the reconstruction and rehabilitation efforts. It should, however, be borne in mind that Mozambique is currently affected by one of the most severe droughts of this century.

8. In May 1992, the United Nations, jointly with the Southern Africa Development Community (SADC), launched a consolidated appeal for the drought emergency in southern Africa for 10 countries in the southern African region, including Mozambique. At the same time, an appeal was launched at Maputo, which presented the priority requirements for the internally displaced and the drought-affected populations.

III. Emergency requirements for 1992/93

9. By December 1990, it was estimated that 1.9 million internally displaced Mozambicans needed emergency assistance, an increase of 600,000 from the 1.4 million persons targeted by the 1990/91 emergency appeal, presented in April 1990. However, subsistence production in the central provinces of Manica and Sofala was severely reduced by continuing drought, which started early in 1971. Joint United Nations/government missions have confirmed that 300,000 additional people in the two provinces are in need of relief food. On the basis of a needs assessment made in November 1991, which covered the crop year 1992/93 (May 1992 to April 1993), it is estimated that of the 4 million internally displaced and war-affected people, 1.8 million depend on relief and about 1.8 million Mozambicans are refugees in neighbouring countries.

10. The drought, together with the prolonged conflict, has doubled the threat of famine and mass starvation facing the Mozambican people. As a result, there are significant population movements towards the coastal areas, secure districts and provincial towns. This is particularly noted along the Beira and Limpopo corridors, two areas that were covered by the partial cease-fire agreement between the Government of Mozambique and the Resistência Nacional Moçambicana (RENAMO) signed at Rome in December 1990.

11. Information supplied by the Provincial Emergency Commissions and data obtained from various organizations working at the local level indicated that the emergency needs had to be reassessed. A joint assessment mission to Mozambique of the Food and Agriculture Organization of the United Nations (FAO) and the World Food Programme (WFP), in March/April 1992, confirmed the almost total failure of the principal cereal crops (maize, rice, sorghum and millet) in the central and southern provinces. Since this was the second consecutive year of drought in the normally surplus provinces of Manica and Sofala, most households had no food or seed stocks.

12. The mission recommended that 1.3 million additional persons be included as beneficiaries of the emergency programme until the end of the next crop season (May 1993). This raised to 3.1 million the total number of persons in need of direct support from the emergency programme in 1992/93. Supplementary feeding and nutritional interventions requiring additional food aid were also recommended.

A. Food aid

13. In October 1991, it was estimated that 267,000 metric tons of relief food would be required for the crop year 1992/93 for a beneficiary population of 1.83 million. However, in April 1992, these estimates were almost doubled, to 460,500 tons, to take into account the drought. This brought the total food aid needs to 1,316,050 tons for 1992/93, including food for market and special feeding programmes.

B. Reserve stocks

14. The various appeals for emergency assistance have emphasized the importance of building up a reserve stock of some 60,000 tons of maize, to expedite action for an adequate response to the rapidly changing situation. Although the establishment of this minimum food reserve has not yet been possible, it would provide a vital back-up in the case of delayed deliveries of pledged food aid or other food supply crises.

15. Since the whole of southern Africa needs to import food grains over the 1992/93 crop year, purchases to establish the buffer stock would have to be made outside the region.

C. Security and logistic constraints

16. The war has stripped the country of much of its economic and social infrastructure. This severely constricts the Government's already limited capacity to respond quickly and effectively to the emergency situation.

17. The enormous task of distributing emergency relief supplies is managed by the Department for the Prevention and Combat of National Disasters, the government agency responsible for the delivery of relief goods to the beneficiary level. The distribution of emergency relief supplies in Mozambique involves the use of ships, boats, trains, trucks and aircraft, all of which have specific limitations and relatively high costs. Road transport capacity, however, remains the most critical capacity constraint, whether for local handling and port clearance, inter-provincial inland deliveries or province-to-district distribution to population centres. While the Department operates a fleet of trucks, the projected quantities of food aid required in 1992/93 would need more than twice the current capacity of the Department for delivery to the beneficiaries. Commercial vehicles must therefore be hired and the distribution mechanism for relief assistance to an expanded beneficiary population adjusted and refined accordingly.

18. However, the most serious constraint on the delivery and distribution of relief supplies is the security situation. At least six Department drivers have been killed in the past year and 11 trucks destroyed in attacks during the first quarter of 1992. Hence, while it is indeed the Government's policy to contract commercial transport services to cover the gap in the Department's transport capacity, the prevailing security situation makes commercial road haulage to some areas in Mozambique an unattractive proposition, particularly in the absence of both insurance cover and compensation. Truck owners, therefore, concentrate their activities in the larger towns or other safe areas.

19. The rapid changes in the security situation also cause difficulties. When the Tete corridor came under attack in early 1991, traffic for Malawi and Minassa and other Mozambican border areas had to be rerouted through Zambia, causing delays in delivery and huge increases in costs.

20. Of the country's 128 districts, a total of 74, with 1.9 million beneficiaries, require convoys with armed escort for supplies to get through. The security conditions constitute a serious limitation on any increase in relief operations. Delays in turn-around time and a resulting decrease in fleet efficiency and tonnage delivered are caused by the need to organize and undertake armed convoys. The number, size and frequency of the convoys is directly related to the number of manned escort vehicles available for this duty. The Government has consistently requested support from the international community to cover the costs of the required protection, vehicles and fuel.

21. As the drought conditions worsen, convoys of food and relief commodities will increasingly be a target for attack in both rural and urban areas. Hence, whatever improvement there may be in the joint efforts of the Department for the Prevention and Combat of National

Disasters and private transporters, it is unlikely that there will be any major increase in the distribution rate unless better security arrangements are in place. For a number of reasons, including its high costs, airlifting is a last resort operation.

22. It is estimated that emergency assistance to Mozambique for the 1992/93 programme will amount to more than US$ 400 million. Transparency and accountability in the use of these funds is a concern of both the Government and donors. Specific problems have arisen with respect to counterpart funds paid on market food aid and the diversion of goods. Many of these problems reflect the very difficult circumstances which exist in Mozambique. However, measures have been introduced which have greatly improved the ability of donors and the Government to monitor the external resources made available.

D. *Health and nutrition*

23. The health sector has to respond to the specific health needs resulting from a prolonged armed conflict, as well as from the current severe and widespread drought. Malnutrition was a cause for concern even before the drought. Now the depletion of the water reserves will contribute to the deterioration of public hygiene and the spread of disease. The drought conditions are likely to cause increases in such illnesses as diarrhoea, cholera, bubonic plague, meningitis, malaria and conjunctivitis.

24. The food shortages resulting from the drought will aggravate the already poor nutritional state of the population. Nutritional surveys are now carried out in all 10 provinces and the results are published in a quarterly bulletin, which is widely circulated among government departments, United Nations organizations, donors and non-governmental organizations. No major starvation crisis was reported in 1991, the first time in three years. None the less, over 90 per cent of the nutritional surveys carried out in 1991 indicated high rates of severe malnutrition. As the drought has become more severe, deaths from hunger and hunger-related diseases have been reported in Manica, Sofala, Inhambane and Gaza provinces.

E. *Water supply and sanitation*

25. The National Rural Water Supply Programme has attempted to build capacity to satisfy the basic potable water requirements of the displaced and returnee populations, and of the rural war-affected population. The provision of clean water to areas where displaced people are concentrated is still a major priority. The Programme has been running parallel programmes for well construction and for the rehabilitation of existing systems, despite major constraints in funding and security. The drought is now compounding the problems of providing safe drinking water. UNDP and a number of non-governmental organizations are involved in giving assistance to displaced and returnee populations in the construction of latrines.

F. *Relief and survival items*

26. Relief and survival items include clothing, blankets, soap, cooking sets, water containers, buckets and tarpaulins. Many displaced persons are virtually destitute, wearing old sacking or even tree bark to cover themselves. This destitution itself adds to the trauma caused by the events which led to their being displaced. The provision of relief and survival items to the displaced and returnees is necessary for hundreds of thousands of families to reconstruct their lives with a minimum of dignity.

G. *Agricultural production*

27. Food crop production in Mozambique shows a chronic deficit because of the continued war situation. The drought has further reduced household-level production. Seed supply for 1992/93 will be a major problem. In December 1991, the needs for the Emergency Seed and Tool Programme were estimated at 11,400 metric tons of seed to benefit 464,000 displaced families. However, the displaced families who should benefit from the seed and tool programme now number 576,000, in addition to 487,000 drought-affected families. The requirements in seeds have consequently increased to almost 26,000 tons, more than double the requirements estimated in December 1991.

28. The need for agricultural hand tools was estimated at 1.9 million units in December 1991. The estimates for hand tool requirements for displaced families have now risen to 3.2 million units. The peasants in many parts of the country have old, worn tools, which makes cultivation extremely difficult. The loss of crops and consequent loss of income because of the drought leaves the peasants without the resources necessary to buy tools for the next crop season. The additional need because of the drought is estimated at 1.3 million units, bringing the total in requirements for hand tools to 3.5 million units.

H. *Returnees*

29. The emergency programme in Mozambique has a comprehensive approach of support to internally displaced persons and returning refugees. Initial support in voluntary repatriation and settlement is provided by the Office of the United Nations High Commissioner for Refugees (UNHCR), in collaboration with the government counterpart agency, the Support Group for Refugees and the Liberation Movement. After the first three months, the multisectoral emergency programme pro-

vides food and domestic items, seeds and tools and support for the re-establishment of social services for both internally displaced people and returning refugees.

30. Under the 1992/93 requirements presented in December 1991, a provisional plan was made by UNHCR for a possible return of 36,000 refugees during the year. The assistance covers basic relief supplies and rehabilitation of returnee transit and settling areas along the border.

31. In the past year, the returnee flow has dropped and in fact many Mozambicans are fleeing to Malawi and Zimbabwe to escape the drought. UNHCR has reported that many are arriving in a very weak and malnourished state with almost no personal belongings. However, given the drought conditions within the region, if the host countries are unable to feed their own populations and food for refugees is reduced, large numbers could begin to return to Mozambique.

IV. International support for emergency needs in Mozambique in 1990/91 and 1991/92

A. *Food aid*

32. In crop season 1990/91 (May 1990 to April 1991), relief food requirements totalled 229,000 metric tons for 1.5 million internally displaced persons and returnees, while market food aid needs were 722,700 tons, for a total of 951,700 tons. 1/ Fifty-eight per cent of the total need was pledged (554,172 tons) while 511,686 tons (54 per cent of the requirements) arrived (including carry-overs from 1989/90). Donor response to relief food aid supplied 87 per cent of the needs (200,332 tons), while only 49 per cent of market food aid (353,850 tons) was pledged.

33. For 1991/92 (May 1991 to April 1992), relief requirements of 270,000 tons for 1.9 million beneficiaries were presented to the Consultative Group meeting in December 1990. An additional 688,775 tons were requested for market food aid, bringing the total to 958,775 tons. Seventy per cent (606,377 tons) of the total need was pledged, an increase of 52,205 tons over 1990/91. Relief food aid pledged increased by 63,045 tons, to 263,377 tons. This increase can be attributed partially to the positive response of the international community to a special drought alert in early 1991, covering the provinces of Sofala and Manica in which two donors pledged an additional 25,000 tons. On the other hand, total market food aid pledges decreased slightly, to 343,500 tons. Arrivals in 1991/92 decreased, to a total of 449,847 tons (including carry-over) or only 52 per cent of the total requirements. Again, the international community responded more positively to relief food aid needs, pledging 95 per cent of the need. Some donors supported shipments

and local purchases of maize and beans in some provinces, thereby reducing transport costs. The European Economic Community (EEC), the United States of America and WFP were the principal donors in this sector.

B. *Logistics*

34. Requirements in the logistics sector were estimated at US$33.9 million in 1990/91 and $25.5 million in 1991/92. These were for internal transport and storage of relief supplies, principally food aid. In 1990/91, $19.4 million was pledged (57 per cent of the requirements). Such underfunding of the logistics sector curtailed relief deliveries. CARE International, with the support of the United States Agency for International Development (USAID), has provided technical assistance to the Logistics Support Unit of the Department for the Prevention and Combat of National Disasters.

35. In the 1992/93 drought emergency programme, donors are requested to meet the costs of delivery of relief food to the provincial capitals or other agreed upon extended delivery points, so as to enable the Department's fleet to concentrate on delivery to the district and community level. Some donors and non-governmental organizations are planning to distribute food directly to beneficiaries.

C. *Agriculture*

36. The distribution of seeds and agricultural hand tools to the internally displaced population and returning refugees is crucial to all self-sufficiency efforts. In 1990/91, 8,400 tons of seeds and 875,000 hand tools were requested for 300,000 targeted beneficiaries in all 10 provinces. This sector received $11.8 million against the initial requirement of $8.1 million. It was thus possible to increase the number of beneficiary families to 392,880.

37. In 1991/92, the programme aimed to reach more families who were able to return to their land, particularly in the populous northern provinces of Zambania and Nampula. Some 530,000 families were targeted and funding for 11,400 tons of seeds and 2 million agricultural hand tools was requested. Much of the seed was purchased locally within Mozambique or through the national seed company. Over $10 million was pledged for seeds (105 per cent of needs). Fund disbursement delays for purchases and deliveries will result in a portion of these seeds and tools contracts being used in the 1992/93 crop season. The tool component was severely

1/ The emergency appeal of 1990/91 did not include 722,800 tons of food aid for market distribution, but in the 1991/92 emergency programme all food aid needs (market and relief) were presented. Therefore both market and relief food needs have been analysed, to make consistent comparisons. The closing reports prepared by the office of the Special Coordinator included all food aid so as to evaluate the complete food security situation.

underfunded, which has caused serious problems in many areas of the country. Only $2.5 million was pledged (58 per cent of requirements), but stock unavailability within the country also limited distribution. Lack of support for internal administration and the transportation of seeds has reduced the efficiency and coordination of the programme. Bilateral agencies, in particular the Norwegian Agency for International Development, the Swedish International Development Authority and USAID, are major donors in this sector. Non-governmental organizations play an important role in all aspects of promoting agricultural recovery.

D. *Health*

38. In 1990/91 the emergency requirements included small projects for the rehabilitation of health services, vital medicines and emergency medical supplies, nutritional rehabilitation, programmes for children in difficult circumstances and support for the Emergency Coordination Unit of the Ministry of Health. A total of $10.4 million was requested and $9.3 million (89 per cent of requirements) was pledged. An additional $561,000 was pledged for related emergency health projects.

39. In 1991/92 the health sector requirements were valued at $6.1 million for provision of medical supplies for the displaced population, of which $5.5 million (68 per cent of requirements) was pledged. Emergency health services are integrated within the national health system and, therefore, donor support is also allocated through bilateral agreements and ongoing development assistance. The United Nations Children's Fund (UNICEF) and the World Health Organization (WHO) are among the main channels of support.

E. *Water*

40. In 1990/91, 10 small drinking water supply projects were presented, for a total value of $910,200; of these, four projects, totalling $328,000, were funded. An additional $655,000 was pledged for rural water supplies in other areas. In 1991/92, three water projects were presented within the emergency programme for a total value of $3 million, and $209,000 was pledged for the projects in Manica, Gaza and Nampula. UNICEF is the lead implementing agency working with the government Rural Water Department.

F. *Education*

41. In 1990/91, $1.2 million was requested for educational materials for internally displaced children and $1.3 million was pledged. In 1991/92 $1.5 million was requested and $2.1 million was pledged for educational materials for free distribution to displaced schoolchildren.

G. *Returnees*

42. The flow of returning refugees has diminished as the security situation along the border areas has become more precarious. In 1990/91, of $6.6 million requested for this programme, $4.5 million was pledged (68 per cent of needs). In 1991/92 the total requirements were estimated at $7.7 million, but because there was little movement of returning refugees support dropped to $3.9 million, or 51 per cent of the requirements. Nevertheless, the institutional capacity must be established within Mozambique to receive the 1.5 million Mozambican refugees in neighbouring countries.

H. *Institutional support for emergency management*

43. External assistance is still required to build up and backstop the Government's capacity to manage the emergency programme at the central and provincial levels. In 1990/91 $3.3 million was requested for technical assistance in emergency planning and management (central and provincial level) and for the Logistics Support Unit of the Department for the Prevention and Combat of National Disasters, operating centrally and in all 10 provinces. Of this, 85 per cent ($2.5 million) was provided. A major UNDP trust project, in cooperation with WFP, to provide United Nations advisers to the Provincial Emergency Commissions has successfully been implemented in Nampula, Sofala, Tete, Manica and Zambézia provinces. UNDP has provided funding for technical support to the National Executive Commission for the Emergency.

44. In 1991/92, $5 million was requested to continue the support and expand provincial level assistance, but only $2.7 million was pledged. The principal donors were Canada, Norway, Sweden and Switzerland, through the United Nations system. USAID supports the Department through CARE International. The Swedish Government provided for UNICEF consultancies and for workshops on logistics and financial management and disaster preparedness.

V. Global development assistance to Mozambique

45. The total value of development assistance disbursed in Mozambique in 1990, as reported to UNDP Maputo, amounted to US$ 1,118 million. This includes humanitarian aid and relief amounting to 15.3 per cent of the total. Total disbursements of development assistance reached a new peak in 1990, 17.4 per cent higher in nominal terms than the value reported in 1989 and double the nominal value of assistance reported in 1983.

A. *Types of development assistance*

46. In 1990, 26.9 per cent of total development assistance disbursements was classified as programme

and budgetary aid and balance-of-payments support. Another 21.4 per cent of disbursements was classified as investment project assistance. Free standing technical cooperation accounted for 19.1 per cent of total disbursements in the reporting year, while 8.2 per cent of disbursements were classified as investment-related technical cooperation. Food aid was estimated to amount to 5.5 per cent of total disbursements. This seems low in view of Mozambique's dependence on food aid for the market sector and free distribution. Disbursements of emergency and relief assistance amounted to 18.6 per cent.

B. *Distribution of assistance*

47. Five major recipient sectors can be identified, accounting for 71.3 per cent of total disbursements, namely, industry (17.7 per cent of total disbursements), humanitarian aid (15.9 per cent), international trade (16.3 per cent), agriculture (12.5 per cent) and transport (9.6 per cent). Despite the large number of donors, most external assistance is provided by a small number of donors, the top 10 accounting for 77.1 per cent. Bilateral donors provided 71.6 per cent of reported external assistance in 1990, the remainder being provided by non-United Nations multilateral organizations (11.1 per cent), the United Nations system (11 per cent) and non-governmental organizations (5.2 per cent).

48. The most important donor in 1990 was Sweden with reported disbursements of US$ 119.2 million, 10.7 per cent of total disbursements in the reporting year, followed by EEC, Italy, the USSR, France, the International Development Association, the United Kingdom of Great Britain and Northern Ireland, the United States of America, Norway and Portugal. Sweden was also the leading donor in 1989 and 8 of the top 10 donors of 1989 are included among the top 10 for 1990. Over the last decade the leading donors have been fairly consistent, with France, Italy, the Netherlands, Norway, Portugal, Sweden and the United Kingdom figuring prominently in development cooperation reports since 1982. Following Mozambique's accession to the International Monetary Fund (IMF) and the World Bank in 1986, assistance from the United States also increased rapidly. Eastern European countries, including the former Soviet Union, did not submit data for the development cooperation reports prior to 1988, though from the late 1970s until 1990 they were major donors. Within the United Nations system, the leading donor was the World Bank, which accounted for 53 per cent of United Nations system disbursements, followed by WFP (13.6 per cent), UNDP (13.4 per cent), IMF (10.4 per cent) and UNICEF (3.6 per cent).

C. *Non-governmental organizations*

49. Owing to poor reporting of development assist-ance activities financed by non-governmental organizations, it is impossible to provide detailed information. In the reporting year 1990, non-governmental organizations provided external assistance totalling $65.1 million, equivalent to 6.2 per cent of total external assistance disbursements. Moreover, data on disbursements financed by non-governmental organizations, including funds from core budgets financed by bilateral agencies, underestimate their importance in development activities within Mozambique, since non-governmental organizations frequently act as executing agents for bilateral and multilateral donor agencies.

50. There is a clear difference in the orientation of development assistance between non-governmental organizations and other sources of external assistance. The available data indicate that 95.4 per cent of disbursements financed by such organizations were provided to the social sectors, compared to 31.4 per cent for all donors. By far the most important sector for non-governmental organizations is humanitarian aid, which accounted for 72.4 per cent of external assistance disbursements financed by those organizations in the reporting year. In this sector, non-governmental organizations account for 27.7 per cent of total disbursements. They were also important sources of finance for projects in the area development sector, where they accounted for 20.7 per cent of all disbursements. Area development is the leading sector for non-governmental organizations development assistance, accounting for 38.9 per cent of all non-humanitarian aid disbursements. Many non-governmental organizations—and bilateral and multilateral agencies involved in the financing of those organizations as executing agencies—believe that their flexibility gives non-governmental organizations a comparative advantage in this sector.

VI. Assistance rendered by United Nations organizations and Member States

A. *United Nations organizations*

United Nations Children's Fund

51. The activities of UNICEF have included the provision of essential drugs, supplementary food, education, and relief supplies for displaced and drought-affected populations. In addition, special projects are in process to enhance rural water supplies and provide for war-traumatized and other children in especially difficult circumstances, and to promote the management and logistical capacities of the Department for the Prevention and Combat of National Disasters at district and provincial level.

United Nations Development Programme

52. The combination of war and drought continues to plague Mozambique and to call for massive relief efforts, including efforts on behalf of the more than 3.5 million displaced persons and millions of others who must depend on international food aid. Coordination of United Nations humanitarian assistance efforts is carried out through the United Nations Special Coordinator for Emergency Relief Operations. This position is held by the UNDP resident representative, and major support for the coordination functions is provided by UNDP.

53. The UNDP resident representative assists the Ministry for Cooperation in the coordination of external aid and technical assistance programmes. In addition, UNDP provides technical assistance to the major coordinating bodies, namely, the Ministry for Cooperation, the Ministry for Planning and the Ministry of Finance and, most recently, in support of the post-war planning exercise coordinated by the National Reconstruction Commission. To assist in the planning and aid coordination at the provincial level, UNDP will also lead the national programme for the decentralization of the planning system. The largest part of the UNDP third country programme has been executed by FAO in agricultural research, training, extension, planning and fisheries.

54. The United Nations Development Fund for Women, with UNDP support, has initiated a pilot project on integrated village development, focusing on access to credit. The United Nations Capital Development Fund focuses on road rehabilitation (to be implemented by the International Labour Organization) and a rural water supply project to be implemented by UNICEF in the northern provinces. Every effort has been made to programme United Nations Volunteers specialists closely with UNDP activities under indicative planning figures as a means of providing cost-effective technical assistance. A major national conference on sustainable development and the environment was assisted by the United Nations Centre for Human Settlements (Habitat) and UNDP. UNDP, the United Nations Population Fund, UNICEF and WFP have worked closely with other United Nations agency teams in the programming and implementing of feeder road programmes and projects in forestry, the emergency programme, population planning and demographic survey, food security, malaria control, post-war planning, rural water supplies, the social action programme, and a maternal and child health and family planning programme. UNDP collaborates with WHO in the national AIDS programme. Finally, UNDP has executed a major industrial policy study with UNDP funding.

United Nations Environment Programme

55. The 1990 Memorandum of Agreement between the United Nations Environment Programme (UNEP) and Mozambique provides the framework within which UNEP has offered substantial assistance for the strengthening of the Environment Division, the Government's principal body for all environmental management efforts. Within this framework, UNEP is providing Mozambique with support in the areas of environmental legislation and coastal zone management. UNEP is also assisting Mozambique in the establishment of an environmental management programme and also in the setting up of a geographic information system.

World Food Programme

56. The World Food Programme has continued to give high priority to providing assistance to Mozambique, both for development purposes and as humanitarian emergency assistance. The current level of WFP assistance amounts to $57.4 million in food aid and logistics support, of which $28.2 million is utilized in the support of primary education and the forestry sector and about $39.2 million for emergency feeding of displaced people.

57. Recognizing the need to provide additional support in the rehabilitation of rural infrastructure such as roads and to improve the food security situation, WFP has formulated two new development projects, which will provide additional assistance amounting to $3.3 million, for a period of four years.

58. In response to the joint United Nations/SADC appeal, WFP is providing additional assistance in food aid and internal transportation costs estimated at $71 million for the crop year 1992/93.

59. In addition to direct food aid and cash support for internal transport, storage and handling, WFP has been playing an important role in providing technical advice to the Government in food aid management and coordination of emergency food aid for relief purposes.

Economic Commission for Africa

60. The Economic Commission for Africa (ECA) will deliver advisory services to Mozambique in response to a request from the Government of that country for the establishment of a structured development information system. It is expected that this will be followed by ECA assistance in implementing such a system, including training of national personnel.

United Nations Centre for Human Settlements (Habitat)

61. Habitat is providing technical assistance to the Government of Mozambique through a UNDP-funded project aimed at developing a long-term programme of support to the urban development and housing sector. The project focuses on the alleviation of urban poverty

through development of the peri-urban settlements which are growing around the urban centres as vast numbers of people, including returnees, converge on the towns. The project will (a) provide assistance for the development of an economic base in those settlements through the use of labour-intensive methods to provide and maintain appropriate infrastructural services, community facilities, improved shelter and urban agriculture; and (b) develop the capacity of local authorities and non-governmental organizations to support local enterprise and create income-generating opportunities.

Food and Agriculture Organization of the United Nations

62. A joint FAO/WFP crop and food supply assessment mission estimated the emergency and other food import requirements of Mozambique as part of the subregional assessment mission during March and April 1992. The report of the mission was transmitted to the international community on 15 April 1992. FAO also provided input to the consolidated United Nations/SADC appeal issued in May 1992 and for the pledging conference held on 1 and 2 June 1992.

63. The FAO Global Information and Early Warning System (GIEWS) continues to monitor the food supply situation in Mozambique and the prospects for the 1992/93 crop, which is to be harvested from March to May 1993.

64. Under its technical cooperation programme, FAO has a project under way on emergency supply of seeds and vegetative materials.

World Health Organization

65. The WHO emergency preparedness programme in Maputo collaborated with the Mozambique health authorities in the training of local health staff, in the preparation for the return of refugees.

66. The organization has supported a number of health-related activities, including the strengthening of health personnel development. Its most recent mission to Mozambique (February 1992) focused on the control of diarrhoeal diseases and acute respiratory infections, on maternal health and safe motherhood, the action programme on essential drugs and on improving case management by health workers in peripheral health facilities.

67. WHO supported the Government of Mozambique in preparing a 12-year health development plan for Manica province and, in connection with the United Nations/SADC drought appeal, participated in the health needs assessment exercise, in collaboration with other United Nations organizations.

B. Member States

Brazil

68. The Governments of Brazil and Mozambique signed an agreement on scientific, technical and technological cooperation in June 1989.

69. The School of Mines of Ouro Preto, Minas Gerais, sent a technical mission to Mozambique from 31 July to 16 August 1991, with a view to evaluating the current situation of the Institute of Geology and Mines of Moatize-Tete.

70. The second follow-up meeting of the Integrated Moatize Coal Project was held at Maputo from 29 October to 1 November 1991 and the Vale do Rio Doce Company formally submitted a pre-viability study on the coal project to the Government of Mozambique. The Brazilian Cooperation Agency also provided support to this project, in coordination with the company, through the designation of a consultant to assist in the strategy for the technological and financial viabilization of the coal project.

71. Under the terms of a bilateral agreement, Brazil admits Mozambican students into Brazilian universities. Currently, there are 76 such students taking graduate and postgraduate courses in Brazil.

China

72. In 1991, China provided Mozambique with relief materials valued at US$ 30,000.

Cuba

73. Cuba has offered to send 76 medical doctors to provide free medical assistance in Mozambique. Of that number, 36 Cuban doctors are already working in different communities in Mozambique.

Denmark

74. Danish emergency assistance to Mozambique in 1991 amounted to DKr 43 million, of which DKr 13 million was channelled through UNHCR and DKr 30 million through Danish non-governmental organizations.

Germany

75. In 1990, official development cooperation with Mozambique amounted to DM 38 million. Of this sum, DM 30 million was for financial cooperation, of which DM 10 million was earmarked for structural adjustment programmes and DM 20 million for projects to promote small and medium industries and for the rehabilitation of the 33 kilovolt substation at Maputo. The remaining DM 8 million for technical cooperation is used to finance projects to promote institutions (Ministry for Cooperation), to help cushion the social impact of the structural adjustment programme by advising the Ministry for Planning, and to promote the private sector.

76. In 1991, a programme totalling DM 68.5 million was agreed upon. This represented an increase of approximately 80 per cent, which made it possible to continue numerous programmes initiated by the former German Democratic Republic. Of this amount, DM 46 million has been committed for financial cooperation, including DM 15 million in quick disbursing funds to support structural adjustment activities. The newly agreed upon projects of financial cooperation benefit the sectors of energy (33 kilovolt transformer station at Nampula), transportation (electrification of the port of Maputo), and social infrastructure (water supply, Mocuba). The DM 20 million committed for technical cooperation is used for measures to strengthen the development bank Banco Popular de Desenvolvimento institutionally and for projects of rural development, health and education. DM 2.5 million serves to support a project to reintegrate Mozambican workers once under contract in the former German Democratic Republic.

77. These funds were complemented in 1990 and 1991 by 7,000 and 7,500 tons, respectively, of wheat, equivalent approximately to DM 1.8 and 1.2 million, respectively, in relief food aid.

78. In addition, five scholarships were financed in each of these two years.

79. In line with the needs of Mozambique, the German Government has in the past made considerable efforts to ease Mozambique's debt load. In 1989, a debt release agreement was concluded for the entire official debt of Mozambique, of DM 180 million accrued under the financial cooperation programme. All new commitments are non-repayable grants.

Norway

80. In 1991, total assistance amounted to about US$70 million, of which the regular bilateral development assistance programme was about $40 million, international humanitarian assistance efforts about $2 million and assistance to refugees and human rights programmes about $2 million.

81. In 1992, total development assistance is projected to reach about $60 million. In addition, humanitarian and refugee assistance will be continued, having reached a total of almost $7 million during the first half of the year. As far as development assistance is concerned, the regular bilateral development assistance programme will amount to $38 million. As a part of this programme, support will be given to rural rehabilitation programmes. The main priority areas for the programme will be energy supply, fisheries, coastal transportation and health. With respect to humanitarian relief efforts, in the first half of the year a little less than $4 million has been disbursed. With respect to assistance to refugees and human rights

programmes in the first half of the year, about $3 million has been disbursed.

Poland

82. Over the years Poland has granted scholarship for university studies to Mozambican citizens. During the present academic year there are 24 students from Mozambique. The annual cost of education of one student is US$4,000.

Saudi Arabia

83. Aid to Mozambique from the Government of Saudi Arabia was 150 tons of dates in the amount of 300,000 Saudi riyals, offered in the year A.H. 1410 (A.D. 1989/90).

Sweden

84. Disaster relief assistance amounting to SKr 118.24 million was allocated during the fiscal year 1990/91. From the country programme, an additional SKr 75 million, approximately, was set aside for this purpose during the same period. Concerning disaster relief for the fiscal year 1991/92, approximately SKr 33 million has been allocated. Disaster and reconstruction assistance within the country programme will amount to approximately SKr 100 million for the fiscal year 1991/92.

Turkey

85. Turkey has sent a draft technical cooperation agreement to Mozambique and proposals for training programmes in Turkey.

United Kingdom of Great Britain and Northern Ireland

1. Programme aid

86. To assist Mozambique in the purchase of essential imported commodities, such as oil, fertilizer, and machine spare parts, the United Kingdom has given £12 million in balance-of-payments support since the beginning of 1991; £7.5 million was transferred in March 1991, the remaining £5 million being transferred in March 1992. Both grants are being managed by the World Bank.

2. Project aid

87. In March 1991 the United Kingdom committed £6.3 million to assist in the rehabilitation of the Matola oil and grain jetties at Maputo port. The difficult security situation, particularly outside the main centres of population, has restricted the opportunities for further investment in new projects.

3. Emergency relief

88. United Kingdom bilateral emergency and small-scale rehabilitation aid commitments to Mozambique and Mozambican refugees in surrounding States, since the adoption of General Assembly resolution 45/227, total £19.28 million, as set out below.

Non-food aid emergency assistance

89. In 1991 we provided £2.166 million in support of our regular emergency programme, mostly channelled through British non-governmental organizations, which provided emergency supplies of seeds, tools, clothes, blankets and cooking utensils to displaced and war-affected people in Mozambique and the surrounding States.

90. So far in 1992 (until 17 June) we have committed £1.6 million of emergency relief in response to the severe drought, for the provision of trucks, seeds and non-cereal food aid.

Small-scale rehabilitation

91. In the 1991/92 financial year, £0.605 million was committed to non-governmental organization projects relating to the rehabilitation of the district and provincial health, agriculture, engineering, water and planning sectors.

92. In 1992 (until 17 June) we committed an additional £0.65 million in support of these continuing pro-

grammes. Of this amount, £500,000 was committed to a UNICEF rural water programme.

Bilateral food aid

93. In 1991 we committed £4 million for the provision of 22,500 tons of cereal food aid, for distribution to internally displaced people in Mozambique and Mozambican refugees in the surrounding States.

94. So far in 1992 we have provided £5.9 million for the purchase of 25,000 tons of cereal food aid for distribution in Mozambique and to Mozambican refugees in Malawi.

95. In 1991 we committed £3.26 million of humanitarian assistance to refugees in surrounding States, £3 million of which was in support of UNHCR programmes, mainly in Malawi.

4. *Technical cooperation*

96. Technical cooperation supports our continuing projects and provides United Kingdom-based training to an annual value of around £1.1 million.

Document 19

Letter dated 23 October 1992 from the Secretary-General to the President of the Security Council on actions taken by his Special Representative in Mozambique towards implementation of the General Peace Agreement

Not issued as a United Nations document; original in French

I have the honour to refer to resolution 782 (1992) adopted on 13 October 1992 by the Security Council on the situation in Mozambique, in which the Council, *inter alia*, approved my recommendations concerning the appointment of an interim Special Representative for Mozambique and the dispatch to Mozambique of a team of up to 25 military observers.

Pursuant to that resolution, I decided that same day to appoint Mr. Aldo Ajello, an Italian national who is a staff member of the United Nations Development Programme (UNDP), to be my interim Special Representative for Mozambique and I asked him to proceed to Maputo in order to assist the parties in setting up the joint machinery which is to be chaired by the United Nations, in finalizing the modalities and conditions for the military arrangements and in carrying out the various other actions which would be required of them at the very beginning of the process. In addition, I assigned to him the tasks described in paragraphs 14 and 15 of the report (S/24642) which I submitted on 9 Oc-

tober to the Security Council concerning the United Nations Operation in Mozambique (ONUMOZ). I also took the necessary steps to dispatch to Mozambique a military team composed of members of existing peace-keeping missions who would be assigned to perform the limited tasks described in paragraph 16 of the above-mentioned report.

The interim Special Representative and the team of 21 military observers arrived in Mozambique on 15 October, the date on which the General Peace Agreement establishing the principles and modalities for the achievement of peace in Mozambique, entered into force following publication in the *Official Gazette* of the legal instruments adopted by the Assembly of the Republic of Mozambique. On 20 October, two teams of six military observers each were deployed to Nampula and Beira. It should be noted that, while the United Nations has established a symbolic presence in Mozambique, as I had recommended in my report, the delays which have occurred in setting up the joint machinery and finalizing the terms of the cease-fire have considerably limited the capacity of ONUMOZ to carry out the tasks assigned to the United Nations under the Rome Agreement.

Since his arrival, the interim Special Representative has met with the President of the Republic of Mozambique, Mr. Chissano, and with Mr. Dhlakama, President of the Resistência Nacional Moçambicana (RENAMO), and has engaged in lengthy exchanges of views with those two leaders concerning various questions relating to the rapid implementation of the Agreement. He has also met with members of the Mozambican Government and representatives of RENAMO, with representatives of the Organization of African Unity, with the ambassadors of the mediator State (Italy) and of the States which participated in the Rome negotiations as observers (France, Portugal, United Kingdom and United States of America), and with other members of the diplomatic community in Maputo. He has also had an opportunity to discuss certain aspects of the implementation of the Rome Agreement with representatives of United Nations agencies and programmes and of major non-governmental organizations which are currently participating in humanitarian assistance activities in Mozambique and which have been assigned to help in the implementation of various aspects of the Peace Agreement relevant to their work.

I am pleased to inform the members of the Council that the Mozambican Government, the leaders of RENAMO and the members of the diplomatic community in Mozambique have welcomed the speed with which the Security Council and the Secretary-General have taken action to support the peace process in Mozambique.

It will be recalled that the two parties undertook to implement specific measures immediately following and, in some cases, even before the entry into force of the Agreement, with a view to activating the joint machinery necessary for the verification and monitoring of the implementation of the provisions of the Agreement. In the meantime, the interim Special Representative has informed me that the necessary conditions do not yet exist for establishing the major commissions (the Supervision and Monitoring Commission, the Cease-fire Commission, the Reintegration Commission and the Joint Commission for the Formation of the Mozambican Defence Force) and that the parties have not yet agreed on the membership of those commissions. This delay is largely attributable to the absence of a RENAMO delegation in Maputo; according to RENAMO, the Government has not yet made the necessary logistical arrangements to enable its representatives to proceed to the capital. Mr. Ajello has emphasized to the two parties the need to meet those requirements as soon as possible.

He has also urged both the Government and RENAMO to reach agreement as soon as possible on the precise locations where their forces are to regroup; on the modalities for verification and monitoring; and on other vital related questions so that the United Nations can assess its needs in terms of human and material resources and so that I can formulate recommendations to the Security Council on the launching of ONUMOZ. It is also essential, as a matter of urgency, to establish, with the cooperation of the Government and RENAMO, mechanisms which would encourage the support of donor countries and strengthen the coordination and delivery of humanitarian assistance provided for in the Rome Agreement.

A concerted effort is essential in order to launch the entire process of the implementation of the General Peace Agreement and I hope that all States concerned, in particular the mediator and observer States, as well as the organizations concerned, will provide every assistance to the parties and to my interim Special Representative in order to resolve the problems which are impeding the effective launching of the peace process.

In the meantime, it has been learned that the Zimbabwean forces began to withdraw from Mozambique on 21 October 1992, as provided for in the operational timetable for the cease-fire contained in section II of Protocol VI of the Agreement. Since the Cease-fire Commission has not yet been established, a reconnaissance team, composed of military observers from Beira, is being dispatched to Chimoio to assess the situation and gather information on the proposed timetable for withdrawal and on the number of men who have actually been withdrawn.

My interim Special Representative is receiving an increasing number of reports from representatives of United Nations agencies and programmes in the various provinces of Mozambique to the effect that the local population, the provincial authorities and the Government and RENAMO forces in various localities are prepared to begin, at the earliest possible date, to implement the Peace Agreement and to disarm their forces and regroup them in the assembly areas. Many people have informed United Nations representatives that they are anxiously awaiting the arrival of United Nations military observers. There have also been frequent reports that Government troops are sharing their food with RENAMO troops and with the population in the areas controlled by RENAMO. RENAMO has begun to clear mines from a number of access routes in those areas in order to facilitate the transport of emergency assistance. Certain routes which previously could not be used for security reasons have now been opened and, in the south and along the coast, there are already large-scale movements of people and goods. The United Nations presence, however symbolic, has thus brought about positive changes in certain provinces.

On the other hand, other events have occurred which are a source of grave concern. Violations of the cease-fire, allegedly committed by both parties, were first reported by the press. Both the Government and RENAMO subsequently addressed official complaints to my interim Special Representative. RENAMO complained about Government troop movements in the Provinces of Nampula, Zambezia and Tete but did not provide the necessary details to substantiate its claims. Conversely, there have been reports of attacks by RENAMO forces on the towns of Angoche and Memba (Province of Nampula) and Maganja de Costa and Lugela (Province of Zambézia). Those violations were subsequently confirmed by representatives of the international community who were in those towns at the time of the attacks. On 22 October, however, the Governor of the Province of Nampula and the Chief of Staff of the Mozambican Armed Forces announced that Government forces had just recaptured Angoche.

According to some reports, RENAMO has indeed launched the largest military operation it has carried out in recent years. It seems, therefore, that there was a major violation of the cease-fire. My interim Special Representative has written to the President of RENAMO emphasizing the extremely negative effect of this military action. He has asked him to provide the necessary security guarantees to enable United Nations military observers to proceed to the areas where the attacks are reported to have taken place. Mr. Ajello has also requested the representatives of the Government and of RENAMO to hold a formal meeting on 26 October in order to discuss various questions relating to the General Peace Agreement, including the composition and establishment of the commissions provided for in the Agreement.

The current situation in Mozambique is therefore critical. I have asked my interim Special Representative to submit to me, at the earliest possible date, detailed recommendations on the human and material resources necessary to carry out the various tasks assigned to the United Nations under the Rome Agreement. In the meantime, the Security Council might wish to issue an appeal to all the parties concerned, requesting them genuinely to unite their efforts with a view to making a start on the implementation of the Agreement.

I should be grateful if you would bring these matters to the attention of the members of the Security Council.

Accept, Sir, the assurances of my highest consideration.

(*Signed*) Boutros BOUTROS-GHALI

Document 20

Statement by the President of the Security Council expressing concern over reports of cease-fire violations in Mozambique

S/24719, 27 October 1992

The Council has taken note of the letter of 23 October 1992 from the Secretary-General to the President of the Security Council concerning the situation in Mozambique. It expresses its gratitude to the Secretary-General and to his interim Special Representative for Mozambique for their efforts to ensure that the United Nations contributes to the implementation of the General Peace Agreement for Mozambique 1/ in accordance with the provisions of this Agreement.

The Council remains deeply concerned by the reports of major violations of the cease-fire in several regions of Mozambique. It calls upon the parties to halt such violations immediately and scrupulously to respect the cease-fire and all the commitments entered into under the Agreement. It also urges the parties to cooperate fully with the interim Special Representative of the Secretary-General, and in particular to take all measures necessary to ensure the safety of United Nations staff in Mozambique.

The Council wishes to reiterate its firm commitment to work towards a lasting peace in Mozambique. In this regard, it urges the parties to respect fully the cease-fire, which is a necessary condition for the speedy establishment of the United Nations Operation in Mozambique and its successful deployment.

1/ *Official Records of the Security Council, Forty-seventh Year, Supplement for October, November and December 1992*, document S/24635, annex.

Document 21

Communiqué dated 20 October 1992 by the Council of Ministers of the Republic of Mozambique concerning the implementation of the General Peace Agreement

S/24724, 28 October 1992

I am transmitting to you herewith the text of a communiqué issued by the Council of Ministers of the Republic of Mozambique on 20 October 1992, concerning the implementation of the General Peace Agreement for Mozambique.

I should be grateful if you would have this letter and its annex circulated as a document of the Security Council.

(*Signed*) Pedro Comissário AFONSO
Ambassador Extraordinary and Plenipotentiary
Permanent Representative to the United Nations

Annex

Communiqué by the Council of Ministers of the Republic of Mozambique

The signing of the General Peace Agreement on 4 October 1992 in Rome by the President of the Republic of Mozambique, Joaquim Alberto Chissano, and by the leader of RENAMO, Afonso Macacho Marceta Dhlakama, has signified for all the Mozambican people and for the international community the end of the war, beginning with the immediate cessation of hostilities between the parties until the formal entry into effect of the cease-fire.

The Assembly of the Republic has unanimously approved the General Peace Agreement, incorporating it into the national law. The publication of the Agreement on 15 October 1992, in the Official Gazette ("Boletim da Republica"), marked the formal start of the cease-fire.

The General Peace Agreement, in its various Protocols, calls for the existence and operation of suitable mechanisms, agreed upon between the parties, concerning the supervision and monitoring of the implementation of the General Peace Agreement, under the chairmanship of the United Nations.

Both parties—the Government and RENAMO—agreed on 15 October 1992 as the date for the entry into effect of the cease-fire, with all the consequences arising therefrom.

In this context, the Secretary-General of the United Nations has appointed his Representative as Chairman of the Commission for Supervision and Monitoring of the General Peace Agreement, who arrived in Maputo on 15 October 1992, as well as the Head of the United Nations Military Observers Team, who arrived in Maputo on 14 October 1992, along with part of the first Team of Observers.

On 15 October 1992, the President of the Republic received in audience the Representative of the United Nations Secretary-General, Mr. Aldo Ajello, whom he advised of the steps that were being taken by the Government with a view to complying with the obligations arising from the General Peace Agreement.

The Secretary-General's Representative was then informed of:

- the composition of the representation of the Government in the various Commissions set forth in the General Peace Agreement;
- the measures taken and under way to facilitate accommodations for the RENAMO members designated to form part of the Commission;
- the measures taken and under way to secure accommodations for the United Nations Observers.

The Head of State asked the Representative of the United Nations Secretary-General to take immediate steps in order to ensure that the Commissions set forth in the General Peace Agreement begin to operate, in order to prevent delays already at the outset.

The Representative of the United Nations Secretary-General informed the Head of State of his availability to travel immediately to Gorongoza and persuade RENAMO's President to send his delegates.

Within the spirit of assuring compliance with the Agreement, the Government also asked RENAMO, through its representative in the COMIVE, to provide information about the date of arrival of its representatives, having been informed that the latter had not left, due to lack of means of transportation between Maringue and Maputo.

Having made arrangements to provide a small plane for the trip, from Maputo and Beira, and while awaiting communication as to the time when it should arrive in Maringue, the Government was informed that the RENAMO delegation was not coming, because RENAMO first wanted to know about the conditions for their accommodations.

Still within the same spirit, on 15 October 1992, the President of the Republic formally communicated to the RENAMO representative in the COMIVE (International

Joint Verification Commission) the answers to the concerns expressed by the RENAMO leaders as to:

– housing
– security
– meals
– identification
– liaison with the media,

assuring that the conditions had been ensured and that the arrangements should follow through.

On 18 October 1992, the RENAMO representative in the COMIVE, in an interview given to the national and international media, released a statement by its organization which makes reference to an alleged movement of the Armed Forces of Mozambique towards zones supposedly under RENAMO's control, affirming that this was due to the lack of willingness on the part of the Government to abide by the Agreement, threatening with retaliation.

It is in this context that on 17 October 1992, armed RENAMO elements attacked, assaulted and occupied the capital of the district of Maganja de Costa; on 18 and 19 October 1992, they attacked, assaulted and occupied the capital of the district of Angoche, and on 19 October 1992, they attacked, assaulted and occupied the capital of the district of Memba, at the same time that concentrations of troops are occurring in various parts of the country, with objectives that are not very clear.

Thus, and taking into account: that the Government has done everything in its power to ensure compliance with the General Peace Agreement, keeping the Representative of the United Nations Secretary-General informed; that the Government has regarded very positively the logistical support that the Armed Forces of Mozambique have been supplying to the RENAMO people when they request it peacefully; that the Government has been encouraging a spirit of reconciliation between the members of the Armed Forces of Mozambique and those of RENAMO.

The Government considers that RENAMO's behaviour, namely:

– Not having itself been represented in the commission set forth in the General Peace Agreement with the task of supervising and monitoring its implementation,

– Launching offensives against civilian targets, in a deliberate strategy of conquest of territories and strategic positions,
– Issuing statements instead of using the agreed-on mechanism as an advance justification for the violations that it set out to commit,

constitutes a grave and systematic violation that seriously jeopardizes the General Peace Agreement.

The actions and attitudes of each party leave no margin for questions about who is willing to comply and will comply and who is determined to violate the General Peace Agreement and, in particular, the cease-fire.

Thus, to the proclaimed and so-welcomed reconciliation of brothers, there are those who wish to oppose or superimpose and perpetuate the rationale and methods of an enemy in open defiance to the Mozambican people and the international community.

The Government has already notified the Representative of the United Nations Secretary-General that RENAMO be ordered to comply with the General Peace Agreement and to conduct its activities in accordance with the parameters set forth therein.

The Government appeals to all Mozambicans so that they may know how to defend the General Peace Agreement, exercising the necessary vigilance against all those who, driven by ambition and by an anti-patriotic and warlike spirit, do everything to jeopardize it. In view of the gravity of the situation, the Government assumes the responsibilities that befall it in the defence and security of the peoples and reserves the right to take the measures it deems suitable to put an end to the violations that have taken place and to restore the conditions for the compliance with and implementation of the General Peace Agreement.

Under the present circumstances, the Armed Forces of Mozambique must continue under a state of alert and readiness in order to drive back any move or attempt to violate the General Peace Agreement.

For Peace, Democracy, Development and National Solidarity.

Maputo, 20 October 1992

Document 22

Statement by President Abdou Diouf of Senegal, in his capacity as Chairman of the Organization of African Unity (OAU), welcoming the signing of the General Peace Agreement for Mozambique

S/24760, 4 November 1992

The Permanent Mission of the Republic of Senegal to the United Nations presents its compliments to the Secretary-General of the Organization and has the honour to transmit to him herewith, for publication as a document of the Security Council, the statement made by the President of the Republic of Senegal, His Excellency Mr. Abdou Diouf, in his capacity as current Chairman of the Organization of African Unity, on the General Peace Agreement for Mozambique.

The Permanent Mission of the Republic of Senegal would be grateful to the Secretary-General for a speedy response to this request.

Annex

Statement by His Excellency Mr. Abdou Diouf, President of the Republic of Senegal and current Chairman of the Organization of African Unity, on the signing of the General Peace Agreement for Mozambique at Rome on 4 October 1992

Africa, whose major concern is to see peace and security in all its regions, welcomed with pride and great joy the signing of the General Peace Agreement for Mozambique on 4 October 1992 at Rome.

This important document, the result of international solidarity and of goodwill on the part of all segments of Mozambican society offers Mozambicans an opportunity to transcend their political and ideological differences and an ideal framework within which to work together, in unity and brotherhood, to rebuild their great country.

This significant step towards reconciliation in Mozambique should be commended, encouraged and supported because it is the way to salvation for the Mozambican people and also a valuable contribution to the establishment of a lasting climate of peace and security in southern Africa.

In my dual capacity as President of Senegal and current Chairman of the Organization of African Unity, I should like to give my full support to these efforts for national reconciliation in Mozambique, to urge all the signatories to the Agreement to persevere on the very responsible course they have chosen and to ask the international community, and the United Nations in particular, to increase their support for this process so as to render it irreversible.

This is also the occasion for me to pay a well-deserved tribute, through the Government and people of Italy, to the international community and to all those who assisted this considerable endeavour.

I ask in particular that all the people of Mozambique, whose dignity and political maturity I should like to emphasize, learn from the lessons of the past and refrain from any action that might jeopardize their wise choice to reconcile and unite with one another in order to promote the economic and social development of their country.

If Africa is to attempt to meet the serious economic and social challenges it faces and regain its true place in the international community, it is absolutely essential that all of its peoples unite within their respective borders, as their cultural and traditional values demand.

It is in this spirit that the Mozambican people must act, and they can surely count on African solidarity and the support of the international community to help their actions succeed.

(Signed) Abdou DIOUF

Document 23

Letter dated 12 November 1992 from Italy concerning the convening of a Donors Conference for Mozambique in Rome

S/24813, 16 November 1992

I have the honour to transmit herewith a note by which the Italian Government, in pursuance of the General Peace Agreement for Mozambique, signed in Rome on 4 October 1992, is convening a Conference to be held in Rome on 15 and 16 December 1992.

I would be grateful if you could have this text

circulated as a document of the Security Council, supplementing document S/24635.

(*Signed*) Vieri TRAXLER
Ambassador

Annex

In order to implement the provisions agreed upon by the parties to the General Peace Agreement for Mozambique, signed in Rome on 4 October 1992 (S/24635, annex), the Italian Government is convening a Conference to be held in Rome on 15 and 16 December 1992.

The Parties to the Peace Agreement, in Protocol VII, have agreed to the following:

"1. The Parties decide to request the Italian Government to convene a conference of donor countries and organizations to finance the electoral process, emergency programmes and programmes for the reintegration of displaced persons, refugees and demobilized soldiers.

"2. The Parties agree to request that, of the funds provided by donor countries, an appropriate share should be placed at the disposal of political parties to finance their activities.

"3. The Parties appeal for the donors conference to be convened no later than 30 days after E-Day. In addition to donor countries and organizations, the Government and RENAMO shall also be invited to send representatives."

The States Members of the United Nations that can consider contributing to the planning and implementation of the aforementioned programmes, according to Protocol VII of the Rome Agreement, are kindly invited to announce their intention to participate in the Rome Donors Conference through the Italian Mission to the United Nations or directly to the Italian Foreign Ministry (D.G. Affari Politici, Uff. X). Pledges may refer to programmes that donor countries may wish to implement bilaterally or in the framework of United Nations development programmes.

Document 24

Letter dated 17 November 1992 from the Secretary-General to Prime Minister Giuliano Amato of Italy requesting deployment of Italian troops in Mozambique

Not issued as a United Nations document

I have asked my interim Special Representative in Mozambique, Mr. Aldo Ajello, to bring this letter to you in person, and to describe to you the reasons for the extremely urgent requests contained in it.

As you are aware, the General Peace Agreement for Mozambique (to which your country has made such a tremendous contribution) provided for the withdrawal of all foreign troops, that is, troops from Malawi and Zimbabwe, within thirty days after the agreement came into force on October 15, 1992. The deadline has therefore already passed, but the foreign troops have not yet withdrawn.

These troops protect the two corridors of Beira and Nacala, which are of vital importance to the two countries involved. The Beira corridor, in particular, contains an especially vulnerable infrastructure, including a railway line and oil pipelines. In addition, the corridors are of enormous logistic importance for Mozambique itself, and, in particular, for the transport of food aid on which the survival of millions depends, both civilians and military. This, in turn, is directly relevant to the success of the

entire operation to support the peace process.

These corridors cross territories that are in part controlled by the Government and in part by RENAMO. The armed forces of both sides are in the process of demobilization, in accordance with the terms of the Peace Agreement. Neither the Government army nor the troops of RENAMO are therefore in a position to control these corridors or keep them secure.

In order to guarantee their security, as well as that of other roads and areas of strategic importance, I intend to obtain the authorization of the Security Council to deploy armed United Nations contingents. Unfortunately, if normal procedures are followed, it will take some three to four months before such troops can be in theatre and operational.

In these circumstances, the withdrawal of the existing foreign troops would leave these vital arteries at the mercy of roaming groups of heavily armed bandits, deserters and irregular militia, who are ready to attack convoys in order to procure food or to sabotage the infrastructure, thereby undermining the peace process.

For political and legal reasons, it will be extremely difficult to extend the presence of the foreign troops for the time needed to bring in the United Nations contingents. The United Nations has no mandate to modify the terms of the Peace Agreement signed in Rome, and the Commission for Supervision and Control, which does have such a mandate, is not in a position to make the required changes because of RENAMO's staunch opposition. For RENAMO, the immediate withdrawal of all foreign troops is a matter of principle that cannot be open to negotiation.

At this stage, the most practical solution appears to be the advance deployment of one logistically self-sufficient battalion, brought in by air within the next two to three weeks, and made available by a Member State until the arrival of the main body of troops approved by the Security Council. My first request is that Italy should be that Member State.

The Peace Agreement also paved the way for a massive relief aid programme to prevent another situation similar to that which is devastating Somalia. This relief programme, in which we are harnessing the resources of every United Nations and voluntary organization in Mozambique, is threatened by the presence of mines on many of the major roads, by the poor condition of these roads after years of enforced neglect, and by the destruc-

tion of some major bridges.

We urgently need the deployment of a self-sufficient engineer battalion to carry out de-mining and road and bridge reconstruction. The urgency of the situation is such that we need the engineer battalion, like the infantry battalion, in two to three weeks. This is my second request.

At the time that the conflict in Bosnia-Herzegovina escalated, Italy generously offered the United Nations the use of a battalion of 1,200 men. For reasons specific to that conflict, I was regrettably unable to accept that offer and the deployment of the Italian battalion did not take place.

If, however, the Government of Italy were able to reiterate such an offer today in the context of Mozambique, and if it were in a position to deploy an infantry and an engineer battalion within the times requested, this would allow us to solve two extremely dangerous and serious problems, and would add a further major contribution to the many already made by Italy in the cause of peace in Mozambique.

Please accept, Mr. Prime Minister, the assurances of my highest consideration.

(*Signed*) Boutros BOUTROS-GHALI

Document 25

Letter dated 1 December 1992 from the Secretary-General to President Chissano on the status of the establishment of ONUMOZ and expressing concern over cease-fire violations in Mozambique

Not issued as a United Nations document

I should like to take this opportunity to thank you personally, as well as the Government of Mozambique, for the cooperation and assistance extended to my interim Special Representative and the team of 25 military observers, who arrived in Mozambique on 15 October, to initiate United Nations activities in support of the General Peace Agreement. I am particularly pleased that, with the cooperation of both parties, all the Commissions and their subsidiary bodies have been established and have commenced their work.

While these developments constitute a hopeful beginning, I am aware that the Government of Mozambique is increasingly concerned about the time-frame of deployment of the major component of the forthcoming United Nations operation. I wish to assure you that the United Nations will do everything possible to meet its

obligations to Mozambique, notwithstanding its current world-wide peace-keeping commitments. It must be borne in mind that we need to give troop-contributing countries adequate lead-time for delivery of logistic *matériel* and equipment in Mozambique. In this regard, our plans to overcome these difficulties in the case of Mozambique were adversely affected by recent developments in Angola. However, pending the adoption of a Security Council resolution on the establishment of the United Nations Operation in Mozambique (ONUMOZ), we are continuing with our efforts to facilitate, as a matter of urgency, the implementation of the peace process. To this end, we are approaching a number of Member States about the availability of their personnel and support for the operation in Mozambique.

My interim Special Representative, Mr. Aldo Ajello,

has been in New York in recent weeks to assist me in the preparation of my report to the Security Council on the establishment of ONUMOZ, including a detailed cost estimate of the operation. This report, which I expect to submit to the Security Council this week, will include an operational plan covering the role of the United Nations in monitoring and guaranteeing the implementation of the General Peace Agreement. Mr. Ajello's contribution to the report has been crucial and his presence in New York most useful in helping me to finalize our plan of action. It is my hope that the Security Council will approve my recommendations shortly so that we may establish ONUMOZ as soon as possible.

With respect to the cease-fire, I am rather concerned that despite the appeal of my interim Special Representative to the parties to refrain from any type of military operation and to settle all disputes related to cease-fire violations in the appropriate commissions, Government troops carried out a number of operations. Mr. Raul Domingos, the Chief of the RENAMO delegation, has furthermore complained to the United Nations about concentrations of Government troops apparently with a view to possible actions. I have been further informed that the Cease-fire Commission has decided to undertake shortly investigations of the alleged violations. In these circumstances, I would like to urge all parties to cease any offensive or counter-offensive actions, to exercise maximum restraint and to refrain from any action which would aggravate the situation.

I have no doubt that I can continue to count on your cooperation and support in the implementation of the General Peace Agreement.

Accept, Mr. President, the assurances of my highest consideration.

(*Signed*) Boutros BOUTROS-GHALI

Document 26

Report of the Secretary-General on ONUMOZ

S/24892, 3 December 1992, and S/24892/Add.1, 9 December 1992

Introduction

1. In my report of 9 October 1992 (S/24642), I conveyed to the Security Council the principal features of the general peace agreement for Mozambique, which is contained in document S/24635, and brought to its attention the role proposed for the United Nations in relation to the peace process. I recommended an immediate plan of action. On 13 October 1992, the Security Council adopted resolution 782 (1992), by which it welcomed the signature of a general peace agreement between the Government of the Republic of Mozambique and the Resistência Nacional Moçambicana (RENAMO), approved the appointment by the Secretary-General of an interim Special Representative and the dispatch to Mozambique of a team of up to 25 military observers, and requested the Secretary-General to report on the establishment of a United Nations Operation in Mozambique (ONUMOZ), including in particular a detailed estimate of the cost of that operation.

I. The current status of the peace process

2. In pursuance of that resolution, I took action the same day to appoint Mr. Aldo Ajello, a national of Italy and a staff member of the United Nations Development Programme (UNDP), as my interim Special Representative for Mozambique, and asked him to proceed to Maputo to assist the parties in setting up the joint machinery, which was to be chaired by the United Nations, in finalizing the modalities and conditions for the military arrangements and in carrying out the various other actions that were required of them at the very beginning of the process. I also entrusted him with the functions described in paragraphs 14 and 15 of my report of 9 October 1992 to the Security Council (S/24642). At the same time, I made arrangements to send to Mozambique a military team whose personnel had been drawn from existing peace-keeping missions and whose limited tasks were described in paragraph 16 of the above-mentioned report.

3. The interim Special Representative and the team of 21 military observers arrived in Mozambique on 15 October 1992, the day when the general peace agreement (hereinafter referred to as "the agreement") came into force, following publication in the *Official Gazette* of the legal instruments adopted by the Assembly of the Republic of Mozambique. On 20 October 1992, two teams of military observers were also deployed to Nampula and Beira.

4. Since his arrival, the interim Special Representative has met on several occasions with the President of Mozambique, Mr. Chissano, as well as with Mr. Dhlakama, President of RENAMO, and has had extensive exchanges with both leaders on various matters

related to the early start of implementation of the agreement. He has also met with members of the Mozambican Government and representatives of RENAMO, representatives of the Organization of African Unity (OAU), and the ambassadors of the mediator State (Italy) and of the observer States at the Rome talks (France, Portugal, United Kingdom of Great Britain and Northern Ireland and United States of America), as well as with other members of the diplomatic community in Maputo. He has, in addition, discussed aspects relating to the implementation of the agreement with representatives of United Nations agencies and programmes and major non-governmental organizations that are currently involved in humanitarian relief effort in Mozambique and that are called upon to assist in carrying out related aspects of the agreement.

5. I am pleased to report that both the Government of Mozambique and the leadership of RENAMO, as well as representatives of the diplomatic community in Mozambique, have expressed their appreciation for the prompt action taken by the Security Council and the Secretary-General.

6. Both parties have committed themselves to undertake immediately after, and in some instances before, the entry into effect of the agreement, specific action to set in motion the joint mechanisms to monitor and verify its implementation. However, no such action had been initiated at the time when the interim Special Representative arrived in Mozambique. Nor had the parties been in direct contact since the signature of the agreement, and RENAMO had no official delegation in the capital. The RENAMO delegation did not wish to move from its headquarters in Gorongosa to Maputo until the Government had provided adequate logistic support, i.e. appropriate housing, transport and communication facilities as foreseen in the agreement. This logistic problem, seemingly marginal, turned out to be a major impediment to the early establishment of the monitoring and verification machinery. Meanwhile, major violations of the cease-fire were reported in various areas of the country, and the parties presented official complaints to the interim Special Representative. A large military operation was reportedly undertaken by RENAMO, which occupied one major town, Angoche, and the villages of Maganja da Costa, Memba and Lugela.

7. In the absence of the machinery foreseen in the agreement for the verification of alleged violations, the interim Special Representative has not been in a position to investigate these incidents. He offered to send United Nations military observers into the areas where military operations had taken place, but this was not possible for lack of agreement between the two parties. I brought these matters to the attention of the Security Council in my letter of 23 October 1992 to its President. The President, in a statement dated 27 October 1992 (S/24719), expressed the Council's deep concern about the reports of major violations of the cease-fire, called upon the parties to halt such violations immediately and urged them to cooperate fully with the interim Special Representative.

8. In order to avoid the escalation of violations, the interim Special Representative called for an informal meeting of the two parties. In a personal letter, he urged Mr. Dhlakama to attend such a meeting, the unsolved logistics problems notwithstanding. He also made a public appeal to both parties. The initiative was successful, and both the Government and RENAMO sent high-level delegations to attend their first meeting in Maputo.

9. Thereafter, the two delegations met on numerous occasions, both bilaterally and together with the interim Special Representative. All conditions and modalities for the establishment of the Commissions foreseen under the agreement were reviewed. The composition of each Commission was extensively discussed and agreement was finally reached. On 4 November 1992, one month after the signature of the agreement, the interim Special Representative was able to appoint the Supervisory and Monitoring Commission, which held its first meeting the same day and appointed the three main subsidiary commissions, the Cease-fire Commission, the Reintegration Commission and the Joint Commission for the Formation of the Mozambican Defence Forces.

10. The Supervisory and Monitoring Commission is composed of government and RENAMO delegations, with representatives of France, Italy, Portugal, the United Kingdom of Great Britain and Northern Ireland, the United States of America and the Organization of African Unity. This Commission is chaired by the United Nations. The Cease-fire Commission is composed of government and RENAMO delegations, with representatives of Botswana, Egypt, France, Italy, Nigeria, Portugal, the United Kingdom and the United States, and is also chaired by the United Nations. The Cease-fire Commission will have subordinate subcommissions in three regional headquarters and also monitoring groups at the assembly areas. The Reintegration Commission is composed of government and RENAMO delegations, with representatives of Denmark, France, Germany, Italy, the Netherlands, Norway, Portugal, South Africa, Spain, Sweden, Switzerland, the United Kingdom, the United States and the European Community (EC) and is chaired by the United Nations. The Joint Commission for the Formation of the Mozambican Defence Forces is composed of government and RENAMO delegations, with representatives of France, Portugal and the United Kingdom. The United Nations has not been requested to take part in this commission.

11. The Supervisory and Monitoring Commission

will guarantee the implementation of the agreement, assume responsibility for authentic interpretation of it, settle any disputes that may arise between the parties and guide and coordinate the activities of the other Commissions. The Cease-fire Commission is responsible for supervising the cease-fire and demobilization. The Reintegration Commission is responsible for the economic and social reintegration of demobilized military personnel. The Joint Commission for the Formation of the Mozambican Defence Forces is responsible for supervising the formation of the new unified armed forces.

12. All Commissions and their subordinate bodies have been established and have begun their work. However, they will require some technical support, including an impartial secretariat, which could best be provided by ONUMOZ. Legal services will also be necessary in order to ensure that the working procedures of the commissions meet international standards and to resolve possible legal disputes. As the composition of the main commissions is multinational and all decisions need to be recorded, translation, secretarial and information services will be required. As for the regional offices of the Cease-fire Commission, transport facilities will be necessary to enable the commissions to carry out their duties on the spot.

13. Meanwhile, the Government has undertaken military operations to retake the four places seized by RENAMO in mid-October (see para. 6 above). The interim Special Representative has continued to urge the two parties to refrain from any type of military operation and to discuss and settle all disputes in the appropriate commissions.

II. Basic assumptions for the United Nations Operation in Mozambique

14. In formulating my recommendations to the Security Council on the establishment of a United Nations Operation in Mozambique (ONUMOZ), I have been guided by three fundamental considerations. The first relates to the trust placed in the United Nations by both parties, as well as by the people of Mozambique. The agreement envisages that the United Nations will provide an impartial and supportive structure to help both parties to break the vicious cycle of violence that has caused so much suffering to Mozambique over the years.

15. The second consideration derives from the breadth of the responsibilities entrusted to the United Nations under the agreement. These will require the involvement of the entire international community, especially United Nations programmes and specialized agencies, and also bilateral entities, intergovernmental agencies and non-governmental organizations, all of which can contribute to the rebuilding and development of a peaceful Mozambique.

16. The third consideration relates to the geography of Mozambique and the country's current condition after 14 years of civil war. It covers an area of 800,000 square kilometres. It is elongated in shape, extending about 1,800 km from north to south, 600 km from east to west in the north and 300 km in the south. Its communications have been devastated by the war. It has been afflicted by the worst drought in decades and food is in short supply. There is an abundance of arms and many armed bandits operate outside the control of the armed forces of either side. Several million Mozambicans are internally displaced or are refugees in neighbouring countries.

17. All these factors have to be taken into account in assessing the human and material resources that ONUMOZ will require. An additional factor is the existence of four transport corridors (the Beira, Limpopo, Nacala and Tete corridors, each providing road, rail and/or pipeline links), which run across Mozambique from the Indian Ocean to land-locked countries to the north and west. These corridors are of critical importance to Mozambique itself, to United Nations humanitarian and other operations in southern Africa and to neighbouring countries. As the civil war intensified, Malawi and Zimbabwe, with the Government of Mozambique's agreement, deployed troops in some of the corridors to assist the Government's forces in keeping them open. With the implementation of the agreement's provisions on the assembly and demobilization of the two sides' forces and on the withdrawal of foreign forces, ONUMOZ will have to assume transitional responsibility for the security of the corridors in order to avoid any vacuum that could be exploited by bandits, pending the formation of the new unified armed forces.

III. Overall framework for the operation

18. In accordance with the agreement, the mandate of ONUMOZ would, if the Security Council agrees, be as follows:

(a) *Political*: to facilitate impartially the implementation of the agreement, in particular by chairing the Supervisory and Monitoring Commission and its subordinate commissions;

(b) *Military*:

(i) To monitor and verify the cease-fire, the separation and concentration of forces, their demobilization and the collection, storage and destruction of weapons;

(ii) To monitor and verify the complete withdrawal of foreign forces;

(iii) To monitor and verify the disbanding of private and irregular armed groups;

(iv) To authorize security arrangements for vital infrastructures; and

(v) To provide security for United Nations and other international activities in support of the peace process, especially in the corridors;

(c) *Electoral*: to provide technical assistance and monitor the entire electoral process;

(d) *Humanitarian*: to coordinate and monitor all humanitarian assistance operations, in particular those relating to refugees, internally displaced persons, demobilized military personnel and the affected local population, and, in this context, to chair the Humanitarian Assistance Committee.

19. The operational concept of ONUMOZ is based on the strong interrelationship between the four components of its mandate. Without sufficient humanitarian aid, and especially food supplies, the security situation in the country may deteriorate and the demobilization process might stall. Without adequate military protection, the humanitarian aid would not reach its destination. Without sufficient progress in the political area, the confidence required for the disarmament and rehabilitation process would not exist. The electoral process, in turn, requires prompt demobilization and formation of the new armed forces, without which the conditions would not exist for successful elections.

20. These strong linkages require a fully integrated approach and strong coordination by the interim Special Representative. The following description of the activities proposed for ONUMOZ in each of its four areas of responsibility should, therefore, be seen as an indivisible and interdependent operational plan.

IV. Operational plan for United Nations observation of military aspects of the agreement

21. The arrangements for the cease-fire and other military aspects of the peace process are set out in detail in Protocol IV to the agreement and were highlighted in my report to the Council of 9 October 1992 (S/24642). This role is similar to that entrusted to the United Nations in other recent cases where the Organization has monitored the implementation of a cease-fire, the separation and concentration of forces, their demobilization and the collection and storage of weapons. In addition, the Cease-fire Commission would also approve plans for dealing with other armed groups, including irregulars, and would authorize security arrangements for vital infrastructure, including the corridors.

22. To ensure credible verification, it would be necessary to obtain from the parties lists of all troops and paramilitary forces, assembled or unassembled, together with details of weapons and ammunition held by them.

There would have to be an agreement on the categories of troops that would be temporarily exempted from the requirement to assemble. Their numbers should be strictly limited and regularly verified. The demobilization process would be initiated and vigorously pursued as soon as troops started to assemble. Arrangements would also be needed for ONUMOZ to control weapons and ammunition in possession of the Government and RENAMO. All arms and ammunition not required for the new armed forces would be destroyed under close supervision of the United Nations. A systematic programme for removal of weapons from the civilian population would also be required from the outset.

23. ONUMOZ's verification function would be carried out mainly by teams of United Nations military observers at the 49 assembly areas in 3 military regions and elsewhere in the field. They would work with, but would remain separate from, the monitoring groups composed of representatives of the two parties at each location. They would observe the manner in which those groups were carrying out their functions in order to verify that the joint monitoring machinery was working effectively. They would respond to requests for assistance and would use their good offices to resolve any problems that might arise within the monitoring groups, conducting their own investigations and patrolling the whole extent of their assembly areas. Teams would also be deployed at airports, ports and other critical areas, including RENAMO headquarters. The security of United Nations personnel would primarily be the responsibility of the parties that controlled the zone where they were present, although in some cases the military observers would be collocated with armed United Nations troops.

24. The military aspects of the United Nations operation in Mozambique would be inescapably linked with the humanitarian effort. The approximately 110,000 soldiers who come to the assembly areas will be disarmed, demobilized and reintegrated into civil society. They will need food and other support as soon as the assembly areas are established, and there should be special provision in the ONUMOZ budget to cover these costs. The refugees and displaced persons who will inevitably gather around the assembly areas will also require food assistance, which will be provided as part of the humanitarian programme. The relief programmes for assembled soldiers and civil populations in the vicinity will need to be closely coordinated, and it will be desirable to avoid population movements towards the assembly areas. Improved accessibility, the de-mining of roads and the organization of secure transport will be important in this context.

25. An ONUMOZ technical unit, staffed by civilian personnel, will assist the interim Special Representative in the implementation of the demobilization

programme and will collaborate closely with a United Nations Office for the Coordination of Humanitarian Assistance (UNOHAC) (see para. 44 below) on its humanitarian aspects. These will include:

(a) The distribution of food, medicine, health care and other essential services to the assembly areas;

(b) The organization of a database, as well as the issue of personal documents for the demobilized;

(c) The supply of civilian clothing and the organization of transport for the ex-combatants when they leave the assembly areas for their homes;

(d) The establishment of a solid link with the provincial and district authorities responsible for the civilian dimension of the demobilization process.

26. The agreement provides for the withdrawal of foreign troops to be initiated following the entry into force of the cease-fire. Simultaneously, the Supervisory and Monitoring Commission, through the Cease-fire Commission, would assume immediate responsibility "for verifying and ensuring security of strategic and trading routes", of which the most important are the corridors described in paragraph 17 above. The withdrawal of foreign troops started after the agreement's entry into force, and two teams of United Nations military observers have been deployed to monitor it. The withdrawal of the remaining foreign troops before alternative security arrangements were in place would leave the corridors at the mercy of roaming groups of heavily armed irregulars. My interim Special Representative has explored several options, but for political and legal reasons, including the clear provisions of the agreement, it would be extremely difficult to extend the presence of the Malawian and Zimbabwean troops.

27. I have given this question much thought. There is an imperative need to continue to ensure the security of the corridors and other key routes and to protect humanitarian convoys using them. There seems to be no alternative but for ONUMOZ to assume this responsibility. For this function it will be necessary to deploy five logistically self-sufficient infantry battalions. In addition, three logistically self-sufficient engineer companies will be needed, supported, as necessary, by mine-clearing and engineering contractors in order to assist in de-mining and road repair and in the destruction of arms and ammunition not required for the new armed forces. These units must be deployed as rapidly as possible in order to permit early completion of the withdrawal of foreign forces.

28. The following additional elements would be part of ONUMOZ's military component and would provide support to the other components of the mission:

(a) A Headquarters company, including a military police platoon;

(b) A military communications unit to ensure secure communications within the entire mission area for all components of ONUMOZ;

(c) A substantial aviation unit to provide a high degree of air mobility in a devastated country where many of the roads have been made impassable. The aviation unit would be responsible for command and liaison, reconnaissance, investigations, medical evacuation and resupply. It would probably be obtained from commercial sources and would consist of up to 24 rotary and fixed-wing aircraft (utility helicopters, light passenger aircraft, medium passenger/cargo aircraft); additional heavy cargo capacity would be obtained, if needed, on a local charter basis;

(d) A military medical unit to support all ONUMOZ components, including a field hospital and medical evacuation capability. The infantry battalions would include integral medical support;

(e) Three logistic companies, as the conditions in Mozambique make it impossible to rely on a civilian resupply system. Each company would consist of a transport platoon, a supply platoon, a fuel, oil and lubricant platoon and a workshop platoon. One would be located at each of the three regional headquarters;

(f) A movement control company.

V. Possible monitoring of the police

29. While the agreement does not provide a specific role for United Nations civilian police in monitoring the neutrality of the Mozambican police, experience elsewhere suggests that this could be desirable in order to inspire confidence that violations of civil liberties, human rights and political freedom will be avoided. Throughout the peace process, but particularly during the electoral campaign, the presence of a United Nations police component could be most useful, although agreement on this point was not reached in the Rome negotiations. If agreed by the two sides, such a component could be headed by an Inspector General, and consist of up to 128 police officers, deployed in the regions and provincial capitals. It would work in close cooperation with the National Police Affairs Commission and provide technical advice to this body as required. I believe that such a unit would be a valuable addition to ONUMOZ and I therefore intend to ask my interim Special Representative to reopen this matter with the parties and seek their concurrence.

VI. Monitoring of the electoral process and the provision of technical assistance for the elections

30. Under the terms of the agreement, legislative and presidential elections will be held simultaneously one year after the date of signature of the agreement. This

period may be extended if it is determined that circumstances exist that preclude its observance. In the light of recent experience in Angola, I believe it to be of critical importance that the elections should not take place until the military aspects of the agreement have been fully implemented. It is also important that the peace process should not be drawn out indefinitely. I have therefore asked the interim Special Representative to give the highest priority to timely implementation of the cease-fire, the assembly, disarmament and demobilization of troops, and the formation of the new armed forces.

31. In the agreement, the parties agreed to invite the United Nations and other organizations and private individuals to observe the elections from the start of the electoral campaign until the new Government's assumption of office. They also agreed to seek technical and material assistance from the United Nations. On the day the agreement was signed, President Chissano formally addressed appropriate requests to me on these matters (S/24635).

32. The terms of reference of ONUMOZ's electoral component would be as follows:

(a) To verify the impartiality of the National Elections Commission and its organs in all aspects and stages of the electoral process;

(b) To verify that political parties and alliances enjoy complete freedom of organization, movement, assembly and expression, without hindrance and intimidation;

(c) To verify that all political parties and alliances have fair access to State mass media and that there is fairness in the allocation of both the hour and duration of radio and television broadcasts;

(d) To verify that the electoral rolls are properly drawn up and that qualified voters are not denied identification and registration cards or the right to vote;

(e) To report to the electoral authorities on complaints, irregularities and interferences reported or observed, and, if necessary, to request the electoral authorities to take action to resolve and rectify them, as well as conducting its own independent investigation of irregularities;

(f) To observe all activities related to the registration of voters, the organization of the poll, the electoral campaign, the poll itself and the counting, computation and announcement of the results;

(g) To participate in the electoral education campaign;

(h) To prepare periodic reports on the evolution of the electoral process, that will be submitted to the Secretary-General through his interim Special Representative.

33. The electoral component would prepare independent reports about the conduct of the elections. It would establish a special relationship with the National Elections Commission.

34. In carrying out its mandate to verify the impartiality of the National Elections Commission and its organs, the electoral component would evaluate the criteria for the appointment of electoral authorities at the regional and provincial levels. The fairness of challenged actions or significant decisions at both the national and the provincial levels would be similarly evaluated.

35. In order to verify that political parties and alliances enjoy complete freedom of organization, movement, assembly and expression without hindrance and intimidation, the electoral component would establish offices in each provincial capital, with an adequate number of observer teams at each of them. The latter would establish contact with political parties and social organizations at the national and local levels and would visit villages and municipalities throughout the country. They would attend all important political rallies and other relevant activities, and verify the observance by all parties of the electoral law and any code of conduct that might be agreed between the parties or established by the electoral authorities. This activity would be reinforced by a public information campaign about electoral activities, ONUMOZ's objectives and the mechanisms established.

36. To verify that all political parties and alliances have fair access to State mass media, the electoral component would verify the distribution of broadcasting time between parties, the content of news broadcasts and the fairness of tariffs. It would also evaluate complaints received on the use of other public resources for political purposes.

37. In carrying out its mandate to verify that the electoral rolls were properly drawn up, the teams would periodically visit registration centres and evaluate complaints received or irregularities observed. The electoral component would accordingly have to be deployed before the beginning of registration.

38. In order to follow up complaints, irregularities and interferences reported or observed, provincial offices would receive complaints and requests presented by political parties or relevant social organizations, analyse their relevance, compile the information on the issues in question and transmit them to the electoral authorities and/or appropriate parties. Significant threats to the fairness of the elections would be carefully investigated and, if necessary, independently reported. A data bank would record the complaints received and analyses of trends would be produced periodically.

39. ONUMOZ would need to include an Electoral Division headed by a Director, with a total of up to 148 international electoral officers (including two consultants), supported by an appropriate number of United Nations volunteers and international and local support

staff. It should have the following structure:

(a) The Office of the Director (Maputo): a unit that would provide overall direction to the Electoral Division. It would maintain contacts with the Government of Mozambique, RENAMO and the National Elections Commission and the main political parties;

(b) Three Regional Offices, each headed by a Regional Coordinator in the southern, central and northern regions;

(c) Provincial Offices each headed by a provincial coordinator assisted by a team of up to 10 Electoral Officers.

40. During the polling itself, the Electoral Division would require the services of up to 1,200 international observers. I have asked the interim Special Representative to seek the cooperation of regional organizations, governments and non-governmental organizations who intend to send election observers to Mozambique, in order to minimize the number of additional observers who will have to be deployed by the United Nations. It should also be possible to draw on United Nations and other international personnel who will already be in Mozambique for non-electoral purposes. All observers would have to have full access to all stages of the poll. With their help, the Electoral Division would develop a projection of results for internal purposes.

41. When a country for the first time prepares for multi-party elections, it is crucial that its electoral authorities have adequate access to technical assistance and material support. The planning and execution of voter registration and polling presents a formidable challenge to national electoral authorities. In Mozambique adequate legal advice, logistical planning and support would be as important as political commitment of the two parties to ensure free and fair elections. A major national as well as international effort would be required. This would encompass a broad range of needs: vehicles, aircraft, communications, voting booths and material, food, tents, salary for registration and electoral brigades. Legal advice on the drafting of an electoral law and technical guidance on the conduct of elections would be especially essential. Technical assistance, if timely, would help to create an orderly and coherent process. In anticipation of the request from the Government referred to in paragraph 31 above, a United Nations technical mission on electoral matters visited Mozambique in September 1992 and established contacts with the Government. It is envisaged that United Nations consultants will continue to cooperate closely with the national electoral authorities.

42. Specific activities of the United Nations in this area will largely occur outside the immediate mandate of ONUMOZ, albeit in close coordination with its electoral component. It is my intention to provide technical assistance to the electoral authorities through the United Nations Development Programme and other existing mechanisms of the United Nations system. These United Nations activities will have to be coordinated closely by my interim Special Representative with those of other intergovernmental bodies, in particular OAU and the European Community, and with bilateral donors. Some of the donors have already sent preparatory teams to the country with a view to elaborating a comprehensive document on electoral support which would be presented to the forthcoming pledging conference in Rome. The United Nations would be ready to play the main coordinating role for the provision of technical assistance to the whole electoral process in Mozambique.

VII. Plan for the United Nations coordination of the humanitarian aspects of the agreement

43. The character and scope of the United Nations ongoing humanitarian assistance programmes in Mozambique require adjustment following the signing of the agreement, in which the parties undertook to facilitate significantly the provision of humanitarian aid to previously inaccessible areas and called on the United Nations to coordinate the provision of all such assistance. Immediately after the signing of the agreement, I accordingly dispatched a humanitarian assistance mission to Mozambique to assess existing United Nations operations in this area and to devise a more effective United Nations response to the intended expansion of humanitarian activities, with emphasis on the development of an appropriate coordination mechanism.

44. As a result, it is my recommendation that ONUMOZ should have a humanitarian component in the form of a United Nations Office for the Coordination of Humanitarian Assistance, which would be established in Maputo, with suboffices at the regional and provincial levels. It would replace the present office of the United Nations Special Coordinator for Emergency Relief Operations. Headed by the Humanitarian Affairs Coordinator, and under the overall authority of my interim Special Representative, it would function as an integrated component of ONUMOZ. To ensure the proper provision and delivery of relief assistance to an expanded beneficiary population in Mozambique, UNOHAC would coordinate the various humanitarian assistance programmes. Operational agencies and the non-governmental aid community would be asked to provide representatives to work within the United Nations Office for the Coordination of Humanitarian Assistance.

45. It is estimated that, as a result of both the war and the continuing drought, the internally displaced population in Mozambique totals some 3 to 4 million people. At present, about 3 million Mozambicans living in accessible areas are receiving humanitarian assistance.

The signing of the agreement has already created access to additional affected areas, many of which are controlled by RENAMO. As a consequence, nearly 270,000 additional beneficiaries are being provided with humanitarian assistance by the United Nations and by the International Committee of the Red Cross (ICRC), under the terms of the Declaration of Rome on the Principles of Humanitarian Assistance of 15 July 1992. Indications are that the number of additional beneficiaries may reach 500,000 in a matter of months.

46. While 1.4 million of the estimated 1.8 million Mozambican refugees living in neighbouring countries receive assistance, the drought is reported to have caused many other Mozambicans to seek refuge there during the past three months. The expected returnee population can thus be estimated at not less than 1.8 million.

47. The United Nations Office for the Coordination of Humanitarian Assistance will also make available food and other relief for distribution to the soldiers in the assembly areas by a technical unit of ONUMOZ, as described in section IV above. Subsequently, humanitarian aid would be required for the reintegration of demobilized troops into their communities.

VIII. Organizational structure of ONUMOZ

48. The organizational structure of ONUMOZ would be as follows:

(a) Mission headquarters and the Office of the interim Special Representative of the Secretary-General, Maputo. The Office will consist of an Executive Director, a Special Assistant, a Political Adviser, an Information Officer, a Planning and Analysis Officer, a Legal Adviser and both international and locally recruited support staff;

(b) A Military Component with headquarters in Maputo, which would include a Military Observer group, five infantry battalions, one engineer battalion, three logistic companies, a Headquarters company, a movement control company, a communications unit, a medical unit and an air unit (probably from commercial sources). The military component would be headed by a Force Commander with the rank of Major General. There would be three regional offices, as set out in section IV above;

(c) If the parties agree, a police component in Maputo, headed by a Chief Police Observer, who would hold the rank of Chief Superintendent or its equivalent, with three regional offices and staff outposted in provincial towns, as set out in section V above;

(d) An electoral component in Maputo, with three regional offices and provincial offices, as set out in section VI above;

(e) An Office for the Coordination of Humanitarian Assistance in Maputo, with 3 regional offices and 10 provincial offices, as set out in section VII above;

(f) An administrative component in Maputo, with three regional offices, providing support in the areas of finance, personnel, procurement, communication, travel, compensation, building management, property control, translation and interpretation, electronic data processing and security.

IX. Observations and recommendations

49. It is a matter of great satisfaction that an end is at last in sight to the cruel war that has ravaged Mozambique for 14 years. Both the Government and RENAMO deserve to be commended for their statesmanship and diplomatic skill and, above all, for their commitment to their people and their country. I very much hope that in the months ahead they will be guided in their actions by the same spirit of national reconciliation and unity. As the people of Mozambique prepare for democratic multi-party elections, they are starting out on a road that can be either divisive or constructive. It is my fervent hope that the spirit of national unity will also shape the electoral process, and that this will be an opportunity for the people of Mozambique to choose freely the leaders who will jointly work for a better future.

50. The mediators and the observers who have so patiently helped to bring about the agreement also deserve the highest praise. I trust that I can count on their continued political and material support as the peace process evolves.

51. The task which the Government and RENAMO have agreed to ask the United Nations to assume is a large and difficult one. The difficulties derive from the size of the country, the devastated state of its infrastructure, the disruption of its economy by war and drought, the limited capacity of the Government to cope with the new tasks arising from the general peace agreement and the complexity of the processes enshrined in the agreement. An additional dimension derives from the critical importance of the Mozambican corridors for so much of southern Africa. To achieve in one year (of which a month and a half have already passed) the assembly, disarmament and demobilization of the two sides' troops, the formation of new armed forces, the resettlement of 5 to 6 million refugees and displaced persons, the provision of humanitarian relief to all parts of the country and the organization and conduct of elections will require a huge and cooperative effort by the Government and RENAMO and by the international community, with the United Nations in the lead.

52. As will be evident from the present report, I feel obliged to recommend that very substantial resources should be made available for this purpose, especially on the military side. This reflects my conviction that it will not be possible in Mozambique to create the conditions

for a successful election unless the military situation has been brought fully under control. If the United Nations is to undertake the responsibilities entrusted to it by the Mozambicans, what has to be done must be done well, and quickly. But however great the resources the United Nations decides to devote to Mozambique, the general peace agreement will not be implemented unless the Mozambican parties make a determined effort in good faith to honour their commitments. The efforts of the United Nations can only be in support of theirs. In the light of recent experiences elsewhere, the recommendations in the present report may be thought to invite the international community to take a risk. I believe that the risk is worth taking; but I cannot disguise that it exists.

53. On this basis, I recommend to the Security Council that it approve the establishment and deployment of ONUMOZ as set out in the present report, and in particular that it agree to:

(a) The establishment of an Office of the interim Special Representative for Mozambique, with up to 12 international Professional staff, 8 international support staff and an adequate number of locally recruited staff;

(b) The deployment of a military component consisting of a Headquarters company and military police platoon; 354 military observers; 5 logistically self-sufficient infantry battalions, each composed of up to 850 personnel; 1 engineer battalion, with contracted assistance as needed; 3 logistic companies; and air, communications, medical and movement control support units;

(c) The deployment of a civilian technical unit to support the logistic tasks relating to the demobilization programme in the assembly areas, with adequate resources;

(d) The deployment, subject to the concurrence of the parties, of 128 police officers to monitor civil liberties and to provide technical advice to the National Police Affairs Commission;

(e) The deployment of an Electoral Division consisting of up to 148 international electoral officers and support staff, from the start of the electoral component of the peace process, followed by the deployment of up to 1,200 international observers for the elections themselves and the periods immediately preceding and following them;

(f) The deployment of 16 international Professional staff to enable the United Nations Office for the Coordination of Humanitarian Assistance to coordinate and monitor all humanitarian assistance within the regions and provinces of Mozambique;

(g) The deployment of up to 28 international Professional staff, up to 100 United Nations Volunteers, up to 124 international support staff and an adequate number of local staff to provide secretariat functions and administrative support to the military, police (if confirmed), electoral and humanitarian components of ONUMOZ, as well as to the commissions chaired by the United Nations.

54. Preliminary cost estimates for ONUMOZ are contained in an addendum to the present report which is being circulated separately.

Addendum (S/24892/Add.1)

1. As stated in paragraph 54 of my main report (S/24892), I indicated that an addendum to the report would be issued which would contain preliminary cost estimates related to the establishment and deployment of a United Nations Operation in Mozambique (ONUMOZ).

2. Based on the operational plan and general assumptions outlined in my main report, it is estimated that an amount of $331.8 million would be required for the period from inception to 31 October 1993. This amount includes the costs of start-up and acquisition of capital equipment. A breakdown of the estimated cost by main objects of expenditure is provided for information purposes in the annex to the present addendum.

3. It would be my recommendation to the General Assembly that, should the Security Council agree to the establishment and deployment of ONUMOZ, the cost relating thereto should be considered as an expense of the Organization to be borne by Member States in accordance with Article 17, paragraph 2, of the Charter of the United Nations and that the assessment to be levied on Member States be credited to a special account to be established for this purpose.

Annex

Cost estimates by objects of expenditure
(For the period from inception to 31 October 1993)
(Thousands of United States dollars)

Objects of expenditure	
1. Military component	
(a) Observers	19 900
(b) Contingent personnel	97 000
(c) Other costs pertaining to contingents	41 100
2. Civilian police	6 900
3. Civilian staff costs	59 700
4. Premises, rental and maintenance	35 200
5. Vehicle operations	11 000
6. Air operations	26 900
7. Communications and other equipment	11 900
8. Miscellaneous supplies, services, freight and support costs	11 200
9. Programme related to former combatants in the assembly areas	11 000
TOTAL	331 800

Document 27

Security Council resolution establishing ONUMOZ

S/RES/797 (1992), 16 December 1992

The Security Council,

Recalling its resolution 782 (1992) of 13 October 1992,

Recalling also the statement of the President of the Security Council of 27 October 1992, 1/

Having considered the report of the Secretary-General of 3 December 1992 on the United Nations Operation in Mozambique, 2/

Stressing the importance it attaches to the General Peace Agreement for Mozambique 3/ and to the fulfilment by the parties in good faith of the obligations contained therein,

Noting the efforts made so far by the Government of Mozambique and the Resistência Nacional Moçambicana to maintain the cease-fire, and expressing concern over the delays in initiating some of the major tasks arising from the Agreement,

Welcoming the appointment by the Secretary-General of an interim Special Representative for Mozambique who will be in overall charge of United Nations activities in support of the Agreement, as well as the dispatch to Mozambique of a team of twenty-five military observers, as approved by resolution 782 (1992),

Noting the intention of the Secretary-General, in this as in other peace-keeping operations, to monitor expenditures carefully during this period of increasing demands on peace-keeping resources,

1. *Approves* the report of the Secretary-General of 3 December 1992 on the United Nations Operation in Mozambique 2/ and the recommendations contained therein;

2. *Decides* to establish a United Nations Operation in Mozambique as proposed by the Secretary-General and in line with the General Peace Agreement for Mozambique, 3/ and requests the Secretary-General in planning and executing the deployment of the Operation to seek economies through, *inter alia*, phased deployment and to report regularly to the Council on what is achieved in this regard;

3. *Also decides* that the Operation is established for a period until 31 October 1993 in order to accomplish the objectives described in the report of the Secretary-General;

4. *Calls upon* the Government of Mozambique and the Resistência Nacional Moçambicana to cooperate fully with the interim Special Representative of the Secretary-General for Mozambique and with the Operation and to respect scrupulously the cease-fire and all the commitments entered into under the Agreement, and stresses that the full respect of these commitments constitutes a necessary condition for the fulfilment by the Operation of its mandate;

5. *Demands* that all parties and others concerned in Mozambique take all measures necessary to ensure the safety of United Nations and all other personnel deployed pursuant to the present and prior resolutions;

6. *Endorses* the approach in paragraphs 30 and 51 of the report of the Secretary-General as regards the timetable for the electoral process, and invites the Secretary-General to consult closely with all the parties on the precise timing of and preparations for the presidential and legislative elections, as well as on a precise timetable for the implementation of the other major aspects of the Agreement, and to report back to the Council on this as soon as possible, and in any event not later than 31 March 1993;

7. *Calls upon* the Government of Mozambique and the Resistência Nacional Moçambicana to finalize as soon as possible, in close coordination with the interim Special Representative of the Secretary-General, organizational and logistical preparations for the demobilization process;

8. *Encourages* Member States to respond positively to requests made to them by the Secretary-General to contribute personnel and equipment to the Operation;

9. *Also encourages* Member States to contribute voluntarily to United Nations activities in support of the Agreement, and requests United Nations programmes and specialized agencies to provide appropriate assistance and support for the implementation of the major tasks arising from the Agreement;

10. *Requests* the Secretary-General to keep the Security Council informed of developments and to submit a further report to the Council by 31 March 1993;

11. *Decides* to remain actively seized of the matter.

1/ S/24719.

2/ *Official Records of the Security Council, Forty-seventh Year, Supplement for October, November and December 1992,* documents S/24892 and Add.1 and Corr.1.

3/ Ibid., document S/24635 and Corr.1, annex.

Document 28

Letter dated 30 December 1992 from Italy transmitting the conclusions of the Donors Conference for Mozambique, held in Rome on 15 and 16 December 1992

S/25044, 4 January 1993

I have the honour to forward to you the summary of conclusions of the Donors Conference for Mozambique, held in Rome on 15 and 16 December 1992.

I would be grateful if you could have the text circulated as a document of the Security Council.

(*Signed*) Mario SCIALOJA
Ambassador
Chargé d'affaires a.i.

ENCLOSURE

Donors Conference for Mozambique
(*Rome, 15-16 December 1992*)

Summary of conclusions submitted by the Chairman of the Conference

1. Upon the invitation of the Italian Government (see S/24813) and in pursuance of Protocol VII attached to the General Peace Agreement for Mozambique, signed in Rome on 4 October 1992 (S/24635), representatives of the United Nations and of the countries and organizations appearing in annex I to the present summary of conclusions met in Rome on 15 and 16 December 1992.

2. The participants reiterated their deep appreciation to the Mozambican parties for effectively promoting peace in their country. They believe that the Rome peace agreement sets an example on the troubled international scene and must therefore meet with the necessary support by the world community.

3. The participants, taking note of relevant decisions of the United Nations as well as of the report of the Secretary-General on the United Nations operation in Mozambique (S/24892 and Corr.1) and of the statement made by his representative, agreed in considering their endeavours in Rome as duly fitting in the general framework of current efforts by the international community to support and sustain the peace agreement for Mozambique.

4. The participants agreed therefore to adhere to the appeal by the Mozambican parties for emergency pledges in areas specified in the above-mentioned Protocol VII: programmes for the reintegration of displaced persons, refugees and demobilized soldiers; and programmes for the setting up of an electoral process.

5. The participants formed two working groups on the reintegration of refugees, displaced persons and demobilized soldiers and on the electoral process, the conclusions of which are attached in annexes II and III to the present summary of conclusions.

6. The participants took note of a document prepared in Maputo with the assistance of the representatives of some participants, which has met with the agreement of the Mozambican parties. They also took note of other documents submitted to the Conference.

7. The participants agreed on the usefulness of attaching herewith, in annex IV to the present summary of conclusions, a summary on the subjects of refugees, the reintegration of refugees, displaced persons and demobilized soldiers, and the electoral process, which derives from the document referred to in paragraph 6 and which is completed by a document provided by the Office of the United Nations High Commissioner for Refugees on Mozambican refugees. This summary is meant to help donors to assess the destination of their pledges and to coordinate interventions by offering suggested fields of action.

8. In the view of the participants, it would be useful to convene in due time in Maputo a United Nations meeting, enlarged with the participation of interested donors, to identify progress in the follow-up of emergency programmes destined to sustain the peace process, as defined by Protocol VII to the general peace agreement.

9. The participants agreed in requesting the Chairman of the Conference to convey the present summary of conclusions and its attachments to the Secretary-General of the United Nations. The list of pledges can be found in annex IV, appendix 2.

10. Participants expressed their gratitude to the Italian Government for convening the Rome Conference and for its generous and important role in promoting the peace process in Mozambique.

Annex I

List of participating countries and organizations

Chairman:

Mr. Carmelo AZZARA, Under-Secretary of State for Foreign Affairs of Italy

Representative of the Secretary-General of the United Nations:

Mr. J. ELIASSON, Under-Secretary-General for Humanitarian Affairs

Government of Mozambique

Resistência Nacional Moçambicana (RENAMO)

Mediators:

Mr. Mario RAFFAELLI
Mr. A. RICCARDI
Mr. Matteo ZUPPI

Countries:

Australia	Holy See	Russian Federation
Austria	Ireland	Senegal
Belgium	Italy	South Africa
Brazil	Japan	Spain
Canada	Kuwait	Sweden
China	Luxembourg	Switzerland
Denmark	Malawi	United Kingdom of
Finland	Netherlands	Great Britain and
France	New Zealand	Northern Ireland
Germany	Norway	United States of America
Greece	Portugal	Zimbabwe

Commission of the European Communities

Specialized agencies of the United Nations:

Office of the United Nations High Commissioner for Refugees (UNHCR)

Food and Agriculture Organization of the United Nations (FAO)

World Food Programme (WFP)

United Nations Development Programme (UNDP)

United Nations Children's Fund (UNICEF)

World Health Organization (WHO)

Other international organizations:

International Committee of the Red Cross (ICRC)

International Federation of Red Cross and Red Crescent Societies (IFRC)

International Organization for Migration (IOM)

World Bank

Commonwealth Secretariat

Non-governmental organizations:

International Council of Voluntary Agencies

Liaison Committee Non-Governmental Organizations—European Community

Association of West European Parliamentarians for Action against Apartheid (AWEPAA)

Annex II

Report of the Working Group on Refugees and Reintegration

Recognizing the interrelationship between assistance to returning refugees, demobilized soldiers and displaced persons,

Deciding to merge the two working groups on refugees and reintegration,

Welcoming the pledges of support made at the Rome Conference on Mozambique,

Taking note of the Conference documentation,

the joint Working Group on Refugees and Reintegration concluded that the following principles should guide international assistance to humanitarian efforts.

1. While recognizing the specific needs of each target group, the Conference concluded that international cooperation should address the needs of all vulnerable groups in priority areas, without discrimination.

2. There should therefore be integration of programmes for the demobilized (after they have left the assembly points), returning refugees, displaced persons and locally affected populations.

3. There is a clear need for the closest and widest coordination at the most decentralized level possible, not only to avoid duplication of efforts and to allow for the most flexible and transparent programming and implementation possible, but also to promote the goals of the general peace agreement through local participation.

4. The United Nations Office for Humanitarian Assistance Coordination, to be established by the Secretary-General pursuant to the general peace agreement, should serve as the follow-up coordinating mechanism to ensure efficient, transparent and flexible programming and should provide overall coordination of United Nations agencies' operations. In particular, the Office for Humanitarian Assistance Coordination is expected to report regularly on the use of contributions and to provide updated requirements based on a periodic reassessment of humanitarian needs. The UNOHAC regroups all the main players involved: the Mozambican parties to the peace agreements; the organizations of the United Nations system; other international organizations; the donors; and the community of non-governmental organizations (NGOs) (both national and international, the latter numbering well over 150).

5. Consideration could be given to expanding the scope of action of the Reintegration Commission to include, in addition to the demobilized, displaced persons and returnees.

6. It is strongly recommended that a trust fund be established under the umbrella of the United Nations, to which interested donors would contribute. The object of this supplementary fund would be for the execution of field activities in support of reintegration. Donors could contribute to the fund as well as use other funding channels and/or provide in-kind assistance such as food or training.

7. There is great urgency in organizing reintegration assistance, owing to the imminent movement of the demobilized, returning refugees and displaced persons.

8. De-mining (to include all activities from mine detection to mine disposal) is a critical element to be addressed from the earliest days.

9. With regard to the demobilized, there is need for a clear delineation of what is to be covered by the peace-keeping operation.

10. The total amount of food aid necessary for all aspects of reintegration should be included in the overall humanitarian budget.

11. Voluntary repatriation is the most desirable solution for refugees and, with 10 per cent of the Mozambican population having refugee status, voluntary repatriation and reintegration are important elements of the national peace process.

12. Countries hosting refugees deserve great appreciation and are called upon to continue to welcome refugees until repatriation is possible.

13. Organized (as opposed to spontaneous) repatriation should not start until minimal basic life-support conditions in Mozambique are ensured, in order to avoid backflows to countries.

14. All interventions should be "people-oriented", i.e., geared to the needs of the beneficiary population in which women and children represent 80 per cent.

Annex III

Report of the Working Group on the Electoral Process

1. The Working Group on the Electoral Process accepted the broad outlines of the budgetary provisions for the organization and conduct of the elections (see annex IV).

2. The Working Group, however, noted that there were no provisions in the budget for funds for the political parties as indicated in section III of paper No. 1. It reiterated that it was very important that equitable fund-ing be provided for this item in order to ensure the success of the electoral process. To this end, the Working Group decided to request the Government of Italy, through the Chairman, to discuss this issue further with the parties concerned in order to work out practical arrangements for implementation.

3. With respect to the budgetary provisions for the electoral process, the Working Group urged the Mozambican parties to expedite action for the establishment of relevant organs and entities, including the Electoral Commission, in order to facilitate the implementation of projects related to the electoral process.

4. The Working Group was informed by the representative of the Secretary-General of the arrangements envisaged by the Secretary-General to verify and monitor the entire electoral process and to provide technical assistance to the Electoral Commission through the United Nations system. The Working Group decided to request the United Nations to be the coordinator of technical assistance for the entire electoral process in Mozambique.

5. In this connection, the Chairman was asked to request the Secretary-General to facilitate the receipt of contributions through the United Nations.

6. It was also agreed to request the United Nations to coordinate a follow-up mechanism to the Donors Conference for Mozambique in cooperation with the donor community and the parties concerned.

7. The Working Group on the Electoral Process stressed the importance of a long-term approach in the electoral field, facilitating capacity-building and dual objectives of the assistance to be provided.

Annex IV

Donors Conference for Mozambique

Summary based on the official document presented by the Government of Mozambique and RENAMO

Rome, 15-16 December 1992

Explanatory note

The amount of external financing required for 1993—up to the elections—was based on the official document presented by the Government of Mozambique together with RENAMO.

The figures were confirmed and agreed upon by the donors at the meeting of the World Bank Consultative Group, held in Paris, on 8 to 10 December 1992.

The estimated costs are presented in Table A and are summarized in the papers attached to the present summary.

The total financing requirements, amounting to $402.9 million do not include emergency and commercial food aid, since it has already been considered at the meeting of the World Bank Consultative Group.

Paper No. 1 describes the financing requirements for the electoral process. The estimated cost of $76.9 million includes $10 million for contingencies. Funds for political parties are not included.

Paper No. 2 describes the financing requirements for the emergency and reintegration programme for displaced persons, returnee population and demobilized soldiers. The financing requirements of $265 million includes $70 million as estimated cost for logistics. In paper No. 2 are also described the activities and financing requirements related to the reintegration of demobilized personnel into civilian life (see appendix to the present summary). The estimated cost of $61 million does not include the Government contribution of $22.5 million and costs related to the 49 assembly areas, which are expected to be covered by the United Nations Operation in Mozambique (ONUMOZ).

Paper No. 3 describes the support to organized refugee repatriation. A total of 100,000 refugees were considered as beneficiaries of an organized repatriation through May to December 1993. The estimated financing requirements of $10.5 million are included in the above-mentioned costs for logistics.

Additional documentation and related costs for repatriation of refugees in 1993—spontaneous or partially assisted—could be presented for discussion by UNHCR during the Conference.

Table A
Implementation of the general peace agreement: financing requirements

	Millions of dollars
Electoral process	76.90
Emergency and reintegration programme for displaced persons, returnee population and demobilized soldiers	326.00
Out of which:	
– Reintegration of demobilized personnel	61.00
– Logistics	59.50
– Support to organized repatriation*	10.50
TOTAL	402.90

*Additional documentation and related costs for repatriation of refugees in 1993—spontaneous or partially assisted—could be presented for discussion by UNHCR during the Conference.

Paper No. 1
Electoral process

Target population: 8 million persons
Estimated cost: $66.9 million
Contingencies: $10.0 million

Note: Funds for political parties are not included.

Electoral process

I. *Foreword*

Protocol III to the general peace agreement (GPA) establishes criteria and procedures for elections as well as supervision and monitoring over execution and final results.

The elections for the President and the National Assembly will take place one year after the GPA has entered into force.

Statistics show that out of a population of 17.1 million in the year 1993, 8 million persons (18-year-old and older) shall be entitled to vote.

II. *Document component*

The official document presented by the two parties foresees the establishment of a specific technical unit (not included in the GPA), which will report to the National Elections Commission and will be in charge of administrative, operational, legal, information and civic education services.

It is estimated that the registration procedures of the voters will begin five months after the GPA enforcement, will take four months and will mobilize 7,000 registration/polling personnel. The draft Electoral Law establishes that citizens should vote where they have registered.

A lump sum of $3.9 million is allocated for the elections education campaign. Maximum objectivity for its proper utilization should be guaranteed. Due to the high rate of illiteracy in the country, utilization of media and broadcasting in local idioms should be provided for.

ONUMOZ shall be responsible to verify that all political parties have fair access to State mass media and broadcasting and it shall also evaluate and monitor the use of other public resources for political purpose.

As the country prepares for the first time ever multiparty elections, it is crucial that its electoral authority be adequately supported with technical assistance, training of the personnel involved in the process and materials.

An adequate level of legal advice, logistical planning and support will be as important as the political commitments of the Government and RENAMO to ensure free and fair elections. For this purpose, the estimated financing requirements are $2 million for training and $2.9 million for technical assistance.

Taking into consideration the fact that Mozambique

covers an area of 800,000 square kilometres and that its communication has been devastated by more than 15 years of civil war, it is of paramount importance to meet the financing requirements necessary to ensure means of transportation for the electoral process. The estimated cost is $21.6 million for air transportation and $9.8 million for surface transportation.

The provisional general budget (see Table B hereafter) is $66.9 million, plus $10 million for contingencies, which is necessary to avert sudden problems in the most delicate phase of the electoral process and to cover, among other things, the cost of fuel supply, the country importing all its fuel.

III. Critical aspects

Due to the chosen electoral system (proportional system with representatives related to the population density) and bearing in mind that over 60 per cent of Mozambicans are lacking identity cards, a registration exercise must precede the elections.

The GPA states that the National Elections Commission should subsidize and support the political parties for their electoral campaign. This component is not included in the provisional general budget. In this respect, an increase of approximately $2 to 5 million of the estimated allowance for the elections education campaign should be envisaged and managed by the United Nations as part of the electoral process.

Wider seems to be the issue of funds for political parties. Protocol II to the GPA provides for guarantee of access to mass media, public funds and facilities.

Protocol VII to the GPA states that RENAMO, immediately after the GPA signature, should act as a political party, subject to registration in accordance with the Electoral Law. It further states that an adequate share of the funds pledged at the Rome Conference should be reserved for the activities of the political parties. The funds should be considered additional to those foreseen for the electoral campaign and possibly made immediately available.

A special and particular (time-limited) commitment by the donors community should be ensured to support the democratic process in Mozambique, even in the absence of international rules on this matter.

A steering committee, composed of the United Nations, the Mozambican Government, RENAMO, donors' representatives, and later integrated by other parties, could be envisaged. The necessary resources, both in kind and in cash, should be provided.

Counterpart funds should be utilized as much as possible; in this regard, special regulations should be established.

Additional support to political parties should be made available through scholarships, both in third countries as well as in Mozambique, together with short courses and seminars on political parties and related disciplines run by neutral rapporteurs.

Table B
Financing requirements

	Millions of dollars
Running costs of electoral organization	8.10
Electoral material	21.60
Air transportation	12.00
Surface transportation	9.80
Civic education	3.90
Training of electoral personnel	2.00
Equipment	1.30
Constituency identification	0.70
Technical assistance	2.90
Food rations, tents, etc.	4.60
Contingencies	10.00
TOTAL	76.90

Note: The above-mentioned financing requirements do not include funds for political parties.

Paper No. 2
Emergency and reintegration programme for displaced persons, returnee population and demobilized soldiers

Target population: 4,566,100 persons
Out of which:
– Displaced and affected persons 3 659 100
– Returnee population 800 000
– Demobilized soldiers and their families 107 000
Estimated cost: $265 million

Emergency and reintegration programme for displaced persons, returnee population and demobilized soldiers

I. Beneficiaries

After the long civil war that Mozambique has been suffering since 1987, it was granted an internationally supported emergency status. After periodical evaluation of the emergency programmes, more adequate strategies to face the situation have been designed.

According to an interministerial committee assisted by United Nations agencies, it is estimated that the actual amount of beneficiaries being supported by ongoing emergency programmes is approximately 4 million people, out of which about 3.7 million people have been affected by drought and civil war. The remaining 300,000 represent the refugee population that is supposed to repatriate by May 1993.

UNHCR data indicate that 500,000 additional Mozambicans could repatriate between May and December 1993, bringing the total amount of returnees to be assisted next year to 800,000.

The GPA has prompted new migratory flows of various ethnic groups back to their areas of origin.

Such migrations are likely to continue throughout next year and could become a major political issue in view of the forthcoming elections. After the GPA, resettlement of a considerable number of returnees and displaced persons may occur.

The present situation, as far as the location of groups and the migratory dynamics are concerned, is shown on the attached maps. [Maps appear on pages 166-167.]

The demobilized soldiers, together with their families, will be reintegrated in the social and productive life of the country.

Therefore, the total target population amounts to approximately 4.6 million persons, out of which 3,693,000 are displaced and affected persons, 800,000 are returnees and 107,000 are demobilized soldiers. Taking into account the families of demobilized soldiers, the target population will increase up to 5 million people. The activities related to the demobilization process are described in appendix 1 to the present summary.

II. *Activities*

The breakdown of programme components, relevant activities and related cost estimates is as follows:

Supply of goods

– Emergency food aid to beneficiaries, totalling up to $55 million, is not included in the budget since it has already been considered at the meeting of the World Bank Consultative Group. This figure takes into account the existing food stocks and the incoming stocks already financed in response to the drought appeal of May 1992. Future needs will be established in May 1993, since they will depend on the results of the 1992/93 crop season.
– Selected seeds and tools for agriculture to be distributed next summer for their utilization in the next agricultural campaigns (March-September 1993). First assistance packages, including clothes and cooking utensils. Estimated cost: $105 million.
– The estimated cost of logistics is $70 million. It includes private transportation, airlift, warehousing, spare parts and related technical assistance.

Provision of basic services and infrastructures

– Primary health care and nutrition services for the affected population in the higher density areas. Estimated cost: $15 million.
– Basic education services, including rehabilitation of related infrastructures, supply of books and materials, one year salaries for teachers in the most affected areas. Estimated cost: $2 million.
– Rural water supply schemes (including small district centres) through implementation of hand-pumping wells and rehabilitation of small water schemes. Estimated cost: $4 million.
– Social activities related to children in difficult circumstances and other vulnerable and marginalized groups. Estimated cost: $2 million.
– Urgent rehabilitation of feeder roads and bridges, essential to facilitate internal migration, distribution of food and first assistance goods, registration and polling associated with the election. Estimated cost: $20 million.
– Implementation of social and productive activities in the most affected areas to support the process of reconciliation among the concerned groups. The activities will require close cooperation and involvement of local authorities and concerned communities. Estimated cost: $45 million.
– Support to refugees' organized repatriation for an amount of $10.5 million is also included in the figure for logistics. The related activities are described in annex II.

Institutional support

Technical assistance and operational support should be planned to properly deal with the reintegration process and the direct support to returnees, displaced persons and demobilized soldiers and their families, involving local authorities, bilateral donors and United Nations agencies. Estimated cost is up to $2 million.

III. *General recommendations for programme management and coordination*

In order to build a solid basis for national reconciliation in Mozambique, relief and humanitarian assistance should be an integral part of the rehabilitation and reconstruction process.

Consistent with this approach the Rome Conference should propose the adoption of the following key strategies:
– Relief operations should be carried out in a general framework of mid-term economic and social rehabilitation.
– The reintegration programme should be directed towards the entire community into which displaced persons, returnees and demobilized soldiers will

resettle, with an even distribution of benefits among the different social groups.

- Programme development should start at the community level, based on available local and human resources. Local organizations (both formal and spontaneous) should be involved in the definition and implementation of the programme.
- Programme activities should avail themselves of existing institutions and related infrastructures without duplicating them or overlapping responsibilities.
- Priority should be given to provinces and districts with high concentration of returnees, displaced persons and demobilized populations.

To implement the above-mentioned strategy, the following management and coordination mechanisms should be envisaged:

- Local governments at district level, local associations, community representatives (including traditional ones) should be responsible for planning, implementing and evaluating programme activities.
- Technical and financial support to the process should be provided by national non-governmental organizations (NGOs) and international cooperation through specific agreements with local governments.
- At the provincial level, existing intersectorial structures assisted by the United Nations Office for Humanitarian Assistance Coordination, NGOs, bilateral and multilateral agencies should be responsible for coordination, supervision and control of the activities undertaken as well as for the implementation of wider or more complex rehabilitation activities.
- At the national level, an interministerial body assisted by the United Nations Office for Humanitarian Assistance Coordination, with the participation of bilateral and multilateral agencies, should be responsible for global programme coordination and supervision as well as for the strengthening of global and sectorial policies and manpower training.
- Periodical plans of action, of a duration of three to four months, should be elaborated at district, provincial and national levels, and follow an agreed standard procedure.
- Programme implementation at different levels should be discussed by the concerned entities in ad hoc seminars to be held at district, provincial and national levels.
- Periodical reports should be prepared by district and province authorities and transmitted through the concerned authorities to the United Nations Office for Humanitarian Assistance Coordination.
- At the international level, a special steering committee, composed of the United Nations organizations, the major donors, should examine periodically the programme implementation and provide global programme guidance.

Table C
Financing requirements

	Millions of dollars
Selected seeds and tools and first assistance packages	105.00
Logistics	70.00
Primary health-care and nutrition	15.00
Education	2.00
Water supply	4.00
Vulnerable groups	2.00
Repair of roads and bridges	20.00
Social and productive activities	45.00
Institutional support	2.00
TOTAL	265.00

Paper No. 3
Support to organized refugee repatriation

Beneficiaries: 100,000 refugees who will return through organized repatriation during the period from May to December 1993.

Total cost: $10,500,000

Note: Additional documentation and related costs for the repatriation of refugees in 1993—spontaneous or partially assisted—could be presented for discussion by UNHCR during the Conference.

Support to organized refugee repatriation

According to United Nations estimates, there are approximately 1.7 million Mozambican refugees. The geographical distribution of the refugees is as follows:

Malawi	1 100 000
South Africa	250 000
	(without refugee status)
Swaziland	25 000
United Republic of Tanzania	72 000
Zambia	24 000
Zimbabwe	230 000
Other countries	1 000
TOTAL	1 702 000

DISPLACED AND AFFECTED PERSONS

September 1992 – Data from the United Nations Special Coordinator
for Emergency Relief Operations

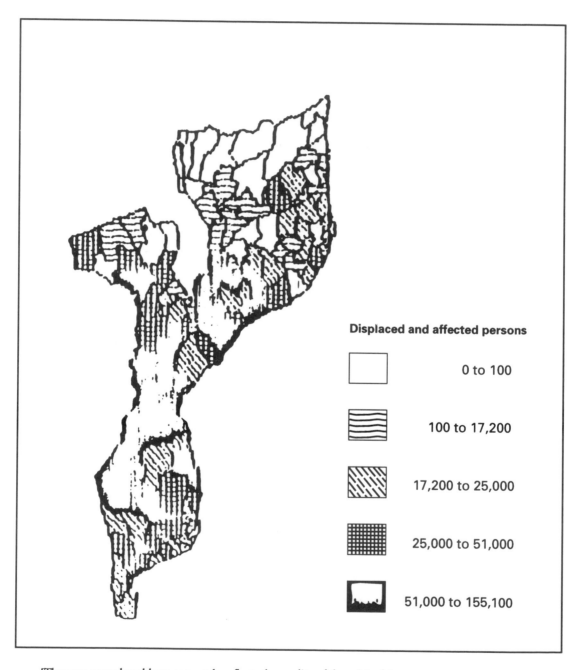

[The map reproduced here accurately reflects the quality of the original.]

RETURNEES

December 1992 – Data from the Office of the United Nations
High Commissioner for Refugees

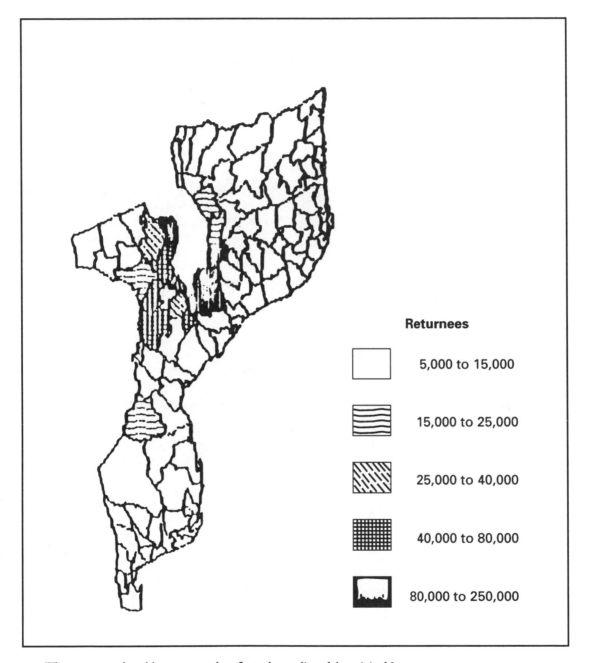

Returnees

5,000 to 15,000

15,000 to 25,000

25,000 to 40,000

40,000 to 80,000

80,000 to 250,000

[The map reproduced here accurately reflects the quality of the original.]

It is estimated that approximately 1,322,000 refugees will repatriate and that their distribution within the different provinces in Mozambique will be as follows:

Cabo Delgado	10 000
Manica (nine districts)	248 000
Niassa (two districts)	40 000
Sofala (three districts)	102 000
Tete (seven districts)	702 000
Zambézia (two districts)	220 000

At the present time it is difficult to foresee how repatriation will take place. It is estimated that a high number of refugees will repatriate spontaneously, without major need for UNHCR assistance.

Approximately 800,000 refugees might return during 1993. Among them about 100,000 could avail themselves of organized repatriation, expected to take place during the period from May to December 1993 (the above-mentioned figures must however be verified after the Rome Conference).

Refugees who remain in the host countries will not be considered in the Rome Conference since they are assisted by ongoing programmes.

I. *Activities*

Activities to be undertaken under the repatriation programme are summarized hereafter.

1. *Gathering of information and preparatory activities within host countries*

These activities include: providing information to refugees on repatriation strategies and procedures; survey of refugees in host countries for the preparation of repatriation, including survey on choice of districts in which refugees want to repatriate; planning of transportation and other activities that may facilitate organized repatriation.

2. *Documentation*

Activities to provide refugees with the proper personal documentation needed for repatriation.

3. *Health*

All refugees who will repatriate through organized schemes will undergo health controls, which will be recorded in an ad hoc personal booklet. During repatriation, health assistance will be provided to all refugees with special assistance given to vulnerable groups. After arrival to the districts of final destination a strict coordination with local health personnel will be ensured.

4. *Distribution of assistance packages*

At the time of departure assistance packages will be given to each repatriating family. Packages could include:

– Food rations for a two-month period
– Materials and equipment to build traditional shelters
– Domestic utensils
– Tools and seeds

The composition of the packages will be defined after the survey mentioned in subsection 1 above.

5. *Transportation*

Road, maritime or railway transportation will be guranteed. Some air transportation can be provided.

6. *Legal assistance*

Legal assistance and activities to ensure the respect of human rights will be provided in the districts of repatriation.

The estimated cost of the above-mentioned activities, which will be carried out during 1993, is $10.5 million. This amount indicates only the additional cost estimated for refugees' organized repatriation necessary to support the peace process in application of the GPA.

The above-mentioned activities should be carried out under the responsibility of UNHCR, which will operate directly or through executing agencies. No transit camps are foreseen. In the case of long journeys, humanized stop-overs will be organized.

II. *Coordination between repatriation and reintegration*

The repatriation process, carried out under the responsibility of UNHCR, will be coordinated with the activities carried out by other United Nations agencies, bilateral cooperation and NGOs. All repatriation activities will be thoroughly planned to guarantee that transportation will take place only after the preliminary reintegration activities necessary for the reception of refugees are implemented in the provinces and districts of final destination.

Reintegration activities for repatriated people are indicated in paper No. 2. At the district level, there will be no special services for refugees/repatriated. In order to facilitate the reconciliation process, emergency assistance, food distribution and provision of basic services should be ensured by local authorities, without discrimination, to all categories of beneficiaries: repatriated, displaced, demobilized and resident population.

Appendix 1
Reintegration of demobilized personnel into civilian life

Beneficiaries: 107,000 demobilized
Financial requirements: $61 million

Reintegration of demobilized personnel into civilian life

I. Foreword

Protocol IV to the GPA regulates the demobilization of Government armed forces and RENAMO military personnel that will not be integrated in the new national army.

The demobilization process has been divided into two stages:

- Phase I, starting with the concentration of troops in the assembly areas and ending with their transportation to the destination of their choice. It includes the surrender of weapons, the feeding, clothing, health care, transportation and severance payment, in addition to the running costs of the Reintegration Commission, and management expenses for the demobilization of civil components.
- Phase II, starting after the transportation of the demobilized to their chosen destinations, including training and other aspects related to their reintegration into social and economic life.

Military personnel from the Government and RENAMO to be demobilized are approximately 107,000.

The estimated cost of the programme is $83.5 million. This figure includes a contribution of $22.5 million to cover six-month severance indemnities to demobilized personnel. The financing requirements are therefore $61 million.

II. Activities

Phase I

The relevant activities and related costs of the programme have been envisaged as follows:

- Food, health care, registration, identification and logistics for the assembly areas. Estimated cost: $10 million.
- Transition to civilian life through distribution of civilian clothes ($1.5 million), transportation to the chosen districts ($24 million), payment of six-

month indemnities ($22.5 million), running costs of the Reintegration Commission ($1.5 million), expenses for coordination of civil components ($0.5 million).

Phase II

Reintegration into social and economic life envisages the following activities:

- Short-term technical training courses and scholarships ($11 million).
- Distribution of kits for micro-entrepreneurial activities ($8.7 million).
- Special programmes for disabled soldiers and vulnerable groups ($4 million).
- Participation to agricultural rehabilitation projects (related costs are included in paper No. 2).

Table D
Financing requirements

		Millions of dollars
Running costs for the assembly areas 1/		10.00
Transition to civilian life:		
Transportation	24.00	
Distribution of clothes 1/	1.50	
Management costs of the Reintegration Commission	1.50	
Demobilization indemnities 2/	22.50	
		49.50
Technical unit management costs		0.50
Social and economic reintegration:		
Technical and professional training	6.50	
Equipment and distribution of kits	9.00	
Scholarships	4.20	
Disabled soldiers	2.10	
Vulnerable groups	1.70	
		23.50
TOTAL 3/		83.50
Financing requirements		61.00

1/ Costs covered by ONUMOZ.
2/ Costs covered by the Government of Mozambique.
3/ Not including de-mining costs estimated at $1,500 per linear kilometre.

	Non-food aid	Food aid 2/
Australia 3/, 7/	1.13	4.52
Austria 6/	2.00	
Belgium	0.16	
Commonwealth Secretariat	0.20	
Canada 3/		15.66
Denmark	8.00	
European Community	71.09	25.96
Finland	1.56	
France	6.00	1.87
Germany	16.60	
Italy	107.53	6.65
Japan 3/	1.00	
Luxembourg	0.19	
Netherlands	13.59	
Norway 3/	8.00	
Portugal 4/	5.23	
South Africa 5/	3.44	
Spain	3.20	
Sweden	22.00	
Switzerland 3/	12.00	

(*continued*)

	Non-food aid	Food aid 2/
United Kingdom 3/, 4/	4.71	
United States	20.00	25.00
Subtotal	307.63	
ONUMOZ	11.05	
TOTAL	318.68	79.66

1/ In the case of pledges expressed in currencies other than dollars, the conversion rate utilized in this list refers to 16 December 1992.
2/ Several donors confirmed in their statements food aid pledges already announced at the meeting of the World Bank Consultative Group (Paris, 8-10 December 1992) and have therefore been reported for record purposes, without any pretension of completeness.
3/ Countries which expressed their willingness to increase their commitments and to communicate their pledges as soon as their respective 1993 budget lines are definitively approved.
4/ Portugal and the United Kingdom have announced a further contribution for the formation of the new Mozambican Army of respectively $15 and 3.14 million.
5/ Estimates only.
6/ Through UNICEF.
7/ Already pledged at the meeting of the World Bank Consultative Group.

*

* *

In addition, the United Nations system (Secretariat and specialized agencies) have indicated that they will pursue emergency assistance for Mozambique in the framework of pertinent United Nations decisions.

Document 29

Letter dated 7 January 1993 from RENAMO President Afonso Dhlakama to the Secretary-General requesting urgent deployment of United Nations troops to Mozambique

Not issued as a United Nations document

As the President of RENAMO, I wish to appeal to you with regard to the implementation of the FRELIMO-RENAMO Peace Accord signed in Rome last October 4, 1992.

It was understood at the time, that with immediate effect, the United Nations would send their peace-keeping forces to oversee the disbanding of both armies and the formation of the country's new Defence Force through to free and fair elections. The Mozambican Security Council has approved the arrival of the UN troops and the announcement has been made that the UN has authorised 7,500 troops and civilians to monitor the cease-fire and election processes in Mozambique.

However, three months have gone by unmonitored and that in itself could constitute the beginning of a new war. RENAMO has no interest in this and thus I appeal to the United Nations who have a mandate in this regard to prevent this from happening.

FRELIMO is violating the conditions established in the Peace Accord by demobilizing 15,000 troops and a further 3,000 SNASP members to reinforce the police force. The police force is being reinforced without any supervision and could act from a strengthened pseudo-military position. Until now, RENAMO has patiently awaited the UN's intervention but these provocations cannot go unnoticed much longer especially because they are being further compounded by incoming millions of dollars from Western Governments and there is no surveillance of how these funds are being utilized. There is nothing stopping FRELIMO from forming its own private army of mercenaries. In Africa money can buy just about anything.

FRELIMO is setting the stage to ensure their stay in power by force if needs be. Whilst RENAMO is not afraid of FRELIMO sabotaging the elections, RENAMO will not partake in the election program until such time as the conditions which guarantee the safety of the population and the process of free and democratic elections, as per the Peace Accord, are adhered to. In the past RENAMO had to resort to the force of arms to bring about the desired change but now we appeal to an Organization such as yourselves, to please take note of the Mozambican case before it is too late and there is a blood bath like in Angola.

We suggest an initial contingent of approximately 65% of your total envoys be sent within this month so the immediate disbanding of the FRELIMO and RENAMO armies, and the formation of the new army, can take place under UN supervision. The present situation constitutes a high security risk as fighting could break out at any given time thus making two years of negotiations for peace in Mozambique and the Agreement which has been achieved a futile exercise. RENAMO does not want this.

Furthermore, the process for elections is being delayed and election date will have to be postponed for RENAMO will not partake in elections until all the agreed conditions are met. Time for a fair political program has to be allowed.

Assured of your understanding and promptness in this matter,

Yours faithfully,

(*Signed*) President Afonso DHLAKAMA

Document 30

Letter dated 22 January 1993 from the Secretary-General to Mr. Dhlakama on the status of the establishment of ONUMOZ

Not issued as a United Nations document

I wish to acknowledge your letter of 7 January 1993 which was delivered to me by hand of Mr. James Jonah, Under-Secretary-General for Political Affairs, upon his return to Headquarters. I was encouraged to learn from his account of the meeting in Gorongosa of your firm determination to see the peace process in Mozambique brought to a successful conclusion.

Immediately after approval by the Security Council of the initial composition of the United Nations Operation in Mozambique (ONUMOZ) on 18 January 1993, I gave instructions to expedite the deployment of its military component. Priority will be given to sending, by the end of next week, some 100 United Nations military observers to verify the first phase of the assembly of Government and RENAMO troops. An ONUMOZ infantry battalion, contributed by Italy, is expected to be installed in Mozambique by mid-February, with the four remaining infantry units to follow shortly thereafter. Plans are underway to fully establish all military elements within two or three months.

As you may be aware, the regrettable delay in the deployment of the first elements of ONUMOZ has been largely due to the late approval by both Mozambican parties of my recommendations about the initial composition of the United Nations military force. The concurrence of RENAMO was received by my interim Special Representative only on 11 January 1993, and I very much hope that RENAMO's reply to my proposal for the second list of troop-contributing countries will be forthcoming shortly.

Meanwhile, it would be important to proceed, without delay, with the first stage of cantonment and demobilization of troops, a crucial element in the peace process.

Please be assured that I will continue to do everything to ensure maximum international support for the peace process in Mozambique. The level of such support will of course be closely coordinated with the steps taken by the Mozambican parties towards full implementation of the Rome Agreements. I would also like to reiterate my conviction about the interrelationship between the various aspects of the peace plan. Without prompt demobilization and formation of the new armed forces, conditions will not exist for successful elections in Mozambique.

Yours sincerely,

(*Signed*) Boutros BOUTROS-GHALI

Document 31

Letter dated 30 January 1993 from Italy's Minister for Foreign Affairs to the Secretary-General on the creation of a trust fund to sustain political parties in Mozambique

Not issued as a United Nations document

I wish to convey to you, also in light of the reports coming from Maputo, the sense of urgency that, in my opinion, should now characterize the operation in Mozambique, an operation which you appropriately suggested with a far-sighted vision of the difficult reality of that country. It is true that the cease-fire continues to be observed; it is urgent, however, to begin the process of demobilization of the armed forces.

In this context, the Italian Government deems it essential to support the process of transformation of RENAMO into a political party. For the time being, this process is proceeding in a positive manner, with the result that the first office of RENAMO has just been inaugurated in Maputo. However, a timely intervention by the U.N. peace-keeping forces remains of utmost importance.

On the one hand, the presence of peace-keeping forces will hopefully serve to provide the most tangible assurance of the compliance by all parties with the Peace Agreement signed in Rome. On the other, I hope that the Organization will soon register the agreement reached by the Mozambican parties, in margin to the recent Conference of Donor Countries in Rome, on the issue of the allocation of funds made available by said Conference in order to finance the electoral process.

In other words, it is necessary to meet the expectations of the Mozambican parties that a trust fund under the United Nations management be created to sustain the political parties at this stage of birth for democracy.

In this connection, the Italian Government wishes to continue to support the peace process in Mozambique in cooperation with the United Nations. I address you in this spirit, aware of the numerous tasks you are currently facing.

With my best regards,
(*Signed*) Emilio COLOMBO

Document 32

Letter dated 10 February 1993 from the Secretary-General to Italy's Minister for Foreign Affairs on the status of the establishment of ONUMOZ and on the General Trust Fund for Electoral Observation

Not issued as a United Nations document

I wish to acknowledge receipt of your letter of 30 January 1993 concerning the United Nations Operation in Mozambique (ONUMOZ). I share your sense of urgency concerning the establishment of ONUMOZ.

For this reason, even before approval of the budget for ONUMOZ, I have decided to expedite the deployment of the military component of the Mission. By the end of this week the United Nations will have more than 100 military observers on the ground and, thanks to the prompt action of your Government, transportation arrangements for the Italian contingent are well underway. I expect that other formed units of United Nations military observers will soon follow. I also secured, through my personal intervention, the agreement of RENAMO to the appointment of Major-General da Silva as Force Commander of ONUMOZ, and he is expected to take up his command shortly.

You have also drawn my attention to the need to meet the expectations of the Mozambican parties that a trust fund be created, under United Nations management, to sustain the political parties at this stage of the birth of democracy.

Based on the advice of the Legal Counsel, we are now in a position to initiate action for the establishment of a trust fund for the electoral process, in the context of the Rome Agreement and the relevant decisions of the Security Council and General Assembly.

In the meantime, the United Nations will welcome arrangements by which contributions can be made through the General Trust Fund for Electoral Observation established in 1992, pursuant to General Assembly resolution 46/137, earmarked for the purposes indicated in Protocol VII of the General Peace Agreement signed in Rome on 4 October 1992.

Please accept, Mr. Minister, the assurances of my highest consideration.

(*Signed*) Boutros BOUTROS-GHALI

Document 33

Report of the Secretary-General on ONUMOZ

S/25518, 2 April 1993

Introduction

1. After considering my report of 3 December 1992 (S/24892 and Corr.1 and Add.1), the Security Council by its resolution 797 (1992) of 16 December 1992 established a United Nations Operation in Mozambique (ONUMOZ). The present report is in response to paragraphs 6 and 10 of that resolution, in which I was requested to keep the Security Council informed of developments, particularly of the timetable for the electoral process, and to submit a further report by 31 March 1993.

2. The specific mandate of ONUMOZ, as set out in paragraph 18 of my report of 3 December 1992 (S/24892) and approved by the Security Council in paragraph 1 of resolution 797 (1992), consists of four distinct but closely related sets of objectives: political, military, electoral and humanitarian. There has been progress in each of these areas, although not always rapidly enough for the demands of the situation.

I. Deployment of the military component of the operation

3. The operational plan for ONUMOZ contained in my previous report to the Security Council provided for verification of cease-fire arrangements and other military aspects of the peace process in Mozambique to be carried out mainly by teams of United Nations military observers. These would work with, but remain separate from, the monitoring groups composed of representatives of the two Mozambican parties at each location. The General Peace Agreement (S/24635, annex) also required that the withdrawal of foreign troops begin upon the entry into force of the cease-fire. The Security Council approved my recommendation that ONUMOZ assume transitional responsibility for security in corridors in order to protect humanitarian convoys using them, until the formation of the Mozambican unified army. The ONUMOZ military component will need to have, in particular, five logistically self-sufficient units to carry out this responsibility.

4. Following the adoption of resolution 797 (1992), there was considerable debate in Mozambique on what it would mean to have United Nations troops present in the country, and especially about the effect on national sovereignty. It was clear that time was needed to overcome uncertainties and resolve disagreements. This also resulted in considerable delay in the approval by both parties of the initial list of troop-contributing countries.

5. Furthermore, Mr. Dhlakama, the President of the Resistência Nacional Moçambicana (RENAMO) wrote me on 7 January 1993 to say that he could not agree to the cantonment and demobilization of RENAMO troops until at least a substantial number of United Nations troops were deployed. He views their presence in certain RENAMO areas as a guarantee that another party could not take advantage of the demobilization of RENAMO forces. This interpretation of the United Nations military contingents' role goes beyond the intention of the original deployment plan and imposes new, unforeseen tasks on United Nations troops. As for the Government, it asked my Special Representative in January for a wider deployment of ONUMOZ forces so that the movements of RENAMO and Government forces could be monitored equally.

6. Following his appointment as Force Commander of ONUMOZ, Major-General Lélio Gonçalves Rodrigues da Silva (Brazil) assumed his duties on 14 February 1993. Meanwhile, the delays in the approval of the list of troop-contributing countries resulted in the rotation of the ONUMOZ military observers only in the third week of January. By that time, only five of the original 25 military observers which had been mandated by Security Council resolution 782 (1992) of 13 October 1992 still remained in Mozambique. However, by mid-March some 154 military observers drawn from 12 countries were deployed at three regional headquarters (Nampula, Beira and Matola) and in Maputo. Of these, some 102 observers have been formed into teams and are ready to take up their assignments immediately in the assembly areas. In the meantime, ONUMOZ military observers are engaged in verification of cease-fire violations and limited monitoring and reconnaissance of the assembly areas. It should be noted, however, that the shortage of aircraft, vehicles, office accommodation and communication equipment limits their activities, for reasons mentioned in paragraph 46 below.

7. With regard to formed military units, much planning and preparation had been done in anticipation of their deployment. In March, reconnaissance parties from various troop-contributing countries inspected their respective deployment areas and completed assessments of their tasks and resources requirements. It is envisaged that infantry battalions will be allocated as follows: Nampula corridor – Bangladesh; Beira corridor – Italy;

Tete corridor – Botswana; Limpopo corridor – Zambia; and National Highway – Uruguay. Support elements of engineers, logistics, movement control, communications, medical and air support will be deployed at ONUMOZ central and regional headquarters.

8. The phased induction plan for United Nations formed units has undergone several major adjustments. There have been administrative delays both within the United Nations, and also by troop-contributing countries. Although I began to approach potential contributors for the Mozambican operation as early as September, the final composition of ONUMOZ military units has not yet been completed. Some countries which several months ago signalled their intention to provide troops to this operation only recently informed the Secretariat of their readiness to dispatch them to Mozambique. I have directed that every effort be made to hasten the deployment of the ONUMOZ military component. The bulk of infantry units will arrive in April, and the full deployment of the force should be complete in May 1993.

9. Meanwhile, a self-sufficient Italian contingent of approximately 1,030, which includes the infantry, a logistical subunit, a medical element and an air wing (which is being provided at no cost to the United Nations), has been completely deployed in the Beira corridor. This contingent became fully operational on 1 April 1993. An advance party of the Bangladeshi contingent has also arrived.

10. A major problem for ONUMOZ military deployment is the lack of freedom of movement. A status of forces agreement has yet to be approved. In its absence, ONUMOZ has to provide advance information on all movements of United Nations military personnel. This requirement imposes restrictions on the effectiveness of the mission.

II. Establishment of assembly areas and demobilization

11. Under the terms of the General Peace Agreement (S/24635, annex), the cease-fire in Mozambique, which came into effect on 15 October 1992, was to be followed rapidly by the separation of the two sides' forces and their concentration in certain assembly areas. Of these, 29 were to be designated for the Government and 20 for RENAMO. Demobilization of those troops who would not serve in the Mozambican Defence Force (FADM) was to begin immediately thereafter. In practice, however, there has been little progress in implementing this crucial aspect of the General Peace Agreement which affects the timetable of the whole peace process.

12. This delay has been caused by several factors. One is that the two parties have not yet provided ONUMOZ with the complete list of troop strength, arms, ammunition, mines and other explosives which was ex-

pected by 15 October 1992. The parties finally agreed that the assembly of troops would proceed in phases. The first phase would be cantonment in seven areas for the Government and five for RENAMO. Both parties, however, have designated their assembly locations not for logistical suitability, but for their importance for control over certain areas. Accordingly, assembly areas have had to be changed, often at the request of the United Nations, because the sites proposed by the parties were inaccessible, without services and water, or may have been mined. Another factor seriously affecting progress is RENAMO's insistence that the assembly and demobilization of its troops will depend on the size and deployment of United Nations forces.

13. At the beginning of January 1993, my Special Representative set up a technical unit to assist in the concentration and demobilization programme. This unit consists of civilian staff seconded from the World Health Organization (WHO), the United Nations Children's Fund (UNICEF), the European Community (EC), the Swiss Development Cooperation Agency and the International Organization for Migration. It will have a team in each assembly area which will act in close cooperation with the teams of military observers. Twelve areas can be opened as soon as logistical support is available.

14. Thanks to substantial donations from the European Community, Norway and Japan, the World Food Programme can now give a basic ration of food to all assembled troops. Arrangements to supply this food have been made. UNICEF will help provide wells, boreholes, pumps and engines and simple non-food items (soap, tarpaulins, blankets, cooking pots). United Nations volunteers should be in each assembly location in a few weeks to organize the logistic support to the assembly areas and to guarantee communication with humanitarian agencies.

15. The technical unit is also preparing for demobilization. Civilian clothes for the demobilized have been procured. Registration procedures for the soldiers have been defined in coordination with the relevant government departments. The International Organization for Migration, in collaboration with the Mozambican Ministry of Transport and Communications, has begun to recruit specialists who will ensure in each province that demobilized soldiers and their families are transported to their places of origin. Thus, from the standpoint of logistical preparations, it would be possible to initiate the first phase of demobilization as soon as the Supervising and Monitoring Commission takes the appropriate decisions.

III. Developing the political process

16. The General Peace Agreement foresaw the creation of a series of commissions to monitor and imple-

ment the objectives set forth in the Agreement. At the invitation of the parties, the United Nations had agreed to chair the Supervisory and Monitoring Commission, as well as two of its subsidiary commissions, the Cease-fire Commission and the Reintegration Commission. The three Commissions were formally established and took up their functions last October shortly after the arrival of my Special Representative in Mozambique.

17. Since my report of 3 December 1992 (S/24892), the Supervisory and Monitoring Commission has held several meetings. Germany has also joined the Commission at the invitation of the parties. As a result, in addition to the two principals—the Government of Mozambique and RENAMO—the Commission comprises the United Nations, the Organization of African Unity (OAU) and six member countries: France, Germany, Italy, Portugal, the United Kingdom of Great Britain and Northern Ireland and the United States of America.

18. It will be recalled that for the political process, the mandate of ONUMOZ as approved by Security Council resolution 797 (1992), and in accordance with the General Peace Agreement, is to facilitate impartially the implementation of the Agreement, particularly by chairing the Supervisory and Monitoring Commission and its subsidiary commissions. The Supervisory and Monitoring Commission has been able to guide and coordinate the work of its subsidiary commissions and to address and resolve disputes which could not be settled at their level. The Supervisory and Monitoring Commission has adopted its own rules of procedure, which also govern the work of its subsidiaries. In addition to the formal meetings, my Special Representative has met on a regular basis with each of the parties individually, as well as with the group of ambassadors representing the member countries on the Supervisory and Monitoring Commission.

19. The Cease-fire Commission has been the most active of the Commissions. Although progress in implementing the cease-fire agreement has been slower than anticipated, the Commission has been able to maintain an ongoing dialogue between the parties on the main issues of its mandate. In January 1993, Cease-fire Commission was expanded to include Zimbabwe and Kenya, bringing the number of invited member countries to 10. However, except in the central region of the country, the subordinate bodies of the Cease-fire Commission, i.e. the regional cease-fire commissions and the assembly area monitoring groups, either have not yet been established or are not fully operational.

20. The Cease-fire Commission has discussed major issues that fall within its mandate. These include the composition and constitution of regional cease-fire commissions and assembly area monitoring groups; alleged violations of the cease-fire, mainly movements of troops by both sides; the nomination and reconnaissance of assembly areas, arrangements for de-mining of 28 priority roads to support the cease-fire agreement as well as humanitarian assistance activities; completion of a national mine-clearing plan; and establishment of a de-mining policy and coordination committee.

21. The discussions of the Cease-fire Commission on the mine-clearing problem have been particularly successful. It is estimated that there are some 2 million mines in Mozambique, some dating back to the colonial era. The Cease-fire Commission established a plan to initiate immediate mine clearing activities on a number of roads that were essential for the provision of humanitarian assistance to affected populations. With the assistance of an expert provided by the United Nations, it also developed a national de-mining policy, setting national priorities and establishing professional standards.

22. One of the appealing features of the plan is its training component in preparation for a mine-clearing school. At a rate of 400 graduates per year, the school will enable some 1,200 to 2,000 Mozambicans, many of them demobilized soldiers, to acquire a skill which, unfortunately, will be in demand for many years to come. Several donor countries have come forward to support the plan financially, and the United Nations has initiated a technical assistance project in response.

23. The Cease-fire Commission has not been able to achieve all its tasks in the time the General Peace Agreement requires. The two parties have not yet supplied the complete list of troop strength, arms, ammunition, mines and other explosives which was expected by 15 October 1992. The plan for the withdrawal of foreign troops, which was to have been declared by 15 October, has not yet been drawn up because of the delay in the arrival of the formed United Nations contingents. As a result, no specific plans for the concentration of troops have been submitted by either party because RENAMO would not start the process before the arrival of the United Nations troops. So far, RENAMO members of the three regional cease-fire commissions have been positioned only in the Central Region (Beira).

24. The Reintegration Commission has been able to hold only one working session. RENAMO has since announced that its delegation to the Commission could not attend the meetings because there was no housing and logistic support for it. However, a series of proposals for the reintegration of demobilized soldiers into civil society have been developed by the United Nations Office for Humanitarian Assistance Coordination and could be implemented once they were reviewed and approved by the Reintegration Commission.

25. The Joint Commission for the Formation of the

Mozambican Defence Force comprises, in addition to the parties, France, Portugal and the United Kingdom. It has not yet had any formal meetings. The parties have so far not even identified their delegations. My Special Representative has repeatedly expressed his concern to the parties that the delay would affect the peace process. However, military delegations from Portugal have visited the country and outlined their potential contribution to the training of the new unified army. The United Kingdom has already prepared facilities in the region to train instructors for the new force. The member countries of the Joint Commission have met recently in Lisbon and planned a unified contribution to the creation of the Defence Force.

26. In addition to the formal meetings of the commissions, my Special Representative has established informal tripartite working meetings with the parties on both political and military subjects. These meetings address questions of common concern so as to agree on working procedures and other related issues.

27. As the work of the commissions chaired by the United Nations progresses, the need for the other commissions has become ever more apparent. The tasks assigned to each of the commissions are often closely related. As a result, the failure of some Commissions to function hampers progress in those already established. In addition, certain questions of paramount importance to the peace process cannot be addressed unless the responsible commissions begin to act without further delay.

28. The National Police Affairs Commission and the National Information Commission have also yet to be established. So far, RENAMO has not been able to identify its representatives of those commissions. The urgency of this matter has become apparent in view of concerns by RENAMO that the Government has integrated military officers and soldiers into the police force. RENAMO's participation in the National Police Affairs Commission would, of course, permit this commission to function and thus to respond to these allegations. Similarly, complaints about human rights violations which should be addressed to these two commissions, as the General Peace Agreement provides, now go unheeded. Furthermore, several of the minor incidents reported to the Cease-fire Commission contained elements of civil crime which should be addressed by the National Police Affairs Commission.

29. Two other commissions whose roles are of major importance for the successful implementation of the Agreement, the National Elections Commission and the National Commission for Administrative Questions, have not yet been established. The delay in creating the National Commission for Administrative Questions has made it impossible to address sensitive issues concerning administration in both Government- and RENAMO-held areas. The implications of the absence of the National Elections Commission are discussed in paragraphs 38 to 44 below.

IV. Humanitarian aid coordination

30. In my report to the Security Council of 3 December 1992 (S/24892), I recommended that ONUMOZ include a United Nations Office for Humanitarian Assistance Coordination (UNOHAC) in Maputo. This would coordinate the international relief effort under the overall authority of the Special Representative. Its Director would also chair the separate Humanitarian Assistance Committee.

31. Following the decision of the Security Council to establish ONUMOZ, the Director of UNOHAC arrived in Maputo on 18 December. As an early step he integrated into UNOHAC the current operations of the United Nations Special Coordinator for Emergency Relief Operations. Since then the Office has filled half of its established posts, and seconded personnel from operational agencies are now part of the staff of UNOHAC.

32. UNOHAC's first task has been to follow up the conclusions and recommendations of the Donors Conference for Mozambique held in Rome on 15 and 16 December 1992. A report on the Conference, which recorded pledges and contributions in the amount of US$ 398.34 million, was circulated to the members of the Council in document S/25044.

33. The Rome meeting also helped to define the objectives of humanitarian assistance to Mozambique. This targets the needs of returning refugees and internally displaced persons, groups in severe distress from drought or acute poverty and demobilized soldiers. The overall goal is to help these groups return to their areas of origin. UNOHAC is now preparing, in consultation with the Government of Mozambique, a consolidated humanitarian assistance programme for 1993-1994, which is intended to describe clearly and completely the use of aid appropriations and the resources pledged at the Rome conference. The programme will be presented to a further donors meeting, probably in May.

34. Although the mid-term prospects are favourable, outside humanitarian assistance will be necessary for the next 18 months. The drought of several years has broken. In the country as a whole, rainfall has recently been above normal. However, the 1993 crop of staple cereals will be much less than normal because seeds and hard tools were lacking in the growing season.

35. Moreover, there are still 1.5 million refugees receiving assistance in neighbouring countries. Spontaneous returns rose sharply in the three months following the

General Peace Agreement. This has now virtually stopped. A further repatriation of 1 million persons may be assisted by the Office of the United Nations High Commissioner for Refugees (UNHCR) in April. Within Mozambique, there are an estimated 3 to 4 million displaced persons.

36. An important humanitarian objective of the humanitarian component of ONUMOZ is, therefore, to help resettlement by promoting essential services at district and community levels. These include support to agricultural production, road repair, water supply and sanitation, health care and education. A second vital purpose is to respond rapidly to humanitarian requirements in RENAMO areas so as to help open up commerce and expand contacts between population groups long isolated by war.

37. To provide supplementary funds for these activities, a United Nations Trust Fund for Humanitarian Assistance to Mozambique has been established by the Department of Humanitarian Affairs. Contributions to the Fund have already been announced for the specific purpose of financing mine-clearing projects, as well as to support the demobilization process and the reintegration of displaced populations.

V. Monitoring of the electoral process and the provision of technical assistance for the elections

38. The General Peace Agreement committed the Government to: establish a National Elections Commission by mid-December 1992; draft and publish an Electoral Law by mid-January 1993 in consultation with RENAMO and other parties and after approval by the Assembly of the Republic; and seek technical and material support for the organization of elections.

39. On 26 March 1993, the Government distributed a draft Electoral Law to RENAMO and other political parties. A Multi-party Conference sponsored by the Government will meet on 20 April to discuss and complete the draft law. Only after this conference will the Government submit the Electoral Law for approval by the Assembly of the Republic and set up the National Elections Commission; there are no firm deadlines for these last two actions.

40. Resolution 797 (1992) gives the United Nations the main coordinating role for technical assistance to the entire electoral process in Mozambique through the United Nations Development Programme (UNDP) and other United Nations agencies. This role was endorsed by the Donors Conference for Mozambique held in Rome on 15 and 16 December. From 29 November to 13 December, a joint mission of the United Nations and the European Community worked with elements of the Government of Mozambique responsible for preparing the electoral process until the National Elections Commission is established.

41. The joint mission revised the overall elections budget and its detailed justification. It also formulated a draft project for integrated support to the electoral process under UNDP coordination. Both this project and the electoral budget were reviewed with the local donor community. In addition, the EC team assisted the Government of Mozambique in revising and finalizing a draft electoral law; prepared a report for the Rome Donors Conference on electoral organization; assessed requirements for logistics, civic education and training; and designed the future organization and functional responsibilities of the Technical Secretariat for the Administration of Elections.

42. UNDP and the EC have since maintained especially close consultations and cooperation in support of the electoral process. The EC has already committed itself to provide significant funds to finance registration materials, and also part of the technical assistance in the elections budget.

43. The timetable for holding the elections is now seriously in question. Relevant aspects of the political, military and humanitarian situations, and of the state of electoral preparations, have been mentioned above. An additional complicating factor is the season of intense rain which lasts from mid-November to late March.

44. It now seems clear that it will not be possible to conduct the elections according to the original timetable, which aimed to complete them during the 1993 dry season. In particular, as I emphasized in my previous report (S/24892), the military situation must be fully under control if we are to create the conditions for a successful election. This in turn depends upon a determined effort by the Mozambican parties to honour fully their commitments. As reported herein, they have yet to do this, although there have been some promising early steps.

VI. Administration, logistics and status-of-forces agreement

45. In various parts of the present report, I have already pointed to some administrative causes for delays in the full deployment of ONUMOZ.

46. The formulation of a budget, given the present uncertain political situation together with the multifaceted components of the mission, proved to be a very complex task and required considerable internal consultations. Since only a relatively limited advance of US$ 9.5 million was made available pending the approval of the whole budget, the purchase of most equipment, as well as the long-term leasing of aircraft and lease of office space, had to be deferred. The lack of an approved

budget also prevented the timely recruitment and deployment of many key personnel.

47. In view of the delays in the timetable of the implementation of various aspects of the General Peace Agreement, the General Assembly decided to appropriate a lump sum amount of US$ 140 million for ONUMOZ for the period from 15 October 1992 through 30 June 1993. Therefore, it is only now that the requisitioning for many items of equipment could start. It is also necessary to emphasize that in order to make optimal and efficient use of resources, ONUMOZ should purchase goods and services, including those related to its de-mining activities, from sources of supply in southern Africa whenever these are more economical than sources of supply elsewhere.

48. Still, these logistic concerns are not the only ones. The mission has experienced serious problems with the provision of office accommodation without cost to the United Nations and of some very basic services to ONUMOZ. The mission has therefore had to attempt to negotiate on the open market, but the results have not usually been very satisfactory, due to the inadequacy of the market itself.

49. Of specific concern to me also is the absence of a status-of-forces agreement on ONUMOZ, which is referred to in paragraph 10 above. Such a draft agreement was prepared on the basis of the model contained in document A/45/594, based upon established practice and drawing extensively upon prior and current agreements. At the present time, the movement of United Nations staff and goods is subject to Mozambican law. Consequently, ONUMOZ is required to obtain authorization for its flights, airport duties have to be paid, vehicles have to be registered locally and local taxes and duties are levied in accordance with national practice. Difficulties are experienced in the operation of ONUMOZ-chartered aircraft.

50. The United Nations is not asking for privileges, exemptions and immunities greater than those which are usually granted by other countries to the Organization in similar circumstances. The current practice regrettably imposes restrictions on the full implementation of ONUMOZ's mandate. Moreover, the approved budget of the mission does not include allowance for customs duties, excise taxes, levies, fees and other charges which the Government, its agents and local authorities are charging ONUMOZ.

VII. Observations

51. The General Peace Agreement signed in Rome consists of a complex series of interlinked agreements. These are to be implemented in stages through coordinated actions of the two parties—the Government of Mozambique and RENAMO—under United Nations verification. Some of the aspects of the peace accords also involve the active participation and support of Member States, and their contributions continue to be invaluable. The peace process is, however, an extremely complicated one. Thus, delay in implementing one element of the General Peace Agreement affects the achievement of others.

52. Any assessment of the current situation must include a number of positive developments. The cease-fire has largely held and the parties have continued to exercise restraint. Mozambique is going through a period without precedent in the past 16 years. After so many years of devastating conflict, there is a strongly felt need for peace. Mozambicans long for a return to the stability that will permit the rehabilitation and reconstruction of their society. I hope that this sentiment will strongly impel the parties to implement the peace accords fully and without further delay.

53. Another positive development relates to the understandings reached on the Zimbabwean and Malawian troops in the country who have been assisting in keeping open the transport corridors which run across Mozambique to neighbouring land-locked countries. The delay in the deployment of ONUMOZ contingents raised concerns at the beginning of the year that the premature withdrawal of these troops might cause the breakdown of the peace process. Fortunately, diplomacy and sound judgement prevailed: arrangements were worked out to permit these troops to remain in the corridors beyond the time specified in the General Peace Agreement.

54. But even if all these developments give cause for satisfaction, there are several reasons for concern which should not be underestimated. Many of the timetables established in the General Peace Agreement proved to be unrealistic. The number of considerable delays has accumulated and there are so far no signs to indicate that this time lost can be recovered quickly or easily. Some time has been lost in forging the necessary support inside the country to implement the Agreement. Continuing deep mistrust has resulted in reluctance to begin assembly and demobilization of troops, and has contributed to the delay in the deployment of United Nations military observers.

55. Another complication was Mr. Dhlakama's insistence that his troops would not assemble unless 65 per cent of the United Nations armed components were deployed and were ensuring stability in areas under RENAMO control. This interpretation obviously goes beyond the provisions of the General Peace Agreement and the operational plan of ONUMOZ. Meanwhile, RENAMO's reluctance to allow timely investigation of alleged cease-fire violations and insistence on keeping certain areas under its control obstruct the freedom of movement of people and goods foreseen in the Agreement.

56. The delays in deployment of ONUMOZ's

formed units also have not been helpful. There are several reasons for such delays, many of a generic nature, which also inhibit other peace-keeping operations. The United Nations clearly needs more rapid and effective means as well as more flexible practices. The example of ONUMOZ also demonstrates the importance of quick responses by troop-contributing countries to United Nations requests. This aspect has become one of the crucial elements the Secretariat is usually faced with at the initial stages of many peace-keeping undertakings.

57. ONUMOZ's logistical problems also arise from the lack of a status of forces agreement. The latter must be finalized quickly so that the mission may freely and effectively carry out its mandate. I have received the personal assurances of Foreign Minister Mocumbi, with whom I met on 31 March, that the agreement will be signed by the Government without further delay.

58. It is essential to have the necessary conditions to allow RENAMO to assume a proper role in the political and social life of Mozambique. This is a serious problem which has to be resolved by the Mozambicans as soon as possible, if the peace process is to succeed. I welcome the cooperative approach of various donor countries which are assisting my Special Representative in his efforts to resolve these difficulties imaginatively and quickly.

59. The timetable for the implementation of the cease-fire arrangements, including the assembly of troops and their demobilization, cannot be delayed any longer. Soldiers should be able to begin returning to civilian life through the programmes envisaged in the General Peace Agreement. The parties must promptly exchange all relevant information concerning the numbers of their troops, their concentration points and assembly areas. To avoid unnecessary hardship for soldiers as well as to mitigate related security and social risks, consideration should be given by the parties to the need for starting the demobilization process before all troops are assembled under United Nations supervision. The main responsibility for the speedy implementation of all these matters related to the cease-fire lies with the Mozambicans themselves.

60. Formation of the new armed forces must also have high priority. I appeal to both parties, and to interested countries which have agreed to assist, to complete as soon as possible all arrangements for the training of the FADM. ONUMOZ is prepared to assist the parties in addressing this and other issues in order to help dispel mistrust and misunderstanding that could threaten the peace process.

61. Security concerns raised by both parties must be addressed without making the peace process hostage to exaggerated complaints or mistrust. The prompt deployment of the ONUMOZ military contingent should help to allay most of these apprehensions. I would be prepared also to consider some adjustments to the military operation by providing additional patrols and observation outside assembly areas and transport corridors, without substantially changing the approved mandate of the mission. ONUMOZ military elements would also undertake, whenever possible, to verify unauthorized internal and cross-border flows of arms and military personnel. However, for the United Nations force to operate effectively, both sides must honour their commitments to guarantee ONUMOZ's freedom of movement and verification capabilities.

62. My Special Representative has, on many occasions, raised the above matters with both parties. Under-Secretary-General James O. C. Jonah also discussed these and other matters with both President Chissano and Mr. Dhlakama when he visited Mozambique last January. On 31 March, I reviewed in detail various aspects of the peace process with Foreign Minister Mocumbi. The two parties have on various occasions, even very recently, reaffirmed their firm commitment to consider peace as an irreversible choice. The possibility of a meeting between President Chissano and Mr. Dhlakama, repeatedly sought by my Special Representative, was recently brought up again by Mr. Dhlakama, and accepted by President Chissano. This meeting, like others in the past, could represent an important opportunity to contribute to the solution of outstanding problems.

63. All the delays and difficulties, however, will seriously affect the timetable previously presented to the Security Council. Although a draft Electoral Law has now been circulated, the delays in doing so will require adjustment of the timetables, particularly the dates for the elections. It is evident that they cannot be held in October 1993 as originally scheduled. I will continue my discussions with the parties on new dates and shall keep the Council informed about this very important matter.

64. Mozambique is now enjoying relative peace. The problems in implementing the General Peace Agreement cannot obscure this fundamental fact. Peace must be sustained and secured. The international community should continue to assist the parties in Mozambique in achieving this goal. Many of the initial problems experienced by the United Nations in establishing ONUMOZ and making it fully operational have now been or will soon be overcome. For my part, I am determined to continue my efforts to accelerate the process of implementation. Despite the many concerns which now preoccupy us all, with the continued goodwill of the parties and the interest and support of the international community, it should be possible in the coming crucial period to build on the progress made so far and firmly implant the peace process in Mozambique, and bring it to a final success.

Document 34

Security Council resolution expressing concern about delays affecting the timetable of the peace process in Mozambique

S/RES/818 (1993), 14 April 1993

The Security Council,

Reaffirming its resolutions 782 (1992) of 13 October 1992 and 797 (1992) of 16 December 1992,

Having considered the report of the Secretary-General of 2 April 1993, 1/

Welcoming the efforts of the Secretary-General to implement fully the mandate entrusted to the United Nations Operation in Mozambique,

Reiterating the importance it attaches to the General Peace Agreement for Mozambique 2/ and to the timely fulfilment by all parties in good faith of the obligations contained therein,

Seriously concerned at delays in the implementation of major aspects of the Agreement,

Noting the efforts of the Government of Mozambique and the Resistência Nacional Moçambicana to maintain the cease-fire,

1. *Takes note with appreciation* of the report of the Secretary-General dated 2 April 1993 1/ and the recommendations contained therein;

2. *Calls upon* the Government of Mozambique and the Resistência Nacional Moçambicana to cooperate fully with the Secretary-General and his Special Representative in the full and timely implementation of the mandate of the United Nations Operation in Mozambique;

3. *Stresses its concern* about the delays and difficulties which are seriously affecting the timetable for implementation of the peace process envisaged in the General Peace Agreement for Mozambique and in the report of the Secretary-General of 3 and 9 December 1992 3/ containing the operational plan for the Operation;

4. *Urges* the Government of Mozambique and the Resistência Nacional Moçambicana to take urgent and determined steps to comply with the commitments they entered into within the framework of the above-mentioned Agreement, in particular with respect to the concentration, assembly and demobilization of their armed troops and the formation of the new unified armed forces;

5. *Also urges* the Government of Mozambique and the Resistência Nacional, in this context, to initiate the training of the first elements of the new Mozambican Defence Forces as soon as possible, and calls upon the countries which have offered assistance to cooperate in this respect, with a view to the earliest possible completion of the arrangements for such training;

6. *Welcomes* the initiatives and readiness of both parties to convene as soon as possible a meeting between the President of the Republic of Mozambique and the President of the Resistência Nacional Moçambicana, in order to address major issues pertaining to peace in Mozambique;

7. *Strongly appeals* to the Resistência Nacional to ensure the effective and uninterrupted functioning of the joint commissions and monitoring mechanisms;

8. *Strongly appeals also* to both the Government of Mozambique and the Resistência Nacional to allow timely investigation of all cease-fire violations and to ensure the freedom of movement of people and goods as foreseen in the General Peace Agreement;

9. *Welcomes* the Secretary-General's intention to ensure prompt deployment of military contingents of the United Nations Operation in Mozambique, and calls upon troop-contributing countries to expedite the dispatch of their troops earmarked for service in the Operation;

10. *Strongly urges* the Government of Mozambique and the Resistência Nacional to finalize, in consultation with the Secretary-General, the precise timetable for the full implementation of the provisions of the General Peace Agreement, including the separation, concentration and demobilization of forces, as well as for the elections;

11. *Stresses* the importance it attaches to the early signature of the status-of-forces agreement between the Government of Mozambique and the United Nations to facilitate the free, efficient and effective operation of the Operation;

12. *Strongly urges* both sides to guarantee the Operation's freedom of movement and verification capabilities pursuant to the commitments made under the General Peace Agreement;

13. *Appreciates* the assistance and pledges made by Member States in support of the peace process, and encourages the donor community to provide appropriate and prompt assistance for the implementation of major aspects of the Agreement;

14. *Requests* the Secretary-General to keep the Security Council informed of developments regarding the full implementation of the provisions of the Agreement,

1/ See *Official Records of the Security Council, Forty-eighth Year, Supplement for April, May and June 1993*, document S/25518.

2/ Ibid., *Forty-seventh Year, Supplement for October, November and December 1992*, document S/24635, annex.

3/ Ibid., documents S/24892 and Add.1.

including on progress in the consultations with the Government of Mozambique and the Resistência Nacional concerning the finalization of the precise timetable for separation, concentration and demobilization of forces, as well as for the elections, and to submit a further report to the Council by 30 June 1993;

15. *Expresses* its confidence in the Special Representative of the Secretary-General and its appreciation for the work he has done to date in coordinating all aspects of the Agreement;

16. *Decides* to remain seized of the matter.

Document 35

Statements made by representatives of the United Kingdom, France, the United States, China, and the Russian Federation during the Security Council's meeting in which resolution 818 (1993) was adopted (extract)

S/PV.3198, 14 April 1993

. . .

Sir David Hannay (United Kingdom): . . .When the General Peace Agreement was signed on 4 October last year, the European Community and its Member States welcomed that signing very warmly and stressed the importance of the Government of Mozambique and of RENAMO carrying out the Agreement in good faith. My Government would like to congratulate both of them on the fact that so far, with one or two minor breakings of the cease-fire, that implementation has indeed been carried out.

But I must confess that, like many other speakers and, indeed, like the representative of the Government of Mozambique, we remain concerned at the very serious delays which the Secretary-General himself mentioned in his report of 2 April. I do not think it would be pointing the finger at anyone to say that there is a certain amount of shared responsibility for that—in the United Nations, the Government of Mozambique and RENAMO.

Be that as it may, the view of my Government, at least, is that this is the moment at which we should try to change gear in this peace-keeping operation and get into high gear now. Because the troops being deployed by the United Nations are arriving, this resolution marks a kind of turning-point in the operation, and we hope that all concerned will see it as such and will now cease to postpone the concentration of troops in the assembly areas, the identification of the assembly areas and so on.

The work of the Commission for the creation of a new united defence force is one of those activities that has lagged behind somewhat. We believe it should be initiated now so that the training can start without delay. It is really crucial that both parties should select and send the first groups of trainees to the facility at Nyanga, where my Government has provided training facilities. I know the Government of Mozambique responded very positively to that quite recently. It is imperative that delayed training should not become in itself an impediment to the formation of the new defence force, which will, in its turn, postpone the process of demobilization.

It is also extremely important, as the resolution makes clear, that the Government of Mozambique should complete the negotiations with the United Nations on a status-of-forces agreement. I welcome very much what the representative of Mozambique had to say on that. I just hope that now the negotiations can be concluded really quickly, because the United Nations Operation in Mozambique (ONUMOZ) does need a status-of-forces agreement if it is to work effectively; and the more troops that are deployed there, the more civilian personnel that are on the ground, the more essential it is to have this status-of-forces agreement.

We are a bit concerned that RENAMO has not so far agreed to participate in the work of the overall peace Commissions in Maputo; or rather, it has agreed to do so in principle, but its members have not come to the capital. We hope that RENAMO will now, without delay, appoint its members to all the Commissions that have been established in accordance with the Peace Agreement. It is really desirable that the President of RENAMO, Mr. Dhlakama, should become available in Maputo, and in that context we welcome very much the call in this resolution for meetings between President Chissano and Mr. Dhlakama, which we feel could make an important contribution to the peace process and its full implementation.

It is clear, I think, from what I have said that a lot remains to be done. But we, for our part, would urge the Government and RENAMO to work together in the spirit of compromise that they showed in the latter stages of the negotiations in the peace process so that they can build on the progress made so far and move forward to the elections which are foreseen. We hope very much that the finalization of the arrangements and the dates for those elections will be accomplished and reported to the Council when next we take this matter up.

. . .

Mr. Mérimée (France) (*interpretation from French*): . . . My delegation welcomes the Council's adoption of this resolution, which testifies to the consistent attention paid by the Council to the implementation of the Rome Agreements.

The situation that has prevailed in Mozambique since the signing of these Agreements gives us certain grounds for satisfaction. The cease-fire is, on the whole, being respected. The country is enjoying a period of calm, which has enabled it to begin to embark upon its reconstruction. My Government would like to pay tribute in this respect to the work done in a few months by the Special Representative of the Secretary-General. The restraint observed so far by the Mozambican parties also deserves our mention and encouragement.

We feel, however, that this situation should be consolidated, and we should not like to see this initial success jeopardized by a delay in the implementation of the Peace Agreement or by unrealistic demands on the part of the Mozambique factions. We would therefore like to express our whole-hearted support for the determination of the Secretary-General to accelerate the deployment of the United Nations Operation in Mozambique (ONUMOZ). But the United Nations must be able to work as effectively as possible. We therefore would urge the parties concerned to facilitate his task by signing a status-of-forces agreement and by granting ONUMOZ personnel full freedom of movement.

The control commissions and machinery created by the Rome Agreements have an important part to play, and they must be made operational as soon as possible. The parties should therefore immediately appoint representatives and cooperate so that these institutions may function effectively. France, which has taken an active part in some of these commissions, will continue to support this process.

In order to promote a lasting peace, it is essential that the military arrangements under the Agreement be fully respected. We therefore call upon the parties to begin immediately regroupment and demobilization operations. The logic of confrontation and distrust must now give way to the logic of peace and reconciliation. The purpose is to give the Mozambican people the possibility of freely choosing their own destiny through free and fair elections.

The United Nations has acted at the request of the parties and will perform its allotted task, but establishing peace and confidence is ultimately the primary responsibility of the Mozambicans themselves. We would like once again to stress this point, as we have done for other United Nations operations. We appeal to the Mozambique parties to show wisdom and realism, and to cooperate in order to ensure the success of the peace process and the reconstruction of the country.

. . .

Ms. Albright (United States of America): . . . The United States has reviewed the Secretary-General's 2 April status report on the United Nations peace-keeping operation in Mozambique and fully endorses its major findings. My Government is aware of the many difficulties that the United Nations Secretariat faced in implementing the operational plan for the United Nations Operation in Mozambique (ONUMOZ) and appreciates the Secretary-General's candor in explaining the reasons for delays in the deployment of ONUMOZ forces.

In this regard, we are pleased to note that these problems are steadily being overcome, and that the first contingent of United Nations Operation in Mozambique (ONUMOZ) peace-keeping forces, an Italian infantry battalion, has now arrived and set up camp in Mozambique.

We welcome the Secretary-General's assurances that every effort is being made to expedite the deployment of the remainder of the ONUMOZ military component, and note, favourably, his estimation that this should be accomplished by the end of May.

We agree completely with the Secretary-General's view that it is now up to the Mozambican Government and to RENAMO to ensure the speedy implementation of the major aspects of the peace accord, especially demobilization of combatants. With the bulk of the infantry units in place by the end of April, demobilization should begin within the next several weeks.

We call upon the Mozambican Government as a matter of high priority to conclude a status-of-forces agreement with the United Nations to facilitate the ONUMOZ mission. At the same time, we urge RENAMO to participate fully in the operations of joint commissions and monitoring mechanisms established under the accord. Both parties should ensure that United Nations personnel have the flexibility and full access that they were guaranteed in Protocol VI of the Agreement of 4 October 1992.

I am pleased to report that the United States has identified significant resources for several aspects of the implementation of the accord, including support for demobilization and elections. We encourage other donors to provide appropriate assistance for the various facets of the transition to peace and democracy.

We should like to make special note of the fine work of the Secretary-General's Special Representative in organizing ONUMOZ and coordinating the various aspects of the peace process under difficult circumstances.

We are confident that we will continue to work with the Mozambican Government, RENAMO and other interested parties to meet the challenges that lie ahead.

. . .

Mr. Chen Jian (China) (*interpretation from Chinese*): . . . In October 1992, thanks to the concerted efforts made by the Mozambique Government and RENAMO, the General Peace Agreement was signed in Rome. This is an important document in ending the civil war and achieving national peace in Mozambique. It not only opens up new prospects for restoring peace and revitalizing the economy in Mozambique, but also has a significant bearing on peace and stability in southern Africa.

At present, Mozambique's peace process is at a crucial historical moment. We have noted that, on the one hand, with United Nations assistance and the joint endeavours of the two Mozambican sides, the peace process has made some progress, while, on the other hand, as is pointed out by the Secretary-General in his report, for various reasons the deployment of the United Nations Operation in Mozambique (ONUMOZ) has met with obstacles, and the implementation of the General Peace Agreement is also faced with difficulties, activities in implementing various timetables are all behind schedule, and it is difficult to hold national elections in Mozambique on time. The Chinese delegation cannot but express its deep concern about this.

Early realization of peace and stability in Mozambique is the ardent expectation of all the African countries as well as the entire international community. We therefore hope the Mozambican Government and RENAMO can promptly resolve their differences through consultations and negotiations and implement comprehensively the General Peace Agreement and the relevant Security Council resolutions. We also hope that ONUMOZ can be deployed as soon as possible. We are glad that the Security Council has just adopted a timely resolution. We believe that the comprehensive implementation of this important resolution will create favourable conditions for Mozambique to engage in national reconciliation and embark on economic development at an early date.

. . .

Mr. Vorontsov (Russian Federation) (*interpretation from Russian*): . . . The Russian delegation supports the draft resolution just adopted by the Council, since we believe that it will lend additional momentum to the performance of the tasks facing the United Nations in conducting the operation in Mozambique. The resolution contains an important appeal to the Government of Mozambique and to RENAMO to cooperate fully with the Secretary-General and his Special Representative in the full and timely implementation of the mandate of ONUMOZ. It is important also for the Secretary-General as soon as possible, in consultation with the Government of Mozambique and RENAMO, to finalize the precise timetable for the full implementation of the provisions of the General Peace Agreement, including the separation, concentration and demobilization of the armed forces of both sides and also the holding of national elections.

We believe that the successful conclusion of the process of a settlement will be helped by the scrupulous observance by the Mozambican parties of the agreed timetable for the implementation of the General Peace Agreement. We welcome the initiatives taken by both sides for the early organization of a meeting between the President of the Republic of Mozambique and the President of RENAMO to discuss the fundamental items involved in the peace settlement in Mozambique.

The Russian delegation expresses the hope that the Government of Mozambique and the leadership of RENAMO will, on the basis of national interests, evince political wisdom and take a constructive approach to finding mutually acceptable solutions to the outstanding questions involved in the settlement, and will work for the establishment of peace and democracy in the country.

The Russian delegation is ready to join the international community in doing everything possible to promote this process.

Document 36

Letter dated 19 June 1993 from Italy's Minister for Foreign Affairs to the Secretary-General on Italy's support for the peace process in Mozambique

Not issued as a United Nations document

In many occasions and on behalf of the United Nations, His Excellency has expressed appreciation for the efforts made by Italy, in the past years, to restore peace in Mozambique, a country ravaged by a harsh civil war. I am aware of the fact that His Excellency regards my Country's endeavors as essential also in this phase preceding the first political elections, and hopes that we show a strong interest in favour of the reconstruction of the country.

It is with great pleasure that I wish to inform His

Excellency that in the past few days, whenever possible, we have further emphasized through significant deeds our interest for Mozambique.

As you may already know, the Under-Secretary of Foreign Affairs, Sen. Azzarà, together with the Under-Secretary-General, Mr. Eliasson, has co-chaired the Conference of Donors Countries. A few days later, the Minister of Defense, the On. Fabbri, visited the country and met with the local Government officials and with the Italian military contingent. Subsequently, I had a meeting in Rome with the leader of RENAMO, Dhaklama, and I tried to convince him, by means of proper pressure, to re-establish a political dialogue with President Chissano, and thus take a step which is essential in order to set a date for the elections. Dhaklama should be returning to Mozambique tomorrow.

Among the many crises afflicting the international scenario and putting a considerable burden on the United Nations, the crisis in Mozambique results in one for which a solution appears to be on the way, while one should not conceal the remaining difficulties.

I share His Excellency's conviction that it is therefore necessary to intensify the efforts made to this day. In this respect, it seems to me that the presence in Mozambique of His Excellency's Special Representative, Mr. Ajello, represents an important element. It is necessary, in my opinion, to strengthen his authority and, consequently, his capacity to operate in Mozambique. I am aware of the fact that His Excellency has been informed of this problem and I hope that He will be able to intervene in the most appropriate way.

While I am looking forward to the opportunity of meeting with His Excellency in Geneva in the next few days, I wish to extend my best regards,

(*Signed*) Beniamino ANDREATTA

Document 37

Report of the Secretary-General on ONUMOZ

S/26034, 30 June 1993

Introduction

1. The present report is submitted in response to paragraph 14 of Security Council resolution 818 (1993) of 14 April 1993, which requested me to keep the Council informed of developments regarding the full implementation of the provisions of the general peace agreement (S/24635, annex), including on progress in consultations with the Government of Mozambique and the Resistência Nacional Moçambicana (RENAMO) concerning the finalization of the precise timetable for the separation, concentration and demobilization of forces, as well as for the elections, and to submit a further report to the Council by 30 June 1993. The present report covers the period up to 25 June 1993, and brings up to date the activities of the United Nations Operation in Mozambique (ONUMOZ) in implementation of the political, military, electoral and humanitarian aspects of its mandate.

2. Since my last report of 2 April 1993 (S/25518), my Special Representative for Mozambique, Mr. Aldo Ajello, has continued his efforts to promote the peace process in the country in consultation with all parties concerned. He reports that, despite numerous difficulties, the Government and RENAMO, with the assistance of the United Nations, can make the peace process succeed, both having repeatedly reiterated their commitment to this end. It is encouraging that, mutual accusations not-withstanding, there have been no major violations of the cease-fire. However, nine months after the signing of the peace agreement, and despite these positive developments, the delays that were previously reported to the Council have not been entirely overcome and, as indicated below, determined efforts by the two parties will be required to ensure that the peace process regains its momentum.

I. Cease-fire arrangements

3. My previous report to the Security Council (S/25518) detailed the various difficulties of a political, administrative and logistical nature that impeded the rapid deployment of the ONUMOZ military component. I am now pleased to inform the members of the Council that, by the beginning of May, all the main infantry battalions of ONUMOZ were fully deployed and its military infrastructure established in all three operational regions. At present, five infantry battalions from Bangladesh, Botswana, Italy, Uruguay and Zambia and support units from Argentina, Bangladesh, India, Italy, Japan and Portugal have been deployed, with a total strength of some 6,100 military personnel. An additional unit, a second engineer company from India, is expected in Mozambique at the beginning of July 1993. Over the last month, ONUMOZ units have been providing security in the Beira, Tete and Limpopo corridors and along national

highway N1 in order to protect humanitarian convoys using them, until the new Mozambican Defence Forces (FADM) become operational. This ONUMOZ presence is a stabilizing factor, and the situation in the country remains generally calm, without armed attacks in the corridors, except for persistent acts of banditry.

4. Further, the withdrawal of foreign troops provided for in the general peace agreement, has been successfully completed. ONUMOZ observers witnessed the repatriation of Zimbabwean troops from the Beira corridor from 11 to 15 April 1993 and the withdrawal of Malawian troops from the Nacala corridor on 9 June 1993.

5. The operational plan of ONUMOZ also envisages that the military component would monitor and verify the cease-fire, the assembly and demobilization of forces in 49 assembly areas (29 for the Government and 20 for RENAMO) and the collection, storage and destruction of weapons. By 25 June 1993, some 260 military observers of the 354 authorized had been deployed to perform these tasks. The remaining military observers are being kept on stand-by in their home countries and will be deployed to Mozambique as soon as the majority of the assembly areas are operational. As a confidence-building measure, it would be also essential to provide additional patrols and observation, which would involve permanent stationing of military personnel outside assembly areas and transport corridors. For this purpose, the strength of the military units is to be brought up to the levels originally envisaged. These steps will ensure effective arrangements for the transportation, storage, and destruction of weapons, as well as to undertake the complex demobilization procedures that have been approved or are being finalized in the joint commissions.

6. Regrettably, more than eight months after the signing of the general peace agreement, the deadlines for the cantonment of government and RENAMO troops have not been met, resulting in a setback to the peace process. Until now, a main cause of delays in this area has been the difficulty in identifying and obtaining government and RENAMO agreement on acceptable sites that would also be logistically accessible to the ONUMOZ personnel responsible for assisting in maintaining them. Yet another condition set by RENAMO was that at least 65 per cent of the ONUMOZ troops should be deployed in order to guarantee security in RENAMO-controlled territories. These problems have been resolved, but the Government and RENAMO are yet to take decisive steps towards assembly and demobilization. Contrary to the understanding of ONUMOZ that this process would be carried out in stages, both parties are now indicating that they will not be ready to proceed until all 49 assembly areas are operational. This implies that the earliest feasible date for full assembly would be early September 1993.

RENAMO recently proposed that government militias and paramilitary formations should be disbanded before troop assembly starts. Neither of the above-mentioned proposals is supported by the provisions of the general peace agreement, and my Special Representative has repeatedly stressed that, while the military situation in Mozambique remains calm, this relative peace will remain fragile until the demobilization is completed and FADM is formed.

7. At present, a total of 13 assembly areas has been approved by the Cease-fire Commission (CCF), 6 of which (3 each for the Government and RENAMO) have been fully prepared and declared ready by ONUMOZ. However, the formal decision to start the process must still be made by the Supervisory and Monitoring Commission (CSC) after the concurrence of the Government and RENAMO is obtained. It is also obvious that there will be many daunting problems involved in the demobilization of several tens of thousands of soldiers and their smooth transition into civilian life. Since mid-April, ONUMOZ military observers have also been involved in the resettlement of some 16,000 government soldiers who were formally demobilized, along with their dependants, prior to the signing of the general peace agreement. The process of registering these soldiers for return to their places of choice began on 17 April 1993 in Maputo province, under ONUMOZ supervision and was concluded on 21 May 1993. By that time, 13,717 soldiers had been registered, more than 7,000 of whom were resettled by 25 June 1993.

8. The active participation and cooperation of the donor community and international financial institutions will be indispensable to assure the success of the reintegration of ex-combatants into civilian life. The United Nations Development Programme (UNDP) and other United Nations programmes and agencies, which are already planning activities in this area, will actively assist in making this a viable project. However, the Government, and Mozambican society itself, must bear the main responsibility for the success of this process. It should be noted here that the unavailability of equipment and supplies for ONUMOZ in the mission area, which must therefore be imported from distant sources, adds substantially to the cost of the operation, besides being very time-consuming. A possible solution might be to authorize ONUMOZ to purchase immediate requirements and to obtain services as far as possible from countries in the region.

9. The status-of-forces agreement between the Government of Mozambique and the United Nations was signed in New York on 14 May 1993. As anticipated in my previous report to the Council, this has greatly facilitated the entire work of ONUMOZ, and especially the deployment of its military component.

II. Formation of Mozambican defence forces

10. Under the terms of the general peace agreement, the formation of the new FADM was to begin immediately after the cease-fire was established and was to be conducted simultaneously with the concentration, disarmament and integration into civilian life of the demobilized personnel. Each side was to contribute an equal number of troops. Delays in this regard have been of particular concern and are linked with delays already pointed out in implementing other major elements of the peace plan. In particular, RENAMO failed to send the first wave of its personnel who were to be trained, together with government personnel, by United Kingdom specialists in the military centre in Nyanga (Zimbabwe). The United Kingdom Government has conveyed to me its disappointment at having to keep its military instructors there for more than five months in anticipation of the arrival of the Mozambican trainees. It is essential, therefore, that RENAMO should urgently take this first step of sending its military personnel to the Nyanga training centre, and I hope that the United Kingdom Government will be in a position to continue to extend its assistance to the training programme.

11. The Joint Commission for the Formation of the Mozambican Defence Force (CCFADM) is expected to start work only in July 1993, the continued delay being primarily attributable to RENAMO's unreadiness to keep its delegation in Maputo (see para. 12 below). To ensure impartiality in the Commission's work, the two parties and the observers have formally requested my Special Representative to assume chairmanship of this important commission and to provide effective secretariat services, which functions were not envisaged by the general peace agreement (see para. 26 below).

III. Political activities

12. The political process in Mozambique continued its chequered course, and limited progress was made between March and the end of May 1993 in the implementation of the general peace agreement. This was due mainly to RENAMO's withdrawal of its delegation from Maputo on the grounds that its members were not provided with proper accommodation, transport and communications facilities. In accordance with protocol III of the general peace agreement, the Government had made several offers to RENAMO of office space and accommodation in Maputo. Subsequently, the Government, in coordination with ONUMOZ, also interceded on RENAMO's behalf with the international community. A trust fund for receiving voluntary contributions and channelling funds to RENAMO was established on 10 May 1993 under rules and procedures conforming to standard United Nations practice. Italy has contributed almost $6 million to the fund, and a number of Member States have announced their intention to contribute. The fund will be used, among other things, to provide RENAMO with office space, accommodation and equipment. Meanwhile, RENAMO is temporarily accommodated in a hotel in Maputo and in 18 houses provided by the Government.

13. At the end of May 1993, RENAMO delegates returned to Maputo to participate first at informal meetings to prepare for the resumption of the work of the commissions, and subsequently at meetings of the joint commissions. The work of CSC and CCF successfully resumed on 3 June 1993, and the Commission for Reintegration (CORE) was convened on 11 June 1993. Both parties recently presented each other with a full list of delegates to all the commissions, including CCFADM, which has since held its first meeting. Also recently, the President of Mozambique appointed members of the National Information Commission (COMINFO) and the Police Affairs Commission (COMPOL).

14. Further, there has been progress in mine clearance. Of a total of $19 million now available, $15 million has been designated for the de-mining of priority roads and a nationwide mine survey; the remaining $4 million will be used to fund other aspects of the nationwide de-mining plan, such as a mine-clearance training facility and a mine-awareness programme.

15. The establishment of two very important bodies, the National Elections Commission (NEC) and the Commission of State Administration, are still pending. The latter is of particular significance, as the RENAMO leadership has declared in public statements that it will not allow members of the Mozambique Liberation Front (FRELIMO) to conduct political, social or economic activities in RENAMO-controlled territory. It should be kept in mind that moves that obstruct the extension of government administration throughout the country would be in violation of the spirit and letter of the general peace agreement. A positive factor is that, after active encouragement from my Special Representative, both President Joaquim Alberto Chissano and Mr. Afonso Macacho Marceta Dhlakama, President of RENAMO, have agreed to meet in Maputo in July 1993.

IV. Preparation for the elections

16. On 26 March 1993, the Government prepared and distributed the text of a draft electoral law to the political parties, and a multi-party consultative meeting to discuss this document was convened on 27 April 1993. However, RENAMO refused to attend the meeting on the grounds that it had not had sufficient time to study the text. The 12 smaller parties, which constitute the

so-called "unarmed opposition", did attend, but walked out after having presented a declaration demanding material and financial support for the establishment of their party headquarters and alleging that there had been insufficient time for them to analyse the draft. These parties also proposed that, before the elections were held, a new Government be established for a transitional period.

17. In the absence of initiatives from any party to break the resulting impasse, several Member States attending the Follow-up Donors' Meeting that was held in Maputo on 8 and 9 June 1993 (see para. 19 below) stressed their concern over the delays in the peace process and urged the parties to resume discussions without delay in order for the elections to be held by October 1994. This made it evident that the international community stands ready to support the peace process, but at the same time is increasingly frustrated by the accumulated delays and considers any further procrastination unacceptable. On 16 June 1993, the Minister of Justice of Mozambique took a step towards breaking the deadlock by inviting all political parties to an informal meeting to set a new date for the discussion of the draft electoral law. An understanding was reached that the parties, including FRELIMO and RENAMO, would reconvene for that purpose during the first half of July 1993. The Government also announced that, in response to the demands of the "unarmed opposition", it had set aside housing for the first three registered parties prepared to move in before the end of June 1993; it also agreed to allocate funds from its 1994 budget to political parties for use during the political campaign. These are positive decisions which, if fully implemented, could make an important contribution to the success of the electoral process.

V. Humanitarian assistance programme

18. The major goal of the humanitarian assistance programme in Mozambique is to address effectively the reintegration needs of all Mozambicans and particularly the humanitarian needs of those who are now returning to resettle in their original communities. It is projected that over 5.5 million Mozambicans will resettle during the next two years. This figure includes about 4 million internally displaced persons, 1.5 million refugees and 370,000 demobilized soldiers and their dependants. This situation has necessitated the programme's shift in emphasis from emergency humanitarian relief towards reintegration and rehabilitation. Support for the repatriation process, the demobilization of armed forces, emergency relief and the restoration of essential services constitute the main components of the current consolidated humanitarian assistance programme for 1993-1994.

19. The details of this programme were presented at the Follow-up Donors' Meeting which, as a sequel to the Donors Conference on Mozambique held in Rome on 15 and 16 December 1992 and on the basis of article VII of the general peace agreement, was convened in Maputo on 8 and 9 June 1993 under the joint chairmanship of the United Nations and the Government of Italy. The implementation of this programme will require $559.6 million for a 12-month period, from May 1993 to April 1994. Against this total requirement, $450 million had been pledged during the Rome Donors Conference and afterwards. Additional pledges totalling $70 million were announced at the Follow-up Donors' Meeting. Having recognized the humanitarian assistance programme as an integral part of the peace process that aims at reconciliation and reconstruction in Mozambique, this meeting also highlighted the complementarity between activities in the humanitarian field and those undertaken in the political area.

20. My Special Representative and the Director of the humanitarian assistance programme, together with the heads of United Nations operational agencies and representatives of the International Committee of the Red Cross (ICRC) in Mozambique, met recently with the leaders of RENAMO to discuss problems related to the provision and distribution of humanitarian relief in RENAMO-controlled areas. It was agreed by all concerned that humanitarian organizations would have unimpeded access to all Mozambicans who are in need of humanitarian assistance and live in areas under RENAMO control. As of 16 June 1993, 19,387 tons of food, 1,729 tons of seed, 1.18 tons of soap and 290,777 units of tools, blankets and other non-food items were distributed in those areas. On 12 June 1993, the Office of the United Nations High Commissioner for Refugees (UNHCR) launched its programme to repatriate Mozambican refugees by organizing the start of the voluntary return of the estimated 250,000 Mozambicans now in Zimbabwe.

VI. New timetable for the peace process

21. The experience of the past several months has demonstrated clearly that the original timetable contained in the general peace agreement, which anticipated that the elections would be held in October 1993, was overambitious and needs to be reviewed in close consultation with the Government and RENAMO. This issue has been raised on numerous occasions by my Special Representative with President Chissano and Mr. Dhlakama. Other interested parties, observer States, United Nations agencies and the donor community in Maputo have also been closely consulted, with a view to determining a realistic deadline for the extension.

22. The core of the new timetable under discussion is the length of time required to complete the demobilization and the formation of the new army, which are

prerequisites for the holding of elections. As envisaged in the adjusted time-frame, the first assembly areas were ready to be opened by 21 June 1993. The timetable also calls for the concentration and demobilization of troops to start on 1 July 1993. During the first two weeks of July 1993, the first group of government and RENAMO soldiers should be sent for training in Nyanga, and the formation of FADM would then begin on 1 September 1993, which would coincide with the opening of the last assembly areas. At the same time, the Electoral Law would be approved by the end of July 1993. Since the registration document, on which the Government insists in the draft Electoral Law, requires the use of photographic equipment and high security grade paper materials for which procurement and delivery will require at least several months, registration will not start before the end of 1993. However, as the rainy season extends from November to March, it is foreseen that the three-month registration period can begin only in April 1994, which would allow the elections to be held by September-October 1994. This would constitute a rather tight schedule, and any major delays would result in a significant postponement of the elections until May-June 1995, after the next rainy season.

23. While the general parameters of the new timetable have been thoroughly discussed, I am still awaiting final agreement from both parties. Meanwhile, during the recent Follow-up Donors' Meeting in Maputo, donors urged the Government and RENAMO to finalize as soon as possible a precise timetable for the full implementation of the provisions of the general peace agreement and stated that they were strongly in favour of holding the elections by October 1994. I hope to be in a position shortly to obtain a firm agreement of the parties to a new timetable, and shall submit my recommendations on the extension of the mandate of ONUMOZ and its financial implications to the Council in due course.

VII. Observations

24. After unfortunate delays between March and May 1993, determined efforts have resulted in forward movement of the peace process in Mozambique. All parties have had time to reflect on their positions. Many positive developments have occurred during the reporting period: the virtually full deployment of ONUMOZ in various regions of the country, the establishment of the Trust Fund to assist RENAMO and the resumption of the work of many of the joint commissions. These, together with a massive international effort in the humanitarian field, with a sharp increase in the return of refugees and displaced persons, have created a firm foundation for advancing the peace process.

25. The fact that the general peace agreement is being implemented, albeit with delays, is clear proof of the desire of the people of Mozambique for the return of peace. However, unless its major provisions are implemented, this promising environment will remain fragile and the future of the country will continue to be uncertain, at best. The United Nations will of course continue to sustain and assist in the implementation of the peace process, but it cannot move it forward by itself. Much would now depend on the two Mozambican parties themselves; their intentions will be increasingly judged by their deeds.

26. It is essential, therefore, that the Government and RENAMO now commit themselves to accelerating the whole peace process in Mozambique. Much time has already been lost; there should be no further delay in finalizing a new and realistic timetable for the implementation of the peace plan. For the plan to succeed, the cantonment and demobilization of troops should start in the coming days and weeks and be completed early in 1994. It would be equally important to ensure that the training of the new army, a vital prerequisite for a democratic and stable environment in Mozambique, be initiated as soon as possible in order to keep the agreed timetable on track. To assist in facilitating this process, I would be ready to accede, with the consent of the Security Council, to the request that ONUMOZ assume chairmanship of CCFADM, on the strict understanding that this would not entail any obligation on the part of the United Nations for training or establishing the new armed forces.

27. The start of preparations for the elections in an atmosphere of tolerance and reconciliation is a matter of high priority. While the international community remains supportive of all positive trends in Mozambique, it would, I am convinced, react negatively to further procrastination by any party or to the introduction of new conditions for proceeding with the implementation of the peace agreement. The scarcity of international resources does not lend itself to sustaining indefinite commitments. There is a pressing need to renew and sustain the momentum towards attaining lasting peace in Mozambique. In such a complex process, it would be inadmissible to allow further postponements. If the Government and RENAMO maintain their political commitment and if the international community is assured that the implementation of the Rome accords would proceed at a brisk pace, the process could succeed and elections could be held not later than October 1994. I do not see any viable alternative.

28. It was opportune that I was able to review the situation in Mozambique with President Chissano on 26 June during the meeting of the Assembly of Heads of State and Government of the Organization of African Unity in Cairo. I am pleased to report to the Council that the President reiterated his commitment to make every effort

to overcome the difficulties and delays encountered, in order to ensure the success of the peace process. I am confident that RENAMO also will endeavour to achieve this vital goal.

29. I would like to take this opportunity to pay tribute to my Special Representative, to the Force Commander, Major General Lelio Gonçalves Rodrigues da Silva, and to the military and civilian personnel of ONUMOZ who are tackling with determination and dedication the difficult task of helping the people of Mozambique to achieve lasting peace and democracy in their country.

Document 38

Security Council resolution approving ONUMOZ chairmanship of the Joint Commission for the Formation of the Mozambican Defence Force (CCFADM) and underlining the importance of holding the elections in Mozambique no later than October 1994

S/RES/850 (1993), 9 July 1993

The Security Council,

Reaffirming its resolutions 782 (1992) of 13 October 1992, 797 (1992) of 16 December 1992 and 818 (1993) of 14 April 1993,

Having considered the report of the Secretary-General of 30 June 1993, 1/

Reiterating the importance it attaches to the General Peace Agreement for Mozambique 2/ and to the timely fulfilment by all parties in good faith of obligations contained therein,

Seriously concerned that the delays in the implementation of major aspects of the Agreement have not been entirely overcome,

Encouraged by the efforts of the Government of Mozambique and the Resistência Nacional Moçambicana to maintain the cease-fire,

Noting with satisfaction the signature of the status-of-forces agreement between the Government of Mozambique and the United Nations, and the full deployment of all the main infantry battalions of the United Nations Operation in Mozambique,

Also noting with satisfaction the successful completion of the withdrawal of Zimbabwean and Malawian troops as provided for in the General Peace Agreement,

1. *Approves* the report of the Secretary-General of 30 June 1993; 1/

2. *Pays tribute* to the Special Representative of the Secretary-General, to the Force Commander of the United Nations Operation in Mozambique and to the military and civilian personnel of the Operation who are tackling with determination and dedication the difficult task of helping the people of Mozambique to achieve lasting peace and democracy in their country;

3. *Welcomes* the progress made to date in the implementation of the provisions of the General Peace Agreement for Mozambique, but stresses its concern that the delays previously reported to the Security Council have not been entirely overcome, in particular with respect to the assembly and demobilization of forces, the formation of the new unified armed forces and finalizing the arrangements for the elections;

4. *Underlines* in this respect the importance it attaches to the holding of the elections no later than October 1994;

5. *Welcomes* the agreement of the parties to the convening of a meeting between the President of the Republic of Mozambique and the President of the Resistência Nacional Moçambicana in Maputo on 17 July 1993 to address major issues pertaining to the implementation of the General Peace Agreement;

6. *Invites* the Government of Mozambique and the Resistência Nacional to cooperate fully with the Secretary-General and his Special Representative in their efforts to promote a resolution of these difficulties and to agree without delay to the revised timetable for the implementation of the provisions of the Agreement on the basis of the general parameters described in paragraphs 21 to 23 of the report of the Secretary-General;

7. *Urges* the Government of Mozambique and the Resistência Nacional to begin, as a matter of urgency, the assembly and demobilization of their forces without waiting for all assembly areas to become operational;

8. *Urges* the Resistência Nacional to dispatch without further delay its military personnel to the military centre in Nyanga, Zimbabwe, for training, together with military personnel of the Government of Mozambique, as the first elements of the new Mozambican Defence Forces;

9. *Approves* the recommendation of the Secretary-

1/ *Official Records of the Security Council, Forty-eighth Year, Supplement for April, May and June 1993*, document S/26034.
2/ Ibid., *Forty-seventh Year, Supplement for October, November and December 1992*, document S/24635, annex.

General that the United Nations Operation in Mozambique should chair the Joint Commission for the Formation of the Mozambican Defence Force, on the strict understanding that this would not entail any obligation on the part of the United Nations for training or establishing the new armed forces, and encourages the Resistência Nacional to participate fully in the work of the Joint Commission;

10. *Stresses* the importance of the early establishment of the Commission for State Administration and the application throughout the country of the provisions of the General Peace Agreement concerning public administration;

11. *Notes with appreciation* the assistance and pledges made by Member States in support of the peace process, and encourages donors to provide appropriate and prompt assistance for the implementation of major aspects of the Agreement;

12. *Also notes with appreciation* the contribution from the Government of Italy to the trust fund described in paragraph 12 of the report of the Secretary-General, and welcomes the intention of a number of other Member States to contribute;

13. *Requests* the Secretary-General to keep the Council informed of developments regarding the full implementation of the provisions of the General Peace Agreement and to submit a report to the Council by 18 August 1993 on the outcome of the discussions on the revised timetable, including for the assembly and demobilization of forces and the formation of the new unified armed forces;

14. *Decides* to remain seized of the matter.

Document 39

Statement by the Secretary-General welcoming the first meeting of President Chissano and Mr. Dhlakama, held on 23 August 1993 in Maputo

UN Press Release SG/SM/5065, 24 August 1993

Secretary-General Boutros Boutros-Ghali welcomes the first meeting, held yesterday in Maputo, between President Joaquim Chissano of Mozambique and Afonso Dhlakama, of the Mozambique National Resistance Movement (RENAMO), which was organized with the assistance of the United Nations.

The Secretary-General trusts that it will have an important confidence-building impact and will facilitate the full and expeditious implementation of all major aspects of the General Peace Agreement on Mozambique. The international community attaches particular significance to this. The Secretary-General earnestly hopes that such dialogue will become an ongoing and action-oriented process, bringing a successful outcome to the peace efforts in the country.

Document 40

Report of the Secretary-General on ONUMOZ

S/26385, 30 August 1993, and S/26385/Add.1, 10 September 1993

Introduction

1. The present report is submitted in response to paragraph 13 of Security Council resolution 850 (1993) of 9 July 1993, which requested me to keep the Council informed of developments regarding the full implementation of the provisions of the general peace agreement (S/24635, annex) and to submit a report to it by 18 August 1993 on the outcome of the discussions on the revised timetable, including the assembly and demobilization of forces and the formation of the unified armed forces. The Council subsequently agreed to my suggestion that the submission of the report be postponed in view of the projected meeting between the President of Mozambique, Mr. Joaquim Chissano, and Mr. Afonso Dhlakama, President of the Resistência Nacional Moçambicana (RENAMO). The present report therefore covers the period up to 25 August 1993 and brings up to date the activities of United Nations Operation in Mozambique (ONUMOZ) in implementing the military, humanitarian, electoral and political aspects of the mandate entrusted to it by the Security Council.

2. The most significant development since my last

report to the Council on 30 June 1993 (S/26034), was the arrival in Maputo, after several postponements, of Mr. Dhlakama, and the start on 21 August 1993 of a series of meetings between him and President Chissano. It is widely expected that these meetings will continue until some form of agreement has been reached on major outstanding issues. The importance of this development cannot be overemphasized. Progress in many major areas of the peace process depends on the successful outcome of these discussions.

I. Military aspects

A. *Deployment of the military component*

3. In my previous report (S/26034), I had informed the Council that the delays that had impeded the rapid deployment of the ONUMOZ military component had been overcome and that, by the beginning of May 1993, the five infantry battalions provided for in my operational plan had been fully deployed along the Beira, Tete, Limpopo and Nacala corridors and along National Highway No. 1. Since then, deployment of all contingents has been completed with the arrival of the Indian engineer company, which is operating in the southern region.

4. At the end of August 1993, the total strength of the formed units, including support elements, was 6,004 as follows:

Argentina	36
Bangladesh	1 363
Botswana	721
India	899
Italy	1 010
Japan	48
Portugal	280
Uruguay	816
Zambia	831

5. As envisaged, operations of the contingents involve mainly the conduct of motorized and air patrols along the corridors, establishing checkpoints and conducting train escorts. United Nations troops have also been involved in escorting road convoys carrying relief food to populations in need in various regions, as well as transporting equipment to assembly areas. In addition, they have carried out repair and reconnaissance of roads, both in populated locations and en route to assembly areas.

6. As of 25 August 1993, 303 of the authorized total number of 354 military observers had arrived in Mozambique. Assisted by troops from the contingents, the observers are now actively involved in the establishment and preparation of assembly areas, conducting inspections and investigations of cease-fire violation complaints.

7. In paragraph 5 of my previous report to the Council (S/26034), I emphasized the need to provide additional patrols and observation, including permanent stationing of military personnel outside transport corridors. I also indicated the need to bring the strength of the military component of ONUMOZ up to the levels originally envisaged. My Special Representative and the Force Commander have now strongly recommended to me the deployment of United Nations troops in Zambézia Province, in addition to the five corridors, in order to ensure security, to provide escort convoys for humanitarian operations, and to facilitate assembly and demobilization of troops in this vast and heavily populated region. I am studying this proposal closely and will present my recommendations on the strengthening of the United Nations military presence in this important province to the Security Council in due course.

B. *Establishment of assembly areas and demobilization*

8. Substantial progress has been made with respect to the establishment of assembly areas for the cantonment of Government and RENAMO troops prior to their demobilization. So far, 34 of the 49 assembly areas have been found acceptable by all sides and have already been approved by the Cease-fire Commission. Of these 34 sites, 26 are designated for government and 8 for RENAMO troops. Teams of ONUMOZ military observers have been deployed in 18 of these 34 approved assembly areas so that the cantonment process may begin as soon as possible. I very much hope the readiness of the United Nations to start receiving troops immediately in the cantonment areas will encourage the parties to begin this process without further delay. At this stage, the process hinges on the success of the meetings between President Chissano and Mr. Dhlakama. As my Special Representative, Mr. Aldo Ajello, has reported to me, Mr. Dhlakama had made it clear that he could not begin demobilization of his troops until the question of administrative control over RENAMO-held areas is resolved. Meanwhile, the Government has indicated its readiness to send its troops to the assembly areas as soon as RENAMO is prepared to do the same.

C. *Cease-fire*

9. Since the signing of the general peace agreement, there have been 47 complaints of cease-fire violations all of which have been investigated by the Cease-fire Commission with the active participation of ONUMOZ. The Commission approved the results of almost half these investigations; some complaints have been dropped, while the results of the remaining cases, which relate

primarily to the question of control and administration of territory, have been transferred to the Supervisory and Monitoring Commission for consideration.

10. The most serious complaints are the following: in late June and early July 1993, RENAMO had detained 27 Mozambican hunters in the area of Salamanga (Maputo Province), claiming that they had been hunting in this RENAMO-controlled area without "RENAMO's permission". After interventions by ONUMOZ, RENAMO released the hunters in the presence of my Special Representative and United Nations military observers. Meanwhile, complaints concerning government encroachment on three villages in Tete Province and on a RENAMO base at the village of Mangole in Gaza Province during the third week of July were filed by RENAMO. While acknowledging that its forces had attempted to dislodge RENAMO from the Tete villages, the Government presented arguments that implied that it reserved the right to use military force in order to reclaim territory that it considered rightfully under its control. In this connection, my Special Representative made a public statement to the effect that disputes of any kind could be resolved only within the mechanisms established under the general peace agreement. Other members of the Supervisory and Monitoring Commission issued a joint statement deploring unilateral action aimed at occupying or reoccupying areas by force. At a subsequent meeting of the Commission, the Government stated that it had no intentions of taking any unilateral action.

11. At the end of July 1993, following the Government's encroachment on the village of Mangole, a statement issued by a senior RENAMO official threatening unspecified retaliatory action against the Government added to the atmosphere of tension. My Special Representative strongly denounced this position.

D. *Formation of the Mozambican Defence Forces*

12. The general peace agreement provided that the formation of the new Mozambican Defence Forces (FADM) was to begin immediately after the cease-fire came into effect and was to be conducted simultaneously with the process of assembly and demobilization of troops so that the new army would be operational by the time elections were held. The process was to be supervised by the Joint Commission for the Formation of the Mozambican Defence Force (CCFADM) which includes, in addition to the parties to the agreement, representatives of France, Portugal and the United Kingdom of Great Britain and Northern Ireland, as statutory members. Shortly after the Security Council adopted resolution 850 (1993), by which it, *inter alia*, agreed to the parties' request that the Joint Commission be placed under the chairmanship of the United Nations. My Special Repre-

sentative convened the first formal meeting of the Joint Commission on 22 July 1993.

13. At that meeting, the Joint Commission approved the Lisbon Declaration by which France, Portugal and the United Kingdom set out the programmes they would offer to assist in the formation of FADM. The Commission decided to initiate the training of instructors for the new Mozambican army immediately by sending 100 officers (50 each from the Government and RENAMO) to the training facility at Nyanga (Zimbabwe) where they arrived on 3 August 1993. After some delays, it is now expected that an additional 440 officers will be dispatched to Nyanga at the beginning of September 1993. I am also pleased to inform the Council that on 13 August 1993, the Joint Commission approved three important documents: the timetable for the formation of the new army; the rules and criteria for the instructors to be trained in Nyanga; and the structure of the high command of the new army. These documents, which were signed at a public ceremony, should have a positive influence on the work of other commissions.

II. Humanitarian assistance programme

14. The comprehensive humanitarian programme is continuing to cover repatriation, demobilization, emergency relief and the restoration of essential services. Its most important goal is to address effectively the reintegration needs of all Mozambicans. In this connection, the programme also focuses on balance-of-payments support for marketed food and agricultural inputs as well as institutional support to strengthen local capacity to manage post-war humanitarian programmes.

15. At the Follow-up Donors' Meeting to the Donors' Conference on Mozambique held in Maputo on 8 and 9 June 1993, considerable concern was expressed about the amount of resources not earmarked. Although some progress has been made in reducing the size of unallocated funds, many donors have yet to indicate the activities or the implementing agencies to which they wish their pledges directed. The United Nations Office for Humanitarian Assistance Coordination (UNOHAC) has recently written to such donors to encourage them to make decisions, so that the implementation of some underfunded activities can go forward. However, even if all commitments were allocated to specific activities, there would still be a net shortfall of some $70 million.

16. The key outstanding needs in the consolidated Humanitarian Assistance Programme are in the following areas and sectors: (a) agriculture, including seeds and tools; (b) multisectoral or area-based programmes, including the reintegration of demobilized soldiers; (c) emergency, including non-food relief, logistics, and the transport of vulnerable groups; (d) the repatriation

operation; (e) institutional support; and (f) balance-of-payments support. In this context, it should be pointed out that access to seeds and tools is essential to a successful return of Mozambicans to the land. Also, the importance of assisting demobilized soldiers to reintegrate into civilian life cannot be overstated.

17. Significant population movements took place during the months of January and February 1993, prior to the secondary planting season. With the main agricultural season beginning in October/November, increased additional population movements are expected. It should be pointed out, however, that for Mozambique as a whole, and within the context of its population of refugees and internally displaced persons, the return of potential resettlers has been relatively slow. One reason for this relatively slow pace of return is the insecurity which potential resettlers feel about the future. Another is the absence of basic services in the areas to which they are expected to return. Without open roads and the bare minimum of economic activity and services, potential resettlers may prefer to wait another year before moving back permanently. The beginning of the demobilization process should, however, send a clear signal that peace is stable and also encourage movement back to the land.

18. However, in certain areas, population movements have recently picked up. Such is the case in Nampula Province where, in contrast to the previously slow rate of resettlement, movement back into RENAMO areas within the province increased considerably from June through August 1993. This increase is due in part to the expansion of assistance from solely relief activities, to include health, water, agricultural inputs and education. Food continues to be delivered to many regions, including many RENAMO areas.

19. Some 326,000 refugees are now back inside Mozambique, a number equal to over 20 per cent of the total of 1.5 million Mozambicans in refuge outside Mozambique at the time the Peace Agreement was signed. More than half of these returnees have moved to the small, exceptionally fertile District of Angonia in Tete Province. The Office of the United Nations High Commissioner for Refugees (UNHCR) has held three transport operations for returning refugees from Zimbabwe, mostly heading for Manica Province. An agreement has now been signed with Swaziland to begin the repatriation of some 24,000 refugees in that country in late August 1993, with the International Organization for Migration handling the transport of the refugees to over 100 different villages and towns inside southern Mozambique.

20. The Commission for Reintegration held its third meeting on 27 July 1993. A series of documents was approved that served to identify the key principles pertaining to the reintegration of demobilized soldiers; impartial treatment of different categories of military personnel; rural orientation; and the use of existing institutions wherever possible. The key programmes identified are in the areas of training and labour-intensive employment creation, owing to the weakness of the formal labour market. This substantial progress resulted from a month of careful and intense preparatory meetings with all concerned.

21. An information programme for the soldiers in the assembly areas was approved; it seeks to encourage the demobilized to return to their rural homes and to re-establish their families as viable economic units. The programme will include precise information for vulnerable groups among the demobilized and general information related to labour-intensive opportunities and training facilities. In this connection, the programme will launch a literacy campaign and make use of radio programmes and local discussion groups.

22. Some progress has been made in the implementation of the mine-clearing programme. A Mine-Clearance Subcommittee has been established to review as well as develop programme and operational details that will be incorporated in proposals for approval by the Cease-fire Commission. Proposals related to a country-wide mine survey and the training of Mozambicans in de-mining and mine-clearance operations are now ready for approval by the Cease-fire Commission.

III. Preparations for the elections

23. The multi-party consultative conference, under the chairmanship of the Minister of Justice of Mozambique, which was suspended on 27 April 1993, resumed its work on 2 August 1993 to discuss the text of the draft electoral law prepared by the Government. All parties, including RENAMO, were in attendance. It had already been agreed that, after the discussion, the Government would present the finalized draft electoral law to the National Assembly for approval and that the document should conform strictly to both the letter and the spirit of the general peace agreement. While the decision of the parties to resume their efforts to discuss the draft electoral law was a positive development, little actual progress has been made in agreeing on a text. In fact, as of 25 August 1993, only 16 of the 284 proposed articles had been considered, with debate breaking down over article 16. This article concerns the composition of the National Electoral Commission, which would be responsible for organizing the parliamentary and presidential elections and should be representative and impartial.

24. According to the Government's original proposals, one third of the members of the National Electoral Commission would be nominated by RENAMO and the remainder by the Government. RENAMO and the parties

which constitute the so-called "unarmed opposition", while accepting the Government's suggestion that the Commission should comprise a total of 21 members, have been claiming more representation for themselves and have made a counter-proposal according to which the Government, RENAMO and the "unarmed opposition" should appoint seven members each. The Government's latest position is that it should appoint 11 members, RENAMO 7, and the unarmed opposition 3 members. Another counter-proposal, put forward by a minor party, suggests that the Commission should consist of 10 members from the Government, 7 from RENAMO, 3 "unarmed opposition" appointees, and an independent chairman.

IV. Political developments

25. Apart from the resumption of the dialogue on the draft electoral law (see sect. III above) and the decision to send officers to Nyanga for training as instructors, an important political development since my last report (S/26034) involves the work of the commissions provided for in the general peace agreement. Since July 1993, all four tripartite commissions chaired by the United Nations have been meeting on a regular basis and approving documents aimed at facilitating and accelerating the peace process.

26. The Supervisory and Monitoring Commission has concentrated on two main issues: the electoral law and guidelines for cease-fire violations. It also considered a document on rules of conduct for the Cease-fire Commission regarding the movement of troops after the signature of the general peace agreement. This document, which separates the military and logistic aspects of such movements from those relating to the administration of territory, has received the full support of the international members of the Supervisory and Monitoring Commission as well as the approval of the Government. RENAMO has requested more time for consultations. Once approved, the document will allow the parties to resolve the problems that arose following the Government's encroachment on three villages in Tete Province, and it is hoped that it will prevent similar situations from occurring in the future. The document also reiterates that all military movements conducted after 4 October 1992 with the purpose of gaining new military positions must be considered as cease-fire violations, and that those troops that had been moved for such purpose should be withdrawn to their previous positions.

27. The Commission for Reintegration has approved key programmes for demobilized soldiers in the areas of training and labour-intensive employment, as well as an information programme for soldiers in the assembly areas. The Commission for Reintegration also decided to recommend to the Supervisory and Monitoring Commission that it extend the activities of the Humanitarian Assistance Committee in accordance with Protocol V, section III, paragraph 5, of the general peace agreement.

28. The general peace agreement also called for four commissions to be established, comprising members of the Government and RENAMO as well as other members appointed as a result of consultations held by the President of Mozambique. Members of three of these commissions have been appointed, and the following bodies have been formally established: the Commission for State Administration, the National Information Commission and the Police Affairs Commission. However, owing to persistent mistrust between the two parties, none of these commissions has yet been convened. RENAMO has objected to the members appointed by President Chissano as well as to the chairpersons selected by him. The establishment of the fourth, the National Electoral Commission, will be determined after the adoption of the draft electoral law (see paras. 23 and 24 above).

29. In his contacts with President Chissano and Mr. Dhlakama, my Special Representative has consistently conveyed to the parties the strong concerns shared by the Security Council and myself that, despite some tangible progress, delays have not been overcome. In particular, he has emphasized to the parties the importance the international community attaches to the holding of the elections in Mozambique no later than October 1994. Obviously, there is an urgent need to agree, without further postponements, on the revised timetable for the implementation of all provisions of the general peace agreement, which was presented by my Special Representative to the parties several months ago. As Council members are aware, the revised timetable takes as its point of departure the resumption of the work of the commissions beginning on 3 June 1993 and concluding 16 months later with the holding of elections in October 1994. The concentration and demobilization of Government and RENAMO troops, to be carried out in stages, is expected to take eight or nine months. The concentration of troops is scheduled to begin in September 1993 and will be followed a month later by the beginning of the demobilization. It is expected that 50 per cent of the soldiers will have been demobilized by January 1994, and the demobilization of troops should be completed by May 1994.

30. Approximately 30,000 soldiers are to be absorbed into the new army and the rest are to return to civilian life. Half the new army is to be operational by May 1994 and formation of the new army should be completed by September 1994. Home transportation of soldiers who will not be part of the new army is to start in October 1993, after demobilization begins, and is to

be concluded by April 1994 in order to enable the demobilized soldiers to register for the elections. Voter registration is expected to take three months and is scheduled to be carried out from April to June 1994. The repatriation of refugees and displaced persons has already begun and is expected to be largely completed by April 1994 so that the resettled population may register in time for the elections.

31. Although the revised schedule has not yet been formally approved by the Supervisory and Monitoring Commission, important progress has been made in key areas. The Government has explicitly agreed to the October 1994 deadline for the holding of the elections, while RENAMO has expressed its implicit agreement. Hence, both parties have agreed in principle to fulfil the overall objective of the general peace agreement within the proposed time-frame. Although some specific modifications have been requested, my Special Representative has made it clear that these should not affect the ultimate goal of holding elections in October 1994.

V. Observations

32. The recent developments in the Mozambican peace process have been encouraging. The most significant of these has been the long overdue start of direct talks between President Chissano and Mr. Dhlakama in Maputo. Although these talks are still under way, they have already instilled a renewed sense of optimism about the prospects for the full and timely implementation of the peace process in Mozambique. There can be no doubt that genuine national reconciliation will be warmly welcomed by all Mozambicans and that it will receive the strong support of the international community.

33. I suggested delaying the submission of the present report expressly in order to be in a position to inform the Council of this event, which not only has special symbolic significance, but is also of substantive importance. As members of the Security Council are aware, President Chissano and Mr. Dhlakama have already announced their intention to meet regularly in the future, and Mr. Dhlakama has agreed to establish a residence in Maputo, dividing his time between the capital and RENAMO headquarters in Maringue. I shall keep the Security Council informed of the progress of the talks. I strongly urge the parties to take this opportunity to turn their current dialogue into an ongoing and action-oriented process aimed at bringing the peace process to a successful outcome. All efforts to this end should stay firmly on the track charted by the general peace agreement.

34. I especially welcome the readiness of RENAMO to accept the principle of a single administration throughout the country. I very much hope that this issue, which is crucial to many elements of the peace process, can be resolved in the coming days, along with the questions concerning the early initiation of the assembly and demobilization process, which are other pressing imperatives. In this context, the timely dispatch of the second group of government and RENAMO military trainees to the Nyanga military facility in Zimbabwe would be a significant advance.

35. It is of vital importance that President Chissano and Mr. Dhlakama reach an understanding on how to break the current deadlock on the composition of the future National Electoral Commission. Several proposals have been put forward; goodwill and determination on the part of all parties involved would help to bridge the already shrinking gap in their respective positions. Having said this, it is my belief that, notwithstanding the present difficulties regarding the establishment of this important commission, work should proceed expeditiously on the drafting of the electoral law so that it may be approved without undue delay, thus making it possible for the elections to be held no later than October 1994, as emphasized in Security Council resolution 850 (1993).

36. There is a pressing need for the two parties formally to approve the revised timetable for the implementation of the peace process. Since most of the elements for the successful movement forward of the peace efforts are in place, I have instructed my Special Representative to follow the above-mentioned plan as closely as possible, and strongly urge the parties to take advantage of the promising situation. The constructive progress achieved recently should not lose its momentum. Furthermore, the demands on the United Nations and its critical financial constraints preclude any further delay or procrastination. The international community, I am confident, would not entertain further attempts to attach conditions to the peace process or to gain more time and obtain further concessions. For its part, the United Nations will continue to support and assist all parties and the people of Mozambique in their endeavours to bring lasting peace and democracy to their country.

Addendum (S/26385/Add.1)

1. As members of the Security Council will recall, in paragraph 33 of my report of 30 August 1993 (S/26385) I emphasized the significance of the direct talks between the President of Mozambique, Mr. Joaquim Chissano, and Mr. Afonso Dhlakama, President of the Resistência Nacional Moçambicana (RENAMO), which began in Maputo on 23 August 1993, and promised to keep the Security Council informed of the progress of the talks. I am now pleased to inform the members of the Council that on 2 September 1993, two major agreements were reached between the Government and RENAMO and an appropriate document was signed on 3 September 1993.

2. The Government of Mozambique and

RENAMO have agreed, in particular, to integrate into the state administration all areas which had been under RENAMO control. This understanding will have major implications for stability in the country and should help to promote national reconciliation.

3. The agreement which will have major consequences for the functioning of ONUMOZ concerns the impartiality of the national police. The parties have agreed to request the United Nations to monitor all police activities in the country, public or private, to monitor the rights and liberties of citizens in Mozambique and to provide technical support to the Police Commission (COMPOL). The proposed United Nations police contingent would be responsible for verifying that all police activities in the country are consistent with the General Peace Agreement (S/24635, annex). The Government has agreed to provide a list of *matériel* in the possession of the police, as well as other information necessary to verify the activities of the police.

4. My Special Representative, Mr. Aldo Ajello, has already begun preliminary consultations with the Government of Mozambique and RENAMO on this matter. It is my intention to send shortly to Mozambique a small survey team of experts and to inform the Security Council in due course of their findings as well as of my final recommendations about the size of the United Nations police component. In this context, I would like to bring to the attention of Council members that, from my Special Representative's initial contacts on this matter, it appears that at least one of the parties has in mind a much larger police force than that envisaged in the initial operational plan for ONUMOZ (S/24892, paras. 29 and 48 (c), and Add.1). While awaiting the experts' recommendation, preparations will be made to commence deployment of the 128 police observers already authorized by the Security Council (S/RES/797 (1992) of 16 December 1992).

5. The Mozambican Government further has indicated that it also will seek the support of the international community in reorganizing its Rapid Intervention Police.

6. President Chissano and Mr. Dhlakama discussed other important issues, including those relating to the impartiality of the press and economic assistance to RENAMO. However, decisions on those issues have been deferred to the next high-level meeting. It is expected that Mr. Dhlakama will again visit Maputo in the beginning of October 1993. In this connection, I would like to reiterate that I am strongly in favour of such meetings becoming an ongoing process. My Special Representative is working with the parties to ensure that the momentum towards the full implementation of the Rome Accords is maintained. It is imperative to immediately begin assembly and demobilization of troops as well as to reach early agreement on the draft electoral law, in order for the elections to be held according to the revised timetable for the implementation of the General Peace Agreement (see S/26835, paras. 29-31). I hope that all Member States concerned would strongly encourage the parties accordingly. No new conditions, preconditions or postponements should be accepted.

Document 41

Letter dated 8 September 1993 from Mozambique transmitting the final document from the 23 August-3 September meeting between President Chissano and Mr. Dhlakama

S/26432, 13 September 1993

Upon instructions from my Government, I have the honour to request that the attached document be circulated as a document of the Security Council.

(*Signed*) Pedro Comissário AFONSO
Ambassador Extraordinary and
Plenipotentiary Permanent Representative
to the United Nations

Annex

Final document from the meeting between the President of the Republic of Mozambique and the President of the Resistência Nacional Moçambicana

3 September 1993

The President of the Republic, Joaquim Alberto Chissano, and the President of the Resistência Nacional

Moçambicana (RENAMO), Afonso Macacho Marceta Dhlakama, meeting in Maputo from 23 August to 3 September 1993, analysed the difficulties related to the questions of territorial administration, the police and the media that have been faced during the process of implementing the General Peace Agreement.

Considering the desire of the parties to respect in full the General Peace Agreement signed in Rome on 4 October 1992 and to achieve a genuine peace in the country based on democracy and national reconciliation;

Considering the need to guarantee a single administration for the country;

Recognizing that the zones under RENAMO administration have specific features;

Recognizing the need to create temporary mechanisms that guarantee the reintegration of the zones under RENAMO administration into the state administration;

Following a lengthy exchange of views on the above-mentioned questions, it was possible to reach the following consensus:

I. *Territorial administration*

With the aim of guaranteeing that the process of reintegrating the zones under RENAMO control into the state administration takes place in a smooth and efficient way and in accordance with the provisions of the General Peace Agreement on the issue;

Considering the need to guarantee observance of the principle of non-discrimination and impartiality in the treatment of all questions to do with the reintegration of these zones;

They decided:

1. The Government shall create the post of adviser to the Governor in the staffing structure of the provincial state apparatus, with the function of advising the Governor on all the questions directly or indirectly to do with the reintegration of the zones under RENAMO control, including socio-economic questions.

2. The Government shall appoint three people in each province, to be nominated by RENAMO, to the advisers' posts.

3. Whenever there is a legal basis the advisers may be dismissed by the Government, in agreement with RENAMO.

The Government will grant dismissal whenever this is requested by RENAMO. In either case RENAMO may nominate other people to replace the dismissed advisers in the terms of No. 2 of this document.

4. The Governor will indicate the director or directors with whom the advisers should work on a case-by-case basis, in the light of the needs or tasks.

5. The provincial directors must give the advisers all the collaboration required for the correct discharge of their duties.

6. Whenever they consider it appropriate, the advisers may propose initiatives and measures or submit opinions to the consideration of the Provincial Governor.

7. All decisions related to the zones under RENAMO control shall be taken with the prior opinion of the adviser, which must be given within the time-limit indicated by the Governor or within a reasonable period of time depending on the circumstances.

8. Decisions on matters related to the zones under RENAMO control that fall within the sphere of authority of the Central Government must be taken with the prior opinion of the Governor's adviser.

9. The advisers are not members of the Government. They are civil servants of the state apparatus who have the specific task defined above.

10. Situations arising in the exercise of the advisory function that are not resolved with the Provincial Governor or with the Central Government will be communicated to the National Administration Commission for consideration and decision.

11. When all the advisers to the Provincial Governors are in place, the Government shall appoint people nominated by RENAMO from among the residents of the zones under its control to fill the state apparatus staff posts in these zones.

Advisers' rights and functioning

12. The advisers shall enjoy the following rights:

- The salary and benefits corresponding to letter E1 of the wage scale in force in the state apparatus;
- Transport during the exercise of their functions;
- Provision of a house to be rented.

13. The Government shall guarantee that the advisers have the necessary working conditions for the satisfactory discharge of their duties.

II. *Police*

1. The parties agreed to request the United Nations to send a police contingent to monitor all police activity in the country, namely the Police of the Republic of Mozambique and others, to monitor respect for citizens' rights and freedoms and to provide technical support to the National Police Affairs Commission (COMPOL).

2. This contingent will also have the mission of verifying that the operations of private protection and security companies respect the General Peace Agreement.

3. The Government undertakes to present a list of all war material possessed by the police and its location in the country, specifying all the data required for controlling the force.

4. The Government undertakes to request support from the international community for the following ends:

(a) The reorganization, training or retraining of the Rapid Intervention Police;

(b) The training and equipping of the Rapid Intervention Police with appropriate weaponry and equipment;

(c) Clarification of the vocation and aims of the Rapid Intervention Police.

5. The provisions set out in point 4 (a), (b) and (c) of this document shall obey internationally acceptable standards.

(*Signed*) Joaquim Alberto CHISSANO
President of the Republic of Mozambique

(*Signed*) Afonso Macacho Marceta DHLAKAMA
President of RENAMO

Document 42

Letter dated 10 September 1993 from the Minister for Foreign Affairs of Mozambique to the Secretary-General on steps taken toward implementation of the General Peace Agreement in Mozambique and requesting United Nations deployment of a contingent of civilian policemen

Not issued as a United Nations document

As it may be recalled, the President of the Republic of Mozambique, His Excellency Joaquim Alberto Chissano, has had the honour to address to Your Excellency a letter dated 4 October 1992 immediately after the signing in Rome, of the General Peace Agreement for Mozambique, requesting the participation of the United Nations in its implementation.

In this regard and in addition to the important briefings provided by the Permanent Representative to the United Nations, Mr. Pedro Comissário Afonso, which have allowed the Organization to follow closely the implementation of the General Peace Agreement, I have the honour to inform you on the latest developments in the implementation of the aforesaid agreement:

- All main Commissions under the Chairmanship of the United Nations are now affectively functioning after a period of inactivity due the circumstances beyond Government's control. It will be recalled that RENAMO Representatives once had decided to suspend their participation in these Commissions for quite a long period of time.

- With the normalization of the situation in Mozambique, refugees and displaced people inside the country have started to move back into their places of origin or to any other places of their choice.

- As envisaged in the Peace Accord, the programme of training of the military instructors who will be responsible for the overall formation of the new national armed forces is under way in the Republic of Zimbabwe.

- The process of demobilization and disarmament of forces is yet to start due the systematic pre-conditions imposed by RENAMO beyond the framework of the Peace Accord.

- A little progress has so far been made in the drafting of the electoral law to be adopted by the Assembly of the Republic in view of the legislative and presidential elections scheduled for October next year. However, intensive consultations are under way between the Government and the oposition, i.e. RENAMO and all other emerging political parties.

With the purpose of removing some of the stumbling blocks which, by and large, have been hindering the smooth implementation of the General Peace Agreement, a series of meetings "tête-à-tête" took place in Maputo from 23 August to 3 September 1993, between the President of the Republic, H.E. Joaquim Alberto Chissano, and the RENAMO leader, Mr. Afonso Dhlakama.

In accordance with the agreement reached in the said meetings, the Government of Mozambique once again submits, through you, this formal request for the United Nations to dispatch a contingent of civilian policemen, whose main task will be:

1. To monitor all police related activities in the country and to provide the National Police Affairs Commission (COMPOL) with the needed technical assistance.

2. To verify that the activities carried out by private security companies are consistent with the General Peace Agreement.

The Government also requests assistance from the international community intended to meet the following requirements:

1. Reorganization, training or updating of the Rapid Intervention Police.

2. Capacity-building and provision to the Rapid

Intervention Police with the appropriate equipment and material.

Finally, on behalf of my Government I would like to seize this opportunity to express my appreciation for the vital role being played by the United Nations, in particular through ONUMOZ, in the whole process of imple-mentation of the General Peace Agreement in Mozam-bique.

Please accept, Excellency, the assurances of my high-est consideration.

(*Signed*) Dr. Pascoal Manuel MOCUMBI

Document 43

Security Council resolution emphasizing the need to respect fully all the provisions of the General Peace Agreement for Mozambique

S/RES/863 (1993), 13 September 1993

The Security Council,

Reaffirming its resolutions 782 (1992) of 13 Octo-ber 1992, 797 (1992) of 16 December 1992, 818 (1993) of 14 April 1993 and 850 (1993) of 9 July 1993,

Having considered the report of the Secretary-General of 30 August and 10 September 1993, 1/

Reiterating the importance it attaches to the General Peace Agreement for Mozambique, 2/ and to the timely fulfilment in good faith by all parties of the obligations contained therein,

Commending the efforts of the Secretary-General, his Special Representative and the personnel of the United Nations Operation in Mozambique to implement fully the mandate entrusted to the Operation and to carry it out to a successful conclusion,

Commending also the role played by the Organiza-tion of African Unity, through the Special Representative of its Secretary-General, in the implementation of the General Peace Agreement,

Noting with satisfaction the recent positive develop-ments in the Mozambican peace process, especially the direct talks in Maputo between the President of Mozambique, Mr. Joaquim Chissano, and the President of the Resistência Nacional Moçambicana, Mr. Alfonso Dhlakama, which led to the agreements signed on 3 September 1993, 3/

Also noting with satisfaction the full deployment of the military component of the Operation and the progress made in the establishment by the Operation of assembly areas,

Stressing the unacceptability of attempts to attach conditions to the peace process, in particular to the assembly and demobilization of troops, or to gain more time or further concessions,

Expressing concern at the continuing delays in the implementation of major aspects of the General Peace Agreement as well as at cases of violations of the cease-fire,

1. *Welcomes* the report of the Secretary-General of 30 August and 10 September 1993; 1/

2. *Emphasizes* the need to respect fully all the provisions of the General Peace Agreement for Mozam-bique, in particular those concerning the cease-fire and the movement of troops;

3. *Reaffirms* the importance it attaches to the hold-ing of elections no later than October 1994;

4. *Strongly urges* the Government of Mozambique and the Resistência Nacional Moçambicana to agree with, and to apply, without further postponement, the revised timetable for the implementation of all provisions of the General Peace Agreement as described in paragraphs 29 to 31 of the report of the Secretary-General, 4/ and appeals to the parties to cooperate fully with the Special Repre-sentative of the Secretary-General in this regard;

5. *Stresses* once again the urgent need for the early initiation of the process of assembly and demobilization of troops, and its continuation, in accordance with the revised timetable without preconditions;

6. *Urges* the Resistência Nacional Moçambicana to join the Government of Mozambique in authorizing immediate assembly of forces, and equally urges that both the Government of Mozambique and the Resistência Nacional immediately thereupon begin demobilization;

7. *Welcomes* the progress made by the Joint Com-mission for the new Mozambican Defence Force, in par-ticular in relation to the training of instructors at Nyanga, and also the progress on mine-clearing;

8. *Deplores* the lack of progress in the multi-party consultative conference, and urges the Resistência Nacional Moçambicana and other political parties to join with the Government of Mozambique in quickly agreeing on an election law, which should include provision for an effective national election commission;

1/ *Official Records of the Security Council, Forty-eighth Year, Supplement for July, August and September 1993,* documents S/26385 and Add.1.
2/ Ibid., *Forty-seventh Year, Supplement for October, November and December 1992,* document S/24635, annex.
3/ Ibid., *Forty-eighth Year, Supplement for July, August and Sep-tember 1993,* document S/26385/Add.1.
4/ Ibid., document S/26385.

9. *Calls on* the Government of Mozambique and the Resistência Nacional to make operational without further delay the Commission for State Administration, the National Information Commission and the Police Affairs Commission;

10. *Commends* the agreements reached in the Maputo talks between the Government of Mozambique and the Resistência Nacional on the reintegration into the state administration of all areas now under the control of the Resistência Nacional as well as on the request for monitoring by the United Nations of all police activities in Mozambique and on undertaking additional tasks, as set out in document S/26385/Add.1;

11. *Requests* the Secretary-General to examine expeditiously the proposal by the Government of Mozambique and the Resistência Nacional for United Nations monitoring of police activities in the country, as set out in document S/26385/Add.1, and welcomes his intention to send a survey team of experts in connection with the proposed United Nations police contingent and to report thereon to the Council;

12. *Urges* the Government of Mozambique and the Resistência Nacional to ensure that the momentum towards implementing the General Peace Agreement in full is maintained so that a just and lasting peace in Mozambique can be established, and to this end encourages the President of Mozambique and the President of the Resistência Nacional Moçambicana to continue their direct talks;

13. *Encourages* the international community to provide appropriate and prompt assistance for the implementation of the humanitarian programme carried out in the framework of the General Peace Agreement, and urges the Government of Mozambique and the Resistência Nacional to continue to facilitate unimpeded access of humanitarian assistance to the civilian population in need;

14. *Requests* the Secretary-General to keep the Council informed of developments regarding the implementation of the provisions of the Agreement and to submit a report on the matter to the Council in good time before 31 October 1993;

15. *Decides* to remain actively seized of the matter.

Document 44

Message of the Secretary-General to the Sant'Egidio Community's Seventh International Meeting of Peoples and Religions in Milan, delivered by the Secretary-General's Special Representative, Ambassador Joseph Verner Reed, on 19 September 1993

Not issued as a United Nations document

...

The work of the Community of Sant'Egidio is exemplary in the field of peace-making. What Sant'Egidio has done and is doing proves that peace-making is not a monopoly of States and statesmen. Indeed, it demonstrates that there are no set formulae for peace-making; even the approach of the Community has varied greatly in different situations. Routes to peace may be many and varied. Sant'Egidio has shown what can be achieved when committed individuals and private groups work steadfastly together to create conditions for peace and reconciliation in situations of conflict.

The Community of Sant'Egidio has developed techniques which are different from, but complementary to, those of professional peacemakers. In Mozambique, the Community worked unobtrusively for years to bring the parties together. It harnessed its own networks. It has been particularly successful in engaging others to contribute to a solution. It deployed its confidential, informal techniques alongside, and in harmony with, the official

work of governments and the intergovernmental bodies. From the Mozambican experience, the term "the Italian formula" has been coined to describe this unique blend of governmental and non-governmental peace-making activity.

Respect for the parties to a conflict, for those involved on the ground, is crucial to the success of this work. The Community believes that, over and above national, political or confessional differences, there is more that unites human beings than divides them. It seeks, through its contacts with leaders of the great religions of the world at meetings such as this, to identify, and build upon, that basic essence of humanity.

In working to put this belief into practice, the Community has also shown skill and sensitivity. It has understood that human beings are not one-dimensional; religious or political leaders who may appear to be intransigent in public may also show feelings of great sensitivity towards their families or friends, to their colleagues or to others who do not totally share their point of view. The

Community has sought to identify these essential, shared, human qualities in the people with whom it works.

Sant'Egidio has taken a close and compassionate interest in the situation of religious and ethnic minorities. In the words of one commentator, it believes that the language of peace should use the grammar of multiethnicity. This truly is a message for our times. Today the voices of hatred and war use the language of ethnic, religious and national exclusion. They must be countered if the world is to avoid a slide into ethnic extremism and micro-nationalism.

Above all, the Community understands the importance of discretion and confidence in peace-making efforts. By having no political or sectarian interest of its own, it is able to deploy its efforts for peace in a climate of confidence.

The Community of Sant'Egidio's work for peace, in sum, is based on a vision. That vision—a vision of a world of tolerance and peace—it shares with the Charter of the United Nations.

We are all working towards the same ends. In the vineyard of peace there should certainly be many labourers; what is certain is that the work is hard. What is equally certain is that many hands are needed to complete it.

The Secretary-General therefore wishes this Meeting every success, not only this weekend, but also in the subsequent endeavours for peace and understanding of all of you who have gathered here.

Document 45

Letter dated 24 September 1993 from Mozambique transmitting a statement of the Mozambique Government's position on Security Council resolution 863 (1993)

S/26511, 1 October 1993

Upon instructions from my Government, I have the honour to request that the attached document be circulated as a document of the Security Council.

(*Signed*) Pedro Comissário AFONSO
Ambassador Extraordinary and Plenipotentiary
Permanent Representative to the United Nations

Annex

Government position on United Nations Security Council resolution 863 (1993) of 13 September 1993

The Government of the Republic of Mozambique has the honour to present its position on resolution 863 (1993) of 13 September 1993 to the distinguished members of the Supervision and Control Commission, and through them to the international community, in the following terms.

The multiple questions raised by the resolution have been matters of concern to the Government for a considerable time. It has been making great efforts to resolve them, unfortunately without success. The Government is thus in total agreement with the appeals and recommendations contained in the resolution, and hopes that they will not yet again become a dead letter.

This resolution recalls the old Latin maxim "pacta sunt servanda" or "AGREEMENTS MUST BE FULFILLED". The importance of the General Peace Agreement (AGP), above all of its implementation, lies in the fact that it interprets and aims to satisfy or at least make viable the interests of the Mozambican people and State, namely socio-economic and cultural development. For this reason the Government identifies with and makes its own every effort towards fulfilling AGP, and highly appreciates all support received to this end.

The Government thus welcomes United Nations Security Council resolution 863 (1993), and salutes the international community that adopted it.

With regard to the content of the resolution, the Government would particularly like to restate its positions in relation to some vitally important questions:

1. *The need to fulfil the provisions of the AGP, above all those relating to the cease-fire and troop movements (paragraph 2 of the resolution)*

The Government remains convinced that the guarantee of success of the peace process, and in consequence of the establishment of a just and lasting peace in Mozambique, lies in the elimination of the subjective and objective factors of war that are still intact on the ground, and that not only serve as a constant threat to the peace that the country is currently essaying, but also make the whole process of pacification and democratization a hostage to weapons and to unstated objectives.

The most obvious manifestations of this serious and worrying situation are the continued training of men outside the framework of training the Mozambican Defence Force (FADM), and the troop movements that have been noted in various parts of the national territory.

The decisive process for eliminating such factors is the cantonment of all troops, in a process guided by the principle of simultaneity, though it may be begun and concretized by territorially delimited phases.

The Government reiterates its readiness to begin this process immediately, as already stated to this Supervision and Control Commission when Security Council resolution 850 (1993) of 9 July 1993 was under consideration, and repeated more recently by the President of the Republic.

2. On demobilization and the formation of the Mozambican Defence Force

Protocol IV.I.i.4 of the General Peace Agreement clearly establishes the principle that demobilization will take place simultaneously with the process of forming FADM, and will conclude when FADM has reached full strength. In this sense, the Government agrees with beginning demobilization as soon as the forces are in assembly points, and continuing it in the terms laid down in the General Peace Agreement.

For the Government, it is fundamental that when demobilization is completed there should already be an army in existence that can take on effective responsibility for the purposes set out in AGP itself, namely defending and safeguarding the country's sovereignty, independence and territorial integrity, protecting the civilian population against crime and all forms of violence in cooperation with the Police Command, intervening and helping in crises and emergencies arising from natural disasters, and supporting reconstruction and development efforts (Protocol IV.I.i.2).

These tasks belong to FADM, and nobody can carry them out in its place.

3. Consultative meeting between the Government and RENAMO and the other parties on the draft Electoral Law

The Government is in full agreement with the position taken by the Security Council on this matter. The total lack of progress in this meeting is due to the existence of forces that are determined to do everything possible to avoid holding elections in 1994. They are forces whose exclusive concern is to win power at any price, even when this signifies defrauding the Mozambican people of their right to self-determination. Going beyond a dismissal of the letter and spirit of what was agreed in Rome concerning the National Elections Commission, they reached the point of wanting to neutralize, handcuff and prevent the Government from assuming its responsibilities, including those relating to organization of the elections. They went as far as trying to transfer the debate of the draft from the appropriate forum in which it was taking place to this Supervision and Control Commission. When this attempt was rejected, they then tried to bring in the United Nations Operation in Mozambique (ONUMOZ) to replace the Government in the chair of the forum. It is these and other attempts, as well as a proliferation of delaying tactics, that have led to the current state of impasse.

The Government is aware that by blocking the discussion of the Draft Electoral Law in this way it is intended to limit or remove the right of Mozambican citizens to elect and be elected in the most free, just and transparent conditions, and to resolve the question of power by means of calculations that have no relation to the will expressed at the polling booths.

That is why the Government considers it imperative to bring this lamentable situation to an end, so that the elections may in fact be held in 1994.

4. On re-timetabling

An initial re-timetabling proposal submitted by ONUMOZ was carefully analysed by the Government, in the light of the General Peace Agreement. The in-depth observations that resulted were communicated to the Chairman of CSC in good time, and he was to continue working sessions with the parties until the new calendar to be formally approved in the Supervision and Control Commission was settled. The Government is still awaiting continuation of the discussion that had meanwhile been adjourned.

Once settled and approved, the timetable must be adhered to rigorously, with no further conditions or preconditions, as stated in the Security Council resolution.

The Government delegation to this Commission considers it useful and opportune to single out the above observations and comments.

Referring back to the appraisal we had occasion to make of Security Council resolution 850 (1993), we would like to register and welcome the evolution represented by the letter and spirit of the current resolution. In view of the difficulties and non-fulfilments that the process of implementing the General Peace Agreement is facing, there is a noteworthy effort to go beyond the indiscriminate distribution of responsibilities. We believe that it is only in this way, using just and objective criteria in its analysis and verdicts, that ONUMOZ will support the Mozambican peace process effectively, and only in this way will it gain respect and credibility, particularly among Mozambicans and in southern Africa.

The Government will continue to do all it can to support and facilitate the task of ONUMOZ.

Document 46

Press briefing by the Secretary-General in Maputo

UN Press Release SG/SM/5133, 20 October 1993

I welcome the international press, and I just want to say that this morning we have been able to produce a breakthrough, and we have had a very constructive and positive meeting with the President of the Republic of Mozambique, with the President of RENAMO, myself and my Special Representative.

We reached agreements on very important points. First, an agreement was reached about the Electoral Commission. As you know, there was a difference of point of view. The Electoral Commission will be composed of 10 members for the Government, seven members for RENAMO and three for the other political parties and one independent chairman. The chairman will be selected by the 20 members of the Commission. If they have a problem reaching a consensus on one name to chair the Commission, they can present a list with up to five names to the President of the Republic, and he will make the final choice. But if the Commission is able to agree on a name, then the Commission will appoint their own chairman.

For the rest of the electoral law, a meeting will be called at the technical level with representatives of all parties. Yesterday, I spent more than one hour with the representatives of all the parties, and I asked them for more cooperation, because we need to create a new momentum in the peace process, and one of the prerequisites for this new momentum—I am not saying the only prerequisite—is the composition of the Electoral Commission.

For the rest of the electoral law, as I told you, a meeting will be called at the technical level with representatives of all parties. The draft of the electoral law, approved by the parties, will be sent to the Council of Ministers for approval before the end of October. In other words, we have 11 days, today being the 20th. And then, when it has been approved by the Council, it will be presented to the National Assembly for final adoption. And I hope that everything will be finished before the end of November.

Another very important subject is the problem of demobilization. Demobilization of paramilitary forces, and militia and irregulars, the dismantling of these forces will start simultaneously with the movement of the first troops to the assembly area and will proceed in parallel with the demobilization process until its completion. And demobilization of troops can start according to this and, what is more important, a new calendar of the different dates of demobilization will be approved before the end of this week.

Then, there was also a problem concerning the three commissions which have been appointed by the President of the Republic. The problems related to the composition of the commissions have been overcome after clarification made by the President of the Republic to the President of RENAMO, and an agreement was reached for the chairmanship of the three commissions.

First, the National Commission for Territorial Administration will have two chairmen, one nominated by the Government and one nominated by RENAMO, and they will work on a rotational basis. Second, the Commission for Information (COMINFO), the chairman will be indicated by RENAMO; and the third commission, the Commission for the Police (COMPOL), the chairman, who has already been appointed by the President of the Republic, will remain. What is more important is that the three commissions will begin to work immediately.

Now, considering the police, I was very frank with the President and the President of RENAMO. I told them that in the United Nations now we have problems due to the number of situations all over the world, due to the fact that we have a financial crisis, and we will not be able to provide immediately the police necessary, in conformity with the Agreement that was concluded in Rome. There were 128, which is the minimum that we agreed. So, considering the possibility of delay in the deployments of the United Nations police contingents, COMPOL, the Commission of Police, could be articulated in local units which would monitor the activity of police in any place where police commands are located. In other words, we will have COMPOL here in Maputo, and observers of COMPOL in the different police posts all over the country.

And, meanwhile, as I promised to President Chissano and the President of RENAMO, I will work to obtain as soon as possible, one, the finance; and, two, the policemen who belong to different countries. They need to speak Portuguese, and it is not easy to find all over the world these police. Assessment about the needs of the United Nations police contingents will be made by a United Nations technical team, which is now in Mozambique and is presently operating to do a complete evaluation of what are the number of police we would need and, what is more important, what would be the cost of these policemen for a period of, let us say, 12 months.

Finally, RENAMO has agreed to approve the documents concerning movements of troops after the signature of the Peace Agreements, presented by my Special

Representative and already approved by the Government. I believe that those steps have been very positive and have created a new momentum in the process of peace.

This new momentum will help me convince the Security Council to continue to give me a mandate to maintain the United Nations presence in Mozambique. This will help me obtain from the different financial institutions all over the world and from the donor countries, from the European Community, more assistance for Mozambique, because Mozambique has reached an agreement and Mozambique is activating the peace process.

Now, the good news I have announced is not the only good news. The other good news is what has happened in Angola, where we have been able to send humanitarian assistance for the first time to different cities, mainly in Cuito and Huambo, and we will do the same with other cities. I was with my Special Representative this morning. We were in contact with Luanda, with Dr. Savimbi, and I have sent with him two personal letters to President Jose Eduardo dos Santos, and to the President of UNITA, Dr. Jonas Savimbi, and I hope that through the contacts that have been established through my personal representative, Blondin Beye, we will be able to resume the talks of Abijan, and we will be able to create a new peace process in Angola, like the peace process which is working now in Mozambique.

May I also mention that I have received my Special Envoy, Ms. Angela King, from South Africa. I have had the occasion to meet the Foreign Minister of South Africa, Pik Botha. I met also the leader of the Pan Africanist Congress of Azania (PAC) and the leader of Inkatha. I have met the leader of the African National Congress of South Africa (ANC), Nelson Mandela, a week ago in New York, and we are following with great attention the evaluation of the situation in South Africa. We are present there. Last week, I obtained a mandate from the Security Council to send additional observers to South Africa, so that we will contribute in a more active way to contain the violence in South Africa.

So let us be optimistic; there is progress in Mozambique, progress in Angola, progress in South Africa. And let us hope that this progress, these successes, will encourage similar successes all over the world, because we are all on the same boat and all of the programmes are interrelated, are interconnected. When we are successful in one place, this success helps us to cope with different other situations. And, when we are not successful in one place, this setback complicates our work in different other situations.

The United Nations is there to help the people of Mozambique, to contribute to the return of refugees, to the rehabilitation, to the reconstruction, to the integration of the people that were fighting each other, and I am sure that my next visit will find a new Mozambique, and that all of us will say that this is a success for the people of Mozambique. But not only for the people of Mozambique, but for the people of Africa, for the people of the world.

Finally, I want to thank my Special Representative here in Maputo and all the team of the United Nations system, the military people, the different agencies. They are doing wonderful work. Their presence there is a good example, and I hope that they will continue for the sake of peace and security, for the sake of progress, for the sake of true democracy in Africa.

Document 47

Security Council resolution extending the mandate of ONUMOZ for an interim period until 5 November 1993

S/RES/879 (1993), 29 October 1993

The Security Council,

Reaffirming its resolutions 782 (1992) of 13 October 1992, 797 (1992) of 16 December 1992, 818 (1993) of 14 April 1993, 850 (1993) of 9 July 1993 and 863 (1993) of 13 September 1993,

Reiterating the importance it attaches to the General Peace Agreement for Mozambique 1/ and to the timely fulfilment by all parties in good faith of obligations contained therein,

1. *Decides*, pending examination of the report of the Secretary-General due under resolution 863 (1993), to extend the mandate of the United Nation Operation in Mozambique for an interim period terminating on 5 November 1993;

2. *Decides* to remain actively seized of the matter.

1/ *Official Records of the Security Council, Forty-seventh Year, Supplement for October, November and December 1992,* document S/24635, annex.

Document 48

Report of the Secretary-General on ONUMOZ

S/26666, 1 November 1993, and S/26666/Add.1, 2 November 1993

Introduction

1. The present report is submitted in response to paragraph 14 of Security Council resolution 863 (1993) of 13 September 1993, which requested me to keep the Council informed of developments regarding the implementation of the provisions of the general peace agreement and to submit a report on the matter to the Council before 31 October 1993. In addition, the Security Council requested me to examine expeditiously the request by the Government of Mozambique and the Resistência Nacional Moçambicana (RENAMO) that the United Nations monitor all police activities in Mozambique. The present report covers the period from my last report of 30 August 1993 to 28 October 1993 and brings up to date the information on activities of the United Nations Operation in Mozambique (ONUMOZ) in the implementation of the political, military and humanitarian aspects of the mandate entrusted to it by the Security Council.

2. I visited Maputo from 17 to 20 October 1993 and had very positive and constructive meetings with the President of Mozambique, Mr. Joaquim Chissano, and Mr. Afonso Dhlakama, President of RENAMO, as well as with leaders of other political parties and representatives of the international community. I am pleased to report that a new momentum has been created in Mozambique, which should help to facilitate the full and timely implementation of the peace agreement.

I. Political developments

A. *General*

3. A number of significant developments have taken place since my report to the Council of 30 August 1993 (S/26385). In accordance with Security Council resolution 863 (1993) of 13 September 1993, and in order to try to break the stalemate in the peace process, I and my Special Representative for Mozambique, Mr. Aldo Ajello, have continued to urge the Government and RENAMO to speed up the implementation of the general peace agreement, particularly with respect to the adoption of the electoral law and the assembly and demobilization of troops.

4. A number of agreements were reached between President Chissano and Mr. Dhlakama during my recent visit to Maputo on outstanding issues that were impeding the peace process. These agreements cover, *inter alia*: (a) the assembly and demobilization of RENAMO and government troops as well as the simultaneous disarmament of paramilitary forces, militia and irregular troops; (b) the composition of the National Elections Commission and the system and timetable for finalizing the electoral law; (c) the chairmanship of the National Commission for Administration, the National Police Affairs Commission and the Commission for Information; (d) the creation of local subcommittees of the National Police Affairs Commission to monitor the activities of the Mozambican police; and (e) the guidelines for the Ceasefire Commission related to the movement of troops after signature of the peace agreement. Following these agreements, the revised timetable with the new dates for assembly and demobilization of troops was approved at a meeting of the Supervisory and Monitoring Commission on 22 October 1993.

B. *Assembly and demobilization of troops*

5. Paragraphs 5 and 6 of Security Council resolution 863 (1993) stressed the urgent need for the early initiation of the process of assembly and demobilization of troops and its continuation in accordance with the revised timetable without preconditions and urged RENAMO to join the Government in authorizing the immediate assembly of troops.

6. As I reported earlier, the Government had indicated its readiness to initiate assembly of troops as soon as RENAMO was prepared to do the same. For a long time, RENAMO had been reluctant to begin assembly and demobilization of troops and had linked various conditions to the process, including the full deployment of the United Nations military contingent, an agreement on the question of administrative control over RENAMO-held areas and the full establishment of United Nations monitoring of police activities as well as on the disarmament of militia and paramilitary groups.

7. During my visit to Maputo, President Chissano and Mr. Dhlakama agreed to begin the movement of their troops to assembly areas in November 1993 and to start demobilization in January 1994. The dismantling of paramilitary forces, militia and irregular troops will be undertaken simultaneously. All troops are to be demobilized by no later than May 1994.

8. In order to facilitate the cantonment and demobilization of troops, the assembly points that are not

ready to receive troops should be approved by both parties and equipped to do so within one month. Since my last report to the Council, the Cease-fire Commission has approved two additional assembly areas, bringing the number of such areas to 36 out of a projected total of 49. The decision on the remaining 13 areas, most of which belong to RENAMO, has been held up owing to the logistical unsuitability of those areas or to political considerations. A number of the outstanding RENAMO sites may indeed need to be moved to different locations. The Government is ready to show flexibility by allowing RENAMO, under certain conditions, to establish assembly areas in zones under its control. Of the 36 approved assembly areas, 26 now belong to the Government (out of a planned total of 29), while 10 belong to RENAMO (out of a projected total of 20); teams of United Nations military observers have already been deployed in 23 of them. Meanwhile, the Government has indicated that it will permit the United Nations to establish a presence in the remaining 12 approved government sites when the number of approved RENAMO assembly areas is in closer proportion to that approved for it.

C. *Preparation for elections*

9. The Security Council, in paragraph 8 of its resolution 863 (1993), urged RENAMO and other political parties to join with the Mozambican Government in quickly agreeing on an electoral law, including provisions for the establishment of an effective National Elections Commission. In this connection, it will be recalled that the multi-party conference on the draft electoral law had reached a deadlock on 3 August 1993 over article 16 (composition of the National Elections Commission). This led to a complete breakdown of discussions, and on 17 September 1993 the conference was finally declared dissolved by its Chairman. Despite various attempts to break the stalemate on article 16 and to find a way of continuing debate on other articles, agreement could not be reached between the Government, RENAMO and the other political parties. Subsequently, the Government declared its intention to finalize the draft law through bilateral consultations with all interested parties. The electoral law must be approved by Parliament no later than November 1993 in order to hold elections by October 1994.

10. On 25 September 1993, RENAMO adopted a declaration reaffirming its commitment to elections in October 1994. However, it suggested that, in view of the short time available, elections could be held without completing the demobilization process. My Special Representative, while welcoming RENAMO's commitment to holding elections in October 1994, underlined that elections without demobilization would be contrary to the peace agreement, and, therefore, unacceptable to the United Nations.

11. As stated earlier, an agreement was reached on the composition of the National Elections Commission during my visit to Maputo. The National Elections Commission will be composed of 10 members from the Government, 7 members from RENAMO, 3 from the other political parties and an independent chairman. The chairman will be selected by the 20 members of the Commission. If the National Elections Commission is unable to come to an agreement on this issue, it will present a list of up to five candidates to President Chissano, who will then make the appointment from the list. All decisions of the National Elections Commission will be taken by consensus.

12. President Chissano and Mr. Dhlakama have also agreed that the rest of the electoral law will be examined at meetings of representatives of all parties at the technical level. Once it is approved by all parties, the draft of the electoral law will be sent to the Council of Ministers for approval before the end of October 1993. The law will then be submitted to the National Assembly for final adoption, which is expected to take place no later than the end of November 1993.

D. *Police*

13. In their agreement of 26 August 1993, President Chissano and Mr. Dhlakama requested the United Nations to monitor all police activities in the country as well as the rights and liberties of citizens of Mozambique (S/26385/Add.1). In pursuance of Security Council resolution 863 (1993), I sent a small survey team of experts to Mozambique to assist me in preparing recommendations about the size and exact requirements of the proposed ONUMOZ police contingent. On 13 October 1993, Mr. Dhlakama issued a declaration in Maringue which stated that he would agree to begin the assembly of RENAMO troops at the end of November, provided that United Nations police observers had begun monitoring Mozambican police activities by that time.

14. In the course of my recent visit to Maputo, I informed President Chissano and Mr. Dhlakama of the serious financial and other constraints that the United Nations is facing. In the circumstances, it would be unrealistic to expect that the requested United Nations police contingent could be deployed at short notice. Given the possibility of delays in the deployment of the contingent, the Government and RENAMO have agreed to establish local subcommittees of the National Police Affairs Commission to monitor police activities throughout the country.

15. In light of this very recent decision, the survey team of United Nations police experts is currently reviewing the police contingent's requirements and I will shortly submit to the Security Council a separate report on its

establishment. Meanwhile, as a contingency measure, I intend, subject to the concurrence of the Council, to proceed with the selection and deployment of the 128 police observers already authorized by the Security Council (see S/24892, paras. 28 and 48 (c), and Add.1 and Security Council resolution 797 (1992).

E. *National Commission for Administration, National Police Affairs Commission and National Commission for Information*

16. Paragraph 9 of Security Council resolution 863 (1993) called on the Government and RENAMO to make operational without further delay the National Police Affairs Commission, the National Commission for Information and the National Commission for Administration. As members of the Council are aware, these Commissions were established and their members and three chairmen were appointed by President Chissano in August 1993. The National Police Affairs Commission and the National Commission for Information are composed of 21 members: six nominated by the Government and six by RENAMO and nine others by the President of Mozambique from Mozambican personalities known for their competence and impartiality. The National Commission for Administration is composed of eight members: four nominated by the Government and four by RENAMO.

17. Since the inauguration of the Commissions, RENAMO had refused to attend their meetings, questioning the impartiality of the nine members appointed by the President to the National Police Affairs Commission and the National Commission for Information, as well as the nomination of the chairmen of all three Commissions. As a result, these Commissions, whose activities are very important for the implementation of the peace agreement, could not become operational. The National Police Affairs Commission and the National Commission for Administration are essential for the implementation of the agreements reached between President Chissano and Mr. Dhlakama in August on a single administration at the provincial and district levels and on the monitoring of police activities.

18. Agreements were also reached on the chairmanship of all three Commissions during my visit to Maputo. The National Commission for Administration will have two chairmen who will work on a rotating basis, one of whom would be nominated by the Government and the other by RENAMO. At the same time, agreements were attained on the chairmanship of the National Police Affairs Commission and the National Commission for Information. After extensive discussion, Mr. Dhlakama also agreed with the proposed composition of these two Commissions. Both the Government and

RENAMO further concurred that the work of the three Commissions would begin immediately.

F. *Timetable for the peace process*

19. In paragraph 4 of its resolution 863 (1993), the Security Council strongly urged the Government and RENAMO to agree and adhere to the revised timetable for the implementation of the general peace agreement without further postponements. The Government had earlier approved the revised timetable and announced its readiness to start the assembly of troops, while RENAMO had reserved its position on the assembly and demobilization of troops. Discussions in informal meetings of the Supervisory and Monitoring Commission on the revised timetable were suspended when the RENAMO delegation returned to its headquarters in September for a meeting of the RENAMO National Council. Subsequently, following the agreements reached between President Chissano and Mr. Dhlakama during my visit, the timetable was finally approved and signed by both parties in a meeting of the Supervisory and Monitoring Commission on 22 October 1993.

20. In accordance with the revised timetable, the concentration of troops in the assembly areas will commence in November 1993, to be followed in January 1994 by the demobilization process. It is expected that 50 per cent of the troops will be demobilized by March 1994, and that the demobilization of troops should be completed by May 1994. Training of officers and soldiers for the new army will begin in November 1993 (training of the infantry instructors at the Nyanga centre in Zimbabwe is already in progress) and is to be completed by August 1994. The new Mozambican Defence Forces should be fully operational by September 1994. Transportation to the places of origin of former soldiers who will not form part of the new army is expected to start in January and to conclude by May 1994 in order to enable the demobilized soldiers to register for elections. Repatriation of refugees and displaced persons has already begun and is expected to be largely completed by April 1994. Voter registration is expected to take three months and has been scheduled from April to June 1994. The electoral campaign will take place from 1 September 1994 until mid-October 1994 after which the elections will take place by the end of October 1994.

II. Military aspects

A. *Deployment of the military component*

21. There has been no substantial change in the deployment of the military component since my last report to the Council (S/26385). As of 21 October 1993, the total strength of the formed units of the military

contingent, including support elements, was 6,021, with contributions from the following countries:

Argentina	36
Bangladesh	1 362
Botswana	723
India	899
Italy	1 043
Japan	48
Portugal	279
Uruguay	814
Zambia	817

22. Also, 196 military personnel served in the Force and regional headquarters of ONUMOZ. The main activities of the formed units continued to be the conduct of extensive air and motorized patrols in the main transport corridors, as well as the maintenance of temporary road checkpoints to monitor road movements. United Nations troops have continued to escort road convoys and trains transporting food supplies to various regions as well as to the assembly areas. In addition, they continued to assist in the repair of major access roads, both those in heavily populated areas and those leading to assembly areas. The troops also guarded important installations such as oil-pumping stations as well as United Nations storage facilities.

23. As of 21 October 1993, 303 of the authorized total of 354 military observers were deployed with ONUMOZ. Assisted by United Nations formed units, the observers continued to conduct inspections and investigations of cease-fire violation complaints. Furthermore, the observers were involved in the establishment and preparation of assembly areas. When the demobilization begins, the role of the military observers will be expanded to include supervision of the collection, storage and disposal of the arms and ammunition of the assembled soldiers.

24. In paragraph 7 of my previous report (S/26385), I noted the need to provide additional patrols and surveillance, including permanent stationing of military personnel outside the main corridors. I also emphasized the need to bring the strength of the military component of ONUMOZ to the originally envisaged level in order to deploy troops in Zambézia Province and to improve security in that region in general, as well as to provide escort for humanitarian assistance convoys. The security situation in the province is still precarious. Because of frequent incidents of banditry, international humanitarian relief organizations are reluctant to operate there. The security situation has also made it very difficult to establish the presence of unarmed United Nations military observers in many areas of this part of the country. I therefore propose to deploy a United Nations infantry unit in Zambézia Province; the implementation

of this proposal would not affect the overall strength of the ONUMOZ military component.

25. A recent increase in incidents of banditry along the main routes, in particular in the southern region, is a matter of particular concern to ONUMOZ. One of the main tasks of ONUMOZ is to assume transitional responsibility for security in the corridors and on other key routes, as well as to protect humanitarian convoys using them. In order to address the immediate security concerns along and around national highway No. 1 to Xai-Xai, national highway No. 2 to Namaacha, the road connecting to Ressano Garcia and other main routes, ONUMOZ is seeking the close cooperation of the Mozambican police. In particular, a task force comprised of government and ONUMOZ representatives has been established to examine general modalities for such cooperation.

26. The demand for ONUMOZ air transport has steadily increased with progress in the implementation of the Agreement. Besides air patrols, there is a growing need for the transport of equipment and United Nations personnel to and from the assembly areas and other points in the various regions, as well as for the transport of Government and RENAMO officers in connection with their training for the new army. I expect that additional requirements for transport of Government and RENAMO soldiers to the assembly areas and their onward travel after demobilization will place an additional burden on the Mission's already overstretched air transport. Meanwhile, out of the 18 helicopters required, only 13 have so far been authorized. Moreover, ONUMOZ requires the further capacity of an extra C-130-type cargo aircraft.

B. *Cease-fire*

27. The Security Council, in paragraph 2 of its resolution 863 (1993), emphasized the need to respect fully all the provisions of the general peace agreement and in particular those concerning the cease-fire and the movement of troops. Since my last report (S/26385), there have been six complaints of alleged cease-fire violations. In the course of inspections conducted by the United Nations, two of those complaints were resolved and two were only partially confirmed, while two were not. On the whole, formally confirmed cease-fire violations have been relatively few and have presented no serious threat to the peace process. Since it resumed its meetings in June 1993, the Cease-fire Commission has reviewed a total number of 59 complaints of alleged cease-fire violations, out of which 27 have been partly or fully substantiated.

28. As noted in my previous report (S/26385), the Government had complained that RENAMO occupied certain areas after the signing of the general peace agree-

ment. These allegations were confirmed by investigations that were conducted by Cease-fire Commission teams comprised of United Nations military observers as well as government and RENAMO representatives. The Cease-fire Commission requested RENAMO to withdraw, but the latter claimed that those troop movements were undertaken mainly for logistical reasons and was reluctant to withdraw. Allegations that the Government had occupied certain areas after the signing of the peace agreement were recently presented to the Cease-fire Commission by RENAMO, and those claims are still under investigation. In some cases, logistical difficulties could serve as a justification for the movement of troops from one location to another. As noted in my previous report (S/26385, para. 26), ONUMOZ had prepared a set of guidelines that draw a distinction between troop movements for military and logistical purposes in order to establish clear criteria for analysing cease-fire violations. The Government has accepted the guidelines. During my visit to Maputo, Mr. Dhlakama finally indicated his readiness to approve the text, which was later signed by both parties in a meeting of the Supervisory and Monitoring Commission on 23 October 1993.

C. Formation of the Mozambican Defence Forces

29. As the Security Council is aware, the training of the first 100 instructors (50 each from the Government and RENAMO) for the new Mozambican Defence Forces was initiated in early August 1993. I am pleased to report that, after some delays in the dispatch of the RENAMO contingent, the additional 440 officers from both parties have now arrived at the Nyanga training centre in Zimbabwe with the assistance of ONUMOZ. The goal of the programme, which is being run by the United Kingdom of Great Britain and Northern Ireland, is to train a corps of officers for the new national army.

30. Furthermore, in accordance with the Lisbon agreement of 19 February 1992, France has agreed to train a company of military engineers, while Portugal will train three companies of special forces and two of marines, as well as provide a course for senior military officers, logisticians and administrative personnel. It is expected that the training of the first logistics unit and the first special forces company will begin in November 1993. The 380 RENAMO soldiers earmarked to participate in this training programme are already assembled at their headquarters in Maringue.

31. On 26 October, following informal tripartite discussions in the Joint Commission for the Formation of the Mozambican Defence Forces, the Commission adopted and signed several important documents: (a) Rules of military discipline of the new Mozambican Defence Forces; (b) the staffing table for the Forces' High Command; (c) the structure of the Forces' Joint General Staff; and (d) the working/instruction uniform of the Forces.

III. Humanitarian assistance programme

32. The humanitarian assistance programme addresses the repatriation of refugees, the demobilization of government and RENAMO troops and their reintegration into society, as well as emergency relief and restoration of essential services in rural areas where returnees and displaced persons are resettling. It also provides for institutional support to Mozambican authorities in charge of emergency management.

33. A year after the signature of the Rome Accord, over 400,000 of the 1.5 million refugees who had found asylum in neighbouring countries have returned to their districts of origin, the vast majority of them from Malawi. In addition to the ongoing operations for returnees from Zambia and Zimbabwe, organized repatriation of some 24,000 refugees from Swaziland began in mid-October 1993.

34. Attention has also focused on the refugee populations in South Africa. With a view to regularizing the status and eventual repatriation of some 250,000 Mozambican refugees in that country, the United Nations High Commissioner for Refugees (UNHCR) concluded a basic agreement with the South African Government and signed on 15 October 1993 in Maputo a tripartite agreement under which the two Governments and UNHCR would cooperate in the repatriation of the refugees concerned.

35. With no major breaches of the cease-fire and good harvests, conditions have also improved for the resettlement of internally displaced persons who, during the civil war, congregated around provincial and district centres. In 1992, there were 4 to 5 million internally displaced persons in Mozambique. It is now estimated that as many as 1.2 million have returned to their home areas. The limited capacity of district administrations to respond to the increased demand for basic services has held back an even larger movement. The situation varies considerably from province to province, with resettlement of displaced persons most advanced in the northern region.

36. Apart from keeping a comprehensive record of the delivery of food and non-food relief supplies to populations living in RENAMO areas, the United Nations Office of Humanitarian Assistance Coordination has instituted in each province humanitarian Assistance Committees as a vehicle for expanding contacts between government officials and RENAMO representatives at the provincial level. In these forums, officers of the Government and RENAMO meet with field workers from United Nations agencies and non-governmental organi-

zations (NGOs) under UNOHAC's chairmanship and carry out joint assessments of the needs of populations in the various districts so that their actions on the ground are coordinated.

37. There has been a significant positive evolution during the past 12 months as regards opening up channels of communication between provincial government agencies and RENAMO authorities, securing access to areas which were earlier out of bounds and obtaining more accurate assessments of the situation prevailing among populations in RENAMO-controlled areas that have not benefited from outside assistance.

38. Where a year ago a seemingly impenetrable wall existed impeding all communication, officials from technical agencies of the Government are now frequently welcomed in districts considered as RENAMO bastions. Thus a recent assessment mission was carried out under the auspices of the United Nations Office of Humanitarian Assistance Coordination in the district of Maringue, the geographical heartland of RENAMO, in the field of health, water supply and sanitation with the participation of several government agencies and NGOs.

39. At the central level, progress has been registered along the same lines. A technical committee continues to meet on a weekly basis to take note of reports of assistance in the preceding week to populations in RENAMO areas and to hear what supplies of food or non-food items are being planned for the coming week. A central tripartite committee on health has also recently been instituted with the participation of officials from the Ministry of Health and RENAMO to make possible the joint planning and implementation of health care programmes.

40. A second mine-clearance operation was launched during the reporting period. In a project jointly financed by Norway and ONUMOZ, 64 demobilized Mozambican soldiers completed their training as deminers and were deployed in the province of Tete, under the supervision of experts from a Norwegian NGO. In the space of two weeks they cleared a minefield near the village of Changara, removing and destroying 124 anti-personnel mines. The mine-clearance teams have now been relocated to the district of Mutara, in the same province, to clear transit roads and tracks used by refugees returning from Malawi.

41. The first pilot project, funded by the Commission of European Communities, in the Sofala province, has been expanded with five additional mine-clearance teams. A number of other projects, for which financing is already secured, still await formal endorsement of the Cease-fire Commission. These include the large-scale operation to clear 28 priority road stretches for the delivery of humanitarian assistance and relief supplies.

42. The mine-clearance plan includes the estab-lishment of a training centre to provide courses in basic mine clearance, mine-clearance supervision, minefield supervising and mine awareness. The project aims to train 1,500 Mozambican deminers, and is now in an advanced stage of preparation. Military instructors provided by several countries will implement this project. Two instructors from the Netherlands are already in the country to assist in the elaboration of operational plans for the project.

43. The Commission for Reintegration held its fourth meeting on 15 October 1993 and approved two programmes for the reintegration of the demobilized soldiers. The first programme is designed to assist demobilized soldiers who choose to farm in their home districts, by providing vegetable seeds, agricultural implements and utensils. The second programme provides the framework for identifying training opportunities for demobilized soldiers as well as financing group training or tuition stipends for single trainees, with a variety of training establishments in the country, over a period of years.

44. The Commission also decided to take early steps to open provincial suboffices of the Commission for Reintegration in those provinces where RENAMO has designated its representatives to the Commission for Reintegration and the Government has made housing available for them. The first Commission for Reintegration suboffices will be opened in the provinces of Sofala and Manica, and others will follow as and when the basic prerequisites are in place. Throughout the reporting period tripartite discussions among government and RENAMO representatives, and chaired by the United Nations Office of Humanitarian Assistance Coordination, have been held with a view to reaching agreement on various employment schemes for demobilized soldiers and officers.

IV. Observations

45. Since my last report to the Council (S/26385) and particularly during my visit to Mozambique, significant progress has been made in removing obstacles which had hitherto impeded the full and timely implementation of the peace agreement. As noted above, major agreements have been reached between the Government and RENAMO on, among other things, the assembly and demobilization of RENAMO and government troops as well as the simultaneous disarmament of paramilitary forces, militia and irregular troops; the composition of the National Elections Commission and the system and timetable for finalizing the Electoral Law; and the creation of local National Police Affairs Commission subcommittees to monitor the activities of the Mozambican police. Agreement on these and other important questions has facilitated the approval by the Supervisory and Moni-

toring Commission of the revised timetable for the implementation of the peace agreement. I would like to pay tribute to the President of the Republic and the President of RENAMO for the wisdom and flexibility they have shown and for putting the interests of the Mozambican people above all other considerations.

46. During my visit to Maputo, I stressed to both President Chissano and Mr. Dhlakama that the United Nations can only facilitate the peace process and that it cannot promote and establish peace without the cooperation of the parties. The political will of the parties to achieve a peaceful settlement must be demonstrated not only with public statements but with concrete action. I also stressed to them that the international community would not invest additional human and material resources and risk lives in peace-keeping operations where such political will did not make a substantive contribution to the peace process. In order to ensure the continued support of the international community in the implementation of the peace process, I urged the two leaders to build on the progress made so that the elections could be held by October 1994, as scheduled.

47. The fulfilment of the terms of the agreements reached by President Chissano and Mr. Dhlakama during my visit to Mozambique, as well as the decisions taken in their earlier meeting last August, would impose a heavy burden on the financial resources of the Mozambican Government. Future agreements on pending matters could also involve additional costs. In order to absorb RENAMO's representatives into the structures of public administration and to integrate them into the society, adequate support from the international community would be required to supplement the limited budgetary resources available.

48. Equally costly will be RENAMO's efforts to transform itself into a political party. In order to facilitate this process, and in accordance with the general peace agreement, protocol 3, paragraph 7, the United Nations has established a trust fund to which some countries have already made contributions. The projected amount of resources for the Fund is US$ 10 million. As at 26 October 1993, a total amount of US$ 5.8 million has been deposited in the Trust Fund account, the main portion of which has been contributed by the Government of Italy. No additional contributions or pledges to the Trust Fund have been received. A minimum of an additional US$ 5 million should be provided.

49. The Trust Fund has helped to solve some of the administrative and logistic problems related to RENAMO's participation in the structures established by the peace agreements. However, there are expenditures associated with the transformation of RENAMO into a political party that cannot be easily met through a United Nations-administered Fund, on account of the rules and procedures that govern their use. The establishment of complementary funding mechanisms and the provision of additional funds would help in resolving such problems. Although the new mechanisms should not be attached to the United Nations, it should not be difficult to establish adequate coordination links with the existing Fund. In addition, it might be necessary to establish another Trust Fund to support the activities of other political parties after the approval of the electoral law and the establishment of the National Elections Commission.

50. Recent developments in Mozambique have placed the peace process on a solid footing and greatly improved the prospects for full and timely implementation of the general peace agreement. I therefore recommend to the Security Council that it extend the existing mandate of ONUMOZ until the holding of elections in October 1994, taking into account the additional considerations contained in paragraphs 15, 24 and 26 above. At the same time, I believe that the status of ONUMOZ should be thoroughly reviewed periodically, at least every three months, and that the further commitment of the international community should be contingent upon clear and timely progress in the implementation of the peace agreement, in accordance with the revised timetable.

51. I wish to place on record my appreciation to my Special Representative, the Force Commander and to the entire staff of ONUMOZ for their dedicated efforts to implement their mandate and bring peace to Mozambique. I should also like to express my appreciation to the NGO community for their valuable contribution in the humanitarian field.

Addendum (S/26666/Add.1)

1. In paragraphs 13 to 15 of my report of 1 November 1993 1/ to the Security Council, I indicated my intention to deploy to ONUMOZ, subject to the concurrence of the Council, 128 police observers which initially had been authorized by it in December 1992. 2/ I also presented additional requirements related to air operations in paragraph 26 of the report.

2. The General Assembly, by its resolution 47/224 C of 14 September 1993, authorized the Secretary-General to enter into commitments in an amount not exceeding $20,000,000 gross per month for the maintenance of ONUMOZ for the period from 1 November 1993 to 28 February 1994. This authorization is subject to the decision of the Security Council to extend the mandate of the Operation beyond 31 October 1993 and to obtaining the prior concurrence of the Advisory Committee on

1/ S/26666.
2/ S/24892 and Add.1 and S/RES/797 (1992).

Administrative and Budgetary Questions for the actual level of commitments to be entered into for the period from 1 November 1993 to 28 February 1994. It provides for 354 military observers, 6,625 contingent personnel, 355 international civilian staff and 506 locally recruited staff.

3. It is estimated that the costs related to the deployment of 128 police observers to ONUMOZ and to additional requirements for transport and air operations would amount to approximately $6,480,000 for the six-month period from 1 November 1993 to 30 April 1994. It is further estimated that the monthly cost thereafter will be approximately $1,405,000. A breakdown of the estimated cost for the six-month period from 1 November 1993 to 30 April 1994, by main categories of expenditure, is provided for information purposes in the annex to the present addendum.

4. It would be my recommendation to the General Assembly that, should the Security Council decide to approve the recommendations contained in my main report relating to the deployment of police observers and to an increase in requirements for air operations, the additional costs relating thereto should be considered an expense of the Organization to be borne by Member States in accordance with Article 17, paragraph 2, of the Charter of the United Nations and that the assessments to be levied on Member States be credited to the ONUMOZ special account.

Annex

Cost estimate of the additional costs to the United Nations for the activities of ONUMOZ
(*Thousands of United States dollars*)

Objects of expenditure	1 November 1993-30 April 1994
1. Civilian police observers	1 743.0
2. Transport operations 3/	1 292.0
3. Air operations	3 445.0
TOTAL	6 480

3/ Provision is made for the purchase of 64 vehicles and related operational costs.

Document 49

Security Council resolution renewing the mandate of ONUMOZ until 5 May 1994

S/RES/882 (1993), 5 November 1993

The Security Council,

Reaffirming its resolution 782 (1992) of 13 October 1992 and all subsequent relevant resolutions,

Having considered the report of the Secretary-General of 1 and 2 November 1993 on the United Nations Operation in Mozambique, 1/

Reiterating the importance it attaches to the General Peace Agreement for Mozambique 2/ and to the timely fulfilment in good faith by all parties of the obligations contained therein,

Commending the efforts of the Secretary-General, his Special Representative and the personnel of the Operation to implement the mandate fully,

Reaffirming its conviction that the resolution of conflict in Mozambique would contribute to peace and stability in the region,

Emphasizing with satisfaction the recent positive developments in the Mozambican peace process, including the direct talks between the President of Mozambique, Mr. Joaquim Chissano, and the President of the Resistência Nacional Moçambicana, Mr. Afonso Dhlakama, and the agreements signed on 3 September 1993,

Stressing with mounting concern the continuing delays in the implementation of the General Peace Agreement which both parties signed,

Stressing once again the unacceptability of attempts to gain more time or further concessions or to attach new conditions to the peace process, and strongly urging the parties not to raise any further issues which might jeopardize the implementation of the Agreement, particularly in light of the commitments entered into during the Secretary-General's recent visit to Mozambique,

1. *Welcomes* the report of the Secretary-General;

2. *Commends* the agreements that were reached between President Chissano and Mr. Dhlakama during the visit of the Secretary-General to Maputo on outstanding issues that were impeding the peace process;

3. *Reaffirms* the vital importance it attaches to the holding of elections no later than October 1994;

4. *Welcomes* the approval by the Mozambican parties of the revised timetable for the implementation of the General Peace Agreement for Mozambique and urges the parties to adhere to it without any delay;

1/ See *Official Records of the Security Council, Forty-eighth Year, Supplement for October, November and December 1993,* documents S/26666 and Add.1.
2/ Ibid., *Forty-seventh Year, Supplement for October, November and December 1992,* document S/24635, annex.

5. *Urges* the Mozambican parties to commence assembly of troops in November 1993 and to initiate demobilization by January 1994 with a view to ensuring the completion of the demobilization process by May 1994 on the basis of the revised timetable;

6. *Notes* the progress made with regard to the formation of the new Mozambican Defence Forces, particularly the commencement of full-scale training in Nyanga, Zimbabwe, of troops from the Government and the Resistência Nacional Moçambicana for the new national army;

7. *Welcomes* the approval of the guidelines for the Cease-fire Commission governing the movement of troops after signature of the General Peace Agreement, and urges the parties to adhere to the guidelines and to cooperate with the United Nations Operation in Mozambique in the efforts to enforce them;

8. *Underlines* the need to make immediately operational the National Commission for Administration, the National Police Affairs Commission and the Commission for Information following the agreements reached recently on their chairmanship;

9. *Authorizes* the Secretary-General to proceed with the selection and deployment of the one hundred twenty-eight United Nations police observers approved by resolution 797 (1992) of 16 December 1992, with a view to deploying them as soon as possible;

10. *Underscores* the importance of the parties making progress on achieving agreed political goals, specifically, the approval of an electoral law and establishment of an electoral commission by 30 November 1993 and the beginning of the concentration of troops in the assembly areas, demobilization of 50 per cent of troops by 31 March 1994, sufficient progress to meet complete demobilization by 31 May 1994, and accelerated progress in training and integrating forces in the new Mozambican Defence Forces so that the process is complete by August 1994;

11. *Calls on* the Government of Mozambique and the Resistência Nacional Moçambicana to build on the progress which has been achieved and to respect fully all the provisions of the General Peace Agreement, in particular those concerning the cease-fire and the movement of troops;

12. *Decides* to renew the mandate of the United Nations Operation in Mozambique for a period of six months, subject to the proviso that the Security Council will review the status of the mandate within ninety days on the basis of a report by the Secretary-General as described in paragraph 13 below;

13. *Requests* the Secretary-General to report by 31 January 1994 and every three months thereafter on whether the parties have made sufficient and tangible progress towards implementing the General Peace Agreement and meeting the timetable laid out in paragraphs 3 and 10 above, and also to report on the situation concerning the implementation of the mandate of the Operation, taking into consideration the need to achieve cost savings to the greatest extent possible, while remaining mindful of the importance of an effective discharge of its mandate;

14. *Appeals* to the international community to provide the necessary financial assistance to facilitate the implementation of the Agreement;

15. *Also appeals* to the international community to make voluntary financial contributions to the trust fund to be set up to support electoral activities of the political parties upon the approval of the electoral law;

16. *Reiterates its encouragement* to the international community to provide appropriate and prompt assistance for the implementation of the humanitarian programme carried out in the framework of the General Peace Agreement, and urges the Government of Mozambique and the Resistência Nacional Moçambicana to facilitate unimpeded access to humanitarian assistance to the civilian population in need;

17. *Calls on* all parties to cooperate with the United Nations High Commissioner for Refugees and other humanitarian agencies operating in Mozambique to facilitate the speedy repatriation and resettlement of refugees and displaced persons;

18. *Decides* to remain actively seized of the matter.

Document 50

Letter dated 15 November 1993 from the Secretary-General to President Chissano on the Secretary-General's visit to Mozambique and the subsequent extension of ONUMOZ's mandate for six more months

Not issued as a United Nations document

I write to express my deep appreciation and thanks for the gracious welcome and the generous hospitality which you afforded me and my delegation during my recent visit to Mozambique.

I am especially grateful for your cooperation in helping to resolve the issues that were impeding implementation of the peace process. As a result of your efforts, and of the agreement reached between the Government and RENAMO during my visit, the Security Council recently voted to extend the mandate of ONUMOZ for a further six months. The extension was made subject to the proviso that the Council would review the status of the mandate within 90 days, based on a report to be submitted to the Council by the Secretary-General. The Council also required that I report every three months thereafter on whether the parties have made sufficient and tangible progress towards implementation of the General Peace Agreement and the holding of elections by October 1994.

I wish to take this opportunity to express to you my personal thanks for the assistance and support that you have given to me, to my Special Representative in Mozambique, Mr. Aldo Ajello, and to all of the members of ONUMOZ, in carrying out the United Nations mandate in Mozambique.

It is vital that together we work to maintain the momemtum that has now been created. I am confident that under your leadership, the goal of building peace and promoting reconciliation in Mozambique will be achieved. I pledge to you my assistance and my strong support.

Please accept, Mr. President, the assurances of my highest consideration.

(Signed) Boutros BOUTROS-GHALI

Document 51

Letter dated 16 November 1993 from the Secretary-General to Mr. Dhlakama on the Secretary-General's visit to Mozambique and the subsequent extension of ONUMOZ's mandate for six more months

Not issued as a United Nations document

I write to express my gratitude for the cooperation you extended during my recent visit to Mozambique, in helping to resolve the issues that were impeding implementation of the peace process.

You will be aware that as a result of the agreement reached between the Government and RENAMO during my visit, the Security Council recently voted to extend the mandate of ONUMOZ for a further six months. The extension was made subject to the proviso that the Council would review the status of the mandate within 90 days, based on a report to be submitted to the Council by the Secretary-General. The Council also required that I report every three months thereafter on whether the parties have made sufficient and tangible progress towards implementation of the General Peace Agreement and the holding of elections by October 1994.

I wish to take this opportunity to express to you my personal thanks for the cooperation and assistance that RENAMO has given to my Special Representative in Mozambique, Mr. Aldo Ajello, and to all of the members of ONUMOZ, in carrying out the United Nations mandate in Mozambique.

It is vital that together we work to maintain the momentum that has now been created, and that we use this momentum to promote the cause of peace and reconciliation in Mozambique. I pledge to you my assistance and my strong support in this endeavour.

Please accept, Excellency, the assurances of my highest consideration.

(Signed) Boutros BOUTROS-GHALI

Document 52

Letter dated 31 December 1993 from the Minister for Foreign Affairs of Mozambique on the crossing of an armed group from Malawi into Mozambique

Not issued as a United Nations document

On behalf of my Government I would like to bring to your attention the disturbing events that took place recently in the border between my country and Malawi.

A few weeks ago, a sizeable number of heavily armed people coming from Malawi crossed the border into Mozambique.

The presence of this armed group is a source of great concern for my Government since it poses a serious threat to the peace process, particularly when it happens at a critical stage of assembling and demobilization of armed forces in the country.

Recalling your recent visit to Mozambique, I believe that you had the opportunity to witness the positive transformations taking place in the region towards the attainment of a durable and long lasting peace. However, the successful outcome of these endeavours calls for strict adherence to the principle of non-violability of States sovereignty and territorial integrity, good neighbourliness and non-interference in the internal affairs of other States.

With my best wishes for 1994,

(Signed) Dr. Pascoal Manuel MOCUMBI

Document 53

Letter dated 14 January 1994 from the Secretary-General to the Minister for Foreign Affairs of Mozambique on a meeting of the Mozambique-Malawi Joint Defence and Security Commission to address the matter of the crossing of an armed group into Mozambique from Malawi

Not issued as a United Nations document

I wish to thank you for your letter of 31 December 1993 in which you informed me that a sizeable number of heavily armed people have, in recent weeks, crossed the border from Malawi into Mozambique. I fully share your concern that, at this critical stage, when the demobilization of troops in Mozambique has begun in earnest, such a development could have negative implications for the peace process.

I am aware that you have copied your letter to my Special Representative in Mozambique, Mr. Ajello, and I assure you that he is following the matter closely. It is also very useful that your are keeping the Ambassadors of the permanent members of the Security Council in your capital informed.

At the same time, I welcome the report that the Government of Malawi has agreed to the proposal of your Government to hold an urgent meeting of the Mozambique-Malawi Joint Defence and Security Commission to discuss the matter. It is my sincere hope that your two Governments will be able to resolve this problem in a way that will avoid any disruption of the peace process in Mozambique.

Please accept, Excellency, the assurances of my highest consideration.

(Signed) Boutros BOUTROS-GHALI

Document 54

Letter dated 14 January 1994 from the Secretary-General to Carlo Azeglio Ciampi, President of the Council of Ministers of Italy, requesting a contribution to the United Nations Trust Fund for assistance to RENAMO

Not issued as a United Nations document

I fully realize that this is not the best moment to raise questions concerning the peace process in Mozambique. Yet, the very role played by Italy during the two years of negotiations between the Mozambican Government and RENAMO, as well as the primary role which the Peace Accords bestow on Italy, lead me to seek your support at a stage which could be critical for the entire peace process in that country.

According to protocol 3, section 7, of the General Peace Agreement, RENAMO is entitled, as the partner of the Government in the peace process, to receive the financial assistance it needs to transform a military organization into a political party. Only RENAMO can avail itself of the status of being the partner in the peace process. Supporting RENAMO in that capacity cannot, therefore, be interpreted as discrimination against other political parties.

Assistance to political parties to meet the costs of the electoral campaign is dealt with in another section of the peace agreement and will be ensured through an ad hoc trust fund. The same peace agreement stipulates that the Mozambican Government will provide the financial assistance required by RENAMO in its capacity as the Government's partner in the peace process, and will appeal to the donor community—and in particular to Italy because of the special role your country played during the entire peace process—in case it lacks the necessary means.

Having found it impossible to make available the financial resources needed, the Mozambican Government has requested, through the United Nations, the support of the international community, and the United Nations has established a Trust Fund for financial assistance to RENAMO to which your country has generously contributed US$5.7 million. Other countries, including the Netherlands, Sweden and Switzerland, made additional contributions which brought the figure to approximately US$7.5 million.

Unfortunately, this effort by the international community, and most especially by your country, has not been able to solve the entire problem. Two issues still need to be addressed. The first is of a quantitative nature: the resources currently available are not sufficient. At least US$1.5 million are needed, as opposed to the US$7.5 million which is at present available. The second issue is of a qualitative nature: the United Nations rules under which Trust Funds are administered are too rigid to meet the needs which stem from the transformation of a military organization into a political party, all the more so in the social and economic context of an African country.

If the RENAMO leader is not enabled to meet the expectations of his supporters, he will lose authority and prestige, and the entire peace process will be destabilized. My Special Representative and the Ambassadors who represent the donor community in Maputo are convinced of the need to set up a more flexible instrument through which to channel about US$300,000 per month until the elections which are due to take place in October. That monthly allowance would be tied to scrupulous implementation of the peace agreement according to the calendar approved by the parties concerned.

Pending the design of adequate instruments which would allow other countries to contribute to the fund, it is absolutely necessary that at least one country make available the resources required to meet the immediate requests from RENAMO, in order to avoid bringing to a halt the demobilization of its troops, which would have damaging effects for the entire peace process.

These are the reasons which lead me to appeal most earnestly to you, in the hope that your Government, which has already expressed on many occasions its interest in Mozambique, will make an additional effort to contribute another US$500,000 towards the above-mentioned objective. Such a contribution, which would need to be managed bilaterally initially, would make it possible to free other contributions from other donor countries. The Government of Mozambique is well informed of the initiative and fully appreciates its value.

I wish to express my warmest appreciation for the support provided by Italy to the various peace initiatives of the United Nations, and to send you my best regards as well as my best wishes for the New Year.

Please accept, Excellency, the assurances of my highest consideration.

(Signed) Boutros BOUTROS-GHALI

Document 55

Report of the Secretary-General on ONUMOZ

S/1994/89 and S/1994/89/Add.1, 28 January 1994, and S/1994/89/Add.2, 1 February 1994

Introduction

1. The present report is submitted in response to paragraph 13 of Security Council resolution 882 (1993) of 5 November 1993, which requested me to report on whether the Government of Mozambique and the Resistência Nacional Moçambicana (RENAMO) had made sufficient and tangible progress towards implementing the timetable concerning the major provisions of the general peace agreement for Mozambique signed on 4 October 1992 in Rome (see S/24635, annex). The Council requested me to report on the situation regarding the implementation of the mandate of the United Nations Operation in Mozambique (ONUMOZ), taking into consideration the need to achieve cost savings to the greatest extent possible, while remaining mindful of the importance of the effective discharge of the mandate.

2. My recommendations on the planned deployment of the ONUMOZ police contingent are contained in an addendum to the present report (S/1994/89/Add.1).

I. Political developments and demobilization of troops

A. *General*

3. A number of important developments have taken place since my report to the Council of 1 November 1993 (S/26666). Most importantly, the long-awaited assembly of troops began on 30 November 1993, and the dismantling of paramilitary forces, militia and irregular troops was initiated on 12 January 1994. The Electoral Law was approved by the Mozambican National Assembly on 9 December 1993, and the National Elections Commission was appointed on 21 January 1994. The National Commission for Administration, the National Police Affairs Commission and the Commission for Information were appointed on 17 November 1993. The President of Mozambique, Mr. Joaquim Chissano, and Mr. Afonso Dhlakama, President of RENAMO, who now maintains permanent residence in Maputo, have met on numerous occasions.

4. On several occasions the two leaders have successfully overcome deadlocked situations in the ongoing negotiations, and their cooperation has led to the timely implementation of many activities called for in the timetable. With the initiation of the cantonment of troops, the peace process has entered into a new phase. However, major problems still remain to be resolved in the immediate future. These include the opening of the remaining 14 assembly areas; initiation and subsequent completion of the actual demobilization; transfer of weapons from assembly areas to regional warehouses; dismantling of the paramilitary forces; provision of financial support for the transformation of RENAMO from a military movement into a political party; and formation of a well-functioning national defence force.

B. *Assembly and demobilization of troops*

5. Paragraph 5 of Security Council resolution 882 (1993) urged the parties to commence assembly of troops in November 1993 and to initiate demobilization by January 1994 with a view to ensuring the completion of the demobilization process by May 1994 in accordance with the timetable signed by the two parties in October 1993. On 30 November 1993, following a series of lengthy negotiations, troop cantonment formally commenced after the ratification by the Supervision and Monitoring Commission of the document entitled "Declaration regarding the opening of assembly areas pursuant to the general peace agreement for Mozambique". In

accordance with the agreement, the initial 20 of the total 49 assembly areas were opened (12 for the Government and 8 for RENAMO), and the assembly of troops ensued. Fifteen additional assembly areas were opened on 20 December 1993. The opening of the remaining 14 sites, which was scheduled for 31 December 1993, has been delayed by a dispute between the two parties over control of the locations proposed for assembly areas in Salamanga and Dunda.

6. During the initial stages of cantonment, government troops assembled in much larger numbers than RENAMO troops. This trend was reversed by mid-December 1993. At this stage, RENAMO has assembled a much larger proportion of the total number of troops than the Government. As of 24 January 1994, 16,609 soldiers have checked into the assembly areas, 9,895 from the Government and 6,714 from RENAMO. This represents 30 per cent of the total number of soldiers expected in the 35 sites open, 22 per cent of the government soldiers and 58 per cent of RENAMO's soldiers. The current imbalance has grown significantly in January 1994, as only a limited number of government soldiers have arrived at the assembly areas during the first half of the month. Although there is evidence that the movement of government soldiers has quickened during the second half of January 1994, such movement is still not sufficient to achieve a better balance.

7. Arms collection has started in most assembly areas. In many cases, however, soldiers arrived in the assembly areas with less than one weapon per soldier on the average, and those weapons were often old and in poor condition. As of 24 January 1994, 11,382 government and 6,200 RENAMO weapons had been registered by ONUMOZ military observers. The transfer to regional warehouses of weapons collected in assembly areas has been delayed owing to political problems raised by the Government at the beginning of the process and subsequently by RENAMO. Storage-capacity for arms in the assembly areas is by now far exceeded, leaving weapons to be stored at unsafe locations and placing at risk not only government and RENAMO soldiers but also United Nations personnel.

8. The movement of soldiers into the assembly area was planned to take place in stages, in careful coordination with the demobilization process, as most assembly areas have the capacity to accommodate only 30 to 50 per cent of the total number of troops at a time. The massive influx of RENAMO troops has led to overcrowding in some areas (almost 211 per cent of capacity at one camp), resulting in shortages of food and other essential items, inadequate lodging and storage facilities and potential health hazards. Delays in the selection of those soldiers who are to be demobilized and those who are to

join the new army further prolong the stay of troops in the assembly areas, thus compounding already existing problems. Food shortages also occurred in assembly areas when the Government did not honour its commitment to supply these areas with dried meat, dried fish and salt. In order to resolve this problem, my Special Representative, Mr. Aldo Ajello, sought support from the World Food Programme (WFP) and the donor community. As a result, WFP increased the rations of basic food items by an average of 25 per cent and the Swedish Government made available US$ 200,000 to cover the provision of the immediate meat and fish needs for the RENAMO assembly areas, while the Government confirmed its commitment to supplying its own assembly areas.

9. There have been a number of incidents of rioting by government soldiers in assembly areas and other locations over demands for back pay. These riots resulted in injuries and the death of two civilians. However, the incidents were resolved as soon as the Government provided the outstanding payments.

10. It was initially planned to provide civilian clothing to the demobilized soldiers at the time of their departure from the assembly areas, while the soldiers who would join the new army would have received only uniforms. However, most of the RENAMO soldiers arrived at the assembly areas literally dressed in rags and hence it became necessary to provide them with clothing at an earlier stage. The Italian Government helped to solve this problem by committing itself to provide civilian clothes for the Government and RENAMO troops who will be joining the new army. This allowed ONU-MOZ to distribute clothes immediately to all the assembled RENAMO soldiers from the existing stocks of civilian clothes.

11. There have been delays in the dismantling of the militia and paramilitary forces, which was scheduled to begin simultaneously with assembly and demobilization of troops. There are approximately 155,600 government military and paramilitary troops in Mozambique, far outnumbering the approximately 80,000 regular government forces. After several attempts to set a deadline for the beginning of this process, the dismantling of the paramilitary groups was initiated on 12 January 1994. The Cease-fire Commission is overseeing the dismantling of the irregular armed groups. This process is very complex and extremely demanding logistically, as the armed elements are widely scattered throughout the country. In addition to the above, there are a total of 15,051 unassembled troops (14,734 for the Government and 317 for RENAMO) in Mozambique according to the information presented by the parties. These troops will not go through the assembly areas but will be demobilized at their present locations.

C. *Preparation for elections*

12. In paragraph 3 of its resolution 882 (1993), the Security Council once again reaffirmed the vital importance it attaches to the holding of elections no later than October 1994. In my previous report (S/26666), I informed the Security Council that agreements had been reached between the Government and RENAMO during my visit to Mozambique from 17 to 20 October 1993, which broke the deadlock on the issues of the composition and chairmanship of the National Elections Commission that had paralysed the debate on the draft electoral law. Subsequent discussions, however, reached an impasse over four other questions: (a) voting rights for expatriate Mozambicans; (b) composition of the provincial and district elections commissions; (c) composition of the Technical Secretariat for Electoral Administration, which will be responsible for the organization of the electoral process; and (d) establishment and composition of an electoral tribunal to serve as final arbiter in all disputes arising from the electoral process.

13. On 26 November 1993, a consensus on the above questions was finally reached after a number of meetings were held between President Chissano and Mr. Dhlakama in consultation with my Special Representative. It was agreed that:

(a) The National Elections Commission would decide whether it was feasible to organize polling for expatriate Mozambicans;

(b) The provincial and district elections commissions would have a chairperson appointed by the Government, a deputy chairperson appointed by RENAMO and one representative from other political parties, with the United Nations represented at the provincial level by two observers;

(c) The Technical Secretariat for Electoral Administration would have a Director-General appointed by the Government and two deputy directors to be nominated by RENAMO and the other opposition parties, respectively. The staff of the Technical Secretariat will be composed of 50 per cent government, 25 per cent opposition and 25 per cent United Nations personnel;

(d) A five-member Electoral Tribunal would be established, composed of two Mozambican judges and three international judges proposed by the United Nations.

14. Following these agreements, the Electoral Law was approved by the Mozambican National Assembly on 9 December 1993, nine days later than envisaged in the timetable. It was promulgated by President Chissano shortly thereafter and entered into force on 12 January 1994. The members of the National Elections Commission were appointed on 21 January 1994 and are now in the process of selecting a suitable chairperson. The General Peace Agreement, in Protocol III, paragraph 7 (a), pre-

scribes that the National Elections Commission shall guarantee the distribution to all parties, without discrimination, of the available subsidies and logistic support for the election campaign. The establishment of a trust fund to support all parties in the electoral process is thus contingent on the functioning of the National Elections Commission.

II. Military aspects

A. *Deployment of the military component*

15. There have been no significant changes in the deployment of the ONUMOZ military elements since my last report to the Security Council (S/26666). The rotation of contingents from Argentina, Botswana, Italy, Japan, Portugal, Uruguay and Zambia was completed smoothly. As of 24 January 1994, against an authorized strength of 6,979, the total strength of the military component, including support elements, was 6,239, with contributions from the following countries:

Argentina	40
Bangladesh	1 433
Botswana	755
Brazil	3
India	919
Italy	1 022
Japan	53
Netherlands	11
Portugal	284
Uruguay	845
Zambia	874

The above figures include 22 military personnel from Bangladesh currently on loan to the United Nations Assistance Mission for Rwanda (UNAMIR) and 1 in New York.

16. United Nations forces continued to carry out extensive operational activities throughout the country. The security of corridors and main roads is being ensured by regular road and aerial patrol as well as by vehicle and train escorts provided by United Nations forces. Furthermore, they are providing security to oil-pumping stations, airports, United Nations warehouses and ONUMOZ headquarters and, more recently, to temporary and permanent arms depots. United Nations forces are also contributing to humanitarian activities in the country by providing engineering and medical assistance. The engineer units continued to conduct road repair and improvement of water supply and were called in to assist in the rehabilitation of the training centres for the Mozambican Defence Force. The increased patrolling by United Nations troops has reduced the number and intensity of banditry incidents along the main routes, especially in the southern and central regions. On several occasions, United Nations armed units successfully negotiated solutions to situations of mutiny.

17. As of 24 January 1994, 330 of the authorized total of 354 military observers were deployed with ONUMOZ. The military observers continued to conduct inspections and investigations into allegations of cease-fire violations and assisted in the establishment and preparation of assembly areas. The observers have supervised the process of cantonment of troops since its inception, including the collection and storage of the weapons and ammunition handed over by government and RENAMO soldiers.

18. Ideally, it would be beneficial to keep much of the present United Nations formed units in Mozambique until the elections are held in October 1994. I am aware, however, of the additional costs associated with the establishment of the sizeable United Nations police presence in the country, which is recommended in my separate report on this matter (S/1994/89/Add.1). At the same time, I also believe that political developments in Mozambique have evolved in such a way as to allow an increasing shift of focus from cease-fire arrangements to general verification of police activities in the country and the respect of civil rights. But while the demobilization of troops is still proceeding, it would not be advisable to reduce the ONUMOZ military component significantly. In May 1994, when this phase will be nearly completed, I intend to begin a gradual cut-back of the Mission's military elements. The Mozambican Defence Force is scheduled to become fully operational by September 1994. By that time, the new Mozambican army will be expected to assume some of the major tasks in the transport corridors that are now performed by ONUMOZ. In my next progress report on ONUMOZ in April 1994, I intend to present to the Security Council reductions as well as estimates of corresponding cost savings.

B. *Cease-fire*

19. On several occasions in the past, the Council called on the Government of Mozambique and RENAMO to respect fully all provisions of the general peace agreement, in particular those concerning the cease-fire and movement of troops. It will be recalled in this connection that the guidelines for movement of troops were signed by the two parties on 23 October 1993. These guidelines have helped the Cease-fire Commission to resolve several cases of cease-fire violations related to the unauthorized movement of troops. RENAMO was for quite some time reluctant to comply with the recommendations of the Cease-fire Commission on two cases,

Dunda and Salamanga, involving movement of RENAMO troops after signature of the general peace agreement. This created complications for the approval of RENAMO assembly areas at these locations as the Government was unwilling to consider the sites until RENAMO's troops had withdrawn from them. RENAMO has now removed its soldiers from Dunda but a dispute remains about the required distance of withdrawal from Salamanga.

20. During the period under review, the Cease-fire Commission received 11 notifications of alleged cease-fire violations. These cases fell into three categories: (a) illegal detention of individuals; (b) alleged movement of troops; and (c) occupation of new positions. None of these violations constituted a serious threat to the cease-fire or to the peace process. Eight cases have been fully resolved and are considered closed. In two cases, the recommendations of the Cease-fire Commission are due to be implemented shortly, while the investigation results of the last case still has to be presented to the Commission.

C. *Formation of the Mozambican Defence Force*

21. Some progress in this area has been made since I last reported to the Council. The training of the 540 instructors by the United Kingdom of Great Britain and Northern Ireland at the training centre at Nyanga (Zimbabwe) was completed by 20 December 1993, and these soldiers were then transported by ONUMOZ to the Dondo training centre in Mozambique on 12 January 1994. They will work with their United Kingdom instructors in training infantry soldiers at the three Mozambican Defence Force training centres. It has been agreed that most of the first group of 5,000 soldiers (half government and half RENAMO) will be transported directly from their present locations without passing through the assembly areas. The infantry training is scheduled to begin on 8 February 1994. The French training of one company of military engineers as well as the Portuguese training of three battalions of special forces and one company of marines and provision of training for senior military officers, logisticians and administrative personnel, which should have begun in November 1993, were delayed as a result of both political and technical problems. Meanwhile, the Supervision and Monitoring Commission approved a total of 19 documents relating to the organization, operating procedures, uniforms, ranking symbols and training of the unified armed forces and other matters. These documents had been elaborated by the Government and RENAMO with substantive assistance provided by Portugal.

22. The Government informed the donor community that it was not in a position to undertake the rehabilitation of the training centres for the new army. Despite the fact that the United Nations has no mandate in this area, my Special Representative intervened in order to speed up the process of the formation of the Mozambican Defence Force, which is an essential element of the peace process. Mr. Ajello has offered all the logistical support that ONUMOZ could provide without incurring additional costs for the ONUMOZ budget and has sought options for funding among the donor community, should this be required. A task force, which included representatives from the Government, RENAMO, the three countries assisting in the formation of the new army (France, Portugal and United Kingdom) and ONUMOZ, was established by the Joint Commission for the Formation of the Mozambican Defence Force to oversee and coordinate the rehabilitation of the training centres. Meanwhile, the Portuguese Government has undertaken to rehabilitate the three centres (Nacala, Catembe and Maputo) for the provision of training by the Portuguese. The Government of Italy has offered to provide $500,000 for the rehabilitation of the remaining training centres should this be required. However, the rehabilitation of the training centres by the Government is in progress, although slightly delayed.

III. Humanitarian assistance programme

23. The facilitation of the return and resettlement of demobilized soldiers into civilian life has been considered an important component of the humanitarian assistance programme, ever since the donors' meeting on Mozambique that was held in Rome in December 1992. Consequently, with the demobilization process well under way, the United Nations Office for Humanitarian Assistance Coordination is now focusing particular attention on its programme for the reintegration of former combatants into civilian life. Through informal tripartite discussions within the Commission for Reintegration, it has been able to secure agreement on a three-pronged strategy that will address the needs of ex-soldiers. An aspect of this strategy deals with the identification of training opportunities within appropriate institutions in Mozambique. The strategy also includes a programme designed to promote self-employment through the provision of occupational kits and credit to qualified persons. Additionally, the strategy seeks to identify employment opportunities in the public and private sectors and the possibility of providing where necessary subsidies to the concerned entities within these sectors, in order to enable them to accept quotas of demobilized soldiers. These three programme components will be tied to an information and referral service that will function at provincial and district levels. The existing provincial commissions for reinte-

gration provide the institutional settings for the operation of such a service.

24. Since the capacity of the Mozambican economy to absorb thousands of new job-seekers leaving military duty is severely limited, donor agencies have been exploring ways and means to ease the problems that could confront ex-soldiers. This has resulted in a proposal to extend the Government severance payment to demobilized soldiers, in support of reintegration.

25. Progress with demobilization and agreement on an election date appear to have stimulated the rate of refugee repatriation and movement of internally displaced persons. It is now estimated that about half of the 4 to 4.5 million people displaced internally by war and drought have returned to their home areas. According to current reports, 621,000 persons or 40 per cent of the original refugee population, have left camps in neighbouring countries for their home districts in Mozambique, most of them spontaneously. Assisted repatriation organized by the Office of the United Nations High Commissioner for Refugees (UNHCR) has continued from Swaziland, Zambia and Zimbabwe, as well as from Malawi, but this constitutes only a fraction of the entire movement of people. In mid-January 1994, the first organized repatriation of 208 refugees took place from South Africa, a cooperative effort of the South African authorities, UNHCR and the International Organization for Migration (IOM).

26. Internally displaced persons and returning refugees make up the bulk of the beneficiaries of free distributions of food and non-food items such as seeds and tools. As may be expected in a year when the number of beneficiaries dropped markedly following a favourable crop season that produced agricultural surpluses in some areas, it has not always been possible to manage the pipeline for food donations without prices being affected in the local cereal markets. In order to counteract the possible negative effect of free food distribution on local production, several agencies have together purchased 62,000 tons of grain from the local market. For instance, WFP alone is making available resources for the purchase of 25,000 tons from local suppliers.

27. An update of the consolidated programme of humanitarian assistance to Mozambique was made public in November 1993. Its principal concerns are the repatriation of refugees, emergency relief of food and non-food items, as well as the restoration of essential services in rural areas where the returnees and displaced people are resettling. It also includes institutional support to Mozambican agencies responsible for emergency management. The revised estimates for priority needs now stand at $609.7 million, an increase of $50 million over a figure projected earlier. This is the result

of an in-depth review of requirements in the health, education and road infrastructure sectors. Similarly, donor commitments for the same period have now reached $559.4 million, a most creditable response by the international community to Mozambican post-war needs. Of this amount, $360.8 million, or 64 per cent, has been committed to special projects that are now in the implementation process.

28. Part of the resources made available by donors as voluntary contributions has been effected through the Trust Fund account established for Mozambique by the Department of Humanitarian Affairs, mainly for programmes in the areas of demobilization, the reintegration of demobilized soldiers and de-mining operations, as well as for multisectoral area-based projects at district and community levels. At the end of December, cumulative pledges to the Department of Humanitarian Affairs and the United Nations Development Programme (UNDP) trust funds stood at $33 million, of which $28 million has been paid in. Project allocations from the trust funds total $20 million, an increase of $15 million since the end of October 1993.

29. Reports on 8 mine accidents since November 1993, recording 21 dead and 15 injured, clearly show that mines continue to pose serious threats to the civilian population. Following an intensive series of tripartite meetings, the national mine-clearance plan of Mozambique was finally approved in December 1993 by the Cease-fire Commission. In order to set priorities for de-mining, a national mine survey is now being carried out by a British non-governmental organization (NGO) and this will, within approximately four months, provide high-quality information on mined roads and areas all over the country. As regards mine clearance, two additional de-mining efforts are about to become operational, one in the province of Sofala financed by the United States Agency for International Development (USAID) and a second in the province of Zambézia funded by the United Kingdom. This brings to four the number of mine-clearance operations now in progress in Mozambique. Contract award is imminent for a fifth project financed jointly from the Department of Humanitarian Affairs Trust Fund and the ONUMOZ budget. In addition, the ONUMOZ mine-clearance training centre, located in Beira, started its first course for 32 Mozambican trainees in mid-January 1994. Four de-mining teams, financed by the European Union, continue to clear the road from Caia to Chemba along the Zambezi River, from Gorongosa to Casa Banana and from Dombe towards Espungabera. Mine clearance in the Mutarara district of Tete Province is continuing by a Norwegian NGO with a team of Mozambican deminers that has recently been increased from 64 to 89 persons.

30. At its meeting on 22 December 1993, the Monitoring and Supervisory Commission decided to reactivate the Humanitarian Assistance Committee, which was established on 16 July 1992 under the declaration of principles guiding the provision of humanitarian assistance to Mozambique (see S/24635, annex). In accordance with the general peace agreement, the future of this Committee, which was chaired by the United Nations, was to be decided in the light of developments, but several subcommittees continued to function as needed. The reactivation of the Committee will now allow these activities to be carried out under a more formal structure.

IV. Observations

31. Significant progress has been made since my last report to the Council (S/26666). However, several serious problems relating to the implementation of the general peace agreement still remain to be addressed by all concerned.

32. The demobilization of the government and RENAMO troops, totalling more than 80,000 soldiers, presents a great challenge to the Mozambican economy and the peace process in the country. For the demobilized soldiers not to become a source of instability, they must have viable economic opportunities, while the troops joining the new army must be incorporated into a well-functioning institution. It should be also emphasized that the success of the proposed reintegration support programme for demobilized soldiers, to be conducted under United Nations auspices, will be entirely dependent upon the generous financial support of the international community.

33. Owing to the hardship of Mozambican army life and to the history of late or non-payment of salaries, it appears that not many soldiers are interested in joining the Mozambican Defence Force at present. In order to attract soldiers to the new army, provision will have to be made for satisfactory conditions of service, including adequate salary, an acceptable quality and quantity of food and decent accommodation. Unless these conditions are met, it would be difficult to expect that the parties would manage to provide the 30,000 personnel envisaged for the new army. I would therefore urge the Government of Mozambique to provide adequate facilities and resources for the soldiers in the Mozambican Defence Force in order to ensure the success of the formation of the new army, which is considered to be an essential element in the implementation of the general peace agreement.

34. The lack of resources available for the transformation of RENAMO into a political party also poses a threat to the peace process. At this stage, the problem has acquired a special dimension and, if left unresolved, could place the peace process in jeopardy. According to protocol III, section 7, of the general peace agreement, RENAMO is entitled to receive the financial assistance necessary to transform itself into a political party. As the Security Council is aware, the Government of Mozambique requested, through the United Nations, the support of the international community to make available the required financial resources. A United Nations-administered trust fund for a projected $10 million has been established.

35. Although this Trust Fund has alleviated some of the administrative and logistic requirements related to RENAMO's participation in the implementation of the provisions of the general peace agreement, it has not entirely solved the problem. The resources currently available are clearly not sufficient. An amount of at least $15 million is needed, as opposed to the $7.5 million currently available. Furthermore, as I indicated in my last report, there are expenditures associated with the transformation of RENAMO into a political party that cannot be easily met through a United Nations-administered Fund, on account of the rules and procedures that govern their use. In close consultation with my Special Representative and members of the donor community, I am presently exploring the possibility of setting up a more flexible funding mechanism. It is envisaged that, subject to the scrupulous and timely implementation of the general peace agreement, an appropriate monthly allowance would be provided to RENAMO under this new mechanism.

36. I am confident that, at this important juncture in the peace process, the United Nations will continue to do its utmost to assist the people of Mozambique. However, in the final analysis, it is the Mozambicans themselves who bear the main responsibility for the success of the implementation of the general peace agreement. The timetable for implementation of the agreement is becoming increasingly tight. It is imperative that the two parties honour their commitments and cooperate closely with the United Nations in overcoming existing obstacles. I trust that the Mozambicans and their leaders are fully aware that the international community will be increasingly reluctant to continue to support this process in the event of further delays.

Addendum (S/1994/89/Add.1)

Introduction

1. As members of the Security Council will recall, in my report of 10 September 1993 (S/26385/Add.1), I informed the Council that, on 3 September 1993, major agreements had been reached between the Government of Mozambique and the Resistência Nacional Moçambicana (RENAMO) as a result of the direct talks between the President of Mozambique, Mr. Joaquim Chissano,

and Mr. Afonso Dhlakama of RENAMO, which took place in August/September 1993. In particular, the parties agreed to request the United Nations to monitor all police activities in the country, public or private, to monitor the rights and liberties of Mozambican citizens and to provide technical support to the National Police Affairs Commission established under the general peace agreement signed in Rome on 4 October 1992 (S/24635, annex). The proposed United Nations police contingent would be responsible for verifying that all police activities in the country are consistent with the general peace agreement. The Government agreed to provide a list of *matériel* in the possession of the police as well as other information necessary to verify its activities. In addition, the Government undertook to request support from the international community on a bilateral basis in order to reorganize and retrain its quick reaction police force. At that time, I indicated my intention to send a small survey team of experts to Mozambique and to inform the Security Council in due course of their findings as well as of my final recommendations about the size of the United Nations police component.

2. As members of the Council are aware, during my visit to Mozambique from 17 to 20 October 1993, police matters, among others, were thoroughly discussed with President Chissano and Mr. Dhlakama. During these discussions, I emphasized to my interlocutors the need to keep various considerations in mind in determining the scope and functions of the proposed contingent. It was stressed that both parties should adopt a cooperative approach in order to maximize the benefit of the presence of United Nations police in the country. I also emphasized that the human and financial capabilities of the United Nations were stretched to the limit; these and other factors would invariably result in delays in deployment. Having this in mind, the parties decided that the National Police Affairs Commission would establish its subcommittees in provinces and districts where Mozambican police activities would be monitored and, if need be, supported by United Nations police observers. I believe that this arrangement could facilitate cooperation among the parties in various parts of the country during the peace process and enhance the activities of the United Nations police component on the ground.

3. It will be recalled that, in paragraph 9 of resolution 882 (1993) of 5 November 1993, the Security Council approved the deployment of 128 police observers as soon as possible. I am pleased to report that 125 observers have already arrived. These initial elements have been deployed in small teams to Maputo and to provincial capitals as an early confidence-building measure, in pursuance of the agreements described in paragraph 1 above.

On 6 January 1994, liaison mechanisms between United Nations police and the National Police Affairs Commission were established. United Nations Operation in Mozambique (ONUMOZ) police observers have visited police stations in various localities to gather information on the personnel and weaponry of the Mozambican police, including that of the quick reaction police. The United Nations police component has so far investigated 14 incidents of alleged politically motivated crimes or civil rights violations. These include the abduction by RENAMO of two police officers on the pretext that they allegedly were plotting to kill Mr. Dhlakama.

4. The present report is based on the extensive work conducted by the survey team of police experts during their visit to Mozambique in October and November 1993, on the numerous consultations held by my Special Representative, Mr. Aldo Ajello, with the Government and RENAMO concerning the mandate, operational concept and size of the ONUMOZ police component, as well as on my personal observations during my visit to Maputo in October 1993.

I. Background

5. In formulating the operational concept of the United Nations police contingent in Mozambique, I have been guided by several basic considerations. It is worth recalling that the country covers a land area of 799,388 square kilometres. It is elongated in shape, about 2,000 km from north to south and 600 km from east to west in the north and 300 km in the south. The population of approximately 16 million people had endured almost 16 years of a devastating civil war, which resulted in approximately 1 million deaths and 4.5 million refugees and displaced persons. The protracted hostilities in Mozambique have disrupted infrastructure to a great degree, contributed to the existence of armed banditry and created conditions for lawlessness in some parts of the countryside. Between May and September 1993 alone, the number of reported crimes in Mozambique included 167 homicides, 726 armed robberies and hundreds of cases of physical assault, rape, etc. Difficulties in the reporting of incidents and continued restrictions on freedom of movement in some areas would suggest that the above statistics do not present a full picture of the crime rate in the country. It is obvious that among their functions, United Nations police observers will need to encourage the Mozambican police to improve the protection of citizens and property.

6. A number of additional factors should also be taken into account. There is no efficient arms control system in place, and estimates put the total number of assorted types of weapons in "non-official" hands at

approximately 1 million. Moreover, 150,000 militia and paramilitary personnel as well as millions of refugees and displaced persons will also have to be reintegrated. Despite all efforts, demobilization of the armed forces will inevitably mean the release of a number of persons who, for various reasons, will not be integrated fully into civilian life. The activities generated by the forthcoming electoral process, including the holding of public meetings, demonstrations and political debates, could deteriorate into violence. Codes of conduct governing political activities must be monitored and human rights and fundamental freedoms will have to be protected during the electoral campaign. The presence of United Nations police observers at political rallies and meetings will be essential to ensure that appropriate arrangements are carried out by the Mozambican police, not only in major provincial cities but throughout the country, including remote locations. The United Nations presence in various localities will therefore be a major confidence-building measure. On the other hand, as the process of free circulation of people and goods and the extension of the State administration gain momentum, the deployment of United Nations monitors throughout the entire territory would produce an additional stabilizing effect, which is essential for the success of the elections.

7. The current strength of the Mozambican police (PRM) is 18,047, with the command structure of national headquarters in Maputo, 11 provincial headquarters and over 200 stations and posts in the districts. There is a quick reaction police force numbering several thousand as well as various private security companies and agencies. It should be noted that on several occasions RENAMO conveyed to my Special Representative its concern at the alleged transfer of combat-trained soldiers to various government police forces. Also, complaints of human rights abuses may increase as political consciousness is raised during the political campaign. Active monitoring by the United Nations could make a substantial contribution to quelling fears of police irregularities.

8. Against this background, it is evident that the operational plan for the United Nations police contingent in Mozambique should be designed to respond suitably to the challenging tasks it is to perform. My Special Representative has discussed with the two parties, and in particular with President Chissano and Mr. Dhlakama of RENAMO, several options for the general set-up of the proposed police element of ONUMOZ. One approach might be to limit the United Nations police presence in the country to a certain predetermined number of teams in each province, totalling several hundred personnel. Another approach might involve the creation of a network covering the most remote corners of the country,

an ideal but ambitious and costly arrangement. In my view, neither of these options is feasible since the former does not adequately reflect the political and security situation currently prevailing in the country, and the latter would involve untenable expense and logistic effort. In his contacts with the parties, therefore, my Special Representative concentrated on what the expert team recommended as an optimum plan for a United Nations police operation in Mozambique, as outlined below.

II. Overall framework for the police operation

9. In accordance with the agreement reached on 3 September 1993 between the Government and RENAMO on the United Nations role in police monitoring and in accordance with the main principles governing the general peace agreement on Mozambique, it is proposed, subject to the agreement of the Council, that the mandate of the ONUMOZ police component (CIVPOL) be as follows:

(a) To monitor all police activities in the country, including those of PRM and any other police and security agencies and verify that their actions are fully consistent with the general peace agreement;

(b) To monitor the respect of rights and civil liberties of Mozambican citizens throughout the country;

(c) To provide technical support to the National Police Commission;

(d) To verify that the activities of private protection and security agencies do not violate the general peace agreement;

(e) To verify the strength and location of the government police forces, their *matériel*, as well as any other information which might be needed in support of the peace process;

(f) To monitor and verify the process of the reorganization and retraining of the quick reaction police and its activities, as well as to verify their weapons and equipment;

(g) To monitor, together with other ONUMOZ components, the proper conduct of the electoral campaign and verify that political rights of individuals, groups and political organizations are respected, in accordance with the general peace agreement and relevant electoral documents.

10. From an operational standpoint, CIVPOL would be a separate component of the Mission under the command of a Chief Police Observer, who would report directly to the Special Representative. At the same time, the new component would complement and work closely with the currently existing electoral, military, humanitarian and administrative components of ONUMOZ. A strong interrelationship with other elements of the Mission will be assured to guarantee the success of CIVPOL's mandate.

III. Operational plan for United Nations monitoring and verification of police-related activities

11. To ensure credible verification, it would be necessary to obtain promptly from the parties all information relevant to carrying out the mandate described in section II above, including on the strength of the police, as well as on the quantity, type and location of *matériel* in their possession. Appropriate liaison arrangements would be established with the national police at the headquarters level in Maputo, at the provincial level and at the district and local (station, post, etc.) levels. Activities of the Mozambican police and private security/protection agencies will be closely monitored by teams of United Nations civilian police observers. They would liaise with established authorities and visit, without restriction, police installations and detention facilities, including prisons.

12. CIVPOL would establish itself at all strategic locations throughout the country. In determining deployment sites, consideration will be given to the ability of ONUMOZ to discharge its responsibilities effectively and to such factors as the need to instil confidence in the public, especially in the context of the electoral process. Arrangements would have to be made to establish a reliable communications network that would link the various levels of CIVPOL as well as enable it to liaise effectively with the Police Commission and its provincial subcommittees. CIVPOL's functions would be carried out by stationing United Nations teams in the vicinity of the Mozambican police stations, posts and by extensive patrolling. In order to monitor certain activities, police observers would be deployed at various national police headquarters. At the same time, ONUMOZ would have unrestricted access to the general public and would be able to gather information as well as to receive complaints from individuals and organizations. CIVPOL would conduct its own investigations, on the basis of such complaints, as well as independently, into politically motivated offences and, when necessary, recommend corrective action. Information about such investigations would be provided promptly to the National Police Affairs Commission and the national authorities.

13. Special attention would be given to the systematic verification of weapons and equipment in the possession of the national police and of private agencies and to monitoring the activities of the quick reaction police force, whose facilities would also be visited on a regular basis; ONUMOZ would also examine the latter's role and structure. Given the scope of arms proliferation among the general population, teams of United Nations police observers would be available to collect any weapons and ammunition that may be surrendered by individuals or irregular forces throughout the country.

14. At the same time, responsibility for the maintenance of law and order will clearly remain with the Government. All violations of the Criminal Code will be investigated by the Mozambican police, with the possibility of parallel investigations being conducted by CIVPOL, when the latter considers it appropriate. It would be essential to ensure a wide understanding among the general public of both what the role of ONUMOZ in police monitoring would be and of what new functions the Mozambican police are to perform in these new circumstances. Within the context of confidence-building measures, United Nations police observers, in coordination with the Government, would also monitor security arrangements for the leadership of RENAMO in its party's capacity as a signatory to the general peace agreement. It may be necessary to familiarize local police with the international concepts of rights, civil liberties and fundamental freedoms, as well as the codes of conduct the political parties might agree to observe during the electoral process. With the concurrence of the Mozambican parties, United Nations police observers would assist the electoral observers of ONUMOZ in monitoring the registration process and the electoral campaign. In this context, they would also monitor security at the polling stations, including the security arrangements for the storage, counting and transporting of ballot papers and other election material.

15. To perform the functions described above, the organizational structure of the ONUMOZ police contingent would be as follows:

(a) The headquarters component, which would be headed by the Chief Police Observer at the rank of Inspector General and would consist of his deputy and chiefs of staff for operations, liaison, investigations, logistics and personnel. A headquarters team would also liaise with and provide technical assistance to the Police Commission;

(b) A special task force stationed in Maputo for the monitoring and verification of the quick reaction police force. This group will also monitor security arrangements for the leadership of RENAMO. In addition, it will be on call to respond to any exigencies that may arise in other parts of the country;

(c) Three compact regional headquarters, whose tasks would primarily be the coordination activities in several provinces. Each of these headquarters will be headed by a regional chief police observer;

(d) Eleven provincial headquarters. Each of these will be headed by a provincial chief police observer and will include a deputy, an operations officer, an investigations officer, a logistics/personnel officer and several patrol and investigation teams, which would cover both the provincial capital and as much of the surrounding area as possible;

(e) One hundred eighty United Nations police stations and posts throughout the country in remote and isolated locations, to be established near government police facilities.

16. Having in mind the various considerations described above and the magnitude of tasks the United Nations police contingent would be called upon to perform, it is proposed that the total strength of the contingent be established at the level of 1,144 police observers (inclusive of the 128 already authorized by Security Council resolution 882 (1993)), with the following breakdown:

(a) The Chief Police Observer, with the rank of Inspector General;

(b) The Deputy Police Observer;

(c) 29 police observers at the component headquarters in Maputo;

(d) 30 police observers comprising a special task force to monitor and evaluate the quick reaction police and to be available for unforeseen exigencies;

(e) 12 police observers in each of the three regional headquarters;

(f) 327 police observers to be deployed at 11 provincial capitals, including those to be formed into stationary and mobile teams to service surrounding areas;

(g) 720 police observers in other locations throughout the country.

17. To the extent possible, United Nations civilian police observers would be colocated with the military and other civilian elements of ONUMOZ and would rely on the existing military and administrative infrastructure of the Mission, including transport and communications facilities. However, given the fact that these elements would be widely spread throughout the country, CIVPOL would require additional support in terms of administrative personnel, such as interpreters and translators, as well as adequate transportation and other equipment, accommodation facilities, etc. It is estimated that a total of 4 international staff and 35 locally recruited personnel would be required.

18. I am fully aware of the challenges involved in setting up such a substantial force and would therefore like to propose that it be deployed progressively. The initial phase, during which the central headquarters and regional and provincial capitals' teams would be fully established, should be completed by mid-March 1994. The second phase would coincide with the voter registration process from April to June 1994, during which up to 70 per cent of CIVPOL's posts and stations

throughout the countryside would become operational. The remainder of the component would be deployed by no later than one month before the beginning of the electoral campaign, which is scheduled to begin on 1 September 1994.

IV. Recommendations

19. As members of the Security Council will recall, I first proposed the establishment of a United Nations police component in ONUMOZ in December 1992. At that time I felt that experience in other similar operations suggested that it would be desirable to deploy a United Nations civilian police to Mozambique in order to inspire confidence that violations of civil liberties, human rights and political freedoms would be avoided. I am pleased to inform the Council that, after extensive discussions, the Government of Mozambique and RENAMO have now agreed to the general concept for the ONUMOZ police contingent. As the peace process moves forward, the presence of a United Nations police element could be most useful, particularly when the national electoral campaign begins.

20. I would like to emphasize that I fully appreciate that the creation of a new component in ONUMOZ places an additional burden on the United Nations and its Member States. The cost estimates for the phased deployment of the police component of ONUMOZ will be issued shortly as a further addendum to the present report. I believe that recent political developments in Mozambique have evolved in such a way so as to allow an increasing shift of focus from the monitoring of ceasefire arrangements to the verification of police activities in the country. In my progress report on ONUMOZ in April, I intend to present to the Security Council my specific proposals about the phased reduction of the military component of the Mission.

21. Mozambique is currently facing one of the most challenging periods in its history, and the events that are taking place there now will determine what develops in the country in the immediate future. The recent, generally positive, developments there deserve the full support of the international community. It should also be recognized that the peace process in Mozambique is only one element in the wider transformation taking place in the entire region of southern Africa. I recommend that the Security Council authorize the establishment of a United Nations police component as a integral part of ONUMOZ with the mandate and deployment described above. I further recommend that Member States consider contributing civilian police personnel to this important undertaking and appeal to them to do so.

Addendum (S/1994/89/Add.2)

1. In my report to the Security Council of 28 January 1994 (S/1994/89/Add.1), I recommended in paragraph 21 that the Council authorize the establishment of a United Nations police component as an integral part of the United Nations Operation in Mozambique (ONUMOZ). The mandate and deployment of the proposed police component would be as set out in paragraphs 9 and 18, respectively. I indicated in paragraph 20 that I would submit a further addendum to the report, in which the cost estimates for the phased deployment of the police component would be presented.

2. It will be recalled that, in paragraph 9 of resolution 882 (1993) of 5 November 1993, the Council approved the deployment of 128 police observers to ONUMOZ as soon as possible. The estimated cost associated with that deployment has previously been submitted to the Council (S/26666/Add.1). It is now estimated that the cost related to the deployment of an additional 1,016 civilian police, as part of an enlarged ONUMOZ police component, would amount to approximately $38,474,000 gross for the period from 15 February to 31 October 1994. A breakdown of the estimated cost by main categories of expenditure is provided for information purposes in the annex to the present addendum.

3. It would be my recommendation to the General Assembly, should the Security Council decide to approve my recommendation for the deployment of an enlarged police component for ONUMOZ, that the additional costs relating thereto should be considered an expense of the Organization to be borne by Member States in accordance with Article 17, paragraph 2, of the Charter of the United Nations and that the assessments to be levied on Member States should be credited to the ONUMOZ special account established for this purpose.

Annex

Cost estimate of the additional costs to the United Nations for the activities of ONUMOZ for the period from 15 February to 31 October 1994
(In thousands of United States dollars)

		Amount
1.	Military personnel costs	-
2.	Civilian personnel costs	
	(a) Civilian police	21 044
	(b) International and local staff	506 a/
3.	Premises/accommodation	4 365
4.	Infrastructure repairs	-
5.	Transport operations	9 389
6.	Air operations	260
7.	Naval operations	-
8.	Communications	698
9.	Other equipment	1 800
10.	Supplies and services	300
11.	Election-related supplies and services	-
12.	Public information programmes	-
13.	Training programmes	-
14.	Mine-clearing programmes	-
15.	Assistance for disarmament and demobilization	-
16.	Air and surface freight	-
17.	Integrated Management Information System	-
18.	Support account for peace-keeping operations	43
19.	Staff assessment	69
	TOTAL	38 474

a/ Provides for 4 international and 35 locally recruited staff.

Document 56

Letter dated 9 February 1994 from the Permanent Representative of Italy to the Secretary-General in response to the request made for a contribution to the Trust Fund for assistance to RENAMO

Not issued as a United Nations document

I refer to your January 14 letter to our President of the Council of Ministers, sent to him from Geneva through Mr. Petrovsky, concerning Mozambique. I am pleased to inform you that, in response to your appeal, the Italian Government is examining ways to continue its concrete support for the transformation of RENAMO into a political party, in accordance with the terms of the peace agreement signed in Rome. In particular, your request for

an additional contribution of 500 thousand dollars, to help implement the demobilization of the RENAMO troops, is being given positive consideration.

This amount would help RENAMO to make the transition from military organization to political party, and in particular to pay for personnel and equipment for its various provincial offices. Utilization of this amount should be decided based on consultations with the United

Nations in Maputo and on the evaluation of RENAMO's individual requests.

As you are aware, this amount supplements the 5.7 million dollars we have already disbursed to the United Nations Trust Fund for financial assistance to RENAMO.

This latest effort by my country is meant to meet RENAMO's immediate needs, pending the set-up of the more flexible instrument mentioned in your letter, which would allow other countries to contribute to the Fund. We earnestly hope that once this new mechanism is in place, you will continue to urge more countries to join in the efforts to help RENAMO become a participant in the democratic process.

The procedures and timetable of this additional Italian contribution will be communicated to you by the President of the Council, Mr. Ciampi, as soon as they have been defined. In the meantime, I thought advance notice of this might be helpful.

Please accept, Mr. Secretary-General, the assurances of my highest consideration.

(*Signed*) F. Paolo FULCI

Document 57

Security Council resolution authorizing the creation of a police component for ONUMOZ

S/RES/898 (1994), 23 February 1994

The Security Council,

Reaffirming its resolution 782 (1992) of 13 October 1992 and all subsequent resolutions,

Having considered the report of the Secretary-General on the United Nations Operation in Mozambique (ONUMOZ) dated 28 January 1994 (S/1994/89 and Add.1 and 2), and having completed the review of the status of ONUMOZ called for in its resolution 882 (1993),

Commending the efforts of the Secretary-General, his Special Representative and the personnel of ONU-MOZ in seeking to implement fully the mandate entrusted to it,

Commending also the role played by the Organization of African Unity (OAU), through the Special Representative of its Secretary-General, in the implementation of the General Peace Agreement for Mozambique (S/24635, annex),

Reiterating the importance it attaches to the General Peace Agreement, and to the timely fulfilment in good faith by all parties of their obligations under the Agreement,

Noting that the people of Mozambique bear the ultimate responsibility for the successful implementation of the General Peace Agreement,

Welcoming recent positive developments in the implementation of the General Peace Agreement, but concerned none the less at delays in its full implementation,

Taking note of the request by the Government of Mozambique and RENAMO concerning the monitoring of all police activities and additional tasks set out in the agreements of 3 September 1993 (S/26432), and of the agreement of both parties to the general concept for the ONUMOZ police contingent,

Stressing the necessity, in this as in other peace-keeping operations, to continue to monitor expenditures carefully during this period of increasing demands on peace-keeping resources, without jeopardizing their purposes,

Noting with appreciation in this context that the Secretary-General, in proposing the establishment of a police component as an integral part of ONUMOZ, has at the same time stated his intention to present specific proposals for the phased reduction of the military component of ONUMOZ, without prejudice to the effective discharge of its mandate, in particular the tasks of its military component,

Reaffirming its conviction that the resolution of the conflict in Mozambique will contribute to peace and security,

1. *Welcomes* the report of the Secretary-General of 28 January 1994;

2. *Authorizes* the establishment of a United Nations police component of up to 1,144 personnel as an integral part of ONUMOZ with the mandate and deployment described in paragraphs 9 to 18 of document S/1994/89/Add.1;

3. *Requests* the Secretary-General, as the police contingent is being deployed, to begin immediately preparing specific proposals for the drawdown of an appropriate number of military personnel with the objective of ensuring there is no increase in the cost of ONUMOZ without prejudice to the effective discharge of its mandate;

4. *Further requests* the Secretary-General to prepare a timetable for (a) the completion of ONUMOZ's mandate, withdrawal of its personnel, and turnover of

any remaining functions to United Nations agencies and programmes by the target date of the end of November 1994, by which time the elected government is expected to have assumed office, and in this context, for (b) the phased drawdown of military forces in the transportation corridors which should begin as soon as feasible and be completed when the new national defence force is operational, and (c) the withdrawal of military observers after demobilization is completed;

5. *Welcomes* recent positive developments in the implementation of the General Peace Agreement including the commencement of the assembly of troops and the dismantling of paramilitary forces, militia and irregular troops, the approval of the electoral law and the appointment of the National Elections Commission and of its chairperson;

6. *Expresses* its concern, however, at the continuing delay in the implementation of some major aspects of the General Peace Agreement, including the commencement of demobilization and the formation of a national defence force and calls upon the parties to work towards the elimination of further delays;

7. *Calls upon* the Government of Mozambique and RENAMO to comply with all the provisions of the General Peace Agreement, in particular those concerning the cease-fire and the cantonment and demobilization of troops, and commends in this respect the commitments made by both President Chissano and Mr. Dhlakama to implement the General Peace Agreement;

8. *Further calls upon* the Government of Mozambique and RENAMO to comply fully and promptly with the decisions of the Monitoring and Supervision Commission;

9. *Encourages* the Government of Mozambique to continue to fulfil its commitments in respect of the provision of logistic support and adequate food, and making outstanding payments, to the troops in the assembly areas and the training centres;

10. *Notes* the recent acceleration in the assembly of the troops of the Government of Mozambique, and calls upon the Government to redouble its efforts to achieve balance between the parties in the cantonment of troops and an expeditious and timely conclusion of this process as called for in the revised timetable;

11. *Underlines* the need for the troops of the Government of Mozambique and RENAMO to hand over all weapons to the United Nations at the assembly areas and for the parties to come to an immediate agreement on the transfer of all weapons to regional depots so as to ensure security in the assembly areas;

12. *Reiterates* the vital importance it attaches to the holding of general elections no later than October 1994 and to the early commencement of electoral regis-tration and other electoral preparations, and *urges* the parties to agree promptly on a specific election date;

13. *Appeals* to the international community to provide the necessary financial assistance to facilitate the implementation of the General Peace Agreement and also to make voluntary financial contributions to the Trust Fund to be set up to support electoral activities of the political parties;

14. *Notes* the Secretary-General's decision to explore the possibility of establishing a more effective mechanism for the provision of resources, disbursement under which is subject to the scrupulous and timely implementation of the General Peace Agreement, as described in paragraph 35 of his report of 28 January 1994;

15. *Welcomes* the proposal to extend the present severance payment scheme to facilitate the reintegration of demobilizing soldiers into civil society and encourages the international community to provide appropriate and prompt assistance for the implementation of this scheme as a complement to the existing efforts made in the framework of the humanitarian assistance programme;

16. *Expresses* its appreciation to the United Kingdom of Great Britain and Northern Ireland, France, Portugal and Italy for their offers of assistance in military training or in rehabilitating the training centres for the new army;

17. *Notes* also with appreciation the response of the international community to the humanitarian assistance needs of Mozambique and encourages the international community to continue to provide appropriate and prompt assistance for the implementation of the humanitarian programme carried out in the framework of the General Peace Agreement;

18. *Urges* all parties to continue to facilitate unimpeded access to humanitarian assistance for the civilian population in need, and also to cooperate with the United Nations High Commissioner for Refugees (UNHCR) and other humanitarian agencies operating in Mozambique to facilitate the speedy repatriation and resettlement of refugees and displaced persons;

19. *Requests* the Secretary-General to ensure maximum economy in the operations of ONUMOZ, while remaining mindful of the importance of an effective discharge of its mandate;

20. *Looks forward* to the next report of the Secretary-General called for in paragraph 13 of resolution 882 (1993) on whether the parties have made sufficient and tangible progress towards implementing the General Peace Agreement and in meeting the timetable set out in paragraphs 3 and 10 of that resolution, on the basis of which it will consider the mandate of ONUMOZ;

21. *Decides* to remain actively seized of the matter.

Document 58

Letter dated 4 March 1994 from the President of the Council of Ministers of Italy to the Secretary-General on Italy's further contribution to the United Nations Trust Fund

Not issued as a United Nations document

I am responding to your kind letter, in which you illustrated to me the financial difficulties presented to the United Nations in guaranteeing the implementation of the Mozambican peace agreement signed in Rome.

We continue to be fully convinced that international support must not fall short in the current moment, when the normalization process has entered a delicate phase and is inclined to open the way—through the difficult operations of demobilizing the troops of the two parties and transforming RENAMO into a political party—to the first free democratic elections, which should give life to the new Mozambique next October.

In accordance with this conviction and the feelings of solidarity and friendship that tie us to the people of Mozambique, I have the pleasure to confirm that the Italian Government has decided, in compliance with your request, to earmark a contribution of 500 thousand dollars to meet the needs of RENAMO mentioned in your letter.

I also wish to communicate that we are examining the possibility of making a further contribution, in addition to the 5.7 million dollars already effected, to meet your appeal concerning the resources targeted for the United Nations Trust Fund for the process of democratization in Mozambique, in the hope that other members of the donor community can quickly add their support.

In expressing my warmest appreciation for the commitment of the United Nations to promoting the building of peace and democracy in Mozambique and in southern Africa, I take this opportunity to convey my most cordial regards.

(Signed) Carlo Azeglio CIAMPI

Document 59

Letter dated 11 March 1994 from the United Nations High Commissioner for Refugees, Sadako Ogata, to the Secretary-General on repatriation of refugees to Mozambique

Not issued as a United Nations document

I have just returned from a two-week mission to southern Africa. I visited Zimbabwe, Swaziland, South Africa and Mozambique. The main purpose of my mission was to assess the conditions under which the voluntary repatriation of Mozambicans is being implemented. This operation is the second largest currently being undertaken by my Office (after former Yugoslavia).

I was pleased to note that the organized repatriation movements from Zimbabwe and Swaziland are running smoothly. I was also satisfied to see the preparations under way in South Africa. Malawi, which I had visited last year, continues to host the largest number of Mozambican refugees. It is expected, however, that spontaneous movements will continue to occur on a large scale in the months to come. UNHCR will make every effort to achieve its ambitious goal of assisting as large a number as possible of Mozambicans to return home before the elections.

The voluntary repatriation of refugees depends on two main factors: security and minimal conditions for reintegration. I was greatly encouraged by the analysis of the peace process that Mr. Ajello kindly shared with me.

This positive impression was further confirmed during my meetings with President Chissano and Mr. Dhlakama. The problem of mines remains, however, a major security concern of the returning refugees. I sincerely hope that UNOMOZ can rapidly undertake demarcation of mined areas as well as de-mining of the access roads to the returnee areas. For our part, we are making all possible efforts to improve the conditions in the areas of return through small scale socio-economic projects. Both in Tete and Maputo provinces I had the pleasure of handing over to the local authorities modest community centers consisting of small schools, clinics and water points.

It is my clear impression that developments in Mozambique are moving in the right direction. It is therefore more important than ever for the United Nations to reinforce its efforts at this crucial juncture. I intend to give the highest priority within UNHCR to this important programme and to engage in active fund-raising.

I am grateful for your understanding and support.

(Signed) Sadako OGATA

Document 60

Letter dated 12 April 1994 from Mozambique concerning the holding of elections

S/1994/419, 12 April 1994

I have the honour to convey to Your Excellency that in accordance with the provisions of the Mozambican Electoral Law, enacted within the framework of the General Peace Agreement for Mozambique, the President of the Republic, H.E. Mr. Joaquim Alberto Chissano, has determined through presidential decree No. 01/94, of 11 April 1994, that the first multi-party elections in Mozambique will be held on 27 and 28 October 1994.

I would like to request Your Excellency to have the text of this letter circulated as a document of the Security Council.

(Signed) Pedro Comissário AFONSO
Ambassador Extraordinary and Plenipotentiary
Permanent Representative to the United Nations

Document 61

Letter dated 21 April 1994 from the President of the Security Council to the Secretary-General regarding the appointment of international members of the Mozambique Electoral Tribunal

S/1994/485, 21 April 1994

I received earlier this month a letter from the Permanent Representative of Mozambique requesting the assistance of the Security Council in the appointment of the international members of the Mozambique Electoral Tribunal as provided for in the Mozambique Electoral Law. The letter advised that the Electoral Law provides that the international members of the tribunal shall be appointed by you on the recommendation of the Security Council.

Ambassador Afonso also called on me and explained that it was the view of his Government that the best assistance that the Security Council could provide on this matter would be for it to forward to you a list of potential candidates from which you could make your selection.

The members of the Council considered this request and agreed that they should facilitate the Mozambique electoral process to the extent they were able. Council members undertook to consider a number of potential candidates and to submit to you such names as they considered appropriate.

Following their consideration of the matter, the members of the Council have asked me to forward to you the attached list of names of persons from which you might wish to choose three persons who would be suitable for appointment as international members of the Mozambique Electoral Tribunal.

(Signed) Colin R. KEATING
President of the Security Council

Annex

Possible candidates for appointment to Mozambique electoral tribunal

Michel COAT (France)
Walter Ramos da COSTA PORTO (Brazil)
Mariano FIALLOS OYANGUREN(Nicaragua)
Juan Ignacio GARCÍA RODRIGUEZ (Chile)
Joao MOREIRA CAMILO (Portugal)

Document 62

Letter dated 27 April 1994 from the Secretary-General to the President of the Security Council on the appointment of international members of the Mozambique Electoral Tribunal

S/1994/514, 28 April 1994

I have the honour to refer to your letter of 21 April conveying the Security Council's request that I choose three persons for appointment as international members of the Mozambique Electoral Tribunal from the list of candidates which you enclosed.

After due consideration of the candidates presented by the Council, I have decided to appoint Michel Coat (France), Mariano Fiallos Oyanguren (Nicaragua) and Joao Moreira Camilo (Portugal) as international members and Walter Ramos da Costa Porto (Brazil) and Juan Ignacio García Rodriguez (Chile) as alternate international members of the Mozambique Electoral Tribunal.

For your information, I enclose a copy of the letter I am sending today to President Joaquim Chissano of Mozambique to apprise him of these appointments.

(Signed) Boutros BOUTROS-GHALI

Annex

Letter dated 25 April 1994 from the Secretary-General addressed to the President of the Republic of Mozambique

I refer to the relevant provision of Article 3b of the Mozambique Electoral Law by which I am required to appoint three judges, at the recommendation of the Security Council, to serve as members of the Mozambique Electoral Tribunal.

I have the honour to inform you that, upon recommendation of the Security Council, it is my intention to appoint Michel Coat (France), Mariano Fiallos Oyanguren (Nicaragua) and Joao Moreira Camilo (Portugal) as international members of the Mozambique Electoral Tribunal. In addition, I will also appoint Walter Ramos da Costa Porto (Brazil) and Juan Ignacio García Rodriguez (Chile) as alternate international members. I enclose their curricula vitae for your information. [Editor's note: The curricula vitae are not reproduced in this book.]

(Signed) Boutros BOUTROS-GHALI

Document 63

Report of the Secretary-General on ONUMOZ

S/1994/511, 28 April 1994

I. Introduction

1. The present report is submitted in pursuance of Security Council resolution 882 (1993) of 5 November 1993, by which the Council extended the mandate of the United Nations Operation in Mozambique (ONUMOZ) for a period of six months. It is also submitted in response to Security Council resolution 898 (1994) of 23 February 1994, by which, in particular, the Council requested me to report on whether the Government of Mozambique and the Resistência Nacional Moçambicana (RENAMO) had made tangible progress in a timely manner towards implementing the provisions of the general peace agreement for Mozambique signed on 4 October 1992 (S/24635). In the latter resolution, the Council further

requested me to begin preparing proposals for the drawdown of an appropriate number of military personnel, to prepare a timetable for the completion of ONUMOZ's mandate and to ensure maximum economy in the operation of ONUMOZ, while remaining mindful of the importance of the effective discharge of its mandate.

II. Political and military aspects

A. *General*

2. A number of important developments have taken place since my last report to the Council on 28 January 1994 (S/1994/89). With the beginning of demobilization on 10 March 1994, the peace process

entered into another critical phase. Fifty-five per cent of government and 81 per cent of RENAMO soldiers have now been cantoned and actual demobilization has begun. The training programme for the new Mozambican Armed Forces (FADM), inaugurated in March 1994, has so far provided training for some 2,000 soldiers. The leaders of FADM, Generals Lagos Lidimo of the Government and Mateus Ngonhamo of RENAMO, were sworn into office on 6 April 1994 as joint high commanders of the new army. .

3. On 11 April, the President of Mozambique, Mr. Joaquim Chissano, announced that the general elections would take place on 27 and 28 October 1994. The National Elections Commission had been inaugurated in February 1994, and its 10 provincial offices were established by the end of March. On 1 March 1994, 30 RENAMO officials signed contracts with the Government to work as advisers to the 10 provincial governors. This arrangement, which was agreed upon by President Chissano and Mr. Afonso Dhlakama, President of RENAMO, during their first meeting in Mozambique in 1993, is one of the key steps in implementing administrative and territorial integration. The advisers will, in particular, facilitate government access to areas formerly controlled by RENAMO that lack basic administrative structures.

4. During the reporting period, President Chissano and Mr. Dhlakama continued to meet regularly. These contacts have contributed greatly to progress in the implementation of the Rome agreement. However, in spite of these positive developments, there still are serious problems that must be urgently addressed and resolved: the slow cantonment of government troops and delays in the demobilization of RENAMO troops, as well as in the formation and training of the new army.

B. *Assembly and demobilization of troops*

5. My last report to the Council indicated that the cantonment of troops had started as scheduled on 30 November 1993. However, the opening of 14 assembly areas was delayed by a dispute between the two parties over control of the locations proposed for assembly areas at Salamanga and Dunda. My Special Representative, Mr. Aldo Ajello, held a series of negotiations that eventually resolved the problem; the total planned number of 49 assembly areas were open and operational by 21 February 1994. Initially, the Government assembled a greater proportion of its soldiers than RENAMO; however, the situation has now been reversed, with RENAMO assembling a proportionally much larger number of soldiers than the Government. As of 18 April 1994, a total of 49,465 soldiers had reported to the assembly areas,

34,012 from the Government and 15,453 from RENAMO. This represents 55 per cent of the soldiers declared by the Government and 81 per cent of those declared by RENAMO.

6. There has been no major increase recently in the movement by the Government of its soldiers to assembly areas. Some of the areas are overcrowded, while others are virtually empty: capacity utilization ranges from a low of 3 per cent to a high of almost 420 per cent. The overcrowding has made the supply of basic goods to these areas an extremely difficult task, which has been aggravated by the lack of adequate air resources. Nevertheless, ONUMOZ has been able to achieve a generally satisfactory level of logistic support to all areas.

7. Because of the delays in demobilization, soldiers have had to remain in the assembly areas for considerably longer periods than originally foreseen. In some of the assembly areas, this situation caused serious tensions among the troops, resulting in 20 violent protests since January 1994. In many instances, government soldiers have not received their pay and, consequently, have refused to be demobilized until arrears due to them are paid. In RENAMO areas, unrealistic promises concerning possible benefits for ex-soldiers were made by commanders. As a result, the present reintegration package does not meet the expectations of some RENAMO soldiers, who have refused to be demobilized. In all cases, ONUMOZ has been working closely with the parties to find solutions and to defuse tensions.

8. Demobilization finally began on 10 March 1994. As of 18 April 1994, a total of 12,756 troops (12,195 government and 561 RENAMO) had been demobilized and transported to the districts of their choice. This corresponds to 20 per cent of government and 3 per cent of RENAMO soldiers expected to check into the assembly areas. On the day of departure from the assembly area, each soldier receives civilian clothing, a demobilization card, a cash sum equivalent to three months' pay and a voucher for an additional three-month subsidy to be paid in the district of residence. As provided for in the reintegration support scheme, each demobilized soldier also receives a reintegration support checkbook providing for an additional 18 months of financial support in the district where he intends to settle. Furthermore, the soldiers receive transport subsidies, rations for two weeks, and packages containing seeds and agricultural tools. Transport is provided for the demobilized, their primary dependants and the soldiers' personal belongings to the district of choice.

9. Although, from a technical point of view, demobilization is proceeding smoothly, the process has been marked by substantial delays. According to the revised timetable, the parties committed themselves to initiate

demobilization in January 1994; the process, however, started only in March and has recently slowed down. In addition, the assembly of remaining troops is now at a near standstill. Unless this trend is reversed, further delays in demobilization will be inevitable. The leaders of both parties are aware of this serious problem. On 8 April 1994, President Chissano met with Mr. Dhlakama and they agreed that the Government would expedite the assembly of its troops and that RENAMO would accelerate the pace of its demobilization.

10. In the meantime, the two parties also agreed that, in addition to moving soldiers into assembly areas for demobilization, a certain number of military personnel would, for practical reasons, remain in their present locations and be demobilized *in situ*. Such locations would include military hospitals, air bases, naval bases and both government and RENAMO military headquarters, for a total of approximately 70 locations. It is estimated that some 17,000 soldiers, including some 4,830 disabled, have to be discharged in this manner. In addition, all military equipment will have to be registered in these sites, with light weapons being immediately transported to regional arms depots. It is planned that heavy equipment will be disabled and remain under the joint custody of a local commander and a United Nations Regional Commander.

11. As of 18 April 1994, 35,536 weapons belonging to government troops and 13,210 belonging to RENAMO troops had been handed over to ONUMOZ military observers. The transfer of weapons from assembly areas to regional arms depots, which had been an issue of major controversy, finally began on 15 March 1994 and is now being carried out on a regular basis. Delays have also accumulated in the disbanding of the 155,600 militia and paramilitary forces. This is due in part to the fact that these forces are scattered throughout the country, with armed elements in virtually all villages. The disbanding is performed by the Government. Verification of the lists of personnel released from duty with paramilitary forces and the collection of surrendered weapons are being done by teams of the Cease-fire Commission. Irregularities in this process that are brought to the attention of the Cease-Fire Commission are immediately investigated. Despite this simplified monitoring method, the implementation of the disbanding of militias has been a logistically complex and demanding task. This was further aggravated by the depletion of ONUMOZ air resources, which brought the process to a standstill at the beginning of March 1994. As of the end of April 1994, 49.5 per cent of the weapons that the Government declared had been assigned to its paramilitary forces had been collected and were in United Nations custody.

C. *Formation of the Mozambican Defence Force*

12. There has been substantial progress in the formation of the Mozambican Defence Force since I last reported to the Council. The formation of the new army is the responsibility of the Government and the Joint Commission for the Formation of the Mozambican Defence Force. Although the general peace agreement did not envisage any role for the United Nations in this aspect of the peace process, the Mozambican parties requested the United Nations to assume chairmanship of the Joint Commission in order to facilitate its functioning; however, the United Nations is not responsible for training or for providing equipment to the new Defence Force. At the same time, the significance of this project for the overall implementation of the peace process cannot be overestimated. In order to facilitate this process, ONUMOZ agreed to provide logistic and transport support for the creation of the new army at no additional cost to the Mission. Voluntary contributions have also been obtained for the rehabilitation of FADM training centres. However, despite all the efforts made by the United Nations, the training process is moving at a slow pace.

13. According to the general peace agreement, FADM would comprise 30,000 troops, 50 per cent of whom should be provided by the Government and 50 per cent by RENAMO. The parties chose France, Portugal and the United Kingdom of Great Britain and Northern Ireland to assist in the training of the new army, and these three countries formulated appropriate programmes in a timely manner. The initial stages of the implementation of these programmes were described in paragraphs 21 and 22 of my last report to the Council (S/1994/89). From the very outset, the programmes have suffered from a lack of financial and other resources. Furthermore, the training programmes as they now stand are designed to train a maximum of 15,000 FADM members before the elections take place. However, President Chissano and Mr. Dhlakama have recently agreed that the elections may take place even if training of all soldiers for the new army has not been completed. This is conditional upon the official formation of the full 30,000-strong army and the commencement of all required training courses before the October elections.

14. In order to find a solution to this difficulty, two options are being considered:

(a) To reduce the number of soldiers to be trained prior to the elections to the 15,000 covered by existing training programmes. Under this option, the formation and training of the remaining units would be completed only after the elections. RENAMO is favourably inclined to this formula, but the Government so far has been reluctant to consider it;

(b)   To retain the number of soldiers to be trained, as planned in the general peace agreement, at the level of 30,000. To make this option viable, it is necessary that additional countries provide assistance to the programme and contribute sufficient human and financial resources to train, by the end of October, 15,000 military personnel who at present have not been designated to receive training. This option seems to be acceptable to both parties.

15.   A quick solution to this problem is essential, not only for the timely formation of the new army, but also for the completion of the demobilization process. If the new army is not entirely formed and placed in training centres, a large number of soldiers will linger in assembly areas. This would prevent these areas from being closed, with serious financial and, in all likelihood, security consequences. A further complication is that the Government has been slow in providing logistical and technical support to the Joint Commission for the Formation of the Mozambican Defence Force as well as to the new army itself.

D.   *Cease-fire*

16.   During the reporting period, there have been no military activities in Mozambique that posed a serious threat to the cease-fire or to the peace process as a whole. However, the Cease-fire Commission received 12 written complaints of alleged cease-fire violations, 8 from RENAMO and 4 from the Government. The complaints fell into two categories: unauthorized presence or misconduct of troops and militia and intimidating or aggressive behaviour by soldiers. Ten complaints were solved and are considered closed, while two cases are still under investigation.

17.   An issue of some concern, however, is the verification of military equipment, particularly heavy equipment, which remains in various military installations. Neither the Government nor RENAMO has so far allowed the United Nations to reconnoitre certain military bases, nor have they provided ONUMOZ with complete lists of military equipment. Government authorities have recently announced that an investigation has been launched concerning an unconfirmed report of the emergence in Zambézia Province of an armed faction that is allegedly advocating the secession of the four northern provinces from Mozambique. Earlier this year, the Government accused a splinter group from Malawi of invading the same area. The Mozambican Government has entered into bilateral discussions with the Government of Malawi for the purpose of ensuring that the border is respected. ONUMOZ is closely monitoring the situation.

E.   *Status of and reductions in the military component of ONUMOZ*

18.   As of 18 April 1994, against an authorized strength of 6,979, the military component, composed of military observers, staff officers and formed units, totalled 5,914 all ranks (see annex).

19.   The United Nations forces continued to carry out operational activities throughout the country, including the maintenance of security in the corridors and along highways and main roads by conducting regular road and aerial patrols as well as by providing train escorts. Furthermore, United Nations troops have provided security to airports, regional depots for weapons collected from both parties, oil-pumping stations, food storage locations and other United Nations installations. ONUMOZ has continued to provide humanitarian assistance to the Mozambican population to the extent possible. Its engineer units assisted in rehabilitating training centres for FADM, as well as in clearing and repairing damage caused by tropical cyclone "Nadia", which struck the northern coast of Mozambique on 24 March 1994.

20.   Three hundred and seventy military observers from 19 countries were deployed with ONUMOZ; 292 of them were based in the 49 assembly areas where they have been supervising the cantonment of troops, their disarmament and subsequent demobilization or transfer to the new army. The military observers are also carrying out the important task of monitoring the cease-fire by conducting inspections and investigations into alleged violations. In addition, the military observers are monitoring the disbanding of paramilitary forces throughout the country. The military observers have gained considerable knowledge of the Mozambican peace process, which in turn enables them to contribute to the efforts to facilitate the implementation of the peace agreement at the local level as well as in the Cease-fire Commission.

21.   It was originally planned to begin a gradual reduction of military observers in June 1994. However, it is now clear that demobilization will not be completed by that time. In addition, the military observers will be called upon to perform essential post-demobilization tasks beyond that date including monitoring and verifying the cease-fire until the newly elected Government takes over, the disposal of collected weapons and ammunition and other verification functions related to the peace process. In these circumstances, I am not in a position to recommend a reduction in the strength of this important element of ONUMOZ at the present stage.

22.   In pursuance of the specific requests made in paragraphs 3 and 4 of Security Council resolution 898 (1994) of 23 February 1994, I am making every effort to ensure that the deployment of the civilian police compo-

nent of ONUMOZ (CIVPOL) will not entail an overall increase in the costs of the Mission, without prejudice to the effective discharge of its mandate. The requested drawdown of the United Nations forces is therefore planned to be implemented as follows:

(a) In accordance with the decision of the Government of Italy, the Italian contingent will be reduced by approximately 800 troops during the month of April 1994. This reduction is already under way. However, the Italian Government has agreed to the retention of the field hospital, a limited logistics element and the necessary security personnel, totalling approximately 200;

(b) A number of ONUMOZ support elements will also be withdrawn or reduced according to their previously scheduled rotation:

	Reduction From	To	Month
Indian engineer company	233	0	May
Indian logistic company	206	0	May
Indian independent engineer company	257	0	July
Indian independent HQ company a/	257	61	May
Bangladesh engineer company b/	250	50	May
Bangladesh movement control unit	24	10	May
Portuguese signals battalion	278	150	May

a/ 41 military police and 20 clerks will be retained.
b/ Some 50 specialists in ordnance disposal will be retained and integrated into the Bangladesh infantry battalion.

23. The drastic reduction of the support units will be partially compensated by the troops' integral logistics systems and some additional civilian support. I would like to pay tribute to the troops who will be leaving the Mission area soon. They have performed admirably under challenging circumstances in Mozambique and have made an important contribution to the difficult task of bringing the peace process forward.

24. As a consequence of this planned reduction, it is intended that the remaining formed units be redeployed as follows:

(a) Two Botswana infantry companies will remain in the Tete corridor;

(b) Two Botswana companies, and possibly the Botswana contingent headquarters, will be redeployed to Chimoio in the Beira corridor;

(c) One Bangladesh company will be moved from Nampula to the Beira corridor. From within that company, one platoon will be stationed in Quelimane (Zambézia Province) to replace a platoon from Botswana.

25. I very much hope that the reduction of support units will not have a negative impact on daily operations.

However, the drawdown in the infantry unit is a cause of concern. Neighbouring countries, to which these corridors are of vital importance as major import/export routes, have already expressed their strong preoccupation about security in them. This concern may be justified, as the reduction of United Nations forces coincides with demobilization of government and RENAMO troops, which in turn is expected to result in an increase in banditry along the main routes. To maintain an adequate level of security, it might be necessary, while reducing the strength of the logistic element, to deploy an additional infantry company to the Beira corridor, and I am approaching potential troop contributors in this regard. Under the circumstances, I do not recommend any further reduction of the military component of ONUMOZ before the elections.

III. Preparation for the elections

26. In paragraph 12 of resolution 898 (1994), the Security Council once again reaffirmed the vital importance it attaches to the holding of elections no later than October 1994. As already mentioned, the dates of the elections have now been set for 27 and 28 October 1994.

27. In paragraph 14 of my previous report (S/1994/89), I informed the Council that the Electoral Law, which was approved by the Mozambican National Assembly on 9 December 1993 and promulgated by President Chissano shortly thereafter, entered into force on 12 January 1994, and that the members of the National Elections Commission were then in the process of selecting a chairperson. On 2 February 1994, they unanimously nominated Mr. Brazão Mazula, who is not associated with any political party, as the Chairman of the National Elections Commission. The Commission officially started functioning on 15 February 1994. It has held a series of working meetings, completed its staffing, established provincial offices and drafted its standing rules of procedure and it is presently opening district offices throughout the country. It has also approved the following timetable for the electoral process:

15 February-31 May:	Selection, briefing and training of registration brigades, preparatory activities for the registration process
1 June-15 August:	Voter registration
16 August-9 September:	Receipt and consideration of claims relating to registration, revision of the electoral rolls and preparations for the electoral campaign
10 September-24 October:	Electoral campaign
27 and 28 October:	Polling

28. The Technical Secretariat for Elections Administration, which is to provide technical support to the National Elections Commission pursuant to the Electoral Law, initiated its activities on 11 February 1994, albeit without a proper legal framework. The government decree that officially established the Technical Secretariat was promulgated on 13 April 1994. As a result, the Technical Secretariat, which is responsible for voter registration, has not yet been able to establish its presence at the provincial and district levels.

29. The Electoral Law provides for the establishment of an Electoral Tribunal to be composed of two national and three international judges, the latter to be appointed by me after receiving nominations from the Security Council. After due consideration of the candidates presented by the Council, I have decided to appoint Michel Coat (France), Mariano Fiallos Oyanguren (Nicaragua) and Joao Moreira Camilo (Portugal) as international members and Walter Ramos da Costa Porto (Brazil) and Juan Ignacio García Rodriguez (Chile) as alternate international members of the Mozambique Electoral Tribunal. I have also written to President Chissano apprising him of these appointments.

30. Resolution 797 (1992) of 16 December 1992 encouraged United Nations programmes and specialized agencies to provide appropriate assistance and support for the implementation of the major tasks arising from the general peace agreement, which would obviously include the preparation of elections. The United Nations is playing a major coordinating role for technical assistance to the entire electoral process in Mozambique. A technical assistance trust fund has been established for this purpose. The financial requirements for the electoral process have been revised down from an original US$ 71 million to US$ 59 million, of which US$ 47 million have already been pledged by the international community. I appeal to donors to bridge the gap of US$ 12 million, as well as to fulfil existing commitments in order to allow the crucial task of voter registration to proceed as scheduled.

31. In May 1993, a trust fund for the implementation of the peace process in Mozambique was established to facilitate the integration of RENAMO in the structures set forth in the peace agreement. The resources provided through this trust fund have assisted the establishment of RENAMO's presence in major cities and its transformation into a political party. However, in addition to the Mozambique Liberation Front (FRELIMO) and RENAMO, 12 other political parties have registered to participate in the elections. Given the fact that these parties have very limited resources available to them, it has been deemed necessary to establish a special trust fund for assistance to registered political parties in Mozam-

bique to enable them to carry out electoral activities. This trust fund has now been established, and I appeal to the donor community to contribute to this important mechanism to ensure the active participation of all eligible parties in the first multi-party elections in Mozambique.

IV. Police activities

32. As members of the Security Council will recall, on 3 September 1993 President Chissano and Mr. Dhlakama agreed to request the United Nations to monitor all police activities in the country, including those of the Mozambican police, to monitor the rights and liberties of Mozambican citizens and to provide technical support to the National Police Affairs Commission created under the general peace agreement. The police component of ONUMOZ, which was established by Security Council resolution 898 (1994) of 23 February, is also mandated to monitor and verify the process of reorganizing and retraining the Quick Reaction Police, to monitor (together with other ONUMOZ components) the proper conduct of the electoral campaign and to perform other functions as described in my report on this matter (S/1994/89/Add.1).

33. I am pleased to report that, as of 18 April 1994, 278 United Nations police observers had already arrived in Mozambique and had been deployed throughout the country. Eighty-seven CIVPOL posts have been identified outside the provincial capitals, which will cover 208 Mozambican police stations and posts. As basic facilities such as accommodation, water and electricity are not available in most of these remote locations, tentage and other necessities had to be obtained to allow these United Nations posts to be fully operational as early as possible. At present, 10 such CIVPOL outposts have been established. Visits to police stations and mobile patrols are regularly carried out to hold discussions with the Mozambican police, to meet the general public and to gather information about police activities, as well as to represent ONUMOZ in the remotest parts of the country.

34. The beneficial confidence-building effect of an increasing CIVPOL deployment is already obvious. The component is maintaining close liaison with the Ministry of the Interior, the Mozambican Police Command, provincial governors and their RENAMO advisers, as well as with other RENAMO representatives, on all police-related matters. However, notwithstanding the agreement of the Government of Mozambique and RENAMO that an enlarged presence of CIVPOL would enhance the peace process, CIVPOL initially faced a number of difficulties in carrying out its mandate, especially as regards access to information and visits to police stations and prisons. In February 1994, a seminar was held with the participation of CIVPOL, the Police Affairs Commission

and the Mozambican police, during which problems of cooperation were discussed and a *modus operandi* was agreed upon. The situation improved following the seminar, particularly at the provincial level, where lack of information about the tasks of CIVPOL seems to have been one of the obstacles.

35. In addition, some difficulties were initially encountered in gaining access to the Quick Reaction Force, a Special Forces Branch of the Mozambican police. As part of the overall reintegration of RENAMO and government-controlled areas, it is foreseen that the Mozambican police will establish police posts in areas controlled by RENAMO. Despite indications from the Mozambican police that it would seek CIVPOL's assistance in this field, its members refused on several occasions to accompany CIVPOL to those locations. In order for CIVPOL to exercise its mandate properly, it is important that it enjoy the full cooperation of the parties. In the relatively short period during which CIVPOL has performed its monitoring functions, it has observed a number of violations of rights and civil liberties. To date, it has investigated 36 cases of misconduct by members of the national police. These cases have subsequently been communicated to the Police Affairs Commission and to the Mozambican Police Command for remedial action, where necessary.

V. Humanitarian assistance programme

36. The United Nations Office for Humanitarian Assistance Coordination (UNOHAC) of ONUMOZ continues to coordinate assistance to internally displaced persons, returnees and ex-soldiers, focusing on their resettlement and full reintegration into Mozambican society. In connection with this priority concern, particular attention is being paid to the implementation of the requisite projects within the social sector, especially in the areas of health, education, water and transport.

37. A reintegration support scheme for demobilizing soldiers has now been added to the overall reintegration programme developed to facilitate re-entry of the demobilized into civilian society. The scheme extends the Government's 6 months' severance payments to ex-soldiers for a further 18 months. A total of US$ 18.1 million has been pledged to this United Nations Development Programme (UNDP)-administered fund by donors who are convinced that a longer reintegration period for the ex-soldiers is prudent. The vocational training programme for demobilized soldiers, along with the distribution of corresponding kits, is expected to begin in June under the auspices of the International Labour Organization (ILO). A job referral and counselling service is being implemented by the International Organization for Migration (IOM).

38. The United Nations mine-clearance programme has suffered significant delays, partially as a result of the slow approval of the national mine-clearance plan by the Cease-fire Commission, but also because the process of identifying and selecting suitable contractors turned out to be protracted. Negotiations have finally been completed for a contract for the clearance of unexploded ordnance and mines blocking 2,000 kilometres of priority roads.

39. Under United Nations auspices, an important road is being cleared near the Malawian border in Zambézia Province, a main route for tens of thousands of returning refugees. The mine-clearance personnel involved have been trained in a project financed by the United Kingdom, which has produced 71 mine clearers so far. Another key road is being cleared in Tete Province and a further 278 mine clearers trained with joint funding from the United Nations and the Norwegian Agency for International Development (NORAD). Through funding made available by the United States Agency for International Development (USAID) and with technical assistance from the United Nations, a further project has trained a first group of 80 mine clearers and 9 dog handlers. They began work in mid-April on a road along the Zambezi River crucial for the return of refugees. The mining of this road leading to Mutarara district, at the juncture of four provinces south of Malawi, had created the country's worst bottleneck for population movements.

40. The United Nations Mine-clearance Training Centre, operating from temporary facilities, commenced its first course for 30 mine-clearance personnel on 4 April 1994. The nationwide survey of mines is also now well on its way, producing detailed information on mined areas and roads.

41. To date, 75 per cent of the 4 million persons who were internally displaced at the time of the signature of the General Peace Agreement in October 1992 have now resettled in rural areas, leaving an estimated 1 million still displaced as of April 1994. One half of the 1.6 million refugees in neighbouring countries at the time of the peace accord have also now returned to Mozambique, with the remaining 800,000 largely expected to return before the planting season in September/October 1994. The organized repatriation by the Office of the United Nations High Commissioner for Refugees (UNHCR) of refugees from South Africa commenced in April and a similar programme for the repatriation of Mozambican refugees from the United Republic of Tanzania and Zambia is scheduled for June and July 1994. Free food distribution is being progressively discontinued in asylum countries and moved to returnees' destinations in Mozambique, to ensure that their move is towards food security and not away from it.

42. Cyclone "Nadia" struck Nampula Province in northern Mozambique on 24 March 1994. The disaster came soon after the recent resettlement of many of the province's internally displaced. Many schools, health posts and roads—already woefully inadequate—were demolished. In the first days following this calamity, UNOHAC, acting under the auspices of the United Nations Emergency Coordinator, organized airlifts of 200 tons of emergency relief supplies provided from the Department of Humanitarian Affairs and government stockpiles and contributions made by bilateral donors, United Nations agencies and non-governmental organizations.

43. The outlook for the coming harvest is only fair as a result of inadequate rainfall in a number of areas and also of the cyclone that destroyed many crops in Nampula Province. These indications point to a probable mix of marketable surpluses and significant food shortages, with redistribution from surplus to deficit areas made difficult by poor marketing networks. A Food and Agriculture Organization of the United Nations (FAO)/World Food Programme (WFP) mission is at present undertaking an assessment of crops and food import needs for the 1994/95 crop year. As part of its continuing food assistance and delivery programme, WFP, together with the European Union and other donors, is purchasing maize in surplus areas for use in relief activities.

44. A total of US$ 50.2 million has been pledged to the Department of Humanitarian Affairs and UNDP trust funds for humanitarian assistance to Mozambique, of which US$ 31 million has been received. Of this amount, $23.8 million has been obligated or disbursed to projects targeting resettling displaced persons, returning refugees and demobilizing soldiers, often through area-based initiatives of benefit to all three groups.

VI. Financial aspects

45. By its resolution 48/250 of 24 March 1994, the General Assembly, *inter alia*, authorized the Secretary-General to enter into commitments for ONUMOZ at a rate not to exceed $26,900,000 gross per month for a period of up to three months beginning 1 May 1994, subject to the decision to be taken by the Security Council in respect of the Operation. This commitment authority is based on the cost estimates for the maintenance of ONUMOZ for the period from 1 May 1994 to 31 October 1994 contained in the Secretary-General's report of 17 January 1994 (A/48/849). In an effort to ensure maximum efficiency and economy, the costs associated with the establishment by the police contingent of ONUMOZ are being met through review of all requirements of the Mission, including those concerning its military component, so as to result in no increase in the cost estimates without prejudice to the effective discharge of the Mission's man-

date. I therefore intend to submit to the General Assembly revised cost estimates for the period from 1 May 1994 to 31 October 1994 within the above-mentioned parameters.

46. As of 20 April 1994, unpaid assessed contributions to the ONUMOZ special account amounted to some $125.6 million for the period from the inception of ONUMOZ up to 30 April 1994. This represents approximately 38 per cent of the total amount assessed on Member States for the Operation.

VII. Observations

47. During the reporting period, a number of important advances were made in the implementation of the peace process in Mozambique. At the same time, some urgent and serious difficulties have continued to hinder the timely completion of the process.

48. The announcement on 11 April 1994 by President Chissano that the general elections will be held on 27 and 28 October 1994 was a significant step forward in the implementation of the peace process. It also signified the intention of the Mozambican parties to adhere to the time-frame set by the Security Council for the completion of the process, and a realization that the international community would not be willing to prolong the process unduly.

49. The political will of the parties, while appreciated, is unfortunately not always translated into the practical steps that must be accomplished to ensure the implementation of the peace process, leading to free and fair elections. Especially worrying are the delays in the assembly of government troops, the demobilization of RENAMO troops and the training of the new armed forces of the country. In addition, the National Elections Commission might face practical difficulties in the very complex process of registration of voters, particularly if it is decided to include Mozambicans living abroad.

50. The commitment of the National Elections Commission to hold the elections in October 1994 was reaffirmed to my Special Adviser, Mr. Ismat Kittani, during his visit to Mozambique in early April 1994. Mr. Kittani held discussions with President Chissano and Mr. Dhlakama and members of other political parties, as well as a number of ministers and political leaders in the country. While commitments were made to accelerate the process, actual progress has not yet met expectations. A number of problems persist in the areas of logistics, finance the identification of party representatives and free access to all districts of Mozambique.

51. Despite these concerns, I have no doubt that free and fair elections are possible, subject to a few minimal conditions. These include free access by the National Elections Commission and its subsidiary bodies to all areas in the country; the widest possible participation of political parties at all levels of the electoral process;

free access to State mass media; full logistical support by the Government and the donor community to the electoral process at the provincial and district levels; and a total and unconditional commitment by all parties to accept the results of the elections, once declared by the National Elections Commission as having been generally free and fair and so confirmed by the United Nations.

52. Considerable progress has been made in resettling internally displaced persons and Mozambican refugees returning from neighbouring countries. The United Nations, in collaboration with other organizations concerned and bilateral donors, will pursue ongoing programmes to assist the remaining 1 million internally displaced persons and 800,000 refugees to be resettled. The mine-clearance programme will be accelerated to ensure that sufficient progress is made in the coming months in the movement of internally displaced persons and returnees and to facilitate the election campaign. The training of mine-clearance personnel, being undertaken by the United Nations and other donor agencies, will be speeded up so that an adequate number of Mozambicans will have been trained to carry out the necessary mine-clearance activities.

53. Continued assistance for these schemes and for the reintegration of demobilized soldiers into civil society is a crucial element in the overall efforts to achieve long-lasting peace in Mozambique. I wish to express my appreciation for the generous support being provided to the humanitarian programmes by many donors and for the commendable work being undertaken in the country by various agencies and organizations.

54. Despite all the challenging tasks that lie ahead, I believe that the major political conditions for the timely completion of this Mission are in place. Meanwhile, ONUMOZ continues to play a vital role in the peace process, which is of increasing importance as the elections draw nearer. I therefore recommend to the Security Council that it extend the existing mandate of ONUMOZ at a reduced strength as described in paragraphs 22, 24 and 25 above until 31 October 1994.

55. I also propose that all military, police and most of the support personnel of the Mission should begin repatriation immediately after the expiration of the mandate. I estimate that this will take up to seven weeks. Subsequently, it is expected that liquidation of the Mission, including the disposal of assets, redeployment of equipment and repatriation of essential administrative staff, will be completed by 31 January 1995. I intend to submit a detailed timetable for the closing down of the Mission in my next report to the Council at the end of July 1994.

56. The peace process in Mozambique has made substantial progress. This was achieved because the parties have resolved to sustain the process and because of the interest and support of the international community. On my part, I am determined to continue my efforts to accelerate the process of implementation and to facilitate the efforts of the Mozambican people to bring it to a final success.

57. I would like to pay tribute to the dedication and professionalism of the staff of ONUMOZ, in particular to my Special Representative, in carrying out the challenging tasks entrusted to them.

Annex

Military and Civilian Personnel
(as at April 1994)

Country	Troops	Head-quarters staff	Military observers	Civilian police
Argentina	36	4	8	
Australia.				16
Bangladesh . . .	1 371	52	30	25
Botswana	736	25	13	
Brazil			27	35
Canada.			15	
Cape Verde. . .			18	
China			10	
Czech Republic			19	
Egypt			20	21
Finland.				5
Guinea-Bissau.			43	25
Hungary.			23	10
India.	894	20	18	
Italy	953	19		
Ireland				20
Japan	48	5		
Jordan				45
Malaysia.			24	35
Netherlands . .		11		
New Zealand .		2		
Norway				9
Portugal	274	3	1	7
Russian Federation . .			19	
Spain			20	14
Sweden.			20	10
Switzerland. . .				1
Uruguay	813	28	34	
United States of America . .		5		
Zambia.	843	22	8	

Document 64

Security Council resolution renewing the mandate of ONUMOZ until 15 November 1994 and urging the Mozambican parties to allow ONUMOZ unimpeded access to the areas under their control

S/RES/916 (1994), 5 May 1994

The Security Council,

Reaffirming its resolution 782 (1992) of 13 October 1992 and all subsequent resolutions,

Having considered the report of the Secretary-General on the United Nations Operation in Mozambique (ONUMOZ) dated 28 April 1994 (S/1994/511),

Reiterating the importance it attaches to the General Peace Agreement for Mozambique (S/24635, annex), and the timely fulfilment in good faith by all parties of their obligations under the Agreement,

Commending the efforts of the Secretary-General, his Special Representative, his Special Adviser and the personnel of ONUMOZ in seeking to implement fully the mandate entrusted to it,

Commending also the role played by the Organization of African Unity (OAU) through the Special Representative of its Secretary-General, in the implementation of the General Peace Agreement,

Reaffirming that the people of Mozambique bear the ultimate responsibility for the successful implementation of the General Peace Agreement,

Reaffirming also its conviction that the resolution of the conflict in Mozambique would contribute to peace and security,

Welcoming the progress made in the implementation of the General Peace Agreement, and in particular the announcement by the President of Mozambique that elections will take place on 27 and 28 October 1994,

Expressing concern none the less at delays in the full implementation of some major aspects of the General Peace Agreement,

Emphasizing the need for the fullest possible cooperation by the Government of Mozambique and RENAMO with ONUMOZ, including with its police component,

1. *Welcomes* the report of the Secretary-General of 28 April 1994;

2. *Welcomes also* the maintenance of the cease-fire, the commencement of demobilization of all forces and the transfer of weapons to regional arms depots, the swearing into office of the High Command and the beginning of the training programme for the new Mozambican Defence Force (FADM);

3. *Welcomes further* the commencement of the deployment of the United Nations police observers as authorized in paragraph 2 of resolution 898 (1994) of

23 February 1994 and stresses the importance it attaches to the fullest cooperation of the parties with the police observers of ONUMOZ;

4. *Urges* all the parties to respect fully their obligations under the General Peace Agreement, especially:

(a) To allow ONUMOZ, including the police observers, unimpeded access to the areas under their control; and

(b) To allow unimpeded access to the areas under their control to all political forces in the country, in order to ensure free political activity in the whole territory of Mozambique;

5. *Notes* in particular the Secretary-General's plan as set out in paragraphs 21 to 25 of his report for the redeployment of ONUMOZ's personnel without prejudice to the effective discharge of its mandate;

6. *Welcomes* the announcement by the President of Mozambique on 11 April 1994 that elections will take place on 27 and 28 October 1994, the inauguration of the National Elections Commission and the establishment of its provincial offices throughout the country; and reiterates the importance it attaches to the elections taking place on these dates with electoral registration commencing on 1 June 1994;

7. *Calls upon* the Mozambican parties to support the electoral process including the work of the National Elections Commission, as described in paragraph 51 of the Secretary-General's report;

8. *Expresses its concern*, however, at continuing delays in the implementation of major aspects of the General Peace Agreement, in particular assembly and demobilization of troops, militia and paramilitary forces, and the formation of the new Mozambican Defence Force in accordance with the revised timetable and in line with paragraph 10 of resolution 882 (1993) of 5 November 1993, and calls upon the parties to comply fully with all the provisions of the General Peace Agreement;

9. *Commends* in this respect the agreement between the President of Mozambique, Mr. Joaquim Chissano, and the President of RENAMO, Mr. Afonso Dhlakama, on 8 April 1994 that the Government of Mozambique would expedite the assembly of its troops and that RENAMO would accelerate the pace of its demobilization;

10. *Urges* the parties to meet the targets of 1 June 1994 for the completion of the assembly of forces and 15 July 1994 for the completion of demobilization;

11. *Underlines* the need for the parties to ensure that ONUMOZ is provided with accurate information on the numbers of troops which remain to be assembled and to allow ONUMOZ access to all their military bases to verify military equipment as well as the number of combatants still outside the assembly areas and to provide ONUMOZ with complete lists of such equipment;

12. *Calls upon* the parties to ensure that the maximum possible number of soldiers are trained for the new Mozambican Defence Force before the elections take place and also calls upon the Government of Mozambique to provide logistical and technical support for the formation of the new Mozambican Defence Force, including regular remuneration for the troops and to begin the transfer of central defence facilities to its command;

13. *Expresses its appreciation* to the United Kingdom of Great Britain and Northern Ireland, France and Portugal for their contribution to the establishment of the new Mozambican Defence Force and to Italy and Zimbabwe for their offers of additional assistance in this regard;

14. *Emphasizes* the importance of progress being made in the area of mine clearance and related training in Mozambique, welcomes the Secretary-General's intention to accelerate the implementation of the United Nations programme in this area and expresses appreciation to those countries which have provided assistance in this regard;

15. *Appeals* to the international community to provide the necessary financial assistance to facilitate the implementation of the General Peace Agreement and also to make voluntary financial contributions to the technical assistance trust fund and the special trust fund for assistance to registered political parties;

16. *Notes with appreciation* the response of the international community to the humanitarian assistance needs of Mozambique and appeals to the international community to continue to provide appropriate and prompt assistance for the implementation of the humanitarian programmes carried out in the framework of the General Peace Agreement;

17. *Reiterates* its encouragement to the international community to provide appropriate and prompt assistance for the implementation of the demobilization scheme as a complement to the existing efforts being made in the framework of the humanitarian assistance programme;

18. *Commends* the efforts of the United Nations, its specialized agencies and other humanitarian agencies operating in Mozambique and urges all Mozambican parties to continue to facilitate their unimpeded access to the civilian population in need and to continue to cooperate with the United Nations High Commissioner for Refugees (UNHCR) and other humanitarian agencies in pursuing ongoing programmes to assist the remaining displaced persons and refugees to be resettled;

19. *Decides* to renew the mandate of ONUMOZ for a final period until 15 November 1994 at the strength described in paragraphs 22, 24 and 25 of the Secretary-General's report of 28 April 1994 subject to the proviso that the Security Council will review the status of the mandate of ONUMOZ by 15 July 1994 based on a report by the Secretary-General as described in paragraph 55 of his report, and also by 5 September 1994 based on a further report by the Secretary-General;

20. *Requests* the Secretary-General to ensure that the Security Council is kept regularly informed on the implementation of the General Peace Agreement, in particular on assembly and demobilization;

21. *Decides* to remain actively seized of the matter.

Document 65

Report of the Secretary-General on ONUMOZ

S/1994/803, 7 July 1994

I. Introduction

1. The present report is submitted pursuant to Security Council resolution 916 (1994) of 5 May 1994 by which the Council extended the mandate of the United Nations Operation in Mozambique (ONUMOZ) for a final period until 15 November 1994, subject to the proviso that the Council would review the status of the mandate of ONUMOZ by 15 July 1994 based on a report by the Secretary-General, and also by 5 September 1994 based on a further report by the Secretary-General. As indicated in paragraph 55 of my last report to the Council (S/1994/511), the present report also elaborates upon the timetable for the closing of ONUMOZ and the withdrawal of the military and civilian personnel of the mission.

II. Major political and military aspects

A. *General*

2. Three and a half months remain before the holding of the first multi-party elections in Mozambique on 27 and 28 October 1994. The preparations for those elections are generally proceeding in accordance with the established timetable. Registration of voters began as scheduled on 1 June 1994 and is progressing satisfactorily.

3. Since my last report to the Council dated 28 April 1994, significant progress has been made in the Mozambican peace process. However, serious problems remain that must be addressed rapidly if the elections are to be held under acceptable conditions. The major concerns now are delays in the completion of the assembly and demobilization of troops belonging to the Government of Mozambique and the Resistência Nacional Moçambicana (RENAMO), as well as delays in the formation of the new Mozambican Defence Force (FADM).

B. *Assembly and demobilization of troops*

4. The Security Council, in its resolution 916 (1994) of 5 May 1994, urged the two Mozambican parties to meet the target dates of 1 June 1994 for the completion of the assembly of forces and 15 July 1994 for the completion of demobilization. While RENAMO accepted the deadlines, the Government declared that it would not be able to meet the target dates set by the Council but would conclude the assembly of its troops by 1 July and their demobilization by 15 August 1994.

5. It will be recalled that in November 1992 the Government had declared that it would send a total of 61,638 troops to its 29 assembly areas. At that time it also indicated that there would be an additional 14,767 soldiers who would be registered outside the assembly areas. The total of government soldiers would thus be 76,405. However, on 21 April 1994, the government delegation to the Cease-fire Commission presented revised and substantially lower figures, indicating that there would be a total of 64,110 government soldiers, 49,630 of whom would be sent to assembly areas and 14,480 of whom would be registered outside such areas. The Government claimed that the discrepancy was attributable to its failure to deduct from the initially estimated total a group of 13,776 soldiers who had been demobilized before the General Peace Agreement was signed. RENAMO did not, however, accept the new figures, and the matter was referred first to the Cease-fire Commission and then to the Supervisory and Monitoring Commission for verification and subsequent decision. On 17 June 1994, following protracted investigations and negotiations, the two parties signed a joint declaration accompanied by two separate statements. Based on the revised estimates, the new overall strength of the government troops was established at 64,466, of which 49,638 are to be registered in assembly areas and 14,828 outside assembly areas. RENAMO agreed to use the revised government figure as a working estimate and as a point of reference, on the condition that it would be verified by the Cease-fire Commission after the assembly of government troops was completed.

6. So far, despite the concerns expressed by my Special Representative and the international community, the assembly of the government troops has not been completed. The 1 July deadline which the Government set for itself has not been met. However, following a request from President Chissano, it has been agreed that 3,476 soldiers who were to be registered in the assembly areas will now be registered and demobilized *in situ*. As of 4 July 1994, the Government still had to assemble 4,517 troops. At the Government's request, ONUMOZ is providing transport to assembly areas for approximately 1,325 soldiers who are located in remote areas of the country. As of 4 July 1994, RENAMO had assembled 17,317 soldiers out of an expected total of 18,241; in a meeting of the Cease-fire Commission it was agreed that 899 RENAMO soldiers based at two locations would not go to the assembly areas but would be demobilized *in situ*. As of 4 July 1994, the Government had demobilized 22,832 soldiers (46 per cent of the expected total), while RENAMO had demobilized 5,138 soldiers (54 per cent of the expected total). A dramatic effort must now be made in order to complete the demobilization process by 15 August 1994.

7. Registration of government troops outside the assembly areas began only on 24 June. But as those soldiers are dispersed at approximately 140 separate locations throughout the country, it is unlikely that their registration and demobilization can be completed by the 15 August deadline. In the meantime, registration of the 4,326 unassembled RENAMO troops began on 25 May and is expected to be concluded shortly. The demobilization of these troops is scheduled to be completed by 15 July.

8. Delays in demobilization and the selection of soldiers for FADM resulted in prolonged waiting periods in assembly areas and led to mounting frustration, demonstrations and rioting by the soldiers. In most cases, they demanded prompt demobilization and payment of salaries in arrears. On a number of occasions, United Nations personnel were attacked and threatened by the soldiers in assembly areas, while food and other supplies were frequently looted. As a precautionary measure, United Nations troops had to be deployed to or around cantonment sites. On 13 June 1994, the Cease-fire Commission approved a plan providing for the closure of all 49

assembly areas, the transfer of all weapons to regional arms depots and the acceleration of the selection of soldiers for the new army. As of 4 July, one Government and three RENAMO assembly areas had already been closed.

9. As of 4 July 1994, a total of 74,858 weapons (59,213 Government and 15,645 RENAMO) had been collected from troops in assembly areas. To date, 87 per cent of the weapons collected have been transported to the regional arms depots. A total of 37,622 weapons out of 49,806 had been collected from the paramilitary forces. Some small caches of weapons have been found at various locations throughout the country. All recovered weapons have been duly registered and transferred to the regional arms depots.

10. On several occasions in the past (see S/1994/511, para. 25), I have indicated my concern with the security situation and the need to have additional United Nations infantry elements in some particularly vulnerable areas of the country. With the repatriation of the main body of the Italian infantry contingent from the central region of Mozambique, I have decided to deploy there in July a self-contained infantry company with a strength of up to 170 personnel, which will be provided by the Government of Brazil. I believe that their presence there will be very important, especially during the critical final stages of demobilization and preparation for the elections.

C. *Formation of the Mozambican Defence Force*

11. In resolution 916 (1994) the Security Council called upon the parties to ensure that the maximum possible number of soldiers were trained for the new Mozambican Defence Force before the elections. The Council also called upon the Government of Mozambique to provide logistical and technical support for the formation of FADM and to initiate the transfer of all central defence facilities to the FADM command. The Government is also responsible for providing regular remuneration to FADM troops.

12. According to the provisions of the general peace agreement, the new Mozambican army is to be composed of 30,000 soldiers, 15,000 from the Government and 15,000 from RENAMO. France, Portugal and the United Kingdom of Great Britain and Northern Ireland agreed to assist the Mozambican Government in training the new army. However, the present training programmes sponsored by the three participating States cover only some 15,000 soldiers. Because of problems encountered in the selection of soldiers for FADM, it now appears unlikely that training of the first group of 15,000 will be concluded by October 1994. As of 4 July 1994, just under 3,000 FADM soldiers had been trained under the above-mentioned programmes. These include the first three infantry battalions totalling 2,223 soldiers, special

forces (350), marines (92), logistics and administration (150), and senior officers (100). Another 1,000 soldiers are currently being trained. In June, 131 Zimbabwean military instructors arrived in Mozambique to assist with infantry training, while Portugal has offered to train an additional 300 soldiers.

13. There are no provisions for training the remaining 15,000 soldiers for FADM. In my last report to the Council (S/1994/511, paras. 13-14) I outlined a number of options which would resolve the problem by phasing the formation of the new army. In my view, it would be preferable for the soldiers covered by the current programmes to be formed prior to the elections, and the second group thereafter. RENAMO is willing to accept this. The Government has put forward a counter-proposal that all 30,000 soldiers be recruited before the elections and half of them trained, while the remainder would be deployed in military centres where they would only receive basic training before the elections. However, in order to realize this option, additional instructors would be needed to assist the Government. Considerable financial resources would also be required to rehabilitate the military centres and to organize the basic training before the end of October. It is doubtful whether the Government could finance and carry out such a programme within the required time-frame. The Government of Italy has been requested to provide assistance in the formation of FADM. While the Government of Italy has undertaken a survey of the possible requirements, it has not as yet formally reacted to the request from the Government of Mozambique.

D. *Cease-fire*

14. During the period under review the cease-fire has been generally respected and military activities did not pose a serious threat either to the peace process or to preparations for the forthcoming elections. A total of four formal complaints were reported to the Cease-fire Commission, all of which are under consideration by the Commission. Three of the cases involve alleged irregularities in the cantonment process. In one case, RENAMO complained about double registration of government soldiers. As a result, the ONUMOZ Technical Unit's data bank has been adjusted to double-check each soldier registered against all soldiers already demobilized. A cross-check found that 260 soldiers had attempted double registration. The Commission is currently deliberating on how to proceed with those cases. The Government lodged two complaints alleging that 89 RENAMO soldiers had left the Lurio assembly area for hostile purposes and that demobilized RENAMO soldiers from the Chinanguanine assembly area had been ordered to return to their former base. A RENAMO allegation that government forces are

undergoing military training in the United Republic of Tanzania has been investigated and the report is currently under review by the Commission.

15. In paragraph 17 of my last report to the Council (S/1994/511), I expressed my concern over the unwillingness of the parties to allow the United Nations to reconnoitre certain military bases and to provide ONUMOZ with complete lists of military equipment. Since then, access has been granted to all military installations designated as locations for unassembled troops. However, the parties have yet to provide the United Nations with updated lists of their military equipment. The general peace agreement provides that biweekly updates of these lists should be presented to the Cease-fire Commission, but the latest submission from both parties was provided in August 1993.

III. Preparation for the elections

16. During the last periodic review the Security Council welcomed the announcement by the President of Mozambique that elections would take place on 27 and 28 October 1994. The Council further reiterated the importance it attached to the elections taking place on these dates, with electoral registration commencing on 1 June 1994.

17. In the October elections, voters will elect both the President of the Republic and the members of the national assembly. The Electoral Law prescribes that the President must be elected by an absolute majority, otherwise a run-off election must be held between the two candidates who received the largest number of votes. The run-off elections must take place between the seventh and the twenty-first day after the publication of the results of the initial ballot, which is to be no later than two weeks after the poll. The term of office for the President and the 250 members of the National Assembly is five years. The National Elections Commission will determine the number of deputies to be elected to the Assembly from each district in proportion to the number of voters registered.

18. The National Elections Commission is the principal body overseeing the electoral process and is assisted in the practical execution of its mandate by the Technical Secretariat for the Administration of the Elections. Provincial and district Elections Commissions and local offices of the Technical Secretariat are now established in all but a few of the 138 provincial districts as well as in the 6 electoral districts which have been established in Maputo. The Electoral Law stipulates that the Mozambique Liberation Front (FRELIMO), RENAMO and other political parties must be represented in all electoral bodies. However, as a result of internal staffing problems, the representation of RENAMO and other parties is low or non-existent in several districts; the transparency of the

electoral process could suffer if this under-representation is not corrected.

19. The overall institutional framework for the elections was completed on 8 June 1994 with the swearing in of the national and international judges for the Electoral Tribunal. The Tribunal will function as a court of appeal against decisions of the National Elections Commission.

20. Training of all electoral elements, voter registration teams and civic education agents was coordinated by the National Elections Commission with technical assistance from the United Nations Development Programme (UNDP) and was concluded at the end of May. Registration of voters began as scheduled on 1 June 1994 and is advancing relatively smoothly. At this stage, approximately 1,500 out of the initially envisaged 1,600 registration teams are fully operational. As of 4 July, at least 2.5 million out of a projected 8 million eligible voters had registered. This has been achieved in spite of significant logistical bottlenecks. Voter registration is scheduled to last 10 weeks but may be extended on an exceptional basis by the National Elections Commission until 12 September 1994, when the electoral campaign is to begin.

21. In paragraph 51 of my last report to the Council (S/1994/511), I expressed my conviction that free and fair elections in Mozambique are possible subject to certain conditions which, I wish to reiterate, are essential to the electoral process. In this context, I have noted with concern that access to a few RENAMO-controlled districts is still impeded. Furthermore, clear rules for access to State mass media, including both radio and television, have yet to be established. As of 4 July 1994, a total of 15 political parties had registered and were participating in the electoral process. RENAMO has not yet officially registered but is participating in the process as a party to the general peace agreement.

22. In my last report, I apprised the Security Council of the situation regarding technical assistance funding for the electoral process and the downward revision of the original budget from US$ 71 million to US$ 59 million. This budget has now been further reduced to $56.3 million. Total pledges towards the election budget now total $52.5 million, including $3.3 million set aside by the Government from the State budget. This leaves a shortfall of $3.8 million. I reiterate my appeal to donors to bridge this gap and urgently honour their earlier commitments in order that preparations for the elections may proceed on schedule. In the meantime, the Mozambican political parties have continuously stressed the need for funds to prepare for the electoral campaign. To date, donors have pledged a total of $3.54 million for the trust fund established to assist registered parties, on the condition that the National Elections Commission establish

rules of procedure and eligibility criteria for the fund. After long delays, the Commission agreed on 28 June 1994 to formulate such criteria.

23. Pursuant to its mandate, the Electoral Division of ONUMOZ is monitoring the entire electoral process; its 148 officers are stationed in provinces and districts as well as in Maputo. Monitoring activities cover voter registration, civic education campaigns, use of the press and activities of political parties and their leaders before and during the electoral campaign. United Nations electoral officers frequently visit and check registration sites and conduct sample counts of registered voters. They also receive complaints from political parties and individuals concerning alleged irregularities in the electoral process. While all complaints are transmitted to the National Elections Commission for follow-up, ONUMOZ is mandated to carry out separate investigations. During the elections on 27 and 28 October, several hundred additional international observers are expected to monitor the polling and the counting of votes throughout the country. A total of 60,000 Mozambican polling officers are to be trained by the National Elections Commission, with assistance from UNDP.

IV. Police activities

24. Of the authorized strength of 1,144 United Nations police observers, 817 had been deployed by 4 July, in accordance with the schedule set out in my last report to the Council of 28 April 1994 (S/1994/511). To date, 29 CIVPOL stations have been established outside provincial and district capitals; 8 of them are in RENAMO-controlled areas. An additional 31 stations are scheduled to open as soon as logistical arrangements are in place. Logistical problems have delayed the establishment of CIVPOL outposts in some areas.

25. The initial reluctance on the part of the authorities of the two parties to cooperate with ONUMOZ civilian police is gradually being overcome. CIVPOL initially encountered difficulties in gaining access to a number of government police stations and was unable to inspect the Quick Reaction Force systematically. Following several discussions with the Minister of the Interior, however, access to the Quick Reaction Force has been granted. Since then, CIVPOL has been given information on the organization, strength, equipment and training of that force.

26. As part of the agreement of 3 September 1993 on the unification of the territorial administration of Mozambique, the two parties decided that the Mozambican police should re-establish posts in areas formerly controlled by RENAMO. RENAMO's political leaders have continuously declared that they would guarantee access to all areas that were under their control, while the national police continues to reiterate its commitment to set up the required posts. However, these commitments have often not been acted upon: in some cases, local RENAMO authorities have denied the government police access, while the latter appears reluctant to extend its posts to former RENAMO areas. This situation is hindering the effective functioning of CIVPOL.

27. ONUMOZ has so far received 47 complaints of misconduct by members of the national police. Thirty-five cases were investigated and fully resolved, while 12 cases are still under investigation. The cases fall mainly into three categories: (a) illegal detention of civilians; (b) abuse of detainees' civil rights; and (c) criminal investigations involving possible political motives. Furthermore, many detainees have complained about the lack of food, water and other necessities in State prisons.

V. Humanitarian assistance programme

28. The coordination of assistance to be provided from now to the end of the year to meet the demands of the humanitarian situation in Mozambique is among the current and major preoccupations of the United Nations. Against the background of the demobilization process and in the light of the continuing return of significant numbers of refugees and internally displaced persons to rural areas, mine-clearance activities as well as agricultural production have also become critical factors in the humanitarian situation. Consequently, the United Nations Office for Humanitarian Assistance Coordination (UNOHAC) of ONUMOZ is now focusing on activities that will effectively address the current situation in a comprehensive manner. Special emphasis is being placed on the implementation of programmes and activities aimed at ensuring the full reintegration and resettlement of returnees and internally displaced persons and demobilizing soldiers within Mozambican society.

29. With the recent completion of the review of the consolidated humanitarian assistance programme, a clearer picture of humanitarian needs for the period from May to December 1994 and related costs has emerged. The provision and distribution of emergency relief in the form of food and non-food items to the various categories of beneficiaries is estimated at US$ 117 million. This covers the distribution of seeds and tools as well as costs related to emergency work in the areas of water supply and health and education in support of overall reintegration programmes in rural areas.

30. For activities related to the repatriation of refugees and the rehabilitation of areas with a large returnee population, an estimated $31 million is required. To date, some 800,000 Mozambican refugees have returned. An additional flow of returnees, estimated at 600,000, is expected before the end of 1994.

31. The reintegration support scheme for demobilized soldiers includes the extension of six months' severance pay from the Government for a further 18 months. With the Government's decision, taken on 23 June 1994, to grant pensions to disabled RENAMO soldiers, the reintegration support scheme was ratified by the Supervising and Monitoring Commission on 24 June 1994. The scheme, together with a programme for training, counselling and job referral to facilitate the re-entry of demobilized soldiers into civilian life, has been established at a cost of $47 million.

32. Although this season's harvest is projected to be better than last season's, the expected reduction in the provision of food relief is smaller than had been hoped for. The increase in areas planted in 1993-1994 as a direct consequence of the cease-fire was countered by inadequate rains and pest infestations, as well as by the scale of destruction caused by cyclone "Nadia" in the northern provinces of the country. The recent Food and Agriculture Organization of the United Nations (FAO)/World Food Programme (WFP) crop and food supply assessment mission has estimated that total cereal imports required during the period from May 1994 to April 1995 will be 600,000 metric tons, which represents a reduction of over 300,000 metric tons from the previous agricultural year.

33. In my last report, I indicated that the implementation of the United Nations mine-clearance programme would be accelerated following delays experienced in its initial phase. The plan to establish a national mine-clearance capacity is now making progress, and it is expected that some 400 Mozambican de-miners will be trained by November 1994. In this regard, the Mine Clearance Training Centre is to be moved from temporary facilities in Beira to more permanent ones in Tete. In the meantime, the national mine survey was completed on 9 June 1994, providing critical details concerning safety of roads and 1,300 confirmed or suspected mined sites. Clearance of 40 kilometres of road in Sofala Province, from Sena to Chiramba, has been completed under a contract with the United States Agency for International Development (USAID). Through a project financed by the United Kingdom, three teams of 68 Mozambican mine clearers are working on the clearance of priority roads in Zambézia. Also, Norwegian People's Aid continues its work in the provinces of Tete and Sofala, having completed the opening of a key route in Zambézia, providing access to an area that has been isolated for many years. That organization, together with a group of 100 mine clearers, is also currently engaged in mine-clearance activities within Maputo province.

34. While persistent efforts will be made to move the humanitarian endeavour in Mozambique towards rehabilitation and reconstruction, the assessment of needs for the period between now and December 1994 indicates the existence of significant emergency-type humanitarian requirements. In this connection, it should be borne in mind that the flow of returnees will continue beyond December 1994, as will other humanitarian programmes, such as mine clearance and the reintegration of demobilized soldiers. At present, UNOHAC is working closely with the Government and RENAMO in order to ensure the sustainability of progress achieved and the coordination of externally funded humanitarian assistance programmes after the elections.

VI. Timetable for the closure of ONUMOZ and withdrawal of civilian and military personnel

35. By paragraph 19 of resolution 916 (1994), the Security Council extended the mandate of ONUMOZ for a final period until 15 November 1994 at the strength described in paragraphs 22, 24 and 25 of my last report (S/1994/511). The withdrawal of ONUMOZ civilian and military personnel is scheduled to begin immediately after the elections on 27 and 28 October 1994 and is scheduled to be concluded before the end of January 1995.

36. Several hundred international electoral observers who are due to arrive in Mozambique approximately 10 days before the October elections are scheduled to be repatriated almost immediately after the poll. The majority of the international staff of the ONUMOZ Electoral Division and the United Nations Volunteers will leave the mission area after the election results are published. Meanwhile, the withdrawal of ONUMOZ police observers is planned to take place in three phases beginning on 10 November 1994 and ending by mid-December, when the last 200 observers from the regional and central headquarters will be repatriated. The withdrawal of the humanitarian component of ONUMOZ is also planned to begin immediately after the elections, with most of the staff of UNOHAC scheduled to leave the mission area by mid-November. A limited number of personnel will remain until the end of November 1994 for handing over activities.

37. The drawdown of the ONUMOZ military component will start on 15 November 1994 and be concluded within 40 days. Preparations for repatriation of each of the major national contingents will take approximately two to three weeks to accomplish; this process will be initiated on 1 November 1994. The tentative withdrawal schedule of infantry units is as follows: the Uruguayan contingent will depart in the period from 18 to 26 November 1994; the Brazilian on 22 and 23 November 1994; the Botswanan on 4 and 5 December 1994; the Bangladeshi from 25 November to 11 December; and

the Zambian in the second half of December 1994. The repatriation of military support units and medical personnel is scheduled to begin on 19 November 1994 and to be completed by 22 December 1994. Until the closure of the mission by the end of January 1995, only a limited number of mostly civilian logisticians and of essential military personnel (specialists and staff officers) would remain in Mozambique.

38. This recommended timetable for withdrawal of personnel is based on the relevant provisions of the general peace agreement. The presence of ONUMOZ would be required until such time as the new Government takes office. The withdrawal plan is thus conditional upon: (a) the successful holding of peaceful, free and fair elections on 27 and 28 October 1994; (b) the announcement of the election results no later than 12 November 1994; and (c) the timely establishment of a new Government. Should a second ballot be required for the election of the President, it might be necessary for the Council to adjust the timetable for the withdrawal of certain elements of ONUMOZ.

VII. Financial aspects

39. As indicated in my report to the General Assembly of 23 May 1994 (A/48/849/Add.1), the estimated financial requirements of ONUMOZ for the period from 1 May to 15 November 1994 amounted to $178,770,900 (gross) and $175,500,100 (net). The Advisory Committee on Administrative and Budgetary Questions, in its report of 24 June 1994 (A/48/956), recommended appropriation and assessment of an additional amount of $111.5 million (gross) for the period from 1 May to 15 November 1994, taking into account the amount of $53.8 million already appropriated and

assessed. However, for the period from inception to 30 June 1994 there are still outstanding assessed contributions for ONUMOZ totalling $153.2 million. As of 30 June 1994, the total amount of outstanding assessed contributions for all peace-keeping operations is $2,100.0 million.

VIII. Observations

40. With the election dates of 27 and 28 October 1994 rapidly approaching, the timetable for the peace process is becoming increasingly tight. While significant progress has been made in many areas, and especially in the electoral sphere, I am concerned by the delays in the assembly and demobilization of troops and in the training and formation of the new army.

41. Both parties to the general peace agreement have repeatedly reiterated their commitment to ensure the conclusion of the demobilization process by the agreed deadlines, but these assurances have not yet been fully translated into action. It is now imperative that the assembly and demobilization of government troops be accelerated dramatically if the established and recently reconfirmed deadline is to be met. If the demobilization of government and RENAMO troops is not completed by the agreed dates, and if a large number of the soldiers selected for FADM are left in assembly areas, there is a danger that three armies will be in existence in Mozambique during the election period. This could pose a serious threat to stability and thus to the holding of free and fair elections and the peaceful formation of the new government. It is therefore imperative that everything possible be done by the parties to speed up the demobilization process.

Document 66

Letter dated 7 July 1994 from Mozambique transmitting a statement of the position of the Government of Mozambique regarding the cantonment of troops

S/1994/806, 9 July 1994

I have the honour to enclose herewith for your consideration, an unofficial translation of the statement by the Head of the Government Delegation to the Cease-Fire Commission (CCF) during its meeting held at Maputo on 4 July 1994, regarding the ongoing peace process in Mozambique.

I would appreciate if you could have the text of this letter and its annex circulated as a document of the Security Council.

Annex
Position of the Government of Mozambique regarding the cantonment of troops
On 4 July 1994, we concluded the cantonment process, with the arrival of the remaining FAM-FPLM troops in the 29 designated assembly areas. There are, however, still 1,325 soldiers and 19 tons of *matériel* whose transportation has been requested to, but not yet granted by, ONUMOZ.

It should be noted that about 3,814 soldiers will remain in their respective barracks, in order to protect military installations and infrastructure. Under the existing agreements within the Cease-fire Commission (CCF), these soldiers are considered as part of the number already cantoned in the assembly areas and whose registration is under way.

As we announce the practical conclusion of the cantonment of Government troops, we deem it appropriate to formally bring to the attention of the CCF some legitimate Government concerns regarding this process.

Until now, the United Nations Operation in Mozambique (ONUMOZ) has exerted considerable, unilateral pressure on the Government for the cantonment of its troops—both through the media and the Security Council—but it has failed to do the same thing with regard to RENAMO.

On the contrary, ONUMOZ stated that RENAMO had concluded its cantonment operations, in contradiction with information contained in its daily reports, which clearly indicates that RENAMO has a considerable number of troops still to be sent to the assembly areas.

The Government deems it necessary that ONUMOZ act with objectivity, avoiding any kind of partiality that might discredit and jeopardize the implementation of the General Peace Agreement, and ultimately the whole peace process.

The cease-fire violations by RENAMO, which have been duly reported by the Government, are a source of great concern. The CCF not only failed to make a final ruling about these violations, but it has also downplayed the seriousness of the incidents by neglecting to make any effort to investigate them. The following such incidents have been duly reported by the Government:

- The presence of a RENAMO battalion in Pandambire;
- Training of soldiers in Gorongosa;
- Movement of a RENAMO batallion from Maringue to Buzua, south of Marromeu.

We must express our concern over the fact that an investigation is yet to be initiated—and is long overdue—into the matter of the reassembly of RENAMO demobilized soldiers in Ngungwe, in spite of a decision already taken in that regard.

About 500 armed RENAMO soldiers have been blocking the road linking Mutarara to Cambulatsitsi, demanding food supplies from ONUMOZ. If, as ONUMOZ has indicated, RENAMO has already cantoned all of its forces in the assembly areas, where do these 500 soldiers come from? How come ONUMOZ is dealing with them without first demanding their cantonment? Isn't this a case of logistical support by ONUMOZ to underground RENAMO forces?

In November 1992, RENAMO had announced that the number of its troops to be sent to the 20 assembly areas reserved for them, was 21,000 men. When we initiated the cantonment process, in November 1993, the ONUMOZ daily reports on the movement of troops stated that the number of RENAMO soldiers that were to be sent to these areas was 19,140. According to recent daily reports, however, the total number of soldiers to be taken to the assembly areas is now 18,421.

We wonder in which sessions of the CCF were such changes in the total number of RENAMO soldiers communicated. Which is in fact, the total number of RENAMO soldiers? How many of them will remain in the centres for non-assembled troops?

We have not been informed of any of that, and apparently, ONUMOZ is not concerned about this. ONUMOZ is acting as if its mission was to control and demand everything from the Government, and not to monitor the implementation of the General Peace Agreement by the parties.

We would like to repeat that making unilateral demands and putting substantial pressure on the Government, while ignoring RENAMO's non-compliance, can seriously jeopardize the peace process.

The Government demands that an end be put to this kind of tolerant behavior, and hopes that ONUMOZ will exert equal pressure on RENAMO for the cantonment and demobilization of its soldiers.

The Government Delegation to the Cease-Fire Commission has clear and precise instructions to seek a quick investigation and clarification of the matters that have already been notified to this body, as well as of the new facts presented in this statement. To accomplish this, we are willing to make all the necessary efforts within the framework of the CCF.

Maputo, 4 July 1994

(*Signed*) Pedro Comissário AFONSO
Ambassador Extraordinary and Plenipotentiary
Permanent Representative to the United Nations

Document 67

Statement by the President of the Security Council expressing concern at continuing delays in the implementation of the General Peace Agreement for Mozambique

S/PRST/1994/35, 19 July 1994

The Security Council notes with appreciation the report of the Secretary-General of 7 July 1994 (S/1994/803) on the United Nations Operation in Mozambique (ONUMOZ). It commends the Special Representative of the Secretary-General and the personnel of ONUMOZ for their efforts in support of the implementation of the General Peace Agreement for Mozambique. They continue to have the full backing of the Council.

The Security Council welcomes the significant progress made in the implementation of the general peace agreement, in particular in the electoral sphere, but remains concerned at continuing delays in the implementation of some major aspects of the Agreement. The Council is especially concerned at the delays which continue to occur in the demobilization of forces and in the formation of the new Mozambican Defence Force (FADM). In this context, the Council reiterates its call in resolution 916 (1994) of 5 May 1994 to the parties to comply fully with all the provisions of the Agreement.

It is essential that the demobilization of all forces is completed by 15 August 1994, as agreed by the parties, and that the difficulties of forming, before the elections, FADM at the strength agreed in the General Peace Agreement are addressed quickly and with flexibility.

The Council is encouraged by the recent announcement of the Mozambican Government's decision to turn over the assets, including equipment and facilities, of the Mozambique Armed Forces (FAM) to FADM by 15 August 1994 and reiterates the importance of the Government providing all necessary support to the establishment of FADM.

The Council underlines the importance to the peace process of the rehabilitation of areas with a large returning population, including through an effective mine-clearance programme. In this regard, it urges that high priority be given to mine-clearance activities and related training.

The Council, in its resolution 916 (1994), decided to renew the mandate of ONUMOZ for a final period until 15 November 1994 and welcomed the announcement by the President of the Republic of Mozambique that elections would take place on 27 and 28 October 1994. It reaffirms the importance it attaches to the elections taking place on these dates and stresses the need for additional decisive steps to that end. In this context, the Council stresses that there is no margin for further delay in demobilization and in the formation of FADM. The Council expects the parties to continue to cooperate with ONUMOZ and with each other to ensure full and timely implementation of the Agreement.

The Council reiterates the importance of the extension of civil administration throughout Mozambique, which is essential for the holding of free and fair elections. In this context, it reaffirms its call to all parties, especially the Resistência Nacional Moçambicana (RENAMO), to allow unimpeded access to the areas under their control to all political forces in the country, in order to ensure free political activity throughout Mozambique.

The Council expresses its intention to endorse the results of the elections provided the United Nations reports them as free and fair and reminds all the Mozambican parties of their obligation under the General Peace Agreement fully to respect the results.

The Council will consider sending a mission, at an appropriate time, to Mozambique to discuss with the parties how best to ensure full and timely implementation of the General Peace Agreement and that the elections take place on the dates agreed and under the conditions set out in the Agreement.

The Council will continue to monitor developments in Mozambique closely and requests the Secretary-General to ensure that it is kept informed on a regular basis.

Document 68

Note by the President of the Security Council on the sending of a mission to Mozambique to convey the Security Council's concern at delays in the implementation of the General Peace Agreement

S/1994/931, 4 August 1994

1. The President of the Security Council has the honour to refer to the statement made by the President of the Council at its 3406th meeting, held on 19 July 1994, in connection with the item entitled "The situation in Mozambique" (S/PRST/1994/35).

2. The statement indicated, in particular, that the Security Council would consider sending a mission, at an appropriate time, to Mozambique to discuss with the parties how best to ensure full and timely implementation of the General Peace Agreement.

3. In accordance with that decision, the President has held consultations with the members of the Council. Following those consultations, the members have agreed that the mission will depart for Mozambique on 6 August 1994, for a duration of approximately five days, and that it will be composed of the following nine members of the Council: Brazil, China, Czech Republic, Djibouti, New Zealand, Nigeria, Oman, the Russian Federation and the United States of America.

The mission will, *inter alia*:

(a) Convey to the leaderships of the Government of Mozambique and Resistência Nacional Moçambicana (RENAMO) the Security Council's concern at the delays in the implementation of major aspects of the General Peace Agreement for Mozambique;

(b) Underline the necessity of completing the demobilization of all forces by 15 August 1994, as agreed by the parties;

(c) Underline the need for the parties to ensure that the elections take place on the dates agreed and under the conditions set out in the agreement;

(d) Stress the intention of the Council to endorse the results of the elections provided the United Nations reports them as free and fair;

(e) Remind all the parties of their obligation under the General Peace Agreement fully to respect the results of the elections;

(f) Stress the full support of the Security Council for the efforts of the Secretary-General and his Special Representative;

(g) Submit to the Council a report of the mission's findings during the visit.

Document 69

Further report of the Secretary-General on ONUMOZ

S/1994/1002, 26 August 1994

I. Introduction

1. The present report is submitted pursuant to Security Council resolution 916 (1994) of 5 May 1994, by which the Council extended the mandate of the United Nations Operation in Mozambique (ONUMOZ) for a final period until 15 November 1994, subject to the proviso that the Council would review the status of the mandate of ONUMOZ by 15 July and by 5 September 1994 based on further reports by the Secretary-General. Further to my report to the Council of 7 July 1994 (S/1994/803), the present report reflects the situation as of 25 August 1994.

2. This report also focuses on issues raised during the mission of the Security Council which visited Mozambique from 7 to 12 August 1994. In my view, the visit had a very positive impact on the peace process, and I fully share many of the observations and recommendations contained in the mission's presentation to the Council made on 18 August 1994.

II. Political and military aspects

A. *General*

3. Since my last report to the Council dated 7 July 1994 (S/1994/803), significant progress has been achieved in the peace process in Mozambique. Several of the difficulties cited in my earlier reports have now been overcome. The process of assembly of soldiers of the Government and the Resistência Nacional Moçambicana (RENAMO) has been concluded, and the demobilization

of these soldiers is almost complete. A number of decisions have been taken with regard to formation of the new army. More than three quarters of the estimated eligible voter population has been registered for elections. Despite the many challenging tasks that lie ahead, I believe that the major political conditions for holding the elections as planned on 27 and 28 October 1994 are in place.

4. At the same time, there is growing concern about the security situation in the country, which has deteriorated in recent months. On the one hand, rioting among soldiers in assembly areas as well as in unassembled locations has become frequent and violent. It has resulted in the setting up of roadblocks and the taking of hostages, as well as demands for immediate demobilization and for the provision of various supplies. I hope that with the imminent completion of the demobilization, many of these problems will be overcome. On the other hand, criminal activity and banditry has increased, raising serious concerns about public safety in the period leading up to, during and immediately after the elections.

B. *Cease-fire*

5. During the period under review, only three complaints of cease-fire violations have been reported to the Cease-fire Commission, two by the Government and one by RENAMO. This brings the total number of complaints since the signing of the general peace agreement to 95. All of these cases have been investigated, and the results were approved by both parties. In general, the cease-fire has been remarkably well respected, and military activities have not posed a serious threat to the cease-fire or to the holding of elections as scheduled.

C. *Assembly and demobilization of troops*

6. The process of assembly of troops has been completed, and the demobilization will be completed shortly. A total of 43,297 Government troops have passed through the 29 Government assembly areas, and 17,466 RENAMO soldiers have passed through the 20 RENAMO assembly areas. It has been an extremely difficult and sometimes dangerous process. In addition, all unassembled troops have been registered. The Government registered a total of 20,919 unassembled troops and RENAMO registered 4,995 unassembled personnel. The closing of assembly areas began on 18 June 1994. As of 22 August, 12 camps out of 49 had been dismantled.

7. The demobilization process was substantially concluded by 22 August 1994, one week after the deadline of 15 August 1994. All documentation has been processed for the limited number of soldiers who still remain in the assembly areas or at unassembled locations. Most of their cases are pending owing to specific circumstances or to last minute registration. Some were sick or absent at the date of demobilization, while others are in the process of being transferred to the new army. The delay in the demobilization process was the result mainly of the increase in the number of soldiers who were to be demobilized following the decision by the Government and RENAMO in the Supervisory and Monitoring Commission on 25 July 1994 that all soldiers who so wished would be demobilized. As of 22 August, a total of 67,155 soldiers (50,596 Government and 16,559 RENAMO) had been demobilized, while 9,226 (5,724 Government and 3,502 RENAMO) were in the process of being demobilized. In the meantime, the Cease-fire Commission approved a plan for follow-up verification of the completion of assembly and demobilization which will commence on 30 August throughout the country.

8. As of 22 August 1994, the date of completion of the demobilization process, a total of 105,009 weapons (87,767 Government and 17,242 RENAMO) had been collected from troops in the assembly areas as well as unassembled locations. As of the same date, a total of 41,471 weapons had been collected from paramilitary forces out of the projected total of 49,806. Despite the demobilization of a much larger number of troops than initially planned, the number of weapons collected by ONUMOZ is below what was expected. Weapons caches were discovered, some of which contained large quantities of arms. Contrary to the rules approved by the Cease-fire Commission, the United Nations was denied permission to collect and disable weapons at unassembled locations on several occasions. This not only delayed the process of disarmament, but also resulted in a number of potentially serious incidents.

D. *Formation of the Mozambican Defence Force*

9. In resolution 916 (1994), the Security Council called upon the parties to ensure that the maximum possible number of soldiers were trained for the new Mozambican Defence Force (FADM) before the elections. The Council also called upon the Government of Mozambique to provide logistical and technical support for the formation of FADM, including regular remuneration for the troops, and to initiate the transfer of all central defence facilities to FADM command. The Council will recall that according to the provisions of the general peace agreement (S/24635 and Corr.1, annex), the new Mozambican Defence Force was to be a volunteer army composed of 30,000 soldiers, 15,000 from the Government and 15,000 from RENAMO ranks. In my last report to the Council, I noted the serious difficulties the parties were facing in forming a new armed force of this size prior to the elections, especially as existing training programmes could accommodate

only 15,000 soldiers. There have been numerous delays in the formation of the new armed forces which were compounded by logistical problems and by a lack of volunteers to join the new army.

10. As of 22 August, only 7,398 soldiers (3,901 Government and 3,497 RENAMO) had joined FADM. At this stage, no more than 10,000 soldiers are expected to join the new army before the elections. So far, 4,276 FADM soldiers have been trained in the various programmes. These include three infantry battalions totalling 1,567, special forces (919), marines (40), logistics and administration (150), senior officers (150) and deminers (100). An additional 2,206 soldiers are currently undergoing training. France, Portugal, the United Kingdom of Great Britain and Northern Ireland and Zimbabwe have been actively contributing to this very important undertaking, while ONUMOZ provided assistance within the scope of its mandate and resources, including transport of soldiers to training centres.

11. The transfer of authority, equipment and infrastructures from the former army to FADM started in mid-July and was formally completed on 16 August 1994. While the military premises and barracks have been accepted for takeover by FADM, information about the present condition of the equipment to be transferred is insufficient at this time. In order to become fully operational, FADM will require additional military equipment and infrastructures. Although protocol IV of the general peace agreement prescribes that the High Command of FADM shall be subordinate to the Joint Commission for the Formation of the Mozambican Defence Forces until the new Government takes office, the present division of authority between the Joint Commission and the Ministry of Defence, which continues to function, remains somewhat unclear.

12. The existence of a viable and fully operational Defence Force is an essential element of stability and security in the country. It is therefore of utmost importance that the continuation of the training of new units be encouraged in every way and that all necessary support be provided for the formation of FADM.

E. Security

13. As already noted, the security situation in Mozambique has deteriorated in recent months. Rioting among soldiers, both inside and outside assembly areas, continued to escalate until early August, when most soldiers had been or were in the process of being demobilized. At the same time, the crime level rose dramatically in both rural and urban areas. The Mozambican police is not properly equipped to control the situation. In spite of the fact that ONUMOZ has stepped up its patrolling and set up checkpoints, in particular along the routes leading from Maputo to Ressano Garcia and to Namaacha, it has so far not been possible to effectively curb the banditry.

F. Status of the military component of the United Nations Operation in Mozambique

14. In accordance with the mandate of ONUMOZ, its military contingents continue to monitor security along the corridors and main routes of the country. At the same time, increasing security problems have necessitated reinforced guarding of United Nations properties and key locations, and a number of ONUMOZ military personnel have been redeployed for this purpose. In paragraph 10 of my last report, I mentioned my intention to deploy a self-contained Brazilian infantry company in Zambézia Province. This company of 170 personnel has now been deployed and is fully operational. With the completion of the demobilization process, ONUMOZ military observers will be actively involved in verifying the demobilization, investigating complaints relating to the ceasefire, verifying weapons caches and monitoring border crossing points, as well as assisting in preparations for the elections. It is my intention, however, to start reducing in September the number of military observers from their mandated strength of 354 officers to approximately 240 before the expiration of the mandate of the mission.

15. It is obvious that the limited scope and mandate of ONUMOZ does not provide and cannot guarantee security and safety in the country. This responsibility lies with the Government, in cooperation with all the Mozambican parties. None the less, in accordance with the overall framework for the Operation (S/24892, sect. III), which was approved by the Security Council in its resolution 797 (1992) of 16 December 1992, ONUMOZ has an important role to play in assisting the Government in providing security to various activities in support of the peace process, especially in strategic routes and around vital installations. I consider it important to step up all ONUMOZ operations aimed at maintaining security and public order, particularly in the crucial period before, during and immediately after the elections. Also, more flexibility is required in the deployment of United Nations troops in order to provide wider coverage of various parts of the country. This could be an important confidence-building measure. I have instructed my Special Representative, Mr. Aldo Ajello, and the Force Commander, Major-General Mohammad Abdus Salam, in consultation with the Government, to undertake appropriate action urgently. In addition, it would be advisable to strengthen the operational capability of ONUMOZ. This includes, especially, strengthening air support resources in order to give the mission more flexibility to respond to unforeseen developments. At the same time, it might be important for the trained FADM units to start

gradual deployment to vital installations in order to ensure a smooth hand-over from ONUMOZ after the elections.

III. Police activities

16. ONUMOZ police functions are another important issue, which is closely related to confidence-building, security and the improvement of the overall political climate in the country. As of 22 August 1994, a total of 905 civilian police (CIVPOL) monitors from 26 countries had been deployed in the mission area. In addition to major cities and towns, CIVPOL has established itself in 44 field posts. However, the Mozambican police has not established its presence in many of the areas formerly controlled by RENAMO. Even in the few areas where the Mozambican police has established itself, it is often not fully operational.

17. The United Nations CIVPOL undertakes constant and extensive patrolling and frequent visits to prisons and other police installations and conducts investigations of complaints alleging political or human rights abuses. Many of the patrols are conducted jointly with the Mozambican police. As of 22 August, CIVPOL had received 91 complaints, 14 of which involved human rights violations. Investigation of 78 of the complaints has been completed, while 13 are still pending. On the basis of the CIVPOL investigations, six cases were referred to the National Commission for Police Affairs for action. Another nine cases, which emerged from independent CIVPOL patrol reports on violations committed by the Mozambican police, were also submitted to the National Commission for Police Affairs for further investigation. The cases continue to fall into three main categories: (a) illegal detention of civilians; (b) abuse of detainees' civil rights; and (c) criminal investigations involving possible political motives. It is a matter of concern that the National Commission for Police Affairs has not yet ruled on the cases referred to it by CIVPOL. Obviously, the deterrent effect of CIVPOL observation would be diluted if no corrective or preventive action follows CIVPOL investigations.

18. In coordination with the Centre for Human Rights, an extensive human rights training programme was organized for CIVPOL monitors. This was the first such programme ever provided to a United Nations civilian police observer force, and has proved very useful to CIVPOL in effectively carrying out its mandated tasks.

IV. Preparations for elections

19. Voter registration, which began on 1 June 1994, was scheduled to conclude on 15 August, but was extended initially until 20 August. The National Assembly decided on 24 August to extend the registration period until 2 September. As a result, the electoral campaign will begin on 22 September and not 12 September. A proposal by the National Elections Commission to allow registration to continue for an additional 10 days and to shorten the political campaign period accordingly is presently being considered by the National Assembly. The extension is being considered because of the serious logistical problems encountered during the initial phases of the registration process and the need to allow refugees and demobilized soldiers more time to register. As of 22 August 1994, it is estimated that a total of around 6.1 million voters had registered out of an estimated voter population of 7,894,850 people. The National Elections Commission lowered the initial estimate of 8.5 million eligible voters, which was based on the 1980 census and was considered inaccurate. At the same time, the National Elections Commission was unable to reach an agreement on voting arrangements for Mozambican citizens living abroad. On 8 August 1994, codes of conduct for presidential candidates and for political parties and rules on access to the State media were approved by the National Elections Commission.

20. During the registration process, voter education was carried out almost exclusively at registration sites by Mozambican civic education personnel. Some voter education activities were undertaken by local and international non-governmental organizations. However, the need for information and education on the electoral process is far greater than what is presently being provided. The National Elections Commission is in need of additional assistance in order to establish efficient public education programmes, including by means of radio broadcasts. ONUMOZ is actively working with the Government and potential donors in this regard.

21. Technical errors in the registration process, such as the improper filling in of registration forms, registration books and voter cards, occurred frequently during the initial phases of the process, resulting in a number of complaints. The irregularities were found to be the result mainly of inadequate experience or training of registration personnel, and were largely overcome when the Technical Secretariat for Electoral Administration issued a series of directives providing guidance to the more than 1,600 registration teams. ONUMOZ is monitoring the electoral registration process with some 120 observers, who continually visit and verify various registration sites. Some political parties, particularly RENAMO, have raised allegations of fraud in the electoral process. Complaints included allegations of using false identification, registration of minors and foreigners, embezzlement of electoral funds, as well as using propaganda to discredit opponents. In many cases, these alle-

gations appeared in the media without proper submission of formal complaints to the National Elections Commission. Most of the complaints, including those investigated independently by ONUMOZ, have not been substantiated.

22. In paragraph 21 of my last report to the Security Council, I noted that certain conditions essential for the holding of free and fair elections had not been met. I am pleased to report that since then, voter registration teams have gained access to all RENAMO-controlled districts. However, logistical problems still exist in areas of difficult accessibility, but these are in the process of being overcome. Unimpeded access by all parties to all areas of the country must be guaranteed.

23. In paragraph 22 of the same report, I drew the attention of the Security Council to a shortfall of US$ 3.8 million in the technical assistance funding for the electoral process. The total budget for this assistance has been increased slightly to US$ 60 million, resulting in a shortfall of US$ 5 million. I reiterate my appeal to donors to bridge this gap in order that preparations for the elections may proceed on schedule. In the meantime, the trust fund for the political parties has now been fully established. Criteria for the disbursement of the fund, as well as procedures for its management, were developed in close consultation with the political parties, the donors and ONUMOZ. Of the total pledges of US$ 3.54 million, only US$ 1.88 million have been received so far, and I urge the donor community to honour their pledges in order to assist all political parties, especially those which are not signatories to the peace agreement, to organize and prepare themselves for active participation in the forthcoming elections. On 19 August 1994, a first disbursement of US$ 50,000 was made to each of the 16 political parties.

24. I also wish to draw the attention of the Security Council to the shortfall in contributions for the trust fund for implementation of the general peace agreement in Mozambique. This fund was established to provide assistance to RENAMO, as one of the parties to the Rome Agreement, in its transition from an armed movement to a political party. Of the US$ 14.6 million already pledged to the fund, which is less than originally expected, only US$ 13.6 million have been received. I appeal to the donors to continue to contribute to this fund.

25. Voting on the election days will take place at about 8,000 polling stations connected in groups to 1,600 polling sites. In order to guarantee the credibility of the electoral process, it is important for the international observation to be as extensive as possible. As requested, the United Nations will undertake sample monitoring. For the actual polling and counting of votes, the United Nations intends to deploy 1,200 electoral observers, as initially planned. However, only 900 observers are covered by the ONUMOZ budget. The remainder will be drawn from existing ONUMOZ staff. The United Nations electoral personnel will be complemented by additional observers provided by Member States, various international organizations, including the European Union and the Association of West European Parliamentarians, and various non-governmental organizations. ONUMOZ intends to coordinate all external verification activities in order to avoid duplication or gaps in the observation process.

26. The most effective way to enhance the credibility of the elections is to ensure that the Mozambican political parties themselves participate extensively in the electoral observation process. Most of the smaller parties, however, do not have the capacity to participate in verification on a large scale. To this end, the parties will need technical and financial support from the donor community. Pledges towards the funding of this important endeavour have already been made by the European Community and the United States Agency for International Development (USAID). A programme aimed at strengthening the capacities of the political parties is presently being developed by ONUMOZ in consultation with donors. I appeal to the international community to provide financial resources for the implementation of this important endeavour.

V. Humanitarian assistance programme

27. The implementation of humanitarian activities continues to proceed along the lines described in my previous report. About 75 per cent of the estimated 3.7 million persons who were internally displaced at the time of signature of the general peace agreement have now been resettled. There are still an estimated 342,000 refugees in neighbouring countries who are expected to return to Mozambique by the end of 1994. The Office of the United Nations High Commissioner for Refugees (UNHCR) has initiated projects aimed at improving living conditions in areas where the returnees are concentrated. These projects are being implemented by non-governmental organizations. With the participation of the International Committee of the Red Cross, Save the Children Fund-United Kingdom, the International Organization for Migration and the World Food Programme, assistance is now being provided in ex-RENAMO areas to children and youths with war experience. Under the overall coordination of the United Nations Children's Fund and the United Nations Office for Humanitarian Assistance Coordination, this assistance is provided to the children while they are in transit centres and will continue until they are reunited with their families.

28. The Reintegration Commission recently approved the creation of a provincial fund to provide small- and medium-sized grants for the employment of ex-soldiers.

The fund will also facilitate their participation in community-based economic activities. With the creation of the provincial fund, the reintegration programme for demobilized soldiers now has four main components. The other three are: the reintegration support scheme, which provides each demobilized soldier with an 18-month subsidy in addition to six months of pay upon demobilization; career counselling and problem-solving services; and the occupational skills development programme, which coordinates reintegration and training programmes and helps provide access to employment opportunities.

29. As I indicated to the Security Council in previous reports, I have been concerned over the inordinate delays experienced in the implementation of the United Nations mine-clearance programme, which comprises four components: the national mines survey, the clearing of mines along 2,000 kilometres of priority roads, the establishment of the Mine-clearance Training Centre and the creation of a national de-mining capacity. The total cost of this programme is US$ 18.5 million, which is met through an allocation of US$ 11 million from within the ONUMOZ budget and by contributions to the trust fund for de-mining activities totalling US$ 7.5 million. At the beginning of 1993, the United Nations Development Programme/Office for Project Services (UNDP/OPS) was given the responsibility of managing the de-mining programme, including the implementation of the survey and the clearing of priority roads, for which US$ 14 million had been allocated. A separate allocation of some US$ 3 million was made for the establishment and operation of the Mine-clearing Training Centre.

30. In view of the concern of the Security Council and my own concern regarding the disappointing pace of implementation of the United Nations mine-clearance programme, I had assured the Council that every effort would be made to accelerate the programme. In May 1994, a plan to accelerate the implementation of the mine-clearance programme was put into place. This programme includes the strengthening of the Mine-clearance Training Centre, the training of Mozambican de-miners, supervisors and instructors, and the creation of a national de-mining authority by November 1994. In order to facilitate the timely implementation of the accelerated programme, the United Nations Office for Humanitarian Assistance Coordination has been reinforced by additional specialized staff dedicated solely to de-mining issues.

31. The national mine survey, which was undertaken by a British non-governmental organization, Halo Trust, has now been completed. The information from this survey has provided the basis for the individual reports of the United Nations Office for Humanitarian Assistance Coordination on mines in the 10 provinces of Mozambique. The UNDP/OPS-implemented project to de-mine 2,000 kilometres of priority roads finally commenced in July 1994. To date, 209 kilometres of roads in Manica Province have been cleared. De-mining activities are also being undertaken by Norwegian People's Aid in Maputo Province, by Halo Trust in Zambézia Province and by Ronco, a USAID contractor, in Sofala Province.

32. Following the decision to move the Mine-clearance Training Centre to a permanent site in Tete, the rehabilitation of the proposed facilities began in mid-June. Although it was originally envisaged that the Centre would become operational by the first week of August, it was not possible to complete the rehabilitation work on time. To date, 119 Mozambican de-miners have been trained by the Centre. In order to accelerate the training programme, the Centre began offering two courses simultaneously, for 60 students each, on 23 August 1994. By the end of November 1994, it is expected that the overall target of training 450 de-miners will have been achieved. The trained Mozambican de-miners will work under the leadership of contracted expatriate supervisors. The first group of expatriate supervisors have arrived and two de-mining teams comprised of trained Mozambican de-miners have been formed. These teams will commence de-mining activities within selected areas of Maputo Province in September 1994. It is expected that at the end of May 1995, Mozambican supervisors trained at the Centre will replace the expatriate supervisors, with additional practical training being provided to them to ensure that adequate competence and safety standards are achieved.

33. The implementation of the de-mining programme will clearly have to continue well beyond the mandate of ONUMOZ. At present, the United Nations Office for Humanitarian Assistance Coordination is performing a number of coordination and management functions. However, proposals regarding the contracting of an organization to provide management training to enable Mozambicans to assume these functions are currently being considered. In addition, consultations are in progress with all concerned in an effort to reach agreement on the most suitable coordination and financing mechanisms to ensure continuity of the de-mining programme after the departure of ONUMOZ.

VI. Closure of the United Nations Operation in Mozambique and withdrawal of civilian and military personnel

34. The Security Council, by its resolution 916 (1994), extended the mandate of ONUMOZ for a final period until 15 November 1994 at the strength described in paragraphs 22, 24 and 25 of my report of 28 April 1994 (S/1994/511). As I noted in paragraph 35 of my last report (S/1994/803), the withdrawal of ONUMOZ civil-

ian and military personnel will begin immediately after the elections and is scheduled to be concluded by the end of January 1995. It will be recalled that in accordance with protocol III of the general peace agreement, the presence of ONUMOZ would be required until such time as the new Government takes office. Thus, the planned withdrawal would obviously depend on: (a) the holding of peaceful, as well as free and fair, elections on 27 and 28 October 1994; (b) the timely announcement of the election results no later than 12 November 1994; and (c) the timely establishment of a new Government. Furthermore, should a second ballot be required for the election of the President, adjustments in the withdrawal schedule might be required.

35. Paragraphs 36 and 37 of my last report also presented a detailed description of various departure schedules. However, after further review of logistic and administrative conditions, slight changes have been introduced to the withdrawal phase of some components. In particular, it is intended that the withdrawal of the staff of the humanitarian component should begin immediately after the elections and be completed by the end of November. By that time, all humanitarian activities extending beyond the mandate of ONUMOZ would be transferred to the Government and/or to other United Nations organizations and agencies.

36. The international electoral observers will depart the mission area immediately after the elections. The withdrawal of the international officers of the ONUMOZ Electoral Division and the United Nations volunteer monitors will commence immediately after the elections; the majority of them will leave after the election results are published and the elections are officially declared free and fair.

37. The withdrawal of ONUMOZ police observers is planned to take place in three phases. Phase one will start on 10 November 1994, when a total of 652 monitors will be withdrawn from various posts throughout the country. Phase two will start on 18 November, when 292 monitors will be withdrawn from the provincial and regional headquarters. Phase three will start on 25 November and will be completed by mid-December, when the 200 monitors at the regional and central headquarters will be withdrawn.

38. The reduction in strength of the ONUMOZ military component will begin on 15 November 1994, as previously planned. The tentative withdrawal schedule now stands as follows: the Bangladesh contingent will depart between 25 November and 12 December 1994; the Botswana contingent on 8 December 1994; the Brazilian company on 27 and 28 November 1994; the Uruguayan contingent from 29 November to 11 December 1994; and the Zambian battalion from 4 to 13 December 1994. The withdrawal of the support units, namely, the Japanese movement control, the Portuguese signals battalion, the Indian headquarters company and the Argentine and Italian hospitals, will begin on 28 November and be completed by the end of December 1994. Until the final closure of the mission by the end of January 1995, only a limited number of civilian logisticians, military specialists, staff officers and a small detachment of infantry to provide security protection to United Nations personnel and property would remain in the country.

VII. Observations

39. The significant progress achieved in the implementation of the peace process in Mozambique since I last reported to the Security Council has been encouraging. With the imminent conclusion of the demobilization of troops, the peace process has reached its final phase—the preparations for and the conduct of the elections. The electoral process itself is progressing well. The most significant role of the United Nations during the next two months will involve technical preparations for elections and assistance in bringing about the conditions necessary for the holding of free and fair elections, as well as in the creation of an environment conducive to a stable and peaceful transition to a democratically elected Government. By all indications, the necessary conditions exist for holding the elections in Mozambique as scheduled.

40. While much will depend on the political will of the Mozambican people and the parties to achieve this goal, a great deal remains to be accomplished in order to ensure that the elections lead to political stability. The Mozambican parties might wish to explore, prior to the elections, the possibility of concluding an arrangement that would enable opposition parties to play a legitimate and meaningful role in the post-electoral period. Such an arrangement could also facilitate the establishment of a government that would ensure the consolidation of peace, political stability and national reconciliation.

41. The transition period that lies ahead for Mozambique will not be an easy one. It will require, above all, statesmanship and a commitment to accommodate various interests. It will be equally important to ensure secure and stable conditions in the country. This will call for a determined effort to continue training and properly equipping a new national army and to upgrade the national police. While the primary responsibilities in this regard rest with the Government, I trust that present and potential donors will provide assistance in those important areas, even after the elections.

42. With the generous assistance of donors, considerable progress has been made in implementing humanitarian programmes in Mozambique. In addition to helping alleviate the suffering of large numbers of vulnerable and disadvantaged persons, the impartial and equitable delivery of humanitarian assistance is contributing

to the overall efforts to achieve national reconciliation after many years of civil war. With the completion of the demobilization of Government and RENAMO soldiers, the implementation of various programmes for the reintegration of demobilized soldiers will be able to proceed more speedily. The progress finally being made in the de-mining programme is overdue but points in the right direction. Bearing in mind the long-term nature of the problem, it will be essential for appropriate financial and other forms of assistance to be provided to the Government to continue with mine-clearance activities after the termination of the mandate of ONUMOZ. I consider it of critical importance that adequate arrangements be put in place for the coordination of all humanitarian and rehabilitation programmes during the transition phase after the departure of ONUMOZ. In this connection, consultations will be held between the United Nations Office for Humanitarian Assistance Coordination and United Nations agencies as well as with the Government and donors to ensure the effective implementation of humanitarian programmes. On the basis of these consultations, proposals will be drawn up for my consideration.

43. I have often stressed that it was up to the people of Mozambique and their leaders to make a determined effort to ensure the full and timely implementation of the Rome agreement and to bring about national reconciliation in the country. I have also urged the international community to continue to contribute generously to various funds and activities aimed at achieving a stable and lasting peace in the country. As the peace process approaches its final leg, it will be incumbent upon all concerned in Mozambique to redouble their efforts to ensure that the elections are conducted in a free and fair manner and that the transitional period promotes national reconciliation and stability. I should also like to remind all parties, once again, of their obligation to respect the results of the elections. The United Nations, for its part, is determined to continue actively to pursue the full implementation of the Rome agreement and to facilitate the efforts of the people of Mozambique to bring it to a successful conclusion.

44. I would like to pay tribute to the dedication and professionalism of the staff of ONUMOZ, in particular to my Special Representative and the Force Commander, in carrying out the challenging tasks entrusted to them.

Document 70

Report of the Security Council Mission to Mozambique of 7 to 12 August 1994

S/1994/1009, 29 August 1994

We, the members of the Security Council Mission established pursuant to the statement made by the President of the Security Council at the 3406th meeting, held on 19 July 1994 (S/PRST/1994/35), have the honour to submit to you herewith the report called for in item (g) of the terms of reference of the Mission set out in the Note by the President of the Security Council dated 4 August 1994 (S/1994/931).

(*Signed*) Ronaldo Mota SARDENBERG (Brazil)

(*Signed*) YANG Xiuping (China)

(*Signed*) Karel KOVANDA (Czech Republic)

(*Signed*) Roble OLHAYE (Djibouti)

(*Signed*) Patrick John RATA (New Zealand)

(*Signed*) Ibrahim A. GAMBARI (Nigeria)
(Chairman)

(*Signed*) Salim Bin Mohammed AL-KHUSSAIBY (Oman)

(*Signed*) Vasiliy S. SIDOROV (Russian Federation)

(*Signed*) Karl F. INDERFURTH (United States of America)

. . .

II. Activities of the Mission

3. The Mission of the Security Council established pursuant to the statement made by the President on 19 July 1994 (S/PRST/1994/35) visited Mozambique from 7 to 12 August 1994, beginning its work in Mozambique on the morning of 8 August.

4. The Mission carried out its work in accordance with the terms of reference decided upon by the Security Council, as contained in the note by the President of the Council (S/1994/931).

5. The Mission's programme of work (see annex I) included meetings with Mr. Joaquim Alberto Chissano, President of the Republic of Mozambique and President of the Frente de Libertação Moçambique (FRELIMO), Mr. Afonso Macacho Marceta Dhlakama, President of the Resistência Nacional Moçambicana (RENAMO), Mr. Pascoal Manuel Mocumbi, Minister for Foreign Affairs of Mozambique, representatives of 16 other registered parties (see annex II), Mr. Aldo Ajello, Special

Representative of the Secretary-General, senior staff of the United Nations Operation in Mozambique (ONUMOZ), heads of government delegations to the peace commissions, the heads of RENAMO delegations to the peace commissions, the Chairman of the National Elections Commission, international members of the peace commissions and ambassadors of Security Council member countries (see annex III), ambassadors of African countries, the representative of the Organization of African Unity (OAU), and representatives of the National Police Affairs Commission, the National Information Commission, the National Commission for Territorial Administration and the United Nations High Commissioner for Refugees (UNHCR).

6. The Mission observed voter registration at a typical registration centre at Matalene. It visited the Training Centre of the New Mozambican Defence Force (FADM) at Manhica and the Mine-clearance Training Centre at Tete. It observed demobilization in RENAMO assembly areas in Nhamacala, at the government assembly area at Chimoio and at General Staff Headquarters at Maputo, where it witnessed the demobilization of President Chissano and other high-ranking government officers. One member of the Mission visited assembly areas and ONUMOZ sections at Mocuba.

7. The Mission touched on all issues affecting the implementation of the general peace agreement, including demobilization, formation of the new army (FADM), issues relating to the elections, security problems in the country before, during and after the elections, humanitarian and refugee issues, mine clearance, the relationship between ONUMOZ and the Government and the role of ONUMOZ after the elections and beyond 15 November. The Mission also heard various requests for assistance.

III. The situation on the ground

A. *Demobilization*

8. In accordance with its terms of reference, the Mission stressed to all interlocutors the necessity of completing the demobilization of all forces by 15 August 1994, as agreed by the parties.

9. The deadline for the demobilization of the Mozambican Armed Forces (FAM) was 15 August 1994. The process of the assembly of troops has concluded and demobilization is expected to be completed shortly.

10. After a number of serious riots and mutinies by soldiers kept for very long periods of time at assembly areas and unassembled locations, on the part of both the Government and RENAMO, owing to delays in the demobilization process, towards the end of July the Government and RENAMO allowed the soldiers themselves to choose between joining the new army and demobiliza-

tion. The great majority of the soldiers chose demobilization and the reintegration support scheme financed by the Government and the international donor community, which is intended to facilitate their reintegration into normal civilian life. Under that plan, the soldiers receive six months of salary from the Government and 18 months' subsidy at salary level from the fund established by the international donor community. The very high degree of demobilization has thus had a negative impact on the number of soldiers available for integration into the new army.

11. Very interestingly, however, a key opposition figure expressed the view that, after the elections, the current lack of sufficient recruits for the new army could be expected to correct itself. In his opinion, having exercised their option for demobilization, severance pay, and the 18-month subsidy at salary level, these ex-soldiers would still be free to return after elections and resume their military careers. This should, it is hoped, enable FADM to achieve at least the target of 15,000 troops relatively quickly.

12. As at 28 August 1994, a total of 70,086 soldiers (52,242 Government and 17,844 RENAMO) had been demobilized and 9,917 were in the process of being demobilized (7,662 on the Government side and 2,250 from RENAMO); 1,624 troops were still in the assembly area, pending resolution of questions relating to their documentation.

B. *New army*

13. Both President Chissano and Mr. Dhlakama stressed the need to have an effective army in place, preferably by the time of the elections. The general peace agreement envisaged the formation of a 30,000-strong unified army before the elections, with 50 per cent of the personnel to be provided by the Government and 50 per cent by RENAMO. However, following delays in cantonment, assembly and demobilization, ONUMOZ proposed that the number of troops to be integrated into FADM before the elections be reduced to 15,000 (to the level covered by the existing training programmes), and to recruit the remainder later. While there was no formal agreement on this proposal, as a result of the riots and mutinies and the low number of FAM soldiers and RENAMO combatants choosing to join the new army, both parties are now prepared to move forward to the elections with whatever the number might be and to deal with the recruitment of the remainder thereafter. As at 28 August 1994, 7,398 had joined the new army. Of this figure, approximately 6,482 soldiers have already been or are being trained.

14. As announced by President Chissano at the 12 August 1994 ceremony for his demobilization as

Commander-in-Chief, and that of other senior officers of FAM, a public ceremony was held on 16 August 1994 for the termination of FAM. In accordance with the general peace agreement, all authority, equipment and structures of FAM were to be transferred to FADM.

15. The Joint Commission for the Formation of the Mozambican Defence Force is responsible for the formation of FADM until the new Government takes office, after which FADM is to be placed under the authority of the Ministry of Defence. The responsibilities of the existing Ministry of Defence until the new Government takes office will have to be clarified.

16. The new army, FADM, lacks necessary funds and equipment, and will not be operational unless these are provided. The Mission was informed that the equipment of the old army was in the process of being transferred to the new army but that a large proportion of it is in poor condition. The weapons of the demobilizing soldiers and combatants were being collected. Some arms caches have been discovered. FADM needs additional equipment and infrastructure.

17. An area of concern is the training capability for the new army following the reduction in the strength of ONUMOZ. The assistance of the international community in building the new army has been requested by both the Government and RENAMO.

18. It was also pointed out that the army could be called upon to play a role in the regional security arrangements currently being discussed and that it would be desirable for it to be trained also for peace-keeping purposes.

19. The Mission has been informed that the Special Representative of the Secretary-General witnessed the demobilization of Mr. Dhlakama at a RENAMO demobilization ceremony held at Meringue on 19 August 1994.

C. *Registration*

20. The Mission was informed that there are an estimated 7.8 million eligible voters in Mozambique, of whom 6.1 million had been registered as at 20 August 1994. But many refugees have not yet returned.

21. The Mission was also informed that, until recently, there had been a limited number of registration brigades and a lack of free movement in the RENAMO-controlled areas because of their slow integration into the civil administration and the existence of land-mines. RENAMO stressed the need to ensure that as many eligible voters as possible are registered.

22. The deadline for registration for all persons was initially extended by five days to 20 August 1994, originally the deadline for special cases only. Under the Electoral Law, extension of the registration period by the competent authorities could not go beyond 12 September 1994, when the election campaign was to have begun. However, by the calculations of the National Elections Commission, the registration period could be extended by no more than five days in order to allow for the conduct of procedures concerning the publication of the results of the census and any challenges thereto. Subsequently, the Mission was informed that, on 23 August 1994, the National Assembly decided to extend the registration period until 2 September 1994.

23. The National Elections Commission decided to intensify the registration process, utilizing existing means. It is, however, experiencing logistical problems, including communications and transportation difficulties. Quick means of transportation, including helicopters, are needed to reach all parts of the country. In a country with a scattered population, there are only two daily newspapers with less than 15,000 copies circulating in two cities, and only two radio stations. The Mission was informed that approximately 5 million persons were expected to vote.

24. The Mission was informed that there was no province or district where registration had not begun but that registration had commenced late in RENAMO-controlled zones.

25. The Mission heard concerns expressed in several quarters about alleged registration irregularities and the fear of election irregularities. Not only must the elections be declared by the United Nations to have been free and fair, they must also be perceived as having been free and fair.

D. *Elections*

26. In accordance with its terms of reference, the Mission stressed to all interlocutors the need for the parties to ensure that the elections take place on the dates agreed and under the conditions set out in the agreement. The Mission reminded the parties of their obligation under the general peace agreement to respect fully the results of the elections, and stressed the intention of the Security Council to endorse the results of the elections provided the United Nations declared them free and fair.

27. President Chissano and Mr. Dhlakama indicated their commitment to holding the elections on 27 and 28 October 1994, as scheduled.

28. The Mission obtained the assurances of the parties of their commitment to the peace process, to the election dates, and to accepting the results of the elections if they are declared free and fair. Mr. Dhlakama stated that the most important thing for RENAMO was the fulfilment of the democratic process and for all parties to make an effort to see that the result was a happy one.

29. Inasmuch as there is the political will to transcend problems, it is the view of the Mission that the elections will be held and the results respected.

30. The difficulties encountered in connection with the elections must be solved. Free access by all the parties to all areas in accordance with the general peace agreement will be necessary so that the elections may be held under acceptable conditions. Concern was raised in several quarters regarding lack of access to areas under RENAMO control for election purposes.

31. Some members of the international community strongly recommend that some form of political accommodation be agreed upon before the elections. Others believe that what is required is a political understanding between the leading parties to the effect that the democratic rules will continue to be observed after the elections are held. It was pointed out that the Government does not support the idea of a Government of national unity. However, it did not rule out the inclusion in the Government of personalities in their individual capacities.

32. In order to ensure a satisfactory level of observation of the elections by the United Nations, it is important that the international community agree to provide a high number of international observers, Mozambique being a vast country, with elections scheduled to take place at about 8,000 polling stations connected in groups to 1,600 polling sites. This effort will be complemented by observers from the Mozambican political parties. In order to strengthen the capacity of these parties to participate in the observation efforts, a programme is being worked out to provide training and financial and logistical support.

E. Civic and voter education

33. The Chairman of the National Elections Commission stressed that in order for the elections to be successful, a strong civic and voter education campaign will have to be undertaken, as well as adequate monitoring of the elections, with representatives of all parties participating fully in the monitoring.

34. The National Elections Commission is in need of assistance to facilitate efficient communication, which will be critical during the elections. Radio and television spots were being utilized but radio reaches less than 30 per cent of the population. The Mission was informed that there were radio transmission problems. ONUMOZ has requested Japan, which had reached agreement with the Government of Mozambique to improve radio broadcasting facilities, to try to boost the transmission capability temporarily. Germany is providing a radio station to RENAMO.

35. As the view was expressed that the elections would not necessarily bring peace, the Mission believes that there is a need to include a component equating elections to peace in the civil education radio programmes.

36. The Mission stressed to all interlocutors that the goal of the peace process is to bring democracy, permanent peace, political stability, real freedom of the press and responsible government to Mozambique.

F. Financing of the parties

37. RENAMO informed the Mission that it needed additional financial means to assist it in connection with the elections. The Mission was informed that not all pledges to the Trust Fund for Implementation of the General Peace Agreement in Mozambique (RENAMO Trust Fund) had been honoured. Of the US$ 14.6 million already pledged only $13.6 million had been received, all of which had been expended. RENAMO also indicated that the European Union had approved funds but that these had not yet been released because of procedural difficulties.

38. The 16 smaller political parties also stressed the need to receive adequate financial support in order to enable them to engage fully in the election process. The Mission has been informed that each of them has now received $50,000 as a first payment from the Trust Fund for the political parties.

G. Security problems in the country before, during and after the elections

39. The deterioration of the security situation throughout the country before, during and immediately after the elections raises serious concern. The Chairman of the National Elections Commission stressed that it was important that the electoral campaign be assured of security and freedom of movement throughout the country.

40. The country will be going into the elections without a fully constituted and properly equipped army. The police are weak, poorly trained and lack the right equipment. On the other hand, thousands of soldiers, whose only skill is the use of weapons, have been demobilized and are without alternative employment. Armed banditry is spreading, especially in the countryside, and the situation may become critical.

41. Under the Chissano-Dhlakama agreement of 3 September 1993, and in accordance with the main principles governing the general peace agreement, the parties agreed to request the United Nations to send a contingent of police, inter alia, to monitor all police activities in the country, to monitor respect for the rights and liberties of Mozambican citizens throughout the country, and to provide technical support to the National Commission for Police Affairs. By resolution 898 (1994), the Security Council authorized the establishment of a United Nations police component as an integral part of ONUMOZ.

42. The Mozambican police is not adequately equipped to deal with public security. There is further

need for international assistance in the field of training and equipping of the Mozambican police.

43. Under the general peace agreement, private and irregular armed groups, which had been formed to fight alongside the government forces against RENAMO, should have been disarmed before the completion of the demobilization process. The Mission was informed that the process of the collection of their weapons is under way. RENAMO raised the question of the need to disband the armed militias before the elections.

H. *Humanitarian and refugee issues*

44. By Security Council resolution 797 (1992), the United Nations Office for Humanitarian Assistance Coordination was transformed into the humanitarian component of ONUMOZ. Humanitarian needs of Mozambique for the period 1992 to 1994 have been estimated at $616 million. The Mission was informed that 87 per cent, or $536 million, of that amount had been made available through the generosity of the international community.

45. The Mission was informed that the humanitarian activities coordinated by the United Nations Office for Humanitarian Assistance Coordination in sectors such as health and agriculture are designed and implemented in a manner intended to cater to the needs of all beneficiary groups, including returnees, internally displaced persons and the demobilized. However, for the demobilized there have been additional and specific programmes designed to facilitate their reintegration into civilian society. These include the Reintegration Support Scheme, a programme for developing occupational skills, a provincial fund to provide small and medium-sized grants for the employment of demobilized soldiers and facilitate their participation in community-based economic activities, and career counselling and problem-solving services.

46. The Mission was also informed that in accordance with the Joint Declaration on the Guiding Principles for Humanitarian Assistance annexed to the general peace agreement, the United Nations Office for Humanitarian Assistance Coordination has also sought to ensure that humanitarian assistance is provided to all who are in need, including those residing in RENAMO-controlled areas. One function of the Office has been to open up the country and currently 40 non-governmental organizations are working in ex-RENAMO areas where formerly only the International Committee of the Red Cross and the World Food Programme operated.

47. The Mission was informed that some 342,000 refugees are still outside Mozambique and that the internally displaced persons who have yet to re-establish themselves in their home areas number 900,000. These facts, together with the continuation of drought conditions in significant areas of Mozambique, suggest that emergency humanitarian assistance will be needed beyond 1994.

48. The social and economic situation in Mozambique is very critical. Changes following in the wake of the peace process, including demobilization and the return of refugees and displaced persons, are increasing social instability. The humanitarian assistance programmes are too limited to address the scope of the problem. In particular, the demobilized could become a source of social unrest for a long time to come. This issue must be carefully reviewed and ways of assisting the present and the new Government in addressing the problem beyond the boundaries of the humanitarian assistance component and the ONUMOZ mandate will have to be sought.

49. The Mission was informed that as a result of an accelerated repatriation of Mozambican refugees nearly 1.1 million refugees had returned by the end of July 1994. It is expected that a further 200,000 will return during September and October 1994, though this will be too late for them to be enfranchised. In June 1994, UNHCR requested, on a humanitarian basis, that the deadline for voter registration of returning refugees be exceptionally extended to as close as possible to the election dates.

I. *Mine clearance*

50. The Mission was informed that there are an estimated 1 million to 2 million mines in Mozambique, spread over some 9,000 areas. The Security Council has stressed in past resolutions the importance it attaches to progress in mine clearance and related training in Mozambique.

51. The Mission was briefed by the Special Representative of the Secretary-General, the Director of the United Nations Office for Humanitarian Assistance Coordination, and other ONUMOZ personnel on the United Nations mine-clearance programme in Mozambique. The programme, which was initiated in 1993, comprises the following components: a National Mine Survey, clearance of mines from 2,000 kilometres of priority roads and the establishment of a Mine Clearance Training Centre. Activities carried out within these components are intended to contribute to the creation of a national mine-clearance capability. The $18.5 million cost of the mine-clearance programme is met from a specific allocation within the ONUMOZ budget ($11 million), and by contributions from the Department of Humanitarian Affairs Trust Fund for De-mining Activities ($7.5 million).

52. Substantial delays in the implementation of

aspects of the mine-clearance programme, and the state of the programme generally, were a source of dismay to the Mission. While the National Mine Survey has been largely completed, there has been only limited progress in the clearing of priority roads, and the Mine-clearance Training Centre is still not fully operational. The Mission was especially concerned to learn during a visit to the Training Centre at Tete that the Centre was experiencing difficulty attracting Mozambican trainees. The lack of resources at the Centre, including such basics as a reliable water supply and medical support unit, was also a cause of concern.

53. An accelerated United Nations programme aimed at creating a domestic mine-clearance capability is now operational in Mozambique. It has the following specific objectives:

(a) Clearance of mines from the 2,000 kilometres of priority roads;

(b) Strengthening of the Mine-clearance Training Centre in order to train 450 Mozambican mine clearers to be deployed in 15 platoons by November 1994;

(c) Building of a supervisory and management structure to cover both field operations and middle management;

(d) Development of a mine survey capability and the training of Mozambican supervisors, instructors and staff for the Mine-clearance Training Centre.

54. The financing of the programme beyond November 1994 deserves serious consideration as the Government of Mozambique is unlikely to be in a position to finance the programme on a long-term basis.

55. A dispensation was being sought by the United Nations Office for Humanitarian Assistance Coordination from United Nations Headquarters to leave the mine-clearing equipment behind.

J. *Requests for assistance*

56. The Mission heard a variety of requests for assistance, which included the following:

(a) The Government would like additional support from the international community in providing the subsidies for the demobilized soldiers;

(b) The Government requested assistance from the international community to equip and train the new army, including with respect to logistics and rehabilitation centres;

(c) The Government requested assistance in the training and equipping of the police force;

(d) The National Elections Commission requested funding for the recruitment of voter registration brigades for deployment in ex-RENAMO areas; additional logistical support, for example, vehicles, aircraft and efficient means of communication throughout the country; assist-

ance to provide civil and voter education; and tents for electoral observers.

K. *The relationship between ONUMOZ and the Government*

57. It was clear to the Mission that there was a certain amount of friction between the Government and ONUMOZ, essentially because of the complexity of the situation in Mozambique. It is in the interest of the parties to ensure that the credibility of ONUMOZ is preserved. The Special Representative of the Secretary-General is of the view that the situation of ONUMOZ benefited from the visit of the Mission.

58. ONUMOZ is pressing to realize the goals of completing its mandate in a timely manner and contributing to the achievement of a successful democratic process. Its energy has lent it a high profile and led to some resentment, to which it should remain sensitive. With events moving rapidly, the Government has occasionally felt overlooked, unconsulted, and even blamed for delays. Overall, ONUMOZ maintains a good level of cooperation with all the parties, including the Government, but must remain sensitive to those perceptions. The situation appears to be under control.

L. *ONUMOZ after the elections and beyond 15 November 1994*

59. Some members of the Mission requested the Special Representative of the Secretary-General to look into the question of which ONUMOZ elements scheduled to be reduced in strength could be kept on until after the elections.

60. Given the manner in which political, security, election and humanitarian events are converging rapidly to a resolution, the Mission felt that ONUMOZ could play a larger, more visible security role in this final period, particularly on the election days. With the lingering tensions and the novelty of elections, every effort must be made to prevent problems. ONUMOZ must deploy its high visibility straight through the election days and, in part, beyond. The United Nations should also have a post-election presence, to be phased out according to the dictates of the near-term situation.

61. In the view of the Government, the United Nations needs to assist Mozambique through a transitional period with a view to its institutional framework becoming fully operational when ONUMOZ ends, so as to ensure that the local framework is capable of effective governance.

IV. Observations and recommendations

62. The Mission formed a positive impression of the pace of the peace process. It maintains a cautious optimism about its prospects.

63. The Mission was satisfied with the pace of demobilization. It noted, however, difficulties relating to the formation of FADM. It emphasizes the importance of a complete transfer of all FAM *matériel* to FADM. The Mission notes the importance of international support for the reintegration programmes for demobilized soldiers. There are problems of resources, in connection with which the parties have appealed to the international community.

64. The Mission is encouraged by the commitment of the parties to hold the elections as scheduled.

65. The Mission believes every effort must be made to ensure the registration process reaches all Mozambicans throughout the country. All zones of the country must be completely open to all citizens in every phase of the electoral process. Training and logistical support will need to be increased to ensure an adequate number of electoral observers. Party observers will require technical assistance. Allegations of electoral irregularities must be submitted through formal channels and acted on expeditiously. There is a need for donor support to meet shortfalls in the electoral budget.

66. The Mission recommends that the Security Council reiterate its call on the parties to respect the results of the elections once declared free and fair by the international community. The Security Council could further encourage the parties to reach an understanding that will promote post-electoral stability and harmony and respect for the rules of democracy.

67. If there was one area of disappointment in an otherwise successful mission, it was that of mine clearance, which was late in starting and has made little progress. This must be rectified, with proper machinery put in place. There should be no attempt whatsoever to disrupt the programme, or to transfer existing resources to another operation. The Mission recommends that the mine-clearing equipment remain in the country.

68. The Mission recommends that the international community assist Mozambique with additional trainers for FADM.

69. The Mission recognizes that the political, social and economic future of the country is entirely dependent on the willingness of the Mozambicans themselves to complete the peace process successfully. At the same time, Mozambique is in dire need of the support of the international community as it continues implementation of the peace process.

70. The Mission was impressed by the dedication, energy and hard work of all the ONUMOZ personnel it encountered. The Mission expresses its thanks to the Special Representative of the Secretary-General for the excellent support given to it in its work.

Annex I

Visit of the Security Council to Mozambique
(7-12 August 1994)

PROGRAMME

Sunday, 7 August

1625 hrs	Arrival at Johannesburg
1700 hrs	Departure from Johannesburg for Maputo
1830 hrs	Arrival at Maputo airport: Mission met by the Special Representative of the Secretary-General

Monday, 8 August

0800 - 0845 hrs	Mission working breakfast
0900 - 1030 hrs	Briefing by the Special Representative of the Secretary-General
1030 - 1145 hrs	International members of the Supervisory and Monitoring Commission
1200 - 1300 hrs	Mr. Pascoal M. Mocumbi, Minister for Foreign Affairs (Ministry of Foreign Affairs)
1315 - 1445 hrs	Lunch
1500 - 1600 hrs	Heads of government delegations to the peace commissions
1630 - 1730 hrs	Heads of RENAMO delegations to the peace commissions
1900 - 2130 hrs	Reception at Polana Hotel hosted by the Ambassador of Nigeria to Mozambique and Mrs. I. J. Udoyen

Tuesday, 9 August

0900 - 1015 hrs	President Chissano (President's office)
1030 - 1145 hrs	Mr. A. Dhlakama (residence of Mr. Dhlakama)
1200 - 1245 hrs	Mr. B. Mazula, Chairman of the National Elections Commission
1300 - 1345 hrs	Lunch
1500 hrs	Departure from Maputo airport for Matalene
1515 - 1545 hrs	Briefing and observation of voter registration at Matalene
1545 hrs	Departure from Matalene for Manhica
1600 - 1700 hrs	Briefing at Manhica FADM training centre

1700 hrs	Departure from Manhica for Maputo
1730 hrs	Arrival at Maputo
1800 hrs	Press briefing
1900 hrs	Reception hosted by Mr. Din Jianduo, Chargé d'affaires of the Embassy of China to Mozambique

Wednesday, 10 August

0800 - 0845 hrs	Breakfast with chief editors of the press
0900 - 1000 hrs	UNHCR and United Nations Office for Humanitarian Assistance Coordination
1000 - 1130 hrs	International members of the peace commissions and ambassadors of Security Council member countries
1130 - 1300 hrs	National Police Affairs Commission, National Information Commission and National Commission for Territorial Administration
1315 - 1445 hrs	Lunch
1500 - 1600 hrs	Political party leaders
1615 - 1715 hrs	Special Representative of the Secretary-General and senior ONUMOZ staff
1730 - 1800 hrs	Meeting on mine clearance with the Deputy Special Representative of the Secretary-General and the Director of the United Nations Office for Humanitarian Assistance Coordination
1900 - 2100 hrs	Reception hosted by the Special Representative of the Secretary-General

Thursday, 11 August

A

0615 hrs	Departure from Maputo for Tete
0915 hrs	Arrival at Tete
0930 - 1030 hrs	Visit to the Mine-clearance Training Centre; briefing by the instructors
1040 hrs	Departure from Tete for Nhamacala
1140 hrs	Arrival at Nhamacala
1140 - 1220 hrs	Visit to the RENAMO assembly area of Nhamacala; observe demobilization
1220 hrs	Departure from Nhamacala for Chimoio
1310 hrs	Arrival at Chimoio
1320 - 1510 hrs	Briefing and lunch with Botswana battalion
1525 - 1615 hrs	Visit to Government assembly area

	of Chimoio; observe demobilization
1630 hrs	Departure from Chimoio for Maputo
1830 hrs	Arrival at Maputo
2130 hrs	Meeting between the Chairman, Mr. Al-Khussaiby, Mr. Olhaye and the ambassadors of Algeria, Angola, Egypt, Malawi, Nigeria, Switzerland, Zaire, Zambia and Zimbabwe, and the representative of OAU

B

0800 hrs	Departure from Maputo for Quelimane
1000 hrs	Arrival at Quelimane
1015 hrs	Departure from Quelimane
1050 hrs	Arrival at Mocuba
1100 - 1200 hrs	Briefing by the Brazilian contingent commander
1200 - 1300 hrs	Lunch with Brazilian contingent
1330 - 1420 hrs	Visit to Mocuba assembly areas and local ONUMOZ sections
1430 hrs	Departure from Mocuba for Quelimane
1505 hrs	Arrival at Quelimane
1515 hrs	Departure from Quelimane for Maputo
1715 hrs	Arrival at Maputo
Participants:	Mr. Ronaldo Mota Sardenberg Mr. Luciano Osorio Rosa Mr. Antonio Ferreira Rocha Brig. A. T. Scheffers, Deputy Force Commander Lt. Col. Alexandra de Mattos Borges Lins Cap. Marinho Pereira Resende Filho Mr. Pelucio Silva

Friday, 12 August

0845 - 1015 hrs	Ceremony for demobilization of President Chissano and other high-ranking Government officers (Estado Maior General)
1320 - 1420 hrs	Debriefing with the Special Representative of the Secretary-General and the Deputy Special Representative of the Secretary-General
1430 - 1500 hrs	Press conference
1515 hrs	Departure from Maputo for Johannesburg

Annex II

Participants in the meeting of the mission with the international members of the peace commissions and ambassadors of Security Council member countries

(Maputo, Wednesday, 10 August 1994)

SECURITY COUNCIL MEMBER COUNTRIES (AMBASSADORS TO MOZAMBIQUE)

Brazil	Luciano Rosa
China	Din Jianduo
Nigeria	Isaiah Udoyen
Russian Federation	Valeri Gamaioun
United States of America	Dennis Jett

INTERNATIONAL MEMBERS OF THE PEACE COMMISSIONS

UNDP	Joana Merlin-Scholtes	(CORE)
OAU	Ahcene Fzeri	(CSC)
European Community	Alvaro Neves da Silva	(CORE)
Botswana	M.P. Lesetedi	(CCF)
Denmark	Stig Barlyng	(CORE)
Egypt	Esmat Abdel Azeem	(CCF)
France	Francis Heude	(CSC, CCF, CORE, CCFADM)
Germany	Helmut Rau	(CSC, CCF, CORE)
Italy	Manfredo Incisa Di Camerana	(CSC, CCF, CORE)
Kenya	Lt. Col. S.M. Chege	(CCF)
Netherlands	Robert A. Vornis	(CORE)
Nigeria	Isaiah J. Udoyen	(CCF)
Norway	Bjoerg Leite	(CORE)
Portugal	Carlos Neves Ferreira	(CSC, CCF, CORE, CCFADM)
South Africa	John Sunde	(CORE)
Spain	Pablo Gomez Olea Bustinza	(CORE)
Sweden	Birgitta Johansson	(CORE)
Switzerland	Conrad Marty	(CORE)
United Kingdom of Great Britain and Northern Ireland	Richard Edis	(CSC, CCF, CORE, CCFADM)
United States of America	Dennis Jett	(CSC, CCF, CORE)
Zimbabwe	John Mayowe	(CCF, CCFADM)

Annex III

List of the 18 registered political parties in Mozambique

FAP–Frente de Ação Patriótica
Raul da Conceição (Secretary-General)

FRELIMO–Frente de Libertaçao de Moçambique
Feliciano Gundana (Secretary-General)

FUMO/PCD–Frente Unida de Moçambique/ Partido da Convergência Democrática
Domingos Arouca (President)
José Manuel Samo Gudo (Secretary-General)

MONAMO/PMSD–Movimento Nacionalista Moçambicano/Partido Moçambicano da Social Democracia
Maximo Dias (Secretary-General)

PACODE–Partido do Congresso Democrático
Vasco Mamboya (President)

PADEMO–Partido Democratico de Moçambique
Wehia Ripua (President)

PALMO–Partido Liberal e Democrático de Moçambique
Martins Luis Bilal (President)

PANADE–Partido Nacional Democrático
Jose Massinga (President)

PANAMO/CDR–Partido Nacional de Moçambique/Centro de Reflexão Democrática
Marcos Juma (President)

PCN–Partido de Convenção Nacional
Lutero Simango (Acting General Coordinator)

PIMO–Partido Independente de Moçambique
Ayacob Sibinde (President)

PPLM–Partido do Progresso Liberal de Moçambique
Neves P. Serrano (President)

PPPM–Partido do Progresso do Povo de Moçambique
Padimbe Kamati (President)

PRD–Partido Renovador Democrático
Maneca Daniel (President)

PT–Partido Trabalhista
Miguel Mabote (President)

RENAMO–Resistência Nacional Moçambicana
Vicente Ululu (Secretary-General)

SOL–Partido Social Liberal e Democrático
Casimiro Nhamitambo (President)

UNAMO–União Nacional Moçambicana
Carlos Reis (President)

Document 71

Statement by the President of the Security Council expressing cautious optimism that Mozambicans will fulfil the goals of the peace process

S/PRST/1994/51, 7 September 1994

The Security Council welcomes the report of the Secretary-General of 26 August 1994 (S/1994/1002) on the United Nations Operation in Mozambique and notes with appreciation the report (S/1994/1009) and oral briefing of the mission it sent to Mozambique to discuss with the parties how best to ensure full and timely implementation of the general peace agreement. It commends the mission for accomplishing its objectives, as set forth by the President of the Council on 4 August 1994 (S/1994/931).

The Security Council is satisfied, at present, with the pace of the peace process, including demobilization of all forces which will be completed shortly. It maintains a cautious optimism that Mozambicans will be able to fulfil the goals of the peace process, achieving democracy, lasting peace, and responsible, representative government in their country.

The Security Council welcomes the fact that the leaders of the main political parties in Mozambique and the National Elections Commission have confirmed their commitments to take all steps necessary to ensure the holding of elections on 27 and 28 October 1994, as scheduled. It underlines the importance of ensuring that the voter registration process reach as many Mozambicans as possible. Those parties who have concerns about the implementation of aspects of the electoral process should pursue them through the National Elections Commission. The Council reiterates its intention to endorse the results of the Mozambican elections provided the United Nations declares them as free and fair and reminds all the parties of their obligation under the General Peace Agreement fully to respect these results as well as the principles of democracy.

The Security Council reaffirms the importance of proceeding as expeditiously as possible with the formation and training of the new Mozambican Defence Force (FADM). It notes with satisfaction that both the Government of Mozambique and RENAMO have accepted the fact that the initial size of FADM will be consistent with

training and recruitment constraints during the pre-election period. It encourages the Government of Mozambique speedily to complete the transfer of the requisite authority and assets from the Mozambique Armed Forces (FAM) to FADM. The Council calls upon Member States to help provide military training and appropriate equipment to the FADM.

The Security Council expresses its appreciation to the Secretary-General for providing a detailed revised timetable for the phased withdrawal of ONUMOZ civilian and military personnel as set out in his report. The Council concurs with the Secretary-General that ONUMOZ should be deployed over a wider area of the country, keeping in mind the need to assist the Government in maintaining security, particularly in the crucial period before, during and immediately after the elections.

The Security Council notes the importance of ensuring that the Mozambican police have the resources required to maintain security in the country, in particular in the post-electoral period. It urges that the Mozambican police be provided with these resources, and calls upon Member States to assist in this regard by contributing to the training and equipment needs of the police.

The Security Council expresses concern at the limited progress made to date in the area of de-mining. It welcomes efforts to revitalize that programme and urges all concerned to accelerate training and mine-clearance activities, and work with the relevant Mozambican authorities towards the establishment of a national de-mining capability, including the possibility of leaving de-mining equipment in Mozambique after the withdrawal of ONUMOZ, subject to the appropriate arrangements.

The Security Council invites the Secretary-General to report on the final disposition of the assets of ONUMOZ within the framework of the withdrawal of ONUMOZ.

The Security Council encourages the parties to continue their efforts in good faith to ensure post-electoral harmony on the basis of the observance of the democratic principles accepted by them in the General Peace Agreement as well as on the basis of the spirit and letter of that Agreement.

The Security Council notes that the post-election period will be an important and delicate time, during which the international community will need to assist the Mozambicans in the rehabilitation and development of their country, and in this regard calls upon the Secretary-General to report to the competent United Nations bodies on what further role the United Nations can perform.

The Council commends the efforts of the Secretary-General and his Special Representative in moving the peace process forward. It expresses its gratitude to the Special Representative of the Secretary-General and his dedicated staff for the assistance rendered to the mission sent by the Security Council to Mozambique.

Document 72

Letter dated 9 September 1994 from the Secretary-General to Italian Prime Minister Silvio Berlusconi on Italy's contribution to operations in Mozambique and to the Trust Fund for the Implementation of the Peace Agreement

Not issued as a United Nations document

I should like to express once again my gratitude for the generous contributions that your Government has made to our operations in Mozambique, and particularly to the Trust Fund for the Implementation of the Peace Agreements. This Fund has been instrumental in allowing the transformation of the Resistência Nacional Moçambicana (RENAMO) into a political party and enabled its full participation in the mechanisms established by the General Peace Agreements.

As you may already be aware, the resources available in this Trust Fund have been exhausted, and we are now facing difficulties in implementing some programmed contributions to the Trust Fund. We have considered various measures and would like to request your consideration of a very efficient solution to the problem.

Italy has contributed funds to the United Nations Office for Humanitarian Assistance Coordination (UNOHAC) Trust Fund which are not currently committed. If you should agree, an amount of US$ 3,000,000 might be transferred from the UNOHAC Trust Fund to the Trust Fund for the Implementation of the Peace Agreement. The UNOHAC Trust Fund could then be replenished at a later date, when funds are available.

We would hope that your Government will consider this proposal favourably, as this would allow us to act immediately and avoid any possibility of jeopardizing the peace process in the crucial days before the elections.

Accept, Excellency, the assurances of my highest consideration.

(Signed) Boutros BOUTROS-GHALI

Document 73

Report of the Secretary-General to the General Assembly on humanitarian and disaster assistance to Mozambique

A/49/387, 16 September 1994

I. Coordination of humanitarian assistance

1. The signing of the general peace agreement in October 1992 and the resulting cease-fire brought to an end more than a decade of armed conflict, which had caused the massive displacement of more than 5 million Mozambicans. Throughout 1992, Mozambique was also affected by the worst regional drought in this century, which provoked additional movements towards provincial and district towns, where there was better access to relief assistance.

2. The peace agreement placed humanitarian assistance firmly within the context of peacemaking and peacekeeping. The Declaration by the Government of the Republic of Mozambique and the Resistência Nacional

Moçambicana (RENAMO) on guiding principles for humanitarian assistance, signed in July 1992 and included as an integral part of the peace accord, specifically called on the United Nations to coordinate the provision of humanitarian assistance to Mozambique. The United Nations Office for Humanitarian Assistance Coordination, which was to function at the field level as the practical expression of the coordination role of the Department of Humanitarian Affairs, was transformed by the Security Council in its resolution 797 (1992) into the humanitarian component of the United Nations Operation in Mozambique (ONUMOZ).

3. Based on the principles of neutrality and freedom of movement, the United Nations Office for Humanitarian Assistance Coordination was to coordinate the expeditious delivery of assistance by United Nations agencies and non-governmental organizations to those in need in affected areas. Humanitarian assistance and continued support for medium- and longer-term development programmes necessary for reconstruction played an important role in the peace-keeping and peacemaking process. Initially, relief assistance spearheaded the opening up of RENAMO areas to facilitate delivery of food, non-food relief items and the start of reconstruction. This cleared the way for the return of internally displaced persons and refugees. Equally important, this process helped to establish and cultivate channels of communication between the Government and RENAMO, especially at local and provincial levels.

4. In line with the mandate of the United Nations Office for Humanitarian Assistance Coordination to ensure neutrality in the distribution of humanitarian assistance, provincial humanitarian assistance committees, chaired by field officers of the United Nations Office for Humanitarian Assistance Coordination, with both Government and RENAMO participation, have been established. These provincial humanitarian assistance committees plan the delivery of food, non-food relief and seeds and tools, as well as promote reconstruction and rehabilitation of basic services. The United Nations Office for Humanitarian Assistance Coordination has initiated tripartite discussions on social services at the central and provincial levels to integrate RENAMO health personnel into the Government's health system and to expand education in ex-RENAMO areas. Meetings of provincial humanitarian assistance committees bring together the Government, RENAMO, non-governmental organizations and the United Nations on a host of issues, as do the sectoral tripartite working groups set up in several provinces. Frequent joint visits to ex-RENAMO areas are helping to speed up rehabilitation of the country's economy and social services. All these efforts also expand the channels of communication which support the reintegra-

tion of all areas into a single administration, as called for in the peace accord.

5. The United Nations Office for Humanitarian Assistance Coordination has endeavoured to create the conditions for greater coordination among the principal actors—the Government, RENAMO, United Nations agencies, donors and non-governmental organizations. Of the 24 Professional staff of the Office at Maputo and in the provinces, 8 were seconded by United Nations agencies, 2 by a multilateral agency and 1 by a major donor, while the remainder were supported by the ONUMOZ budget. Ten field assistants from the United Nations Volunteers were assigned to different parts of the country, while the staff of many other organizations have worked on numerous projects together with personnel of the United Nations Office for Humanitarian Assistance Coordination. Another area in which multi-agency coordination efforts have resulted in clear benefits is in putting together the information needed to work together better. Because they are acting in concert, the Government, RENAMO, donors, agencies and implementors are able to combine their information into a global picture of the needs and each individual organization's response. Substantial progress has been made by the United Nations Office for Humanitarian Assistance Coordination in consolidating such information into reports on indicators and a geography of human needs and responses throughout the country.

6. The management of emergency interventions and the transition to reconstruction and rehabilitation requires coordination by government institutions to ensure that assistance responds to priority needs. The National Executive Commission on the Emergency is responsible for coordination at the central level, while the provincial emergency commissions are focal points in the provinces. The Department for the Prevention and Combat of Natural Disasters is the operational relief agency with offices in all provinces. At the national and provincial levels, that Department and the government unit that provides support to refugees are active participants within the coordinating mechanisms of the United Nations Office for Humanitarian Assistance Coordination. Emergency response units were set up within ministries with major responsibilities for humanitarian assistance such as health, education and social welfare. These entities had combined needs of US$ 18 million for institutional support during 1993/94, against which there were commitments of $8.7 million and obligations for disbursement of $7.9 million by the programme year's end in April 1994. The United Nations Office for Humanitarian Assistance Coordination is working closely with national institutions to ensure that the roles and responsibilities deemed necessary to continue after the departure of ONUMOZ are

passed on to appropriate government institutions or United Nations agencies.

II. Humanitarian assistance programmes: 1992 to 1994

A. *Mobilization and allocation of resources*

7. The outline for humanitarian assistance programmes emerged from the donors conference held at Rome in December 1992. The conference produced a draft set of financial requirements for post-war programming in support of the resettlement and reintegration of the returning refugees, internally displaced persons and demobilized soldiers, along with initial pledges from the international community. Support for the electoral process was also discussed.

8. On that basis, the United Nations Office for Humanitarian Assistance Coordination, in conjunction with both the Government and RENAMO, developed a consolidated humanitarian assistance programme for the period May 1993 to April 1994, with requirements of $560 million. The relief needs of the immediate post-war period were covered by the 1992/93 Mozambique drought emergency appeal, which totalled $457 million, of which $315 million, or 62 per cent, was pledged. A follow-up meeting with donors, also chaired by the United Nations and Italy, was held at Maputo in June 1993. Subsequently, the humanitarian assistance programme has been continually updated in response to changing needs.

9. An updated consolidated humanitarian assistance programme was presented in November 1993 in conjunction with the World Bank Consultative Group meeting in Paris. The most important change at that time was the doubling of needs for the health sector to $52 million, mainly to cover requirements for rural health care, which had gone beyond what was originally foreseen. Since the update was produced, a reintegration support scheme has been set up to pay subsidies to ex-soldiers for over 18 months, as well as other important training and reintegration programmes for that important target group, creating additional requirements of $23 million. The response of the international community to the consolidated programme has been excellent. Firm commitments totalling $536 million have been made, representing 87 per cent of the programme's target of $616 million by the end of April 1994.

10. With regard to implementation of humanitarian activities, $455 million, or 85 per cent of commitments, had been disbursed or obligated for disbursement by 30 April 1994. However, there are still many outstanding and new needs to be met during the remainder of 1994, mainly for emergency relief and reintegration

schemes. These are presented in a consolidated humanitarian assistance programme for the eight months from May to December 1994. In this regard, $47 million are required to fund special programmes for the reintegration of demobilized soldiers and $51 million to deliver humanitarian support for reintegration in rural areas, mainly in the form of seeds and tools, health, water, education and a vulnerable groups programme. Another $66 million is required for emergency relief, including food, non-food and internal migration assistance and special relief in the wake of cyclone Nadia, while a further $31 million is required for the refugee repatriation operation.

11. Although a large portion of these needs and activities indicate the existence of significant emergency humanitarian requirements, the consolidated humanitarian assistance programme for 1994 attempts to move the humanitarian endeavour in Mozambique towards rehabilitation and reconstruction. In this sense, it is to provide a link to the medium- and longer-term development assistance provided by the World Bank, United Nations agencies and bilateral donors.

12. Commitments of a total of $51 million have been made to the trust funds that are administered by the Department of Humanitarian Affairs and the United Nations Development Programme (UNDP) to support the activities defined in the consolidated humanitarian assistance programme. While these funds are under 10 per cent of the overall programme for 1993/94, they have facilitated a flexible response by the donor community to the particularly urgent needs which emerge, often unpredictably, in a complex situation.

13. Funds from both the Department of Humanitarian Affairs and the UNDP trust funds have been applied to important aspects of the demobilization programme, including provision of food, transportation, clothing, seeds and tools. The trust fund of the Department of Humanitarian Affairs has allocated $20.7 million to multi-sectoral initiatives that target the reintegration of internally displaced persons and refugees, mine clearance, transport of the most vulnerable to their home communities and the provision of seeds and tools and other items. A total of $9 million has already been received by the UNDP trust fund for reintegration programmes for ex-soldiers, including the reintegration support scheme.

14. While the response of the international community has created the foundation on which rehabilitation and sustainable development can be built, assistance with the planning, coordination and monitoring of national reconstruction will be required in order to maximize the use of available resources. In short, the support given to humanitarian programmes during the peace process must now be translated into firm commitments aimed at ensuring durable development.

B. *Food aid*

15. At the time of the peace agreement, there were 3.1 million displaced and drought-affected Mozambicans and 1.2 million refugees in neighbouring countries who were receiving food aid. The peace agreement opened up possibilities for getting relief to inaccessible areas, thereby averting the threat of widespread famine. Against 460,000 tons of relief food aid (maize, beans, oil) requested in the 1992/93 Mozambique drought emergency appeal, 554,000 tons were pledged. These commitments ensured sufficient carry-over stocks to meet the food aid needs for the massive resettlement that began immediately after the cease-fire went into effect in mid-October 1992.

16. As a result of increased agricultural production, the projected number of people to be assisted for the 1993/94 period dropped to a monthly average of 1.8 million beneficiaries, taking into account returning refugees and resettling internally displaced families. The required 336,000 tons of food were covered by arrivals of food committed in 1992, as well as contributions from May 1993 to April 1994. Donors have channelled relief food aid through the United Nations (the World Food Programme (WFP)) or non-governmental organizations. Food aid deliveries to RENAMO areas increased steadily because roads were being opened and mines cleared, particularly in Sofala Province. The United Nations Office for Humanitarian Assistance Coordination recorded 74,000 tons distributed to 78 districts from the signing of the peace agreement through May 1994. There are more than 30 national and international non-governmental organizations involved in distribution in those areas.

17. A joint Food and Agriculture Organization of the United Nations (FAO)/WFP crop and food supply assessment mission to Mozambique visited all provinces in April 1994. The mission reported that overall food aid requirements for the 1994/95 marketing year will would be 495,000 tons of cereal and 100,000 tons of pulse. To meet these requirements, imports of 182,000 tons of cereal are recommended for emergency relief assistance, along with an additional 313,000 tons of cereal to be imported for commercial marketing. The remainder of food requirements should be covered by local production, mainly of cassava.

18. The number of people in need of food assistance during the 1994/95 period will include 457,000 war- and drought-affected persons, 118,000 demobilized soldiers and their dependants, and 547,000 returnees expected up to May 1995. This works out to a monthly average of 1.1 million beneficiaries over the 12 months from May 1994 to April 1995, compared to 1.8 million over the previous 12 months and 3.1 million at the time of the signing of the peace agreement. In 1994/95, the inclusion of demobilized soldiers and their dependents so

as to assist in their reintegration into civilian life is important in the context of reinforcing the climate for a durable peace.

19. World Food Programme assistance to Mozambique during the period 1992-1994 reached 500,000 tons of food commodities, with handling and internal transport costs valued at $232 million. World Food Programme assistance covered about 60 per cent of the total emergency food requirements, with the remainder coming principally from the United States of America, the European Union, Canada, Germany, the United Kingdom of Great Britain and Northern Ireland, the Netherlands, Switzerland and Norway. In order to address the problem of food delivery to inaccessible areas, the World Food Programme established a special logistics unit—UNILOG—in October 1992. While its initial primary responsibility was delivery of assistance to RENAMO-controlled areas, it has expanded into other areas, including all the assembly areas for the demobilization of soldiers.

20. Decreasing free food distributions is a priority to be accomplished through food-for-work schemes during the transition from emergency to development, as part of the peace-building process. The involvement of non-governmental organizations in a coordinated reduction of free food distribution will be important for the success of this effort. Local purchasing of food commodities by the donor community should be adopted so as to protect local markets from excessive food aid and to redistribute products from surplus to deficit areas.

21. Nutritional rehabilitation programmes were a major priority and concern at the time of the signing of the peace agreement. Widespread malnutrition as a result of war and drought had been documented throughout the country, thereby requiring supplemental feeding programmes on a significant scale. With increased food aid coverage as well as improved household-level food production since the signing of the peace agreement, average national nutritional levels have returned to normal after the emergency and drought. A total of 5,000 tons of commodities of high nutritional value have been requested in 1994/95 for nutritional intervention programmes and hospital feeding in areas where pockets of malnutrition exist.

22. Market food aid needs were determined to be 417,000 tons of cereal for the 1993/94 marketing year. However, arrivals registered by the Ministry of Commerce through April 1994 totalled only 161,500 tons, owing to delayed arrivals, to the fact that many pledges were rolled over to 1994/95, to some local surpluses of maize and to the transfer of food stocks from market aid to emergency relief.

23. The FAO/WFP crop and food supply assess-

ment mission estimated market food needs at 227,000 tons of maize, 85,000 tons of wheat and 40,000 tons of rice for the coming marketing year, in order to support and stabilize markets in deficit areas. However, these needs are not included in the consolidated humanitarian assistance programme for 1994, as market food aid is now considered to be a regular programme not linked to emergency relief and humanitarian assistance needs.

24. The importation of other non-food items such as seeds and tools was included within the 1993/94 consolidated humanitarian assistance programme, for which $1.5 million had been committed and disbursed by the end of the programme year on 30 April 1994. This category of support is also no longer included within the 1994 humanitarian assistance programme.

C. Non-food relief items

25. The distribution of non-food relief items targets the most vulnerable persons in previously inaccessible areas and resettling displaced persons who lack basic household necessities. A total of $6.5 million was pledged during the 1992/93 period, while $12.2 million was pledged for this category of assistance within the 1993/94 consolidated humanitarian assistance programme. More than 1 million relief and survival items have been distributed to the most needy persons since the signing of the peace agreement.

26. The distribution of humanitarian assistance to ex-RENAMO areas has been a priority during the 1993/94 programme year, supplying numerous areas that had been impossible or difficult to reach for many years. More than 20 agencies have been involved in the distribution of close to 450,000 non-food relief items such as blankets, clothing, soap and kitchen utensils in 37 districts over the period from October 1992 to April 1994.

27. The emergency stockpile project, operated by the Department of Humanitarian Affairs in cooperation with the Government emergency relief agency, has contributed substantially to the relief and survival of populations in both Government and ex-RENAMO areas. Various items, including zinc roofing sheets, clothing sets, blankets, kitchen sets and tents, have been distributed. In special cases, small generators and water tanks have also been provided. A total of 508 tons of these items was distributed to 185,000 beneficiaries in 1993, and the plan is to continue to deliver such items throughout 1994 using commitments that have been carried over from the previous year. Following the destruction caused by cyclone Nadia, the emergency stockpile project of the Department of Humanitarian Affairs provided 58 tons of relief items. It is estimated that 150,000 persons beyond the reach of the emergency stockpile project will need relief and survival items valued at $3.8 million.

D. Transportation of internally displaced persons

28. The resettlement of internally displaced persons is characterized by spontaneous movement, with only a small portion requiring assistance. By May 1994, over 40,000 internally displaced persons had been transported and resettled with assistance from the International Organization of Migration (IOM). Only 140,000 (4 per cent) out of the total of 3.7 million displaced persons are expected to require transport. Past experience has shown that, overall, 28 per cent of the internally displaced leave the province of their present residence, with 18 per cent moving to a neighbouring province and 10 per cent going to a distant province. The majority, 72 per cent, move to another district within the province they are in.

29. To facilitate family reunification and long distance travel arrangements, a network of IOM-supervised transit centres has been established throughout the country. Considerable energy has been devoted to coordination with non-governmental organizations and other partners who have the capacity to ensure that resettling persons have the basic conditions necessary for their successful reinstallation. In cases where no organization is available to meet a particular need, IOM intervenes directly.

30. Financial needs within the 1993/94 consolidated humanitarian assistance programme were calculated at $7.4 million of which $2.5 million have been committed, including $2.3 million, which have been obligated for disbursement. After a review of needs and lower-than-expected average transport costs, financial requirements to cover the transportation of an additional 100,000 persons over the period from May to December 1994 have been calculated at $2.7 million.

E. Repatriation of refugees

31. Between the signing of the general peace agreement in October 1992 and the end of June 1994, the Office of the United Nations High Commissioner for Refugees (UNHCR) estimated that 867,000 Mozambican refugees had already returned. Most have returned spontaneously, but 40,000 were brought back in organized repatriations from Zimbabwe, Zambia, Swaziland and South Africa.

32. In 1994, UNHCR entered into the second phase of its programme to step up the repatriation of the 725,000 refugees still residing in six neighbouring countries. The movements were accelerated after the April harvest and are expected to continue to be heavy until the beginning of the next planting season in September/October 1994, with lighter movements following in November and December. At least another 350,000 refugees are expected to return by the end of the year. It is expected that the remaining refugee population still re-

siding in the countries of asylum at the end of 1994 will be repatriated during 1995. This will particularly concern South Africa, which, in December 1994, will still host a significant number of Mozambican refugees.

33. UNHCR has estimated the total cost of the Mozambique repatriation and reintegration operation in all involved countries at $203 million over the three-year period from 1993 to 1995. The first appeal was launched in May 1993, for which UNHCR received contributions amounting to $52 million. In February 1994, UNHCR appealed for $103 million for the 1994 portion of the programme. The budget required for Mozambique alone from May to December 1994 is estimated at $51 million, including $26 million in repatriation costs, $22 million for the reintegration of returnees and a further $2.5 million required for support to the government unit responsible for refugees.

34. During 1993, cross border coordination mechanisms were established at the field level, including joint assessment missions and regular coordination meetings with operational partners. District authorities of asylum countries met regularly with officials from Mozambique, UNHCR, IOM, WFP and non-governmental organizations to decide on operational and logistics issues with a direct bearing on the acceleration and coordination of the various repatriation exercises. Within the overall repatriation operation of UNHCR, IOM handles the transport of refugees in the organized repatriations from South Africa, Swaziland, Tanzania and Malawi. WFP closely coordinates programming on the transfer of food supplies from countries of asylum to Mozambique, while non-governmental organizations implement much of the actual reintegration programmes.

35. UNHCR has elaborated a reintegration strategy and is now discussing it with the appropriate Mozambican authorities, with the aim of incorporating the strategy into the national planning process. While continuing to finance quick impact projects in the areas that receive refugees, UNHCR will also be phasing out its activities where reintegration programmes have been, or will soon be, completed.

F. *Support for reintegration*

36. Even during the war, considerable international assistance was provided for the provision of basic services to the displaced populations. Emergency relief must respond to immediate needs while at the same time building the foundation for longer-term development. Seed and tool distribution, health services, primary school education and water supply projects formed an important part of the Mozambique emergency programme before the signing of the peace agreement.

37. The signing of the peace agreement set off large-scale population movements, which continue today. Since October 1992, more than 2.7 million internally displaced persons have resettled within the country, while an additional 867,000 refugees have returned from neighbouring countries. This has created an enormous pressure to expand the delivery of services to areas that had been virtually abandoned for up to a decade. The first waves of resettlers moved into relatively close and secure areas, often sending only one family member at first if their destination was more remote. Now that demobilization has begun, confidence is increasing among resettlers. Border areas are being cleared of land-mines which will further stimulate movements of both refugees and displaced persons.

38. United Nations agencies, bilateral donors and non-governmental organizations have supported many initiatives to rehabilitate social infrastructure as the first phase of longer-term reconstruction. Many were area-based programmes concentrated in the provinces of Manica, Zambézia, Nampula and Tete. UNHCR has supported the resettlement of returning refugees by rehabilitating basic services in major areas of return under its quick impact programme, implemented through 20 non-governmental organizations.

39. Reintegration of internally displaced persons, returning refugees and, most recently, demobilized soldiers and their families, must take place within their communities. More than 30 organizations started area-based programmes in the most affected areas during 1993/94. Tete, Manica and Zambézia have benefited the most from these initiatives, since they are the areas most affected by the influx of resettling families. Niassa Province will be receiving an increased influx of returnees, as will Inhambane and Cabo Delgado. These provinces have few non-governmental organizations supporting community-based development programmes and will therefore require increases in such assistance in 1994.

40. In the 1993/94 consolidated humanitarian assistance programme, $23 million was committed and $19 million obligated for disbursement for these activities. Many of these projects will continue throughout 1994 and into 1995, focusing on the community as a whole without differentiating among categories of beneficiaries. Increasing food production through the distribution of seeds and tools is a common element of such projects, as is the rehabilitation of social infrastructure. Such programmes should fall within the national planning process in the future. Therefore, although continued support is clearly needed, these activities are no longer included in the consolidated humanitarian assistance programme for May to December 1994. These needs were presented to the international community at the 1993

Consultative Group meeting in Paris, and revised needs will be presented by the Government in December 1994.

1. *Agriculture*

41. The agricultural season in Mozambique starts in October/November and goes through April/May. The war and drought seriously affected local food supplies and reduced the number of livestock from 2 million to a few hundred thousand. The focus of the rehabilitation programme has been to supply basic agricultural inputs to the family sector, which produces most staple foods in the country. The signing of the peace agreement in October 1992 opened up the possibility of getting seeds and agricultural hand tools to areas that had previously been inaccessible. A total of 16,600 tons of seed and over 1 million tools were distributed in 1992/93 to the affected rural areas, including RENAMO-controlled areas. The principal donors were Norway, Sweden, the United Kingdom, the United States and the European Economic Community. This expanded seed distribution accounted for the increased agricultural production, which reduced significantly the food aid requirements.

42. Given the resettlement of over 3 million Mozambicans, the seed requirements for 1993/94 were doubled, as was the response from the international community. The 1993/94 crop season was marked by the most ambitious seed and tool distribution operation ever undertaken in Mozambique. Consistent with Mozambique's policy of promoting household-level food security, the operation oversaw the distribution of 33,000 tons of seed and nearly 5 million tools to over 1 million beneficiary families.

43. Seeds and tools were distributed in 45 districts, including ex-RENAMO zones, some for the first time. Beneficiaries were able to open up new lands for cultivation, or at least replenish exhausted seed stocks. Refugees returning from Malawi, Zimbabwe, Zambia and Tanzania also received seeds and tools, mainly at transit centres, but sometimes at their final destinations. The province of Tete alone, which had the most returnees, was covered by some 300 distribution points. The major donors for this effort included Denmark, Germany, Italy, Norway, Portugal, South Africa, Sweden, the United Kingdom, the United States and EEC. Non-governmental organizations were the major implementing partners in this endeavour. Seeds provided in 1993/94 should have been sufficient to cover about 1.1 million hectares, using a generous estimate of the amount of seed needed per hectare.

44. Despite substantial inputs in the 1993/94 agricultural campaign, crop production has been seriously affected by erratic rainfall and dry spells during critical weeks. As a result, the much larger area planted this year will yield a slightly smaller harvest of maize and cassava than the year before. Maize production is estimated at 527,000 tons, or 1 per cent below last year, and cassava production at 3,295,000 tons, or 6 per cent below last year. The reduction in maize production has seriously undermined the much better harvests of other cereals and pulses, resulting in a net increase in total production of only 7 per cent overall, as forecast in the report of the FAO/WFP crop and food supply assessment mission.

45. Estimates for the 1994/95 crop season have been made after considering the various population groups in need of agricultural inputs. These include internally displaced persons going back to their original places, returnee families, demobilizing soldiers, victims of cyclone Nadia and drought-affected populations. It is estimated that a total of 550,000 families will require assistance in the form of seeds and tools. Calculations are made at the rate of 25 kilograms of seed and 5 tools per family. The estimated cost of the programme is $17.6 million, including $14.6 million for seeds and $3 million for tools.

2. *Health*

46. Between 30 and 50 per cent of rural health facilities were looted, destroyed or forced to close during the war. Before the signing of the peace agreement, rehabilitation projects focused on the existing health facilities, especially those damaged during hostilities. After the peace accord, the Government, donors and implementing agencies prioritized the reactivation of essential services in rural areas where the resettlement of the population is taking place.

47. In 1992/93, the assistance in the health areas focused on emergency services, vaccination campaigns and supply of vital drugs and medicines. Of the $7.2 million required, $5.7 million was pledged by Norway, Sweden, Switzerland, the United States, EEC and WHO. The expansion of the rural health network in the post-conflict situation is a prerequisite for increasing health service coverage. Many new areas have become accessible where no health care was previously delivered. As of July 1994, at least 37 agencies and non-governmental organizations were operating in ex-RENAMO areas in 51 districts. This expansion of services should continue throughout 1994 as accessibility increases and stability is consolidated. Special programmes are being developed to assist in the integration of RENAMO health workers and services into the national health system. The updated 1993/94 consolidated humanitarian assistance programme defined priority needs totalling $52 million for health. Of this, $33 million was committed, including $19 million obligated for disbursement, by the close of the programme year. Over $18 million of the total was committed to rural health care and rehabilitation. Much of this programming will carry over throughout 1994.

48. The National Reconstruction Plan has targeted some 220 primary health units for rehabilitation or reconstruction in 1994, a target which it appears will be

reached. More than 30 agencies and non-governmental organizations are currently involved in the rehabilitation of the health network countrywide. For instance, 23 health posts have already been rehabilitated in border districts to support the reintegration of returnees, and several more are targeted for rehabilitation under UNHCR's quick impact programme in 1994/95. Increased drug availability needs to be ensured through an extended distribution network. Drug requirements of $9 million were included in the 1993/94 consolidated programme, including the supply of essential drug programme (EDP) kits to primary health units in rural areas, as well as drugs for specific programmes such as leprosy and tuberculosis or in response to epidemics such as cholera or dysentery. These needs will continue throughout 1994, in particular for EDP kits. Overall requirements of close to $24 million must be met through import support programmes and bilateral or multilateral agreements.

49. Just under 20,000 cholera cases were reported in 1993, down from more than 30,000 in 1992, but this has been offset by an outbreak of dysentery in all provinces in 1993; 47,000 cases were reported. WHO has assisted the Ministry of Health in epidemiological monitoring and in the provision of cholera drug kits. Support has also been given to strengthen the emergency management capacity of the Ministry.

50. Denmark, Switzerland and UNICEF, in particular, are supporting the recurrent health budget and channelling funds to provincial authorities. A decentralization programme has been put in place that aims at improving the allocation and use of resources at the provincial level by strengthening provincial health management. The health portion of the 1994 consolidated humanitarian assistance programme has defined only additional needs to support the resettlement in rural areas of internally displaced families, returning refugees and demobilized soldiers—needs which are not already contemplated within national reconstruction or sectoral investment plans. These additional requirements have been assessed at $12 million for the period from May to December 1994. They reflect emergency needs for recurrent expenditure in the expanded health network, as well as increased demand for services. Some funds have been allocated for the reactivation of health units in underserved rural areas, including ex-RENAMO areas not targeted in other plans. Funds are also allocated for training activities targeting RENAMO health workers, in order to facilitate the integration of RENAMO health services into the national health system.

3. Water

51. The war in Mozambique had a disastrous effect on the provision of water, especially in rural areas. The situation was compounded by the 1991/92 drought, which left many shallow wells dry and further reduced the water supply for the rural population. The 1992/93 Mozambique drought emergency appeal placed a major priority on expansion of water sources. Of the $8.2 million requested for priority water supply schemes, there were pledges for $7.4 million. UNICEF was the primary implementer, utilizing funds from Canada, the Netherlands, Sweden, the United Kingdom, the United States and from its own sources.

52. The target for 1993/95 is to provide a total of about 6,000 new or rehabilitated water sources (2,000 per year) to support the resettlement process, including the placement of hand pumps on existing wells that lack them. At the beginning of 1993 this appeared to be a fairly realistic target, with substantial sums promised for the purchase of drilling rigs and vehicles. However, the calculation of financial requirements in the water sector for 1993/94 totalling $14.4 million was based on the national cost per well constructed and excluded the considerable overhead of the non-governmental organizations, which received most of the funding and then subcontracted with the national rural water company, PRONAR, to do the work. More than 50 per cent of the requirements was for equipment such as vehicles and drilling rigs needed to dig and drill larger numbers of wells and boreholes.

53. Of the $14.4 million required for the water sector in the consolidated humanitarian programme for 1993/94, some $12.9 million had been committed by donors as of the close of the programme year, and virtually all of it obligated for disbursement. Most of the money will be spent by the end of 1994, with only one or two projects continuing into early 1995. Without investment in equipment, little more can be accomplished in the second half of 1994 than was done in the same period in 1993. Needs for May to December 1994 total $13.4 million, including $11 million needed for the procurement of equipment, drilling rigs and trucks.

4. Education and social welfare

54. The reopening of schools is a major component of national reconstruction in both Government and ex-RENAMO areas. Less than half of Mozambique's children aged 6 to 11 attend school. The situation is even more serious because many displaced persons and returnees are returning to rural areas, where the majority of primary schools were destroyed or closed during the war. About 1.2 million students and 20,000 teachers were forced out of the schools between 1983 and 1991. Tete Province was the most affected, with 98 per cent of its primary schools closed or destroyed. During the war, support for education concentrated on the supply of school books and materials for the displaced children.

55. The humanitarian assistance programme in-

cluded a requirement of $9.5 million for classroom construction, kits for teachers and pupils and support to provincial authorities. Donors had committed $4.2 million by the closing of the programme year at the end of April 1994. Rural school reconstruction is also included in medium-term reconstruction programmes supported by the World Bank, UNICEF, UNDP, WFP and other United Nations and bilateral agencies. Most area-based programmes of non-governmental organizations also include school reconstruction.

56. At least 200,000 children of primary school age have returned to their home districts since the peace accord, increasing demands on the much-reduced infrastructure. Data on ex-RENAMO areas indicate that the situation there is at least as bad as in Government areas, and at times much worse. In some localities and districts most of the schools require either major renovation or complete reconstruction. Support for the education sector during 1993/94 concentrated on renovation or construction of schools and classrooms. In the six provinces for which the United Nations Office for Humanitarian Assistance Coordination has reliable data, more than 40 organizations will renovate or construct a total of 456 schools, or 790 classrooms, by the end of 1994. Few donors and implementors, however, have made provisions for school books and furniture, the construction of teachers' houses or for improvement of the quality of education. Such support is urgently required, since fiscal constraints prevent such start-up costs from being absorbed by the Government's budget.

57. Tete Province, where the influx of returning refugees is greatest, has received the most support during 1993/94, with 171 schools and 121 classrooms renovated or built. During 1993, UNHCR, which supported the primary schooling of Mozambican refugees in Malawi, financed the reconstruction of 87 classrooms in border districts inside Tete Province. With this level of expansion there is intense pressure to increase the number of teachers, creating additional demands on overstretched public budgets. For the remainder of 1994, the consolidated humanitarian assistance programme has targeted start-up costs for schools in resettled areas, such as kits for teachers, building materials for teachers' houses, support for the upgrading of teachers at the provincial and district levels, and the provision of pedagogical supervision, bicycles, textbooks and sports equipment. Total costs are estimated at $3.2 million. Bilateral donors are encouraged to cover these additional recurrent expenditures, especially the salaries of teachers, when they are supporting the construction of school buildings.

5. Road rehabilitation

58. Road rehabilitation is necessary for the postwar resettlement. The National Directorate of Roads and Bridges within the Ministry of Construction and Water is in charge of road reconstruction and has identified priority roads for repair throughout the country. Funding requirements for this sector in the consolidated programme of 1993/94 were estimated at $35 million. As at 30 April 1994, commitments exceeded these requirements by $14 million. Since this funding will cover work well into 1995, the sector is not included in the 1994 consolidated humanitarian assistance programme. However, the road sector requires long-term planning. There is still a shortfall of $25 million against plans from now until early 1996.

59. Roads to be rehabilitated with financing from Germany include 838 km in Tete Province and 1,049 km in Manica. The International Development Agency (IDA) is funding the rehabilitation of 547 km in Nampula Province, 1,084 km in Niassa and 824 km in Cabo Delgado. The Swedish International Development Agency and IDA are supporting the rehabilitation of 528 km in Inhambane Province, 485 km in Maputo Province and 966 km in Gaza Province. The National Directorate of Roads and Bridges has put out tenders for this work. Contractors have already been selected for 746 km of road works funded by the United States Agency for International Development (USAID) in the Zambezi Valley. Work began in April, covering Tete, Sofala and Zambézia Provinces including rehabilitation of the Sena bridge. Twelve non-governmental organizations are involved in road repairs in six provinces, complementing work in other sectors by providing access to the project sites and facilitating food and other deliveries. UNHCR has supported 267 km of road repairs for the benefit of returning refugees.

6. Reintegration of demobilized soldiers

60. During 1994, programmes to support the reintegration of demobilizing Government and RENAMO soldiers into their home communities were developed under United Nations coordination, with substantial support from the international community. The reintegration of demobilized soldiers begins with the actual demobilization process. Once the soldiers arrive in the assembly areas they benefit from an information programme on social reintegration which was designed to prepare them for civilian life. The Ministry of Finance, with the support of the Technical Unit of ONUMOZ for demobilization, has paid subsidies to all demobilized soldiers and cooperation has been excellent.

61. The first task has been the transport of the demobilized soldiers to their destination. IOM is transporting the soldiers with eligible family members and personal belongings from the assembly areas to their places of resettlement. Once established in their district of choice, ex-soldiers benefit from other general support

programmes, including the provision of seeds and tools and access to emergency food distribution. It is anticipated that many who return to rural areas will subsequently also benefit from area-based programmes and labour-intensive projects. Institutionally, the central-level Commission for Reintegration has been operational for over a year and has established 11 provincial commissions for reintegration. IOM has implemented an information and referral service to support all the provincial commissions by linking demobilized soldiers to reintegration programmes and providing them with counselling and information.

62. Other programmes being prepared for demobilized soldiers include an extended cash payment scheme, small economic activity promotion through the provision of vocational kits and training and a quick-action community-based fund. The extended cash payment or reintegration support scheme provides a subsidy for 18 months, based on actual salary levels. The reintegration support scheme, implemented by UNDP, commences upon completion of the Government's six-month subsidy programme, giving each demobilized soldier a total of two years of subsidies. The payments are made through the local branch of the Banco Popular de Desenvolvimento, which has the greatest national coverage. While the reintegration support scheme is designed to respond to the immediate needs of the demobilized soldier, the project for economic activity promotion is more developmental. The $3 million start-up budget will finance several sub-projects concentrating on training and vocational kits. The training fund is for vocational and entrepreneurial training by supporting institutions, with payments based on quotas for the enrolment of ex-soldiers. Vocational kits of tools and basic equipment will be provided to supplement the training. Demobilized soldiers with the aptitude and interest may also be assisted in accessing existing credit schemes.

63. The International Labour Organization (ILO), through a UNDP trust fund, will provide technical support for training and the provision of kits. ILO will also provide a management component to facilitate coordination of the principal activities of the Commission for Reintegration. Finally, a provincial fund for the reintegration of demobilized soldiers is being prepared. This fund will be managed at the provincial level to promote community-oriented development projects to enable quick responses to social friction involving demobilized soldiers. Job creation is the primary concern, channelled through multilateral organizations such as IOM, as well as bilateral agencies and non-governmental organizations. A lesson drawn from the experience of other countries is that the social and economic reintegration of demobilized soldiers requires both quick action projects

and longer-term efforts. The majority of these programmes are expected to last 18 months, with funding requirements totalling $47 million. Over $30 million have been committed, with the largest shortfall being for vocational training, kits and the provincial fund.

7. *Mine clearance*

64. It is estimated that there are up to 2 million uncleared land-mines scattered throughout Mozambique. Following the signing of the peace agreement, the United Nations was asked to provide assistance for mine-clearance activities and for the establishment of a national de-mining capacity. Accordingly, the Security Council approved mine clearance as part of the ONUMOZ mandate. A total of $11 million was set aside in the ONUMOZ budget for this purpose, and a further $7.5 million was contributed to the trust fund of the Department of Humanitarian Affairs by Italy, the Netherlands and Sweden. The mine-clearance programme includes information, survey, training, clearance and coordination elements. In addition, Mozambique has benefited from some bilateral assistance for dealing with the land-mine problem.

65. Overall management of the Mozambique mine-clearance programme was originally assigned to UNDP in October 1993 as part of its mine-clearance project in Mozambique. Regrettably, inordinate delays were experienced in the implementation of the programme. In May 1994, an accelerated six-month plan was put into place and the United Nations Office for Humanitarian Assistance Coordination assumed responsibility to ensure that the objectives of the ONUMOZ mandate in the area of mine clearance could be realized in a timely manner. For this purpose, a Deputy Director of the United Nations Office for Humanitarian Assistance Coordination was appointed to take charge of the coordination and management of the de-mining programme.

66. The British non-governmental organization, Halo Trust, was contracted by UNDP to carry out a national survey of the mine situation, with funding from the trust fund of the Department of Humanitarian Affairs. The cost of the survey, which was completed in July 1994, was $420,000. The results of the survey have been published by the United Nations Office for Humanitarian Assistance Coordination. UNDP/Office for Project Services (OPS) also contracted for the clearance of 2,000 kilometres of priority roads in Manica and Sofala Provinces at a cost of $4.8 million. Funding for this contract was provided from ONUMOZ and the trust fund of the Department of Humanitarian Affairs and activities began in July 1994. The clearance of a further 2,000 kilometres of priority roads in the central region is being carried out by the RONCO company, with funding provided by USAID. Under both contracts, Mozambican personnel

are being trained to carry out the de-mining work, and trained mine-detector dogs are used as part of the process.

67. The Norwegian non-governmental organization Norwegian People's Aid, funded by the Government of Norway, first started operating in Tete Province clearing tracks and areas to facilitate the return of refugees from Malawi. The Norwegian People's Aid has now expanded its operation to Maputo Province and other border provinces, with additional funding provided by ONUMOZ. The Norwegian People's Aid has trained some 300 Mozambican de-miners. Halo Trust, in a project separate from its national survey and funded by the Government of the United Kingdom, has trained three teams of Mozambican de-miners and is working in Zambézia Province, clearing routes that are important in connection with the work of other British non-governmental organizations. UNHCR has been carrying out a mine-awareness education campaign, including the training of mine-awareness instructors in countries of asylum, and is cooperating with non-governmental organizations on mine-awareness both through direct instruction and a mass media campaign. UNICEF is also carrying out mine-awareness education inside Mozambique as a component of its other educational programmes.

68. The Mine-clearance Training Centre was originally established by ONUMOZ at Beira, but was subsequently relocated to Tete. It is staffed by military personnel provided as instructors by Australia, Bangladesh, the Netherlands and New Zealand. Under the accelerated plan, the Centre will have trained 450 Mozambican de-miners and supervisors, surveyors and instructors by the end of November 1994. The project is funded by ONUMOZ. The facility will be taken over by the Government of Mozambique as part of its de-mining programme after the ONUMOZ mandate is completed. The United Nations-trained de-miners will be deployed in 15 teams to carry out de-mining activities. Equipment for the teams has been provided by ONUMOZ. Commercial supervisors have also been contracted to supervise the teams in the field, but they will eventually be replaced as Mozambican supervisors become available. The first teams should be deployed by mid-September to undertake de-mining in Maputo Province, one of the most severely affected in Mozambique.

69. The clearance of the land-mines, which are impeding the economic and social development of Mozambique, will require a number of years. It is hoped that the Mozambican national capacity can eventually encompass all of the Mozambicans who have been engaged in mine-awareness and clearance efforts. The establishment of a national government entity, which is to assume responsibility for the de-mining programmes upon the expiry of the ONUMOZ mandate, has unfortunately also suffered delays. Additional technical and financial assistance will clearly be required after November 1994. Before that time, however, required managerial capacities must be created and a management training programme should be in place that would provide operational and financial management capacities and thus set the stage for the eventual assumption of full responsibility by the Government of Mozambique.

G. *United Nations support for development activities*

70. Mozambique is one of the largest recipients of foreign aid in Africa. According to data compiled by the UNDP Country Office for its *Development Cooperation Report 1991*, total reported external assistance amounted to $991 million in 1991 ($1,066 million in 1990), corresponding to $69 per capita. In 1991 (the last year for which UNDP produced a Development Cooperation Report), 33 per cent of total external assistance disbursements were classified as programme/budgetary aid and balance-of-payments support; 26 per cent as technical cooperation; 21.9 per cent as food aid and emergency relief assistance; and 19.2 per cent as investment project assistance. Bilateral donors accounted for 63.8 per cent of total disbursements reported to UNDP for 1991, the United Nations system for 17.2 per cent, other multilateral organizations for 13.3 per cent and non-governmental organizations for 5.8 per cent.

71. The 1993 Consultative Group meeting, organized by the World Bank, estimated external financing requirements for 1994 to be $1,089 million, excluding $405 million in debt relief, but including the special programmes stemming from the implementation of the peace agreement dealing with demobilization, de-mining, reintegration, resettlement, elections and non-food relief items. A total of $1,043 million was pledged at the Consultative Group meeting by the donor community. Mozambique is an active borrower from the International Development Association (IDA) facility of the World Bank. A total of 20 projects are currently being implemented with loans from the World Bank.

72. The net indicative planning figure (IPF) resources of the UNDP Fourth Country Programme 1993-1997 ($90.5 million) are targeted at strengthening institutional and human capacities in support of the transition processes and national programmes of Mozambique. The country programme areas of concentration are: poverty alleviation and post-war rehabilitation; economic and financial management; and environment and natural resources management. With regard to national reconstruction, besides ongoing assistance to reconstruction planning, UNDP is engaged in supporting Mozambique in several initiatives that specifically target poverty alleviation, post-war rehabilitation

and facilitation of resettlement and reintegration of displaced people, returning refugees and demobilized troops in the rural areas into the productive process. With respect to UNDP-administered funds, the United Nations Development Fund for Women (UNIFEM) is funding a successful pilot project in integrated village development for increased food production by women that focuses on access to rural credit. Involvement of the United Nations Capital Development Fund (UNCDF) in Mozambique dates only from 1989 and concentrates on feeder-road rehabilitation implemented by ILO and rural water supply projects implemented by UNICEF in the northern provinces. UNV specialists have been closely linked with IPF activities as a means of providing cost-effective technical assistance.

73. WFP assistance to Mozambique during the period 1992-1994 has been predominantly for returnees, displaced people, drought-affected families and demobilized soldiers. During this period, WFP provided 500,000 tons of various commodities and related transport and handling costs worth $232 million. WFP has also been involved in the support of various developmental activities. The main areas of concentration continue to be assistance to the social sectors, education, health, rehabilitation of feeder roads and support to basic urban services in Maputo City. WFP assistance during the period under review amounted to $37 million. A new development project, which gives major emphasis to rehabilitation of health and school facilities, is being prepared with the World Bank as an interface between emergency and development, to begin in early 1995.

74. For several years, UNHCR had a very limited programme of assistance for spontaneous returnees from neighbouring countries of asylum. Encouraged by the peace negotiations between the Government and RENAMO, UNHCR started preparations in 1992 for an integrated regional plan of action for the repatriation of 1.5 million refugees. A memorandum of understanding between the Government of Mozambique and UNHCR was signed in March 1993 which provided the overall framework for repatriation activities inside Mozambique. UNHCR estimated the total cost of the operation for the period 1993-1995 as $203 million, of which $100 million is for activities within Mozambique.

75. UNICEF support for development activities in the 1992-1994 period covers the sectors of health and nutrition, water and sanitation, education, rural development, children in difficult circumstances, information and social planning. Health programmes include maternal and child health, primary health care, essential drugs programmes, health education, nutrition and the rehabilitation of rural health infrastructures. The water programmes are designed to increase the number of clean water sources, primarily in rural areas. Area-based rural development programmes are concentrated in six districts in Inhambane, Manica and Zambézia Provinces.

76. The programme of the Food and Agriculture Organization of the United Nations (FAO) over the period 1992-1994 totalled $12 million, with additional support from UNDP of $8.7 million. The largest project is the development of an eight-year national family sector agricultural programme to begin in 1995. Other areas of importance have been early warning systems for food security, forestry and fisheries management, aquaculture training and extension, and the supply of root crop vegetative material for resettling families.

77. The Third Country Programme 1992-1994 of the United Nations Population Fund (UNFPA) aims to assist the Government in achieving more balanced population trends and distribution in maternal and infant mortality and morbidity through continuing improvement in the quality and coverage of maternal and child health and family planning services and promoting the status of women through the elimination of practices that hinder their participation in population and development activities.

78. The United Nations Industrial Development Organization (UNIDO) has been assisting the Government, with funding from UNDP, to define an industrial development policy. UNIDO funded and executed a project to formulate an environmentally sustainable industrial development programme in Mozambique. During 1992/93, an important area of activity was the promotion and development of small-scale industries through the execution of a UNDP-funded pilot project in Nampula Province.

79. Within the framework of the Global Programme on AIDS, the World Health Organization (WHO) has been supporting the national AIDS control programme since its inception in 1988. Through the regular budget of $4.2 million for the period 1992-1995, WHO is supporting the Mozambican Health Ministry through a number of health programmes in the area of development assistance.

80. The United Nations Educational, Scientific and Cultural Organization (UNESCO) is reinforcing its programmes in the country through policy and technical support to the national educational authorities. Educational projects are being designed within the framework of the education sector development strategy. In particular, initiatives are under way to assist Mozambican refugees returning from Malawi and Zimbabwe. Furthermore, negotiations are currently under way with the European Union in order to secure funding for education rehabilitation in Mozambique (emergency school reconstruction and supplies).

III. Assistance to the victims of cyclone Nadia

81. Cyclone Nadia hit Mozambique in March 1994, affecting several northern provinces. The province of Nampula was hardest hit, with 13 districts suffering heavy damage. More than 900,000 persons either lost their crops or housing according to an assessment mission of the Department of Humanitarian Affairs following the cyclone. The recorded death toll was 52, with 316 people injured. The disaster regrettably came soon after the war's end, and after the recent resettlement of many of the provinces' internally displaced. Many schools, health posts and roads—already woefully inadequate—were demolished. Power and water supplies were cut off to urban and peri-urban areas as a result of the destruction of electricity, water pump and piping networks.

82. In the first days following this calamity, the United Nations Office for Humanitarian Assistance Coordination, with the logistical support of ONUMOZ, organized flights of 200 tons of emergency relief supplies provided from the Department of Humanitarian Affairs and government stockpiles, as well as by non-governmental organizations and bilateral donors. In addition to food, medicines, relief and survival items, roofing sheets, tubes and generators were transported to the affected areas.

83. The damage to the cashew trees, which are the foundation of the rural cash economy, will have an impact for many years. In the affected areas, damage to the trees was between 80 and 90 per cent, and it will take from five to eight years for new trees to become productive after they are planted. Relief and reconstruction in the wake of the cyclone is well under way. Immediate food assistance was required for 80,000 persons. A total of $2.3 million of relief assistance was requested to supplement ongoing humanitarian programmes in the affected areas. By September 1994, donations totalling $1.6 million had been made available by donor Governments and United Nations agencies.

IV. Information provided by Member States

84. In addition to information provided in various parts of this report on humanitarian assistance provided by donor Governments, the following information has been made available by Member States to the Secretariat.

Denmark

85. In 1993, a total of 42 million Danish kroner in humanitarian grants was provided, out of which 25 million was channelled through United Nations agencies and non-governmental organizations. By mid-1994, a grant of 2.1 million Danish kroner was provided for relief operations following the damage caused by cyclone Nadia. Furthermore, 13 million Danish kroner are being granted through Danish non-governmental organizations this year, and it is also expected that 6 million Danish kroner will be channelled through UNHCR to assist refugees and displaced persons. Additionally, a special allocation of 50 million Danish kroner was made to support demobilization and reintegration efforts and rehabilitation activities.

Finland

86. During 1993, humanitarian assistance valued at 5 million Fmk was provided through various humanitarian organizations.

Germany

87. For the reporting period, relief supplies with a total value of 1 million DM were provided through United Nations agencies and non-governmental organizations. A total of 129.3 million DM was provided for various reconstruction and reintegration programmes in 1993, with a further 4.5 million DM having been provided thus far in 1994. Food aid, with a total value of 18 million DM, has also been supplied.

Namibia

88. A contribution of $1,000 has been made to the United Nations trust fund for Mozambique and arrangements are currently being made for a contribution to be made to the 1994 appeal for the repatriation and reintegration of Mozambican refugees of UNHCR.

Norway

89. Donations amounting to a total of 17.7 million Norwegian kroner have been made available through United Nations agencies and non-governmental organizations.

Portugal

90. Within the framework of the donors conference held at Rome in December 1992, a total of $4.5 million has been granted for reintegration programmes, including rehabilitation activities, reintegration of demobilized soldiers and emergency food aid. In addition, a sum of $2.7 million has been raised for projects in the health and education sectors in Mozambique and Angola to be implemented by non-governmental organizations.

Spain

91. Following the damage caused by cyclone Nadia, relief items valued at 16 million pesetas have been provided.

92. In 1993, assistance provided to Mozambique amounted to 9.1 million Swiss francs, with a further 5.5 million having been provided in the first six months of 1994. Resources have been channelled through the International Committee of the Red Cross, United Nations agencies and non-governmental organizations.

93. During the financial year 1 April 1994 to 31 March 1994, the United Kingdom spent over 30 million pounds sterling on bilateral assistance to Mozambique, covering balance-of-payment support, project aid, technical assistance and humanitarian aid.

Document 74

Report of the Secretary-General on ONUMOZ

S/1994/1196, 21 October 1994

I. Introduction

1. Two years after the signing of the General Peace Agreement for Mozambique in Rome on 4 October 1992, important results have been achieved in maintaining peace in Mozambique and preparing for the country's first multi-party elections. Despite the many difficulties encountered in this formidable process, Mozambique is now ready to hold these elections as scheduled, on 27 and 28 October 1994. Although the Security Council has not specifically requested an additional report, the present report is presented in order to bring the Council up to date, on the eve of the elections, on the latest developments in Mozambique.

II. Current status of the peace process and preparations for the elections

2. Significant progress has been achieved on all fronts since my last report to the Security Council on 26 August 1994 (S/1994/1002). Having reviewed the status of the peace process, I believe that essential conditions now exist for holding free and fair elections. Despite some apparent tension in recent weeks, there has been no violation of the cease-fire for many months; voter registration has concluded in an orderly manner; and the electoral campaign is now in its most active phase. More than 75,000 soldiers have been demobilized and a unified army comprising approximately 10,000 soldiers has been formed. The number of incidents of violent rioting in the country has significantly decreased and the political situation is relatively calm. These are important achievements.

3. On the negative side, however, the atmosphere during the electoral campaign has been tense and armed banditry has become widespread. This situation is exacerbated by the continuing proliferation of weapons despite the fact that, as of 11 October 1994, 111,539 weapons had been collected from troops of the two parties and 43,491 from the paramilitary forces.

4. After two extensions, voter registration, which started on 1 June 1994, ended on 2 September, with 6,396,061 voters having been registered. This represents 81 per cent of an estimated eligible population of 7,894,850. Some technical errors occurred during the initial phases of the registration process, but these were primarily a result of a lack of clear instructions to, or training of, the registration teams. This situation was corrected upon the issuance of necessary instructions by the electoral authorities. During the registration period, the United Nations Operation in Mozambique (ONUMOZ) received 83 complaints of irregularities, of which 34 were subsequently submitted to the National Elections Commission. ONUMOZ considers that these complaints should not seriously affect the overall electoral process.

5. After verifying the authenticity of supporting documentation, the National Elections Commission announced on 13 September 1994 that the applications of 12 presidential candidates had been accepted. One application was rejected by the Commission owing to a lack of the required number of endorsing signatures. The Commission accredited 14 political parties and coalitions to participate in the legislative elections. A total of 3,117 candidates will compete for the 250 seats in the National Assembly.

6. Because of the extension of the registration period, the electoral campaign did not begin formally until 22 September, 10 days later than initially planned. Although it started in a calm and constructive atmosphere, the campaign has become marred by an increasing volume of disturbances, inflammatory rhetoric and, in some cases, even physical attacks. In particular, several rallies of the Mozambique Liberation Front (FRELIMO) and the Resistência Nacional Moçambicana (RENAMO) and their leaders have been disrupted by clashes between their supporters

and militants of opposing parties. ONUMOZ neverthe-less believes that these incidents, despite their gravity, have not so far posed a serious threat to the democratic nature and fairness of the electoral process. Some public pronouncements made by certain candidates, however, could cast doubt on their commitment to accept the results of the elections. This is unfortunate and worrying.

7. In paragraph 23 of my previous report (S/1994/1002), I informed the Security Council of the situation regarding the funding of technical assistance for the electoral process and the Trust Fund for Assistance to Registered Political Parties. As of 17 October, the short-fall had still not been fully met. I appeal strongly to donors to honour their commitments and urgently bridge the existing funding gap.

8. The planning and execution of the actual voting presents a formidable challenge to the national electoral authorities and to the United Nations. Many of the organizational and logistical problems encountered during preparations for the verification of the poll have been overcome but there are still major needs in such areas as logistic support to election officials, transportation and communications.

9. ONUMOZ, United Nations agencies operating in Mozambique and non-governmental organizations, together with the national electoral authorities, have cooperated in putting together and executing an elaborate operational plan. During the two-day poll, voters will cast their ballots at approximately 7,300 electoral stations grouped in 2,700 polling sites throughout the country. ONUMOZ will observe and verify the polling and the counting of votes in all provinces with the help of approximately 2,100 United Nations electoral observers. Of this number, 570 observers will be provided by Member States and 279 will come from various United Nations headquarters. ONUMOZ will contribute 934 observers from its ranks, while the diplomatic community in Maputo and non-governmental organizations operating in Mozambique will second 278 personnel to serve as United Nations electoral observers. ONUMOZ will also work closely with the European Union, which will field 200 observers. In addition, several organizations, including the Organization of African Unity (OAU) and the Association of European Parliamentarians for Southern Africa, will provide observers, who will be either incor-porated in the ONUMOZ electoral teams or assisted, to the extent possible, by the Mission.

10. In paragraph 26 of my previous report (S/1994/1002), I emphasized that the most effective way to enhance the credibility of the elections was to ensure that the Mozambican political parties themselves partici-pated extensively in electoral observation. The Govern-ment of the United States of America has funded a

programme which was designed by ONUMOZ and which is presently being implemented by the International Republican Institute, the International Organization for Migration (IOM), and a non-governmental organization, Cooperative for American Relief Everywhere, Inc. (CARE). This programme, which provides training and financial benefits for up to 35,000 monitors from Mozambican parties, will help to ensure effective obser-vation of the elections by the parties at all polling stations. In a parallel programme funded by the Trust Fund for Assistance to Registered Political Parties, 78 repre-sentatives from all of the Mozambican parties are under-going computer training in order to enable them to verify the processing of election results at both the provincial and national levels.

11. Although the electoral process is generally pro-gressing well, I am concerned that there are still so many uncollected weapons and munitions throughout the country, including in undeclared and so far unverified depots. This problem has been exacerbated by the parties' lack of cooperation in the verification of some military bases and certain police installations, including those of the Quick Reaction Police. I trust that the Government and RENAMO recognize the critical importance of these and other verification activities for the confidence-building which is so vital for the success of the elections. I urge them to honour their commitments and to cooper-ate with ONUMOZ in implementing its mandate. It will be equally important to pursue this issue after the elec-tions, as a major element in the overall security situation in the country. In addition, the training of the new Mozambique Defence Forces and the upgrading of the national police will need to be vigorously pursued.

III. Observations

12. The people of Mozambique are to be congratu-lated for maintaining peace in their country and preparing themselves for the presidential and legislative elections which will bring closer the goals of achieving democracy, lasting peace and representative government.

13. There is an obvious risk that political tempera-tures will rise before and immediately after the poll. Particular caution and statesmanship will be required at this time. I am confident that the people of Mozambique possess the ability to consolidate peace and stability, especially during the very important transitional period after the elections. I am encouraged by repeated affirma-tions by FRELIMO, RENAMO and other competing parties of their commitment to the peace process and to a democratic future for Mozambique. It has been clear for the last two years that the resumption of conflict, or any outbreaks of violence or attempts to challenge the results of the elections as verified by ONUMOZ, would

provoke a very negative and strong reaction from the people of Mozambique and from the international community.

14. The future of Mozambique lies in the hands of its people and their leaders. I encourage them to maintain a constructive dialogue and to do all that is necessary to ensure that the elections are held in a secure and free atmosphere and that the post-election period will foster peace, stability and national reconciliation. The United Nations will continue to support and facilitate efforts to that end. In particular, efforts must continue to ensure post-electoral harmony by forging a national consensus, if not an agreement, about the democratic future of the country. This goal can only be achieved if account is taken both of the vital interests of all the parties involved in the peace process and of the role they can play in the country's future. The world will be watching Mozambique closely before and after the elections.

15. It will be important for the international community to continue to assist Mozambicans in the rehabilitation and reconstruction of their country. As called upon by the Security Council, I will, in due course, present to the competent bodies of this Organization my recommendations on the future role that the United Nations can play in these areas. Also, in a post-election submission to the Council, I will report on the disposition of the assets of ONUMOZ and on the withdrawal of the Mission, as set forth in paragraphs 34 to 38 of my previous report (S/1994/1002).

Document 75

Statement by the President of the Security Council appealing for a calm and responsible election process in Mozambique

S/PRST/1994/61, 21 October 1994

The Security Council has been following closely the progress made by the Government of Mozambique and the Resistência Nacional Moçambicana (RENAMO) towards the implementation of the general peace agreement for Mozambique. It commends them and the people of Mozambique for what has been achieved.

The Security Council believes that the necessary conditions have now been established for the holding of free and fair elections on 27 and 28 October 1994 under effective national and international monitoring. These elections, by providing the Mozambican people with an opportunity fully to exercise their right to vote, hold out the prospect of securing for them lasting peace, stability and democracy.

The Security Council appeals to all concerned to ensure that the election campaign and the subsequent voting are conducted in a calm and responsible manner; that the elections are held freely and fairly; that those in authority act with complete impartiality in order to avoid any allegation of fraud; and that the election days and their aftermath are characterized by the absence of violence or the threat of violence. It also appeals to all parties to respect the safety and security of the officials of the National Elections Commission and the international election observers and to assist them to carry out their mandate.

The Security Council reiterates its intention to endorse the results of the elections should the United Nations declare them free and fair, and reminds the parties of their obligation, under the general peace agreement, fully to abide by the results.

The Security Council trusts that the parties will be guided, after the elections, by the spirit of reconciliation as well as the principles of democracy and the need to work together in harmony to reconstruct their country, thereby enabling the international community to continue to support Mozambique as it pursues rehabilitation and reconstruction.

The Security Council takes this opportunity to express its appreciation to the Secretary-General, his Special Representative and the personnel of the United Nations Operation in Mozambique (ONUMOZ) and calls upon the parties to continue to cooperate with them to ensure the fulfilment of the ONUMOZ mandate, including verification of their complete demobilization and disarmament.

Document 76

Letter dated 27 October 1994 from Zimbabwe transmitting the final communiqué of the Summit Meeting of the Frontline States held in Harare, Zimbabwe, on 25 October 1994

Not issued as a United Nations document

The Permanent Mission of the Republic of Zimbabwe to the United Nations presents its compliments to the Office of the Secretary-General of the United Nations and has the honour to attach herewith a Final Communiqué of the Summit Meeting of the Frontline States held in Harare, Zimbabwe, on Tuesday 25 October 1994.

The Permanent Mission of the Republic of Zimbabwe to the United Nations avails itself of this opportunity of renewing to the Office of the Secretary-General of the United Nations the assurances of its highest consideration.

Final communiqué of the Summit Meeting of the Frontline States held in Harare, Zimbabwe, Tuesday, 25 October, 1994

1. The Summit Meeting of the Heads of State and Government and Heads of Delegation of the Frontline States and Lesotho, Malawi and Swaziland was held in Harare, Republic of Zimbabwe, on 25 October 1994.

2. Participating in the Summit were:

(i) His Excellency Mr. Robert G. Mugabe, President of the Republic of Zimbabwe and Chairman of the Frontline States.

(ii) His Excellency Sir Ketumile Masire, President of the Republic of Botswana.

(iii) His Excellency Mr. Joaquim Chissano, President of the Republic of Mozambique.

(iv) His Excellency Mr. Ali Hassan Mwinyi, President of the United Republic of Tanzania.

(v) His Excellency Mr. Sam Nujoma, President of the Republic of Namibia.

(vi) His Excellency Mr. Frederick J.T. Chiluba, President of the Republic of Zambia.

(vii) His Excellency Mr. Bakili Muluzi, President of the Republic of Malawi.

(viii) The Right Honourable Dr. Ntsu Mokhehle, Prime Minister of the Kingdom of Lesotho.

(ix) The Honourable Prince Mbilini, Prime Minister of the Kingdom of Swaziland.

(x) The Honourable Dr. Antonio Pitra Neto, Minister of Public Administration of the Republic of Angola.

(xi) The Honourable Mr. Aziz Pahad, Deputy Minister of Foreign Affairs of the Republic of South Africa.

Mozambique

3. The Summit was briefed by His Excellency Mr. Joaquim Chissano, the President of the Republic of Mozambique, on the problems and prospects of the implementation of the Rome Peace Accords and the impending 27-28 October 1994 Mozambican multi-party elections.

4. The Summit noted with satisfaction that the electoral campaign has taken place in an orderly and peaceful manner and expressed the hope that the forthcoming elections shall be free and fair, thus consolidating national unity, democracy and reconciliation in Mozambique.

5. The Summit considered imperative strict respect for the letter and spirit of the General Peace Accords, which should remain the fundamental norm of the whole process for both signatories as well as for the international community.

6. The Summit considered that the fundamental conditions for the holding of free and fair elections are already in place.

7. The Summit called on all Mozambican parties to accept the results of the 27-28 October 1994 democratic elections, once they have been declared free and fair, and further reaffirmed the commitment of Southern African States to accept the decision of the Mozambican people in those elections.

8. The Summit rejected the imposition of any political system of government from outside. The Summit called upon the international community to prevent and condemn in the strongest terms, interference by foreign interests that could compromise the implementation of the Mozambican peace process.

9. The Summit made a firm commitment to support the government that emerges from a free and fair election in Mozambique and to harness the resources of the region for the consolidation of democratic order, peace, stability and prosperity of the people of Mozambique.

10. The Summit resolved to continue to monitor the

situation in Mozambique and to be ready to take appropriate and timely action if the situation so demands. The Summit further urged the international community to support the reconstruction and development of Mozambique which are prerequisites for peace and democracy, not only in that country, but in the region as a whole.

11. The Summit noted, with satisfaction, the important role played by the United Nations in building up the peace process in Mozambique and the Rome Accords. The Summit called upon the United Nations to complete its mandate in a manner that will consolidate peace in Mozambique.

Angola

12. The Summit was briefed by the Honourable Dr. Antonio Pitra Neto on the grave social, military and political situation in Angola, and in particular on the negotiations in Lusaka between the Government and UNITA.

Document 77

Statement by the Secretary-General emphasizing that Mozambique's elections must proceed as planned

UN Press Release SG/SM/5456, 27 October 1994

The Secretary-General has been informed by his Special Representative that difficulties have been encountered during the first day of elections in Mozambique. The Secretary-General woud like to emphasize that elections must go ahead as planned and agreed by the parties. It is essential that the parties must fully honour their commitments in this regard. In the event of questions being raised about the electoral process, the Secretary-General would like to draw the attention of the parties to the fact that there is a mechanism already in place to address such issues. The Secretary-General looks forward to the satisfactory conclusion of the elections in which the international community and the United Nations have invested so much.

Document 78

Message from the President of the Security Council urging RENAMO to reconsider its decision to withdraw from the elections

UN Press Release SC/5922, 27 October 1994

I have been asked by the members of the Security Council to appeal to you most earnestly to reconsider your decision to withdraw RENAMO from the elections currently taking place in Mozambique. Appropriate procedures are in place through the National Elections Commission whereby any concern RENAMO may have can be addressed.

In its statement of 21 October 1994, the Security Council expressed its satisfaction at the progress made by both parties towards implementation of the General Peace Agreement, and its support for the elections which have now begun in an orderly atmosphere. It noted that these elections hold out for the people of your country the prospect of securing lasting peace, stability and democracy. On behalf of the members of the Security Council, I urge your party not to put this opportunity in peril.

Document 79

Joint declaration issued in Maputo on 28 October 1994 by the international members of the Supervisory and Monitoring Commission, welcoming the decision of RENAMO President Afonso Dhlakama to participate fully in the elections

Not issued as a United Nations document

1. The Chairman of the CSC, the Special Representative of the Secretary-General of the United Nations, Dr. Aldo Ajello, and the international members of the Supervisory and Monitoring Commission (CSC) have noted with concern the list of alleged electoral irregularities submitted to the National Elections Commission (CNE) by RENAMO and certain other Opposition parties on 26 October 1994.

2. The CSC members recognise that thus far the CNE has not been able to satisfy RENAMO and other Opposition parties about the issues they have raised. The CSC members note that a number of potentially serious irregularities have been identified by RENAMO and undertake to make every effort to ensure that these complaints are fully investigated and, where possible, resolved prior to the completion of polling.

3. Considering their responsibility to help ensure the full and timely implementation of the General Peace Agreement, the CSC members wish to remind all parties concerned that any evidence of significant electoral fraud will prevent the elections from being declared free and fair by them. They urge that the difficulties that have until now prevented the full participation of all parties in the elections be swiftly resolved in a spirit of reconciliation and an atmosphere of mutual respect.

4. The CSC members warmly welcome the decision of the President of RENAMO, Mr. Afonso Dhlakama, to participate fully in elections in spite of the serious reservations expressed by RENAMO in recent days.

5. The CSC members note that provision has been made in the Electoral Law for the voting period to be extended to three days if necessary. They recommend that the CNE should adopt a flexible approach to ensure that sufficient time is made available to allow a high voter turnout and the resolution of as many difficulties and potential irregularities as possible before the polls close.

Maputo, 28 October 1994

Aldo AJELLO
Special Representative of the Secretary-General
of the United Nations

Ahcene FZERI
Ambassador Extraordinary and Plenipotentiary
Organization of African Unity

Robert PUISSANT
Ambassador Extraordinary and Plenipotentiary
Embassy of the Republic of France

Helmut RAU
Ambassador Extraordinary and Plenipotentiary
Embassy of the Federal Republic of Germany

Manfredo INCISA DI CAMERANA
Ambassador Extraordinary and Plenipotentiary
Embassy of the Republic of Italy

Manuel LOPES DA COSTA
Ambassador Extraordinary and Plenipotentiary
Embassy of the Republic of Portugal

Richard EDIS
Ambassador Extraordinary and Plenipotentiary
Embassy of the United Kingdom of Great Britain
and Northern Ireland

Dennis C. JETT
Ambassador Extraordinary and Plenipotentiary
Embassy of the United States of America

Document 80

Letter dated 9 November 1994 from the Secretary-General to the President of the Security Council recommending a technical extension of the mandate of ONUMOZ

S/1994/1282, 11 November 1994

As members of the Security Council are aware, the first multi-party elections in Mozambique were conducted on 27, 28 and 29 October 1994.

In his preliminary statement of 2 November 1994 (see annex), my Special Representative, Mr. Aldo Ajello, emphasized that the polling process had been peaceful and had been conducted in a well-organized manner, with few technical problems. With the assistance of approximately 2,300 international electoral observers, the United Nations monitored the polling, during which no reports of major irregularities, incidents or breaches of the Electoral Law of Mozambique were received. It was emphasized that following the completion of the counting of votes, the Special Representative would be in a position to make an official pronouncement on behalf of the United Nations concerning the fairness of the entire electoral process. Similar statements were made by the European Union election observation mission in Mozambique and by the Special Representative of the Organization of African Unity in Mozambique. I would like to take this opportunity to pay tribute to the people of Mozambique as well as to all the staff of the United Nations Operation in Mozambique (ONUMOZ) for this remarkable achievement.

Since the polling was extended for an additional day until 29 October 1994, the deadline for the publication of the final electoral results is now set for 13 November 1994. According to article 275 of the Electoral Law, the investiture of the Assembly of the Republic is to take place within 15 days of the publication of the election results. On the assumption that it will take 15 days to complete this entire process and that a second round of presidential elections is not required, the swearing in of the President should take place by 10 December 1994. Article 274 of the Electoral Law provides that the President of the Republic should assume office within eight days of the above investiture. The swearing in of the President would also be considered as the date the new Government takes office.

It will be recalled that, by its resolution 916 (1994) of 5 May 1994, the Security Council decided to renew the mandate of ONUMOZ for a final period until 15 November 1994 at the strength described in paragraphs 22, 24 and 25 of my report to the Council of 28 April 1994 (S/1994/511), subject to the proviso that the Council would further review the status of the mission periodically. Such reviews were conducted on several occasions, on the basis of submissions presented to the Security Council and of the report of the Security Council mission which visited Mozambique from 7 to 12 August 1994 (S/1994/1009).

In several of my reports to the Security Council, most recently in paragraph 34 of my report dated 26 August 1994 (S/1994/1002), I indicated that the withdrawal of ONUMOZ would begin after the elections and would be concluded by the end of January 1995. In that report, I also mentioned that, in accordance with the provisions of the general peace agreement, the presence of the United Nations in Mozambique would be required until such time as the new Government takes office. It was also stressed that the planned withdrawal of ONUMOZ was contingent on the holding of peaceful, free and fair elections, the timely announcement of the results of the elections and the subsequent establishment of the new Government.

Having the above considerations in mind, I recommend that the mandate of ONUMOZ be extended for technical reasons until such time as the new Government is installed. This is expected to take place by 15 December 1994. During this period, ONUMOZ would continue its present functions of good offices, as well as its verification and monitoring activities, as mandated by the Security Council in its relevant resolutions on Mozambique. This recommendation is made on the understanding that the overall framework for the drawdown of ONUMOZ, as set forth in paragraphs 34 to 38 of my report of 26 August 1994 (S/1994/1002), would remain in effect, with appropriate adjustments to be made to the withdrawal schedule of United Nations military and police personnel; in particular, there will be a need to extend the duration of the withdrawal of some United Nations military and police observers. It is expected that the above adjustments will have no significant financial implications for the Organization.

I would be grateful if you would bring this matter to the attention of the members of the Security Council.

(*Signed*) Boutros BOUTROS-GHALI

Annex

Preliminary statement by the Special Representative
of the Secretary-General for Mozambique
Maputo, 2 November 1994

Elections in the Republic of Mozambique,
27-29 October 1994

1. At 1800 hours on the evening of 29 October 1994, after being extended to a third day, the polling period of the first-ever multi-party elections in Mozambique was concluded. As I speak, the counting of the ballots for both the presidential and the legislative elections is in full process.

2. The voting has taken place peacefully, in a well-organized manner marked by very few technical problems. The United Nations, through its more than 2,300 international observers, has received no information about any major irregularity, incident or breach of the Electoral Law which could have adversely affected the validity of the elections.

3. Ballots were cast in all districts and all provinces at a total of 7,244 polling stations. Throughout the country, the process was carried out in a calm and positive atmosphere. The voters, the electoral authorities and the political parties all demonstrated their commitment to the success of the elections. In particular, the three days of voting have been characterized by a remarkable absence of violence, intimidation and coercion.

4. The polling began on schedule on Thursday, 27 October. Owing to logistical problems and the delayed arrival of material, some polling stations opened late on the first day and, in a few isolated cases, polling stations did not open at all that day. These problems were resolved on the second day, and the extension of the polling by one day offered ample opportunity to all those who wished to exercise their right to vote.

5. The initial reservation by the Resistência Nacional Moçambicana (RENAMO) to participate in the elections created some confusion on the first day of voting. However, the guarantees of close monitoring by the international community, which brought RENAMO back into the process, as well as the additional voting day ensured that the situation did not unduly affect the polling process. During the entire voting period, RENAMO party monitors continued to verify the voting at most polling stations together with their counterparts from the other political parties.

6. There was a massive voter turnout nationwide. In some provinces, more than 90 per cent of the registered voters went to the polls. The overcrowding on the first day of polling created temporary disruptions at some polling stations. But there were no serious incidents and order was quickly restored everywhere. The voters showed exemplary patience, often waiting for more than half a day to contribute their part to the building of multi-party democracy in their country.

7. Because the announcement of the third day of voting was made only late into the second polling day, the news did not reach some remote voting stations. As a result, these stations began the counting of the ballots after closing the polls on the evening of 28 October. When the information was received, most polling stations returned the ballots to the boxes, which were resealed—all in the presence of the party monitors—and voting continued the next day. In a few instances, voting did not occur on the third day, but it is unlikely that voters who had wished to vote were unable to do so.

8. The United Nations observation would not support any possible claim of fraud or intimidation, or any other patterns of incidents that could have affected the credibility of the elections. Indeed, the voting can be described as having been carried out peacefully and with integrity.

9. I wish to express my warmest tribute to the people of Mozambique, who once again proved their commitment to democracy and a strong will to live in peace and harmony. Whatever the outcome of the voting, they are the main protagonists of the peace process and outright winners of these elections.

10. Let me congratulate the National Elections Commission, and in particular its President, Mr. Brazão Mazula, for the excellent job done in arranging the polling. I also wish to praise the political parties and candidates, who, through their conduct during the polling, have demonstrated their seriousness in participating in the process of democratization of their country.

11. Finally, I thank the international community, the non-governmental organizations as well as the personnel of ONUMOZ for their active participation in the observation efforts on those three memorable days in the history of Mozambique.

12. As I mentioned earlier, the electoral process will only be over when the counting process is completed. ONUMOZ will continue to be vigilant throughout this last important phase. Following the completion of the count, I shall be in a position to make an official pronouncement on behalf of the United Nations in respect of the freedom and fairness of the entire electoral process.

Document 81

Security Council resolution extending the mandate of ONUMOZ until 15 December 1994 at the latest

S/RES/957 (1994), 15 November 1994

The Security Council,

Reaffirming its resolution 782 (1992) of 13 October 1992 and all subsequent relevant resolutions,

Taking note of the letter from the Secretary-General to the President of the Security Council on the United Nations Operation in Mozambique (ONUMOZ) dated 9 November 1994 (S/1994/1282),

Having considered the report of the Secretary-General on ONUMOZ dated 26 August 1994 (S/1994/1002),

Having considered also the report of the Security Council Mission to Mozambique, dated 29 August 1994 (S/1994/1009),

Commending the efforts of the Secretary-General, his Special Representative and all the staff of ONUMOZ,

1. *Welcomes* the elections that took place in Mozambique on 27, 28 and 29 October 1994 in accordance with the General Peace Agreement;

2. *Reiterates* its intention to endorse the results of the elections should the United Nations declare them free and fair and calls upon all Mozambican parties to accept and fully abide by the results of the elections;

3. *Also calls upon* all Mozambican parties to complete the process of national reconciliation based, as provided for in the General Peace Agreement, on a system of multi-party democracy and the observance of democratic principles which will ensure lasting peace and political stability;

4. *Decides* to extend the existing mandate of ONUMOZ until the new Government of Mozambique takes office, as recommended by the Secretary-General in his letter of 9 November 1994, but not later than 15 December 1994, and authorizes ONUMOZ, in particular a limited number of civilian logisticians, mine-clearance and training personnel, military specialists, staff officers and a small detachment of infantry, to complete its residual operations prior to its withdrawal on or before 31 January 1995;

5. *Requests* the Secretary-General to advise the Security Council when the installation of the new government has been accomplished;

6. *Approves* the withdrawal schedule as described by the Secretary-General in his report of 26 August 1994 and in his letter of 9 November 1994 for the safe and orderly withdrawal of all ONUMOZ military and civilian personnel before 31 January 1995;

7. *Invites* the Secretary-General to submit in timely fashion a final report on the termination of ONUMOZ;

8. *Decides* to remain actively seized of the matter.

Document 82

Statement by the Special Representative of the Secretary-General declaring the Mozambique elections free and fair

UN Press Release SG/SM/5488, 19 November 1994

The results of the first multi-party elections in Mozambique were announced today by the National Elections Commission. In accordance with the provisions of the General Peace Agreement, the United Nations has observed the entire electoral process. This included the initial preparations for the elections, the registration of voters, the electoral campaign, the polling from 27 to 29 October 1994 as well as the counting of votes.

The electoral process has been characterized by the impartiality, the dedication and the high degree of professionalism displayed by the electoral authorities. It has been distinguished by the strong commitment of the political players to let the principles of democracy prevail.

And it has confirmed the will of the Mozambican people to live in peace and harmony.

Problems have occurred, irregularities were recorded and disruptions did take place. However, throughout the entire process there has been no event or series of events which could affect the overall credibility of the elections.

The registration of voters, after being extended twice, was concluded on 2 September 1994 with 81 per cent of the estimated voter population registered. Initial administrative problems and technical errors were corrected by the Technical Secretariat for Electoral Administration. Some political parties alleged intimidation, fraud and irregularities, such as false identification, registration of minors and foreigners as well as misuse of electoral funds. Only a limited number of cases could be substantiated.

The electoral campaign formally started on 22 September, 10 days later than initially planned due to the extension of the registration period. With very few exceptions, political rallies proceeded peacefully and the parties were able to campaign freely.

Civic education was carried out in an impartial manner by Mozambicans specifically trained for this purpose. Despite the recognized insufficiency of the civic education campaign, the high turnout of voters during the polling days demonstrated that most Mozambicans were informed about the process.

As I noted in my preliminary statement, the polling was carried out peacefully and with integrity. RENAMO's initial reservation about participation in the elections was overcome by guarantees of close monitoring of the process by the international community. The United Nations Operation in Mozambique (ONUMOZ) carefully examined all the complaints, allegations and concerns presented by RENAMO and other political parties.

In accordance with the Electoral Law, the results of the national count were to be announced within 15 days of the close of the polls. However, the counting process took longer than initially foreseen. This was mainly due to the need to ensure absolute accuracy and transparency under the scrutiny of political party monitors and United Nations observers. In addition, mathematical errors complicated the computerization of the data at the provincial level. Yet, the counting process was carried out in an orderly manner and our observation confirms the credibility of the results as publicized today.

On behalf of the United Nations, I therefore declare that the elections held in Mozambique from 27 to 29 October 1994 were free and fair. The outcome of the Presidential elections and the composition of the new Assembly of the Republic reflect the will of the Mozambican voters.

The future of Mozambique lies in the hands of the Mozambican people and their leaders. I am sure that they will be able to join their energies, creativity and capabilities in a common endeavour to meet the challenges of reconstruction and development and to ensure lasting peace, stability and national reconciliation.

Document 83

Statement by the Secretary-General congratulating the people and the leaders of Mozambique on the elections

UN Press Release SG/SM/5489, 19 November 1994

The people of Mozambique have exercised their right of voting in the presidential and parliamentary elections in a calm and peaceful atmosphere. The Chairman of the National Elections Commission has today announced the results of the elections. My Special Representative has, in turn, declared that, notwithstanding some irregularities, the elections were free and fair.

I wish to take this opportunity to congratulate the people and the leaders of Mozambique on this successful outcome. I call on all Mozambicans now to begin the task of national reconciliation and to ensure that peace and stability prevail in their country and region.

Document 84

Security Council resolution calling upon all Mozambican parties to stand by their obligation to accept the results of the elections

S/RES/960 (1994), 21 November 1994

The Security Council,

Reaffirming its resolution 782 (1992) and all subsequent relevant resolutions,

Expressing its appreciation for the efforts of the Secretary-General, his Special Representative and the United Nations Operation in Mozambique and its staff for ensuring the successful completion of the electoral process,

1. *Welcomes* the elections that took place in Mozambique on 27, 28 and 29 October 1994 in accordance with the General Peace Agreement;

2. *Welcomes also* the statement of the Special Representative of the Secretary-General of 19 November

1994 (SG/SM/5488) on the results of the elections, declaring them free and fair;

    3. *Endorses* the results of these elections;

    4. *Calls upon* all Mozambican parties to stand by their obligation to accept and fully abide by the results of the elections;

    5. *Also calls* upon all Mozambican parties to continue the process of national reconciliation based, as provided for in the General Peace Agreement, on a system of multi-party democracy and the observance of democratic principles which will ensure lasting peace and political stability;

    6. *Urges* all States and relevant international organizations to contribute actively to the reconstruction and rehabilitation of Mozambique;

    7. *Decides* to remain seized of the matter.

Document 85

Statement by the President of the General Assembly expressing satisfaction with the smooth conduct of the Mozambican elections

UN Press Release GA/8816, 21 November 1994

At the conclusion of the electoral process which took place in Mozambique, and following the announcement by the National Elections Commission of the results of these first multi-party electoral consultations, Amara Essy, President of the United Nations General Assembly, wishes to express his deep satisfaction with the smooth conduct of the elections and the peaceful climate which prevailed during them.

    The President of the General Assembly is convinced that these elections have enabled Mozambique to move irreversibly along the road to democracy and that the Mozambican people will now be able to launch and win the only battle worth fighting, namely, the battle for the reconstruction and economic and social development of Mozambique and for the achievement of the well-being of the people of Mozambique.

    The President of the General Assembly reiterates his appreciation and congratulations to the Special Representative of the Secretary-General for Mozambique, and to all persons of good will who helped to find a solution to the crisis in Mozambique.

Document 86

Letter dated 30 November 1994 from the Minister for Foreign Affairs of Mozambique to the Secretary-General

Not issued as a United Nations document

The signing of the General Peace Agreement for Mozambique in Rome, on 4 October 1992, marked the launching of a new era in the history of my country. Indeed, over the last two years of the implementation of the Rome Agreement, remarkable events have taken place, culminating with the holding of the first multi-party general elections on 27, 28 and 29 October 1994.

    The people of Mozambique and my Government welcomed the unanimously adopted Security Council resolution 960 (1994) on 21 November, which, *inter alia*, endorsed the results of the elections, declared them free and fair and urged all States and relevant international organizations to contribute actively to the reconstruction and rehabilitation of Mozambique.

    By its resolution 957 (1994) of 15 November 1994 the Security Council, *inter alia*, decided to extend the existing mandate of ONUMOZ until the new Government of Mozambique takes office, but not later than 15 December 1994, and authorized the ONUMOZ to complete its residual operations prior to its withdrawal on or before 31 January 1995.

    On behalf of the people and Government of Mozambique, I wish to seize this opportunity to pay tribute to Your Excellency for the outstanding efforts you have made for the success of this operation.

    Through you, I wish to express my Government's gratitude to your Special Representative, Mr. Aldo Ajello, for the significant role he has played in the implementation of the Rome Agreement and to all those men and women who have contributed for the success of the United Nations Operation in Mozambique.

As the United Nations Operation in Mozambique (ONUMOZ) is winding up and a new chapter in the history of my country is beginning, I look forward to a continued presence of the United Nations in Mozambique through its Specialized Agencies and relevant Organs. I wish to pledge our firm determination to continue working with you in the years ahead.

Please accept, Mr. Secretary-General, the assurances of my highest consideration.

(*Signed*) Dr. Pascoal Manuel MOCUMBI

Document 87

Letter dated 13 December 1994 from the Secretary-General to the Minister for Foreign Affairs of Mozambique on the end of the ONUMOZ mandate and congratulating the leaders and the people of Mozambique on the successful implementation of the General Peace Agreement

Not issued as a United Nations document

Thank you for your kind letter dated 30 November 1994. It is indeed gratifying that, two years after the historic signing in Rome on 4 October 1992 of the General Peace Agreement, the United Nations Operation in Mozambique (ONUMOZ) has successfully concluded its political mandate. With the inauguration of President Joaquim Chissano on 9 December 1994, the relevant provisions of Security Council resolution 957 (1994) concerning the extension of ONUMOZ have been fulfilled, and the Mission is now proceeding with residual activities.

I would like to congratulate you warmly on the successful implementation of the main provisions of the Rome Agreement which have culminated in the holding of free and fair elections in Mozambique in late October this year. This remarkable achievement is attributable foremost to the people of Mozambique and their leaders, who have demonstrated their determination to move toward peace, stability and reconciliation. Your Excellency's expression of gratitude for the outstanding effort made by the Organization and, in particular, for the role played by my Special Representative and the personnel of ONUMOZ in promoting the peace process in Mozambique is a source of deep satisfaction.

I would like to take this opportunity to express my appreciation for the cooperation Your Excellency's Government has extended to ONUMOZ during the last two years, and convey to your Government and the people of Mozambique my best wishes for the earliest resolution, in pursuance of the General Peace Agreement, of all issues which remain outstanding.

I would like to assure you that the United Nations will continue to assist Mozambique in strengthening the national reconciliation process, its new democratic institutions, as well as its economic and social integration.

Accept, Excellency, the assurances of my highest consideration.

(*Signed*) Boutros BOUTROS-GHALI

Document 88

Statement by the President of the Security Council welcoming the installation of the President of Mozambique and the inauguration of the new Assembly

S/PRST/1994/80, 14 December 1994

The Security Council welcomes the installation of the President of the Republic of Mozambique and the inauguration of the new Assembly of the Republic of Mozam- bique following the first Mozambican multi-party elections, as provided for in the General Peace Agreement, that were held on 27, 28 and 29 October 1994, which were declared as having been free and fair and were endorsed by the Council in its resolution 960 (1994) of 21 November 1994.

The Security Council congratulates the people and the parties of Mozambique for their peaceful fulfilment of the goals set out in the General Peace Agreement. It encourages them to continue their efforts in good faith to ensure post-election harmony on the basis, *inter alia*, of the observance of democratic principles. It believes that, with the new governmental structure in place, the foundations have been laid to secure lasting peace, stability, national reconciliation and democracy.

The Security Council commends the Secretary-General, his Special Representative and the United Nations Operation in Mozambique (ONUMOZ) and its staff for their fulfilment of the mandate of ONUMOZ and for their efforts in assisting the successful achievement of the objectives of the General Peace Agreement.

The Security Council notes that, ONUMOZ having completed its mission, its mandate has come to an end and ONUMOZ will be finally withdrawn from Mozambique by 31 January 1995 in accordance with resolution 957 (1994) of 15 November 1994. In this connection, it looks forward to the Secretary-General's report on the final disposition of the assets of ONUMOZ within the framework of the withdrawal of ONUMOZ, as requested in its statement of 7 September 1994 (S/PRST/1994/51). In that context, it also expresses the hope that effective arrangements for the disposition and, as appropriate, the destruction of weapons and the establishment, with the assistance of the United Nations, of a national de-mining capability will be in place prior to the final withdrawal of ONUMOZ, and that consideration will be given to leaving de-mining and other equipment in Mozambique after the withdrawal, subject to the appropriate arrangements.

The Security Council emphasizes that the post-election period will be an important and delicate time, during which there is a continuing need for the international community to assist the Government and people of Mozambique in the reconstruction and redevelopment of their country. It notes the intention of the Secretary-General to report to the competent United Nations bodies on future United Nations activities in Mozambique. It urges all States and relevant international organizations to contribute actively to these efforts.

Document 89

General Assembly resolution concerning assistance to Mozambique

A/RES/49/21 D, 20 December 1994

The General Assembly,

Recalling Security Council resolutions 386 (1976) of 17 March 1976 and 782 (1992) of 13 October 1992,

Recalling also its relevant resolutions, in particular resolution 45/227 of 21 December 1990 and resolution 47/42 of 9 December 1992, in which it urged the international community to respond effectively and generously to the call for assistance to Mozambique,

Reaffirming the principles for humanitarian assistance contained in the annex to its resolution 46/182 of 19 December 1991,

Recalling further its resolution 48/7 of 19 October 1993 on assistance in mine clearance, and noting with great concern the proliferation of land-mines in areas that had been the scene of war in Mozambique,

Bearing in mind the donors conference held at Rome in December 1992 and the follow-up meeting held at Maputo in June 1993, the main objective of which was to mobilize resources for post-war programming in support of the resettlement and reintegration of returning refugees, internally displaced persons and demobilized soldiers,

Bearing in mind also the Paris Declaration and the Programme of Action for the Least Developed Countries for the 1990s, 1/ adopted by the Second United Nations Conference on the Least Developed Countries on 14 September 1990,

Stressing the need for continuing support for humanitarian assistance in view of the ongoing process of repatriation, resettlement and reintegration of the returning refugees, internally displaced persons and demobilized soldiers,

Stressing also that Mozambique is emerging from a devastating war and that a proper response to the current situation in the country requires substantial international assistance provided in a comprehensive and integrated manner and linking humanitarian assistance with economic aid for national reconstruction and development,

Noting with gratitude the mobilization and allocation by relevant organizations of the United Nations system and intergovernmental and non-governmental organizations of resources for a post-war consolidated humanitarian assistance programme for Mozambique,

Welcoming the role played by all parties and the people of Mozambique in general in the implementation of the General Peace Agreement for Mozambique, signed at Rome on 4 October 1992, 2/ whose main goals are the establishment of lasting peace, the enhancement of democracy and the promotion of national reconciliation in that country,

Having considered the report of the Secretary-General of 16 September 1994 on assistance to Mozambique, 3/

1. *Takes note* of the report of the Secretary-General;

2. *Expresses its gratitude* to all States and intergovernmental and non-governmental organizations that have rendered assistance to Mozambique;

3. *Notes with appreciation* that a mine-clearance programme is under way in Mozambique, with the support of the United Nations, in close cooperation with Governments and intergovernmental and non-governmental organizations, and urges the international community to continue to provide the needed assistance for the accomplishment of the mine-clearance programme in that country;

4. *Commends* the people of Mozambique for their diligence and tireless efforts in pursuit of lasting peace and stability in that country;

5. *Expresses its satisfaction* at the successful implementation of the General Peace Agreement for Mozambique, which has created favourable conditions for the establishment of lasting peace, the enhancement of democracy, the promotion of national reconciliation and the implementation of a programme of national reconstruction and development for Mozambique;

6. *Welcomes* the successful implementation of the

General Peace Agreement, which culminated in the holding of multi-party elections in October 1994 in that country;

7. *Calls upon* the international community and intergovernmental and non-governmental organizations to continue to render their generous assistance to Mozambique in the form of financial, material and technical support for the repatriation of refugees and the resettlement and reintegration of the returning refugees, internally displaced persons and demobilized soldiers;

8. *Appeals* to the international community to extend its support to the Government and people of Mozambique in order to establish lasting peace and democracy and to promote an effective programme of national reconstruction and development in that country;

9. *Requests* the Secretary-General, in close cooperation with the Government of Mozambique:

(a) To continue his efforts to mobilize international assistance for the national reconstruction and development of Mozambique;

(b) To ensure the coordination of the work of the United Nations system for an adequate response to the humanitarian assistance and development needs of Mozambique;

(c) To prepare a report on international assistance for the national reconstruction and development of Mozambique for submission to the General Assembly at its fifty-first session.

1/ A/CONF.147/18, part one.
2/ See *Official Records of the Security Council, Forty-seventh Year, Supplement for October, November and December 1992*, document S/24635, annex.
3/ A/49/387.

Document 90

Final report of the Secretary-General on ONUMOZ

S/1994/1449, 23 December 1994

I. Introduction

1. The present report is submitted pursuant to Security Council resolution 957 (1994) of 15 November 1994, in which the Council invited me to submit a final report on the termination of the United Nations Operation in Mozambique (ONUMOZ). The present report summarizes the status of implementation of the General Peace Agreement (S/24635, annex) as at 9 December 1994, the date of expiry of the mandate of ONUMOZ. It also provides updated information on the withdrawal of ONUMOZ personnel.

II. Political and military aspects

A. General

2. The mandate given to ONUMOZ two years ago by the Security Council in its resolution 797 (1992) of 16 December 1992 has now been successfully accomplished. ONUMOZ has verified and monitored the implementation of the General Peace Agreement, signed on 4 October 1992 at Rome, from the establishment of the initial implementation structures to the assembly of approximately 92,000 troops and the demobilization of 80,000 of them. It coordinated and monitored humani-

tarian assistance operations, provided technical assistance to and verified the entire electoral process, culminating in the holding of free and fair elections on 27 to 29 October 1994. It assisted in the formation of the new joint army of almost 12,000 troops and, in accordance with Security Council resolution 898 (1994) of 23 February 1994, monitored the activities of the Mozambican national police.

3. The last meeting of the Supervisory and Monitoring Commission (CSC) was held on 6 December 1994. At that meeting, the chairmen of the Cease-fire Commission (CCF), the Joint Commission for the Formation of the Mozambican Defence Force (CCFADM), the Commission for Reintegration (CORE), the National Police Affairs Commission (COMPOL) and the National Information Commission (COMINFO), submitted their final reports on the work of their commissions. On 7 December 1994, in a ceremony at the President's Office, my Special Representative, Mr. Aldo Ajello, handed those reports to Mr. Joaquim Alberto Chissano, the President-elect, thus formally concluding the work of the Commissions.

4. The new Assembly of the Republic was installed on 8 December 1994. The election of its Chairman became the subject of controversy when delegates from the Frente de Libertação de Moçambique (FRELIMO) insisted on open voting, while the opposition demanded secret balloting. The opposition walked out after a lengthy debate, and the FRELIMO candidate, Mr. Eduardo Joaquim Mulembwe, was elected Chairman.

5. The newly elected President of Mozambique was inaugurated on 9 December 1994. He appointed his Government on 16 December 1994. In accordance with paragraph 4 of Security Council resolution 957 (1994), those events marked the expiry of the mandate of ONUMOZ. My Special Representative left Mozambique on 13 December 1994.

B. *Elections*

6. The Mozambican peace process culminated in the holding of presidential and legislative elections on 27 to 29 October 1994. Twelve candidates participated in the presidential election and 14 political parties and coalitions in the legislative election. On the eve of the elections, the Resistência Nacional Moçambicana (RENAMO) announced its withdrawal from the poll. Following the intervention of the international community, including a message from the President of the Security Council, the active involvement of the Secretary-General in international efforts, as well as guarantees by ONUMOZ and the international members of the CSC that the electoral process would be closely monitored, RENAMO decided to participate. Although the uncertainty about RENAMO's intentions created some confu-

sion on the first day of voting, there were no major disruptions and polling continued smoothly on the second and third days.

7. In accordance with its mandate, ONUMOZ monitored and verified the entire electoral process while also providing necessary logistic support. The elections were conducted in a peaceful and orderly manner. ONUMOZ has examined all complaints, allegations and concerns brought before it by the political parties and individuals. Although some irregularities were recorded, most were of an administrative nature, and no event or series of events occurred that could have had an adverse effect on the overall outcome of the elections. I would like to pay tribute to the electoral authorities of Mozambique for the efficient and impartial organization of all aspects of the electoral process. I would also like to thank the international community and those organizations, programmes and agencies, particularly the United Nations Development Programme (UNDP), whose financial and technical assistance to the Mozambican authorities made it possible to hold the elections in such an exemplary manner. My preliminary assessment of the conduct of the voting was conveyed to the Security Council in a letter dated 11 November 1994 (S/1994/1282).

8. On 19 November 1994, the Chairman of the National Elections Commission (NEC) announced the results of the elections. The incumbent President, Mr. Chissano, received 2,633,740 votes, amounting to 53.3 per cent of those cast in the presidential election. The leader of RENAMO, Mr. Afonso Macacho Marceta Dhlakama, received 1,666,965 votes, or 33.7 per cent. The candidate receiving the third largest number of votes (2.9 per cent) was Mr. Wehia Ripua of the Partido Democrático de Moçambique (PADEMO). A total of 5,402,940 persons, representing 87.9 per cent of all registered voters, participated in the presidential election. Blank votes amounted to 5.8 per cent, while 2.8 per cent were considered invalid by the NEC. In the legislative election, FRELIMO received the largest share of the votes with 2,115,793 (44.3 per cent), followed by RENAMO with 1,803,506 votes (37.8 per cent) and the União Democrática (UD) with 245,793 votes (5.2 per cent). Those three parties will have the following share of the new Parliament's 250 seats: FRELIMO – 129, RENAMO – 109 and UD – 12.

9. Immediately after the announcement of the election results, my Special Representative declared the elections free and fair, based on the reports of the United Nations observers. A copy of Mr. Ajello's statement was distributed to members of the Council, which unanimously endorsed the results in its resolution 960 (1994) of 21 November 1994. All Mozambican political parties have accepted the results.

C. *Assembly and demobilization of troops*

10. As was noted in my earlier reports to the Security Council, the demobilization of government and RENAMO troops was substantially concluded by 22 August 1994, and completion of the process was formally declared by the CSC shortly thereafter. A total of 91,691 (67,042 Government and 24,649 RENAMO) soldiers had been registered by ONUMOZ. Some 78,078 soldiers (57,540 government and 20,538 RENAMO) were demobilized, while some of the remainder joined the new army.

11. ONUMOZ collected from the military and paramilitary forces, as well as from the general population, a total of 189,827 weapons, 43,491 of which belonged to the paramilitary forces. A limited amount of arms, ammunition and explosives was destroyed, while the remainder was transferred to the new Mozambican Defence Force (FADM). There is concern about their safe keeping and I very much hope that the Government of Mozambique will take all necessary measures in that regard as soon as possible, destroying or otherwise disposing of all weapons that will not be needed for the FADM and the national police.

12. The post-demobilization verification, by teams comprising representatives of the Government, RENAMO and ONUMOZ, began on 30 August 1994. The parties declared to the CCF for verification a total of 722 former military positions or depots (435 government and 287 RENAMO). In accordance with the procedures approved by the CCF, the teams also verified any information provided to the United Nations by the parties or by any other source, related to the presence of troops, undeclared arms depots or caches. As a result of those activities, substantial numbers of weapons were found, including tanks, anti-aircraft guns, mines, armoured personnel carriers and mortar bombs. In addition, a small number of previously unregistered military personnel were identified at some government and RENAMO bases.

13. Because of delays in demobilization, as well as the parties' initial reluctance to participate fully in the verification mechanism, the process lagged behind the original schedule. It was not possible, therefore, to complete the verification of weapons before the expiry of the ONUMOZ mandate. As at 9 December 1994, United Nations teams had verified a total of 754 government and RENAMO locations, consisting of 432 (out of 435) declared government locations, 67 undeclared government locations, 171 (out of 287) locations declared by RENAMO and 79 undeclared RENAMO locations. A total of 22,069 weapons and large amounts of ammunition were found during the verification process.

D. *Formation of the Mozambican Defence Force*

14. The General Peace Agreement did not initially foresee a role for the United Nations in the formation of

the new army. However, at the request of both the Government and RENAMO, the Security Council, by its resolution 850 (1993) of 9 July 1993, approved my recommendation that ONUMOZ chair the CCFADM.

15. On 25 July 1994, the parties agreed that instead of forming a new army of 30,000 soldiers before the elections, as envisaged in the General Peace Agreement, the FADM would be composed of troops who volunteered to join. As at 9 December 1994, a total of 11,579 soldiers had enlisted in the Force. With the assistance of France, Portugal and the United Kingdom of Great Britain and Northern Ireland, the following units had been trained: six infantry battalions, three special forces battalions, one company of marines, two units of logistic specialists and one company of sappers. In addition, a number of officers had received leadership training, while one group of military police instructors had undergone training abroad. Additional support to the training of the FADM was provided by Zimbabwe, and Italy contributed financially to the rehabilitation of the training centres.

16. Some of the trained FADM units are not yet fully operational, mainly as a result of financial and logistical constraints. A number of units are being trained under the supervision of FADM officers, while others are providing much-needed security at weapons depots.

E. *Withdrawal of the military component of ONUMOZ*

17. The withdrawal of the military component has proceeded in accordance with the plan described in paragraphs 34 to 38 of my report of 26 August 1994 (S/1994/1002). It began on 15 November 1994 and is scheduled to be completed by 31 January 1995. As at 18 December 1994, 2,966 military contingent and headquarters personnel had departed from the mission area, with 1,184 remaining. Of the 322 military observers, 165 had left. The Mission is currently proceeding with residual operations, as per paragraph 4 of Security Council resolution 957 (1994).

18. A limited force of four infantry companies, two from Bangladesh and two from Zambia, the Argentinian field hospital, a skeleton headquarters staff, de-mining personnel and a small number of military observers have been retained to assist in the residual operations and the liquidation phase of the Mission, during which they will gradually be repatriated. The infantry units will provide security for United Nations personnel and protection of United Nations property, where necessary.

III. Police activities

19. Pursuant to Security Council resolution 898 (1994) of 23 February 1994, a total of 1,086 United

Nations civilian police (CIVPOL) from 29 countries were deployed to the mission area. As planned, United Nations CIVPOL established 83 field posts (68 in government- and 15 in formerly RENAMO-controlled areas) in addition to its regional and provincial headquarters. This wide deployment facilitated CIVPOL's close monitoring of the activities of the Mozambican police throughout the country. However, despite the agreement of 3 September 1993 between President Chissano and Mr. Dhlakama on the unification of the territorial administration, the Mozambican police did not establish posts or become operational in the areas formerly held by RENAMO. CIVPOL activities in those areas were thus restricted.

20. CIVPOL investigated 511 complaints, of which 61 were related to human rights violations. Regrettably, the cases of human rights violations investigated, documented and forwarded by CIVPOL to COMPOL for action did not result in the expected disciplinary or preventive action. The issue was raised on several occasions with COMPOL and the Mozambican police, as the absence of corrective or preventive measures reduced the impact of the CIVPOL investigations. The 3 September 1993 agreement between President Chissano and Mr. Dhlakama requested that a United Nations police contingent observe all police activities and verify the strength and location of the police force. However, the Government delayed CIVPOL access to some police training centres, to the facilities of the Rapid Reaction Police and to those of the Presidential Guard until two weeks before the elections.

21. At the same time, in accordance with its mandate, CIVPOL was able to monitor, together with other ONUMOZ components, the conduct of the entire electoral campaign and to assist in the verification of the political rights of individuals, groups and political organizations. In addition, during the voting and counting processes, 565 civilian police served as electoral observers.

22. The first group of 32 United Nations police observers left Mozambique on 17 November 1994. As at 18 December 1994, 566 observers had been withdrawn. The remainder will leave Mozambique between 19 and 31 December 1994, except for about 20 who will remain in the mission area until mid-January.

IV. Humanitarian assistance programme

23. ONUMOZ was entrusted with the mandate to coordinate and monitor all humanitarian assistance operations, in particular those relating to refugees, internally displaced persons, demobilized military personnel and the affected local population, and, in that context, to chair the Humanitarian Assistance Committee. The General Peace Agreement set out two objectives for international humanitarian assistance: firstly, it was to serve as an instrument of reconciliation; secondly, it was to assist the return of persons displaced by war and famine. Out of a target population of 6.5 million, approximately 4.3 million people have now returned to their original areas of residence; this includes 3 million internally displaced people, 1.1 million returnees and approximately 200,000 ex-combatants and their dependants.

24. When the General Peace Agreement was signed, a large area of Mozambique was inaccessible for delivery of relief assistance. ONUMOZ humanitarian efforts, mainly through the provincial humanitarian assistance committees, contributed significantly to the opening of those regions. It thus became possible for humanitarian organizations to deliver relief supplies to vulnerable communities. Currently, emergency assistance is distributed by over 40 organizations to beneficiaries at more than 300 delivery points within previously inaccessible areas.

25. The Coordinated Programme of Assistance, which was developed in cooperation with the donor community and the two major parties, placed emphasis on the restoration of essential services in rural areas, particularly for the returning refugees. The international community contributed directly more than 78 per cent of the approximately $650 million required to meet Mozambique's needs for humanitarian assistance during the period of the ONUMOZ mandate. United Nations organizations and agencies, international public and non-governmental organizations, as well as a number of Mozambican entities, played an essential role in the design and implementation of both the individual and the overall humanitarian programmes.

26. At the time of the establishment of ONUMOZ, 80 per cent of the primary schools in Mozambique had either been closed or destroyed and the availability of other social services was minimal. With the help of the Office of the United Nations High Commissioner for Refugees (UNHCR) and a number of non-governmental organizations, more than 700 primary schools and 250 health facilities have been built in rural areas. A joint project of the World Bank and the World Food Programme (WFP) will reconstruct another 310 health posts. In addition, approximately 2,000 wells have been opened or rehabilitated and the national Programme for Rural Water Supply (PRONAR), in concert with its major operational and funding partner, the United Nations Children's Fund (UNICEF), is engaged in a programme that aims to provide one water source per 500 people. In addition, WFP and local authorities have worked together to distribute increasing amounts of seed throughout the country.

27. Since some 20,000 more government and RENAMO soldiers than the originally envisaged 57,103

were demobilized, the budget for the Reintegration Support Scheme increased to $31.9 million, of which $27.6 million has been pledged and only $8.9 million received. The scheme, which is being implemented by UNDP, includes cash payments, vocational training, promotion of small-scale economic activities and credit facilities for the demobilized soldiers. It is essential for the successful reintegration of the ex-combatants into civilian life. I strongly appeal to donors to contribute to this important scheme, to honour their existing pledges and to help meet the shortfall in pledges of $4.3 million.

28. As a result of the slow start of the original United Nations de-mining programme, a new and accelerated programme was put in place in June 1994. Its ultimate goal is the creation of a national Mozambican mine-clearance capacity. By the end of the mandate of ONUMOZ, the programme had been able to train 450 Mozambicans to man 10 de-mining teams, which are currently operating in the southern areas of Maputo province. They have cleared some 40,000 square metres and disabled over 555 mines. The programme has also achieved a significant number of other goals: 20 Mozambicans were trained as de-mining team supervisors; an additional 16 Mozambicans have completed training as minefield surveyors; and others have been trained for work as paramedics, explosive ordnance disposal specialists and logisticians, and for general administrative and other functions.

29. To date, the accelerated de-mining programme has relied exclusively on funds from the ONUMOZ budget and on personnel provided by the Governments of Australia, Bangladesh, Germany, the Netherlands and New Zealand. The programme is expected to continue through November 1995. In that context, arrangements need to be put in place to ensure that the future requirements of the programme regarding equipment and transport are met. It is understood that, for its continuation through November 1995, the programme will have to rely principally on obligations under the current ONUMOZ budget. It is hoped that the period of time between now and November 1995 will be sufficient for the Government of Mozambique and others concerned to reach a final determination regarding the future of the de-mining programme.

30. In July 1994, UNDP and the Office for Project Services contracted LONRHO, a commercial firm, to clear mines from 2,000 kilometres of priority roads in the provinces of Sofala and Manica. Having so far completed work on over 1,644 kilometres, LONRHO is expected to fulfil its contractual obligations by January 1995. A team of 100 de-miners from the HALO trust, a British non-governmental organization, began de-mining activities in May 1994 and has cleared some 50 kilometres of roads and an area of some 125,000 square metres, mainly in

the province of Zambézia. RONCO, a commercial firm contracted by the United States Agency for International Development (USAID), has cleared over 1,000 kilometres of roads in Manica and Sofala, while the non-governmental organization Norwegian People's Aid is working in the provinces of Maputo and Tete where it has so far cleared 48 kilometres of roads, as well as an area totalling 1,276,211 square metres.

31. All parties concerned with de-mining in Mozambique share the view that there is a need for the establishment of an entity at the national level to provide the various de-mining organizations and companies with policy orientation, operational standards and coherence. At present, it is envisaged that the capacity required for such an entity will be built through a donor-supported UNDP project.

V. Liquidation of the assets of the United Nations Operation in Mozambique

32. In the eighth paragraph of the statement on Mozambique issued by its President on 7 September 1994 (S/PRST/1994/51), the Security Council invited me to report on the final disposition of the assets of ONUMOZ within the framework of its withdrawal. That request was reiterated in a subsequent presidential statement dated 14 December (S/PRST/1994/80). At present, ONUMOZ capital assets total $20.82 million and fall into four major categories, as follows: (a) vehicles, $11.53 million; (b) communications equipment, stores and generators, $5.45 million; (c) building and engineering equipment and stores, $0.72 million; and (d) general services, stores and equipment, $3.12 million.

33. The liquidation of ONUMOZ assets was initiated immediately after the elections. The process is guided by the following principles and policies, listed in order of priority: (a) equipment that conforms to established standards or is compatible with existing equipment will be redeployed to other United Nations operations or placed in reserve for use by future missions; (b) other equipment will be transferred to United Nations organizations, as well as to national and international non-governmental organizations already operating in Mozambique or in the process of establishing a presence there, upon request and against appropriate credit to the ONUMOZ Special Account; (c) commercial disposal within the country in accordance with standard United Nations procedures; and (d) any remaining assets or installations that cannot be dismantled will be donated to the new Government of Mozambique. This also refers to airfield installations as well as to mine-clearing equipment. With regard to the latter, the Mission will be guided by the statement of the President of the Security Council of 7 September 1994

(S/PRST/1994/51), which indicated the need to leave de-mining equipment in Mozambique after the withdrawal of ONUMOZ, subject to the appropriate arrangements. Negotiations are under way to arrange for the transfer of ONUMOZ de-mining equipment to a national entity that would be established to pursue such activities.

34. With the official closure of ONUMOZ planned to take place by the end of January 1995, it will be necessary to retain in Mozambique, primarily in the capital, for approximately one to two months, a small number of United Nations civilian logisticians to deal with outstanding boards of inquiry, the disposition of property and equipment, and other long-term activities. Thereafter, I will be in a position to present to the competent United Nations bodies a report on the liquidation of ONUMOZ assets.

VI. Observations

35. Two years after the signing of the General Peace Agreement the mandate of ONUMOZ has been accomplished: the peace process in Mozambique has come to a successful conclusion. This remarkable achievement can be attributed to several key factors: the strong commitment to peace and reconciliation demonstrated by the Mozambican people and their leaders; the political pragmatism shown by the parties to the General Peace Agreement; the clarity of the ONUMOZ mandate and the consistent support provided by the Security Council; and the international community's significant political, financial and technical support of the peace process. The success of the operation represents an example of what can be achieved through the United Nations when all forces join together in one common endeavour towards a common goal.

36. Although all major aspects of the General Peace Agreement and the ONUMOZ mandate have been implemented, some issues remain to be pursued. These include the existence of arms caches in the country and the safe keeping of weapons collected by ONUMOZ; the incomplete integration of the territorial administration; and the continued presence of mines throughout the country. It will also be essential to continue to train and equip the FADM properly and to upgrade the national police. Mozambique's democratic institutions must also be strengthened and economic and social reconstruction promoted in order to ensure that peace, democracy and development can be sustained. I trust that the new Government of Mozambique will give due attention to these important matters and that the Security Council, the United Nations system and the international community will consider positively any requests for assistance that the Government might make.

37. Finally, I would like to pay a well-deserved tribute to my Special Representative and to all the staff of ONUMOZ for the dedication and professionalism they demonstrated in the fulfilment of their assignments. They contributed to the successful outcome in Mozambique in an outstanding manner and deserve the appreciation of all.

Document 91

Letter dated 26 January 1995 from President Chissano to the Secretary-General on the successful conclusion of ONUMOZ's mandate

Not issued as a United Nations document

After the successful implementation of the General Peace Agreement for Mozambique, it is gratifying to say that in a few days the United Nations Operation in Mozambique (ONUMOZ) will conclude its historic mission in my country.

Due to its magnitude the task was far from easy, but the mission was remarkably a successful one by virtue of the spirit of diligence and determination that endured among all participants throughout this process.

The people of Mozambique are conscious of the crucial role played by the United Nations in the whole peace process in Mozambique. Our people, therefore, remain indebted to all those men and women who spared no efforts in helping Mozambique to become again a home of peace in our planet.

Security Council resolution 960 (1994) of 21 November, endorsing, *inter alia*, the results of the elections on one hand, and, urging all states and relevant International Organizations to contribute actively in the reconstruction and rehabilitation of Mozambique, on the other, is a precious instrument at this point in time when the new government is embarking in concerted efforts in order to meet the challenges of national reconstruction in this country.

Notwithstanding the successful conclusion of the ONUMOZ mission, we look forward to a continued presence of the United Nations in Mozambique through its specialized agencies and we wish to pledge our readiness to continue to fully cooperate with you for the success of the tasks entrusted to the United Nations Organization.

Finally, on behalf of the people and government of Mozambique, I wish to seize this opportunity to pay tribute to Your Excellency and, through you, to all those who contributed for the success of the United Nations Operation in Mozambique.

Please accept, Excellency, the assurances of my highest consideration.

(*Signed*) Joaquim Alberto CHISSANO

Document 92

Statements made by the Minister for Foreign Affairs and Cooperation of Mozambique and the representatives of Botswana, Germany, the Russian Federation, Italy, the United Kingdom, China, the United States, France, Brazil and Portugal at the final Security Council meeting on Mozambique (extract)

S/PV.3494, 27 January 1995

...

Mr. Simão (Mozambique): Today's meeting is the last of a series of Security Council meetings on Mozambique during the past two years. We are honoured to participate in today's deliberations, especially because we are assembled not to express our concerns over outstanding issues but, rather, to say that at last our collective mission has been successfully accomplished, despite all the hurdles we encountered in the process.

We are therefore happy to congratulate ourselves on the completion of a major, delicate but successful United Nations peace-keeping operation. It is now time for a final assessment of the whole process, so as to draw lessons that will certainly help the United Nations address similar operations in future and to collectively exchange views on the United Nations Operation in Mozambique and on how best we can enhance the role of the United Nations in peace-keeping operations.

In a few days, in pursuance of Security Council resolution 957 (1994) of 14 November 1994, the United Nations Operation in Mozambique will have completed all its activities and withdrawn from Mozambique.

As the Council is aware, in fulfilment of the provisions of the General Peace Agreement for Mozambique, the first multi-party general elections were held from 27 to 29 October 1994. These elections have been regarded by the international community and by this body as an example of the political maturity of the Mozambican people. We take great pride in the distinction thus conferred on our people. It gives us renewed energy and the confidence to overcome future challenges. My Government recognizes the significant role played by the Security Council in the success of these first general elections in my country and regards them as the real foundation for the establishment of a multi-party democratic society in Mozambique.

At the completion of this process, a new Assembly of the Republic, consisting of 250 deputies from the three political parties that obtained the most votes, was inaugurated on 8 December. Subsequently—on the following day—President Chissano was sworn in as the first President elected by universal suffrage.

These very important steps marked the beginning of a new era in the history of Mozambique. This is an era in which political pluralism, national reconciliation and peaceful coexistence between Mozambicans will have to be ensured in order to enable lasting peace to be attained in our country. Indeed, it is within the framework of multi-party democracy that a presidential forum, composed of a variety of distinguished political figures, will be created to enhance the national reconciliation process and the consolidation of democracy. We are entering an era in which violence and the use or threat of the use of force will be replaced by political dialogue and tolerance; an era in which the right to agree or disagree with one another must be respected by each and every person.

In other words, this is an era in which respect for human rights and fundamental freedoms will constitute the cornerstone of our society. In his inaugural address, President Chissano committed himself to doing all in his power to attain these objectives, so that the peace we celebrate today may endure for ever. He further emphasized, *inter alia*, that

"As I begin my mandate as President of the Republic, I declare my solemn commitment that I shall always be the President of all Mozambicans. I shall guarantee to all Mozambicans equal rights and freedoms, enshrined in the Constitution and in law. I shall respect the will of the majority and shall pay due attention to the rights of minorities in order that the enjoyment of freedom and rights shall never again be restricted or threatened by intolerance, discrimination or acts of aggression."

In summary, we have entered an era in which Mozambicans will learn to live together in harmony and will concentrate their efforts on healing the wounds resulting from so many years of conflict and destruction.

As we begin this new phase in our democratic process, we look forward to addressing the challenges ahead of us. Currently, the Government is engaged in the preparation of the budget, whose approval by the Assembly of the Republic is scheduled to take place in March. To this end, President Chissano, in his annual address to the diplomatic community accredited in Mozambique, launched an appeal to the donor community for its continued involvement in the process of national reconstruction. He further stressed his conviction that the implementation of the Economic and Social Rehabilitation Programme launched by the Government in 1987, having shown encouraging trends and significant progress during the last year, can register even better results now that our country is enjoying a climate of peace, provided it is supported by the international community. We sincerely hope that the forthcoming Consultative Group meeting, scheduled for March in Paris, will be in line with the expectations of our people by responding positively to the country's needs.

My Government attaches great importance to the promotion of the wider involvement of both the national and the foreign private sectors in the implementation of undertakings that can generate employment and contribute to the solution of the economic and social problems facing us today. In this connection, the Government has recently carried out a thorough review of the legislation on foreign investment, so as to simplify the legal proceedings in order to provide substantial incentives for foreign investment. In addition, my Government will continue to require international assistance in addressing vital issues pertaining to the reintegration of demobilized soldiers, returnees and displaced persons, as well as in taking actions aimed at eradicating poverty. These initiatives must be complemented by other actions aimed at promoting rural development and restoring primary health-care services in both urban and rural areas.

The ongoing de-mining programme will play an important role in the fulfilment of the Government's priorities in the years to come. If we are to consolidate the normalization of life in rural areas, increase food production and facilitate the movement of people and goods throughout the country, it is essential that the issue of land-mines be addressed with high resolve. In this connection, I wish to take this opportunity to express our gratitude to all those who have assisted and continue to assist my Government in carrying out this very important initiative. I had a very positive talk on this issue this morning with Mr. Peter Hansen, the Under-Secretary-General for Humanitarian Affairs.

Those are, in summary, some of my Government's priorities. However, in order to maintain and further strengthen a truly democratic society, whose foundations have been established as a result of our recently held general elections, it is essential to ensure the adequate functioning of democratic institutions.

Accordingly, my Government regards it as of great importance to strengthen national institutions responsible for the maintenance of peace, tranquility and public order in our country as well as to ensure that the road on which we have just embarked is not blocked owing to lack of means. I have in mind the issue of the formation of the Mozambican Defence Force (FADM)—an issue which is yet to be fully addressed—and the strengthening of the role of the national police in ensuring, and its capacity to ensure, public safety. Moreover, we are determined to strengthen the judicial system so as to consolidate a real state of law.

The consolidation of the judicial system has been recognized as one of the most important elements in ensuring and guaranteeing the existence of true democracy in a country like ours—and I believe, in all developing countries—and in ensuring a system of checks and balances as well as transparency and accountability in the management of national affairs. Furthermore, there is general consensus that if we are to ensure true democracy in Mozambique, then we must create and consolidate a permanent electoral body which can guarantee the adequate supervision and monitoring of future elections. This should be an institution that is respected for its professionalism and transparency, and that thereby enjoys the necessary support of all political parties inside the country.

Those are some of the main areas where we believe the support of the Security Council is crucial. In this connection, my Government very greatly appreciates the assurances given by the Secretary-General in his recent letter to my predecessor—now Prime Minister—His Excellency Mr. Pascoal Manuel Mocumbi, in which the Secretary-General indicated that despite the withdrawal of the United Nations Operation in Mozambique (ONUMOZ), the United Nations will continue to assist Mozambique in strengthening the national reconstruction process and its new democratic institutions, as well as in its economic and social integration. We in Mozambique look forward to actively participating in and contributing to the materialization of these assurances.

I should like to seize this opportunity, as I speak today on the subject of economic and social integration, to draw the Council's attention to the growing concern over a possible threat to our fragile peace that might result from the consequences of a new and renewed drought in Mozambique and in the southern African region as whole.

My Government appreciates most sincerely the roles which the Security Council and the international community as a whole have played in helping us mitigate the devastating consequences of man-made and natural calamities which have ravaged our region. Nevertheless, I do believe it is my duty to encourage the Council to keep this issue under permanent review. As a matter of fact, human lives have already been lost in Mozambique as a result of the drought that is afflicting an ever-greater number of areas of my country.

For those reasons, my Government believes that the holding of the first multi-party general elections and the withdrawal of the United Nations Operation in Mozambique should not be regarded as ends in themselves. They are only the culmination of an important phase of the whole peace process and the beginning of a new and more challenging one. In our opinion, the need for the international community to continue to assist the people and the Government of Mozambique in consolidating peace and stability is more acute than ever before.

The presence of the United Nations Operation in Mozambique offers me an excellent opportunity to refer briefly to the overall issue of peace-keeping operations. Our vision—and, I am certain, that of many others among us today—is that peace-keeping forces will be successful only if they enjoy the support of the parties involved. On the other hand, they must strictly adhere to fundamental principles outlined by the General Assembly and respect their respective terms of reference as approved by the Security Council and in line with the agreement reached by the parties. In particular, as my predecessor argued in his statement to the General Assembly at its forty-ninth session:

> "Where there is a Government, even with weak institutions, peace-keeping missions should work in close cooperation ... with the local authorities and respect and strengthen those institutions, rather than try to weaken or undermine them." (*Official Records of the General Assembly, Forty-ninth Session, Plenary Meetings, 15th meeting*, p. 37)

Those observations remain valid today. I believe it is important to underline them because, as the Secretary-General indicated in his "Agenda for Peace", the State is and must remain the foundation-stone of the work of the United Nations.

In the case of the United Nations Operation in Mozambique, we congratulate ourselves on its excellent and smooth communication with the Secretary-General and his Special Representative during the whole process. The existence of adequate communication is vital for the success of peace-keeping operations, for it helps to solve problems and crises as they arise. Above all, communication helps to restore confidence between the United Nations and the parties whenever necessary. To this end, may I recall the Secretary-General's visits to Mozambique at a time when the whole peace process seemed to be deadlocked, and of the Security Council's Mission at a time when it appeared unclear to the international community whether elections would be held as scheduled. Thanks to communication, we were able to resolve all difficulties and to bring the peace process to the successful conclusion we all celebrate today.

The consolidation of peace in Mozambique constitutes a significant contribution to peace in the southern African region, where we witnessed in 1994 significant developments in many of its countries. The holding of multi-party general elections in a number of countries of the region has been the central element of the ongoing democratic transformation we are experiencing.

The recent signing of the Lusaka Protocol between the Government of the Republic of Angola and UNITA constitutes a significant contribution to efforts for peace in our region. We sincerely wish to encourage both parties to take maximum advantage of the momentum created in Lusaka and to work together for a better future in their country. May I take this opportunity to underline the importance we attach to the early deployment of the third United Nations Angola Verification Mission (UNAVEM III). Our recent experience in this regard has shown that the sooner such a verification mechanism is established and deployed, the better for the success of the peace process. I would therefore urge the Council to look into this matter more diligently and expeditiously.

These developments lead us to believe in lasting peace and security in Mozambique and in southern Africa as a whole. My Government wishes to encourage all members of the Council to work towards this objective.

. . .

Mr. Legwaila (Botswana): I have the special honour and privilege to speak on behalf of the 11 States members of the Southern African Development Community (SADC): Angola, Lesotho, Malawi, Mozambique, Namibia, South Africa, Swaziland, the United Republic of Tanzania, Zambia, Zimbabwe and my own country, Botswana.

. . .

It is with immense joy that we salute the people of Mozambique and all their political leaders for doing what is right for their country. We salute their determination and strong commitment to fostering national reconciliation, peace and democracy. We especially admire their tenacious adherence to the General Peace Agreement signed on 4 October 1992, the orderly manner in which they conducted the elections and the respect they so clearly demonstrated for the verdict of the people of Mozambique. This has given Mozambique the best hope for durable freedom, democracy and peace. We have every confidence that the newly elected leadership will rise to the challenge and put the country on a firm footing in the furtherance of the aspirations reposed in them by the electorate.

The success story of Mozambique cannot be told without acknowledging the pivotal role played by the United Nations and the international community as a whole. The patience and goodwill so amply demonstrated by the Security Council over a period of two difficult years have enabled the people of Mozambique to sustain the peace process to its logical conclusion. The 10 resolutions adopted by the Council, as well as all presidential statements issued subsequent to the signing of the General Peace Agreement, contributed in no small measure to the success of the peace process.

We also owe a debt of gratitude to the Secretary-General and his Special Representative, Mr. Ajello, for the tireless efforts they deployed to ensure that the United Nations Operation in Mozambique (ONUMOZ) would achieve the glorious success it has achieved. The devotion and sacrifices of the men and women who served with ONUMOZ deserve our special appreciation and applause. The ONUMOZ success story is the story of the productive quality of their professionalism, which has crowned the United Nations peacemaking and peace-keeping exertions with success stories elsewhere.

The recurring theme of post-conflict peace-building—that there is an inexorable link between peace and development—has great significance and relevance for Mozambique. The daunting task of reconstruction and rehabilitation in Mozambique has begun. A durable basis for peace and security in that war-ravaged country lies in the social and economic uplifting of its people; and the international community is called upon to assist. The end of the mandate of the United Nations Operation in Mozambique (ONUMOZ) and its complete withdrawal should not signal the end of this assistance. Continuous support should be given for social and economic development to ensure that there is no reversal of the gains made so far.

The response of the international community to the reintegration support scheme has so far been positive, and we hope that the momentum can be maintained, even accelerated. There is clearly an urgent need for enhanced cooperation with the Mozambican authorities in the reintegration of ex-combatants into civilian life. We trust that existing pledges of assistance will be honoured so that the Government can commence in earnest the process of training and equipping these men and women with technical skills for alternative employment.

In addition, as in many other areas recovering from the vicissitudes of armed conflict, the territory of Mozambique is littered with anti-personnel land-mines. The idea that the mine-clearing equipment currently in use in Mozambique should be left behind when ONUMOZ finally withdraws is most welcome, and we hope that it will find favour with the relevant organs of the United Nations. Land-mines, as we all know, are a menace to humanity. Mozambique needs to be rid of these indiscriminate tools of war so that its people can go about their daily lives and enjoy their new-found democratic rights in total freedom.

The leaders of southern Africa are working very hard to ensure that our region is not subjected to another war, or wars, after the resolution of conflicts in Mozambique, South Africa and Angola. The attainment of peace and democracy in Mozambique has consolidated the fundamental political changes which have swept the subregion in the past five years. It is our hope that the people of the sister Republic of Angola will soon see the end of the conflict that has marred their lives for so long and will join the people of Mozambique in celebrating the onset of real peace.

. . .

Let me conclude by daring to hope that peace and democracy will flourish in Mozambique and that the destructive conflict from which the Mozambican nation has just emerged will be banished for ever.

Mr. Graf zu Rantzau (Germany): . . . Only two years after the General Peace Agreement was signed on 4 October 1992, its main goals have been achieved: a cease-fire, the dissolution and disarmament of the Government and RENAMO troops, the establishment of a joint defence force, the repatriation and reintegration of approximately 5 million refugees and internally displaced persons, and the holding of the first general presidential and parliamentary elections.

Even if the original time-frame turned out to be too ambitious and had to be changed, in the end a number of factors were decisive for the success of ONUMOZ. The most important prerequisite for the success of the peace process was the desire for peace on both sides. A continuation of the civil war, which could not have been won by military efforts, would have further devastated an already exhausted country. Both parties to the conflict realized this.

Even the most favourable circumstances, however, cannot prevent the development of crisis situations that threaten to derail the peace process. Tribute is due the Special Representative of the Secretary-General, Mr. Aldo Ajello, for his tireless efforts to find creative solutions to the various unexpected difficulties along the way.

We would further like to mention the Supervisory and Monitoring Commission, whose task was to guarantee the implementation of the Peace Agreement and compliance with the timetable and with the cease-fire. The active role played in the Commission by its international members, jointly with the representative of the United Nations, has turned it into an effective instrument to further the peace process. We should think about including similar mechanisms in future peace-keeping missions as well.

An important prerequisite for the implementation of the Rome Agreement was the establishment of the United Nations Trust Fund to provide logistical support. Its significance cannot be overestimated, since it enabled the opposition to participate in the peace process on an equal economic footing.

Even a success story may include some lessons to be learned. I want to mention just a few.

Peace-keeping operations will be even more successful when they embrace the principle of lean management. This holds true not only for Headquarters but also for the individual operations on site. Efficient management includes transparency and cost-effectiveness in the handling of tender offers.

The Mozambican experience demonstrates the importance of guaranteeing freedom of movement in the country for civilians and returnees from the very start of the mission. In order to ensure this, the mission should be capable of executing police tasks from the outset. The verification of the disarmament of conflicting parties should be concluded by the end of the mandate of a peace-keeping operation.

After almost 20 years of turmoil and suffering, the people of Mozambique now have the chance to build a better future for themselves. No one expects the road ahead to be easy. The weapons arsenals of both former conflicting parties, arsenals that still exist in Mozambique, remain a cause for concern. The reconstruction of democratic institutions will continue to require political and material support from the international community.

Considering all that has been achieved in the last two years, however, we feel that we have reason to be optimistic about the future of Mozambique. I would therefore request Minister Simão to assure his people of our continued solidarity.

. . .

Mr. Lavrov (Russian Federation) (*interpretation from Russian*) . . . We sincerely congratulate the people and the leaders of Mozambique on the successful holding of the first multi-party elections in the history of that country and the creation of a democratic coalition Government. This important event is a worthy culmination of Mozambique's progress along the difficult road to peace and consent and has marked the end of a lengthy period of destructive internecine conflict that brought untold suffering to the people of that country. The Russian Federation actively promoted the peace process in Mozambique and wishes the people and the Government of that friendly country, to which we are solidly linked by many years of fruitful cooperation, further success in creating a stable, democratic and flourishing State.

The successful implementation of the large-scale and complex task of effecting a political settlement in Mozambique was made possible by the consistent support of the international community and the staunch resolve of the Mozambicans themselves to break out of the vicious circle of violence and confrontation. An important and instructive role in this regard was played by President Chissano and the leaders of the Mozambican political parties, who, displaying a rare degree of political courage and statesmanlike wisdom and restraint, were able, for the sake of the higher interests of their country, to rise above the differences that had separated them for years and embark on the course of national reconciliation. We are convinced that this approach is the most reliable guarantee of success in carrying out the difficult tasks of the post-conflict stage in Mozambique.

We would also like to express our gratitude to the personnel of the United Nations Operation in Mozambique (ONUMOZ) and the Special Representative of the Secretary-General, Mr. Ajello, for their skilful and determined efforts to bring the peace process in Mozambique to success. This became an important component in the consolidation of stability and security in the southern African region as a whole. The success of the complex and large-scale Operation in Mozambique is one of the most impressive examples of the real capacities of the United Nations in the field of peace-making.

During the three-year mandate of ONUMOZ, a great deal of meaningful and useful experience has been gained, which we believe deserves thorough study in order to further enhance the effectiveness of United Nations peace-keeping operations. In this connection, we look forward to the presentation of the Secretary-General's report containing an analysis of the lessons learned from the United Nations Operation in Mozambique. We are quite certain it will be an important contribution to our future work.

Mr. Fulci (Italy): . . . The United Nations Peace-keeping Operation in Mozambique marks a milestone in the history of our Organization's peace-keeping activities.

This Operation is already often being cited as one of the true success stories of the United Nations in the application of the pertinent provisions of the Charter, which the founding fathers conceived of as a way to end the tensions and conflicts that have marked the history of this century. The Italian people, our Parliament and our Government are deeply gratified by the outcome of the process begun in Rome two years ago, and we are proud to have had a role in making it possible. Of course, it was a long, extremely difficult and complex negotiation, and sincere homage must be paid to both parties—the Government and RENAMO—and to all those who contributed to the final success through their tenacity, good faith and, above all, sincere willingness to compromise. Our colleague here at the United Nations, Ambassador Pedro Comissário Afonso, also lent a very skilful hand from New York, and we should acknowledge that.

But good offices and mediation alone would not have sufficed; military and financial commitments were equally necessary. In this regard, allow me to cite only three figures concerning the Italian contribution to Mozambique. To monitor observance of the peace agreements, together with other United Nations troops, my country deployed in Mozambique a total of 4,700 men, 650 vehicles and 11 aircraft, a contribution amounting to roughly $300 million, only a fraction of which was reimbursed by the United Nations.

Equally significant were the voluntary contributions—another $110 million—through bilateral and multilateral channels; and this does not include additional bilateral economic assistance.

Of course, the elections were the key element in the peace process, and we must again congratulate the Mozambican Government and RENAMO on keeping to their agreement and making possible what many had considered impossible: fair, impartial and free elections, with an 88 per cent participation rate by Mozambican voters.

In the long term, some of the key aspects of ONU-MOZ will represent a point of reference for other peace-keeping operations. A careful study of the presence and activity of the United Nations in Mozambique could contribute, we believe, to the deeper reflection currently under way on United Nations peace-keeping activities, in connection with the Secretary-General's recent important Supplement to the Agenda for Peace.

We also should remember that individuals play a crucial role in operations of this type. The professionalism, experience, negotiating talent and personal qualities of those involved—of the Special Representative of the Secretary-General, for instance—often can mean the difference between success and failure. From this perspective, we must pay tribute once again to the political stature and leadership of the Mozambican leaders, and also to the Secretary-General's Special Representative, Aldo Ajello, and to all the on-site representatives of the donor countries, who operated at all times in close and effective coordination.

We should never tire of reminding ourselves that peace and development go hand in hand. They are the two sides of the same coin: there can be no peace without development, and no development without peace. I am glad to assure the Foreign Minister that Italy intends to continue in Mozambique to play a role on the front line of this phase of consolidating democracy and stability, which are so closely linked to economic development. The seeds of democracy in Mozambique will take root, but they are still fragile and in need of care. The stabilization of political institutions, in the meantime, will constitute a vital premise for the economic and social development to which the country so rightly aspires.

In this perspective, we believe that two fundamental conditions must be fulfilled. First, the international community must continue to maintain a high level of commitment to helping Mozambique, even when that country is no longer on the map of crisis areas. Secondly, a true policy of national reconciliation must continue to prevail in that country, one that would allow everybody to participate on an equal footing in its democratic life and institutions.

Let me conclude by wishing every success to Foreign Minister Simão and to the new, freely and democratically elected Government of Mozambique. It is our most sincere hope that the consolidation of freedom, democracy and development in Mozambique will set a shining example for other countries that, unfortunately, are still affected by civil war and internal strife.

...

Sir David Hannay (United Kingdom): . . . The holding of free and fair elections in Mozambique in October last year represented a historic achievement for the people of Mozambique and for the international community. We pay tribute to the people of Mozambique, whose will for peace overcame all the obstacles, and who exercised their right to vote in such impressive numbers and in such a responsible manner.

The United Nations Operation in Mozambique (ONUMOZ) has been a success of which the United Nations can be justly proud. Its peace-keepers, military observers and civilian police made a vital contribution to the sustaining of peace and security throughout the country as it made the difficult transition from civil war to multi-party democracy. The Electoral Division and the many international and national electoral observers contributed to the effectiveness and credibility of the electoral process. My Government warmly congratulates the

Secretary-General, his Special Representative, Mr. Aldo Ajello, and the thousands of men and women who worked within the United Nations Operation in Mozambique on their skill and dedication. It is important that the lessons learned and the experience gained from ONUMOZ be put to good use in other United Nations peace-keeping operations.

The United Kingdom is proud to have played its part in support of the peace process, including bilaterally through assisting in the formation and training of the new armed forces and the provision of electoral observers, and through the assistance offered by the European Union, about which the Permanent Representative of France, speaking later in this debate on behalf of the European Union, will say more. The United Kingdom will, to the best of its ability, continue to support the people of Mozambique in their efforts to reconstruct the economic and social base of their country.

The international community has done much to help the people of Mozambique over the last two years, and its assistance will not come to an end when ONUMOZ is terminated on 31 January. But it can only help. It cannot determine the future of Mozambique; only Mozambicans can do that. If they show the same spirit of national reconciliation as they amply demonstrated in the two years from the signing of the Rome Accords to the holding of the elections, then the future will be bright. We look to both the Government and the democratic Opposition in Mozambique to work closely together to this end. If they do so, they can be assured of the full backing of the international community.

In conclusion, I would offer one New Year resolution to the new democratically elected Government of Mozambique—namely, that never again should this Council have on its agenda, as we have today, an item entitled "The situation in Mozambique". That would indeed be an achievement for the Government and people of Mozambique and for this Council.

Mr. Li Zhaoxing (China) (*interpretation from Chinese*): ... The Chinese and African peoples share identical or similar historical experiences. China has all along been following closely the developments in Africa. We deeply sympathize with the conflict-torn African continent in the post-cold-war era and with its people for the suffering caused by conflicts. It has been an important component of China's foreign policy to support the African people in their endeavour to achieve lasting peace and strengthen friendly relations of cooperation with all African other countries.

His Excellency Mr. Qian Qichen, the Vice-Premier and Foreign Minister of China, is now visiting Africa. In his meetings with leaders of African States, he said that the disintegration of the bipolar world has made a huge impact on Africa, which greatly needs an environment of peace, unity and stability. China attaches importance to Africa and supports the just demands and reasonable stand of African countries in international affairs. This is just what we are doing at the United Nations, including the Security Council.

Mozambique has now set out on the road of consolidating peace, the road of economic rehabilitation and reconstruction, following the successful elections and the establishment of a new Government. The success in the Mozambican peace process has shown us that, even if there are numerous difficulties and hardships the conflicting parties can turn hostility into friendship and achieve the peace and stability to which the people ardently aspire, as long as, acting in their overall national interests, they have the necessary political will and persevere to achieve a political settlement through peaceful negotiations.

The international community—particularly the United Nations and donor countries—has made tremendous efforts and put in enormous resources for the settlement of the conflict in Mozambique. China not only participated in the United Nations Operation in Mozambique (ONUMOZ), but also sent monitors to the elections in Mozambique. While engaged in in-depth discussions of the Secretary-General's "Supplement to an Agenda for Peace" (S/1995/1), people are summarizing the experience gained in ONUMOZ, which they hope will bring some inspiration and guidance to many other United Nations peace-keeping operations. In our view, the key to the success of ONUMOZ lies in the observance of the purposes and principles of the Charter and the adherence to the principles proven effective in traditional peace-keeping operations. That success was also dependent on the unswerving support of the international community, including that of the United Nations and the Security Council.

The Mozambican people are now faced with the arduous task of economic reconstruction, which calls for constant strong support from the international community. The Chinese Government and people will, as always, do whatever they can to help the Mozambican Government and people overcome the current difficulties and achieve economic and social development.

Mr. Inderfurth (United States of America): ... This is an auspicious occasion. We mark the closing of one chapter in the history of Mozambique and the opening of another. The long-running conflict, and the United Nations peace-keeping operation it spawned, have drawn to a close. A new, democratic, cooperative future opens up before the Mozambicans, who have shown courage and fortitude in pursuing this new path.

The peace-keeping operation in Mozambique was one of the largest and most successful in United Nations history. Its success was due to the combined efforts of the Mozambican people, the member States of the international community, and the men and women of the United Nations. Each of these—from the most powerful to the least, from the leaders of Mozambique's political parties to the poorest citizen walking to a ballot box in the countryside, from senior officials in this grand building to the youngest private in a blue helmet who guarded a lonely road-crossing in the bush—all can be proud of what their work together has accomplished.

Of course, no operation runs perfectly and there are important lessons to be learned from the United Nations experience in Mozambique. But the final result, ending years of bloodshed in a peaceful election, refutes the arguments of those who claim that United Nations peace-keeping is a needless expenditure of money and blood with nothing to show for it. The United Nations Operation in Mozambique (ONUMOZ) demonstrates that, with commitment and determination, peace-keeping can work, assisting the transition from the horrors of war to the blessing of peace. After ONUMOZ has fulfilled its mandate and completed its withdrawal, the United Nations still has a role to play in Mozambique. The war-damaged infrastructure and economy of that country will require international assistance. Other residual effects of the war must be dealt with, including the thousands upon thousands of anti-personnel land-mines that still pose a threat to the civilian population and will hold back economic recovery for years to come. Also, the amount of arms and weapons which the United Nations has collected from demobilizing soldiers or found in hidden arms caches concerns us. We hope that the United Nations and the newly elected Government of Mozambique will collaborate in the destruction or disabling of these weapons, so that they do not find their way into the black market, and from there into neighbouring countries which themselves are trying to keep their fledgling democracies intact. We urge the Government of Mozambique to attend to this item urgently.

The reconstruction and rehabilitation of Mozambique can now go forward. My country will be there to help. We must bear in mind, however, that hopes for national unity and recovery can be realized only if Mozambique remains committed to democracy, economic reform and national reconciliation.

The critical work of reconciliation in Mozambique is far from over. Soldiers laying down their arms and citizens voting in an election are merely steps along the path: big steps—important steps—yes; but not the end of the journey. The Government and the people of Mozambique must continue this journey, including the process of political dialogue and reconciliation between the Government and the opposition. The people of Mozambique

and the international community have invested too much to leave the work unfinished.

The United Nations has limited financial and human resources. But when the people of Mozambique asked for assistance it was willingly given. Now the international community will watch carefully to see how the people of Mozambique build on this investment. We all have a stake in continued peaceful progress in Mozambique. The people and the Government owe it not only to themselves but to all of us to forge ahead along the path we have helped them lay out. We believe they can do it. We look forward to following their progress and celebrating further milestones along the way.

. . .

Mr. Mérimée (France) (*interpretation from French*): I have the honour of speaking on behalf of the European Union.

. . .

In the past year, after nearly 20 years of conflict, Mozambique has experienced notable events. For the people of Mozambique, the elections held on 27 to 29 October 1994 were a decisive step forward and the culmination of the lengthy peace process that had started in earnest with the signing of the Rome Agreement on 4 October 1992.

In all, 88 per cent of the 6.4 million Mozambicans who had registered to vote went to the polls over three days to elect their President and their legislators. This shows how eager the Mozambicans, voting for the first time, were to turn a new page in their history.

This success resulted from a set of factors that deserve to be emphasized. First, the tale of Mozambique would not have had this happy ending without the determination to succeed displayed by the President of Mozambique, Mr. Chissano, and the President of RENAMO, Mr. Dhlakama, both of whom were motivated and encouraged by the Mozambican people's desire for peace.

Secondly, the European Union wishes to pay tribute to all who participated in the United Nations Operation in Mozambique (ONUMOZ), and in particular to the Special Representative of the Secretary-General, Mr. Aldo Ajello, who supported the efforts of the Mozambicans to make the elections succeed by adapting ONUMOZ to the situation as required.

Finally, we must emphasize that the management of the case of Mozambique was exemplary with respect to efforts by the countries of the region and by the troop-contributing countries, and with respect to the involvement of donors in the process of implementing the Peace Agreement.

The European Union spared no effort on the Community-wide and bilateral levels to enable us today to say that the United Nations Operation in Mozambique has been a complete success. Suffice it to recall that 80 per cent of the election expenses were defrayed by the European Union, which during the balloting provided 200 observers in addition to those serving as United Nations international observers.

The European Union intends to continue its Community-wide and bilateral efforts to promote peace-building in Mozambique. In its resolution 957 (1994) of 15 November 1994, the Security Council set 31 January 1995 for the withdrawal of ONUMOZ. Clearly, the Mozambicans will not be abandoned after that date. United Nations specialized agencies will replace the blue helmets to coordinate the development and growth of the country in order to consolidate the new peace. We appeal to the Secretary-General to ensure that this takes place.

It is for that very purpose that the European Union will continue its assistance. All Mozambicans must be able to see their ballot transformed into a road map to democracy and progress.

In that connection, the European Union attaches great importance to true national reconciliation. We hope that sincere cooperation between the majority and the opposition will be among the new Government's priorities. We think the opposition ought to be represented both at the governmental and at the local level. The European Union stresses that peace in Mozambique deserves participation by all Mozambicans in its consolidation.

More broadly speaking, the European Union notes that the success of the operation in Mozambique, following the elections in South Africa, is a source of encouragement for the process of democratization and progress throughout southern Africa. We hope that Angola will follow Mozambique's example and soon rejoin the ranks of democratic countries advancing towards political renewal and economic and social development.

. . .

Mr. Valle (Brazil): For more than two years, the Security Council has followed with keen interest and concern the evolution of the situation in Mozambique. My delegation is extremely pleased that the Security Council has decided to hold a debate on an issue the outcome of which has been very much welcomed by the entire international community. Gathered here today, in a far different atmosphere and with a clearly different purpose, the Council is considering the conclusion of the United Nations Operation in Mozambique (ONUMOZ).

First of all, I would like to welcome very warmly His Excellency Mr. Leonardo Santos Simão, Minister of Foreign Affairs and Cooperation of Mozambique, and thank him for the very comprehensive statement he made. His thorough analysis of the situation clearly demonstrates the magnitude of the achievements attained by the imple-

mentation of the Rome peace accord. My delegation was particularly impressed by his words, in the light of the huge challenges facing his Government in the reconstruction and rehabilitation of his country.

It is a known fact that Brazil feels very closely linked to Mozambique, given our common historical, cultural and ancestral ties. We maintain with that sister country an intense relationship that both Governments have been continuously nurturing over a long period of time. With the successful conclusion of the peace process, as provided for in the accords of 1992, our relations are bound to grow even closer at a moment when Mozambique takes decisive strides on the path of peace, stability and economic and social development.

The meeting today should result in an appraisal of the collective effort of the international community towards ensuring peace and stability in a country ravaged by conflict for well over a decade. The accomplishment of the Operation just concluded has decisively contributed to the elimination of the horrors of war and the creation of an environment allowing political negotiation to prevail over confrontation, and understanding over suspicion.

There is no better way to successfully conclude a peace process than to abide by the wishes of the people. The general elections held in October 1994 represent a milestone for the country. The elections were conducted in a remarkably peaceful and orderly manner. The massive participation of voters, just shy of 90 per cent, clearly indicates the desire of an entire people to actively participate in the shaping of the future of their country. It also signifies the strong will of Mozambicans to start a new period in their history, leaving behind war and suffering. It should also be noted, as pointed out by the Secretary-General in his report, that all Mozambican political parties have accepted the results of the elections. This is an obvious indication that peace, stability and democracy are part of an irreversible process in Mozambique, dispelling the fears of some Member States that the elections might not be free and fair.

My Government has consistently supported the United Nations efforts to bring peace to Mozambique, both as a member of the Security Council in the biennium 1993-1994, when the Council was actively seized of the matter, and as a troop contributor to the United Nations Operation in Mozambique (ONUMOZ). A Brazilian military officer, General Lélio Rodrigues, had the privilege of being the first force commander of ONUMOZ. Later, in 1994, Brazil sent an infantry company that was deployed in the region of Zambézia and contributed actively to the process of assembly of troops and demobilization.

We have also consistently stressed our position that

ONUMOZ, as well as any other peace-keeping operation of the Organization, should be established and deployed in the name of the United Nations as a whole, and not of the Security Council alone. My delegation has repeatedly underscored the two main policy principles that have guided our position. First, peace-keeping operations must be aimed at contributing to alleviating tensions and promoting peace in regional conflicts that pose a threat to peace and stability. Secondly, peace-keeping operations must be absolutely impartial if they are to implement their mandates successfully. These operations constitute an important means to assist in the implementation of agreements to which the parties have freely committed themselves.

The success story of ONUMOZ allows us to draw some conclusions on ongoing and future United Nations efforts in the field of peace-keeping. To be effective, these operations have to be adequately staffed and equipped; delays in their deployment are to be avoided at all costs.

Most important is the need to persevere in the search for peace when the commitment to national reconciliation prevails among the parties. No precipitate reduction or withdrawal of the personnel of any operation should occur without prior determination of the impact on the operation's capability to discharge its mandate successfully.

In the specific case of Mozambique, fortunately, the Council in its wisdom avoided a premature reduction of the military component of ONUMOZ at a crucial moment in the peace process, when demobilization was still under way and the formation of the new defence force had barely begun. We have always stressed that if peace has its costs, the absence of peace is even costlier.

Peace in Mozambique was possible because of a combination of domestic and international factors. The Special Representative of the Secretary-General, together with the force commander and all the personnel of ONUMOZ—military, civil police and civilian staff— deserve our recognition for the successful conclusion of the mission.

Although the support provided by the international community was substantial and decisive, the Operation owes its success to the unequivocal commitment to peace of the people of Mozambique as a whole and, in particular, that of President Joaquim Chissano. My delegation pays its sincerest tribute to his leadership, political wisdom and true statesmanship, which played a vital role in the successful conclusion of the peace process. Our recognition is extended to the people of Mozambique, who must receive the ultimate praise for the success story of ONUMOZ.

Finally, we would like to express our hope that the successful trend which started in South Africa, has now been repeated in Mozambique and is being extended to

Angola can indeed spread northward in Africa and, hopefully, to other peace-keeping operations in troubled areas in other continents.

As we witness the dawning of a new era in Mozambique, the international community should, in order to reaffirm its commitment to the welfare of that country and of the entire subregion, shift its efforts from peace-making to reconstruction, rehabilitation and development in Mozambique. Brazil stands ready to continue to do its part.

. . .

Mr. Catarino (Portugal): . . . I need not remind the Council of the special relationship that exists between Portugal and Mozambique, resulting from historical ties consolidated during the course of centuries, which today is embodied in the profound friendship between the two peoples and in the close cooperation between the two countries. It was therefore with a profound sense of pleasure that Portugal witnessed the positive manner in which the peace process in Mozambique was carried out.

Portugal played an active role throughout the process, from the very beginning. As an observer of the peace negotiations, we participated fully in the process that led to the signing of the General Peace Agreement. We then contributed significantly to its implementation on the ground. We took part in all the international commissions created by the General Peace Agreement, as well as in the Joint Commission for the formation of the armed forces of Mozambique. Portugal was entrusted with the task of forming three battalions of special forces, one company of marines and a number of logistics units.

In addition, Portugal has supported the organic and conceptual reorganization of the armed forces through the dispatch to Mozambique of a specialized team composed of 100 officers and non-commissioned officers. Without a doubt, our common language and the profound mutual understanding between our peoples were decisive factors in the success of these actions.

Portugal also actively participated in ONUMOZ, both in its command structure and by sending a communications battalion which guaranteed, with great technical competence I might add, the communications network of that Operation throughout the implementation of the peace process. We also deployed close to 60 police officers to the ONUMOZ contingent of civilian police observers, which played a crucial role in the successful outcome of the peace process.

A Portuguese judge was one of the members of the electoral tribunal. Portugal was also present in the international monitoring effort through the deployment of 42 observers, 30 of whom were part of EUMOZ, the electoral monitoring operation of the European Union established following a proposal put forward by my country.

The Portuguese Government has always held that only through the full implementation of the General Peace Agreement will the parties be able successfully to complete the process designed to bring to an end the suffering of a people burdened by many years of war. At a decisive moment, the Mozambican people showed in a civil and serene manner through an impressive turnout at the polls that, regardless of whom they voted for, they fundamentally desired peace. The political leaders of Mozambique, encouraged by the positive examples in the region, also contributed towards bringing about the tide of stability that has emerged. The outcome of the peace process in Mozambique represents a further step towards the development and progress of a democratic southern Africa.

Naturally, the role of the United Nations in this process has been crucial. At this point, I should like to pay tribute to the efforts of the Secretary-General, Mr. Boutros-Ghali, and in particular to his Special Representative, Mr. Aldo Ajello, who always found a way out at critical moments in a process that demanded not only a mediatory role but also one of bringing the parties closer together and promoting understanding between them.

I would be committing an injustice if I did not equally pay tribute here to the work carried out by this body, the Security Council, which, throughout the peace process, showed in a clear manner the importance placed by the international community in, and its commitment to, a successful implementation of the General Peace Agreement. At a very delicate stage of the process, the Security Council did not hesitate to send a mission to Mozambique, which enhanced the impact and credibility of ONUMOZ, as well as a better understanding of the manner of ensuring the full implementation of the General Peace Agreement within the established time-frame.

It is true that the role of the international community has been extremely important over the last two years. It should not, however, end here. We have witnessed the process of pacification and democratization of Mozambique. It is now essential to support the consolidation of democracy. This will be the only way of guaranteeing, over the long term, the fruition of the investment made by the international community.

We therefore appeal to the international community to maintain its efforts now and to support, at both the bilateral and the multilateral levels, the reconstruction and development of Mozambique in such a way as to guarantee the consolidation of peace and democracy in that country.

The recent positive developments that have occurred in the region have had a positive influence on the choices made by the Mozambicans. Similarly, there can be no doubt that the consolidation of peace and democracy in Mozambique will contribute significantly to regional stability.

It is therefore necessary to continue on the path of the process, already under way, of the reconciliation of the Mozambican family and of an institutionalized democracy, in which all can contribute usefully to the development of the country in an atmosphere of mutual respect and observance of democratic principles. This evolution will also depend on the Mozambican people's perception of their future prospects. It is therefore essential that the international community provide the necessary assistance which ensure these prospects of progress and sustainable development, particularly through the international financial institutions.

On our part, we remain committed to taking on a front-line role in helping in the reconstruction of Mozambique. In this context, I should like to point out that Portugal's largest foreign-investment project relates to the Cahora Bassa dam, an enormous undertaking which we hope will come to benefit in a significant manner, particularly in the key sector of energy, the economy of Mozambique, as well as those of other countries in the region.

Nearly 18 years of civil war certainly planted some seeds of mistrust. We are confident that the continued effort and commitment of the international community and the political and civil maturity already shown by the Mozambicans will prevent those seeds from taking root and will allow Mozambique to live in a new era of peace and prosperity.

V Subject index to documents

[This subject index to the documents reproduced in this book should be used in conjunction with the index on pages 316-321. A complete listing of the documents indexed below appears on pages 83-89.]

A

Administration.
See: Financing. Public administration.

Agreement on partial cease-fire in Mozambique (1992).
– Document 1

Agriculture.
– Documents 18, 73

Aid coordination.
– Documents 12-15, 26, 28, 33, 73
See also: Coordination within UN system.
Development assistance.

Aid programmes.
See: Aid coordination. Development assistance.
Displaced persons. Emergency relief. Food aid.
Humanitarian assistance. Military assistance.
Refugees.

Amato, Giuliano.
– Document 24

Andreatta, Beniamino.
– Document 36

Armaments.
– Document 64
See also: Armed forces. Military demobilization.

Armed forces.
– Documents 1, 24, 29-30, 32, 34-35, 37-38, 45, 49,
55, 57, 63-67, 69-70, 90
See also: Military activity. Military demobilization.
Military personnel. Rapid deployment forces. Troop
withdrawal.

Armed incidents.
See: Military activity.

B

Berlusconi, Silvio.
– Document 72

Border incidents.
See: Military activity.

Boutros-Ghali, Boutros.
– Documents 2-11, 14-15, 19, 24-26, 29-32, 36,
38-39, 42, 44, 46, 49-56, 58-59, 64, 72, 77, 81,
83, 86-87, 91

Budget contributions.
See: Financial assistance. Financing. Humanitarian
Assistance. Trust funds.

C

Cease-fire violations.
– Documents 19, 20, 21, 25, 34, 45, 55

Cease-fires.
– Documents 1, 6-7, 9-13, 19-21, 25-28, 34-35, 37,
40, 42-43, 45, 48-49, 55, 57, 63-66, 68-71, 74, 90

Chissano, Joaquim Alberto.
– Documents 2-3, 6-9, 12, 14, 25, 41, 50, 91

Ciampi, Garlo Azeglio.
– Documents 54, 58

Civil and political rights.
– Document 12
See also: Freedom of movement. Police.

Civilian persons.
– Documents 49, 57, 63-65, 81

Coalition governments.
See: Political parties.

Colombo, Emilio.
– Documents 31-32

Commissions.
– Documents 10, 12-13, 21, 26, 33, 37-38, 40, 43,
45, 48, 55, 63, 65-66, 69, 79

Community health services.
See: Health services.

Community of Sant'Egidio.
– Documents 2, 12, 44

Conflict resolution.
See: Dispute settlement. Negotiation.

Coordination within UN system.
– Documents 18, 73, 89
See also: Aid coordination.

D

Demobilization.
See: Military demobilization.

Democracy.
– Documents 81, 84, 89

Detained persons.
– Document 12

Development assistance.
– Documents 18, 73, 89, 92
See also: Aid coordination. Humanitarian Assistance. Reconstruction.

Dhlakama, Afonso.
– Documents 12, 15, 29-30, 36, 41, 51

Disarmament.
See: Armaments. Military demobilization. Verification.

Disaster relief.
See: Emergency relief. Relief transport.

Displaced persons.
– Documents 12, 18, 23, 28, 37, 48-49, 57, 63-64, 73, 89
See also: Humanitarian assistance.

Dispute settlement.
– Documents 12, 17, 20-23
See also: Negotiation.

Donors Conference for Mozambique (1992): Rome.
– Documents 23, 28, 73, 89

E

Economic assistance.
See: Development assistance. Emergency relief. Financial assistance. Humanitarian assistance. Military assistance. Reconstruction.

Election campaigns.
See: Election law. Elections.

Election districts.
See: Elections.

Election law.
– Documents 12, 40, 43, 45-46, 49, 57, 79, 82
See also: Elections.

Election verification.
See: Electoral assistance.

Elections.
– Documents 4, 12-13, 23, 26-29, 31-38, 40, 43, 45-46, 48-49, 55, 57-58, 60-61, 63-65, 67-71, 74-86, 88-90, 92
See also: Election law. Voter registration.

Electoral assistance.
– Documents 2, 4-8, 10, 12-13, 26, 33, 46, 61, 63, 65, 69, 74-75, 80-82, 84, 88, 90, 92

Electoral Tribunal.
– Documents 61-62

Emergency relief.
– Documents 18, 23, 28, 73
See also: Humanitarian assistance. Refugees.

Equipment and supplies.
– Documents 64, 90

F

Financial assistance.
– Documents 34, 38, 49, 57, 64

Financing.
– Documents 23, 26, 28, 46, 55, 70

Food aid.
– Documents 10, 14-15, 18, 73

France—Military assistance.
– Documents 57, 64

Freedom of movement.
– Documents 34-35, 64

Frente de Libertãçao de Moçambique (FRELIMO).
– Documents 37, 48

Front-line States.
– Document 76

G

General Peace Agreement for Mozambique (1992).
– Documents 2-3, 6-7, 9-12, 16-17, 19-28, 34-35, 37-38, 41-43, 45, 48-49, 55, 57, 63-64, 66-68, 70, 75-76, 78-82, 84, 86-89, 92

H

Health services.
– Documents 18, 73

Human rights.
See: Civil and political rights.

R

Rapid deployment forces.
– Document 42

Reconstruction.
– Documents 17, 36, 73, 75, 84, 89, 92

Refugees.
– Documents 12, 18, 23, 28, 37, 46, 49, 57, 59, 64, 70, 73, 89
See also: Displaced persons. Humanitarian assistance. Repatriation.

Relief transport.
– Documents 14-15, 19
See also: Humanitarian assistance. Transport corridors.

Repatriation.
– Documents 12, 18, 28, 46, 49, 57, 59, 63, 73
See also: Refugees.

Resettlement.
– Documents 35, 49, 57, 63-64, 67, 89

Resistência Nacional Moçambicana (RENAMO)
– Documents 1-3, 10-12, 16, 19, 21, 26-27, 30-31, 34-35, 37-39, 41, 43, 45-46, 48-49, 54-58, 63-64, 66-68, 72-73, 78-80, 82, 92

S

Sanitation.
See: Water supply and sanitation.

Social integration.
– Document 73

Special missions.
– Documents 5-8, 10, 16, 21, 68, 70

Staff security.
– Documents 20, 27, 75

T

Technical cooperation.
See: Aid coordination. Development assistance. Election verification.

Training programmes.
– Documents 34-35, 37, 49, 57, 63-64

Transport corridors.
– Documents 1, 24, 26, 33, 37, 40, 63
See also: Humanitarian assistance. Relief transport.

Troop deployment.
– Document 24-27, 29-30, 32-33, 40, 55, 63, 69-71

Troop withdrawal.
– Documents 12, 19, 24, 26, 37, 46, 48, 55, 65-66, 69, 71, 81, 88, 90, 92
See also: Armed forces. Military demobilization.

Trust funds.
– Documents 31-32, 38, 49, 54, 56-58, 63-65, 69-70, 72
See also: Electoral assistance. Political parties.

U

UN.
– Documents 10-11

UN. General Assembly. President.
– Document 85

UN. Security Council.
– Documents 61, 81

UN. Security Council Mission.
– Documents 68, 70

UN. Special Representative for Mozambique.
– Documents 13, 16, 19, 21, 25-27, 34-38, 80, 82, 84, 92

UN Development Programme
– Documents 18, 33, 55, 63, 65, 69, 73, 90

UN High Commissioner for Refugees.
– Documents 28, 49, 57, 59, 64, 73

UN Operation in Mozambique.
– Documents 13, 20-21, 25-26, 30-35, 37-38, 40, 45, 47-51, 55, 57, 63-72, 74-75, 80-82, 86-88, 90-92

UN Operation in Mozambique—Budget Contributions.
– Documents 63, 65

UN Operation in Mozambique—Establishment.
– Documents 16, 27

UN Operation in Mozambique—Financing.
– Documents 26, 55

United Kingdom—Military assistance.
– Documents 57, 64

V

Voter registration.
– Documents 57, 64
See also: Electoral assistance. Elections.

Voting.
See also: Electoral assistance. Elections.

W

Water supply and sanitation.
– Documents 18, 73

Working groups.
– Document 28

World Food Programme
– Documents 18, 73

Z

Zimbabwe—Armed forces.
– Document 1

Zimbabwe—Military assistance.
– Documents 26, 49, 64

VI Index

[*The numbers following the entries refer to paragraph numbers in the Introduction.*]

H

Halo Trust, 182
Health services, 178
Homoine massacre, 26
Hostages, 143
Human rights, 5, 14, 157-158
    training, 158
Humanitarian assistance, 3, 9, 11,
    36, 55-57, 82, 84, 95, 102,
    161-162, 165, 168-173, 178,
    186, 188, 237, 242.
    See also Emergency assistance

I

ICRC.
    See International Committee
    of the Red Cross
Income distribution, 34
Independence movements, 13-16,
    34
Information services, 175
Inhambane Province, 20, 22
    massacres, 26
Inhaminga, 28
International Committee of the
    Red Cross, 56-57, 166, 177,
    182
International Organization for
    Migration, 207
International Republican Institute,
    207
Italy, 44-45, 51, 90, 104, 166,
    181, 204-205

J

Joint Commission for the
    Formation of the
    Mozambican Defence Force,
    71, 80, 93, 96, 108-109, 146,
    233
Joint FAM-Zimbabwean Force, 25
Joint Political Declaration (1992),
    59
Joint Verification Commission
    (JVC), 46

K

Kenya, 38, 44, 65

L

Land-mines, 31, 94, 103, 131,
    180, 198, 216, 242-244.
    See also Mine clearance
Lidimo, Lagos
    (Lieutenant-General), 149
Limpopo transport corridor, 21,
    35, 46, 100

M

Machel, Samora, 16, 23, 25
Malawi, 21, 30, 38, 44, 65, 83,
    92, 103, 168
    armed forces, 83, 92, 101
Manica Province, 20, 25
    military activity, 30
    refugee return, 168
Manjacaze massacre, 26
Maputo City, 8, 22, 25, 43, 46,
    57, 77-79, 96-97, 112,
    118-119, 123-124, 166, 187,
    209, 217, 221, 224, 229
Maputo Province, 26, 31, 35, 97, 110
    civilian police deployment, 157
    refugee return, 168
    troop deployment, 93, 100
Maringue, 78, 80, 96, 170
Masire, Sir Ketumile, 58
Massacres, 26
Matola Province
    troop deployment, 93
Matsangaissa, Andre, 18
Mazula, Brazão, 194, 228
Mediators, 23, 44-45, 51, 61, 78
Military activity, 24, 28-31, 46-47,
    110
Military observers, 55, 77-78, 83,
    85, 91, 93, 100-102, 116,
    130-132, 153-156, 171, 232,
    235
Military training, 17-18, 20,
    108-109, 113, 147-148,
    242-243
Mine clearance, 8, 55, 95, 128, 148,
    170, 173, 181-184, 187, 242.
    See also Land-mines
MNR.
    See Resistência Nacional
    Moçambicana

M

Mocumbi, Pascoal Manuel, 113
MONAMO/PMSD.
    See Movimento Nacionalista
    Moçambicano/Partido
    Moçambicano da Social
    Democracia
Mondlane, Eduardo
    assassination, 15
Movimento Nacional da
    Resistência de Moçambique
    (MNR).
    See Resistência Nacional
    Moçambicana
Movimento Nacionalista
    Moçambicano/Partido
    Moçambicano da Social
    Democracia, 212
Mozambican Defence Force, 5,
    108-109, 122, 144, 147-149
Mozambican National Resistance.
    See Resistência Nacional
    Moçambicana
Mozambican police, 5, 10, 64, 71,
    96, 114, 120, 157-159, 224,
    243
Mozambique Armed Forces,
    24-26, 135-136, 138-140,
    144, 146-147, 149.
    See also Armed forces
Mozambique Armed
    Forces–Zimbabwean Force,
    25
Mugabe, Robert, 58

N

Nacala transport corridor, 21, 83,
    100-101
Nampula Province, 26, 78, 143,
    185, 202
    troop deployment, 93
National Assembly, 91, 201-202,
    223, 233
National Commission on
    Administration, 72, 112, 121,
    161, 171
National Elections Commission,
    72, 105, 115, 120-121, 191,
    194-196, 199-200, 206,
    217-218, 222-224, 227-228.
    See also Electoral commissions

foreign assistance to, 20, 23
Gaza Province, 20, 31
General Peace Agreement for
    Mozambique (1992), 4-5, 59,
    75, 98
Government recognition, 49, 61
headquarters, 25, 79
humanitarian assistance, 9, 56-57,
    162, 165-166, 169-173, 188
Inhambane Province, 20, 26
Inhaminga, 28
leadership, 18, 41
Manica Province, 20
Maputo Province, 31, 97
military activity, 24, 28-29, 31,
    36, 46-47, 110
military group, 13, 17, 20
Nampula Province, 26
negotiation, 23, 37-40, 42-45,
    54, 96, 126
Niassa Province, 26
political party, 3-4, 8, 53, 58,
    104, 203-204, 206, 228,
    240
Sofala Province, 20, 28
Tete Province, 24, 26
troop demobilization, 92, 94,
    117, 128, 131-140, 143-144,
    150-151, 174, 177
trust fund for, 3-4, 97, 104,
    106, 204-205
Zambézia Province, 24
Riccardi, Andrea, 45
Rome accords.
    See General Peace Agreement
    for Mozambique

S

Salam, Mohammad Abdus, 136
Sant'Egidio.
    See Community of Sant'Egidio
Save the Children Fund, 177
Schools, 30, 179
Severance payments, 129, 137,
    145, 175
Sofala Province, 20, 25, 28, 78, 143,
    170, 202
    military activity, 20, 25, 30
    refugee return, 168

South Africa, 13, 17, 20, 23, 27,
    38, 40, 65, 73, 168, 241
Southern Africa, 2, 46, 73, 82, 84,
    162, 241
Southern Rhodesia, 13, 17-18, 20.
    See also Zimbabwe
STAE.
    See Technical Secretariat for
    the Organization of the
    Elections
State Administration Commission,
    105
Supervisory and Monitoring
    Commission, 63, 67, 69-70,
    80-81, 95-96, 105, 110-111,
    122, 125, 139, 191, 203,
    221-222, 233, 239

T

Tanzania.
    See United Republic of
    Tanzania
Technical assistance, 195-196,
    198, 208
Technical Secretariat for the
    Organization of the Elections,
    192
Tete Province, 9, 24, 26, 110, 143,
    179-180, 183
    military activity, 24, 26, 30
    refugee return, 165, 168
Tete transport corridor, 36, 100
Training
    elections, 86, 195, 197,
        207-208, 216
    human rights, 158
    military, 17-18, 20, 108-109,
        113, 147-148, 242-243
Transitional Government, 16
Transport corridors, 5, 21, 46-47,
    82-83, 92, 100-101, 154,
    162, 171
    Beira, 21, 25, 30, 35, 46, 83,
        90, 101, 155
    Limpopo, 21, 35, 46
    Nacala, 21, 83, 101
    Route Number 1, 26, 100
    Tete, 36, 100
Transport infrastructure, 17, 21,
    102, 180

Troop cantonment, 94, 116, 128,
    134-135, 140, 142.
    See also Assembly areas
Troop demobilization, 3, 8, 11, 85,
    89, 92, 94, 98, 108, 116-117,
    120, 122, 126-130, 133-134,
    136-140, 142-144, 156, 166,
    173-177, 237, 241-243
    verification, 68, 124, 150, 152-153
Troop deployment
    UN Operation in Mozambique,
        8, 83, 90, 92-93, 100-101,
        142, 155
Troop withdrawal, 66, 83, 90, 92,
    101, 154
Troop-contributing States, 90,
    100-102, 109, 118, 154
Trust funds, 3-4, 97, 104, 106,
    166, 204-206, 208
    UN Trust Fund for Assistance to
        Registered Political Parties in
        Mozambique, 206, 208
    UN Trust Fund for
        Humanitarian Affairs, 166
    UN Trust Fund for the
        Implementation of the Peace
        Agreement in Mozambique,
        104, 106, 204-205

U

UD.
    See União Democrática
UN
    commission chairmanship, 7,
        81, 108-109, 113, 239
    electoral verification, 51, 54, 85,
        214, 226
    humanitarian assistance, 11, 84,
        162, 165, 186
    negotiation, 38-39
    peace process implementation,
        11, 53, 59, 63, 65, 67-68, 70,
        82, 123, 125
    peace-keeping operation, 62,
        73-75, 77, 91, 188, 237, 240
    property, 154, 235
    role, 1-2, 4-6, 12, 50, 54, 64,
        66, 69, 240
    staff, 142, 235
    See also Trust funds

United Nations publications of related interest

The following UN publications may be obtained from the addresses indicated below, or at your local distributor:

An Agenda for Peace
Second edition, 1995
By Boutros Boutros-Ghali,
Secretary-General of the United Nations
E.95.I.15   92-1-100555-8   155 pp. $7.50

An Agenda for Development
By Boutros Boutros-Ghali,
Secretary-General of the United Nations
E.95.I.16   92-1-100556-6   132 pp. $7.50

Building Peace and Development, 1994
Annual Report on the Work of the Organization
By Boutros Boutros-Ghali,
Secretary-General of the United Nations
E.95.I.3   92-1-100541-8   299 pp. $9.95

New Dimensions of Arms Regulation and
Disarmament in the Post–Cold War Era
By Boutros Boutros-Ghali,
Secretary-General of the United Nations
E.93.IX.8   92-1-142192-6   53 pp. $9.95

Basic Facts About the United Nations
E.93.I.2   92-1-100499-3   290 pp. $5.00

Demographic Yearbook, Vol. 44
B.94.XIII.1   92-1-051083-6   1992   823 pp.
$125.00

Disarmament—New Realities:
Disarmament, Peace-Building and Global
Security
E.93.IX.14   92-1-142199-3   397 pp. $35.00

United Nations Disarmament Yearbook, Vol. 18
E.94.IX.1   92-1-142204-3   1993   419 pp.
$50.00

Statistical Yearbook, 39th Edition
B.94.XVII.1 H   92-1-061159-4   1992/93
1,174 pp. $110.00

Women: Challenges to the Year 2000
E.91.I.21   92-1-100458-6   96 pp. $12.95

World Economic and Social Survey 1994
E.94.II.C.1   92-1-109128-4   308 pp. $55.00

World Investment Report 1994—
Transnational Corporations, Employment
and the Workplace
E.94.II.A.14   92-1-104435-9   446 pp.
$45.00

Yearbook of the United Nations, Vol. 47
E.94.I.1   0-7923-3077-3   1993   1,428 pp.
$150.00

The United Nations Blue Books Series

The United Nations and Apartheid, 1948-1994
E.95.I.7   92-1-100546-9   565 pp. $29.95

The United Nations and Cambodia, 1991-1995
E.95.I.9   92-1-100548-5   352 pp. $29.95

The United Nations and Nuclear Non-Proliferation
E.95.I.17   92-1-100557-4   199 pp. $29.95

The United Nations and El Salvador, 1990-1995
E.95.I.12   92-1-100552-3   611 pp. $29.95

United Nations Publications
2 United Nations Plaza, Room DC2-853
New York, NY 10017
United States of America
Tel.: (212) 963-8302; 1 (800) 253-9646
Fax: (212) 963-3489

United Nations Publications
Sales Office and Bookshop
CH-1211 Geneva 10
Switzerland
Tel.: 41 (22) 917-26-13;
        41 (22) 917-26-14
Fax: 41 (22) 917-00-27

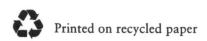 Printed on recycled paper